Interstitial Law-Making in Public International Law: A Study of Environmental Impact Assessments

International Environmental Law

Series Editor

Makane Moïse Mbengue

VOLUME 17

The titles published in this series are listed at *brill.com/iel*

Interstitial Law-Making in Public International Law: A Study of Environmental Impact Assessments

By

Viviane Meunier-Rubel

BRILL
NIJHOFF

LEIDEN | BOSTON

Library of Congress Cataloging-in-Publication Data

Names: Meunier-Rubel, Viviane, author.
Title: Interstitial law-making in public international law : a study of environmental impact assessments / by Viviane Meunier-Rubel.
Description: Leiden ; Boston : Brill Nijhoff, [2022] | Series: International environmental law, 1873-6599 ; volume 17 | Based on author's thesis (doctoral - Yale Law School, 2018). | Includes bibliographical references and index. | Summary: "Environmental Impact Assessment (eia) requirements are quasi-universal. Praised as the core of the international legal response to ensure environmental protection, this procedure is an information tool for better public decision-making, which can contribute to empowering individuals and civic groups. Based on the historical background of the relevant norms and on case studies, Interstitial Law-Making in International Law: A Study of Environmental Impact Assessments verifies whether the role of procedure in secreting substantive law may be fulfilled in the distinctive legal system of public international law, while appraising how eia requirements have been conceived and implemented as regards to encouraging all international actors to behave in an environmentally conscious way, in a world of heterogeneous political regimes"– Provided by publisher.
Identifiers: LCCN 2021058284 (print) | LCCN 2021058285 (ebook) | ISBN 9789004467576 (hardback) | ISBN 9789004467583 (ebook)
Subjects: LCSH: Environmental impact analysis–Law and legislation. | Environmental law, International.
Classification: LCC K3585 .M48 2022 (print) | LCC K3585 (ebook) | DDC 344.04/6–dc23/eng/20220131
LC record available at https://lccn.loc.gov/2021058284
LC ebook record available at https://lccn.loc.gov/2021058285

Typeface for the Latin, Greek, and Cyrillic scripts: "Brill". See and download: brill.com/brill-typeface.

ISSN 1873-6599
ISBN 978-90-04-46757-6 (hardback)
ISBN 978-90-04-46758-3 (e-book)

This book is printed on acid-free paper and produced in a sustainable manner.

This book is based on the author's award winning doctoral dissertation which received the Yale Law School's Ambrose Gherini Prize for best paper in the field of international law (2018)

Contents

Appendices

Abstract

Almost all UN member states now have some type of Environmental Impact Assessment (EIA) requirements, often combined with international, regional or bilateral agreements. EIA provisions have been highly praised as being at the core of the international legal response to ensure environmental protection. Their salient features characterize the evolution of public international law; they are soft law provisions of a preventive and procedural nature, involving public participation, aimed at achieving a common interest. EIA is an information tool for better public decision-making, which can contribute to empowering individuals and civic groups. In addition to the 1991 Convention on Environmental Impact Assessment in a Transboundary Context (Espoo Convention), the 1998 Convention on Access to Information, Public Participation in Decision-Making and Access to Justice in Environmental Matters (Aarhus Convention) formally expressed the possibility for all potential users of international law to become participants in the international legal system.

Within the framework of the New Haven School, this book is based on Henry Sumner Maine's apothegm, "substantive law has at first the look of being gradually secreted in the interstices of procedure".[1] It has two related objectives: to study whether the role of procedure in secreting substantive law may be fulfilled in the idiosyncratic legal system of public international law, while appraising how EIA requirements have been conceived and have been implemented as regards encouraging all international actors to behave in an environmentally conscious way, in a world of heterogeneous political regimes.

The New Haven School emphasizes that law is not a fixed set of traditional rules, but a continuous and dynamic process of authoritative decisions, in which a wide array of actors participate. EIAs have facilitated the empowerment of individuals and the creation of transnational environmental networks. As it appears in the case studies, and despite their critics, EIAs have chalked up substantial successes and achievements. In the search of symbols expressive of common aspirations around the world, and of sentiments for crystallizing the public order of the world community, EIAs appear to play such a role. It has been a common cultural experience from which have emerged common symbols and practices, essential for world unity. As Mahnoush Arsanjani

1 HENRY SUMNER MAINE, DISSERTATIONS ON EARLY LAW AND CUSTOM 389 (John Murray. 1883).

underlines, "[t]he most striking aspects of these common symbols are related to the value and the place of the individual vis-a-vis others and vis-a-vis their governments".[2]

As procedural rules, EIA requirements have equipped individuals with tools to express their preferred social choices, and have tended to fight off arbitrariness, in order for the confrontation of competing interests to unfold within expectations of effective norms of environmental protection, in view of sustainable development worldwide. In the words of Michael Reisman, "civic enforcement will have achieved a significant victory if it sustains expectations of the effectiveness of certain norms, even though, in particular cases, it has not succeeded in securing the full implementation of those norms. And civic enforcement will become a major strut of international order if it can, by recruiting more and more private individuals, mobilize increasing support for the basic prescriptions of a world order of human dignity".[3] EIA norms have exemplified this victory. They are now expected to be effective, and to support demands for sustainable development. Recommendations follow with regard to improving the timing of EIAs, follow-up programs, the organization of public participation, as well as the role of financial institutions.

---

2 Mahnoush H. Arsanjani, *The Uses and Abuses of Illusion in International Politics, in* LOOKING TO THE FUTURE – ESSAYS IN INTERNATIONAL LAW IN HONOR OF W. MICHAEL REISMAN 58 (Mahnoush H. Arsanjani, et al. eds., 2011).

3 W. Michael Reisman, *Making International Humanitarian Law Effective: the Case for Civic Enforcement, in* THE UNITED NATIONS: A REASSESSMENT – SANCTIONS, PEACEKEEPING, AND HUMANITARIAN ASSISTANCE 37–38 (John M. Paxman & George T. Boggs eds., 1973).

Foreword

A technological and science-based civilization has the capacity – and the imperatives – to mount large-scale initiatives that impact the environment. A rational program to protect the environment is one which anticipates the impacts that such initiatives will have; if the initiatives do not promise to be environmentally neutral, their costs and benefits can be weighed in advance and alternatives may be invented. Because the environment is a common resource on which all members of the community depend, procedures for deciding on projects which may impact the environment should be as democratic as possible, for public participation, while a value in itself, also enables the mobilization of sectors of the public for the defense of the environment. And in as much as the environment knows no boundaries, procedures should allow for transnational participation.

Among the repertory of techniques for making rational decisions about those initiatives, the environmental impact assessment or EIA is the most widespread. The forerunner of EIA practice was the United States' National Environmental Policy Act of 1970. It has been followed by comparable legislation in almost all members of the United Nations and, because of the transboundary effects of many initiatives, its place in international law has been confirmed by the International Court of Justice.

That said, there is a world of difference between the prescription of policy and its actual application. Legal systems have no shortage of *lex imperfecta* and *lex simulata:* legislative exercises which look effective and pay lip service to the common interest but are actually intended to be virtually hollow, containing only the seeds of their own ineffectiveness. Viviane Meunier-Rubel, an international legal scholar committed to procedures enhancing sound environmental decisions in a public order of human dignity, insists on asking whether the EIAs really are mere "paper tigers" or whether they can play a "significant determinative role in environmental protection and international law making". She traces the history, diffusion and practice of EIAs transnationally before focusing, in granular detail, on three transnational cases: the Vuotos dam and reservoir project for hydropower in Finland; an extra-high voltage power line between France and Spain as part of the development of the European power grid; and the Upper Mekong Navigation Improvement project.

Sir Henry Maine famously said of the Common Law that it seems to secrete substantive law in the "interstices of procedure". So too EIAs. Though the outcomes of these cases vary, Ms. Meunier-Rubel shows that the EIA has emerged as a common procedural experience which can empower individuals to participate in transnational environmental networks. It is not a panacea. Its success depends, among other things, on a politically open context, access to accurate data and, even then, it is part of a larger decision process which can corrupt its outcomes. But if perfection is unattainable, a sound public order is the better for the effort.

Readers of this brilliantly written and ground-breaking book will find that Meunier-Rubel's guarded optimism is warranted and one hopes that many will be inspired to apply her methodology and her insights for the benefit of the earth's environment.

Michael Reisman
Yale Law School
New Haven, Connecticut – U.S.A.
July 6, 2021

Acknowledgements

My doctoral dissertation, upon which this book is based, would not have seen the light without the inspiration, guidance and patience kindly provided by my supervisor, W. Michael Reisman. I am deeply grateful for his inestimable teaching and for the example he has set. My heartfelt thanks also to my co-supervisor, Daniel C. Esty, for his instruction, time and advice, as well as to Lea Brilmayer and Oona A. Hathaway, all members of my JSD committee at Yale Law School, from which support my work profited during my residence there, and to which I extend my thanks. All along the way, Maria Z. Dino showed warm encouragement, of which I am appreciative. I am thankful to Cina Santos as well, whose thoughtfulness greatly eased the process. My research was immensely facilitated by the efficacy and kindness of the Lillian Goldman Law Library staff, whom I thank, along with various other libraries and archives departments. This book vastly benefited from the great many persons I interviewed, or whose help and insight I solicited, all of whom I thank here again. I also wish to thank the anonymous reviewers for Brill/Nijhoff. Lastly, I am grateful to my husband for his infinite encouragement and patience, to my mother for her love and education, to my family and friends.

Illustrations

References are to pages

Charts

Figures

Maps

Acronyms

AC	Alternative Current
ACFTA	ASEAN-China Free Trade Area (or CAFTA – China-ASEAN Free Trade Area)
ADB	Asian Development Bank
ADEME	Agence De l'Environnement et de la Maîtrise de l'Energie
AE	Autorité Environnementale
AEPS	Arctic Environmental Protection Strategy
AIIB	Asian Infrastructure Investment Bank
ASEAN	Association of Southeast Asian Nations
ATCM	Antarctic Treaty Consultative Meeting
BO	Boletín Oficial
CAFTA	China-ASEAN Free Trade Area (or ACFTA – ASEAN-China Free Trade Area)
CBD	Convention on Biological Diversity
CEAA	Canadian Environmental Assessment Act
CEE	Comprehensive Environmental Evaluation (Antarctic Environmental Protocol)
CEQ	Council on Environmental Quality (in the US)
CERCLA	Comprehensive Environmental Response, Compensation, and Liability
CESI	Centro Elettrotecnico Sperimentale Italiano
CGEDD	Conseil Général de l'Environnement et du Développement Durable
CJEC	Court of Justice of the European Communities
CJEU	Court of Justice of the European Union
CNDP	Commission Nationale du Débat Public
CoP	Conference of the Parties
CPDP	Commission Particulière du Débat Public
CSCE	Conference on Security and Cooperation
CSR	Corporate Social Responsibility
DC	Direct Current
DDE	Direction Départementale de l'Equipement
DRAE	Délégation Régionale à l'Architecture et à l'Environnement
DREAL	Direction Régionale de l'Environnement, de l'Aménagement et du Logement
DUP	Déclaration d'Utilité Publique
DWT	Deadweight Ton
EA	Environmental Assessment
EBRD	European Bank for Reconstruction and Development
EC	European Communities
ECAFE	(UN) Economic Commission for Asia and the Far East

ECE	European Commission for Europe
ECJ	European Court of Justice
EDF	Electricité de France
EEA	European Economic Area
EEC	European Economic Community
EEPR	European Energy Program for Recovery
EEZ	Exclusive Economic Zone
EGAT	Electricity Generating Authority of Thailand
EHV	Extra High Voltage
EHVDC	Extra High Voltage in Direct Current
EIA	Environmental Impact Assessment
EIB	European Investment Bank
EIS	Environmental Impact Statement (US NEPA)
ELD	Environmental Liability Directive
EMF	ElectroMagnetic Field
ENTSOE	European Network of Transmission System Operators
EP	Equator Principles
EPA	Environmental Protection Act (Finland)
EPE	European Principles for the Environment
EPFI	Equator Principles Financial Institutions
EPL	Environmental Protection Law (Lao PDR)
ESCAP	(UN) Economic and Social Commission for Asia and the Pacific
ESF	Environmental and Social Framework (World Bank)
ESIA	Environmental and Social Impact Assessment
ESMF	Environmental and Social Management Framework (WB)
ETA	Euskadi Ta Askatasuna, *i.e.* Basque country and freedom
EU	European Union
FANC	Finnish Association for Nature Conservation
FME	Finnish Ministry of the Environment
FNE	France Nature Environnement
GDP	Gross Domestic Product
GEA	Global Environmental Assessment Project
GEF	Global Environment Facility
GWh	Gigawatt hours (unit of energy representing one billion watt hours)
GMP	Genetically Modified Plant
GMS	Greater Mekong Subregion
HELCOM	Helsinki Commission (full name: Baltic Marine Environment Protection Commission)
HV	High Voltage
Hz	Hertz

IA	Impact Assessment
IAIA	International Association for Impact Assessment
IBRD	International Bank of Reconstruction and Development (WB Group)
ICJ	International Court of Justice
IDA	International Development Association (World Bank Group)
IEE	Initial Environmental Evaluation (in the Antarctic Environmental Protocol)
IEM	Internal Energy Market (European Union)
IFC	International Finance Corporation (World Bank Group)
IFI	International Financial Institution
IIL	Institute of International Law
ILA	International Law Association
ILC	International Law Commission
ILO	International Labour Organisation
ILR	International Law Reports
IMF	International Monetary Fund
IO	International Organization
IP	Inspection Panel
ITLOS	International Tribunal for the Law of the Sea
IUCN	International Union for Conservation of Nature
JCCCN	Joint Committee on Coordination of Commercial Navigation on the Lancang-Mekong River
JO	Journal Officiel
KHO	Korkein hallinto-oikeus (Supreme Administrative Court of Finland)
kV	Kilovolt
LEL	Lender Environmental Liability
LMC	Lower Mekong Cooperation Mechanism
LMI	Lower Mekong Initiative
LPRP	Lao People's Revolutionary Party (formerly Pathet Lao)
LRSA	Living River Siam Association (formerly SEARIN)
M-POWER	Mekong Program on Water, Environment and Resilience
MC	Mekong Committee
MDB	Multilateral Development Bank
MFMP	Multilateral Fund for the Montreal Protocol
MNC	Multinational Corporations
MoNRE	Ministry of Natural Resources and Environment (Thailand)
MOP	Meeting of the Parties
MP	Member of Parliament
MRC	Mekong River Commission
MRC JC	Mekong River Commission Joint Committee

MRCS	Mekong River Commission Secretariat
MW	Mega Watts
NAAEC	North American Agreement on Environmental Cooperation
NABU	Nature And Biodiversity Conservation Union (Germany)
NACEC	North American Commission for Environmental Cooperation
NADB	North American Development Bank
NAFTA	North American Free Trade Area
NATO	North Atlantic Treaty Organization
NDB	New Development Bank
NDF	Northern Development Foundation
NDIA	National Defense Industrial Association
NEB	National Environment Board (Thailand)
NEPA	(US) National Environmental Policy Act
NEPC	Nordic Environmental Protection Convention
NEQA	National Environmental Quality Act (Thailand)
NGO	Non-Governmental Organization
NMC	National Mekong Committee
OECD	Organization for Economic Cooperation and Development
PGM	Plantes Génétiquement Modifiées
PNPCA	(MRC) Procedures for Notification, Prior Consultation and Agreement
PPA	Power Purchase Agreement
PRP	Potentially Responsible Parties
REE	Red Eléctrica de España
RTE	Réseau de Transport d'Electricité
SAC	Supreme Administrative Court
SCI	Site of Community Importance (Natura 2000 network in the EU)
SEA	Strategic Environmental Assessment
SEARIN	Southeast Asia International Rivers Network (now LRSA)
SEPA	Swedish Environmental Protection Agency (Naturvårdsverket)
SESA	Strategic Environmental and Social Assessment
SOM	Senior Official Meeting
SPA	Special Protection Area (Natura 2000 network in the EU)
SRI	Socially Responsible Investment
SSNC	Swedish Society for Nature Conservation
STEA	Science, Technology and Environment Agency (Lao PDR)
TEIA	Transboundary Environmental Impact Assessment
TERRA	Towards Ecological Recovery and Regional Alliance
TEU	Treaty on European Union
TK	Traditional Knowledge
TSO	Transmission System Operator

TWG	Technical Working Group (implementation of the Navigation Agreement)
UCPTE	Union pour la Coordination de la Production et de la Transmission d'Electricité
UFEPTE	Union Franco-Espagnole Pour la coordination de la Production et du Transport d'Electricité
UFIPTE	Union Franco-Ibérique Pour la coordination de la Production et du Transport d'Electricité
UMNIP	Upper Mekong Navigation Improvement Project
UN	United Nations
UN GAOR	United Nations General Assembly Official Records
UNCED	United Nations Conference on Environment and Development (Rio)
UNCHE	United Nations Conference on the Human Environment (Stockholm)
UNCLOS	United Nations Convention on the Law of the Sea
UNECE	United Nations Economic Commission for Europe
UNEP	United Nations Environmental Program
UNFCCC	United Nations Framework Convention on Climate Change
UNGA	United Nations General Assembly
UNIPEDE	Union Internationale des Producteurs et Distributeurs d'Electricité
UNTS	United Nations Treaty Series
US	United States
USAID	United States Agency for International Development
VATT	Valtion Taloudellinen Tutkimuskeskus (Finnish Institute for Economic Research)
WB	World Bank
WCD	Word Commission on Dams
WSSD	World Summit on Sustainable Development (Johannesburg)

Table of Cases

References are to pages

Finland

France

United States

Thailand

European Community

International Courts and Tribunals

Table of Treaties and Other International Instruments

References are to pages

Treaties

Other International Instruments

European Secondary Legislation

CHAPTER 1

Introduction

> *Law is frequently conceived of as fixed and stable, and of course the principles of natural law are assumed to be permanent. But law is actually a dynamic process, and its components are far less certain than popularly supposed. As for international law, it is particularly volatile, presenting especially daunting intellectual and moral challenges to the lawyers who practice it.*[1]

> *Le propre du juriste est d'avoir égard à tous les points de vue (…) La procédure importe au droit beaucoup plus que le matériel de textes préexistants. Elle est le moyen de l'invention du droit.* [2]

∴

A great mystery remains unresolved until this day: the collapse, between 750 and 1050, of the Lowland Maya Classic-period civilization. Scientists now seem to agree on an environmental hypothesis. Even though diverse factors can explain each regional collapse, only one is common to the whole Lowland Maya civilization, one that explains why the populations left this extensive area: an environmental disaster. Their prosperity rested on their agricultural system. However, the production of stucco, which was the most treasured building and decorative component, led to massive deforestation. Stucco requires a lengthy warming of limestone, obtained by burning considerable quantities of wood. Deforestation led to irreversible erosion, which ruined the agricultural system, and ushered in the end of the sacred royalty. Class status rivalries, for power

---

1 W. Michael Reisman, *On the Causes of Uncertainty and Volatility in International Law, in* THE SHIFTING ALLOCATION OF AUTHORITY IN INTERNATIONAL LAW: CONSIDERING SOVEREIGNTY, SUPREMACY AND SUBSIDIARITY – ESSAYS IN HONOUR OF PROFESSOR RUTH LAPIDOTH 33 (Tomer Broude & Yuval Shany eds., 2008).

2 MICHEL VILLEY, PHILOSOPHIE DU DROIT (DÉFINITIONS ET FINS DU DROIT – LES MOYENS DU DROIT) 209–210 (Dalloz Réédition ed. 2001). "What is characteristic of a lawyer is that they consider every point of view (…) Procedure is significantly more important to lawmaking than pre-existing rules. Thanks to procedure, law is created." (author's translation).

 DOI:10.1163/9789004467583_002

and prestige, had provoked an escalation of displays of splendor and wealth in order to attract allegiances.[3] City-states competed by waging wars, but also, and mostly, through a profusion of temples, palaces, monuments, public squares and other sites that could be used for magnificent and expensive rituals to regain the favors of divinities. Power was thought to be of divine origin. It rested on spectacular ceremonies organized in imposing architectural settings, grandiose funeral cults, splendidly carved and engraved monuments, and the required rewards of diverse networks. Furthermore, overpopulation, due to increased workforce demand, worsened the environmental crisis because of the limited supply of natural resources.[4] Afterwards, in the 11th century, Mayas erected new cities in Yucatán, north of the deserted central lowlands, and set up a new political regime, *multepal*, which signifies "to govern collectively", or "to rule jointly".[5]

1 Environmental Degradation and EIA Rationale

> *In consequence of this primary mutual hostility of human beings, civilized society is perpetually threatened with disintegration. The interest of work in common would not hold it together; instinctual passions are stronger than reasonable interests.*[6]

Today, the accelerating rate of environmental damage is an even more predominant trend. This trend has extended to the global level and has been

3 Arthur Demarest, *The Collapse of the Classic Maya Kingdoms of the Southwestern Petén: Implications for the End of Classic Maya Civilization, in* MILLENARY MAYA SOCIETIES, PAST CRISES AND RESILIENCE (PAPERS FROM THE INTERNATIONAL COLLOQUIUM – MUSÉE DU QUAI BRANLY, PARIS, JULY 1–2, 2011) 27, 40 (Marie-Charlotte Arnauld & Alain Breton eds., 2013).

4 Arthur Demarest, *The end of Classic Maya Civilization: collapse, transition and transformation, in* ANCIENT MAYA: THE RISE AND FALL OF A RAINFOREST CIVILIZATION 240–274 (2005); JARED DIAMOND, COLLAPSE, HOW SOCIETIES CHOOSE TO FAIL OR SUCCEED 157–177 (Viking. 2005); B. L. Turner II & Jeremy A. Sabloff, *Classic Period collapse of the Central Maya Lowlands: Insights about human-environment relationships for sustainability*, 109 PNAS 13908 (2012).

5 Ernesto Arredondo Leiva, *Une perspective sociopolitique de la guerre maya, in* MAYA – DE L'AUBE AU CREPUSCULE 75 (2011); ROBERT J. SHARER, THE ANCIENT MAYA 404–405 (Stanford University Press 5th ed. 1994); GRANT D. JONES, THE CONQUEST OF THE LAST MAYA KINGDOM 104–106 (Stanford University Press. 1998).

6 SIGMUND FREUD, CIVILIZATION AND ITS DISCONTENTS 104–105 (James Strachey trans., W. W. Norton & Company. 1929).

compounded by potentially highly destructive technologies. Environmental misconduct is leading to rapid ecological degradation, with immediate consequences for human beings. Epigenetics, a new biomedical field, has established that, far from slow and distant genetic evolution, human beings can be immediately marked and shaped by their environment, be it pollution, food, viruses, etc., in the form of chemical imprints carried by the genome, and that can be transmitted to their progeny as well. Damaging the environment that sustains human life may pertain either to a syndrome of omnipotence, of blind aggressiveness, self-destructiveness,[7] or indifference to legacy. Published in France in 1956, *The Roots of Heaven* by Romain Gary was one of the first novels of the modern era inspired by environmental concerns in the face of human hubris. In his book, Gary presented the external, physical world as imposing desirable limitations. In an interactive dynamic, if nature is to be domesticated, it also domesticates our destructive impulses. Lynton K. Caldwell, a principal architect of the National Environmental Policy Act in the United States, later echoed Gary: "Science demonstrates the dynamic interconnectedness of Earth, biosphere and sociosphere. It also confirms the limits to life and Earth within which mankind's interests, risks, and futures are encompassed".[8] To counteract the destructive trend, environmental policies are based on sustainable development,[9] on the human instinct of survival, and the ability to decide for the long-term, i.e. on rationality. "Rationality draws on various means of control: the environment (physical resistance of the surroundings to desire and imagination), practice (verifying activity), culture (reference to common knowledge), other people (do you see the same thing as me?), the cortex (memory, logical operations). In other words, rationality is corrective".[10] For these reasons, sustainable development is most often sought

7 Daniel Cohen evokes an actual instance of collective suicide (DANIEL COHEN, LA PROSPERITE DU VICE, UNE INTRODUCTION (INQUIETE) A L'ECONOMIE 225 (Albin Michel. 2009).

8 Lynton K. Caldwell, *Is World Law an Emerging Reality? Environmental Law in a Transnational World*, 10 COLO. J. INT'L ENVTL. L. & POL'Y 227, 230 (1999).

9 "Looking further ahead, the long-term reference point is sustainability of development. Decisions taken over the next generation – decisions that can be informed by EA processes – may well determine whether society becomes a sustainable one, or whether it overshoots resource and environmental thresholds". (BARRY SADLER, INTERNATIONAL STUDY OF THE EFFECTIVENESS OF ENVIRONMENTAL ASSESSMENT – FINAL REPORT – ENVIRONMENTAL ASSESSMENT IN A CHANGING WORLD: EVALUATING PRACTICE TO IMPROVE PERFORMANCE Executive Summary (p. v) (Canadian Environmental Assessment Agency – International Association for Impact Assessment. 1996)).

10 EDGAR MORIN, SEVEN COMPLEX LESSONS IN EDUCATION FOR THE FUTURE 6–7 (UNESCO. 1999).

through procedural obligations, i.e. rationalized decision-making processes, as epitomized in the environmental impact assessment procedure.

Common misconceptions and fears about sustainable development are often misguided. Some companies successfully mix profits with environmental protection, even in the face of scarce natural resources and penniless consumers for some. They develop thriving business models because they proactively turn constraints into opportunities through innovation, actively shape their business environments, and instill sustainability in their company culture.[11] For instance, in Hong Kong, train operator MTR Corporation has successfully linked sustainability and risk management.[12] The company has built a sophisticated framework – a Sustainable Competitive Advantage model – to guide its actions. In particular, several environmental impact assessment reports have been mandatory for every project to develop a new rail line. Furthermore, MTR Corporation has measured the impacts of these projects both before *and* after the construction stage, also a rare policy.[13] More generally, sustainable development has been identified as an inescapable business megatrend (akin to recent and past large-scale changes such as electrification, mass production, information and communication technology …).[14] Being mindful of the economic advantages of sustainable development allows us to strike an otherwise elusive balance between economic interests and environmental protection: instead of attempting to attract investors with short-term and ill-advised

---

11 WORLD ECONOMIC FORUM & BOSTON CONSULTING GROUP, REDEFINING THE FUTURE OF GROWTH: THE NEW SUSTAINABILITY CHAMPIONS 7 & 10 (World Economic Forum – Boston Consulting Group. 2011).

12 Mass Transit Railway Corporation Ltd. (MTR Corporation) was established in 1975 as a government-owned statutory corporation. On 5 October 2000, MTR Corporation was privatized.

13 WORLD ECONOMIC FORUM & BOSTON CONSULTING GROUP, *supra* note 11 at 12. Hong Kong has demonstrated impressively sound project development capabilities; another example with strong stakeholder participation is *Hong Kong 2030: Planning Vision and Strategy report to assess the Territorial Development Strategy*, mentioned *in* CASSANDRA WESOLOWSKI, ENVIRONMENTAL ASSESSMENTS AND STAKEHOLDER INVOLVEMENT 177 (2006). Whether Hong Kong will continue on this path under the ever-tightening Chinese political regime remains to be seen.

14 David A. Lubin & Daniel C. Esty, *The Sustainability Imperative – Lessons for leaders from previous game-changing megatrends*, 88 HARVARD BUSINESS REVIEW 42 (2010). See also DANIEL C. ESTY & ANDREW WINSTON, GREEN TO GOLD: HOW SMART COMPANIES USE ENVIRONMENTAL STRATEGY TO INNOVATE, CREATE VALUE, AND BUILD COMPETITIVE ADVANTAGE (Yale University Press (revised and updated edition from Wiley in 2009). 2006); DANIEL C. ESTY & P.J. SIMMONS, GREEN TO GOLD BUSINESS PLAYBOOK: HOW TO IMPLEMENT SUSTAINABILITY PRACTICES FOR BOTTOM-LINE RESULTS IN EVERY BUSINESS FUNCTION (John Wiley & Sons, Inc. 2011).

policies, comprehensive environmental regulations should be strengthened.[15] Lastly, large companies are often fearful of detrimental publicity, which can be another incentive to conform to environmental regulations. Sustainable development has been accompanied by the correlative global trend of Socially Responsible Investment (SRI), of which Environmental Impact Assessment (EIA) "is a fundamental component",[16] and the more general concept of Environmental, Social and Governance principles (ESG). In the United States for instance, in 2020, SRI represented a third of the total US assets under professional management, an increase of 42% since 2018.[17] At present and on the global scale, ESG-dedicated funds represent US$1.2 trillion, i.e. around a 2% share of the market. More than 90% of these funds were located in Europe and North America in 2018, but have attracted growing interest in Asia.[18] Overall, as a long-term trend, assets under management using sustainable investing strategies have consistently shown a dramatic growth, which is quite remarkable even if from a very low base. Whether it is only virtue-signaling (greenwashing) or actual sustainable investments remains under scrutiny.

To achieve environmental protection and sustainable development, prevention has been widely acknowledged as preferable to remedy, for several reasons:[19] reparation is often pointless because of irreversible damage;

---

15 See, for instance, the dissenting judgment of Lord Walker of Gestingthorpe in *Belize Alliance of Conservation Non-Governmental Org. v. Dept. of Env't*, [29 January 2004] UKPC 6 (Belize), para. 120: "Belize has enacted comprehensive legislation for environmental protection and direct foreign investment, if it has serious environmental implications, must comply with that legislation. The rule of law must not be sacrificed to foreign investment, however desirable (indeed, recent history shows that in many parts of the world respect for the rule of law is an incentive, and disrespect for the rule of law can be a severe deterrent, to foreign investment). It is no answer to the erroneous geology in the EIA to say that the dam design would not necessarily have been different. The people of Belize are entitled to be properly informed about any proposals for alterations in the dam design before the project is approved and before work continues with its construction".

16 Kees Bastmeijer & Timo Koivurova, *Transboundary Environmental Impact Assessment: An Introduction, in* THEORY AND PRACTICE OF TRANSBOUNDARY IMPACT ASSESSMENT 23 (Kees Bastmeijer & Timo Koivurova eds., 2008).

17 And from 1995 to 2020, sustainable investing increased more than 25-fold, a compound annual growth rate of 14% (US SIF FOUNDATION, REPORT ON US SUSTAINABLE AND IMPACT INVESTING TRENDS 1 (2020)).

18 JP Morgan Research, *Why COVID-19 Could Prove to Be a Major Turning Point for ESG Investing*, July 2020.

19 As stated since the beginning of the environmental movement. See, for instance, RICHARD B. BILDER, THE SETTLEMENT OF DISPUTES IN THE FIELD OF THE INTERNATIONAL LAW OF THE ENVIRONMENT 224–226 (Hague Academy of International Law ed., Martinus Nijhoff. 1975).

there are significant hurdles in tracing the chain of responsibilities; courts may struggle with highly technical evidence;[20] it is typically not state practice to engage another state's responsibility for transboundary harm, as the Chernobyl accident blatantly demonstrated, after which states simply entered into negotiations on new multilateral treaties, aiming to prevent the occurrence of similar events.[21] Only once has a state pursued another in respect to the latter's responsibility for transboundary pollution – the *Trail Smelter* Arbitration, between the United States and Canada.[22] Nevertheless, this case is not conclusive, since Canada had admitted its liability in advance. States are reluctant to establish a precedent that could be used against the claimant in the future. They are very cautious about preserving their sovereignty and margin of action. Furthermore, because of the complexity of global environmental issues and causal interdependence in this field, there is little space for absolute innocence.[23] Prevention and the necessity of rationalized decision-processes are the reasons why EIA was developed and became the first modern environmental law norm.

---

20 See *Kleppe v. Sierra Club,* 427 US 390, 412, 96 S.Ct. 2718, 2731, 49 L.Ed.2d 576 (1976); *Baltimore Gas & Electric Co. v. Natural Resources Defense Council, Inc.,* 462 US 87, 103, 103 S.Ct. 2246, 2255, 76 L.Ed.2d 437 (1983); *Marsh* v. *Oregon Natural Resources Council,* 490 US 360, 361, 377 (1989); *Monsanto v. Geertson* 561 US 139, 130 S.Ct. 2743, 2763 (2010); *Pulp Mills on the River Uruguay* (*Argentina v. Uruguay*), Judgment, 2010 ICJ Reports 14, at para. 168 (20 April).

21 Convention on Early Notification of a Nuclear Accident (Vienna) 26 September 1986, 1439 UNTS 275, 25 ILM 1370 (1986), in force 27 October 1986; Convention on Assistance in the Case of a Nuclear Accident or Radiological Emergency (Vienna) 26 September 1986, 25 ILM 1377 (1986), 1457 UNTS 133, in force 26 February 1987.

22 3 RIAA 1911 (1938), 35 AM. J. INT'L L. 684 (1941). James R. Allum, *"An Outcrop of Hell": History, Environment, and the Politics of the Trail Smelter Dispute, in* TRANSBOUNDARY HARM IN INTERNATIONAL LAW: LESSONS FROM THE TRAIL SMELTER ARBITRATION (2009). The *Trail Smelter* Arbitration, "it must be said, still stands in splendid isolation as a basis for a customary rule on transborder pollution" (Oscar Schachter, *The Greening of International Law, in* HUMANITÉ ET DROIT INTERNATIONAL: MÉLANGES RENÉ-JEAN DUPUY 273 (1991)). Despite its diverse reassertions, the Trail Smelter principle has remained elusive in practice (TRANSBOUNDARY POLLUTION – EVOLVING ISSUES OF INTERNATIONAL LAW AND POLICY (S. Jayakumar, et al. eds., 2015)).

23 "We are so much at the roots of everything that we cannot keep claiming innocence (…) Aware of a limitless power, of an infinite responsibility and, at the same time, of how little we know" (François Ewald, *L'expérience de la responsabilité, in* DE QUOI SOMMES-NOUS RESPONSABLES? HUITIÈME FORUM LE MONDE LE MANS 31 (Thomas Ferenczi & Etienne Balibar eds., 1997) (author's translation).

2 Definition of EIA

According to the Convention on Environmental Impact Assessment in a Transboundary Context (hereinafter the Espoo Convention), an environmental impact assessment is a national procedure, with public participation, for evaluating the likely impact of a proposed activity on the environment.[24] EIA is not only a document, but an institutionalized decision process, which should achieve three related goals: provide decision-makers with relevant information on the environmental consequences of proposed activities, and their alternatives; provide a mechanism for ensuring the participation of potentially affected persons in the decision-making process; lead to decisions which take that information into account.[25] In the course of this book, I will thus refer to the term "EIA" either as the assessment itself, or more broadly as the decision-making process that includes such assessment – the determination made as regards its necessity, the assessment, its circulation, the informal or formal participatory processes at any given time, and the follow-up and post-monitoring processes.

Before the adoption of stand-alone EIA requirements, the core issue of environmental policies was their fragmented and disjointed character. Obligations were separately defined within the diverse regulations applicable to each sectoral permit. There was no comprehensive approach. For the first time, autonomous EIA statutes and treaties have imposed a holistic view of environmental risk assessments. Then, the ultimate decision is generally not constrained by substantive obligations, which can be viewed as a shortcoming. However, it also means that the protected interests cannot be defined away, because what triggers an EIA is an all-encompassing concern, of a preventive nature, constituted by the imminence of a potential harm done to the environment, not the potential violation of specific substantive standards.

Moreover, EIA requirements have dramatically improved the possibilities of public participation. Environmental information has become more readily available to citizens, and EIA obligations have provided formal opportunities for affected populations and civic groups to participate in project development. In a manner comparable to the judicial process, EIA – i.e. a rationalistic process characterized by transparency, deliberations, accountability – confers

---

24 Convention on Environmental Impact Assessment in a Transboundary Context (Espoo), Article 1(vi), 25 February 1991, 30 ILM 802 (1991), in force 10 September 1997.

25 PHILIPPE SANDS, ET AL., PRINCIPLES OF INTERNATIONAL ENVIRONMENTAL LAW 657 (4th ed. 2018).

legitimacy on decisions taken by unelected officials, if properly designed and implemented.[26] Because scientific information is indispensable, but not sufficient, as it is uncertain and variable in quality, not to mention incomplete and costly, there can be no single definitive answer at the end of the EIA process, but a legitimate one nonetheless, which will reflect public values and arbitrate among diverging interests – i.e. a political decision.[27]

3 Origins and History of EIA

Success will be achieved only when the preservation of nature is forcefully demanded by the public itself[28]

3.1 *National Environmental Policy Act* (NEPA)

EIA originated in the United States, as a public policy passed in reaction to social pressure.[29] The public had become increasingly alarmed at the environmental consequences of human endeavors. In 1970, the National Environmental

26 "It is not at all necessary (...) to ascribe to judges the wisdom of philosopher kings. The capacity of judges to give meaning to public values turns not on some personal moral expertise, of which they have none, but on process that limits their exercise of power. One feature of that process is the dialogue judges must conduct; they must listen to all grievances, hear a wide range of interests, speak back and also assume individual responsibility to what they say." (OWEN M. FISS, THE LAW AS IT COULD BE 54–55 (2003)).

27 Lynton K. Caldwell, *Analysis–Assessment–Decision: the Anatomy of Rational Policymaking*, 9 IMPACT ASSESSMENT 81, 81 (1991).

28 Mervyn Hugh Cowie, delegate of Kenya at the International Conference for the Preservation of Fauna and Flora of Africa, held in Bukavu, Congo, 26–31 October 1953 (author's translation). Cowie (1909–1996) was a conservationist, the founder and first director of the National Parks in Kenya.

29 "NEPA was the outcome of a complex network of happenings. First there was a strong tradition for conservation, fostered by groups like the Sierra Club (founded 1892) and the National Audubon Society (1905). (...) there were zealots with a mission (like Rachel Carson) and administrators with vision (like Steward Udall). There were well publicized examples of the lack of foresight in using new technology, which acted as flashpoints to set off a chain reaction in public opinion. (...) The politicians then realized that the public conscience was ahead of them, so they lost no time in catching up and taking a lead. (...) and the wave of enthusiasm about public participation in great issues (such as civil rights, medicare and environment) led to powerful and effective lobbies, and ultimately to Henry M. Jackson's Bill S1075 in February 1969." (Eric Ashby, *Background to environmental impact assessment*, *in* ENVIRONMENTAL IMPACT ASSESSMENT 5 (Timothy O'Riordan & Richard D. Hey eds., 1976)).

Policy Act (NEPA) was adopted.[30] NEPA introduced EIA as an action-forcing mechanism, to press environmental concerns into public decision-making processes. Since then, EIA requirements have been adopted worldwide, with NEPA serving as the original model. They have spread to different levels of government and regulations, and to private sector projects. The initial emphasis on the environmental consequences of projects has since been enlarged to embrace socio-economic effects, not only of projects, but also of policies, programs, plans, technologies,[31] and regulations. Preventive in nature, EIAs are viewed as the major regulatory tool in the environmental field. In the US, where EIA requirements first appeared, public awareness had been raised in great part thanks to Rachel Carson, in her seminal book, *Silent Spring* (published in 1962), which described the grave consequences of the absence of preliminary studies:

> It is not my contention that chemical insecticides must never be used. I do contend that we have put poisonous and biologically potent chemicals indiscriminately into the hands of persons largely or wholly ignorant of their potentials for harm. We have subjected enormous numbers of people to contact with these poisons, without their consent and often without their knowledge. (...) I contend, furthermore, that we have allowed these chemicals to be used with little or no advance investigation of their effects on soil, water, wildlife, and man himself. Future generations are unlikely to condone our lack of prudent concern for the integrity of the natural world that supports all life.[32]

Beginning in the 1960's, when most material needs were being fulfilled thanks to economic prosperity, the consumerist society lost some of its attractiveness, yielding to renewed spiritual quests. Mainstream political culture adopted a

---

30 National Environmental Policy Act, enacted in 1969 and signed into law on 1 January 1970 by President Richard Nixon (42 USC §4321 et seq. (1969)).

31 EIAs have spread, not only to different types of decision-making processes, but also to research conduct. For instance, geoengineers adopted a regulatory framework in March 2010. The Asilomar International Conference on Climate Intervention Technologies aimed to minimize the risks associated with scientific research on climate intervention or climate geoengineering, and focused on the development of risk reduction guidelines for climate intervention experiments. According to the Oxford Principles, geoengineers agreed on having independent EIA undertaken beforehand, with public participation (Steve Rayner, et al., *The Oxford Principles*, 121 CLIMATIC CHANGE 499 (2013)).

32 RACHEL CARSON, SILENT SPRING 12–13 (First Mariner Books 2002) (1962). Carson (1907–1964) was a writer and a marine biologist with the US Fish and Wildlife Service.

post-materialist values paradigm,[33] and "environmental quality was an integral part of this new search of a higher standard of living".[34] *Silent Spring* caught the attention of the greater public, and raised ampler awareness about chemical pollution and the necessity of environmental protection. Academic contributions were fostered subsequently, and other seminal works resonated profoundly, such as *The Tragedy of the Commons*.[35] Associations began to form, like the World Wildlife Fund (1961), the Environmental Defense Fund (1967), or the Natural Resources Defense Council (1969).[36] In addition, several conspicuous ecological disasters further shifted the attention to the issue of pollution. In January and February 1969, two oil spills five and a half miles off the coast of Santa Barbara (California) coated thirty miles of beaches, and killed thousands of seabirds, fish and other animals. John Whitaker, the principal adviser on environmental issues to President Nixon, believed the oil spill "was comparable to tossing a match into a gasoline tank: it exploded into the environmental revolution, and the press fanned the flame to keep the issue burning brightly".[37]

Actions and associations were at that time focused mainly on separate, specific issues. NEPA addressed this segmented thinking, which is inherently problematic because ecosystems are interconnected, and environmental public policies must be envisaged in a comprehensive manner. NEPA's legislative history underscores this challenge, i.e. citizen groups' strong tendency to focus on a single issue. "Citizens may not always organize themselves to protect an environmental *system*. One group may be interested only in visual pollution, while another is interested in noise, and it is an unfortunate fact of life that

33 RONALD INGLEHART, THE SILENT REVOLUTION – CHANGING VALUES AND POLITICAL STYLES AMONG WESTERN PUBLICS (Princeton University Press. 1977).

34 SAMUEL P. HAYS & BARBARA D. HAYS, BEAUTY, HEALTH, AND PERMANENCE – ENVIRONMENTAL POLITICS IN THE UNITED STATES, 1955–1985 4 (Cambridge University Press. 1987).

35 Garrett Hardin, *The Tragedy of the Commons*, 162 SCIENCE 1243 (1968).

36 The Sierra Club, the oldest, largest and most influential environmental association in the United States, had been founded long before, on 28 May 1892 in San Francisco, by the conservationist and preservationist John Muir. Robert Underwood Johnson had worked with Muir on the successful campaign to create a larger Yosemite National Park. In 1889, Johnson and Muir began thinking of constituting an association for the protection of the Sierra Nevada, which was done eventually with the help of professors from Berkeley and Stanford.

37 JOHN C. WHITAKER, STRIKING A BALANCE: ENVIRONMENT AND NATURAL RESOURCES POLICY IN THE NIXON-FORD YEARS 264 (Berkeley American Enterprise Institute for Public Policy Research. 1976).

the normal resolution of a pollution problem is to push it into another area which may not be so vigorously defended (...) What we need is groups with a *total* environmental concern".[38] Environmental associations did not even participate in the legislative process leading to NEPA. "There was no sense of a unified approach at that time"; there was also a deep distrust of the government, and very few environmental associations knew how to work with government entities then.[39] In addition, fragmented decision-making has been more advantageous to powerful lobbies.[40] Lynton Caldwell was one of the first scholars to argue for harmonizing environmental principles, the tools to implement them, and a holistic view of decision-making, which he integrated into NEPA.[41] Caldwell was an advisor to Senator Henry M. Jackson, and one of the main authors of NEPA, including the staggered addition of EIA under the name of the Environmental Impact Statement (EIS). NEPA's genesis occurred within Congress, in response to a perception of national interest. In the US Senate, the bill for a National Environmental Policy Act was introduced by Henry M. Jackson. Remarkably, Jackson's provision that every citizen had a right to a healthy environment was rejected.[42] NEPA became procedural

38 FRANK M. POTTER, *Progress Means Pollution: An Idea Whose Time Has Come – and Gone*, THE ENVIRONMENTAL DECADE – ACTION PROPOSALS FOR THE 1970'S, 91ST CONGRESS, HR App. 4 342, 344 (1970); also *in* Air pollution – 1970, Part 4. US Senate, Hearings before the Subcommittee on Air and Water Pollution of the Committee on Public Works, 91st Congress, 2nd session on S. 3229, S. 3466 [and] S. 3546, 26 March 1970, page 1199–1200.

39 Lynton K. Caldwell, *An Interview with Lynton Caldwell on the National Environmental Policy Act (NEPA)*, 5 ENVTL. PRAC. 281, 282 (2003).

40 MATTHEW J. LINDSTROM & ZACHARY A. SMITH, THE NATIONAL ENVIRONMENTAL POLICY ACT: JUDICIAL MISCONSTRUCTION, LEGISLATIVE INDIFFERENCE, AND EXECUTIVE NEGLECT 22 (Texas A&M University Press. 2002). This beneficial relationship between interest groups, civil servants, and members of legislative committees has been described as an "iron triangle", regarding each favored program and office. See RANDALL B. RIPLEY & GRACE A. FRANKLIN, CONGRESS, THE BUREAUCRACY, AND PUBLIC POLICY (Brooks/Cole Pub Co 5th ed. 1990) (1976).

41 LINDSTROM & SMITH, 23. 2002. See Lynton Caldwell's 1964 article (unpublished), *Making Environmental Concepts Operational: A Checklist of Criteria for Environmental Planning* (cited *in* LYNTON K. CALDWELL, THE NATIONAL ENVIRONMENTAL POLICY ACT: AN AGENDA FOR THE FUTURE 59–61 (Indiana University Press. 1998)).

42 LINDSTROM & SMITH, 48. 2002. See also diverse suggestions for an amendment to the Constitution for environmental protection *in* Rutherford H. Platt, *Toward Constitutional Recognition of the Environment*, 56 ABAJ 1061 (1970). Debating possibilities of substantial provisions for a healthy environment: Edward F. Roberts, *Right to a Decent Environment; E=MC2 Environment Equals Man Times Courts Redoubling their Efforts*, 55 CORNELL L. REV. 674 (1970).

in nature. "[T]he genius of NEPA lies in its linkage of mandatory procedure to substantive policy criteria and in the pressure it brings upon administrative agencies to consider scientific evidence in their planning and decision-making".[43] A prominent and early advocate of environmentalism, Senator Edmund S. Muskie firmly insisted on the essential role of public participation, in contrast to Jackson, the bill's sponsor, who trusted self-policing by federal agencies. Thanks to Muskie's objections, the EIS requirement was added to the compromise bill.[44] NEPA was crucial because it dealt "with environmental problems on a preventive and an anticipatory basis", a radical departure from a crisis mentality that focused on reclaiming "our resources from past abuses".[45] For all major federal actions, NEPA mandated the introduction of a broad set of environmental goals, institutionalized a uniform action-forcing mechanism to ensure compliance with these ecological goals, required that public participation be part of the decision-making process, and established the Council on Environmental Quality (CEQ) within the Executive Office of the President, charged with developing policies consistent with NEPA's objectives and with the implementation of NEPA.[46] There was no opposition to the bill, because legislators wished to be perceived as pollution fighters in face of the overwhelming wave of public concern.[47] NEPA was "the Sherman Act of environmental law",[48] the first major US environmental law, a national declaration of policy for the protection of the environment, including an action-forcing mechanism, the Environmental Impact Statement (EIS). When NEPA was passed, Richard Nixon proclaimed "the nineteen-seventies absolutely must be the years when America pays its debt to the past by reclaiming the purity of its air, its waters and our living environment. It is literally now or never".[49] Congress' rejection of a formal right to a healthy environment notwithstanding, NEPA was drafted

---

43 LYNTON K. CALDWELL, SCIENCE AND THE NATIONAL ENVIRONMENTAL POLICY ACT: REDIRECTING POLICY THROUGH PROCEDURAL REFORM (University of Alabama Press. 1982).

44 LINDSTROM & SMITH, 45. 2002; Jim Kershner, *NEPA, the National Environmental Policy Act* (2011) at http://www.historylink.org/File/9903 (accessed 17 June 2021).

45 115 CONG. REC. 40,416 (1969) (remarks of Sen. Jackson, the bill's sponsor).

46 LINDSTROM & SMITH, 18. 2002.

47 Caldwell, ENVTL. PRAC., 281 (2003).

48 WILLIAM H. RODGERS, HANDBOOK ON ENVIRONMENTAL LAW 697 (West Publishing. 1977).

49 *Nixon Promises an Urgent Fight to End Pollution – 'Now or Never' Effort*, THE NEW YORK TIMES, 2 January 1970.

in lyrical terms,[50] and declared as "our basic national charter for protection of the environment",[51] a statute in form, a constitution in spirit.[52]

NEPA was the result of compromise and represented a broad consensus.[53] Because no substantive rights could then be obtained despite much hope,[54] progressive advocates settled for procedural protections, which embodied a revolution in values: environmental considerations integrated into economic development, and public participation into decision-making processes. The US Supreme Court confirmed these expectations, finding that NEPA would "inevitably bring pressure to bear on agencies to respond to the needs of environmental quality".[55] By 1973, Richard Nixon had turned away from the environment, reducing the corresponding budgets, but NEPA remained in place and developed in unexpected ways: the cornerstone of NEPA's procedural protections became the environmental impact statement,[56] even though the EIS was added as an afterthought and to reach a compromise.

---

50 As reflected by the Oxford Dictionary of American Legal Quotations, which includes nine entries under "Environmental Law", three of which are quotations from NEPA, the only environmental statute to be included (FRED R. SHAPIRO, THE OXFORD DICTIONARY OF AMERICAN LEGAL QUOTATIONS 123–124 (Oxford University Press. 1993)).

51 40 CFR 1500.1 Purpose (a).

52 "A statement of environmental policy is more than a statement of what we believe as a people and as a Nation. It establishes priorities and gives expression to our national goals and aspirations; it serves a constitutional function in that people may refer to it for guidance in making decisions where environmental values are found to be in conflict with other values" (115 Cong. Rec. S7815 (daily ed. 10 July 1969)), cited in (along with a detailed review of NEPA's legislative history): Eva H. Hanks & John L. Hanks, *An Environmental Bill of Rights: The Citizen Suit and the National Environmental Policy Act of 1969*, 24 RUTGERS L. REV. 230, 245 (1970). Painting NEPA as "the centerpiece of US environmental law", see Michael C. Blumm, *A Primer on Environmental Law and Some Directions for the Future*, 11 VA. ENVTL. L.J. 381, 382 (1992). Depicting NEPA as "the most important environmental legislation" (but rather critical otherwise), see Arthur W. Murphy, *The National Environmental Policy Act and the Licensing Process: Environmentalist Magna Carta or Agency Coup de Grace?* 72 COLUM. L. REV. 963, 965 (1972).

53 Nevertheless, tactical ability was still preferred to pass the bill with no further amendment in the Senate, by having it voted on during the morning hour, a period reserved for routine matters (LINDSTROM & SMITH, 40. 2002.).

54 *Ely v. Velde*, 451 F.2d 1130, 1139 (4th Cir. 1971) (refusing argument that the Constitution guarantees a habitable environment). See also *Tanner v. Armco Steel Corp.*, 340 F. Supp. 532, 535 (SD Tex. 1972); *Environmental Defense Fund v. Corps of Eng'rs*, 325 F. Supp. 728, 739 (ED Ark. 1971), aff'd, 470 F.2d 289 (8th Cir. 1972), cert. denied, 412 US 931 (1973).

55 *Robertson v. Methow Valley Citizens Council*, 490 US 332, 349 (1989) (citing 115 Cong. Rec. 30, 40425 (1969) (remarks of Sen. Muskie)).

56 *Young v. GSA*, 99 F.Supp. 2d 59, 67 (DDC 2000).

3.2 *On the International Plane*

Interestingly, the only thing Lynton Caldwell would have done differently is a more specific formulation for overseas applications of NEPA.[57] With regard to international relations, in 1928, Max Huber, the sole arbitrator of the *Island of Palmas* case, had stated that the exclusive right to territorial sovereignty "has corollary a duty: the obligation to protect within the territory the rights of other states, in particular their right to integrity and inviolability in peace and in war".[58] In 1941, in the *Trail Smelter* case, the tribunal found "that under the principles of international law, as well as the law of the United States, no state has the right to use or permit the use of its territory in such a manner as to cause injury by fumes in or to the territory of another or the properties or persons therein, when the case is of serious consequence and the injury is established by clear and convincing evidence".[59] This major environmental case established some fundamental principles in international environmental law, which were later to be proclaimed in the Stockholm and Rio Declarations,[60] and reaffirmed by the International Court of Justice.[61] If the activities of a country negatively impact the territory of a neighboring state, they must cease and compensation is due, a principle which can be traced back to Roman law (*sic utere tuo ut alienum non laedas*). However, in our global, interconnected world, where every activity has far-reaching consequences, how do we implement this principle? The difficulties and risks of taking projects of a hazardous activity to an international tribunal in an anticipatory manner must be carefully ascertained.[62] To enjoin a state in advance, and particularly a state that

---

57 "So much depends on who is in power and how they want to interpret it. The only difference I would have made, given today's climate, is with regard to overseas applications – more specific policy covering what American corporations and the military can do overseas, for example. These are areas where the State Department and Defense Department tend to drag their feet." (Caldwell, ENVTL. PRAC., 283 (2003)).

58 *US v. Neth.*, 2 RIAA 829, 839 (1928).

59 *Trail Smelter Arbitration* (US v. Can.) 3 RIAA 1911 (1938), 35 AM. J. INT'L L. 684, 716 (1941).

60 Principle 21 of the Declaration of the United Nations Conference on the Human Environment, 16 June 1972, UN Doc. A/Conf.48/14/Rev.1, 11 ILM 1416 (1972) (the Stockholm Declaration). Principle 2 of the Rio Declaration on Environment and Development, 14 June 1992, UN Doc. A/CONF.151/26 (vol. I), 31 ILM 874 (1992), where the word "developmental" was added to the previous formulation of the Stockholm declaration.

61 *Legality of the Threat or Use of Nuclear Weapons*, Advisory Opinion, ICJ Reports 1996 226, at para. 29, p. 242 (8 July). Re-affirmed in *Gabčíkovo-Nagymaros Project (Hungary / Slovakia)*, Judgment, 1997 ICJ Reports 7, at para. 53 (25 September).

62 See for a recently successful instance: *Aerial Herbicide Spraying (Ecuador v. Colombia)*, Order, 2013 ICJ Reports 278 (13 September), and the analysis of Alan Boyle, *Transboundary air pollution: a tale of two paradigms*, *in* TRANSBOUNDARY POLLUTION – EVOLVING

has a different political regime, might be counterproductive to the international system. Lawsuits are not the optimal solution. In 1991, the ILC Draft Code of Crimes against the Peace and Security of Mankind, as provisionally adopted, encompassed environmental offences (for universal jurisdiction), but they disappeared from the final ILC Draft Code adopted in 1996.[63] Consequently, international agreements in environmental law have mainly rested on consultation and negotiation requirements, of a soft law nature (weak compliance and liability mechanisms), as set out as early as the mid-20th century, in the pioneering *Lake Lanoux* case:

> consideration must be given to all interests, whatever their nature, which may be affected by the works undertaken even if they do not amount to a right. (…) The second question is to determine the procedure whereby these interests can be safeguarded. Although this procedure necessarily involves negotiations, it cannot be reduced to purely formal requirements, such as taking note of complaints, protests, or expressions of regret submitted by the lower riparian state. The tribunal considers that the upper riparian state, under the rules of good faith, has an obligation to take into consideration the various interests concerned, to seek to give them every satisfaction compatible with the pursuit of its own interest and to show that it has, in this matter, a real desire to reconcile the interests of the other riparian with its own.[64]

In the words of Francisco de Vitoria, the protection of the environment is by definition a common good for the whole world (*bonum commune totius orbis*). On the international plane, the current protection of common interests has partly taken the form of EIA, which arose in particular from the due diligence principle. EIA is a preventive and collaborative tool. The obligation of due

---

ISSUES OF INTERNATIONAL LAW AND POLICY (S. Jayakumar, et al. eds., 2015). Boyle was counsel for Ecuador.

63 Draft Code of Crimes against the Peace and Security of Mankind, *in* Report of the International Law Commission, forty-third session, UN GAOR, 46th Sess., Supp. No. 10, UN Doc. A/46/10 (1991). The Draft Code begins on page 79. See Article 26 – *Willful and Severe Damage to the Environment* (page 107). Draft Code of Crimes against the Peace and Security of Mankind, *in* Report of the International Law Commission, forty-eighth session, UN GAOR, 51st Sess., Supp. No. 10 at 9, UN Doc. A/51/10 (1996).

64 *Lac Lanoux Arbitration* (France v. Spain), para. 22 (16 Nov. 1957), 24 ILR 101, 12 RIAA 281, translated in English *in* 1974 Y.B. INT'L L. COMM'N, VOL. II, PT. II, 194–9. See also the case of the *Land Reclamation in and around the Straits of Johor* (Malaysia v. Singapore), Provisional Measures, Order of 8 October 2003, ITLOS Reports 2003, p. 10.

diligence includes preventive and minimization measures as the appropriate standard for the conduct of states,[65] which requires notification and consultation. In fulfilling their due diligence duty, states must base their project permits on EIAs.[66] Due diligence obligations have been proceduralized. Since the global emergence of ecological awareness in the 1970's, it has been widely repeated that comprehensive and objective assessments as well as monitoring are key to environmental protection and sustainable development.

Before states engage in potentially harmful activities, acceptable levels of risks must be determined. This determination is context-dependent. Consequently, a state must properly study the environmental impact of its project, including the interests of the affected populations. Both in the domestic and transboundary contexts, EIA is purely informative in nature, because each decision is complex and unique; competing interests are best addressed and resolved through good faith consultation. The multiplication of national EIA requirements has applied pressure to adopt an international instrument, and integrate transboundary impacts and actors in the decision-making process. As a result, the main environmental management procedure for transboundary impacts is governed by the 1991 Espoo Convention,[67] which applies to forty-five parties (as of 2021), all UNECE members. Since 2014, non-UNECE countries can become parties to the convention.[68]

If there were no EIA requirement, i.e. if there were no compulsory procedure to ensure that the relevant information be produced in comprehensive and intelligible ways, the duty to notify and consult with other states and all affected populations would be rather futile, for lack of adequate, readily available, widely understandable and useful information. For this reason, even when an EIA is not specifically prescribed, some consider that it is an obligation nonetheless, because EIAs are indispensable to fulfill general obligations like the duty to inform and due diligence.[69] Hence, the best policy is to adhere

65 ILC Commentary on the Draft Articles on Prevention of Transboundary Harm from Hazardous Activities, para. (7) under Article 3 (p. 391–392), *in* Report of the International Law Commission, fifty-third session, UN GAOR, 56th Sess., Supp. No. 10 at 370, UN Doc. A/56/10 (2001) (hereinafter the 2001 Draft Articles on Transboundary Harm).

66 The Espoo Convention; Article 7 of the 2001 ILC Draft Articles on Transboundary Harm.

67 Convention on Environmental Impact Assessment in a Transboundary Context (Espoo) 25 February 1991, 30 ILM 802 (1991), in force 10 September 1997 (hereinafter the Espoo Convention).

68 See *infra* chapter 2, page 48 et seq., and notes 105, 106.

69 International Law Association, Report of the Sixtieth Conference held at Montreal in 1982, p. 174, Para. 12, Dietrich Rauschning, rapporteur on the legal aspects of the conservation of the environment.

to principles of notification and consultation. This part of international law has made major strides, but much remains to be accomplished. "[T]o say that a state has no right to injure the environment of another seems quixotic in the face of the great variety of transborder environmental harms that occur every day".[70]

4 EIA Reception and Appraisal

EIAs have been the object of significant praise, domestically and internationally. "NEPA uniquely provided openness in decision-making, calling for collaboration and a holistic approach, and provided an overarching statement about the need to address the environment. (…) The beauty of NEPA is its breadth".[71]

4.1 *Assessment of EIA Efficiency*

> *The notion of effectiveness as some sort of absolute measure is untenable* [72]

In a 2004 survey of staff from the US Department of Defense, the Department of the Interior, and the Forest Service, most respondents felt that NEPA added value to a project.[73] In the eyes of many, EIAs resulted in reaching better decisions. They have been presented as one of the most successful policy

70 Oscar Schachter, *The Emergence of International Environmental Law*, 44 J. INT'L AFF. 457, 463 (1991). This statement still rings true today.

71 Nancy Sutley, Chairperson of the Council on Environmental Quality (from 2009 to 2014), *in* Noelle Straub, *CEQ chief urges agencies to take fresh approach to NEPA*, THE NEW YORK TIMES, 23 March 2009. At the outset, NEPA's impact was enhanced beyond initial expectations (Daniel A. Dreyfus & Helen M. Ingram, *The National Environmental Policy Act: A View of Intent and Practice*, 16 NAT. RESOURCES J. 243, 243 (1976)).

72 Matthew Cashmore, et al., *Introduction: The effectiveness of impact assessment instruments*, 27 IMPACT ASSESSMENT AND PROJECT APPRAISAL 91, 93 (2009).

73 *Fast Tracking NEPA Documents – Tools to Overcome Schedule Delays*, available at https://ndiastorage.blob.core.usgovcloudapi.net/ndia/2004/enviro/sessions/session9/king2.ppt, accessed 17 June 2021. The survey was conducted by Tetra Tech, Inc., for presentation at the 30th NDIA Environmental Energy Symposium and Exhibition. See also LINDA LUTHER, CRS REPORT FOR CONGRESS – THE NATIONAL ENVIRONMENTAL POLICY ACT: BACKGROUND AND IMPLEMENTATION 30 (2007); SERGE TAYLOR, MAKING BUREAUCRACIES THINK – THE ENVIRONMENTAL IMPACT STATEMENT STRATEGY OF ADMINISTRATIVE REFORM (Stanford University Press. 1984), who had previously observed how rapidly NEPA had had a significant effect on the decisions made by the Corps of Engineers and the Forest Service.

innovations of the 20th century, widely and rapidly adopted.[74] EIAs are said to bring the best expertise to the decision-making process, especially from those who are directly concerned.[75] NEPA has fundamentally changed the capacity of influence of participants in environmental policy-making. Since the beginning, there have been hopes of incremental changes based in particular on a select group of individuals trained in environmental analysis that permeated the agencies, allowing for heightened environmental value in agency decision-making.[76] More generally, praise and hope are based on the dynamic, informative, and educative process induced by EIA. Even when studies are pessimistic about EIA outcomes, they usually end on a hopeful and optimistic note, often because of this longer-term benefit. Although the importance of EIA has not been disputed, serious criticism has surfaced since the outset of EIA. A recurrent critique, especially in times of economic and financial crisis, can be readily addressed: the cost of EIA.[77] Strong opposition to EIA legislation at the beginning ("the procedure is too costly and too long") has continued unabated to the present day.[78] These critiques usually significantly underestimate the costs of environmental damage incurred because of hasty and ill-informed decisions. Be that as it may, procedures could undeniably be improved in terms of cost-efficiency, as the case studies displayed in this book will show.

---

74 SADLER, 1 & 24. 1996.

75 EPA, Final Guidance For Incorporating Environmental Justice Concerns *in* EPA's NEPA Compliance Analyses, Chap. 4 (US Environmental Protection Agency. 1998); Luke W. Cole, *Legal Services, Public Participation, and Environmental Justice*, 29 CLEARINGHOUSE REV. 449, 454 (1995), describing inhabitants as "home-grown experts".

76 "Because NEPA was not designed to control specific kinds or sources of pollution, its benefit to society is difficult to quantify. The act was designed primarily to institutionalize in the federal government an anticipatory concern for the quality of the human environment, that is, an attitude, a heightened state of environmental awareness that, unlike pollution abatement, is measurable only subjectively and qualitatively" (Council on Environmental Quality: The Twentieth Annual Report of the Council on Environmental Quality Together with the President's Message to Congress 15 (CEQ. 1990)).

77 In the US, in the mid-1990's, the median cost of an EIS was US$ 2.7 million (over sixteen EISS) *in* NATIONAL ACADEMY OF PUBLIC ADMINISTRATION, MANAGING NEPA AT THE DEPARTMENT OF ENERGY, at Point IV C. (DOE. 1998), available at https://energy.gov/nepa/downloads/managing-nepa-department-energy-0 (accessed 17 June 2021). In 2013, the median cost was US$ 1.7 million (but only over four EISS) *in* UNITED STATES GOVERNMENT ACCOUNTABILITY OFFICE, NATIONAL ENVIRONMENTAL POLICY ACT – LITTLE INFORMATION EXISTS ON NEPA ANALYSES 12 § GAO-14-369 (GAO. 2014).

78 See for instance the position of the United Kingdom about the EIA directive *in No Environmental Assessment?* 7 ENVIRONMENTAL POLICY AND LAW 20 (1981). See also David Annandale & Ross Taplin, *Is environmental impact assessment regulation a 'burden' to private firms?* 23 ENVIRON. IMPACT ASSESS. REV. 383 (2003).

More broadly, while EIAs are commonly viewed as an improvement in terms of scrutiny and inclusion of environmental concerns in decision-making processes, their accomplishments may appear especially commendatory with regard to past negligence and failures. However, their benefits could still be enhanced with regard to present sustainable development objectives. Decision-making is by definition characterized by a choice between several possibilities. Consequently, alternatives are naturally at the core of the EIA procedure, but there appear to be grave deficiencies in identifying and presenting all the available options. "The focus on EIA documentation and the consent decision is said to create a perception that EIA is simply a bureaucratic, perfunctory step in obtaining development consent".[79] The priority has often been that the EIA be done rather than anything being done by it.[80] Decades after its first adoption, some critics described the "state-of-the-art" EIA as an uneven blend of planning theory, traditional scientific theory, discipline-specific social, economic and biological theories, evaluation theories and procedures, public policy and organizational theories, with the conceptual whole amounting to decidedly less than the sum of all its parts.[81] Furthermore, because of their lack of substantive requirements, EIA regulations have been criticized as suffering from their emphasis on procedure. Some have pessimistically asserted that Senator Muskie's concerns about a toothless NEPA (or any EIA legislation for that matter) were still viable today, in that "as long as an agency complies with the EIS procedural requirements in NEPA, final decisions on whether to proceed with the proposed action are left up to the agency".[82]

Confronted with these critiques, can EIA effectiveness be assessed? The task is elusive. The effectiveness of EIAs has always been difficult to evaluate.[83] For

79 Matthew Cashmore, *The role of science in environmental impact assessment: process and procedure versus purpose in the development of theory*, 24 ENVIRONMENTAL IMPACT ASSESSMENT REVIEW 403, 410 (2004).

80 Geoffrey T. McDonald, *Going beyond environmental impact assessment: Environmental input to planning and design*, 15 ENVIRON. IMPACT ASSESS. REV. 483, 485 (1995); A. L. Brown & R. C. Hill, *Decision-scoping: making EA learn how the design process works*, 10 PROJECT APPRAISAL 223, 224 (1995).

81 David P. Lawrence, *The need for EIA theory-building*, 17 ENVIRON. IMPACT ASSES. REV. 79, 79–80 (1997).

82 LINDSTROM & SMITH, 46. 2002.

83 SADLER, 40,45. 1996; Matthew Cashmore, et al., *The interminable issue of effectiveness: substantive purposes, outcomes and research challenges in the advancement of environmental impact assessment theory*, 22 IMPACT ASSESS. PROJ. APPRAIS. 295 (2004). About the difficulties to assess the efficiency of public participation: Nicolas Ulibarri, et al., *How does stakeholder involvement affect environmental impact assessment?* 79 ENVIRON. IMPACT ASSESS. REV. 106309 (2019).

instance, the average duration of an EIA is documented only with difficulty.[84] Often, it is plainly acknowledged that determining the effectiveness of NEPA, for example, is arduous,[85] if not impossible. Far from such a clear assertion, other studies have ambiguously concluded that there was no obvious trend in the number or significance of the modifications that were brought to the projects under consideration.[86] While EIAs have been in use for fifty years, their effectiveness in the global sphere has only recently become the focus of social science research, and the very possibility of their evaluation is still questioned or, again, emphasized as extremely difficult. Even a significant undertaking like the Global Environmental Assessment Project (GEA) began by underlining the related hurdles.[87] If any influence is detected, no clear conclusion is drawn.[88] There seems to be little empirical evidence of EIAs' efficiency, probably due to the fact that the focus of inquiry has not been broad enough.

4.2 *EIAs are Procedural in Nature, with Public Participation at Their Core*

> *Starting from the premise that law should serve human beings, the New Haven School anchors its policy-oriented search for a world public order of human dignity in the universe of human aspirations* [89]

When critics of EIAs underline a lack of clear evidence of effectiveness or of substantive requirements, they tend to ignore the real intent of EIA legislations, which reach far beyond the dichotomy of procedure v. substance. Decision-making is a complex process, the result of a fine balance between competing interests, which is best left to the political realm. In addition to

---

84 There is very little data available on EIA timelines, which makes it easier for critics of the EIA process to claim that EIAs are both lengthy and costly (Garry Middle & Isaac Middle, *Professional Practice – The inefficiency of environmental impact assessment: reality or myth?* 28(2) IMPACT ASSESS. PROJ. APPRAIS. 159, 160, 163 (2010)).

85 JAMES RASBAND, et al., NATURAL RESOURCES – LAW AND POLICY 282 (2009).

86 Adam Barker & Christopher Wood, *An Evaluation of EIA System Performance in Eight EU Countries*, 19 ENVIRONMENTAL IMPACT ASSESSMENT REVIEW 387 (1999).

87 ASSESSMENTS OF REGIONAL AND GLOBAL ENVIRONMENTAL RISKS – DESIGNING PROCESSES FOR THE EFFECTIVE USE OF SCIENCE IN DECISIONMAKING (Alexander E. Farrell & Jill Jäger eds., 2006). GLOBAL ENVIRONMENTAL ASSESSMENTS – INFORMATION AND INFLUENCE (Ronald B. Mitchell, et al. eds., 2006).

88 SADLER, 52. 1996.

89 W. Michael Reisman, et al., *The New Haven School: A Brief Introduction*, 32 YALE J.INT'L L. 575, 579–580 (2007).

specific, measurable direct effects, effectiveness should be defined in terms of the relevant parties' mutual increase in understanding and knowledge.[90] As a result, consultation and participation are an integral, indispensable part of the EIA process, in the broader context of democratic legitimacy.[91] Thanks to the opportunities that they formally provide, EIA requirements impose, facilitate, and nurture the empowerment and participation of individuals and civic groups in the legal process, as defined by the New Haven School – a communication process. For "the EIA process operates in an open-ended, decision-making context. It is taken forward and influenced by the actions of numerous participants. The outcomes of the process are not always clear or apparent. In these circumstances, cause-effect relationships cannot be easily measured or quantified; and often, proponents and opponents of EIA differently interpret the utility of the process".[92] EIA requirements are intrinsically designed to enable a wider participation in public policy choices in the complex domain of sustainable development. "Questions of influence and effectiveness can [then] also be approached via a focus on the various networks created through scenario development processes",[93] as we will see in the following chapters with the case studies. The New Haven School emphasizes that law is not a fixed set of traditional rules, but a continuous and dynamic process of authoritative decisions, in which a wide array of actors participate.[94] EIA is an informational tool that can contribute to enabling widespread civic empowerment.

Public participation and the inclusion of public values into environmental impact studies are considered to be two of the main functions of EIA, and a source of their worldwide appeal.[95] What constitutes public participation

---

90 Arja Huttunen, *The effectiveness of public participation in the environmental impact assessment process – a case study of the projected Sierilä hydropower station at Oikarainen, northern Finland*, 16:2 ACTA BOREALIA: A NORDIC JOURNAL OF CIRCUMPOLAR SOCIETIES 27, 37 (1999).

91 James P. Boggs, *Procedural vs. Substantive in NEPA Law: Cutting the Gordian Knot*, 15 THE ENVIRONMENTAL PROFESSIONAL 25 (1993); NEIL CRAIK, THE INTERNATIONAL LAW OF ENVIRONMENTAL IMPACT ASSESSMENT, PROCESS, SUBSTANCE AND INTEGRATION 35–36 (Cambridge University Press. 2008).

92 SADLER, 38. 1996.

93 Simone Pulver & Stacy D. VanDeveer, *"Thinking about Tomorrows": Scenarios, Global Environmental, Politics, and Social Science Scholarship*, 9 GLOBAL ENVIRONMENTAL POLITICS 1, 10 (2009).

94 Reisman, et al., YALE J.INT'L L., 578 (2007); W. Michael Reisman, *1995 Siebenthaler Lecture – A Jurisprudence from the Perspective of the "Political Superior"*, 23 N. KY. L. REV. 605 (1995).

95 Judith Petts, *Public Participation and Environmental Impact Assessment, in* HANDBOOK OF ENVIRONMENTAL IMPACT ASSESSMENT 145–146, 152, 170, (Judith Petts ed. 1999);

has been the subject of some debate. For the purposes of this book, however, I understand public participation as "any form of interaction between government and corporate actors and the public that occurs as part of EIA processes".[96] EIA and its associated learning process is one of the most important and useful tools in empowering local communities, including their disadvantaged or marginalized members, to exercise increased control over their region, environment, and future development. The numerous advantages of public participation and its virtuous cycle have long been recognized. Information sharing, consultations, transparency, accountability, collective involvement, access to local knowledge, identification of all the possible alternatives, and legitimacy of the decision ... all tend to avert costly and lengthy litigation, promoting broadly-based individual and social learning, enabling the transition to sustainability, bolstering the democratic foundations of society. The concept of social and organizational learning is a dynamic process. EIA is a process aimed at a projection of risks and changes, the study of alternatives, to ensure that decision makers are truly considering all possibilities, a project-level decision instrument, often carried out amidst political and public controversy. EIAs are employed to publicly back, object to, or mitigate potentially or overtly contentious projects. They aim at better-informed decisions, which then have the potential to be widely accepted.

Limited resources and time constraints are the inescapable reality of EIAs.[97] In the domain of project development, and contrary to common conceptions of scientific research on which EIAs rely, predictions of potential impacts must be made, alternatives must be compared, a decision must be taken. EIA is at the crossroads between science and public values, generating civic science.[98]

Rob Sippe, *Criteria and Standards for Assessing Significant Impact*, *in* HANDBOOK OF ENVIRONMENTAL IMPACT ASSESSMENT 74–92 (Judith Petts ed. 1999).

96 Ciaran O'Faircheallaigh, *Public participation and environmental impact assessment: Purposes, implications, and lessons for public policy making*, 30 ENVIRONMENTAL IMPACT ASSESSMENT REVIEW 19, 20 (2010). See also Barry Barton, *Underlying Concepts and Theoretical Issues in Public Participation in Resources Development*, *in* HUMAN RIGHTS IN NATURAL RESOURCE DEVELOPMENT: PUBLIC PARTICIPATION IN THE SUSTAINABLE DEVELOPMENT OF MINING AND ENERGY RESOURCES 78 (Donald M. Zillman, et al. eds., 2002).

97 "Environmental impact assessments (EIAs) are produced for use in the real world", Robert B. Beattie, *Everything you already know about EIA (But don't often admit)*, 15 ENVIRON. IMPACT ASSESS. REV. 109, 109 (1995). See also William Dickerson & Joseph Montgomery, *Substantive Scientific and Technical Guidance for NEPA Analysis: Pitfalls in the Real World*, 15 THE ENVIRONMENTAL PROFESSIONAL 7, 7 (1993).

98 "The notion of civic science serves as an umbrella for various attempts to increase public participation in the production and use of scientific knowledge (...) Civic science hosts many ambitions, such as enhancing public understanding of science, increasing citizen

EIA has continued to flourish because it is adaptable and "can accommodate diverse biophysical, socio-economic and geopolitical realities".[99] Their flexibility is an ideal feature that allows them to adapt to the singularity of each project, and to include different fields of analysis (scientific, socio-economic, geopolitical ...). This flexibility of procedural requirements is essential, confronted as we are with ever-new problems in a world in constant evolution. Wrapped in an undeserved mantle of supposed objectivity, EIAs are in truth advocacy documents.[100] They can be seen as a scenario, knowledge production processes, as "boundary objects" that link different, but intersecting social worlds;[101] in other words, as "spheres of 'co-production,' where knowledge and social order are produced simultaneously".[102] Consequently, there have been high hopes about the Espoo Convention, seen as instrumental in shifting decision-making from central governments to a transnational EIA system.[103] The Espoo Convention has created new possibilities for transnational issues to be voiced. In lieu of a clash between the political identity of nation-states, rather, dispersed interest groups and governmental authorities may confront their value choices beyond national interests. Instances of this phenomenon are illustrated by the following case studies.[104] "[T]here is a movement that expands public participation beyond political boundaries, such that procedural rights of individuals become internationally promoted to the point of establishing participation rights in the hands of *ex juris* individuals".[105] Confronted with the subjective

---

participation, diversifying representation in, and promoting democratization of science" (Karin Bäckstrand, *Civic Science for Sustainability: Reframing the Role of Experts, Policy-Makers and Citizens in Environmental Governance*, 3 GLOB. ENVIRON. POLIT. 24, 24–25 (2003)).

99 Cashmore, ENVIRONMENTAL IMPACT ASSESSMENT REVIEW, 406 (2004).

100 Beattie, ENVIRON. IMPACT ASSESS. REV., 113 (1995).

101 Susan Leigh Star & James R. Griesemer, *Institutional Ecology, 'Translations' and Boundary Objects: Amateurs and Professionals in Berkeley's Museum of Vertebrate Zoology*, 1907–39, 19 SOC. STUD. SCI. 387 (1989). As boundary objects, they are "both plastic enough to adapt to local needs and the constraints of the several parties employing them, yet robust enough to maintain a common identity across sites. They are weakly structured in common use, and become strongly structured in individualistic use" (id. at 393).

102 Pulver & VanDeveer, *supra* note 93 at 9. See also BRUNO LATOUR, SCIENCE IN ACTION – HOW TO FOLLOW SCIENTISTS AND ENGINEERS THROUGH SOCIETY (Harvard University Press. 1987).

103 Timo Koivurova, *The Transnational EIA Procedure of the Espoo Convention*, 8 FINNISH Y.B. INT'L L. 161, 198 (1997).

104 See *infra* chapters 4–6. With respect to the Vuotos case, see also Koivurova, FINNISH Y.B. INT'L L., 198–199 (1997).

105 William A. Tilleman, *Public Participation in the Environmental Impact Assessment Process: A Comparative Study of Impact Assessment in Canada, The United States, and the European Community*, 33 COLUM. J. TRANSNAT'L L. 337, 421 (1995).

nature of development planning, the main concern with EIA is to ensure scientific accuracy and public participation, striking a balance when integrating value judgments into an information provision model. However, much of the time, regulations and practice instead separate the two by requiring consultations only after the final EIA report, as we will see in the following chapters. This distinction runs contrary to the nature of EIA: in addition to the inevitable biases of the diverse participants, there is an inherent and fundamental scientific uncertainty, which is itself worsened by the EIA constraints in terms of time and budget; in other words, "mandated science cannot be value-free and univocal".[106] Consequently, no legitimate reason warrants excluding public participation from the very beginning of the EIA process, quite the contrary.

5 Overview of the Book

Lynton Caldwell forewarned in clear terms: "I do not underestimate the scientific and technical difficulties that may be encountered in impact analysis and assessment. But I continue to believe that the greater problem in the effective use of this procedure is in the opinions of people regarding how decisions should be made and what values should receive priority".[107]

Even in relatively recent research about EIA, conclusions have been drawn in terms of expectancy: "EIA processes create a decision-making environment that *will* promote outcomes that are based on accepted principles, and not solely on an aggregation of interests", with a parallel acknowledgement that political sensitivities hinder the achievement of acceptable solutions.[108] Out of the five main problematic issues identified in 1996, all five of them seem to still remain current as of today.[109] Should we dismiss EIA provisions as "paper tigers", or do they have a significant, determinative role in environmental protection and international law-making?

With this in mind, I have undertaken three case studies, all related to infrastructure in the energy field, as well as in the transportation domain

106 Brenda Lee, et al., *Values and Science in Impact Assessment*, 23 ENVIRONMENTS 93 (1995). See also Brian Wynne, *Uncertainty and environmental learning – Reconceiving science and policy in the preventive paradigm*, 2 GLOB. ENVIRON. CHANGE 111 (1992).

107 Caldwell, IMPACT ASSESSMENT, 86 (1991).

108 CRAIK, 203. 2008. (emphasis added).

109 SADLER, 41. 1996. This report listed to what an EIA should apply (screening phase), how it should be undertaken, what it should address (scoping phase), result in, and provide the basis for.

with respect to the last one. The first case study narrates a large dam/reservoir project for hydropower purposes in Finland, the birthplace of the Espoo Convention, with impacts on Swedish waters. The second describes an extra-high voltage power line project between France and Spain, as part of the development of the European power grid. The third case study tells the too little-known story of the Upper Mekong Navigation Improvement Project (UMNIP), which attempted to transform the tumultuous Mekong River into a large navigation canal between China and Thailand, through Myanmar and Laos, in parallel with the development of hydropower on the same river and its tributaries.

Today, EIA provisions are highly praised as being at the core of the international legal response to ensure environmental protection. Their salient features characterize the evolution of public international law; they are soft law provisions of a preventive and procedural nature, involving public participation, aimed at achieving a common interest. Contrary to those who argue that substantial requirements are needed to supplement the EIA procedure, my hypothesis is that procedure leads to substantial achievements in international environmental law. This book has two related objectives: to study whether the role of procedure in secreting substantive law may be fulfilled in the idiosyncratic legal system of public international law, while appraising how EIA requirements have been conceived and have been implemented as regards encouraging all international actors to behave in an environmentally conscious way, in a world of heterogeneous political regimes.

CHAPTER 2

Sources and Structure of International Environmental Impact Assessment Prescriptions

> *What must exist in order for us to speak of a legal system is not a formal enforcer but an expectation accompanying a belief that there is a "right" way to act, that someone, possibly even the injured party, may properly respond, in ways that might otherwise be improper, to infractions of that expectation. It is this factor that helps sustain the norm. The durability of norms through time is what makes law, including microlaw, significant in our lives.* [1]

In its first part, this chapter surveys the evolution of the sources of international Environmental Impact Assessment (EIA) provisions as a matter of positive law. The second part of the chapter is an overview of the common structure presented by EIA prescriptions.

1 Sources of International EIA Prescriptions

According to the Convention on Environmental Impact Assessment in a Transboundary Context (hereinafter the Espoo Convention), EIA is a *national* procedure for evaluating the likely impact of a proposed activity on the environment.[2] EIA-related international agreements have usually referred to domestic provisions for detailed requirements. The harmonization of these

---

1 W. MICHAEL REISMAN, LAW IN BRIEF ENCOUNTERS 13 (Yale University Press. 1999). See also Daniel Bodansky, *Prologue to a Theory of Non-Treaty Norms*, *in* LOOKING TO THE FUTURE – ESSAYS IN INTERNATIONAL LAW IN HONOR OF W. MICHAEL REISMAN (Mahnoush H. Arsanjani, et al. eds., 2011); CRAIK, 88. 2008.

2 Convention on Environmental Impact Assessment in a Transboundary Context (Espoo) Article 1(vi), 25 February 1991, 30 ILM 802 (1991), in force 10 September 1997.

 | DOI:10.1163/9789004467583_003

requirements at the international level is still in process.[3] Another notable characteristic of EIA provisions is their reciprocal influence. Lastly and most importantly, it is essential to bear in mind the role and the contribution of this vast set of EIA norms to the law-making process: as the three case studies will show in chapters 4 to 6, they have generated community expectations of what has become the appropriate behavior and the procedure to follow in project development.

Sovereign states have been reluctant to regulate the assessment of transboundary impacts of their activities by way of multilateral treaties, for instance in the case of non-navigational uses of freshwater resources. Historically, the 1923 Convention on Hydraulic Power stands as an exception.[4] The convention recognized the sovereign right to develop natural resources (Article 1), but affirmed that states shall consult with each other, and try to reach an agreement if there were some potential transboundary impacts (Articles 2 and 4). It emphasized the necessity of studying the impacts of development projects, and the need to reach agreements purely on a scientific and technical basis.[5] The convention was also groundbreaking in that it even included the necessity of taking into account cumulative impacts (Article 2, Para. 1), a provision which has often been a debated requisite otherwise, to this day. However, none of the parties to the convention were neighboring states with a common

3 About the necessity of the development and the effective implementation of international environmental law faced as we are with "a considerable number and variety of principles and rules with different degrees of legal value", see the Institute of International Law (IIL), Resolution on Procedures for the Adoption and Implementation of Rules in the Field of Environment, Strasbourg Session, 4 September 1997 (Eighth Commission, Rapporteur: Felipe Paolillo).

4 Convention relating to the Development of Hydraulic Power affecting more than one State (Geneva) 9 December 1923 (League of Nations Treaty Series, Vol. 36. Geneva, UN Publications, page 77), in force 30 June 1925, signed by seventeen states: Austria, Belgium, The British Empire (with New Zealand), Bulgaria, Chile, Denmark, The Free City of Danzig, France, Greece, Hungary, Italy, Lithuania, Poland, Kingdom of the Serbs, Croats and Slovenes, Siam, and Uruguay, but ratified by ten only. Adopted by the International Law Association (ILA) at its fifty-second conference, held in Helsinki in August 1966 (Report of the Committee on the Uses of the Waters of International Rivers (London, International Law Association, 1967). See GEORGES SAUSER-HALL, L'UTILISATION INDUSTRIELLE DES FLEUVES INTERNATIONAUX 536–538, Recueil des cours / Collected Courses, Volume 83 (Hague Academy of International Law. 1953).

5 Article 5: "The technical methods adopted in the agreements referred to in the foregoing articles shall, within the limits of the national legislation of the various countries, be based exclusively upon considerations which might legitimately be taken into account in analogous cases of development of hydraulic power affecting only one State, without reference to any political frontier".

interest in shared water resources. Hence, the convention was never applied. Nevertheless, it served as a model for the 1933 Montevideo Declaration, about which Mexico made a general reservation, and to which the United States refrained from giving approval,[6] but which served in turn as a model for later related agreements in South America.[7]

EIA was first introduced in the United States, by the National Environmental Policy Act (NEPA), enacted by Congress in December 1969 and signed into law by President Richard M. Nixon on 1 January 1970.[8] Public concern about environmental degradation had been steadily growing, notably fueled by works like Rachel Carson's seminal book, *Silent Spring* (published in 1962), which challenged the indifference of the scientific community of the day. "In comprehending the importance of environmental degradation, the public was the path breaker – generally ahead of Congress, and far ahead of the White House".[9] EIA spread rapidly to the international sphere and to other domestic legislation. According to the latest survey (published in 2019), 183 jurisdictions out of 197 are endowed with the EIA norm,[10] often combined with international, regional or bilateral agreements. Over fifty years, since NEPA, EIA has been steadily and universally acknowledged as one of the main environmental protection mechanisms.

6 Declaration concerning the Industrial and Agricultural Use of International Rivers, Seventh Conference of American States, Resolution LXXII (Montevideo, 24 December 1933), *in* DANTE A. CAPONERA, THE LAW OF INTERNATIONAL WATER RESOURCES 204–205 § 23 (FAO. 1980).

7 Lilian del Castillo-Laborde, *Sovereignty and Equitable Utilization: A Regional Implementation Summary*, *in* A HISTORY OF WATER, VOL. 2: SOVEREIGNTY AND INTERNATIONAL WATER LAW 362–366 (Terje Tvedt, et al. eds., 2015). On the duty to consult, see the 1957 *Lac Lanoux* Arbitration, *supra* page 15.

8 National Environmental Policy Act, 42 USC §4321 et seq. (1969).

9 Lynton K. Caldwell, *NEPA Revisited: A Call for a Constitutional Amendment*, 6 THE ENVIRONMENTAL FORUM 18, 18 (1989).

10 Tseming Yang, *The Emergence of the Environmental Impact Assessment Duty as a Global Legal Norm and General Principle of Law*, 70 HASTINGS LAW JOURNAL 525 (2019). According to Yang, only six countries have no EIA requirements (Eritrea, Nauru, Singapore, Suriname, and South Sudan); Singapore has no general EIA requirement, but appears to engage in EIA in specific contexts. In South Sudan, an Environmental Protection bill was drafted in 2013, but has not been approved yet (at http://www.eia.nl/en/countries/af/south+sudan/EIA, accessed 17 June 2021). Before 2019, the most comprehensive survey dated back to 1998, and had already identified 120 systems with some type of EIA mechanisms (ANNIE DONELLY, ET AL., A DIRECTORY OF IMPACT ASSESSMENT GUIDELINES (IIED – WRI – IUCN 2nd ed. 1998)). See also a recent overview conducted by the UNEP, ASSESSING ENVIRONMENTAL IMPACTS – A GLOBAL REVIEW OF LEGISLATION (2018).

In 2001, the International Law Commission (ILC) Draft Articles on Prevention of Transboundary Harm from Hazardous Activities noted "the practice of requiring an environmental impact assessment has become very prevalent in order to assess whether a particular activity has the potential of causing significant transboundary harm".[11] Ten years later, in 2010, the International Court of Justice (ICJ) observed:

> the obligation to protect and preserve, under Article 41 (a) of the Statute, has to be interpreted in accordance with a practice, which in recent years has gained so much acceptance among States that it may now be considered a requirement under general international law to undertake an environmental impact assessment where there is a risk that the proposed industrial activity may have a significant adverse impact in a transboundary context, in particular, on a shared resource. Moreover, due diligence, and the duty of vigilance and prevention which it implies, would not be considered to have been exercised, if a party planning works liable to affect the regime of the river or the quality of its waters did not undertake an environmental impact assessment on the potential effects of such works.[12]

The ICJ considered "that an environmental impact assessment must be conducted prior to the implementation of a project", and that post-monitoring was necessary ("once operations have started and, where necessary, throughout the life of the project, continuous monitoring of its effects on the environment shall be undertaken").[13] Five years later, the ICJ confirmed its stance in the *Costa-Rica v. Nicaragua* case, adding that, in the event the EIA confirms the existence of a risk of significant transboundary harm, the state of origin is required to notify and consult in good faith with the affected state, in accordance with its due diligence obligation. Its statement has been seen as a rare summary of the state of general international law with respect to the protection of the environment:

---

11 Article 7, Commentary (4) (page 403). Regarding the 2001 Draft Articles on Transboundary Harm, see also *infra* pages 39–40.

12 *Pulp Mills on the River Uruguay* (*Argentina* v. *Uruguay*), Judgment, 2010 ICJ Reports 14, at para. 204 (20 April). For earlier recognitions of the place of EIA in customary law, see the dissenting opinions in the *Request for an Examination of the Situation in accordance with Paragraph 63 of the Court's Judgment of 20 December 1974 in the Nuclear Tests* (*New Zealand v. France*) *Case*, Order, 1995 ICJ Reports 288 (22 September): Judge Weeramantry (pages 342–345), and Ad Hoc Judge Palmer (page 411, para. 87, and page 412, para. 91).

13 Id., at para. 205.

> Thus, to fulfil its obligation to exercise due diligence in preventing significant transboundary environmental harm, a State must, before embarking on an activity having the potential adversely to affect the environment of another State, ascertain if there is a risk of significant transboundary harm, which would trigger the requirement to carry out an environmental impact assessment. (...)
>
> If the environmental impact assessment confirms that there is a risk of significant transboundary harm, the State planning to undertake the activity is required, in conformity with its due diligence obligation, to notify and consult in good faith with the potentially affected State, where that is necessary to determine the appropriate measures to prevent or mitigate that risk.[14]

The International Tribunal for the Law of the Sea (ITLOS) also "stressed that the obligation to conduct an environmental impact assessment is a direct obligation under the convention and a general obligation under customary international law".[15]

1.1 *Domestic Origins of* EIA *Prescriptions*

EIA originated in domestic legal systems in the 1970's, upon which international EIA norms were modeled. Notably, as regards the implementation of EIA prescriptions, international norms refer back to domestic systems, which also include international considerations. As well as other instruments, the landmark convention regarding Transboundary EIA (TEIA), the Espoo Convention, defines environmental impact assessment as "a national procedure".[16] The International Court of Justice observed "that it is for each State to determine in its domestic legislation or in the authorization process for the project, the specific content of the environmental impact assessment required in each case,

14 *Certain Activities Carried Out by Nicaragua in the Border Area* (*Costa Rica v. Nicaragua*) *and Construction of a Road in Costa Rica along the San Juan River* (*Nicaragua v. Costa Rica*), Judgment, 2015 ICJ Reports 665, at para. 104 (16 December). See also PIERRE-MARIE DUPUY & JORGE E. VIÑUALES, INTERNATIONAL ENVIRONMENTAL LAW 62–63 (2nd ed. 2018).

15 *Responsibilities and obligations of States with respect to activities in the Area*, Advisory Opinion, 1 February 2011, ITLOS Reports 2011, page 10, para. 147 & 148.

16 Article 1(vi). See also Principle 17 of the Rio Declaration; Goals 2, 3, and Principle 4 of the 1987 UNEP Goals and Principles of EIA; World Bank, *ESS1. Assessment and Management of Environmental and Social Risks and Impacts*, *in* ENVIRONMENTAL AND SOCIAL FRAMEWORK – SETTING ENVIRONMENTAL AND SOCIAL STANDARDS FOR INVESTMENT PROJECT FINANCING 25 (2016).

having regard to the nature and magnitude of the proposed development and its likely adverse impact on the environment as well as to the need to exercise due diligence in conducting such an assessment".[17] According to the due diligence principle, states must observe preventive duties, such as EIA, if there is a likely significant adverse transboundary impact. The crucial role of preventive obligations and domestic law with respect to transboundary impacts has long been emphasized.[18] National EIA procedures have often extended to transboundary impacts, rather than setting up a separate assessment process. A regular review of implementation of the Espoo Convention, carried out since 2003, has revealed that the majority of the forty-five parties have had domestic legislation in place fulfilling their obligations under the convention, that there has been a continuous increase in the application of the convention and, to a lesser extent, in the development of bilateral and multilateral agreements to support its implementation.[19] The necessity of identifying transboundary impacts was recognized in a number of domestic EIA systems, either regarding activities within the territory of the state, or in connection with its own agencies.[20] Extraterritorial application of environmental statutes is all the more necessary that international law is plagued with ineffective enforcement mechanisms.

In the US, NEPA appears silent with respect to its application to projects with effects abroad, but there is evidence of implicit congressional intent, in line with NEPA's goals, as revealed by the statutory construction (NEPA applies to *all* agencies), and by the legislative history, as reflected by the following quotes for instance:

17 *Pulp Mills on the River Uruguay (Argentina v. Uruguay)*, Judgment, 2010 ICJ Reports 2010 14, at paragraph 205 (p. 83–84) (20 April). Tilleman, COLUM. J. TRANSNAT'L L., 351 (1995). See, more generally, about the application of domestic EIA beyond the state: CRAIK, 45 et seq. 2008.

18 See Peter H. Sand, *The Role of Domestic Procedures in Transnational Environmental Disputes*, *in* LEGAL ASPECTS OF TRANSFRONTIER POLLUTION (OECD. 1977).

19 See, for the latest review, UNECE, FIFTH REVIEW OF IMPLEMENTATION OF THE CONVENTION ON ENVIRONMENTAL IMPACT ASSESSMENT IN A TRANSBOUNDARY CONTEXT (2013–2015) (UN. 2018). See Article 8 and Appendix VI of the Espoo Convention about bilateral and multilateral cooperation.

20 It is now common for states to require EIA for international development projects undertaken by their national development agencies. In the US, see USAID Environmental Procedures Regulation, 22 CFR 216, §216.6 and §216.7. In Canada, see Global Affairs Canada (formerly Canadian International Development Agency), at http://international.gc.ca/world-monde/funding-financement/environment_handbook-manuel_environnement.aspx?lang=eng#a4 (accessed 17 June 2021).

> Although the influence of the US policy will be limited outside of its own borders, the global character of ecological relationships must be the guide for domestic activities. Ecological considerations should be infused into all international relations.[21]

> The international aspects are clearly a major part of the questions which the Council would have to confront.[22]

> Implicit in this section [102(2)] is the understanding that the international implications of our current activities will also be considered, inseparable as they are from the purely national consequences of our actions.[23]

> What is involved is a congressional declaration that we do not intend, as a government or as a people, to initiate actions which endanger the continued existence or the health of mankind: That we will not intentionally initiate actions which will do irreparable damage to the air, land, and water which support life on earth.[24]

However, the lack of clear intent led to some controversy, since, in the absence of clearly expressed congressional intent, there is an ordinary presumption against the extraterritorial application of a US statute.[25] Combined with the fact that the presumption was rather weak at first, especially since NEPA does not transgress any accepted principles of international law, the application of EIA obligations to transboundary impacts was seen as fairly obvious by the courts,[26] in keeping with their approach to extra-jurisdictional effects in

---

21 CONGRESSIONAL WHITE PAPER ON A NATIONAL POLICY FOR THE ENVIRONMENT, 115 Cong. Rec. 29,078, 29,081–82 (1969).

22 HR Rep. No. 91-378, 91st Cong., 1st Sess., at 7 (1969).

23 Id., at 9.

24 Conference Report on NEPA (115 Cong. Rec. 40,415, 40,416 (1969). In addition to these four quotes, see Joan R. Goldfarb, *Extraterritorial Compliance with NEPA amid the Current Wave of Environmental Alarm*, 18 B.C. ENVTL. AFF. L. REV. 543 (1991), and Karen A. Klick, *The Extraterritorial Reach of NEPA's EIS Requirement after Environmental Defense Fund v. Massey*, 44 AM. U.L. REV. 291 (1994), which cite also the Senate Hearings (*Hearings on S. 1075, S. 237, and S. 1752 Before the Senate Comm. on Interior and Insular Affairs*, 91st Cong., 1st Sess. 118 (1969)), and some congressional committee oversight hearings (House Comm. on Merchant Marine and Fisheries, Administration of the National Environmental Policy Act, HR Rep. No. 92-316, 92d Cong., 1st Sess. (1971).

25 *Murray v. The Schooner Charming Betsy*, 6 US (2 Cranch) 64 (1804).

26 For instance, NEPA was deemed applicable to a proposed oil pipeline in Alaska, with the inclusion of the assessment of the impacts in Canada in consequence (*Wilderness Society v. Morton*, 463 F 2d 1261 (DC Cir. 1972); or of the impacts in Canada of a dam project

general.[27] In 1976, the Council on Environmental Quality (CEQ) stated that NEPA did apply extraterritorially.[28] In 1979, President Carter decided to further clarify the application of NEPA to transboundary impacts by an executive order, which required the consideration of transboundary impacts abroad or in the global commons areas, but in a rather limited fashion. Furthermore, Section 3–1 excluded that the order constituted a cause of action. Consequently, Executive Order 12,114 was rather ineffective.[29] In 1997, the CEQ released another memo to "clarify the applicability of NEPA to proposed federal actions in the US that may have transboundary effects".[30] The CEQ indicated that the potential for transboundary impacts should be identified during the scoping process (i.e. the determination of the issues that the EIA must cover[31]). In the case of potential transboundary impacts, the CEQ recommended that the agencies with relevant expertise in the affected state be notified, but provided no further details. Since the resurgence of the presumption against extraterritoriality,[32] US courts have gradually focused on whether the application of NEPA would encroach on the sovereignty of another state.[33] Until

---

situated in Washington State (*Swinomish Tribal Community v. Federal Energy Regulation Commission*, 627 F 2d 499 (DC Cir. 1980)). In both cases, Canadian entities were granted standing in the US courts to challenge the adequacy of the EIS.

27 See *Cathcart v. Snohomish County*, 96 Wash.2d 201, 634 P.2d 853 (1981), which held that the adequacy of an EIS is a question of law, and "mandates that extra-jurisdictional effects be addressed and mitigated, when possible. *Save A Valuable Environment v. Bothell*, 89 Wash.2d 862, 576 P.2d 401 (1978). In *Save*, an EIS was considered deficient, and the zoning approval invalidated, because the EIS failed to address the extra-jurisdictional consequences of a proposed shopping center". (p. 209; p. 858–859).

28 US Council on Environmental Quality, Memorandum on the Application of the EIS Requirement to Environmental Impacts Abroad of Major Federal Actions (1976), 42 Fed. Reg. 61,068 (1977).

29 Exec. Order No. 12,114, 3 CFR 356 (1980), reprinted in 18 ILM 154 (1979), para. 2–3(a) and (b).

30 CEQ, Memorandum to Heads of Agencies on the Application of NEPA to Proposed Federal Actions in the U.S. with Transboundary Effects (1 July 1997), at https://energy.gov/nepa/downloads/guidance-application-nepa-proposed-federal-actions-united-states-transboundary (accessed 17 June 2021). CEQ guidance documents are not binding on agencies, but the US Supreme Court has upheld the right of the CEQ to interpret NEPA, and has held that CEQ guidelines should be given "substantial deference" (*Andrus v. Sierra Club*, 442 US 347, 358 (1979); see also *Robertson v. Methow Valley Citizens Council*, 490 US 332, 334 (1989)).

31 See *infra* page 67 et seq. (2. Scoping – Impact analysis – Report preparation).

32 In *EEOC* v. *Arabian Am. Oil Co. (Aramco)*, 499 US 244 (1991), the Supreme Court applied the presumption for the first time in nearly forty years (see Randall S. Abate, *Dawn of a New Era in the Extraterritorial Application of U.S. Environmental Statutes: A Proposal for an Integrated Judicial Standard Based on the Continuum of Context*, 31 COLUMB. J. ENVTL. L. 87 (2006)).

33 See *Environmental Defense Fund, Inc. v. Massey*, 986 F.2d 528, 536 (DC Cir. 1993), deciding that NEPA is applicable to projects with effects in the Antarctic: "Section 102(2)(C), on

the Trump Administration (2016 – 2020), the CEQ had consistently asserted that NEPA applies extraterritorially, but on 16 July 2020, it released its final rule, the first major revisions to NEPA regulations since 1978, titled "Update to the Regulations Implementing the Procedural Provisions of the National Environmental Policy Act" (85 FR 43304), according to which NEPA does not apply to "agency activities or decisions with effects located entirely outside of the jurisdiction of the United States" (Paragraph 1508.1(q)(1)(i)). Since the election of President Joseph R. Biden in November 2020, the survival of this CEQ final rule is uncertain. Either it will be repealed by the new administration, or under the Congressional Review Act, or it will be challenged in court.

In the wake of the United States, other jurisdictions have adopted a similar approach to TEIA. For instance, Canada and the European Union (EU) have acknowledged their necessity early on.[34] Various examples of TEIA were conducted before the adoption of treaty obligations.[35] However, on a closer look, Canada adopted a rather ambivalent approach. In principle, whether or not the project is subject to the federal EIA process, the government can intervene in case of potential transboundary impacts. Under the 1992 Canadian Environmental Assessment Act (CEAA), this decision was in its discretion; the minister of the environment could decide to refer the matter to mediation or a review panel.[36] Like NEPA in the US, CEAA did not go into detail about

---

its face, is clearly not limited to actions of federal agencies that have significant environmental effects within US borders" and "Congress, when enacting NEPA, was concerned with worldwide as well as domestic problems facing the environment"; *Natural Resources Defense Council v. Department of the Navy*, 2002 WL 32095131 (CD Cal. 2002) (NEPA is applicable to sonar tests in high seas and EEZ); *Center for Biological Diversity v. National Science Foundation*, 2002 WL 31548073 (ND Cal. 2002), finding that NEPA is applicable to projects in the Gulf of California, considered as the high seas, since such projects do not impinge on the sovereignty of Mexico; *Born Free U.S.A v. Norton*, 2003 US Dist. LEXIS 13770 (DDC 2003), refusing to apply NEPA to the import of eleven elephants: "the Court is not dealing with environmental effects in a no-man's land such as Antarctica, where the US has some real measure of control; (…) this Court is not inclined to take the step of requiring [the Fish and Wildlife Service] to conduct an environmental analysis aimed at second-guessing the validity of Swaziland's determination" (at 38–39).

34 In Canada, see 1984 Environmental Assessment and Review Process (EARP) Guidelines Order, SOR/84-467, s. 4(1)(a); In the EU, see Council Directive 85/337/EEC of 27 June 1985 on the assessment of the effects of certain public and private projects on the environment, Article 7 (OJ L 175, 5 July 1985, p. 40–48) (hereinafter the EIA Directive).

35 UNECE, CURRENT POLICIES, STRATEGIES, AND ASPECTS OF ENVIRONMENTAL IMPACT ASSESSMENT IN A TRANSBOUNDARY CONTEXT (UNITED NATIONS. 1996), at 19–20 (enumerating several examples of the application of domestic EIA processes to transboundary impacts before the Espoo Convention). See also the *Vuotos* case in Finland (*infra* chapter 4).

36 See 1992 CEAA, s. 47 (International environmental effects).

notification of transboundary impacts, such as identification of the points of contact, involvement of the public. Besides, the possibility to petition the environment minister to initiate a transboundary proceeding under Section 47 of the 1992 CEAA was limited to provincial governments, and foreign governments or subdivisions thereof. NGOs and affected individuals were not included. This procedure was never used.[37] In 2012, the CEAA was revised and the obligation, for the responsible authority, to offer to consult and cooperate in case of impacts outside Canada was formulated even more tersely.[38] The experience in Europe, prior to the Espoo Convention, was quite similar in that the 1985 EIA Directive recognized the importance of assessing transboundary impacts (Article 7). States of origin were required to notify affected states, but no details were provided as regards implementation. Consequently, there was an uneven application of those requirements.[39] Moreover, domestic TEIA requirements have usually had severe limitations that reside in their discretionary nature and the lack of reciprocity that may ensue. The EIA procedures of the state of origin will apply, as opposed to those of the affected state, hence the need for coordination and harmonization at a supranational level. This harmonization process has occurred in different settings.

International EIA prescriptions will be presented below under the common categorization of soft law and hard law.

1.2 *Soft Law Instruments*

Environmental assessment was evoked in some recommendations of the *Action Plan for the Human Environment*, adopted by the 1972 United Nations Conference on the Human Environment (UNCHE).[40] The parallel *Stockholm Declaration* listed many important principles, such as the responsibility of

---

37 DAVID R. BOYD, UNNATURAL LAW: RETHINKING CANADIAN ENVIRONMENTAL LAW AND POLICY 154 (UBC Press. 2011).

38 Canadian Environmental Assessment Act, 2012, Sections 2(1), 5(1)(b) and 18 combined. For a general, critical appraisal of the 2012 CEAA, see Robert B. Gibson, *In full retreat: the Canadian government's new environmental assessment law undoes decades of progress*, 30 IMPACT ASSESS. PROJ. APPRAIS. 179 (2012). In 2019, the CEAA was replaced by the Impact Assessment Act (SC 2019, c. 28, s. 1), which barely mentions any international aspect of a project. It simply states that the environment minister and the minister of foreign affairs may implement any international agreement to which Canada is a party (Section 114).

39 For instance, impacts to non-member states or to the global commons were not included; in the United Kingdom, the TEIA requirements of the 1985 EIA directive were not transposed until 1999 (see the Town and Country Planning (EIA) (England and Wales) Regulations 1999, SI 1999 No. 293).

40 Recommendations 51 and 61 (United Nations Conference on the Human Environment (Stockholm) 16 June 1972, UN Doc. A/Conf.48/14/Rev.1 (1972), 11 ILM 1416 (1972)).

states to respect the environment of other states and the global commons areas,[41] but did not include the necessity of EIA: Principle 20 simply encouraged scientific research and development, and the free flow of scientific information and experience. The subsequent creation (on 5 June 1972) of the United Nations Environmental Program (UNEP) would prove an essential element of the further development of EIA requirements. Later that same year, the United Nations General Assembly revived an earlier draft of the Stockholm Declaration, i.e. Draft Principle 20 that provided a less equivocal EIA requirement. During the UNCHE, some developing countries (Brazil in particular) had objected to Draft Principle 20, because they viewed the obligation to consult as a possibility to prevent or delay their development projects. Brazil and Uruguay had then proposed that Draft Principle 20 be simply referred to the UNGA for consideration.[42] Draft Principle 20 provided that "relevant information must be supplied by states on activities or developments within their jurisdiction or under their control whenever they believe, or have reason to believe, that such information is needed to avoid the risk of significant adverse effects on the environment in areas beyond their national jurisdiction".[43] The UN revived the draft principle in a diluted form: in December 1972, *UNGA Resolution 2995* recognized that official and public knowledge of technical data should be provided with regard to planned activities in order to prevent significant transboundary harm, but without delaying or impeding the use of natural resources.[44]

---

41 Principle 21: "States have, in accordance with the Charter of the United Nations and the principles of international law, the sovereign right to exploit their own resources pursuant to their own environmental policies, and the responsibility to ensure that activities within their jurisdiction or control do not cause damage to the environment of other States or of areas beyond the limits of national jurisdiction". This principle echoes the *Trail Smelter Arbitration* (US v. Canada) 3 RIAA 1911 (1938), 35 AM. J. INT'L L. 684 (1941).

42 Brazil took a particularly active role in leading the developing world at the Stockholm Conference, because of its immense rainforests, which gave it power and interest in the outcome of the conference. Brazil blocked Draft Principle 20 for essentially short-term political reasons, because it was then enmeshed in a dispute with Argentina that could have invoked the principle against Brazil (STEVEN BERNSTEIN, THE COMPROMISE OF LIBERAL ENVIRONMENTALISM 36 and 43, note 12 (Columbia University Press. 2012). See Report of the United Nations Conference on the Human Environment (Stockholm) 16 June 1972, UN Doc. A/Conf.48/14/Rev.1 (1972), Annex II (Report of the Working Group on the Declaration on the Human Environment, para. 6); Louis B. Sohn, *The Stockholm Declaration on the Human Environment*, 14 HARV. INT'L L. J. 423, 499 (1973)).

43 UN Doc. A/Conf.48/4, Annex, Para. 20, at 4 (1972), reproduced in Sohn, *supra* note 42 at 496.

44 Co-operation between States in the Field of the Environment, UNGA Resolution 2995 (XXVII), UN GAOR, 27th Sess., 15 December 1972, Supp. No. 30 (1972) at 42.

Following NEPA, the United States took on an important role in promoting the adoption of EIA requirements at the international level. Even if their efforts failed to lead to a global EIA treaty, they were influential in the gradual adoption of EIA recommendations and commitments worldwide. In 1977, Senator Claiborne Pell introduced a bill in the US Senate, calling for the negotiation of a treaty on international environmental assessments. The US Senate passed Resolution 49 on 21 July 1978, including the draft treaty, which would apply to state and non-state actors, in cases where some significant adverse effects can be expected on the territory of another state, or on global commons area, with an EIA submitted to both the affected state and UNEP for consultations.[45] At the same time the bill was introduced in the US Senate, the North Atlantic Alliance (or North Atlantic Treaty Organization (NATO)) passed a similar resolution, urging its state members to sign a treaty requiring international environmental analyses of major national projects with significant effects in other nations or in the global commons.[46] No global treaty has been signed as of yet, nor has the role assigned to UNEP as regards the global commons been pursued.

In 1978, the UN Environment Program (UNEP) adopted the Principles on Conservation and Harmonious Utilization of Natural Resources Shared by Two or More States (*UNEP Draft Principles of Conduct*), which state the no-harm principle (Principle 3), provide for EIA in Principle 4 (in case of activities that may pose a risk of significant environmental impact), and for exchange of information and consultation in Principle 5. The UNEP Draft Principles of Conduct apply only to state actors, which can seek the assistance of international institutions (Principle 10).[47]

The 1982 United Nations *World Charter for Nature* is more comprehensive than the UNEP Draft Principles of Conduct. The threshold is lower. The charter applies to activities that may simply disturb nature rather than requiring the probability of significant impacts.[48]

---

45 The bill was introduced on 24 January 1977. Senate Resolution 49 was passed on 21 July 1978 (17 ILM 1082 (1978); 124 Cong. Rec. 22,204 (1978)) (hereinafter the 1978 US Senate Resolution).

46 North Atlantic Assembly, Resolution No. 74 on International Environmental Analysis of Major National Projects, Twenty-third Meeting (Paris) September 1977, Report of the US Delegation, at 340 (US Government Printing Office. 1977) (hereinafter the NATO Resolution). Also mentioned by Claiborne Pell to the US Senate, *in* 124 Cong. Rec. 22,205–22,206 (1978).

47 UN Doc. UNEP/GC.6/17 (1978), 17 ILM 1091 (1978).

48 See Articles 11(b), (c), 16, 23 of the World Charter for Nature, 28 October 1982, UN GA Res. 37/7, UN GAOR, 37th Sess., UN Doc. A/Res/37/7 (1982), 22 ILM 455 (1983).

That same year, a UNEP Working Group of Experts on Environmental Law was created to prepare more elaborate recommendations on EIAs. In 1984, in Washington DC, the United States hosted the first meeting of the Working Group, and Senator Claiborne Pell delivered an address. Concomitantly, the European Communities were in the process of adopting their EIA Directive.[49] In 1987, the *UNEP Goals and Principles of Environmental Impact Assessment* provided guidelines for the establishment of detailed EIA stipulations, notably the inclusion of international considerations within domestic legislations (transboundary impacts, notification and consultation with affected states).[50] The influence of NEPA, the 1978 US Senate Resolution, and the 1985 EIA Directive is manifest in the UNEP EIA Goals and Principles. They offer several means of ascertaining whether an activity will have a significant effect on the environment: either an initial environmental evaluation (like in NEPA), or pre-established lists of activities, list of areas or resources where significant effects are likely, and the use of further criteria to confirm significance[51] (as in the 1985 EIA Directive). The composition of the EIA is quasi-identical to an Environmental Impact Statement (EIS) in NEPA, including an indication of transboundary impacts on the territory of another state, or in the global commons[52] (like in the 1978 US Senate Resolution or the NATO Resolution). No mandatory consultation is recommended. Consultations take place only if agreed upon by concerned states, probably because of some residual concerns from developing countries already expressed at the UNCHE, and as displayed in UNGA Resolution 2995. Like NEPA, the UNEP EIA Goals and Principles require a brief, non- technical summary of the EIA,[53] in order to facilitate public participation. Review and comments by the public and other agencies are recommended, as well as a written final decision with stated grounds.[54]

In 1987, the World Commission on Environment and Development, established by the United Nations, released its report (*Our Common Future*, also

---

49 See *infra* page 45 et seq.

50 See Goals 2 and 3 of the UNEP Goals and Principles of Environmental Impact Assessment, UNEP Res. GC 14/25, 14th Sess. (1987), endorsed by UN GA Res. 42/184, UN GAOR, 42nd Sess., UN Doc. A/Res/42/184 (1987) (hereinafter the UNEP Goals and Principles). They were amended in 2004. HUSSEIN ABAZA, ET AL., ENVIRONMENTAL IMPACT ASSESSMENT AND STRATEGIC ENVIRONMENTAL ASSESSMENT: TOWARDS AN INTEGRATED APPROACH (UNEP. 2004).

51 See Principle 2 accompanied by an official note.

52 See Principle 4.

53 Principle 4 (h).

54 Principles 7–9.

known as the Brundtland Report),[55] which led to the convening of the 1992 United Nations Conference on Environment and Development in Rio de Janeiro (UNCED, also known as the Earth Summit). In the *Rio Declaration*, the UNCED confirmed the necessity of EIA for sustainable development, which is also the stated objective of the UNEP Goals and Principles and the Espoo Convention. The UNCED emphasized the transboundary and participatory nature of EIA. Principle 17 of the Rio Declaration is based on EU and Nordic states' drafts, and was clearly influenced by the 1985 EIA Directive, the Espoo Convention and the Antarctic Environmental Protocol.[56] Principle 17 states "environmental impact assessment, as a national instrument, shall be undertaken for proposed activities that are likely to have a significant adverse impact on the environment and are subject to a decision of a competent national authority". It does not discriminate between domestic and international settings. If an activity is likely to have a significant adverse environmental impact, even if only on the territory of a single state, an EIA is necessary. If there are some potentially significant transboundary impacts, Principle 19 declares "states shall provide prior and timely notification and relevant information to potentially affected States on activities that may have a significant adverse transboundary environmental effect and shall consult with those States at an early stage and in good faith", which must be read in conjunction with Principle 2 (the no-harm principle). EIAs are also cited repeatedly in *Agenda 21* (the UNCED action plan).

Ten years later, in 2002, the *World Summit on Sustainable Development* (WSSD) further advanced the UNCED EIA requirements, by calling for integrated and multi-sectoral approaches.[57] In 2001, the *ILC Draft Articles on Prevention of Transboundary Harm from Hazardous Activities* were conceived in the wake of the UNCED output. In case of an activity that involves risks of significant transboundary harm (Article 1), any decision in respect of the authorization of this activity must be based on an assessment of the possible transboundary harm caused by that activity, including any EIA (Article 7). The ILC commentary to its draft articles noted that the requirement of assessment of adverse

55 UNGA A/RES/38/161 (1983) for the establishment of the WCED. WORLD COMMISSION ON ENVIRONMENT AND DEVELOPMENT, OUR COMMON FUTURE (Oxford University Press. 1987).

56 Jorge E. Viñuales, *The Rio Declaration on Environment and Development*, *in* THE RIO DECLARATION ON ENVIRONMENT AND DEVELOPMENT: A COMMENTARY 43 (Jorge E. Viñuales ed. 2015).

57 See Paragraphs 18(e), 19(e), 36 and 62(h) of the Plan of Implementation of the World Summit on Sustainable Development, *in* Report of the World Summit on Sustainable Development (Johannesburg) 26 August – 4 September 2002, UN Doc. A/Conf.199/20 (hereinafter the WSSD Plan of Implementation).

effects of activities had been incorporated in many international agreements, and that "the practice of requiring an environmental impact assessment had become very prevalent".[58] Some other codification efforts also included provisions related to EIA, such as the *2002 ILA New Delhi Declaration*,[59] and the *1997 IIL Resolution on Environment.* In 1997, the Institute of International Law (IIL) emphasized the importance of the prevention and precautionary principles, as linked to the requirements of the sustainable development of human societies. The IIL adopted a Resolution on Environment with environmental impact assessment listed among the first general principles,[60] where the IIL also deemed important to underline that "the obligation to prevent damage exists independently of any obligation to make reparation" (Article 9), which is an essential distinction to bear in mind when it comes to enforcing procedural obligations such as EIA.[61] In another resolution adopted the same day, the Institute of International Law also observed that "both responsibility and liability have in addition to the traditional role of ensuring restoration and compensation that of enhancing prevention of environmental damage",[62] and also underlined the duty of conducting transboundary EIA (Article 29).

Another source of soft law EIA requirements is provided by some *guidelines adopted by treaty bodies,* which are non-binding, but which provide further guidance for the implementation of EIA requirements, particularly in view of the specificities of each treaty and, in some instances, in connection with other related treaties. For example, the Antarctic Treaty Consultative Meeting,[63] the Meeting of the Parties to the Espoo Convention,[64] and the Conference

---

58 See *supra* note 11.

59 See Section 4(2) of the New Delhi Declaration of Principles of International Law Relating to Sustainable Development, International Law Association (ILA), ILA Resolution 3/2002, 6 April 2002, UN Doc. A/CONF.199/8 (9 August 2002).

60 See Para. 2 of the Preamble, Articles 5 and 6 of the IIL Resolution on the Environment (Strasbourg, 4 September 1997 – Eighth Commission, Rapporteur: Luigi Ferrari Bravo).

61 See *infra* page 126 et seq.

62 Para. 5 of the Preamble of the IIL Resolution on Responsibility and Liability under International Law for Environmental Damage (Strasbourg, 4 September 1997 – Eighth Commission, Rapporteur: Francisco Orrego Vicuña).

63 Guidelines for Environmental Impact Assessment in Antarctica, adopted by Resolution 1 (1999), replaced by Resolution 4 (2005) updated by Resolution 1 (2016).

64 Guidance on Public Participation in Environmental Impact Assessment in a Transboundary Context, Meeting of the Parties to the Convention on Environmental Impact Assessment in a Transboundary Context, Report of the Third Meeting, 4 June 2004, UN Doc. ECE/MP.EIA/6, Decision III/8; Guidance on Good Practice and on Bilateral and Multilateral Agreements, Meeting of the Parties to the Convention on Environmental Impact Assessment in a Transboundary Context, Report of the Third Meeting, 4 June 2004, UN Doc. ECE/MP.EIA/6, Decision III/4.

of the Parties under the Convention on Biological Diversity (CBD)[65] adopted guidelines to assist developers in the preparation of EIA (in matters of methodology or public participation for instance, or the incorporation of the substantial objectives of the treaty – protection of the Antarctic environment, biodiversity – at each stage of the EIA process), and to promote sub-regional cooperation and consistency. Some guidelines were also added to the earlier conventions that were originally devoid of EIA requirement (such as the 1971 Ramsar Convention for instance[66]).

Lastly, the Arctic states adopted a set of guidelines in the absence of a treaty commitment to conduct EIA. Unlike the global commons status of the Antarctic, several different treaties apply to the Arctic, as it is the subject of the exclusive jurisdiction of eight states.[67] It is inhabited and its resources can be exploited. Six of the eight Arctic states are parties to the Espoo Convention

65 Guidelines for Incorporating Biodiversity-Related Issues into Environmental Impact Assessment Legislation and/or Processes and in Strategic Environmental Assessment, Report of the Sixth Meeting of the Conference of the Parties to the Convention on Biological Diversity, COP 6 Decision VI.7 (The Hague, Netherlands, 7–19 April 2002) (UN Doc. UNEP/CBD/COP/6/7). Revised guidelines were issued in 2006 (COP 8 Decision VIII.28, UNEP/CBD/COP/DEC/VIII/28). The EIA/SEA Guidelines of the CBD refer to substantive criteria in other international environmental treaties, such as the Convention on the Conservation of Migratory Species of Wild Animals (Bonn), 23 June 1979, 19 ILM 15 (1980), in force 1 November 1983 (hereinafter the 1979 Bonn Convention), and the Convention on Wetlands of International Importance especially as Waterfowl Habitat (Ramsar) 2 February 1971, 11 ILM 963 (1972), in force 21 December 1975 (hereinafter the 1971 Ramsar Convention). See also The 1971 Ramsar Convention and impact assessment: strategic, environmental and social, Resolution VII.16 of the Conference of the Parties to the 1971 Ramsar Convention (7th Meeting of the Conference of the Parties, San José, Costa Rica, 10–18 May 1999).

66 In 1980, Recommendation 1.6 on Assessment of Wetland Values requested that, in case of any projected large-scale wetland transformation, the decision not be taken until an assessment of all the values involved has been made, and ecologists be included in the planning process. It also requested that international funding agencies and bilateral and multilateral development aid should finance such assessments (1st Meeting of the Conference of the Contracting Parties, Cagliari, Italy, 24–29 November 1980). Recommendation 6.2 on Environmental impact assessment called on the parties to integrate environmental considerations in relation to wetlands into planning decisions in a clear and publicly transparent manner, invited them and national and international organizations to submit available guidelines on environmental appraisal and EIA relevant to wetlands, requested the drafting of EIA guidelines (6th Meeting of the Conference of the Contracting Parties, Brisbane, Australia, 19–27 March 1996). See also Resolution VII.16 (1999), Resolution VIII.9 (2002), and Resolution X.17 (2008).

67 The Arctic states are Canada, Denmark, Finland, Iceland, Norway, Russia, Sweden and the United States. See Timo Koivurova, *Increasing Relevance of Treaties: The Case of the Arctic*, AJIL UNBOUND (2014).

(The Russian Federation and the United States are not). In 1991, in a harmonization effort regarding environmental issues, the Arctic states concluded the Arctic Environmental Protection Strategy (AEPS), a formally non-binding instrument. Subsequently, in 1996, the Arctic states established the Arctic Council, as an umbrella organization to administer the AEPS and coordinate Arctic cooperation. Under the auspices of the AEPS, the *1997 Guidelines for Environmental Impact Assessment in the Arctic* (hereinafter the Arctic EIA Guidelines) were developed.[68]

1.3 *Treaties and Other Binding Instruments*

1.3.1 General EIA Prescriptions

With regard to transboundary EIA (TEIA), treaties and other binding instruments followed soon after NEPA. The first was the *Nordic Environmental Protection Convention* (hereinafter the NEPC) in 1974, between Denmark, Finland, Norway, and Sweden.[69]

The NEPC was followed by *UNEP regional seas conventions* (the first one was the 1976 Barcelona Convention),[70] and the *United Nations Convention on the*

68 Guidelines for Environmental Impact Assessment in the Arctic, adopted by the Arctic Council in the 1997 Alta Declaration on the Arctic Environmental Protection Strategy (available at https://www.unece.org/fileadmin/DAM/env/eia/documents/EIAguides/Arctic_EIA_guide.pdf, accessed 17 June 2021).

69 Stockholm, 19 February 1974, 13 ILM 511 (1974), in force 5 October 1976. See Article 6 for TEIA. A first possibility of participation by foreign public authorities had been granted the year before by the Danish Environment Protection Act, Act No. 372 of 13 June 1973 on Environment Protection, Lovtidende A XXXIV 1088 (1973) (English summary in 23 FOOD AND AGRICULTURAL LEGISLATION 81 (1974), and in 40 INT'L REV. ADMINISTRATIVE SCIENCES 200 (1974)). See also *infra* chapter 4, page 141.

70 Convention for the Protection of the Mediterranean Sea Against Pollution, Annex III, B.9 and C, (Barcelona) 16 February 1976, in force 12 February 1978; Kuwait Regional Convention for Co-operation on the Protection of the Marine Environment from Pollution (Kuwait) 24 April 1978, 1140 UNTS 133, 17 ILM 511 (1978), in force 1 July 1979. The Kuwait Convention is a framework convention, accompanied by an Action Plan with EIA provisions (Art. III(b) of the convention, providing for the formulation and adoption of further protocols); Convention for Co-operation in the Protection and Development of the Marine and Coastal Environment of the West and Central African Region, Art. 13, (Abidjan) 23 March 1981, 20 ILM 746 (1981), in force 5 August 1984; Convention for the Protection of the Marine Environment and Coastal Area of the South-East Pacific, Art. 8, (Lima) 12 November 1981, IELMT 981:85, in force 19 May 1986; Regional Convention for the Conservation of the Red Sea and Gulf of Aden Environment, Art. XI, (Jeddah) 14 February 1982, 9 EPL 56 (1982), in force 20 August 1985; Convention for the Protection and Development of the Marine Environment of the Wider Caribbean Region, Art. 12, (Cartagena de Indias) 24 March 1983, 22 ILM 221 (1983), in force 11 October 1986; Convention for the Protection of the Natural Resources and Environment of the South Pacific Region, Art. 16, (Noumea) 25 November 1986, 26 ILM 38 (1987), in force 22 August 1990; Convention on the Protection of the Black

Law of the Sea (hereinafter UNCLOS), which was adopted in 1982, after nine years of negotiation.[71] Norway had proposed to include a provision on EIA at the onset of the UNCLOS negotiations (in 1973), without any vigorous opposition.[72] This draft provision became Article 206 of UNCLOS. EIA is also required in relation to the deep-sea bed area, according to Article 165, paragraph 2(d). The authoritative Virginia Commentary describes Article 206 of UNCLOS as similar to NEPA, and as an essential part of a comprehensive environmental management system, a particular application of the no-harm principle stated in Article 194, paragraph 2.[73]

Many other international agreements prescribe explicit or indirect general obligations on environmental impact assessment, such as those regulating the atmospheric emissions of nitrogen oxide,[74] occupational health,[75] asbestos use,[76] transboundary movements of waste,[77] industrial accidents,[78] the energy sector,[79] protection of mountainous areas,[80] protection of some migratory

---

Sea against Pollution, Art. XV(5), (Bucharest) 21 April 1992, 32 ILM 1101 (1993), in force 15 January 1994 (the Bucharest Convention); Convention for Cooperation in the Protection and Sustainable Development of the Marine and Coastal Environment of The Northeast Pacific, Art. 6(2)(b), 10(2)(b) and 12(1)(c), (Antigua) 18 February 2002, not yet in force.

71 United Nations Convention on the Law of the Sea (Montego Bay) 10 December 1982, 21 ILM 1261 (1982), in force 16 November 1994.

72 See working paper submitted by Norway (A/AC.138/SC.III/L.43 (1973, mimeo)), Art. XV. MYRON H. NORDQUIST, UNITED NATIONS CONVENTION ON THE LAW OF THE SEA: A COMMENTARY 122 (para. 206.2) (Myron H. Nordquist, et al. eds., Martinus Nijhoff. 1991).

73 Id. at 122 (para. 206.1).

74 Protocol to the 1979 Convention on long-range transboundary air pollution concerning the control of emissions of nitrogen oxides or their transboundary fluxes, Article 6, (Sofia) 31 October 1988, 28 ILM 214 (1988), in force 14 February 1991.

75 ILO Convention concerning Occupational Health Services, Article 5, (Geneva) 25 June 1985, in force 17 February 1988.

76 ILO Convention (No. 162) concerning Safety in the Use of Asbestos, Article 1.2, (Geneva), 24 June 1986, 2 SMTE 359, in force 16 June 1989.

77 Convention on the Control of Transboundary Movements of Hazardous Wastes and their Disposal, Article 4.2.f. and Annex V.A, (Basel), 22 March 1989, 28 ILM 657 (1989), in force 5 May 1992.

78 Convention on the Transboundary Effects of Industrial Accidents, signed in Helsinki on 17 March 1992 by twenty-six UNECE member countries and the European Union, in force 19 April 2000 (31 ILM 1330 (1992)). As of August 2021, there were forty-one contracting parties. See Article 4 and Annex III.

79 Energy Charter Treaty (Lisbon) 17 December 1994, 33 ILM 360 (1995), in force 16 April 1998. At present, the treaty has been signed or acceded to by fifty-four states, the European Union and Euratom. See Article 19. See also Articles 3(7) and 8(2)(b) of the Energy Charter Protocol on Energy Efficiency and Related Environmental Aspects (same dates and reference as the Energy Charter Treaty).

80 The Framework Convention on the Protection and Sustainable Development of the Carpathians was adopted and signed by seven parties (Czech Republic, Hungary, Poland,

species,[81] public participation in environmental matters.[82] A few treaties have some more detailed requirements, such as the approval of projects under the regime of the Clean Development Mechanism within the United Nations Framework Convention on Climate Change.[83]

1.3.2 Regional Instruments

In 1985, two regional instruments were adopted: the ASEAN Agreement and the EIA Directive in the European Community.

The 1985 *ASEAN Agreement*[84] was rather limited and has not entered into force yet. One short provision about EIA (Article 14) stated in general terms that (emphasis added):

> (1) The Contracting Parties undertake that proposals for any activity which may significantly affect the natural environment shall *as far as possible* be subjected to an assessment of their consequences before they are adopted, and they shall take into consideration the results of this assessment in their decision-making process.
> (2) In those cases where any such activities are undertaken, the Contracting Parties shall plan and carry them out so as to overcome

Romania, Serbia, Slovak Republic, Ukraine) on 27 May 2003 in Kiev, Ukraine, in force 4 January 2006. See its Articles 12 and 13. See also, Declaration on Environment and Sustainable Development in the Carpathian and Danube Region, Article 2, (Bucharest) 30 April 2001; Protocole d'application de la Convention Alpine de 1991 dans le Domaine de la Protection de la Nature et de l'Entretien des Paysages, Article 9, 20 December 1994. Protocole d'application de la Convention Alpine de 1991 dans le domaine de l'énergie Protocole Energie, articles 12 and 15, (Bled) 16 October 1998; Protocole d'application de La Convention Alpine de 1991 dans le domaine des transports, Protocole Transports, Article 8, (Lucerne) 31 October 2000. All three protocols' signatories are: Austria, France, Germany, Italy, Liechtenstein, Monaco, Slovenia, Switzerland, and the EU.

81 1979 Bonn Convention, article V(5)(l) and (n).

82 Convention on Access to Information, Public Participation in Decision-Making and Access to Justice in Environmental Matters, Article 6.2(e) and Annex I, Article 20, (Aarhus) 25 June 1998, 38 ILM 517 (1999), in force 30 October 2001 (hereinafter the Aarhus Convention).

83 Modalities and Procedures for a Clean Development Mechanism defined by Article 12 of the Kyoto Protocol (Decision 17/CP.7, UNFCCC, 7th session of the Conference of the Parties (Marrakesh, 2001), UN Doc. FCCC/CP/2001/13/Add.2, page 20).

84 ASEAN Agreement on the Conservation of Nature and Natural Resources (Kuala Lumpur) 9 July 1985, 15 EPL 1964 (1985). At the time, the ASEAN was composed of six state members: Indonesia, Malaysia, the Philippines, Singapore, Thailand, and Brunei. Since then, as of 2021, Vietnam, Laos, Myanmar and Cambodia have joined the ASEAN.

> or minimize any assessed adverse effects and shall monitor such effects with a view to taking remedial action as appropriate.

Article 14 combined with Article 12(3) could be interpreted as indicating a TEIA requirement.[85]

In the context of a different political structure, the *1985 EIA Directive*[86] was significantly more detailed and far-reaching, but its implementation still proved difficult at times, for the same usual reasons – for instance, EIAS would slow or even stop industrial development, and lead to time-consuming litigation[87]. The directive was the first EC incursion into the planning field, and has had a significant influence on the decision-making processes of EU state members. For this reason, there had been a notable delay between the European Commission's original proposal (the first preliminary draft directive was produced in 1977) and the adoption of the directive in 1985.[88] The EIA Directive initially introduced some brief provisions about TEIA (in Article 7), which were expanded in 1997, in the amended directive that was passed to implement the Espoo Convention. In 1997, according to the new Article 7, member states became responsible for the detailed arrangements for implementing the requirements of the Espoo Convention. Following the Aarhus Convention,[89] Directive 2003/35/EC has further amended Article 7 in regard to public participation. EU law provided impetus to the development of the Espoo Convention, although with some differences as regards their respective content. The amended and codified EIA Directive now implements nearly all of the requirements of the Espoo Convention with regard to TEIA.[90] It

85 Article 12(3): "[The Contracting Parties] shall, where appropriate, coordinate their land use planning with a view to conserving and managing natural resources of significant importance for two or several Contracting Parties".

86 Directive 85/337/EEC on the assessment of the effects of certain public and private projects on the environment (OJ L175, 5 July 1985, p. 40).

87 See for instance the position of the UK government *in No Environmental Assessment?* 7 ENVIRONMENTAL POLICY AND LAW 20 (1981).

88 CHRISTOPHER WOOD, ENVIRONMENTAL IMPACT ASSESSMENT: A COMPARATIVE REVIEW 34 (Prentice Hall 2nd ed. 2003).

89 See *supra* note 82.

90 The initial 1985 EIA Directive and its three amendments (in 1997, 2003, 2009) have been repealed and codified by Directive 2011/92/EU of the European Parliament and of the Council of 13 December 2011 on the assessment of the effects of certain public and private projects on the environment (OJ L 26, 28 January 2012, p. 1–21), itself amended in 2014 by Directive 2014/52/EU. The initial numbering of the articles has remained quasi-identical. Since 2003, further amendments and codification have not brought any significant change to Article 7.

even provides for an additional obligation, which is absent from the Espoo Convention: the affected states are required to inform their own public when they receive the final decision (Article 9.2).

When international treaties are drafted in ambiguous terms, such that the extent of their obligations is indeterminate, they appear to leave states with broad discretion.[91] However, there has been an evolution toward more precise language, mandatory terms, and a level of commitment that echoes EIA requirements in the domestic systems of parties to international agreements (see for instance the evolution of UNEP regional seas conventions[92]). There is one notable exception to this evolution, i.e. the watercourse treaties. The 1992 UNECE Convention on the Protection and Use of Transboundary Watercourses and Lakes (*the Water Convention*) simply mentions EIA as one of the measures that state parties shall apply in order to prevent, control, and reduce transboundary impact.[93] The 1997 United Nations Convention on the Law of the Non-Navigational Uses of International Watercourses (*the UN Watercourses Convention*) mentions EIA as a simple source of technical data and information.[94] If a party is not otherwise required to conduct an EIA, the UN Watercourses Convention does not provide for an EIA obligation. After lengthy debates, the framework convention, which is considered a reference in international water law, appears to have subordinated the no-harm principle to the principle of equitable and reasonable utilization.[95]

---

91 See, for instance, United Nations Convention on Biological Diversity, Art. 14, (Rio de Janeiro) 5 June 1992, 31 ILM 822 (1992), in force 29 December 1993, where the EIA obligation is nuanced by the phrase "as far as possible and as appropriate"; UNCLOS, Art. 206 ("as far as practicable"), see *supra* pages 42–43.

92 See, for instance, Article 7 of the Convention on the Protection of the Marine Environment of the Baltic Sea Area (Helsinki) 9 April 1992, BNA 35: 0401, in force 17 January 2000 (the Helsinki Convention) as amended (the last amendments entered into force on 1 July 2014)); Article XV(5) of the Bucharest Convention. There are some exceptions: Articles 6 and 12 of a specific protocol to the Bucharest Convention concerning land-based marine pollution, adopted 7 April 2009, not yet in force; Article 17.1 of the Framework Convention for the Protection of the Marine Environment of the Caspian Sea (Tehran) 4 November 2003, 44 ILM 1 (2005), in force 12 August 2006.

93 Articles 3(1)(h) and 9(2)(j) of the Water Convention (Helsinki, 17 March 1992, 31 ILM 1312 (1992), in force 6 October 1996). Article 4.6 of its Protocol on Water and Health (London, 17 June 1999, in force 4 August 2005).

94 Article 12 of the UN Watercourses Convention (New York, 21 May 1997, 36 ILM 700 (1997), in force 17 August 2014). As of August 2021, there were thirty-seven parties to the convention. States that are traversed by the Mekong River are not party to this convention, save for Vietnam only (see *infra* chapter 6).

95 Salman M.A. Salman, *The Future of International Water Law: Regional Approaches to Shared Watercourses? in* LOOKING TO THE FUTURE – ESSAYS IN INTERNATIONAL

1.3.3 The Espoo Convention and the Antarctic Environmental Protocol

Nonetheless, even if the level of formal commitment has increased, albeit with a few exceptions, EIA obligations are still formulated mostly in general terms, because the details of the conduct of an EIA fall back on domestic legislation, as evoked by the definition of an EIA in the Espoo Convention: EIA is a national procedure.[96] There are only two formally binding treaties with detailed EIA requirements: the Espoo Convention and the Antarctic Environmental Protocol. And only the Espoo Convention could become a global transboundary EIA treaty.[97]

The negotiations that led to the *Espoo Convention* began in the 1970's. They were conducted by the UN Economic Commission for Europe (UNECE), a United Nations organization set up to facilitate cooperation between Eastern and Western European countries, Canada and the United States. Originally, national EIA legislations, the 1974 NEPC, and an OECD recommendation issued in 1977 constituted an impulse for the Espoo Convention.[98] In 1975, the Conference on Security and Cooperation in Europe (CSCE) marked a notable step of the *détente* period. The CSCE had the foresight to include in its final act some references to the environment. Two specific topics were assigned to the UNECE in relation to transboundary environmental issues – the long-range transmission of air pollutants, and the concept of EIA. However, the creation of a group of experts on the topic of EIA was delayed for seven years, until 1982. Then, the 1985 EIA Directive, the 1987 UNEP Goals and Principles, and the Brundtland Report all had significant influence on the UNECE. They triggered the revival of discussions on EIA. The UNECE Group of Experts decided to hold a seminar in Warsaw, in September 1987, which was the first substantial sign of progress within the UNECE in more than ten years.[99] Robert G. Connelly, chair

---

LAW IN HONOR OF W. MICHAEL REISMAN 908, 913–915 (Mahnoush H. Arsanjani, et al. eds., 2011).

96 See also, for instance, Article 14(1)(a) of the Convention on Biological Diversity; Article 4(1)(f) of the United Nations Framework Climate Change Convention (New York) 9 May 1992, 1771 UNTS 107, in force 24 March 1994 (UNFCCC).

97 See *infra* note 107.

98 OECD Recommendation on the Implementation of a Regime of Equal Right of Access and Non-discrimination in Relation to Transfrontier Pollution, C(77) 28 (Final), 16 ILM 977 (1977). See Jonas Ebbesson, *Innovative Elements and Expected Effectiveness of the 1991 EIA Convention*, 19 ENVIRON. IMPACT ASSESS. REV. 47, 49 (1999); Mikael Hilden & Eeva Rebekka Furman, *Assessment across borders – Stumbling blocks and options in the practical implementation of the Espoo Convention*, 21 ENVIRON. IMPACT ASSESS. REV. 537, 538 (2001).

99 Robert G. Connelly, *The UN Convention on EIA in a Transboundary Context: A Historical Perspective*, 19 ENVIRON. IMPACT ASSESS. REV. 37, 39 (1999).

of the UNECE Working Group and rapporteur for the topic "EIA in Specific Circumstances", suggested TEIA requirements. His suggestion was met with incredulity at first, because it was seen as inconsistent with state sovereignty. TEIA was a controversial issue,[100] but throughout the sessions of the working group, the United States, Canada and the Nordic countries were very active in trying to advance the proposed TEIA Convention.[101] The convention was finally signed in Espoo (Finland), on 25 February 1991.[102]

The Espoo Convention is a framework convention that is based on the 1985 EIA Directive, but which establishes more arduous requirements. There are substantive goals assigned to the EIA requirements, such as sustainable development and the no-harm principle.[103] At first, the Espoo Convention was a regional convention for UNECE members only. In February 2001, non-UNECE members were allowed to become parties upon approval by the Meeting of the Parties (at present, there are forty-five parties to the convention, all UNECE members[104]). The 2001 amendment has come into force in 2014, but is not yet operational.[105] There has been some interest from non-UNECE countries in joining the Espoo Convention.[106] Thus, the Espoo Convention could

100 Id. at.39. Robert G. Connelly was a Canadian civil engineer who had joined the Canadian Federal Government as an advisor in environmental affairs, specialized in EIA. In the 1990's, Connelly was Vice-President, then President of the Canadian Environmental Assessment Agency.

101 See *infra* chapter 4 for the role of Finland in the negotiations.

102 Convention on Environmental Impact Assessment in a Transboundary Context (Espoo) 25 February 1991, 30 ILM 802 (1991), in force 10 September 1997. As of 2021, there were forty-five parties to the Espoo Convention.

103 See Preamble and Article 2 (1).

104 Malta was the latest state to become a party, after accession, on 20 October 2010. The United States, Russia and Iceland have not ratified the convention. "Iceland's reasons (...) are said to be the impracticality of TEA procedures due to the country's location and the fact that priorities need to be established for a country with such a small civil service" (Pamela Lesser & Timo Koivurova, *Impact Assessment and the New Arctic Geo-Environment, in* ARCTIC MARINE GOVERNANCE, OPPORTUNITIES FOR TRANSATLANTIC COOPERATION 196 (Elizabeth Tedsen, et al. eds., 2014)). Nevertheless, TEIAs in the European Economic Area (EEA) are required under Icelandic national law (Article 19 of the 1993 EIA Act, now Article 18 of the 2000 EIA Act).

105 First Amendment to the Espoo Convention, Meeting of the Parties, 27 February 2001, Decision II/14, UN Doc. ECE/MP.EIA/4, in force 26 August 2014. Some ratifications are still missing for the amendment to become operational, however (Art. 17 as amended, with its new Para. 3).

106 Wiek Schrage & Nick Bonvoisin, *Transboundary impact assessment: frameworks, experiences and challenges*, 26 IMPACT ASSESSMENT AND PROJECT APPRAISAL 234, 236 (2008).

become the basis for a global transboundary EIA treaty.[107] With respect to its subject-matter, the convention applies to transboundary impacts, defined as not "exclusively of a global nature" (Articles 1 (viii) and 2. 1). It applies to a broad range of impacts (Article 1(vii)), which signifies that it can apply concomitantly with other environmental instruments. Some of these instruments clearly refer to the Espoo Convention, such as the Helsinki Convention.[108] Under the Espoo Convention, in 2001, the Meeting of the Parties established an Implementation Committee "for the review of compliance by the parties with their obligations under the convention with a view to assisting them fully to meet their commitments".[109] The committee meets and reports on its activities once a year. It is composed of eight members, elected each year.[110] The review of compliance is characterized "as a non-adversarial and assistance-oriented procedure".[111] The main role of the Implementation Committee is to review submissions made by one or more parties to the Espoo Convention regarding non-compliance by a party with its obligations. Even though the possibility of a public trigger was considered,[112] this possibility remained controversial and the parties ultimately decided against it. Non-state actors

107 John H. Knox, *Assessing the Candidates for a Global Treaty on Transboundary Environmental Impact Assessment*, 12 NYU ENVT'L LJ 153 (2003); Timo Koivurova, *Could the Espoo Convention Become a Global Regime for Environmental Impact Assessment and Strategic Environmental Assessment? in* TRANSBOUNDARY ENVIRONMENTAL GOVERNANCE – INLAND, COASTAL AND MARINE PERSPECTIVES (Robin Warner & Simon Marsden eds., 2012).

108 1992 Convention on the Protection of the Marine Environment of the Baltic Sea Area, Article 7 (1) and (2), which also refers to the EIA Directive. See also Article 14 of the CBD, and Article 6 of the 2002 Protocol to the Bucharest Convention. See, more generally: David M. Dzidzornu, *Environmental Impact Assessment Procedure Through the Conventions*, 10 EUR. ENVT'L L. REV. 15, 23 (2001).

109 Report of the Second Meeting (Sofia), 26–27 February 2001, Decision II/4, Review of Compliance (ECE/MP.EIA/4). See also Article 14 bis of the convention, introduced by the second amendment to the convention (Decision III/7 of the Meeting of the Parties, 4 June 2004, UN Doc. ECE/MP.EIA/6, in force 23 October 2017).

110 Report of the Second Meeting, Decision II/4 (ECE/MP.EIA/4), Appendix to Annex IV (p. 73).

111 Espoo Convention, Article 14bis (introduced by the second amendment, which was adopted on 4 June 2004, and came into force on 23 October 2017 (ECE/MP.EIA/6, Annex VII, Decision III/7, 3.(f)).

112 Jerzy Jendrośka, *Practice and Relevant Cases that emerged in the Context of the Espoo Convention Implementation Committee, in* NON-COMPLIANCE PROCEDURES AND MECHANISMS AND THE EFFECTIVENESS OF INTERNATIONAL ENVIRONMENTAL AGREEMENTS 323, 329–331 (Tullio Treves, et al. eds., 2009). Jendrośka was a member of the Implementation Committee from 2008 to 2011.

cannot formerly initiate the compliance procedure under the Implementation Committee. Only parties to the convention can bring a complaint.[113] However, the Operating Rules of the Implementation Committee allow non-state actors to submit information to the committee if a state is failing to comply with the Espoo Convention. The committee can then decide to act on its own initiative.[114] In addition, NGOs have the right to participate in the meetings of the Conferences of the Parties (CoP), on which occasions they may submit information about cases of non-compliance. Such information may be equivalent to an indirect trigger of the non-compliance procedure when the CoP conveys this information to the appropriate compliance bodies.[115] Along with only one other convention, the Espoo Convention Implementation Committee holds some of its meetings in open session.[116] Upon the review of the complaint, the Implementation Committee can then make recommendations to the Meeting of the Parties.

The other binding agreement with detailed EIA requirements, the *Antarctic Environmental Protocol*, applies to a global commons area without any state's sovereign territory, and devoid of any economic activity. The Environmental Protocol, adopted within the framework of the Antarctic Treaty in 1991, rules on the comprehensive protection of the Antarctic environment, and defines Antarctica "as a natural reserve, devoted to peace and science" (Article 2).[117] EIA is the main instrument of environmental management of the Antarctic,

113 Article 5 of Structure and functions of the Implementation Committee and procedures for review of compliance, Annex to Decision III/2 of the 3rd Meeting of the Parties, Cavtat, June 2004 (ECE/MP.EIA/6).

114 Rule 15 of the Operating Rules (Annex to Decision IV/2 of the Meeting of the Parties, ECE/MP.EIA/10). The term "any other source" is open-ended, and shall abide by the criteria listed in Rule 15, Para.2 (Jendrośka, 330–331. 2009.) The Espoo Convention website provides a special form for the members of the public, NGOs, and all other non-parties, so that they can submit information to the committee (at https://www.unece.org/env/eia/implementation/implementation_committee_meetings.html, accessed 17 June 2021).

115 Francesca Romanin Jacur, *Triggering Non-Compliance Procedures*, *in* NON-COMPLIANCE PROCEDURES AND MECHANISMS, AND THE EFFECTIVENESS OF INTERNATIONAL ENVIRONMENTAL AGREEMENTS 381 (Tullio Treves, et al. eds., 2009).

116 The other convention is the Convention on the Protection and Use of Transboundary Watercourses and International Lakes (the Water Convention).

117 Protocol on Environmental Protection to the Antarctic Treaty (Madrid) 4 October 1991, 30 ILM 1461 (1991), in force 14 January 1998. The Antarctic Treaty was signed in Washington on 1 December 1959 by twelve countries (Argentina, Australia, Belgium, Chile, France, Japan, New Zealand, Norway, South Africa, the USSR, the United Kingdom, and the United States), 402 UNTS 71, 19 ILM 860 (1980), in force 23 June 1961. At present, the total number of parties to the treaty is fifty-four.

based on the no-harm principle. Once an activity has a minor or transitory impact, as opposed to the typically higher threshold of a significant impact, an EIA is required (Article 8(1)).

Both the Espoo Convention and the Antarctic Environmental Protocol establish detailed rules for EIAs, in order to ensure some minimum common requirements, hence some reciprocity between the parties. Indeed, towards reciprocity, the necessity to go beyond the non-discrimination principle is evident in the case of countries with strong EIA requirements, but whose neighboring countries have weaker ones. In such a case, there is an imbalance in environmental management between them. For instance, in 1993, the three members of the North American Agreement on Environmental Cooperation (NAAEC), the environmental side agreement to NAFTA, assembled a draft agreement on transboundary EIA based on the principle of non-discrimination. The lack of reciprocity created difficulties. Canada and the United States have enacted federal EIA legislation that applies only to federal projects or approvals. Mexico's national EIA legislation applies to a wider array of activities, which means that Mexico would be compelled to consult with the United States in more instances than the latter, which led to a deadlock.[118] Consequently, a minimum of reciprocal and common requirements is necessary for a successful TEIA agreement.

1.4 *EIA Prescriptions in Developing Countries*

The origins of EIA in many developing countries contrast with the origins of EIA legislation in North America and in Europe. In the United States, NEPA responded to civil society pressure for introducing environmental concerns and transparency into decision-making processes. In Central and Eastern Europe, the impetus for belonging to the European Union led to compliance with norms in effect in the EU (the EIA Directive and the Espoo Convention). In many developing countries, the development of EIA requirements first resulted from the pressure of international institutions, notably development banks.[119] Only then did some countries later develop further EIA legislation for

118 1993 Draft North American Agreement on Transboundary Environmental Impact Assessment, published in 1997 (on file with the North American Commission for Environmental Cooperation). See John H. Knox, *The Myth and Reality of Transboundary Environmental Impact Assessment*, 96 AJIL 291, 305 et seq. (2002).

119 Ann Hironaka & Evan Schofer, *Decoupling in the Environmental Arena: The Case of Environmental Impact Assessments*, *in* ORGANIZATIONS, POLICY AND THE NATURAL ENVIRONMENT: INSTITUTIONAL AND STRATEGIC PERSPECTIVES (Andrew Hoffmann ed. 2002).

domestic reasons directly linked to the advantages of EIA in terms of environmental protection.[120] Already by the mid-1990's, about two-thirds of the developing countries had enacted EIA requirements.[121] At first, EIA requirements were incorporated into a broader environmental protection act and did not set out detailed procedural requirements. Even though specific EIA legislation has continued to expand, it is still often of a general nature. Consequently, legal requirements for EIAs are frequently lenient and opaque. Typically, developing countries apply EIA prescriptions to a narrower range of projects (screening phase) that address fewer issues (scoping phase). The inadequacy of EIA legislation in developing countries has flowed in great part from the fact that they were modeled upon regulations in Western nations, which typically enjoy more elaborate bureaucracies, open decision-making processes, decentralized political structures, higher literacy rates, and better communication and transportation infrastructure. Moreover, as regards transboundary EIAs, some EIA systems were adopted independently, and have been quite diverse from one country to the other. For all these reasons, it is difficult for the affected public and/or the affected states to obtain a proper TEIA, unless there are external constraints, such as the avenues provided by the development banks. At the moment, existing detailed EIA systems tend to be found in the requirements of international financial institutions and development-assistance agencies. They also operate with the involvement of external NGOs, which now leads us to the regulations of International Organizations, an examination of which will be presented in the following section.

1.5 *International Organizations*

International Organizations (IOs), composed of individual states, have provided an indication of what states consider good EIA practice.[122] In order to promote sustainable development successfully and ensure the efficiency of legal reforms, environmental policy, as embodied in rigorous project development procedures, needed to be extended to, and introduced into the financial

120 MOHAMMAD A. BEKHECHI & JEAN-ROGER MERCIER, THE LEGAL AND REGULATORY FRAMEWORK FOR ENVIRONMENTAL IMPACT ASSESSMENTS – A STUDY OF SELECTED COUNTRIES IN SUB-SAHARAN AFRICA (The World Bank. 2002).

121 CHRISTOPHER WOOD, ENVIRONMENTAL IMPACT ASSESSMENT IN DEVELOPING COUNTRIES: AN OVERVIEW (CONFERENCE ON NEW DIRECTIONS IN IMPACT ASSESSMENT FOR DEVELOPMENT: METHODS AND PRACTICE) 3 (EIA Centre, School of Planning and Landscape, University of Manchester. 2003).

122 See the *Gabčíkovo – Nagymaros* case, where Vice-President Weeramantry cited the World Bank practice as evidence of state practice (1997 ICJ Rep. 7, at 111 (25 September)).

services sector. With regard to Multilateral Development Banks (MDBs),[123] the World Bank (WB) and regional banks are international organizations established by international treaty. Consequently, they are subjects of international law and, as such, capable of possessing international rights and duties.[124] Apart from two recent exceptions (the European Bank for Reconstruction and Development – EBRD, and the binational North American Development Bank – NADB), environmental policy is not included in the charters of MDBs. The World Bank's mandate evolved from initial support of the reconstruction of Europe to its later promoting development throughout the world. Development was then understood as a purely economic notion. NGOs as well as influential member states, such as the United States, uttered strong criticism toward the WB's environmentally unsound lending activities. They built external pressure that has led to progressive improvement.[125] Two trends emerged. The first, of convergence: MDBs have consulted each other to harmonize their rules, considered as an ensemble of standardized practices. The second, of improvement: faced as they were with increasing demands of accountability, MDBs have also made efforts to improve their standards, applicable at all phases of the development projects. In 1980, the World Bank and five regional

123 Some of the major multilateral financial institutions are the African Development Bank (AfDB), the Asian Development Bank (ADB), the Asian Infrastructure Investment Bank (AIIB), the European Bank for Reconstruction and Development (EBRD), the European Investment Bank (EIB), the Inter-American Development Bank (IDB), the International Bank for Reconstruction and Development (IBRD), the International Finance Corporation (IFC) and the Multilateral Investment Guarantee Agency (the last three are part of the World Bank Group).

124 *Reparation for Injuries Suffered in the Service of the United Nations*, Advisory Opinion, 1949 ICJ Reports 174, at 178–179 (11 April). *Interpretation of the Agreement of 25 March 1951 between the WHO and Egypt*, Order, 1980 ICJ Reports 73, at 89–90 (6 June). Mahnoush H. Arsanjani, *Claims Against International Organizations: Quis custodiet ipsos custodes*, 7 YALE JOURNAL OF WORLD PUBLIC ORDER 131 (1981); Emmanuel Gaillard & Isabelle Pingel-Lenuzza, *International Organisations and Immunity from Jurisdiction: to Restrict or to Bypass*, 51 INTERNATIONAL AND COMPARATIVE LAW QUARTERLY 1 (2002).

125 Ian A. Bowles & Cyril F. Kormos, *Environmental Reform at the World Bank: The Role of the U.S. Congress*, 35 VA. J. INT'L L. 777 (1995); Stephen J. Macekura, *Leveraging the Lenders: The Quest for Environmental Impact Statements in the United States and the World Bank, in* OF LIMITS AND GROWTH – THE RISE OF GLOBAL SUSTAINABLE DEVELOPMENT IN THE TWENTIETH CENTURY (2015). See also the US International Institutions Act as amended by the 1989 International Development and Finance Act (also known as the *Pelosi Amendment*), which requires the representative of the US in each MDB not to vote in favor of proposals with potentially significant environmental impacts, unless an EIA has been made available at least 120 days in advance to the board, affected groups and local NGOs, with prior notice of its availability (22 USC § 262m-7).

development banks adopted a set of rules pertaining to the provision of financial resources in view of sustainable development, including an EIA requirement.[126] Development is now defined as *sustainable development*.[127] Not only did MDBs come to the realization that non-economic factors entail economic consequences, but also, as significant international actors of a legal system, that they could not remain isolated from the sea change occurring in international public policy as regards the meaning of development and the necessity of good governance for enhanced legitimacy. For this reason, the World Bank and other MDBs have expressly adopted a sustainable development mandate,[128] which meant a challenge not only to translate this mandate into specific policies and concrete, measurable actions, but also, and more broadly, to redefine their role and to diminish their autonomy in a comprehensive and global policy shift towards greater accountability.[129] This shift led to a convergence of MDB practice and to normative changes. The mandate of two newer development banks, the European Bank for Reconstruction and Development and the North American Development Bank, expressly stipulates political, economic and environmental goals.[130]

---

126 The World Bank, five regional development banks (the African Development Bank, the Arab Bank for Economic Development in Africa, the Asian Development Bank, the Caribbean Development Bank, the Inter-American Development Bank), the EU, the OAS, UNEP, and UNDP adopted a Declaration of Environmental Policies and Procedures Relating to Economic Development (1 February 1980, 19 ILM 524 (1980)).

127 UNGA Res. 47/191, Institutional arrangements to follow up the United Nations Conference on Environment and Development (A/Res/47/191), 22 December 1992, Para. 23.

128 See, for instance, World Bank, Making Development Sustainable: The World Bank Group and the Environment (1994); Advancing Sustainable Development: The World Bank and Agenda 21 (1997); Making Sustainable Commitments. An Environment Strategy for the World Bank, 17 July 2001. DAVID FREESTONE, THE WORLD BANK AND SUSTAINABLE DEVELOPMENT – LEGAL ESSAYS (Martinus Nijhoff. 2013). See also ASIAN DEVELOPMENT BANK, THE BANK'S MEDIUM-TERM STRATEGIC FRAMEWORK (1995–1998), Manila, President's Office (Asian Development Bank. 1995).

129 Gunther Handl, *The Legal Mandate of Multilateral Development Banks as Agents for Change Toward Sustainable Development*, 92 AJIL 642, 645 (1998).

130 EBRD: Agreement Establishing the European Bank for Reconstruction and Development, Articles 1 and 2, (London) 29 May 1990, 29 ILM 1077 (1990), in force 28 March 1991. NADB: Agreement Between the Government of the United States of America and the Government of the United Mexican States Concerning the Establishment of a Border Environment Cooperation Commission and a North American Development Bank, Article 1 of Chapters I and II, (Mexico City) 18 November 1993, 32 ILM 1545 (1993), in force 1 January 1994. To this day, the charters of the EBRD and the NADB are the only two charters that contain an environmental mandate.

A larger aspect of these normative changes is community expectations: multilateral environmental treaties that embody fundamental general concerns, with the support of a majority of states and other international actors, generate expectations of compliance from IOs as well, whether or not they are parties to these treaties, as law-making is a process of communication.[131] A related and specific normative change is that, as the implementing agency/trustee of the Multilateral Fund for the Montreal Protocol (MFMP),[132] and in accordance with the Global Environment Facility (GEF) program,[133] the World Bank can no longer provide funding for projects that violate the objectives of these treaties, even to countries that are not parties to them, and regardless of whether MFMP or GEF funds are involved. Nor can regional development banks, if they act as executing agencies for the World Bank and the UNEP in the management of GEF-funded projects. They cannot support projects "that would run counter to the objectives of the ... conventions which [they are] formally committed to implement".[134] Hence, the World Bank is supposed to undertake its extended

131 "Expectations about appropriate behavior, some explicit, some at levels of consciousness so deep that people are not aware of them, are shaped in all of these processes of communication. If one is to understand and influence international law-making, plainly one must address the process in its rich totality", W. Michael Reisman, *International Lawmaking: A Process of Communication*, 75 AM. SOC'Y INT'L L. PROC. 101, 107 (1981). "A new norm cannot emerge without both practice and opinio juris; and an existing norm does not die without the great majority of states engaging in both a contrary practice and withdrawing their opinio juris", ROSALYN HIGGINS, PROBLEMS AND PROCESS: INTERNATIONAL LAW AND HOW WE USE IT 22 (Oxford University Press. 1994). "these latter decisions, those taken in accordance with community expectations and enforced by organized community coercion, (...) are, from the perspectives we recommend, most appropriately called "law"", Myres S. McDougal, *Jurisprudence for a Free Society*, 1 GEORGIA LAW REVIEW 1, 4 (1966). Handl, AJIL, 660–661 (1998). See *infra* chapter 3.

132 The Protocol on Substances that Deplete the Ozone Layer (Montreal, 16 September 1987, 26 ILM 1541 (1987), in force 1 January 1989) aims at reducing these substances. To date, the Montreal Protocol is the only UN treaty signed and ratified by all UN members.

133 The GEF was established in 1990, and restructured in 1994 (Instrument Establishing the Global Environment Facility (Geneva) 16 March 1994, 33 ILM 1273 (1994), and its subsequent amendments). The GEF is a mechanism for international cooperation in view of providing new and additional grant and concessional funding to meet the agreed incremental costs of measures to achieve agreed global environmental benefits in climate change, biodiversity, international waters, and ozone layer depletion (Para. 2). Also eligible for funding are the agreed incremental costs of activities concerning land degradation, primarily desertification and deforestation (Para. 3).

134 Peter H. Sand, *The Potential Impact of the Global Environment Facility of the World Bank, UNDP and UNEP*, *in* ENFORCING ENVIRONMENTAL STANDARDS: ECONOMIC MECHANISMS AS VIABLE MEANS? 496 (Rüdiger Wolfrum ed. 1996). Sand is a former legal adviser for environmental affairs at the World Bank.

development mandate in compliance with any international environmental instrument to which the borrower is a party, as well as other international environmental prescriptions that apply to the World Bank.[135]

In practice, in the late 1980's, the World Bank undertook significant restructuring itself, and created an Environment Department (in 1987). In the same decade, the contours of its environmental mandate were also shaped by the adoption of several internal environmental safeguard policies and procedures,[136] including one on EIA which has served as the umbrella policy since 1989. In response to criticism, the World Bank then amended its requirements. Operational Policy (OP) 4.01 and Bank Procedure (BP) 4.01 state the current requirements for any project undertaken prior to October 2018.[137] Recently, the World Bank reformed its environmental policy for investment project financing. In August 2016, it adopted a new Environmental and Social Framework (ESF) that replaced the previous one (in particular OP/BP4.01 for EIA), and has been applied to all new development projects since it went into effect, on 1 October 2018 (in parallel with the first generation of safeguards that have stayed in place for older and ongoing projects until the latter come to an end).[138] The World Bank has been heavily criticized for shifting the responsibility to enforce environmental requirements back to borrowers when the bank deems that applicable national laws achieve "objectives materially consistent" with its own set of rules.[139] The risk appears to be that the World Bank may rely too

135 Handl, AJIL, 651–653 (1998).

136 First, in the mid-1980's, they were adopted under the form of Operational Manual Statements (OMSs) and Operations Policy Notes (OPNs). After 1987, they were progressively enacted in Operational Directives (ODs). In the early 1990's, they were gradually converted into Operational Policies (OPs), Bank Procedures (BPs), and Good Practices (GPs). A clear distinction has been established between OPs and BPs, which are mandatory for WB staff, and the GPs, which are simply advisory.

137 Operational Directive 4.00 (1989), then Operational Directive 4.01 (1991), then Operational Policy 4.01 (OP 4.01) since 1999, as amended.

138 In 2001, the World Bank's directors decided to embark upon a new environment strategy, which was finalized on 4 August 2016, by the adoption of a new Environmental and Social Framework (ESF). See in particular ESS1 Assessment and Management of Environmental and Social Risks and Impacts, completed by a new WB Directive, the Environment and Social Directive for Investment Project Financing, effective January 2020. The previous WB safeguards will run in parallel to the new ESF for projects approved before the launch of the new ESF, for an estimated seven years (at https://www.worldbank.org/en/projects-operations/environmental-and-social-framework, accessed 17 June 2021).

139 Para. 9, 12(b), 13 ... of the Environmental and Social Policy for Investment Project Financing. See Press Release, *NGO Response to the World Bank's Proposed environmental and social Framework: Proposed World Bank Standards Represent Dangerous Set-back to Key Environmental and Social Protections* (2016).

heavily on the information provided by the borrower in making this determination in these cases. Furthermore, during the preparatory consultations, WB stakeholders had emphasized that the new policy should apply to all IDA and IBRD activities, including development policy loans, program for results, and technical assistance.[140] However, the new policy applies only to investment lending (with the inclusion of financial intermediaries), not to a wider range of the bank's financing products. The new ESF aims at further harmonizing the World Bank's environmental protections with other development institutions. If the ambition of the new ESF is commendable, building capacity is a long road. Regardless, the Bank seems to rush into allowing additional leeway to borrowing countries. At the moment, it is thus feared that the general trend be a relaxation of environmental requirements due to new competition, notably from the Asian Infrastructure Investment Bank.[141]

The objective of the World Bank's environmental policies is to help ensure that bank-financed projects are "environmentally sound and sustainable, and thus to improve decision-making".[142] To achieve this objective, the World Bank resorts to environmental assessment (EA) instruments, which include EIA, regional or sectoral environmental assessment, environmental audit, hazard or risk assessment, environmental management plans, and an Environmental and Social Management Framework (ESMF).[143] In 1999, the World Bank also adopted some guidelines (Pollution Prevention and Abatement Handbook), where there is an express linkage of EA processes to substantive environmental standards and objectives. In these guidelines, the Bank's requirements are detailed and apply to screening, identification of adverse impacts, gaps in knowledge, analysis of alternatives, and public consultation at both the scoping stage and once a draft EA document has been prepared.[144]

---

140 World Bank, *Review and Update of the World Bank's Environmental and Social Safeguard Policies – Summary of input submitted by stakeholders*, Question 1, Coverage and Relevance, point 2; Q6, Coverage; Q6, Internal reforms, t 1; Q9, Coverage (October 2012-April 2013).

141 Natalie Bugalski, *The Demise of Accountability at the World Bank?* 31 AM. U. INT'L L. REV. 1 (2016); Kathryn D. Priester, *Safeguard Reforms at the World Bank: Mutual Accountability or a Race to the Bottom?* 32 GEO. INT'L ENVTL. L. REV. 599 (2020). For a rather confident point of view as regards the future role of the World Bank, see Philipp Dann & Michael Riegner, *The World's Bank Environmental and Social Safeguards and the evolution of global order*, 32 LJIL 537 (2019). See also *infra* chapter 6, page 306 et seq.

142 OP 4.01, Para. 1 and Annex A (definitions).

143 OP 4.01, Para. 7.

144 The Pollution Prevention and Abatement Handbook, World Bank Group, pages 22–26, with a description of the Bank's EA process (at http://documents.worldbank.org/curated/en/758631468314701365/Pollution-prevention-and-abatement-handbook-1998-toward-cleaner-production, accessed 17 June 2021).

The World Bank also resorts to Inspection Panel reviews that ensure compliance with its requirements. The Inspection Panel was established in 1993. It was an innovation at the time, as an independent compliance mechanism for individuals and communities who believe that they have been, or are likely to be, adversely affected by a WB-funded project. The Inspection Panel assesses allegations of harm to people or the environment, and reviews whether the World Bank followed its policies and procedures. Upon review of a complaint, the Inspection Panel may recommend further investigations, which it conducts once the investigation has been authorized by the Board of Executive Directors. At present , EA is the most frequent basis for complaints filed with the Inspection Panel (83% of all complaints).[145]

All MDBs have endeavored to institute similar safeguard systems, either individually, or collectively.[146] In the 1990's, when the share of the World Bank-financed projects diminished, other major funders were encouraged to adopt similar obligations. A first step toward harmonization approach has been the UNEP Financial Initiative, a partnership between the United Nations Environment Programme and the global financial sector, created in the wake of the 1992 Earth Summit in order to promote sustainable finance. The UNEP Financial Initiative includes over two hundred financial institutions. Their latest proposal is the Principles for Responsible Banking, adopted in 2019. The International Finance Corporation (IFC) also initiated discussions with private sector financial institutions, which led to the adoption of the Equator Principles in 2003. The Equator Principles (EP) lay out a risk management framework for determining, assessing and managing environmental and social risks in project development. They are primarily intended to provide a minimum standard for due diligence, in view of responsible risk decision-making processes within the private sector. Currently, 111 Equator Principles Financial Institutions (EPFI) in 37 countries have officially adopted the EP, covering the majority of international project finance debt within developed and emerging markets.[147] Other major funders include the bilateral and multilateral agencies.

---

145 At https://www.inspectionpanel.org/panel-cases/data, accessed 17 June 2021. See also *infra* chapter 6, page 299 et seq. On how aid assistance improved prior to 1993, with some developments still relevant presently, see David A. Wirth, *Legitimacy, Accountability, and Partnership: A Model for Advocacy on Third World Environmental Issues*, 100 Yale L.J. 2645 (1991).

146 HARVEY HIMBERG, REPORT – COMPARATIVE REVIEW OF MULTILATERAL DEVELOPMENT BANK SAFEGUARD SYSTEMS (2015).

147 At http://www.equator-principles.com (accessed 17 June 2021). See also the European Principles for the Environment (EPE), adopted on 30 May 2006, by the Council of Europe

In 2003, the OECD, for instance, agreed to strengthen common approaches to environmental concerns and officially supported export credits, of which many apply to major projects in developing countries.[148] The latest version of the assessment procedures, adopted in 2012 and amended in 2016, resemble the Equator Principles.[149]

The OECD Common Approaches, the EP, and MDBs have promoted convergence around common environmental and social standards. More generally, MDBs, multilateral agencies, and private banks alike are bound by international legal obligations relative to sustainable development and the protection of the environment[150] for the same reasons stated above, i.e. community expectations of appropriate behavior.

2 Generalized Structure Common to Domestic EIA Systems, Adopted by International EIA Prescriptions

A review of EIA systems reveals the common structure of EIA requirements. An EIA usually conforms to the following main steps:

1. Screening
2. Scoping – Impact analysis – Report preparation
3. Notification – Consultations
4. Public participation
5. Final decision
6. Follow-up programs

Development Bank, EBRD, European Investment Bank, Nordic Environment Finance Corporation, and Nordic Investment Bank.

148 OECD Recommendation on Common Approaches on Environment and Officially Supported Export Credits, 18 December 2003, C(2003)236 and C/M(2003)29.

149 Recommendation of the Council on Common Approaches for Officially Supported Export Credits and Environmental and Social Due Diligence (The "Common Approaches") 28 June 2012 – C(2012)101, Amended on 6 April 2016 – C(2016)38.

150 Handl, AJIL, 664–665 (1998). See also *infra* chapter 6, page 296 et seq.

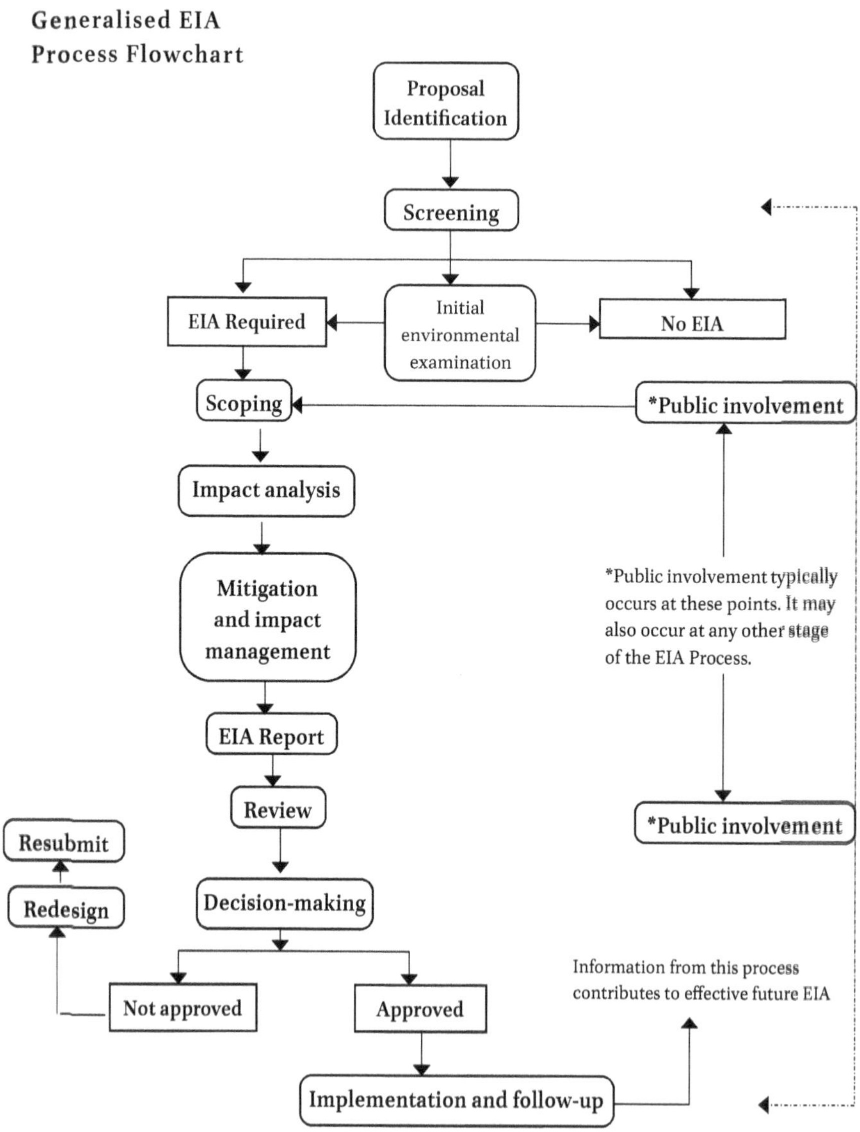

CHART 1 Generalized EIA Process Flow chart
(UNEP, ENVIRONMENTAL IMPACT ASSESSMENT TRAINING RESOURCE MANUAL Section E – Topic 1, page 114 (UNEP 2nd ed. 2002). ILLUSTRATION REPRODUCTION COURTESY OF THE UNEP. See two similar flowcharts *infra* pages 85–86)

Because they state procedural obligations, NEPA, the EIA Directive, and the Espoo Convention describe their purposes and underlying values and principles.[151] Apart from a few EIA systems, EIA legislation frequently affirms its policy goals and a clear connection between EIA and these goals.[152] Then, as a planning tool, an EIA should naturally start as early as possible in the decision-making process. NEPA emphasizes that "agencies shall integrate the NEPA process with other planning at the earliest possible time to ensure that planning and decisions reflect environmental values, to avoid delays later in the process, and to head off potential conflicts".[153] For the World Bank, it also starts "at the earliest stage of the project cycle",[154] as well as for the EBRD.[155] Regrettably, the EIA Directive does not specify when the EIA process should start.

2.1 *Screening*

The practice of EIA has been focused on the project level, and more particularly on major projects. The proper definition of a threshold is paramount, otherwise scores of projects are regularly allowed to pass as proposed.

2.1.1 Initial Range of Activities Captured by EIA Prescriptions

In federal states, there is a combination of federal and state regulations, which usually do not perfectly overlap. In the United States, according to NEPA, an EIS must be prepared for all major federal actions. The range of activities encompassed by NEPA is broad, but excludes purely private activities (i.e. activities that are not financed, assisted, nor regulated by a federal agency), or those subject only to sub-state government oversight. In the United States and Canada, the gap is not always supplemented by EIA requirements at the state level, particularly in states that border an international frontier.[156]

---

151 42 US Code § 4321; EIA Directive, Preamble, Para. 2, referencing Art. 130R of the Treaty Establishing the European Community, OJ C325; Espoo Convention, Preamble.

152 See, for example, Canadian Environmental Assessment Act, 2012 (S.C. 2012, c. 19, s. 52), Article 4; Canadian Impact Assessment Act, 2019 (S.C. 2019, c. 28, s. 1), Article 6; Part XII of the UNCLOS, which addresses marine pollution. It states a general obligation to protect and preserve the marine environment in Article 192, which is developed in Article 194 (Article 206, about EIA, belongs to Part XII).

153 40 CFR § 1501.2. See also § 1501.1(a).

154 BP 4.01, Point 2. ESS1, Annex 1, Para. 4, 7; ES Policy for IPF, Para. 3(b), 26, 53.

155 EBRD, 2014 ESP (Performance Requirement 6, Para. 8). For projects initiated after 1 January 2020, 2019 ESP (PR 6, Para. 8).

156 In the US, twenty states have NEPA-like environmental planning requirements, the list of which can be found at https://ceq.doe.gov/laws-regulations/states.html (accessed 17 June 2021). Among the four states that border Mexico, only one, California, is on the list. Among the thirteen that border Canada, more than half are not on the list (Alaska, Idaho, New Hampshire, North Dakota, Maine, Michigan, Ohio, Pennsylvania, Vermont).

In other jurisdictions, like in the European Union countries or Mexico, EIA provisions identify areas of *prima facie* application, without any consideration for the administrative authority in charge of the authorization. EIA legislation applies to public and private projects in industrial sectors or categories of activities that are presumed to produce significant adverse transboundary impacts.[157] An ex-ante classification of projects establishes significance in the gradation of impacts, as presumed or excluded.[158] The EIA Directive lists activities that are automatically subject to an EIA.[159] Another instance is the Equator Principles (EP), which apply to all industry sectors and to four financial products.[160]

2.1.2 Projects That May Potentially Cause a Significant Environmental Effect

> *Environmental significance is an unashamedly anthropocentric concept. When applied in EIA decision-making, it uses judgements and values equally with, or to a greater extent than, science- based criteria and standards* [161]

Depending on the legislation under consideration, either for activities not automatically subject to an EIA (listed in the Annex I of the EIA Directive for instance), nor categorically excluded, or for any activity (Article 2.2 of the Espoo Convention), a two-step screening is necessary, i.e. a review of the activities listed in the applicable legislation, then a determination of significance in regard to their potential impacts. The threshold of significance is the most common in international, regional, and domestic EIA regulations (UNEP EIA Goals and Principles, the Espoo Convention, the CBD, the US-Canada Air Quality Agreement, the UNEP regional seas agreements, the UNCLOS (along with substantial pollution[162]), the EIA Directive, NEPA, CEAA, Mexico, Finland,

157 In Mexico, see Chapter 2 of *Reglamento de la Ley General del Equilibrio Ecológico y Protección Ambiental en Materia de Evaluaciones de Impacto Ambiental*, Mexico DF, 30 May 2000. EIA Directive, Article 4.1 and Annex I. The EIA Directive has adopted a broad definition of project. It "means the execution of construction works or of other installations or schemes, or other interventions in the natural surroundings and landscape including those involving the extraction of mineral resources" (Article 1.2.(a)).

158 See, for instance: NEPA, Section 1508.4; the 2007 Exclusion List Regulations (SOR/2007–108) pursuant to Subparagraph 59(c)(ii) of the 1992 CEAA.

159 EIA Directive, Article 4.1. and Annex I.

160 Equator Principles (July 2020), Scope (page 5) (at https://equator-principles.com/app/uploads/The-Equator-Principles_EP4_July2020.pdf, accessed 17 June 2021).

161 Sippe, 75. 1999.

162 Article 206: "When States have reasonable grounds for believing that planned activities under their jurisdiction or control may cause *substantial pollution of or significant and harmful changes to the marine environment*, they shall, as far as practicable, assess the

Sweden, France, Spain, China, Laos, Thailand, Cambodia, Vietnam …[163]). There are few exceptions to the choice of significant impact as the EIA threshold. One such exception is the Antarctic Environmental Protocol, because it applies to a specific area, which led to the choice of a lower threshold – an EIA is required if an activity has at least a "minor or transitory impact".[164] The Equator Principles also impose a lower threshold. They resort to the threshold of a significant adverse impact (Category A), but also to a threshold of a limited adverse impact (Category B). For Category A and, as appropriate, Category B Projects, the Assessment Documentation needs to include an Environmental and Social Impact Assessment (ESIA).[165]

World Bank procedures call for screening of proposed projects to determine which type of assessment is required. For projects that began before October 2018, there are three categories: projects in Category A require a full EIA; those in Category B require environmental analysis and case-by-case determination; projects in Category C require neither.[166] For new projects since October 2018, all of them must undergo an EIA, but the WB and the borrower agree to resort to the WB's ESF on a case-by-case basis (ESS1, Para. 7 et seq., and Para. 14 et seq.). For subprojects, there are four categories of risk (high, substantial, moderate, or low), with a broad range of criteria to determine the risk level on a case-by-case basis, not only upon first examination, but with regular reviews all along the project life cycle.[167] As for the level of obligations that the risk level triggers, a high-risk project requires an EIA in accordance with the ESF. If a project rates at any of the other risk levels, the borrower's domestic laws apply, under the supervision of the World Bank. In other words, the new ESF has reverted back to when the borrower was principally in charge of the whole project. Whether or not the World Bank will exercise proper supervision remains to be seen.[168]

The EBRD's categorization is slightly different: Category A Projects require a full EIA (a list of indicative Category A projects is provided). For Category B Projects, environmental and social appraisal requirements may vary,

---

potential effects of such activities on the marine environment and shall communicate reports of the results of such assessments in the manner provided in article 205". (emphasis added).

163 To cite only a few countries, among which those that will be the object of the subsequent case studies (see *infra* chapters 4 to 6).

164 Art. 8(1).

165 Equator Principles (July 2020), Principles 1 and 2.

166 WB OP 4.01, Point 8.

167 See WB Environmental and Social Policy for Investment Project Financing, Para. 20 and 21, and Environmental and Social Directive for IPF, Section III(C).

168 ESS1 Para. 19 *et seq.*, Environmental and Social Policy for Investment Project Financing, Para. 23 et seq.

depending on the project, and are determined by the EBRD on a case-by-case basis. The impacts of Category C Projects can readily be addressed through limited environmental and social appraisal.[169]

An identical threshold – a significant impact – could be seen as a welcome occurrence at all levels in order to facilitate the implementation of EIA requirements. With this in mind, NEPA, UNEP, the Espoo Convention, as well as a few others, attempted to define significance,[170] but determining whether the threshold has been met is usually done on a case-by-case basis.[171] Indeed, a flexible interpretation of the concept of environmental significance has been essential to the rapid worldwide spread of EIA as a public-policy tool. This concept can thus be adapted to different jurisdictional cultures.[172]

In the European Union, until 2014, member states enjoyed a rather large margin of appreciation for projects that belong to the second category (those that are not automatically subject to an EIA). They could decide to evaluate significance on a case-by-case basis, or by resorting to thresholds and criteria listed in Annex III of the EIA Directive. The Court of Justice of the European Communities (CJEC) would condemn member states that abused this possibility.[173] The 2014 amendments to the EIA Directive have reduced this margin of appreciation, by adding a step to the determination procedure. The developer is required to provide information on the characteristics of the project, on its

169 Environmental and Social Policy, Appendix II, and Environmental and Social Procedures, Point 3.3.1 (at https://www.ebrd.com/what-we-do/strategies-and-policies.html, accessed 17 June 2021).

170 For NEPA, see 40 CFR §1508.27 (*"Significantly* as used in NEPA requires considerations of both context and intensity". Context and intensity are then described); UNEP Draft Principles of Conduct: the expression "significantly affect" means "any appreciable effects on a shared natural resource and excludes *de minimis* effects" (Definition Section); Specific Methodologies and Criteria to Determine the Significance of Adversary Transboundary Impact (Report by the Espoo Convention Secretariat, CEP/WG.3/R.6, 1995); 1996 Cuixmala Model Draft Treaty for the Protection of the Environment and the Natural Resources of North America, Article 2.7 (*in* Alberto Szekely, et al., *Cuixmala Model Draft Treaty for the Protection of the Environment and the Natural Resources of North America*, 36 NATURAL RESOURCES JOURNAL 3 (1996)).

171 See, for instance, the Antarctic Treaty System where the EIA guidelines were adopted in part to facilitate the case-by-case determination. The parties noted that a "determination of the status of activities was context dependent, based on value judgments and information available at the time". The United States "commented that the focus of the discussion should not be on developing prescriptive definitions but rather on providing guidance for making determinations" (Final Report of the Twenty First Antarctic Treaty Consultative Meeting (Christchurch, 19–26 May 1997), Para. 22 (p. 10–11)).

172 Sippe, 74 et seq. 1999.

173 CJEC, 2 May 1996, Case C-133/94, *Commission v. Belgium*, ECLI:EU:C:1996:181 (see, in the same vein, regarding the determination required by the Habitats Directive, CJEC, 6 April 2000, Case C-256/98, *Commission v. France*, ECLI:EU:C:2000:192).

likely significant effects on the environment (the detailed list of information to be provided is specified in Annex IIA), and on mitigation measures (Article 4.4). The competent authority must then make its determination available to the public, stating its main reasons to require or not an EIA, within a period of time not exceeding ninety days from the day the information has been provided (Article 4.5). In other words, the 2014 amendments added the necessity of a preliminary assessment, of the sort that already existed in other instruments (for instance, NEPA requires an Environmental Assessment (EA) for all proposed actions, and the Antarctic Environmental Protocol requires a similar preliminary assessment[174]). It has been a welcome addition, because the environmental impacts can be apprehended only if there has been a preliminary evaluation.[175] In order to address the ambiguity of the significance threshold, most jurisdictions have required that the responsible authority conduct a preliminary assessment in order to determine whether an activity has the potential to cause significant environmental effects, in which case a full EIA will be required (of which the official name varies – Comprehensive Environmental Evaluation (CEE), Environmental Impact Assessment (EIA), Environmental Impact Statement (EIS) …). Under the regime of the 1991 Antarctic Protocol, there is yet another intermediary assessment, the Initial Environmental Evaluation (IEE – if the activity may have a minor or transitory impact as determined by the preliminary assessment). The IEE is conducted by the responsible authority alone, as a self-assessment tool, but each party is supposed to transmit an annual list of its IEEs and the decisions that ensued (Article 6).

In order to determine environmental significance, some jurisdictions resort to criteria or factors in the screening process when an EIA is not automatically required, and to determine if it should be.[176]

The Espoo Convention resorts to both a list of activities and criteria simultaneously. A state "of origin shall ensure that in accordance with the provisions of this convention an environmental impact assessment is undertaken prior to a decision to authorize or undertake a proposed activity listed in Appendix I that is likely to cause a significant adverse transboundary impact" (Article 2(3)). Appendix I lists a vast array of both public and private sector projects, generally of a large scale. An initial decision is necessary to determine whether an activity listed in Appendix I is likely to cause significant adverse

174 NEPA: 40 CFR 1501.4(b) and (c), and 1508.9 (EA for all actions except those that are categorically excluded).
Antarctic Environmental Protocol: Art. 8 and Annex I, Art. 1.

175 EVE TRUILHÉ-MARENGO, DROIT DE L'ENVIRONNEMENT DE L'UNION EUROPÉENNE 216 (Larcier. 2015).

176 EIA Directive, Annex III. CEQ Regulations, 40 CFR § 1508.27.

environmental impact. If two state parties disagree about the significance of a proposed activity that belongs to the list in Appendix I, they can resort to the Inquiry Procedure (detailed in Appendix IV). An independent inquiry commission will scientifically determine if the threshold has been met, and will issue recommendations.[177] It is a cooperative process, which includes the continued exchange of information, and which is supposed to bring about reasoned decisions, respectful of the no-harm principle.[178] For the activities not included in Appendix I, parties are only required to enter into discussions on whether the proposed activity is likely to cause a significant adverse transboundary impact. General guidance for identifying criteria to determine significant adverse impact is set forth in Appendix III.[179] However, in the case of a disagreement, the inquiry procedure is not available. It is available only in the case of a disagreement as to whether an activity included in the list of Appendix I may cause a significant adverse environmental impact.

Other international EIA instruments address the difficulties associated with screening by providing guidelines. For instance, both the Convention on Biological Diversity (CBD) and the Ramsar Convention EIA Guidelines recommend that screening criteria include biodiversity measures, provide detailed examples of how to proceed, and refer to applicable national, regional and international instruments.[180] The Arctic EIA Guidelines also emphasize that the decision to conduct an EIA for a project should take into account the special geo-biological and atmospheric conditions in the Arctic. They strongly

177 Article 3, and Appendix IV, Para. 2 and 14.

178 To this day, the inquiry procedure has been invoked on one occasion, by Romania on 19 August 2004, with respect to the Danube-Black Sea Deep Water Navigation Canal in the Ukrainian part of the Danube Delta (Bystroe Canal Project). In July 2006, the Inquiry Commission, composed of three scientific experts and the Secretary to the Espoo Convention, unanimously concluded that the project would have a significant adverse transboundary impact and made some recommendations: a bilateral research program addressing the gaps in scientific information and knowledge, to contribute to a realistic evaluation of the navigation route and adequate mitigation measures (https://unece.org/environment-policyenvironmental-assessment/inquiry-commission, accessed 17 August 2021).

179 Article 2(5) and Appendix III.

180 CBD Voluntary guidelines on biodiversity-inclusive impact assessment, Preamble (4) and Annex B (1), COP 8 – Decision VIII/28, 20–31 March 2006, UN Doc. UNEP/CBD/COP/DEC/VIII/28 (hereinafter the CBD Voluntary guidelines on biodiversity-inclusive impact assessment). Ramsar Convention EIA Guidelines, adopted at the 8th Meeting of the Conference of the Contracting Parties to the Convention on Wetlands, Valencia, Spain, 18–26 November 2002, by Resolution VIII.9, in connection with the CBD EIA Guidelines (the first set of CBD guidelines, adopted in April 2002 (COP 6, Decision VI/7, UNEP/CBD/COP/6/7)).

recommend Arctic-specific thresholds and sensitivity criteria, and provide lists in this regard. They also refer to related instruments.[181]

In domestic or regional settings, disputes about whether there is a potential significant adverse impact are subject to judicial review,[182] but courts have been reluctant to question the expertise of administrative agencies in this matter. In the international sphere, the reliance on common standards is thus even more necessary.[183] However, sovereign states still continue to insist on a case-by-case determination, which has the advantage of ensuring the persistence of EIA systems.

2.2 *Scoping – Impact Analysis – Report Preparation*

2.2.1 Scoping

For reasons of time and budget constraints, which are typical of project developments, scoping aims at balancing comprehensiveness and efficiency, by concentrating the EIA on the issues that are most likely to have a significant impact on the environment. However, the exclusion of some issues from an EIA has proved difficult because of the threat of litigation, the reluctance of environmental groups, and the high levels of scientific uncertainty in the environmental field.

An EIA is supposed to include a description of the purpose and need for the proposed action, of the project itself, of the affected environment, a thorough examination of the environmental consequences of the planned action, the alternatives to this action, mitigation measures, and a non-technical summary.[184] The Espoo Convention adds to this list an explicit indication of predictive methods and underlying assumptions as well as the relevant environmental data that was used, an identification of gaps in knowledge and uncertainties encountered in compiling the required information and, where appropriate, an outline for monitoring and for management programs and any plans for post-project analysis. The list that results from Article 4 and Appendix II of the Espoo Convention is similar to the requirements for a CEE under the Antarctic Environmental Protocol regime (Article 3 of Annex I).

The scoping process serves in part to identify reasonable alternatives. The potential range of reasonable alternatives may include alternatives outside the mandate of the lead agency, as well as the no-action alternative.[185] The

181 Pages 6, 11–12, and Appendix II.

182 See, for instance, the abundant case-law of the Court of Justice of the European Union (TRUILHÉ-MARENGO, 216–220. 2015).

183 CRAIK, 134 & 137–138. 2008.

184 See, for instance, the EIA Directive, Article 5.1.

185 For instance, in the US, see 40 CFR § 1502.14 (c) and (d).

comparison of alternatives is essential for determining whether or not the planned project and its impacts are acceptable. According to the CEQ, this requirement is "the heart of the EIS (...) providing a clear basis for choice among options by the decision-maker and the public".[186] The International Law Commission also acknowledged the importance of alternatives.[187] Comparing alternatives and their environmental, economic, and social consequences is all the more important in the absence of explicit standards. The comparison of alternatives is the only possible comparison and evaluation. It is required in many instruments. The World Bank requires that all alternatives be included, along with their systematic comparison.[188] However, the Espoo Convention requires consideration of alternatives only "where appropriate" (Appendix II(b)). This has been interpreted as a reference to domestic EIA systems and to the principle of non-discrimination.[189] The application of this principle is not problematic when there are similar domestic EIA systems, such as in the UNECE area, where the Espoo Convention applies at present.[190] However, provisions based on the non-discrimination principle may contradict the aspirations of the Espoo Convention to become a global treaty, as the difficulties of the NAAEC with the 1993 Draft North American Agreement on Transboundary Environmental Impact Assessment exemplify.[191]

International EIA prescriptions usually refer to national laws with respect to scoping procedures, except for the Antarctic Environmental Protocol, which naturally stands apart because of the specificity of the Antarctic area. However, even if the 1991 Antarctic Protocol details the scoping procedures for IEE and CEE (Articles 2 and 3 of Annex I), it does not include the obligation to consult other parties at the scoping stage. Few, if any, EIA instruments require consultations at this stage, which has proved problematic.

2.2.2 Impact Analysis

The Espoo Convention, the Antarctic Environmental Protocol and the World Bank broadly define the notion of impact, which, for instance, includes for

186 CEQ NEPA Regulations, p. 477, under 40 CFR § 1502.14. See also 42 USC § 4332(C)(iii); *Calvert Cliffs' Co-ordinating Committee Inc. v. United States Atomic Energy Commission*, 449 F.2d 1109 (DC Cir. 1971) at 1128.

187 Article 10 of the 2001 Draft Articles on Transboundary Harm.

188 World Bank BP 4.01, Para. 19; WB ESS1, Para. 24 and Annex 1, Para. 13(g). See also EIA Directive, Article 5.1(d).

189 CRAIK, 139–140. 2008.

190 See WOOD, 139. 2003, who has observed some uniformity in the consideration of alternatives among the seven EIA systems that he examined.

191 See *supra* page 51.

the former the consideration of effects on human health and safety, flora, fauna, soil, air, water, climate, landscape and historical monuments or other physical structures, or the interaction among these factors. It also includes effects on cultural heritage or socio-economic conditions resulting from alterations to those factors.[192] However, the Espoo Convention does not require the assessment of the cumulative impacts of proposed activities (in combination with other existing activities or planned projects), unlike the Antarctic Environmental Protocol,[193] the UNEP EIA Goals and Principles (Principle 4(d)), the World Bank (ESS1 Para. 23), and some domestic EIA requirements.[194] Much could be achieved if the necessity to examine cumulative impacts was expanded.[195]

In addition to a list of minimum procedural requirements, international EIA instruments may add, more systematically, the geographical extension of EIA beyond the state (transboundary EIA), or the assessment of impacts on issues of common concern, or the impacts that fall under diverse applicable protection regimes (e.g. biological diversity or climate change).

2.2.3 Report Preparation

The responsibility for preparing the report is often delegated to the project proponent (or developer, according to the different terminologies), who frequently is a private entity.[196] For projects financed by the World Bank, if the EIA is the responsibility of the borrower, the bank usually assists and monitors the EIA process, then reviews the EIA and the impacts themselves in order to ensure consistency with the bank's policies.[197] The EBRD goes further: the

192 Espoo Convention, Art. 1(vii); see also the Antarctic Environmental Protocol, Articles 3(1) and (2); World Bank, OP 4.01, Para. 3 and 4; WB ES Policy for IPF, Para. 4.

193 Article 3(2)(c)(ii).

194 See, for example, the 2012 Canadian Environmental Assessment Act, Section 4(1)(i) and section 19(1)(a); CEQ, CONSIDERING CUMULATIVE IMPACTS UNDER THE NATIONAL ENVIRONMENTAL POLICY ACT (Washington DC: CEQ, 1997). In France, an EIA had to include cumulative impacts (Act No. 2010–788 of 12 July 2010, Art. 230 – Article L. 122–3 of the Environment Code), but this requirement was recently suppressed in the new Article L. 122–3 (*Ordonnance No. 2016–1058, 3 août 2016*). However, Article R. 122–5.II.5°(e) of the Environment Code (modified in August 2016) still requires that an EIA include cumulative impacts.

195 WOOD, 370. 2003.

196 EIA Directive, Article 1(g)(i), and Article 5(1). The proponent is called a "developer" in the directive, defined "as the applicant for authorization for a private project or the public authority which initiates a project" (Article 1(b)); In the case of NEPA, the lead federal agency is responsible for its implementation.

197 OP 4.01, Points 4 and 5.

client is only required to provide the necessary information, perhaps some studies, but the bank undertakes the appraisal.[198] However, when the project proponent is not in charge of the project appraisal, there is a discontinuity of project design and EIA, which contradicts the necessity to incorporate the study of impacts as early as possible in project development.

As a matter of principle, the costs of an EIA are borne by the developer. In the case of a project financed by a development bank, the borrower usually asks the bank for financial aid.

The Espoo Convention makes no explicit provision concerning the author of the EIA report. For the EBRD as well as all other MDBS, the EIA "is expected primarily to be conducted by independent consultants or other third-party experts".[199] The importance of independent experts with no financial ties is paramount, but it does not appear as clearly in legal requirements. NEPA requires that professional integrity be ensured, and the names and qualities of the preparers stated.[200] Only in 2014 was the EIA Directive amended to require the use of competent experts, but there is still no mention of independence (it was also added that the competent authority should ensure that it has the sufficient expertise to examine the EIA).[201] Despite the inevitable variations in competence levels of consultant firms and other EIA experts, most countries do not include a related provision that specifies how the necessary level of competence is to be secured. Thus, the main selection criterion to choose among consultancy firms has been an established reputation. Some forms of accreditation of EIA experts or codes of practice are being introduced in

---

198 EBRD 2015 EIA Procedures, Point 3.2, and Table 1.

199 EBRD 2015 EIA Procedures, Point 3.4.3; see also World Bank OP 4.01, Point 4; the World Bank recently came back on its policy on this point. For new projects, it now requires an independent consultant on a case-by-case basis, depending on the evaluation of the risk and only to assist the borrower in the EIA (ES Policy for IPF, Para. 35).

200 40 CFR § 1502.24 and 40 CFR § 1502.17.

201 Directive 2014/52/EU of 16 April 2014, amending Directive 2011/92/EU, Preamble Para. 33, Article 5.3(a) and (b). See, for instance, the case of France where the independence of experts is still only a matter of recommendations. A national commission for deontology and alerts in health and environmental matters was created in 2013, and eventually installed in 2017 (Act No. 2013–316 of 16 April 2013, *relative à l'indépendance de l'expertise en matière de santé et d'environnement et à la protection des lanceurs d'alerte*; Governmental Decree No. 2014–1629 of 26 December 2014 regarding its composition and functioning; Ministerial Decree of 10 October 2016 regarding the appointment of its members; Ministerial Decree of 20 January 2017 regarding the appointment of its president); Marianne Moliner-Dubost, *La loi sur l'indépendance de l'expertise en matière de santé et d'environnement et la protection des lanceurs d'alerte: un titre prometteur mais un contenu décevant*, 38 REVUE JURIDIQUE DE L'ENVIRONNEMENT 415 (2013).

some countries.[202] In the EU, following some concerns regarding the quality of the EIA reports,[203] the European Commission had proposed a mandatory accreditation system, but the European Parliament feared that it would be too expensive an obligation for member states to bear. According to the European Parliament, EIA review and independence are adequately ensured, even without a system of recognized experts, because of the following safeguards: in addition to the obligation that the report be prepared by competent experts, the quality of the EIA will result from the expertise of the competent authority that will review the EIA. Tentative guarantees to avoid conflicts of interest were introduced as well: when the competent authority is also the developer of the project, they must perform their respective duties with complete independence.[204]

In the face of a general reluctance to regulate in matters of competence and independence of experts, proper quality control of EIA reports can be ensured by a conjunction of different verifications, measures and requirements: accreditation of consultants, independent consultants, independent external review or expert assistance, guidelines, codes of practice, up to date data banks and analyses, mandatory scoping, public participation.

NEPA insists on an interdisciplinary approach that should be adopted when preparing the EIS,[205] and requires that methodologies be identified and compared.[206] Then, in order to facilitate the fulfillment of its goal, an EIA needs to be easily readable. To this end, NEPA goes into remarkable detail, as only

202 Australia (voluntary code of practice), the United Kingdom (Institute of Environmental Management and Assessment (IEMA), a non-mandatory registration system), India (NABET, an accreditation scheme). For a list of examples of EIA expert accreditation, see NETHERLANDS COMMISSION FOR ENVIRONMENTAL ASSESSMENT, EIA ACCREDITATION: WHAT AND HOW? (NCEA. 2014). See also Rob Verheem, *How to strengthen the independence of IA reviewers and practitioners*, 39 IMPACT ASSESS. PROJ. APPRAIS. 80 (2021).

203 Commission of the European Communities, Report from the Commission to the Council, the European Parliament, the European Economic and Social Committee and the Committee of the Regions on the application and effectiveness of the EIA Directive (Directive 85/337/EEC, as amended by Directives 97/11/EC and 2003/35/EC) (COM(2009) 378 final) Para. 3.2.1. page 6 (2009); European Commission, Results of the consultation on the review of the EIA Directive (European Commission. 2010). The results of the public consultation showed that 53% were in favor of a quality control mechanism.

204 EIA Directive, Para. 25 of the Preamble and Article 9a (since the 2014 Amendment). For the legislative history, see Jan Bouckaert, *Revised European Directive on EIA for projects* (2014), at https://www.stibbe.com/en/news/2014/may/revised-european-directive-on-environmental-impact-assessment-eia-for-projects (accessed 17 June 2021).

205 40 CFR § 1501.2(a); § 1502.6; § 1507.2(a); see also 42 USC 4332(A).

206 40 CFR § 1502.24.

domestic regulations can. It requires that the EIS itself (not just the executive summary) be written in plain language and make use of appropriate graphics, in order to be understood by decision-makers and the public.[207] Agencies are encouraged to use a recommended format, which is especially detailed for the EIA cover sheet.[208] NEPA also sets a limit to the size of the EIS (150 pages maximum, or, in case of exceptionally complex or large projects, 300 pages maximum), and of the executive summary (15 pages maximum).[209] Time limits depend on the individual project, but must be set up by the responsible agency.[210]

2.3 *Notification – Consultations*

2.3.1 Notification

At the other stages of the EIA process (such as the content of the report for instance), domestic and international rules can be indistinct (as seen above), but at the notification stage, there are some specific rules with regard to transboundary impacts. According to Article 3.1 of the Espoo Convention, "for a proposed activity listed in Appendix I that is likely to cause a significant adverse transboundary impact, the Party of origin shall, for the purposes of ensuring adequate and effective consultations under Article 5, notify any Party which it considers may be an affected Party as early as possible and no later than when informing its own public about that proposed activity". The EIA Directive establishes a similar obligation (Article 7.1). In a transboundary context, notification can be triggered by more specific geographical criteria. For instance, the US-Canada Air Quality Agreement imposes on each party an obligation to notify the other party if new sources of air pollution are located within 100 kilometers (62 miles) of the US-Canada border.[211] Under UNCLOS (of which the United States is not party), the obligation of notification is executed by the

207 40 CFR § 1502.8.

208 40 CFR § 1502.10 and 1502.11.

209 40 CFR § 1500.4(a) and 1502.2(c) (general provisions); 1501.7(b)(1) (size limit is a requirement that needs to be taken into account as early as the scoping phase); 1502.7 (EIS); 1502.12 (summary).

210 40 CFR § 1501.8.

211 Agreement between the United States and Canada on Air Quality (Ottawa) 13 March 1991, 30 ILM 676 (1991), in force 13 March 1991, Art. V(1) and (3), respectively. "The 100-km notification zone matches the proposed notification zone set out in the draft transboundary EIA agreement prepared by the NACEC, showing a degree of commensurability between the proposed NACEC EIA process and the transboundary air quality regime between the US and Canada" (CRAIK, 143 (FN 45). 2008.) NACEC stands for North American Commission for Environmental Cooperation.

transmittal of the EIA report to "the competent international organizations" (Article 205), which in turn will make the report available to all states. UNEP was evoked to serve as one such international organization, but these international organizations have yet to be identified. The most obvious candidates are the regional sea commissions set up under the regional sea conventions, but in the absence of a formal designation, state parties only need to notify by way of publication.[212] All state parties are notified, not merely the states that are directly affected, an obligation that underlines the global nature of the marine environment.[213] However, a state that is directly affected should be particularly notified in light of the preventive purpose of UNCLOS (Articles 192 and 194), its regionalized approach to marine management, the obligation to cooperate and to notify set out in Article 198 (in case of an imminent or actual damage).[214] When it comes to the global commons, the most progressive system is set out in the Antarctic Environmental Protocol, according to which state parties are required to transmit a draft CEE to all the other parties, and to the Committee for Environmental Protection.[215] Both the Committee and the Antarctic Treaty Consultative Meeting review and circulate the draft CEE in their turn. The draft CEE must also be publicly available (the internet considerably eased the circulation of such documents). However, there is no formal non-state participation in the EIA review process.

In the international sphere, the question has been raised regarding who should be the beneficiary of notification and consultation requirements: states alone, affected individuals within states, international organizations, NGOs ...? According to Article 3.8 of the Espoo Convention, the public of the affected state shall be informed and be provided with opportunities to comment on, or object to the proposed activity. To facilitate the required notification, a standard format for transmitting notification was adopted early on.[216] Each state party provides designated points of contact.[217]

212 Id. at 145. For instance, the Commission on the Protection of the Black Sea Against Pollution established under the Bucharest Convention (Articles XV(5) and XVII), or the Baltic Marine Environment Protection Commission under the 1992 Helsinki Convention (Articles 7 and 19).

213 NORDQUIST, para. 205–3. 1991.

214 CRAIK, 145–146. 2008.

215 Antarctic Environmental Protocol, Annex I, Art. 3(3).

216 Decision 1/4 of the First Meeting of the Parties to the Espoo Convention, 27 March 1998, UN Doc. ECE/MP.EIA/1998/4.

217 Decision 1/3 of the First Meeting of the Parties to the Espoo Convention, 30 March 1998, UN Doc. ECE/MP.EIA/1998/3. See updated list of points of contact at http://www.unece.org/env/eia/points_of_contact.html (accessed 17 June 2021).

As for the content of the notification, the Espoo Convention goes beyond the non-discrimination principle, which is reflected in Articles 2.6 and 3, by requiring a minimum level of information, notification and involvement by application of the duty to cooperate, the duty to exchange information, and the no-harm principle (Articles 3, 5 and 6). Article 3 is long and detailed. It lists what the notification must include at a minimum: information on the proposed activity, including any available information on its possible transboundary impact; the nature of the possible decision; and an indication of a reasonable time within which a response under Article 3.3 is required, taking into account the nature of the proposed activity; notification may include the information set out in Article 3.5 (the information that the affected state shall provide if it wishes to participate in the authorization process). If the affected state chooses to participate in the EIA process, Article 3.6. also requires that it provide information at the request of the party of origin.

2.3.2 Consultations

The obligation to notify affected states is associated with the obligation of the state of origin to then consult with the affected state (Articles 3 and 5 in the Espoo Convention). While almost every EIA system includes some form of consultations, they differ significantly in terms of how these consultations take place, and when they are required to begin. They are seldom required at the screening and scoping stages, despite their importance.[218] Early consultations make it possible to focus the EIA at the beginning of the decision-making process, to identify all the issues and alternatives, to have the most relevant and complete information, and to take into consideration all the concerns of the affected public.[219] However, before the completion of the EIA

218 As emphasized in SADLER, para. 5(2) (page 114 et seq.). 1996.

219 See, for instance, how explicit the Arctic EIA Guidelines are in this regard, page 15: "Clearly, one of the most important features in Arctic assessment is the early and full involvement of indigenous people and other local communities, who hold special knowledge of the Arctic. Public participation in scoping is necessary for the efficient use of this knowledge. Without public participation, it is virtually impossible to cover the full range of diverse and complex values and viewpoints typical of the Arctic inhabitants. The participation of the public could lead to a negotiated agreement between the researchers and indigenous or other local communities so that information can be shared in an organized and acceptable way, and the roles and responsibilities of all parties can be described clearly.

Public involvement in determining the scope of assessments is useful especially for controversial activities. Scoping may identify problems or conflicts, which can be alleviated or solved while the proposed project is still being developed. Scoping may also be used to coordinate actions of the various agencies involved in the assessment and decision-making processes.

report, consultations are most commonly conducted on a voluntary basis. Under NEPA for instance, consultations are a formal requirement only after the preparation of the draft EIS report.[220] In the Espoo Convention, the obligation to consult also comes into effect after the completion of the EIA report, which must be sent along with notification, and on which consultations will be based. Neil Craik has observed that, in the Espoo Convention, the obligation to consult with the public of an affected state, which is based on the non-discrimination principle, may occur earlier than the obligation to consult the authorities of the affected state under Article 5. Articles 2.6 and 3.1 require that source states ensure that the opportunity provided to the public of the affected state is equivalent to that provided to the public of the state of origin. Consequently, if the source state consults its own public during scoping, the public of the affected state also has the right to participate at this early stage of the EIA process. Thus, occasionally, the non-discrimination principle can have the effect of increasing the minimal requirements,[221] contrary to its usual effect.

2.4 *Public Participation*

Almost every EIA system includes some form of public participation, which is one of its fundamental components. Under the Espoo Convention, public participation from both the state of origin and the affected state is an important element of transboundary EIAs.[222] Consequently, the convention includes obligations of states towards other states, and of states directly towards the public. During the negotiations that led to the Espoo Convention, the role of public participation and equal treatment for the public in each state was the most contentious issue, long unresolved.[223] According to Article 1(x), the public is defined as "one or more natural or legal persons and, in accordance with national legislation or practice, their associations, organizations or groups". The second part of the article, which acknowledges the role and importance of NGOs and other representative groups, results from the first amendment to the

---

An open process while determining the scope of an EIA is also a crucial first step towards building mutual confidence in fair environmental assessment and problem-solving, and ultimately in a fair decision-making process".

See also EBRD 2019 ESP, Performance Requirement 7, Para. 12; PR 10, Para. 2, 8, 20, and 23.

220 40 CFR § 1503.

221 CRAIK, 143. 2008. Also discussed in Knox, AJIL, 314 (2002).

222 Espoo Convention, Articles 2.2, 2.6, 3.8 and 4.2.

223 Connelly, ENVIRON. IMPACT ASSESS. REV., 41 (1999).

convention (adopted in 2001), which entered into force only recently, in 2014.[224] In some guidelines, the third Meeting of the Parties to the Espoo Convention has explained the importance of public participation, and expressly referred to the Aarhus Convention and domestic legislations ("to the discretion of the Parties") for detailed requirements.[225] It was explained that

> When governments enable the public to participate in decision-making, they help meet society's goal of sustainable and environmentally sound development [by timely disclosure of relevant information]. Public participation in environmental decision-making and, in particular, in EIA, may lead to some benefits in these processes. As a result of public participation, the process of decision-making, up to and including the final decision, becomes more transparent and legitimate. Public debate on proposed activities among all interested groups at an early stage of decision-making may prevent or mitigate conflicts and adverse environmental consequences of the decisions with transboundary impacts.[226]

In 2001, the second Meeting of the Parties to the Espoo Convention had already highlighted the extensive political role and the democratic values of public participation in EIA in a transboundary context. They help "to develop civil society and democracy".[227]

The preamble to the Convention on Access to Information, Public Participation in Decision-Making and Access to Justice in Environmental Matters (the Aarhus Convention[228]) contains the same premises. The Aarhus Convention, adopted under the auspices of the UNECE, similarly to the

---

224 1st amendment to the Espoo Convention, Report of the Second Meeting of the Parties (27 February 2001), Decision II/14, Annex XIV (ECE/MP.EIA/4), in force 26 August 2014: "Wishing to modify the Espoo Convention with a view to clarifying that the public that may participate in procedures under the convention includes civil society and, in particular, nongovernmental organizations".

225 See Points 1.1 (§3) and 1.3 (§9) of the Guidance on Public Participation in Environmental Impact Assessment in a Transboundary Context, Report of the Third Meeting of the Parties (4 June 2004), Decision III/8, Annex VIII, page 98 (ECE/MP.EIA/6). See also UNECE, GUIDANCE ON THE PRACTICAL APPLICATION OF THE ESPOO CONVENTION 15 (United Nations (ECE/MP.EIA/8). 2006).

226 Guidance on Public Participation in Environmental Impact Assessment in a Transboundary Context, *supra* note 225, at Point 1.1 (para. 2).

227 Draft Guidance on Public Participation in Environmental Impact Assessment in a Transboundary Context, 2nd MOP (2001), Decision II/3, Annex, Para. 8(b).

228 Aarhus, Denmark, 25 June 1998, 38 ILM 517 (1999), in force 30 October 2001. At present, there are forty-seven parties to the Aarhus Convention.

Espoo Convention, is a treaty that directly provides individuals with participatory rights in environmental decision-making processes. Interestingly, the parties agreed to apply the Aarhus principles to international organizations (Article 3.7). The EBRD is the only international financial institution to have implemented Article 3.7 and to have committed to take into account the Aarhus Convention, two years after the latter was signed.[229] Like the Espoo Convention, the Aarhus Convention applies the non-discrimination principle along with a set of minimum standards, but it provides for more detailed obligations in matters of notification, comments and transmittal of relevant information. Like the Espoo Convention, the Aarhus Convention lists activities that trigger compulsory public participation, but the list found in the Aarhus Convention is more comprehensive.[230] The Aarhus Convention is aimed at environmental decision-making in a broader sense. The state of origin is required to notify and extend participation rights to the public regardless of transboundary impacts. The right to participate in environmental decision-making is extended to the "public concerned," which is defined as "the public affected or likely to be affected by, or having an interest in, the environmental decision-making; non-governmental organizations promoting environmental protection and meeting any requirements under national law shall be deemed to have an interest" (Article 2.5). Consequently, the threshold in the Aarhus Convention is lower than in the Espoo Convention (public likely to be affected versus significant adverse environmental impact), and guarantees public participation even when the Espoo Convention does not apply. According to Jonas Ebbesson, the Aarhus Convention also applies when and if resources and services are privatized because of its broad conception of public authority.[231]

229 The EBRD committed to "take into account the Aarhus Convention, the general spirit, purpose and ultimate goals of which are subscribed to by the EBRD in the implementation of its Environmental Policy, along with other relevant international conventions" (EBRD, *Public Information Policy* (PIP) (2000), para. 1(d) *in* ANDREA BIANCHI, NON-STATE ACTORS AND INTERNATIONAL LAW note 75 (Routledge. 2009)). Since then, the most recent public information policies of the EBRD have been rephrased slightly more vaguely, firstly in 2014: "The EBRD recognises the importance of the principles, purpose and ultimate goals of the UNECE Aarhus Convention", then in 2019: "The EBRD recognises the developments made to advance the recognition and exercise of the right to access information as a human right and the importance of the principles, purpose and ultimate goals" of the Aarhus Convention (Section I of the 2019 Access to Information Policy – at http://www.ebrd.com/what-we-do/strategies-and-policies/public-information-policy.html (accessed 17 June 2021).

230 Aarhus Convention, Art. 6.1(a) and Annex I.

231 Jonas Ebbesson, *Public Participation and Privatisation in Environmental Matters: An Assessment of the Aarhus Convention*, 4 ERASMUS LAW REVIEW 71 (2011).

Surprisingly, there is no explicit connection between the Espoo and the Aarhus conventions, despite a proposal to this effect during the negotiations of the latter,[232] and despite the fact that the Espoo Convention clearly provides for public participation as a major requirement (Article 2.2).[233] Similarly, no explicit link had been made between Principle 10 and Principle 17 of the Rio Declaration, despite the fact that "the inclusion of strong public participation principles, including the use of environmental impact assessments as set out in Principle 17, was one of the primary objectives of the United States, the European Community, Canada, and the Nordic Countries".[234] Perhaps is this an additional illustration of the contentious character of public participation. Without a formalized combination of their provisions, the Espoo Convention and Aarhus conventions are distinct and autonomous treaties, a broad current trend in multilateral environmental instruments.[235] However, the two conventions do interact because of the overlapping membership,[236] as well as some substantive connections, which in turn result eventually in some reciprocal influence.[237] Furthermore, if not with the Espoo Convention *per se*, there are

232 "During the drafting of the Aarhus convention, a bracketed article was included that indeed related the participatory notions to EIA procedures. However, in the final version, this explicit connection was eliminated. Considering that the convention was negotiated within the same international forum as the Espoo convention, it is surprising that the explicit connection between public participation and EIAs failed to be adopted" (Jonas Ebbesson, *The Notion of Public Participation in International Environmental Law*, 8 YB. INT'L ENV.L. 51, 88 (1998).) The Espoo Convention is only mentioned once, among other treaties, in the preamble (at Paragraph 23), and provisions on public participation in national EIA procedures are incidentally mentioned in Annex I, Paragraph 20.

233 See also the comments of the ECE Executive Secretary Gerald Hinteregger on the adoption of the Espoo Convention: "This is a major achievement in combating pollution and it will cause significant changes in environmental legislation within many of the signing nations ... Not only will it force all signing nations to establish an environmental impact assessment procedure, but it will allow governments and the public from other nations to participate in that process from the start" *in* Laura Carlan Battle, *A Transnational Perspective on Extending Nepa: The Convention on Environmental Impact Assessment in a Transboundary Context*, 5 DUKE ENV L & POL'Y F 1, 4 (1995).

234 Jeffrey Kovar, a member of the US delegation to the Rio Conference, *in* Jeffrey D. Kovar, *A Short Guide to the Rio Declaration*, 4 COLO. J. INT'L ENVTL. L. & POL'Y 119, 131 (1993).

235 See Robin R. Churchill & Geir Ulfstein, *Autonomous Institutional Arrangements in Multilateral Environmental Agreements: A Little-Noticed Phenomenon in International Law*, 94 AMERICAN JOURNAL OF INTERNATIONAL LAW 623 (2000).

236 As of August 2021, only 1 out of the 45 parties to the Espoo Convention was not a party to the Aarhus Convention (Canada). Only 3 out of the 47 parties to the Aarhus Convention were not parties to the Espoo Convention (Georgia, Tajikistan, Turkmenistan).

237 See Jonas Ebbesson, *A Modest Contribution to Environmental Democracy and Justice in Transboundary Contexts: The Combined Impact of the Espoo Convention and Aarhus Convention*, 20 RECIEL 248 (2011).

explicit connections between the Aarhus Convention and EIA procedures (NEPA similarly intertwines access to information and public participation[238]). The Aarhus Convention applies to any activity for which there is a domestic EIA requirement that involves public participation,[239] which is advantageous if the domestic requirements fall below the minimum standards set by the Aarhus Convention, and also if the Espoo Convention does not apply to the proposed activity. Lastly, because of its specific focus, the Aarhus Convention imposes notification to the public, but not to states. However, there are overlaps with other international instruments. Moreover, one can surmise that the public in the affected areas will in turn inform the public authorities of their country.

International EIA provisions acknowledge the specificity and the crucial importance of traditional knowledge from indigenous people and other environmentally vulnerable groups,[240] which needs to be incorporated into scientific data and methodologies. The Arctic EIA Guidelines also emphasize the coordinating role that could be given to transnational groups, such as the Inuit Circumpolar Conference, the Saami Council and the Indigenous Peoples Secretariat.[241]

With regard to the timing of public participation, the affected public should participate in every stage of the EIA process – screening, scoping, review, and comments. It should participate as early as possible, at the screening phase, or at least at the scoping phase, in order to provide timely information and to avoid potential conflicts. Under NEPA, the agency in charge of a project shall invite the public to participate in the scoping process.[242] Under the EIA Directive, the precise moment where public participation begins is left to the discretion of member states, but the public must be informed early on in the environmental decision-making procedures and, at the latest, as soon as some minimal information can reasonably be provided (Article 6.2, which lists the said information). In the case of the World Bank, the borrower should consult with the affected public as early as possible, and at least twice for Category A Projects: shortly after screening (and before the terms of reference of an EA have been determined), and once a draft EA report has been prepared. In its

---

238 40 CFR §1500.1 (b).

239 Article 6, and Annex I.

240 Principle 22 of the Rio Declaration. See also the Arctic EIA Guidelines, page 37; 2006 CBD Voluntary guidelines on biodiversity-inclusive impact assessment. On the rights and status of indigenous people, see Siegfried Wiessner, *Rights and Status of Indigenous Peoples: A Global Comparative and International Legal Analysis*, 12 HARV. HUM. RTS. J. 57 (1999). See also *infra*, chapter 3, page 121 et seq.

241 Arctic Guidelines, page 41.

242 40 CFR § 1501.7(a)1.

new ESF, the World Bank simply recognizes the importance of early consultation with stakeholders, the precise timing of which will be determined on a case-by-case basis.[243]

Under these regulations, the public should be able to participate early and meaningfully, thanks to procedures that guarantee a satisfying degree of participation (such as hearings). Under NEPA, the public is invited to comment on the draft EIS.[244] The public has access to information during the course of NEPA procedures.[245] Under the Espoo Convention, the public of the affected state shall be invited to comment no later than the public of the state of origin, as an application of the non-discrimination principle (Article 3.1 and 3.8). Since 2014, the amended EIA Directive has gone beyond the previous and vague requirement of a reasonable time for the public to participate: the timeframes for consultations shall not be shorter than thirty days (Article 6.7).

Lastly, as regards the results of public participation, in NEPA, the responsible authority prepares the final EIS in which it must respond to all the comments according to the rule of reason, i.e. considering the salience of the comments.[246] Until recently, the EIA Directive was utterly silent in this regard. In 2014, it established an obligation at a later stage, since there is no obligation to consult before the EIA report. It is only when a decision has been reached that the public (and in case of transboundary impacts, the affected state) should be informed of the manner in which the results of their consultation have been taken into account in the final decision (Article 9.1(b)). The objective is to ensure that the decision be taken and justified based on the information provided by other agencies, states and the public.

2.5 *Final Decision*

In all jurisdictions, a consistent and logical principle is that the EIA process must have been completed before a final decision is made.[247] The assumption regarding EIA is that an informed and participatory decision-making process will produce environmentally sound decisions. EIA obligations are procedural

243 OP 4.01, Paragraph 14. For new projects since October 2018: ES Policy for IPF, Para. 53; ESS1 Annex 1, Para. 4; ESS10, Para. 22.

244 40 CFR § 1503.1(a)4.

245 40 CFR § 1506.6.

246 40 CFR § 1503.4. *Marsh v. Ore. Natural Res. Counc.*, 490 US 360, 370–374 (1989); William Murray Tabb, *Environmental Impact Assessment in the European Community: Shaping International Norms*, 73 TULANE LAW REVIEW 923, 944 and 958–959 (1999).

247 See, for instance, Espoo Convention, Article 2.3; EIA Directive, Articles 2.1 and 8a.1.(a); NEPA, 40 CFR §1506.10(b); World Bank OP 4.01, Point 5; EBRD, 2014 ESP, Points 29 and 30, and 2015 Environmental Procedures, Point 2.

in nature, and generally do not impose substantive environmental norms or objectives. These objectives are supposed to be attained through exchange of information and mutual consultations. Consequently, in its final decision, the state of origin is required, if not to conform with the recommendations of the EIA, at least to take due account of the outcome of the EIA, including the EIA documentation, comments received from the public of the affected state and from the affected state authorities, and state-to-state consultations.[248] To verify the fulfillment of this due-diligence duty, the Espoo Convention requires that the state of origin provides the affected state, not only with its final decision, but also with the reasons and considerations on which it is based (Article 6.2). Since 2014, the EIA Directive similarly requires that the decision (approval or refusal) states its reasons and conditions, along with a description of the project, mitigation measures, and monitoring programs, if needed (Article 8a). Until then, the EIA Directive only required that the results of consultations and the information gathered should be duly taken into account (Article 8). Article 8a was specifically added to address what the final decision should contain. Other international EIA instruments contain similar procedural obligations. In the end, the state proposing the activity remains free to decide, provided that the decision be justified. The Antarctic EIA system, like all the others, places reliance on the expected outcome of consultations and reasoned decisions.

The EIA Directive requires that the competent authority take its decision within a reasonable period of time (Article 8a.5). The Espoo Convention is silent in this regard.

If new information comes to light after a final decision has been made, but before work has commenced, the Espoo Convention requires that it be disclosed. It also requires consultations on whether the decision needs to be revised, if a party so requests (Article 6.3).The two criteria that trigger the obligation of disclosure and consultation are formulated in rather general terms: work has not commenced, and the information must potentially affect the decision. In regard to the latter criterion, the Espoo Convention does not require a supplemental EIA, unlike NEPA,[249] and leaves its determination to state discretion. There is no such obligation of disclosure in the Antarctic Environmental Protocol, where the focus is exclusively on prevention, careful and comprehensive planning.

---

248 Espoo Convention, Art. 6.1.

249 40 CFR § 1502.9(c). A supplemental EIS is required when the information is relevant, which is determined by the application of the rule of reason (*Marsh v. Oregon Natural Resources Council*, 490 US 360 at 370–374 (1989)).

Because of the potential liability of the lender for the environmental consequences of its activities, the EBRD adopted the use of environmental covenants, included in its decisions to grant loans, by which the bank obtains assurances that the environmental requirements specified in the financing agreements will be met prior to effectiveness or disbursement of funds,[250] and during the EBRD's supervision of the implementation of a loan.[251] The EBRD followed in the footsteps of the World Bank, which had adopted such covenants as early as in the 1970's.[252]

More generally, there has been a noticeable tendency to establish continuous obligations on states to verify that their activities do not cause significant adverse transboundary impacts.[253]

2.6 *Follow-up Programs*

EIAs *per se* are a one-time event, a planning tool limited to the project development phase before a final decision is made. However, verifying the implementation of the conditions set out in the project authorization is imperative, as is the collection of long-term data through follow-up programs. These data help to assess the accuracy of the impact predictions, the effectiveness of mitigation measures, and the identification of deficiencies. Monitoring programs suggest ways of improving EIA methodology and procedures. The growing inclusion of continuous monitoring responds to the criticism that EIA processes excessively rely on limited predictive capabilities, which may prove inaccurate or outdated.[254] Monitoring is necessary during the project planning and operation, and after the project has been completed. Consequently, developers may be required to conduct an adaptive management procedure (i.e. to continuously adapt their project, then their activity) whenever there is new information, in order to address and reduce unpredicted environmental impacts. UNCLOS requires continuous monitoring (Article 204), as an obligation distinct from,

250 EBRD Procedures for Environmental and Social Appraisal and Monitoring of Investment Projects, 10 July 2015, Para. 3.6.2; Gregory Rose, *The Year in Review – Reports from Organizations – Regional Development Bank: the EBRD*, 3 YB.INT'L ENV.L. 544, 545 (1992).

251 See *infra* note 262.

252 Mohammad A. Bekhechi, *Some Observations Regarding Environmental Covenants and Conditionalities in World Bank Lending Activities*, *in* MAX PLANCK YEARBOOK OF UNITED NATIONS LAW (Jochen A. Frowein & Rüdiger Wolfrum eds., 1999).

253 See, for instance, the case of the *Gabčíkovo-Nagymaros Project* (*Hungary v. Slovenia*), Judgment, 1997 ICJ Rep. 7 (25 September), reprinted in 37 ILM 162 (1998), and the case of the *Bystroe Canal Project* (Romania, Ukraine) as submitted to the Implementation Committee of the Espoo Convention in 2004 and 2007 (EIA/IC/S/1 and EIA/IC/S/1 *bis*).

254 Bradley C. Karkkainen, *Toward a Smarter NEPA: Monitoring and Managing Government's Environmental Performance*, 102 COLUM. L. REV. 903, 927 (2002).

but closely related to EIA.[255] In 1997, Judge Weeramantry, in his separate opinion to the *Gabčíkovo-Nagymaros* case, evoked the obligation of continual monitoring in respect of the no-harm principle.[256] The requirement of continuous programs has continually increased.[257] In the United States, follow-up programs were not originally part of NEPA. They are now voluntary, as a way of increasing the efficiency of NEPA.[258] The 2019 Canadian Impact Assessment Act expressly requires follow-up programs,[259] as does the EIA Directive (a requirement in place since 2014[260]). The Espoo Convention lets the parties determine and agree if post-project analysis must be carried out. Article 7 and Appendix V combined describe the objectives as follows:

> (a) Monitoring compliance with the conditions as set out in the authorization or approval of the activity and the effectiveness of mitigation measures,
> (b) Review of an impact for proper management and in order to cope with uncertainties,
> (c) Verification of past predictions in order to transfer experience to future activities of the same type.

Article 7.2 of the Espoo Convention also states that:

> When, as a result of post-project analysis, the Party of origin or the affected Party has reasonable grounds for concluding that there is a significant adverse transboundary impact or factors have been discovered which may result in such an impact, it shall immediately inform the other Party. The concerned Parties shall then consult on necessary measures to reduce or eliminate the impact.

This provision flows from the no-harm principle, applied here beyond the planning stage of an activity. The Antarctic Environmental Protocol also contains

255 NORDQUIST, para. 204-1. 1991.

256 (1997) ICJ Rep 7 at 111. See also para. 112 of the judgment.

257 See CBD EIA Voluntary Guidelines, for which the monitoring stage is a fundamental component of EIA (para. 5(g) and 44–50); the Arctic EIA Guidelines, p. 27–29; *Case Concerning Land Reclamation by Singapore in and around the Straits of Johor (Malaysia v. Singapore)*, Award, (2005) XXVII RIAA 133, 1 September 2005, Permanent Court of Arbitration, Settlement Agreement, para. C.9.b.

258 32 CFR § 615.15 (h) through (l), and 40 CFR § 1505.2(c) and § 1505.3.

259 Articles 2, 6(1)(n), 22(1)(k), 63(4)(b); the 2012 CEAA already required follow-up programs (Articles 19(1)(e); 43(1)(d)(i); 53(4)(b). Definition in Article 2(1)).

260 Article 8a.4.

mandatory requirements for post-project analysis, the details of which depend on the presence of a CEE (Art. 5), or an IEE (Art. 2(2)). Here, monitoring is limited to assessing the actual impacts of an activity in order to adapt it, if necessary. The 1991 Antarctic Protocol does not consider monitoring as a way of improving EIA methodology, which has been criticized.[261] The World Bank and the EBRD also require that EIAs include follow-up programs.[262]

3 Conclusion

The existence of EIA and TEIA prescriptions has been widely recognized and established, albeit inconsistently. The specific requirements that these obligations involve, and the articulation between all the EIA-related instruments, have been in dispute. In the European Union, EIA prescriptions mutually overlap and reinforce each other. In the international sphere, some treaties refer to other treaties and to domestic provisions for more detailed EIA rules.[263] There is a clear tendency toward harmonization. For example, Canada applied the transboundary EIA provisions of CEAA to non-parties to the Espoo Convention, such as the United States.[264] The United States has based the application of NEPA to transboundary impacts on customary law, such as the duty to prevent harm and the duty to notify.[265] In all jurisdictions, EIA prescriptions of all natures and at all levels have developed dynamically, but much progress remains to be made.

261 New Zealand reported to the Meeting of the Parties that: "The terms "minor" and "transitory" are interpreted by the Treaty Parties in their implementation of Annex I and a great deal of experience in producing IEEs and CEEs has accumulated. Many IEEs and CEEs have been presented as Information Papers at the ATCM meetings. However, there is at present no systematic approach to utilizing and learning from this experience" (XX ATCM/INF 2, *Developing an Understanding of Minor and Transitory*, submitted by New Zealand, 29 March 1996 (cited *in* Donald R. Rothwell, *Polar Environmental Protection and International Law: The 1991 Antarctic Protocol*, 11 EJIL 591, 600 (2000)).

262 World Bank OP 4.01, Para. 13 and 19; BP 4.01, Para. 19–23. 2015 EBRD EIA Procedures, Para. 3.6.1 and Table 2 – Key roles and responsibilities during environmental and social monitoring of project implementation (page 10); 2019 ESP, Para. 29 et. seq.

263 This is examined in a series of informal UNECE reports looking at the interaction of the Espoo Convention with other treaties (available at www.unece.org/env/eia/resources/faq.html#Interact, accessed 17 June 2021).

264 Canadian Environmental Assessment Act, SC 1992, c. 37, as amended, s. 47. How TEIAs will be conducted under the new Impact Assessment Act, where TEIA requirements were reduced, remains to be seen (see *supra* note 38).

265 CEQ Guidance on the Application of NEPA to Proposed Federal Actions in the United States with Transboundary Effects, issued on 1 July 1997, available at https://energy.gov/nepa/downloads/guidance-application-nepa-proposed-federal-actions-united-states-transboundary (accessed 17 June 2021). About the new CEQ rule released in July 2020 and its uncertain future, see *supra* page 34 et seq.

Flow-chart of the stages of an assessment according to the Convention

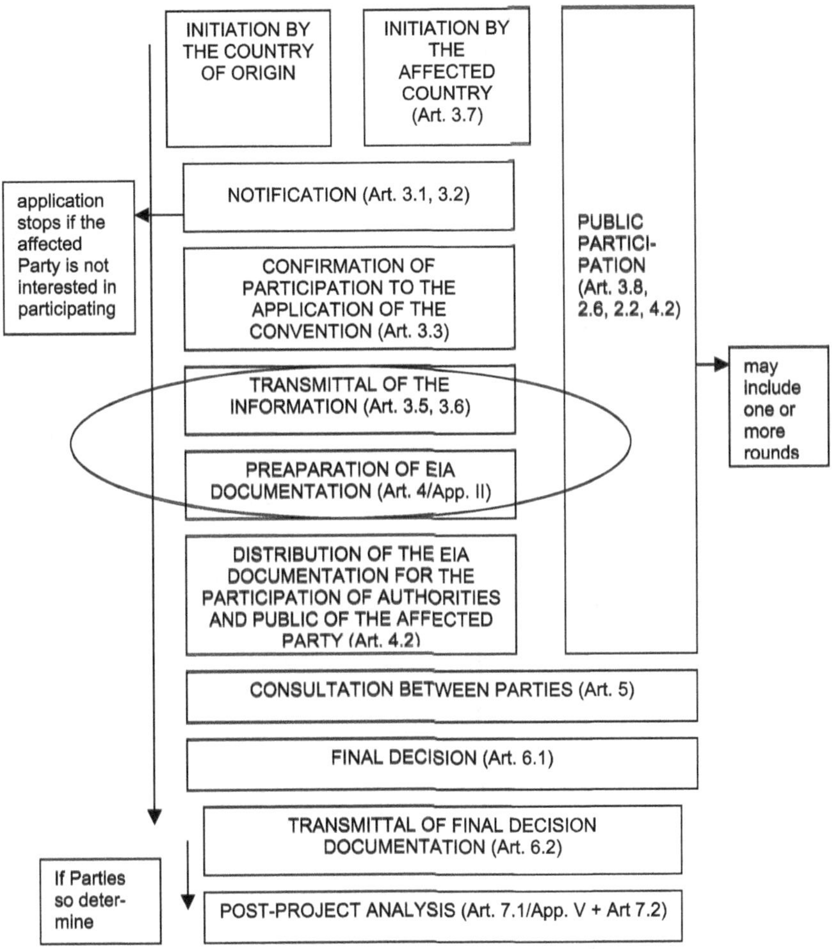

CHART 2 Flow chart of the stages of an assessment according to the Espoo Convention (UNECE, *Guidance on the Practical Application of the Espoo Convention* 10 (United Nations (ECE/MP.EIA/8). 2006))

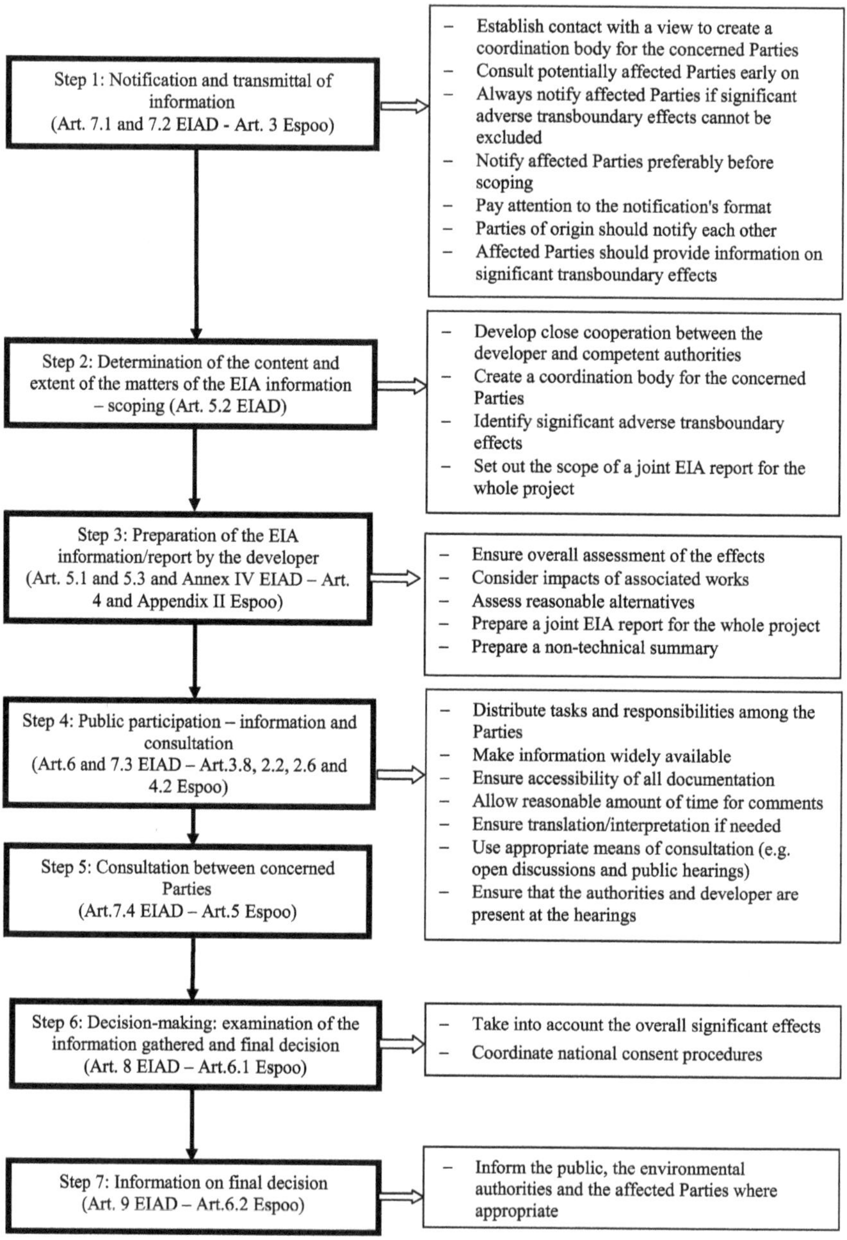

CHART 3 Flow chart of the transboundary EIA procedure and summary of guidance based upon the Espoo Convention, the EU directive, and best practice (European Commission, *Guidance on the Application of the Environmental Impact Assessment Procedure for Large-scale Transboundary Projects* 5 (European Union. 2013))

CHAPTER 3

The Role of EIAs in Public International Law

Substantive law has at first the look of being gradually secreted in the interstices of procedure.[1]

The individual sees himself, first and foremost, as a member of a group such as the nation-state rather than as an individual actor, with potentialities for influence varying from context to context. As long as this self-perception persists, the realistic individual in mass society is extremely unlikely to consider himself as anything other than a spectator or audience member. Hence, a fundamental intellectual task in preparation for political activity in any international enforcement program is the rediscovery, the recapture, of the self. Once this internal process commences, the individual may begin to explore the many arenas in which he can maximize his effectiveness as a political actor. (…) *the individual must begin to view himself as a participating architect.*[2]

∴

1 EIA and the Dynamics of International Law

The Environmental Impact Assessment (EIA) is a potent information tool aimed at better public decision-making, which can contribute to empowering individuals and civic groups. In addition to the 1991 Espoo Convention, the 1998 Aarhus Convention formally expressed the possibility for anyone to be integrated in the dynamics of the international legal system, in the wake of a trend that has gradually identified users, rather than subjects of international law.[3] As an all-encompassing term, *users* appropriately evokes the different

1 HENRY SUMNER MAINE, DISSERTATIONS ON EARLY LAW AND CUSTOM 389 (John Murray. 1883).

2 W. Michael Reisman, *Making International Humanitarian Law Effective: the Case for Civic Enforcement*, *in* THE UNITED NATIONS: A REASSESSMENT – SANCTIONS, PEACEKEEPING, AND HUMANITARIAN ASSISTANCE 33 (John M. Paxman & George T. Boggs eds., 1973).

3 Emmanuel Roucounas, *The Users of International Law*, *in* LOOKING TO THE FUTURE – ESSAYS IN INTERNATIONAL LAW IN HONOR OF W. MICHAEL REISMAN 220 (Mahnoush

 | DOI:10.1163/9789004467583_004

roles that any person may take on, consciously or not, including the role of a political actor, a participating architect in the law-making process. The Aarhus Convention requires public participation in the assessment of activities likely to have environmental impacts, as a duty of member states and a right of individuals and their associations, early in the decision-making process, "when all options are open and effective public participation can take place".[4] In this view, EIA provides the means for clarifying one's standpoint, as it encompasses different perspectives.[5] It has the required characteristics to provide meaningful assistance to the intelligence function as described by the New Haven School, i.e. gathering, processing, and disseminating information relevant to making social choices. In environmental law in general, and in the following case studies in particular (chapters 4 to 6), individuals and Non-Governmental Organizations (NGOs), not public authorities, were the first to use intelligence to invoke and promote environmental protection and sustainable development, pressure for better decisions in this regard, and ultimately have better environmental legal norms and policies adopted. Sustainable development is procedural in essence.[6] The exact nature, mechanisms and effects of EIA procedures need to be clarified, which is the subject-matter of this book.

More than sixty years ago, Myres McDougal proposed the then-radical idea that states were not the only subjects of international law. He exposed

---

H. Arsanjani, et al. eds., 2011). Roucounas explains the passage from the individual as a remote addressee of international law and a solitary person, to *non-state actors* or *participants*, and eventually to *users* as the all-encompassing term for which Roucounas convincingly advocates. See also Michel Virally, *Panorama du droit international contemporain*, 183 RECUEIL DES COURS 25 (1983); Louis Sohn, *Making International Law User-Friendly*, *in* INTERNATIONAL LAW AS A LANGUAGE FOR INTERNATIONAL RELATIONS: PROCEEDINGS OF THE UNITED NATIONS CONGRESS ON INTERNATIONAL LAW, NEW YORK 411 et seq. (1996); ROSALYN HIGGINS, THEMES AND THEORIES: SELECTED ESSAYS, SPEECHES, AND WRITINGS IN INTERNATIONAL LAW 73–90 (Oxford University Press. 2009).

4 Articles 6 to 8, especially Article 6.4.

5 Alan Diduck & Bruce Mitchell, *Learning, Public Involvement and Environmental Assessment: A Canadian Case Study*, 5 JOURNAL OF ENVIRONMENTAL ASSESSMENT POLICY AND MANAGEMENT 339, 351–354 (2003). See also "EIA lies at the crossroad where economic, environmental, and social values intersect. Balancing these values requires a holistic approach, a collaborative effort between governments, business sectors, and the public. In order to achieve lasting environmental protection and sustainable economic growth and development, public participation must figure prominently in the EIA process". (Jesse L. Moorman & Zhang Ge, *Promoting and Strengthening Public Participation in China's Environmental Impact Assessment Process: Comparing China's EIA Law and U.S. NEPA*, 8 VT. J. ENVTL. L. 281 (2007)).

6 CRAIK, 80. 2008; Alan Boyle, *The Gabcikovo-Nagymaros Case: New Law in Old Bottles*, 8 YBIEL 13, 18 (1997).

the reality of the latter as a process of decisions in which a much wider range of actors participated – individuals, international organizations, transnational corporations (or multinational corporations), NGOs, gangs, etc.[7] Myres McDougal and Harold Lasswell combined their home disciplines – law for the former, political science and psychology for the latter. Together with Michael Reisman, they established the New Haven School, which has realistically defined law-making – or the prescribing of policy as authoritative for a community – as a process of communication. Any form that this communication can take must be examined to identify what the law is.[8] Law-making communications have a particularity: rather than transmitting a single message, they carry simultaneously three co-ordinate communication flows in a fashion akin to the coaxial cables of telephonic communications: the policy content, the authority signal, and the control intention. All three flows must be continuous for a prescription to endure.[9] The second component (the authority signal) relates to the authority of the communicators, with which the relevant audience endows them, consciously or not. Thanks to this authority conferred upon them, the communicators become the appropriate lawmakers.[10] The third flow (the control intention) involves an indispensable component to law-making: power, defined as the capacity and willingness to make a preferential expression effective. From the standpoint of a jurisprudence of insight and empowerment,[11] a decision is a more complex process than a judge applying rules to a specific dispute in an organized setting. In order to identify and influence decisions in all settings, a jurist must resort to a more detailed concept of decision functions. Lasswell analyzed the decision process into seven component functions:[12]

(1) *intelligence*, or the gathering, processing, and dissemination of information relevant to making social choices;

---

7 W. Michael Reisman, *The Democratization of Contemporary International Law-Making Processes and the Differentiation of their Application*, *in* DEVELOPMENTS OF INTERNATIONAL LAW IN TREATY MAKING 19 (Rüdiger Wolfrum & Volker Röben eds., 2005).

8 Reisman, AM. SOC'Y INT'L L. PROC., 105 (1981).

9 W. MICHAEL REISMAN, THE QUEST FOR WORLD ORDER AND HUMAN DIGNITY IN THE TWENTY-FIRST CENTURY: CONSTITUTIVE PROCESS AND INDIVIDUAL COMMITMENT 141 (Hague Academy of International Law. 2013).

10 Id. at 144–146.

11 Siegfried Wiessner, *Michael Reisman, Human Dignity, and the Law*, *in* LOOKING TO THE FUTURE – ESSAYS IN INTERNATIONAL LAW IN HONOR OF W. MICHAEL REISMAN 21 (Mahnoush H. Arsanjani, et al. eds., 2011).

12 Reisman, The Democratization of Contemporary International Law-Making Processes and the Differentiation of their Application 19–20. 2005; Myres S. McDougal, et al., *The World Constitutive Process of Authoritative Decision*, 19 J. LEGAL EDUC. 253, 261 (1967).

(2) *promotion*, or the processes by which individual or collective awareness of a discrepancy between a desirable state and one that is or is about to take place gradually leads to a demand for some type of community intervention and regulation;
(3) *prescription*, or law-making, which occurs when actors, with varying degrees of authority, select and install certain preferences about policy as community law. This may be accomplished by a legislature or some other organized lawmaker; but it is usually, and, especially in international law, largely accomplished in informal and sometimes even chaotic processes whose outcomes are generally referred to as "custom";
(4) *invocation*, or the provisional characterization of a certain action as inconsistent with a prescription or law that has been established, accompanied by the demand that an appropriate community institution act;
(5) *application*, or the organization of the facts of a particular dispute, the specification of a norm or norms that apply, and the fashioning of a mandatory formulation. When this takes place in a court, it is called a judgment, but it also occurs in informal, unorganized situations;
(6) *termination* or the abrogation of existing norms and the social arrangements based upon them, the development of transitional regimes and, where appropriate or necessary, the design of compensation programs for those who have made good-faith value investments on the expectation that the old regime would continue; and
(7) *appraisal*, or the evaluation of the aggregate performance of all decision functions in terms of community requirements.[13]

Within the continuous dynamics of decision-making processes, EIA serves the appraisal function and the intelligence function in particular, as an information tool for better decisions. The intelligence function comprises the gathering, evaluation, and dissemination of information relevant to decision-making, and may include predictions based on such information, as well as planning for future contingencies.[14] Information must be oriented towards identifying and solving problems. All three tasks – collecting, processing, disseminating – are equally important. Considering the immense and ever-increasing volume of available information, Myres McDougal, Harold Lasswell and Michael

13 REISMAN, The Quest for World Order and Human Dignity in the Twenty-first Century: Constitutive Process and Individual Commitment 175–176. 2013.

14 Myres S. McDougal, et al., *The Intelligence Function and World Public Order*, 46 TEMPLE LAW QUATERLY 365, 365, 447 (1973). See also Reisman, N. KY. L. REV., 612 (1995); McDougal, et al., J. LEGAL EDUC., 261 (1967).

Reisman were prescient in their early warning about the importance of selectivity and economy in processing this information.[15] For this purpose, an EIA is an effective tool for collecting, processing, and presenting information in an appropriately organized fashion. EIA generates and collects the necessary information in a readily available format that can be easily circulated.[16] Thanks to this centralized and accessible information, EIA can help individuals to see themselves and to act as participants in the constitutive law-making process. Not only decision-makers, but also any stakeholder that so desires, can inform themselves and act upon this information. "The conception that the dignity of every human individual includes a right to participate in all value processes finds repeated expression in contemporary international law. Such participation ultimately depends upon relatively unrestricted access to pertinent intelligence by all who seek it".[17] Even in authoritarian political regimes where intelligence is usually retained in the hands of the governing elites, EIA requirements may allow a breach of this secrecy. "Even quite closed and technocratic EA processes can be broken open if the public becomes aware of the project and begins to mobilize against it".[18] Even when the official EIA is erroneous, the *UMNIP* case shows that it constitutes a useful base upon which the affected populations can build their opposition and develop communication strategies (see chapter 6). The *Vuotos* and the *Interconnection* cases are another example of how pressure groups can demonstrate that the information upon which public authorities based their decision is inaccurate, which harms the legitimacy of the project at stake, and exposes its real motives, along with its long-term effects (see chapters 4 and 5). Any decision is based on choices that

15 "The body of potentially relevant information is so enormous, and the man hours of attention are so few, that one of the principal criteria of a sound intelligence operation refers to selectivity. [...] The intelligence needs of the contemporary world constitutive process are enormous; the scope is spatially coterminous with the very limits of the earth-space arena, extends temporally from the distant past into a future whose foreseeability is a function of man's capacity to engage in systematic prediction, and ranges over every critical value process in diverse and changing contexts. But resource allocation for the intelligence process is necessarily limited". (McDougal, et al., TEMPLE LAW QUATERLY, 373–374 and 377–378 (1973)).

16 See *supra* chapter 2 (pages 71–72), about the detailed requirements of NEPA for instance: 40 CFR § 1502.8: EISs "shall be written in plain language and may use appropriate graphics so that decision-makers and the public can readily understand them. Agencies should employ writers of clear prose or editors to write, review, or edit statements".

17 McDougal, et al., TEMPLE LAW QUATERLY, 396 (1973).

18 John F. Devlin & Nonita T. Yap, *Contentious politics in environmental assessment: blocked projects and winning coalitions*, 26 IMPACT ASSESSMENT AND PROJECT APPRAISAL 17, 19 (2008).

will need to be explained to those it affects and who protest it. "We are concerned with authoritative decision; our interest in intelligence derives from the dependence of rational decision on knowledge. Our task is to identify the optimum procedures for gathering, processing and disseminating intelligence for constitutive and public order decision".[19] EIA can be such a procedure, hence a vehicle for individual and community empowerment, whether to fully participate meaningfully in project development, or simply to oppose governments and corporations as regards prejudicial plans for the exploitation of natural resources.[20]

When determining what international law prescribes in this domain, as in any other, the critical question is the content of the actual expectations of politically relevant individuals and groups.[21] In this regard, for instance, an officer of the US Army Corps of Engineers said that the practice of EIA would continue even if the Corps were no longer required by law to undertake EIA. "Why? Because the public now expects it".[22] EIA is all the more expected that it is a straightforward and common-sense requirement.[23] Thus, EIAs are a general expectation that will be verified in the following case studies. "Expectations about appropriate behavior, some explicit, some at levels of consciousness so deep that people are not aware of them, are shaped in all of these processes of communication. If one is to understand and influence international lawmaking, plainly one must address the process in its rich totality".[24]

Individuals created (…) the environmental movement.[25]

As in the human rights domain, environmental protection has been promoted by private initiatives. For instance, NEPA, which introduced EIA for the first

19 McDougal, et al., TEMPLE LAW QUATERLY, 365 (1973).

20 Harvey A. Feit, *Re-cognizing Co-management as Co-governance: Visions and Histories of Conservation at James Bay*, 47 ANTHROPOLOGICA 267, 269 (2005).

21 REISMAN, The Quest for World Order and Human Dignity in the Twenty-first Century: Constitutive Process and Individual Commitment 150. 2013.

22 Lynton K. Caldwell, *Understanding Impact Analysis: Technical Process, Administrative Reform, Policy Principle, in* POLICY THROUGH IMPACT ASSESSMENT – INSTITUTIONALIZED ANALYSIS AS A POLICY STRATEGY 10 (Robert V. Bartlett ed. 1989).

23 Michel Prieur, *Le respect de l'environnement et les études d'impact*, 2 REVUE JURIDIQUE DE L'ENVIRONNEMENT 103 (1981). CRAIK, 27 and 88. 2008.

24 Reisman, AM. SOC'Y INT'L L. PROC., 107 (1981).

25 W. Michael Reisman, *The View from the New Haven School of International Law*, 86 AM. SOC'Y INT'L. L. PROC. 118, 125 (1992).

time, was adopted in the United States because of pressure from civil society.[26] In the three case studies considered in this book, individuals and pressure groups promoted their preferred policies, acting as users of international law and aspirants in the process. The word *aspirant* here means individuals and groups that seek to participate in authoritative processes of a community with the aim of achieving influence or lawful control.[27] They may be pressure groups of different sorts, or individuals. EIA is destined to serve efficiently in both authoritarian and democratic regimes, albeit in different fashions. In authoritarian states, even if the EIA is defective, it can serve as a base for protests. When pressure groups are forbidden or suppressed, or when activists are imprisoned or killed, it generates international protests and draws attention; "it seems safe to say that if the protests have rarely succeeded in vindicating the position of aspirants, they have nonetheless sustained a general international demand for the continuation of this norm".[28] At the other end of the spectrum, in democratic states with a high consensus about the necessity of environmental protection, such as Scandinavian states, EIA may serve as an additional and potent aid to public participation. The law-making process and its mix of policy content, authority signals and control intentions depend on the community where one operates. Where there is a high sense of a collective purpose, with a shared understanding of the common interests, there is less need for control intentions.[29] Scandinavia can serve as an illustration, where "[c]onsensual circumstances appear to facilitate a relatively informal use of EIA".[30] In the *Vuotos* case for instance, the Espoo Convention, which prescribes Transboundary EIAS (TEIAS), was applied by Finland before its entry into force (see *infra* chapter 4). EIA, as display of information and solicitation of

26 Caldwell, THE ENVIRONMENTAL FORUM, 18 (1989). See also Ashby, 5. 1976. See *supra* chapter 2 and the origins of NEPA, page 8 et seq.

27 W. Michael Reisman & Eisuke Suzuki, *Recognition and Social Change in International Law: A Prologue for Decision-making*, *in* TOWARD WORLD ORDER AND HUMAN DIGNITY: ESSAYS IN HONOR OF MYRES S. MCDOUGAL 424 (W. Michael Reisman & Burns H. Weston eds., 1976).

28 Id. at 425.

29 Reisman, AM. SOC'Y INT'L L. PROC., 112 (1981).

30 Caldwell, Understanding Impact Analysis: Technical Process, Administrative Reform, Policy Principle 12. 1989. *Scandinavia* here is understood as the Nordic Countries (Denmark, Finland, Iceland, Norway, Sweden). See, for instance, Finland, which has diligently applied the Espoo Convention (to thirty-eight projects as of the end of 2010) *in* TIMO KOIVUROVA, ET AL., VALTIOIDEN RAJAT YLITTÄVIEN YMPÄRISTÖVAIKUTUSTEN ARVIOINTI SUOMESSA – YVA-LAIN TOIMIVUUS KANSAINVÄLISTÄ KUULEMISTA KOSKEVIEN VELVOITTEIDEN NÄKÖKULMASTA (EIA IN A TRANSBOUNDARY CONTEXT IN FINLAND) 11 (Finnish Ministry of the Environment. 2012).

participation, can then help to motivate and empower individuals in democracies, especially when individuals tend to be hesitant and skeptical about their potential role. Key to understanding how EIAs are conducted and used is understanding how aspirants feel empowered and decide to act. This investigation is centered on the circumstances under which EIA bears meaningful results, i.e. not simply that an EIA was produced, but that it had a mitigation and/or empowerment effect. Benefits from the process induced by EIA may be quite difficult to evaluate,[31] as it is by definition a process that attempts at introducing a fundamental change in values. Nonetheless, EIA, being a communication process,[32] has all the characteristics of a potent tool to influence the decision-making process and, more generally, the law-making process.

2 The Procedural Nature of EIA, in View of a Rational and Political Decision, Not Only a Scientific Report

The main trait is that EIA is a procedure, rather similar to a trial, where different opinions are confronted. In both cases, the consideration of all points of view is paramount. Ultimately, the decision is, or should be, the product of this collective operation. More broadly, EIA pertains to law as a process of communication, in which anyone who so wishes may participate. Procedure then matters more to law than preexisting rules: through procedure, law is being made.[33] However, faced as we are with environmental threats, hope has been focused on science, considered as the source of all the answers. International environmental law does depend on accurate and state of the art scientific knowledge, especially for transnational audiences.[34] Nevertheless, gathering and analyzing accurate scientific data is only the first phase of an EIA. EIAS cannot be scientific reports only. They need to encompass a broader analysis of the project, including the social impacts, through consultations and debates, resulting in a choice of values and potential risks. A harsh reality is quite often observed: there is no real debate, no real consultations, no discussion

31 For an analysis of the difficulties of studying the effects of an EIA and the objectives of such a study, see Ismo Pölönen, et al., *The effectiveness of the Finnish EIA system – What works, what doesn't, and what could be improved?* 31 ENVIRONMENTAL IMPACT ASSESSMENT REVIEW 120, 122 and 127 (2011); Tonis Poder & Tiit Lukki, *A critical review of checklist-based evaluation of environmental impact statements*, 29(1) IMPACT ASSESSMENT AND PROJECT APPRAISAL 27 (2011). See *supra* page 17 et seq.

32 Farrell & Jäger (eds.), 1. 2006.

33 VILLEY, 209, 210. 2001. See Maine's quote *supra* page 87.

34 McDougal, et al., TEMPLE LAW QUATERLY, 389, 413–414 (1973).

of alternatives, no meaningful process. According to some, political deliberations proportionate to the current environmental challenges have yet to take place.[35] This reveals how little is still known about EIAs, or how underestimated they may still be.

At present, when an EIA is actually conducted, the results seem to fall between two poles. On the one hand, it may be a hastily drafted document prepared after the decision was taken, done only to comply with an official requirement, detached from any concrete action or results, legitimating *ex post* the decision at stake.[36] On the other hand, albeit quite rarely, it is a process achieving public participation and informed decisions for the common good. In-between, there are longer-term, incremental effects. The goal of this book is to elucidate how EIAs contribute to law-making processes. Particularly in the international sphere, where there is no hierarchically structured authority, nor coercive measures to implement what has been decided, EIAs are capable of generating authoritative decisions, as a process of communication.

2.1 *EIA or the Reintroduction of Dialectics and Discourse*

> *Knowledge about environmental problems has expanded rapidly in recent decades (…) Yet too often scientific information has not been transformed into effective and appropriate policies to protect the global environment (…) global environmental assessments are more likely to be influential if the process is perceived not only as scientifically credible but also as salient to policy concerns and as generated through legitimate means. (…) although the content of the assessment clearly matters, its influence is often determined more by the process that generated it and by external factors affecting the receptiveness of different audiences.*[37]

EIA is an information tool, which leads to the reintroduction of dialectics as a legitimate means for effectively participating in the law-making process. As Neil Craik emphasizes, the advantage of EIAs is that they do not confront state sovereignty directly,[38] but instead establish a participative process. However, debates and misunderstandings about discourse illustrate the reluctance to engage in an open and inclusive decision-making process. By discourse, I mean

35 Editorial, *Paniques environnementales*, ESPRIT 4 (2010).
36 Knox, AJIL, (2002).
37 Mitchell, et al. (eds.), back cover. 2006. (emphasis added).
38 "The self-regulatory nature of EIA processes is well suited to international governance as it imposes low costs on state sovereignty" CRAIK, 244. 2008.

the exchange of views, organized in a legitimate fashion, which precedes and leads to a decision. Legitimacy is key to an efficient decision-making process. In public international law, because of the specificities of supranational governance as compared to domestic democratic regimes (mainly, a more distant link to elections), other foundations for legitimacy are needed. EIAs can be seen as being based on three interacting forms of legitimacy – procedural legitimacy, substantive legitimacy, and scientific legitimacy.[39] Procedural legitimacy predominates, since it is the basis of the other forms of legitimacy.[40] "Procedural rigor is especially important in the international policy domain, where the lack of democratic underpinnings and political accountability requires special focus".[41] More generally, in all kinds of fora, EIAs may participate in "the return of discourse", as understood by Michel Foucault. As Foucault argued, the universal fear of the unknown, of the unexpected and the uncontrolled leads to the suppression of discourse in many cases.[42] Reference to a preexisting reality, or to an author, an expert, an external authority who is thought to know best is preferred instead. Western culture has secured the elision of the reality of discourse, so that it takes as little room as possible between thought and its public expression, so that discourse appears as only the external appearance of thought, confused with public speech in the end, and eliminated.[43] Discourse tends to be eliminated whenever power is at stake. Real discourse necessarily follows procedural rules, which preclude unilateral will and unilateral power.[44] The will to harness the latter had consequently narrowed the place of procedural rules.

39 Id. at 244–251.

40 "Procedural rigor plays a special role in legitimizing governance and the exercise of power because it reinforces and enhances each of the other five sources of legitimacy" (Daniel C. Esty, *Good Governance at the Supranational Scale: Globalizing Administrative Law*, 115 YALE L. J. 1490, 1522 (2006)). The other five sources of legitimacy are democratic legitimacy, results-based legitimacy, order-based legitimacy, systemic legitimacy, and deliberative legitimacy.

41 Id. at. 1522. See also Daniel Bodansky, *Legitimacy*, *in* THE OXFORD HANDBOOK OF INTERNATIONAL ENVIRONMENTAL LAW 704 et seq. (Daniel Bodansky, et al. eds., 2008).

42 "There is undoubtedly in our society, and I would not be surprised to see it in others, though taking different forms and modes, a profound logophobia, a sort of dumb fear of these events, of this mass of spoken things, of everything that could possibly be violent, discontinuous, querulous, disordered even and perilous in it, of the incessant, disorderly buzzing of discourse". Michel Foucault, *The Discourse on Language*, *in* THE ARCHAEOLOGY OF KNOWLEDGE & THE DISCOURSE ON LANGUAGE 228–229 (Rupert Swyer trans., Pantheon Books. 1972).

43 Id. at 227.

44 Id. at 216.

However, discourse was eventually reintroduced, notably through soft law. Paradoxically, soft law was first used to respond to a sovereignty issue: states were concerned to preserve their power when undertaking commitments. Soft law can take the form of what Michael Reisman describes as *lex imperfecta*, i.e. "putative statutory instruments which have been structured, either textually or contextually, so as to be practically unenforceable".[45] EIA obligations, when they lack precise timing, public participation requirements or enforcement mechanisms – in other words, when there is a weak or absent control intention, which they often do, are an instance of *lex imperfecta*. This imperfect law, or "law without teeth", is not wholly without effect. As described below,[46] EIA requirements, as an official norm, are now part of the myth system (as opposed to the operational code). As such, they generate expectations. When these expectations are not met by the ruling elites, the discrepancy can be denounced by way of invocation, hence the multifold role of EIA – as an intelligence tool and/or as a base for invocation and promotion of appropriate environmental decisions and policies.

2.1.1 Reasons and Incentives to Act

Clear motivations geared toward environmental protection and sustainable development are indispensable for EIAs to be properly conducted by project proponents, competent authorities and experts, for EIA requirements to be properly enforced by courts, and for EIAs to attract the indispensable public participation. There are numerous and varied obstacles to overcome. Even though EIA is now a worldwide requirement, and environmental protection a global common interest, the world is still composed of competing sovereignties, a mixture of democratic and authoritarian states, at different economic stages, which is a major obstacle to the necessary environmental policy harmonization emphasized by the Espoo Convention.[47] Despite its aspiration to be a global treaty, this convention has so far applied only to a region where prior political and economic integration has allowed such harmonization. As a result, even though environmental awareness emerged in the 1970's, and although environmental protection has expanded and permeated the public

45 W. Michael Reisman, *The Concept and Functions of Soft Law in International Politics, in* ESSAYS IN HONOUR OF JUDGE TASLIM OLAWALE ELIAS 141 (Emmanuel G. Bello & Bola A. Ajibola eds., 1992); W. MICHAEL REISMAN, FOLDED LIES 29–31 (Free Press. 1979). See also W. Michael Reisman, *A Hard Look at Soft Law*, 82 AM. SOC'Y INT'L L. PROC. 373 (1988).

46 See *infra* page 112 et seq.

47 Article 11(2)(a).

policy discourse ever since, concrete actions and results are still difficult and slow to achieve on the global scale and in certain regions. Consequently, the tragedy of the commons and the free rider problem have remained problematic issues. In his short essay, scientist Garrett Hardin declared that the solution was not technical, but legal.[48] Paradoxically enough, this statement came from a biologist, in a time of triumphant and all-encompassing science. Hardin emphasized the futility of appeals to conscience and guilt. Rather, to act meaningfully signifies reaching an agreement on an arrangement of values, in order to avoid exhausting the resources on which humanity depends. It would seem that some civilizations have ended because of their ignorance or dismissal of environmental problems,[49] but their disappearance was geographically circumscribed. The contemporary stakes of environmental protection are planetary. In addition to economic integration, it may fundamentally be a matter of a convergence of defining interests, which, in the environment protection domain, are rather obvious: for the first time, countries the world over in principle share the same fundamental interests.

However, to share a common interest may not be sufficient for citizens or populations to unite their effort and overcome their innate rivalry.[50] For a dialectical engagement to be instantiated, within the framework of an EIA, meaningful participation of the stakeholders is of the essence. EIAs provide an opportunity to have citizens participate in the decision-making process when

48 Hardin *supra* chapter 1, note 35. Hardin explained in particular how Adam Smith's theory of the invisible hand was rebutted in 1833 by W. F. Lloyd, on whose lectures Hardin based his developments (WILLIAM FORSTER LLOYD, TWO LECTURES ON THE CHECKS TO POPULATION, Oxford University Press. 1833).

49 "Increased climate variability from ~AD 250–600 coincided with the demise of the Western Roman Empire and the turmoil of the Migration Period. Historical circumstances may challenge recent political and fiscal reluctance to mitigate projected climate change [...] The rise and fall of past civilizations have been associated with environmental change, mainly due to effects on water supply and agricultural productivity, human health and civil conflict" (Ulf Büntgen, et al., *2500 Years of European Climate Variability and Human Susceptibility*, SCIENCEXPRESS 1 (2011)). See also the end of the Lowland Maya civilization (*supra* page 1), and more generally JARED DIAMOND, COLLAPSE, HOW SOCIETIES CHOOSE TO FAIL OR SUCCEED (Viking. 2005).

50 "(...) if [Weber] chose what in his own terms he called scientific truth, it was because this truth was universal and, as such, constituted the proper grounds and domicile of a community of minds, across political boundaries and through the centuries. The cult of vitalistic values and the affirmation of the will to power result in the denial of universality: rivalry among rather than community of individuals would then constitute the essence of humanity". Raymond Aron, *Max Weber and Modern Social Science, in* HISTORY, TRUTH, LIBERTY – SELECTED WRITINGS OF RAYMOND ARON 361 (Franciszek Draus ed. 1985). See also *infra* page 102.

it comes to their environment. EIAs need to be well designed, and public participation is imperative in order to achieve the ultimate goals of the process. A community of interests, undeniable in the environmental domain, is not sufficient to create a nation, let alone global citizenship.[51] Only a real sentiment, a willingness to live together is capable of creating a legal system in which every day, every citizen agrees to live by, endorse and promote the rules by which they materialize this will.[52] This willingness can materialize through mutual consultations in the international domain, provided that concerned citizens recognize this personal dimension of sovereignty to which they are all contributors,[53] and provided that they can act upon their concerns. Having citizens realize that they are all part of the legal dynamics, even in the seemingly most inconsequential matters,[54] can prove difficult.

When considering a general reluctance to act, social pressure seems to eventually bring about public participation. For instance, in the United States, a strong sense of community and considerable social pressure prevail. Mobilization and civic actions are quite frequent. In this regard, the US Supreme Court emphasized the extent to which American citizens are involved in their country's life, and how they, as such citizens, define the country.[55] In Scandinavia, there is a similar sense of community (see *infra* chapter 4). In more hierarchical and centralized states, deliberative democracy is rather more difficult to develop. When a country is organized very hierarchically, incentives for regular public participation are quite naturally feeble. In addition, in environmental matters as in many others, the independence of NGOs may be difficult to maintain over time, as they gain importance (see *infra* chapter 5). Still, when reluctance to participate is overcome, stakeholders can then inform, and be fully informed so that they may participate meaningfully, hence the essential importance of communities. Real participatory democracy

---

51 "Do interests suffice to make a nation? I do not think so. Communities of interest determine commercial treaties. However, sentiment features in the making of nations. A nation is a body and soul at the same time. A *Zollverein* [customs union], by contrast, is never a fatherland". (ERNEST RENAN, WHAT IS A NATION? (Ethan Rundell trans., 1882)).

52 "A nation is therefore a great solidarity constituted by the feeling of sacrifices made and those that one is still disposed to make. It presupposes a past but is reiterated in the present by a tangible fact: consent, the clearly expressed desire to continue a common life. A nation's existence is (please excuse the metaphor) a daily plebiscite, just as an individual's existence is a perpetual affirmation of life." (Ibid.).

53 "The citizens themselves are sovereign", *Perez v. Brownell*, 356 US 44, 65 (1958) (Warren C.J., Black J., Douglas J. dissenting).

54 REISMAN, Law in Brief Encounters. 1999.

55 "Citizenship in this Nation is a part of a cooperative affair. Its citizenry is the country and the country is its citizenry", *Afroyim v. Rusk*, 387 US 253, 268 (1967).

can emerge only among people who feel they share a common fate and if they believe that they can contribute to decide this fate. Then, they also realize that they cannot delegate this responsibility to others, experts included.[56]

Furthermore, on the international plane, as Harold Lasswell has emphasized, "the prerequisite of a stable order in the world is a universal body of symbols and practices".[57] Lasswell underlined the importance of material unity; in particular, there must be sufficient tangible inducements to unity.[58] In this view, the role of multilateral development banks (MDBS) for instance can be crucial. To many, their procedures for project development and decision-making are perceived as the model to follow, which put domestic systems under increased pressure to meet international standards. Combined with the entitlement effects of human rights instruments, "the practices of international organizations contribute to the creation of the common culture that Lasswell saw as vital for securing world unity".[59] These practices and the findings of the various MDB review mechanisms participate to interstitial law-making and soft law.[60]

Along with contributing substantially to the decision-making process, what is also important is that the affected public communicate its preferred policy and outcome, and contribute substantially to the law-making process. It is as much about influencing the decision, as about having the latter accepted and its risks collectively assumed. A legitimate decision, reached thanks to public participation, build general trust because individuals and civic groups have participated, which may help to spare lawsuits. Moreover, the public interest is complex to define, as it is more complex than the simple addition of private interests. Consequently, the best way to identify the public interest is through an adequate public debate rather than an a priori, unilateral top-down opinion. Because of the diversity of individual interests, and the necessity to

56 Vincent Descombes, *Comment agir en citoyen?* ESPRIT 178, 195 (2011). See also "Democracy (…) is asking people's opinion while at the same time giving them the means to know what they are being asked about" (CLAUDE ROY, LE RIVAGE DES JOURS 138 (Gallimard. 1992)) (author's translation).

57 Harold D. Lasswell, *In Quest of a Myth: the Problem of World Unity, in* WORLD POLITICS AND PERSONAL INSECURITY 181 (1935).

58 Id. at 182–183.

59 Mahnoush H. Arsanjani, *The Uses and Abuses of Illusion in International Politics, in* LOOKING TO THE FUTURE – ESSAYS IN INTERNATIONAL LAW IN HONOR OF W. MICHAEL REISMAN 58–59 (Mahnoush H. Arsanjani, et al. eds., 2011).

60 Alix Gowlland Gualtieri, *The Environmental Accountability of the World Bank to Non-State Actors: Insights from the Inspection Panel,* 72 BRITISH YEARBOOK OF INTERNATIONAL LAW 213, 251–252 (2001). Regarding the crucial role of MDBS, see *infra* chapter 6, page 296 et seq.

balance market economy with regulation, the common good may be best achieved by setting up incentives based on widely disseminated information, which would in turn create a sense of responsibility.[61] Information delivered through a well-calibrated procedure helps to counteract cognitive biases, the force of emotions and the taint of particular circumstances.[62] Moreover, often, dialectics generates an outcome that no parties involved quite expected, an alternative solution that no one had thought of at first.[63]

In democracies, where freedom of expression is guaranteed and opportunities to choose and to act have become more and more numerous over time, EIAs are thus designed from the perspective of the political superior, in John Austin's terms.[64] This is to say that it is designed for anyone who is aware of their possibilities to make and promote their own choices. For Austin, law is the body of rules that must be obeyed for fear of a sanction. This implies, for positivists, simply looking for what the rules are and their articulation. In this context, civil disobedience is justified only with difficulty. However, this is only one perspective, that of the political inferior's. "The perspective of those at the upper end of Austin's dyad, the political superior was ignored or excluded from the definition of law".[65] Instead of considering that, in a democracy, anyone may be, depending on the circumstances, a political superior or a political inferior, many choose to believe that law does not allow for choice, but is merely the result of the commands of the political superior, i.e. someone else designated as the elite. That may be the reason why public participation is rather scarce even when a participative decision-making process, such as EIA, is in place. Firstly, EIAs are rarely fully and properly conducted. In all jurisdictions, only projects of a certain size trigger the obligation to carry out an EIA. Secondly, the manner in which the public is involved sheds light upon the limited extent of public participation.[66]

However difficult any choice and any decision might be, living with dignity requires being able to take charge of one's responsibilities and possession of one's place in the community in a meaningful fashion. The New Haven School emphasizes how, ultimately, subjective values inevitably preside over any

61 JEAN TIROLE, ECONOMIE DU BIEN COMMUN 15 (PUF. 2016).

62 An age-old issue, already evoked by Aristotle. See the numerous writings of Daniel Kahneman, Amos Tversky, Olivier Sibony.

63 Neil Craik emphasizes that "underlying interests can be altered through interactions" CRAIK, 252, see also 260. 2008.

64 Reisman, N. KY. L. REV., 605 (1995).

65 Id. at. 605.

66 O'Faircheallaigh, ENVIRONMENTAL IMPACT ASSESSMENT REVIEW, 19–20 (2010); Pölönen, et al., ENVIRONMENTAL IMPACT ASSESSMENT REVIEW, 126 (2011).

choice in this process. As Raymond Aron argued, along similar lines: "It is not the subjectivity and relativity of scientific knowledge that make choice necessary but, rather, the *partial* character of scientific truths and the *plurality* of values".[67] Lynton K. Caldwell, who drafted the discrete EIS provision in NEPA (called the action-forcing clause), observed that "deficiencies in our understanding of human behavior account for much of the ineffectiveness of our laws",[68] seemingly in echo of Harold D. Lasswell who observed about psychoanalysis that it would greatly improve his understanding of human choices and interactions.[69] EIA is an empowering tool, but which may be disregarded because a common reaction is to instinctively pull the blankets over one's head "to avoid the cold reality of dawn",[70] afraid of fully taking responsibility, unaware of one's potential. Understanding the central and common traits of the human psyche helps us to understand how EIAs and their potentialities are, or could be, used.

Spinoza claimed that, in a republic, all are supposed to be educated and enlightened. Consequently, no absurd decisions can realistically be made because the authorities must decide for the benefit of all, lest they be removed from power. By their very number, the people composing the majority of the population make it almost impossible for absurd decisions to be reached.[71] For this reason, EIA requirements prescribe a decision-making process with public participation aiming at ensuring the common good. Spinoza emphasized the importance of the role of every single citizen:

> [I argue that liberty] ought always to be enjoyed, and that it cannot be denied without great peril to the peace and much damage to the well-being of the whole commonwealth. In the demonstration of this

67 Aron, 339. 1985. Aron further writes: "the impatience of a man of action who demands of science the knowledge of means and consequences but who knows in advance that it will not free him from the obligation to choose, because the gods are many and the values contradictory." (id. at 341).

68 Caldwell, COLO. J. INT'L ENVTL. L. & POL'Y, 230 (1999).

69 Letter to Anna P. and Linden Lasswell, 3 December 1928, cited *in* RODNEY MUTH, et al., HAROLD D. LASSWELL: AN ANNOTATED BIBLIOGRAPHY 10 (New Haven Press · Kluwer Academic Publishers. 1990). H. D. Lasswell engaged in psychoanalysis with Theodor Reik, in Vienna.

70 REISMAN, Folded Lies 23. 1979. See also *infra* page 112 et seq.

71 "absurdities are less to be apprehended in a democracy; for it is next to impossible that the majority of an assembly, especially if it be numerous, should yield to one foolish person, or agree to any foolish or pernicious thing" (SPINOZA, THEOLOGICO-POLITICAL TREATISE (Robert Willis trans., Trübner & Co. 1862)), available at https://en.wikisource.org/wiki/Theologico-Political_Treatise_1862/Preface, accessed 17 June 2021.

> principle, I begin with a summary of the natural rights of man, which I show *extend as far as the desires and power of the individual extend*, and that no one is bound by natural law to live according to the pleasure of another, but that everyone is by natural title the rightful asserter of his own independence.[72]

History is made individually, by every citizen rather than being the exclusive product of elites, by everyone at the base rather than by only a few at the top. To what extent do citizens really exercise their natural rights, and how is it integrated with the rest of the decision-making processes? To see how psychological dispositions play into environmental issues, studies about how scientific information is conveyed and received show that people usually do not feel directly concerned; they do not believe, or have difficulties acknowledging, that they might have an impact on a global phenomenon. People naturally distance themselves from the problem (think, for instance, of climate change, perhaps the best documented issue). Coping by denial – the instinctive pulling of the blankets over one's head – is often observed. Even confronted with scientific certainty, individuals may feel disconnected from the urgency of required action. Instead, the emotional processing of information manifests itself by attribute substitution, recency of events in memory, insensitivity to bias in external samples of information, fixation on irrelevant information, discounting the importance of future events, and many others … all possibly summed up by a denial and renunciation attitude.[73] A political scientist explains inaction towards climate change by the fact that it "has become an ideologically polarizing issue. It taps into deep personal identities and causes what Dan Kahan (…) calls "protective cognition"[[74]] – we judge things in part on whether we see ourselves as rugged individualists mastering nature or as members of interconnected societies who live in harmony with the environment. Powerful special interests like the coal and oil industries have learned how to halt movement on climate policy by exploiting the fear people feel when their identities are threatened".[75] Consequently, to focus better on the

---

72 Id. at preface (emphasis added).

73 Ben R. Newell & Andrew J. Pitman, *The Psychology of Global Warming – Improving the Fit between the Science and the Message*, 91 BULLETIN OF AMERICAN METEOROLOGICAL SOCIETY 1003, 1007 (2010).

74 Dan Kahan, *Fixing the Communications Failure*, 463 NATURE 296 (2010). See also, by the same author, *Climate-Science Communication and the Measurement Problem*, 36 ADVANCES IN POL. PSYCH. 1 (2015).

75 Thomas Homer-Dixon, *Disaster at the Top of the World*, THE NEW YORK TIMES, 22 August 2010.

issues at stake, the New Haven School addresses the question of perspective by calling for an indispensable clarification of standpoint and for self-calibration when addressing any issue.[76] In this regard, Georg Simmel would add to Kahan's analysis that individuals no longer belong to only one social circle, but to several,[77] which may bring about a less biased, less ethnocentric self in the long run, more naturally inclined to clarify his or her standpoint for a better self-calibration.

2.1.2 Conceptual Tools for Mapping the Relevant Processes

When meaningful public participation is achieved, an EIA responds to Hardin's concern, i.e. finding ways to legitimate the required authority of both the custodians and the corrective feedbacks.[78] At the opposite end of the spectrum, in illiberal democracies or authoritarian regimes where the sense of local communities tends to be strangled by the central state, public participation in an EIA is reduced to a deceptive display.[79] In this case, an EIA takes on another

76 Reisman, AM. SOC'Y INT'L. L. PROC., 120 (1992). See also Germaine Tillion, *Vivre pour comprendre*, LE MONDE DIPLOMATIQUE, April 2009: "Once in a while, some rare and tormented souls have a natural ability to comprehend others' experience, but most people know and comprehend only what they themselves have experienced. The reverse is also true. To know oneself well, one must know how to consider one's own experience with a fresh look, to adopt a perspective outside one's self. Some cruel mistakes could be avoided if we expanded this double reference system" (author's translation).

77 GEORG SIMMEL, SOCIOLOGIE, ETUDES SUR LES FORMES DE LA SOCIALISATION 414 et seq. (Lilyane Deroche-Gurcel & Sibylle Muller trans., Puf. 2010).

78 "The laws of our society follow the pattern of ancient ethics, and therefore are poorly suited to governing a complex, crowded, changeable world. Our epicyclic solution is to augment statutory law with administrative law. Since it is practically impossible to spell out all the conditions under which it is safe to burn trash in the back yard or to run an automobile without smog-control, by law we delegate the details to bureaus. The result is administrative law, which is rightly feared for an ancient reason – *Quis custodiet ipsos custodes*? – "Who shall watch the watchers themselves?" John Adams said that we must have "a government of laws and not men". Bureau administrators, trying to evaluate the morality of acts in the total system, are singularly liable to corruption, producing a government by men, not laws. Prohibition is easy to legislate (though not necessarily to enforce); but how do we legislate temperance? Experience indicates that it can be accomplished best through the mediation of administrative law. We limit possibilities unnecessarily if we suppose that the sentiment of *Quis custodiet* denies us the use of administrative law. We should rather retain the phrase as a perpetual reminder of fearful dangers we cannot avoid. *The great challenge facing us now is to invent the corrective feedbacks that are needed to keep custodians honest. We must find ways to legitimate the needed authority of both the custodians and the corrective feedbacks*". (Hardin, SCIENCE, 1245–1246 (1968). (emphasis added)).

79 See *infra* chapter 6.

role: as the embodiment of the discrepancy between the myth system (official EIA requirements) and the operational code (defective EIA), it becomes a tangible base for protests and civic actions.

For any person willing to participate, the New Haven School identified seven decision functions – intelligence, promotion, prescription, invocation, application, termination, appraisal[80] – each of them presenting distinctive opportunities to make choices, with four intellectual tasks to carry out so as to choose best: clarification of standpoint, careful selection of focal lenses, a map of community processes, a praxis of choice-making. The approach of the New Haven School has been designed to understand and shape law in all contexts, from the local to the planetary, and is especially empowering for individuals not associated with the state.[81] Procedure, such as EIA, serves policy goals as interstitial law-making. The New Haven School has developed tools in order to bring about changes in public and civic order that will make them more closely approximate the goals of human dignity.[82] EIA requirements were first put in place by legislation, the purpose of which was to establish a national policy that would encourage productive and enjoyable harmony between man and his environment, and to promote efforts that would prevent or eliminate damage to the environment and biosphere, and stimulate the health and welfare of humankind.[83] EIAs are now widely acknowledged as communication processes, not just as scientific reports.[84] To thoroughly understand their effectiveness or their potential, it is thus critical to understand the respective process that is used. EIAs need to include the participation of stakeholders, either directly or through valid representation – which begs the question of the legitimacy of this representation. Then, it is a matter of arrangements of values and policies, all the more necessary in the complex domain of sustainable development, which raises multidimensional and long-term questions. EIA requirements may overcome the current predominant criteria of strict efficacy (cost-benefit analysis) as the gauge of policy and normative choices at the expense of the necessary arrangements of values.[85] Law is policy, and the

80 See *supra* page 89 et seq.

81 Reisman, et al., YALE J.INT'L L., 577 (2007).

82 Id. at 576.

83 NEPA, Sec. 2 (42 USC § 4321).

84 Farrell & Jäger (eds.), 2, 3, 278. 2006; Ronald B. Mitchell, et al., *Information and Influence*, *in* GLOBAL ENVIRONMENTAL ASSESSMENTS – INFORMATION AND INFLUENCE 308, 324–328 (Ronald B. Mitchell, et al. eds., 2006).

85 Douglas A. Kysar, *It Might Have Been: Risk, Precaution, and Opportunity Costs*, 22 J. LAND. USE & ENVTL. LAW 1 (2006). Susan Rose-Ackerman, *Étude d'impact et analyse coûts-avantages : qu'impliquent- elles pour l'élaboration des politiques publiques et les réformes*

New Haven School, as a policy-oriented approach, provides a set of conceptual tools for mapping the relevant processes by identifying the participants, their perspectives, the situations in which they interact, their bases of power, their strategies, and the aggregate outcomes of the process of interaction,[86] which, when applied to the analysis of the EIA process, can help to achieve optimum environmental policies.

In parallel with the clarification of their standpoint, participants need to be well informed. "Unless the audience has an appreciation of the naturally disputative and accretive character of science, its resolution of a conflict may not be a balanced and informed weighting of the sides. Alternative resolutions are doubting the probity of the disputants, siding with the most assertive (or colorful or optimistic or certain), or deciding that "anything goes" and that "my guess is as good as yours"".[87] This brings to mind Simone de Beauvoir's observation about Manichaean views held by those who do not participate in the decision-making process, or who may be ill-informed. Indeed, when one commits to action, as Beauvoir notes, one comes to realize how nuanced and complex reality always is, contrary to how simple it may be perceived when one remains passive.[88] Furthermore, we operate in a complex world where the profusion of information, its rapid diffusion as well as its wide availability, lead to the fragmentation of this information. In post-industrial societies, mass media tend to arbitrarily select and associate events that they present as cause and effect. This technique – the cinematographic effect – has simplified

---

législatives? 140 Revue française d'administration publique 787 (Viviane Meunier-Rubel trans., 2011); Susan Rose-Ackerman, *Putting Cost-Benefit Analysis in Its Place: Rethinking Regulatory Review*, 65 U. Miami L. Rev. 335 (2011).

86 Reisman, et al., YALE J.INT'L L., 577 (2007).

87 Baruch Fischhoff, *Hot air: The psychology of Co-induced climatic change, in* COGNITION, SOCIAL BEHAVIOR, AND THE ENVIRONMENT 178 (John H. Harvey ed., 1981).

88 "The individual who acts accepts responsibility for good and evil just like the others, he knows that it is up to him to define ends, to see that they triumph; in action he experiences the ambiguity of all solutions; justice and injustice, gains and losses, are inextricably intermingled. But whoever is passive puts himself on the sidelines and refuses to pose, even in thought, ethical problems: good must be realized, and if it is not, there is wrongdoing for which the guilty must be punished. Like the child, [the individual that remains passive] imagines good and evil in simple storybook images; Manichaeism reassures the mind by eliminating the anguish of choice; deciding between one scourge and a lesser one, between a benefit today and a greater benefit tomorrow, having to define by oneself what is defeat and what is victory: this means taking terrible risks" (SIMONE DE BEAUVOIR, THE SECOND SEX 733 (Constance Borde & Sheila Malovany-Chevallier trans., Vintage Books. 2011)).

the perception of reality, in truth significantly more complex and nuanced.[89] Hence the necessity of clarifying standpoints, well-conducted EIAs with all pertinent information, consultations and debates, to then decide in the most enlightened way on what risks count as acceptable. In other words, in order to motivate people to act, and then to best address the many possibilities that exist and to best choose among them, participation of all the stakeholders and appropriate communication are required. This is a very general process.[90] "Culture is human nature" according to Marshall Sahlins, for whom an individual cannot truly exist before or apart from his or her interactions with society.[91] Hence the necessary, essentially collegial, consensual, deliberative aspect of a proper decision-making process such as the EIA procedure. Human beings are always evolving, "human nature is a *becoming*, rather than an always-already being".[92] The value of procedure unveils: a social relationship, an experiment through which all stakeholders are informed, consulted, inform in their turn, choose, mitigate and assume the collective consequences of a project, in the dynamic process of law-making.

2.1.3 The Legal Process

The continuous process of communicating is what constitutes the legal process. Roman jurists did not decide by syllogisms, or deductions imposed by pre-established rules, but by controversies that led to probable truths with as wide

89 Reisman, N. KY. L. REV., 613–615 (1995). See also Monica Hakimi, *The Media as Participants in the International Legal Process*, 16 DUKE JOURNAL OF COMPARATIVE & INTERNATIONAL LAW 1 (2006).

90 "What is the meaning of conversation? According to Montaigne, to converse is to dispute for the sake of truth, the common cause. Victory is indifferent. What matters is the quality of the exchange and the progress made in gaining wisdom about life". (author's translation – ALAIN FINKIELKRAUT, UN CŒUR INTELLIGENT, LECTURES 114 (Stock / Flammarion. 2009); Michel de Montaigne, *De l'art de conférer*, *in* LES ESSAIS (Villey & Saulnier. 1588)).

91 MARSHALL SAHLINS, THE WESTERN ILLUSION OF HUMAN NATURE 104 et seq. (Prickly Paradigm Press. 2008). Françoise Dolto was of the same opinion, who thus criticized Descartes for declaring "I think therefore I am" in the sense that a person does not take her place all by herself, but in relation to others (FRANÇOISE DOLTO & GÉRARD SÉVÉRIN, L'EVANGILE AU RISQUE DE LA PSYCHANALYSE, TOME I 165 (Seuil. 1977)). Language was naturally developed because of the defining necessity for human beings to be in relation with each other, what Aristotle phrased as man is a political animal: "it is clear that the city-state is a natural growth, and that man is by nature a political animal". (Politics, *in* Book 1, section 1253a). See also DANTE ALIGHIERI, THE DIVINE COMEDY, at https://digitaldante.columbia.edu (accessed 17 June 2021).

92 SAHLINS, *supra* note 91 at 107.

as possible an accord of the expressed opinions.[93] Henry Maine's famous apothegm emphasizes the pivotal place of procedure in early legal systems: "substantive law has at first the look of being gradually secreted in the interstices of procedure".[94] In this particular respect, a comparison has been drawn between Roman law and common law; until the 19th century, procedural formalities dominated common law thinking.[95] In the same vein as the New Haven School in the United States, Chaïm Perelman and the Brussels School emphasized that dialectics still defines legal reasoning today.[96] Michel Villey described the nature and evolution of dialectics as follows:

> Is it not the ultimate fate of dialectics, grounded in uncertain opinions, to remain in uncertainty? (…) Exchanges of views must always (…) lead to a solution, but how to reach this end? The art of dialectics came to an apogee in the Middle Ages. In the disputed questions of Scholasticism, it is the role of the *master* to *end* (*concludere*): not the necessary conclusion of a syllogism, but the end of a debate. (…) The worth of the results should not be overstated. Throughout the process that leads to the conclusion, how many factors of uncertainty! The choice of actors, "authorities", where only *qualitative* criteria can be used, as opposed to

93 Michel Villey, *Liminaire – Données historiques, in* ARCHIVES DE PHILOSOPHIE DU DROIT – LA LOGIQUE DU DROIT (1966). See also: "searching for law is a collective task. As a matter of fact, it is polyphonic (…) Light will come from a joust between opposing pleas. Controversy was the ultimate place where law was created" (author's translation – Michel Villey, *Histoire de la logique juridique, in* ANNALES DE LA FACULTÉ DE DROIT DE TOULOUSE – TOME XV 76 (1967)). In Roman law, for most of the duration of the Republic, law was developed more through procedure than through legislation and its interpretation (PETER STEIN, ROMAN LAW IN EUROPEAN HISTORY 8 and 126 (Cambridge University Press. 1999)).

94 SUMNER MAINE, 389. 1883.

95 FREDERICK MAITLAND & FREDERIC WILLIAM POLLOCK, HISTORY OF ENGLISH LAW BEFORE THE TIME OF EDWARD I 558 et seq. § II (Cambridge University Press. 1898). The process of Roman law's development was replicated in England, where Chancery organized itself based on a procedural tradition – a system of forms of action, or writ system (JOHN H. LANGBEIN, et al., HISTORY OF THE COMMON LAW, THE DEVELOPMENT OF ANGLO-AMERICAN LEGAL INSTITUTIONS (Aspen Publishers – Wolters Kluwer. 2009). See also THEODORE PLUCKNETT, A CONCISE HISTORY OF THE COMMON LAW 361 (Butterworth 4th ed. 1948); F.W. MAITLAND, THE FORMS OF ACTION AT COMMON LAW (A.H. Chaytor & W.J. Whittaker, eds. Cambridge. 1909); J. H. BAKER, AN INTRODUCTION TO ENGLISH LEGAL HISTORY (Butterworths 4th ed. 2002).

96 CHAÏM PERELMAN & LUCIE OLBRECHTS-TYTECA, THE NEW RHETORIC: A TREATISE ON ARGUMENTATION (John Wilkinson & Purcell Weaver trans., University of Notre Dame Press. 1969).

> scientific and rigorously measurable ones, even for the choice of the master to end the debate, which is wholly at her discretion. However, her decision is a reasoned one. It is *informed* by the debate, during which, in the context of a regulated procedure, the various aspects of the disputed issue have been reviewed, hence providing the highest and most complete perspective ('Golden Mean' [Aristotle]). Dialectics unites these two moments: dialogue and decision. If they were to be dissociated, dialectics would disappear. Then dialogue, left to itself, without order and without end, would be sterile, incapable of leading to anything except the refusal of *skeptics* to conclude. Deprived of their reasons, decisions would be nothing more than an *arbitrary* choice by the authorities.[97]

In light of these developments about dialectics, EIA requirements can be seen as their reintroduction into project development. EIA provisions require protection of the common interest, the consideration of a particular situation and decision by a procedural operation.

Consequently, the ultimate purpose of the EIA process, which is fundamentally a communication process, goes beyond providing the necessary information about environmental impacts in order to make an enlightened decision; it is also ultimately to attract as many as possible to the cause of the project once the latter is decided. Ultimately, the majority of the stakeholders agree to run the risks altogether, after having made a deliberative and informed decision. In this sense, EIA is a political process. It enhances the actual and perceived fairness of actions ultimately decided.[98] EIAs have a social function, i.e. they reflect on the political desirability of the available choice[99] in the larger context of participatory democracy. Consequently, the expectations generated by EIA requirements have often led to the adoption of Strategic Environmental Assessment requirements (SEA), i.e. EIA applied to a higher level of decision-making: policies, plans and programs.[100] They also led, in France for instance,

97 VILLEY, Philosophie du droit (Définitions et fins du droit – Les moyens du droit) 201. 2001 (author's translation).

98 EPA, FINAL GUIDANCE FOR INCORPORATING ENVIRONMENTAL JUSTICE CONCERNS IN EPA'S NEPA COMPLIANCE ANALYSES Chap. 4 (US Environmental Protection Agency. 1998).

99 Jorge E. Viñuales, *Legal Techniques for Dealing with Scientific Uncertainty in Environmental Law*, 43 VAND. J. TRANSNAT'L L. 437, 471 (2010). See also Leslye A. Herrmann, *Injunctions for NEPA Violations: Balancing the Equities*, 59 U. CHI. L. REV. 1263, 1267 (1992): "The EIS process is public and resembles rulemaking".

100 See Directive 2001/42/EC of the European Parliament and of the Council of 27 June 2001 on the assessment of the effects of certain plans and programmes on the environment, OJ L 197, 21 July 2001, p. 30–37 (the SEA Directive).

to the impact assessment (IA) of bills,[101] which extended the IA process to all statutory drafting in an attempt to improve the quality of the legislative corpus and reduce its inflation – a formal return to basic and common sense requirements.[102]

Information and consultation, within neutral and independent frameworks and institutions, with a clearly identified target audience and decision-maker(s), are key to an efficient process. Because of scientific uncertainty, EIAs aim at establishing acceptable levels of unpredictability. The precautionary principle is ultimately more a collective decision to take risks rather than allowing only a few to be informed and decide. It is a question of having as much information and as many stakeholders involved in the decision-making process as possible. That is why the precautionary principle exists in tandem with public participation.[103] There must be a reasonable discussion and then a reasoned choice, as defined by Max Weber,[104] lest the formal debate legitimate, not the decision, but only itself.[105] For that purpose, balance and timing are key – balance between all the participants and the issues to address, timing as to the start of public participation, duration of the consultation phase, and the moment to come to a conclusion and to take the decision.[106] The final decision is only the most apparent outcome of the process that was followed. There are larger dynamics at play. The appropriate process guarantees the best decision, in an ongoing legitimate debate of which informed and responsible citizens

101 Article 8 of *Loi organique* No. 2009-403, 15 April 2009.

102 See, more generally, Guy Carcassonne, *Penser la loi*, 114 POUVOIRS 39 (2005).

103 See, for instance, Articles 5 and 7 of the 2004 French Environment Charter, included in the preamble of the French Constitution. See also "This lack of baseline data often leads to high levels of uncertainty in predicting impacts during EIAs and reliance on modelling to predict impacts. As a result, decisions on acceptability are risk-based and the precautionary principle gets expressed in terms of adaptability of management responses rather than waiting until sufficient information has become available to complete the EIA. The dilemma for the EPA is to determine at what point sufficient data is available so that the level of uncertainty about predicting impacts becomes acceptable. In these cases, much of the time taken in these phases of the EIA relates to establishing acceptable levels of uncertainty" (Middle & Middle, IMPACT ASSESS. PROJ. APPRAIS., 167 (2010)).

104 "But it would be wrong to present science and arbitrary decisions as alternative options. Between the rational proposition – valid for all, because it can be demonstrated according to methods that apply to all – and the choice made by each individual alone, without binding anyone else, there is room for a reasonable decision, i.e. a decision founded on reason, although it may run contrary to the interests of a few." (Aron, 366. 1985).

105 Philippe Muray, *Il faudrait ne jamais … in* ESSAIS – EXORCISMES SPIRITUELS IV – MODERNE CONTRE MODERNE (2003).

106 "It takes time to come to a conclusion" (Jacques Lacan, *Le moment de conclure*, avant-dernier séminaire (XXV), 1977–1978 – author's translation).

are part. Some are ready, occasionally, to renounce having their views prevail as long as they are represented. Process permits all concerns to be voiced, lest they be ignored or brushed aside, only to reappear in a more violent form.

Scientific data and analysis is the first component of EIAs, but it is only one of many. If EIAs are presented as purely scientific documents, stakeholders will expect scientific rigor and completeness, which poses a substantial risk of frustration and anger. At the same time, professional experts that claim a scientific character for their studies assert objectivity as a way of discouraging critical discussion by the lay public. In reality, EIAs are not exclusively scientific, but are ridden with value judgments, and highly political. Professional experts must acknowledge and clearly state their assumptions in order for their studies to be useful tools, including external input, in order to redirect the public to the economic or the political arena.[107] Members of the International Association for Impact Assessment (IAIA) (mostly consultants and government employees) were surveyed in 2008 and demonstrated what Robert Beattie has denounced, i.e. the misleading claim of an objective, scientific rationale as the sole component of an EIA. IAIA members contested the reality of predominant political influences. The IAIA survey seems to show uneasiness about the art of EIA, i.e. a complex process that is designed to accommodate competing values or interests. Practitioners do not appear to easily combine the art and science of EIA – technical expertise and public debate and aspirations.[108]

Max Weber argues that we must renounce responsibility if we opt for conviction, and vice versa, because scientific arguments alone cannot justify a radical political choice. The choice to make is, precisely, political in nature, based on values, and values *per se* cannot be proven. Importantly, a practical decision does not need to be proven true. Such a decision can have positive or negative effects, but it cannot be true or false because there is a difference in categories, between determining what exists, which pertains to the domain of science, and deciding on a course of action, which belongs to the domain of politics.[109] Thus, only through a process that permits the confrontation of all opinions will it be possible to achieve the best possible informed and legitimate decision. However, the EIA process seems to be excessively state-centered, and public input has been too secondary. On the domestic level, it has often been observed that the decision-making process is often closed to the public.[110] In a

107 Beattie, ENVIRON. IMPACT ASSESS. REV., 111–113 (1995).

108 Angus Morrison-Saunders & Barry Sadler, *The art and science of impact assessment: results of a survey of IAIA members*, 28(1) IMPACT ASSESSMENT AND PROJECT APPRAISAL 77 (2010).

109 Descombes, *supra* note 56 at 181.

110 Dzidzornu, EUR. ENVT'L L. REV., 19–21 (2001).

public report on the efficacy of EIAs, it was clearly stated that decisions were made behind closed doors.[111] In France for instance, as of 2014, the appraisal of substantial amendments had yet to be conducted,[112] and, more generally, IAs had not yet permeated the habits of the public administration. Since then, the actual appraisals have been criticized for two main reasons: their tardiness and their poor quality.[113]

To the disengaged observer, EIAs appear to be at the core of the tensions between the myth system and the operational code, as described by Michael Reisman.[114] The normative myth system is the ensemble of official norms as opposed, though not systematically, to the operational code, which is the effective behavior of sufficiently numerous and relevant actors of a community. Even when formal law is not applied or not sanctioned, it embodies key values and influences the operational code, to which the normative myth system remains the reference.[115] Social stability perdures in case of unsanctioned discrepancies between the myth system and the operational code because these discrepancies are either accepted or ignored. In the former case (if they are accepted), formal law must be completed by a study of the socially proper behavior in order to determine what the law is. In the latter case (if discrepancies are ignored), when independent and empowered actors become aware of

111 SADLER, 16. 1996.

112 Introduced in 2009, Article 98-1 of the bylaws of the National Assembly was passed in application of a constitutional reform (Article 15 of *loi organique* No. 2009-403, 15 April 2009, *relative à l'application des articles 34-1, 39 et 44 de la Constitution*). As of 2014, Article 98-1 had not been applied yet – no evaluation of a proposed amendment to a bill had been conducted (LAURE DE LA RAUDIÈRE & RÉGIS JUANICO, RAPPORT D'INFORMATION SUR LA SIMPLIFICATION LÉGISLATIVE: MIEUX LÉGIFÉRER, MIEUX ÉVALUER: QUINZE PROPOSITIONS POUR AMÉLIORER LA FABRIQUE DE LA LOI 94 (Assemblée nationale. 2014)).

113 See, for instance, CONSEIL ÉCONOMIQUE SOCIAL ET ENVIRONNEMENTAL & JEAN-LOUIS CABRESPINES, ETUDE D'IMPACT: MIEUX ÉVALUER POUR MIEUX LÉGIFÉRER 119 (Délégation à la prospective et à l'évaluation des politiques publiques. Conseil économique, social et environnemental. 2019).

114 REISMAN, Folded Lies 15–36. 1979; REISMAN, The Quest for World Order and Human Dignity in the Twenty-first Century: Constitutive Process and Individual Commitment 95–104. 2013.

115 Michael Reisman quotes La Rochefoucauld in this regard: "hypocrisy is the homage vice pays to virtue" (FRANÇOIS DE LA ROCHEFOUCAULD, MAXIMES ET RÉFLEXIONS MORALES 223 (page 54) (Didot. 1796). Even if some protested the accuracy of this maxim (see Jean-Jacques Rousseau, *Réponse au Roi de Pologne, Duc de Lorraine, sur la réfutation faite par ce prince de son discours, in* ŒUVRES – DISCOURS 87–88, (1751)), Reisman emphasizes that homage *is* owed, and something should be paid (REISMAN, Folded Lies 29. 1979).

these discrepancies (or do no longer accept them) and test them against the standards of the myth system, dissensions can erupt, leading to instability and then possibly change. Consequently, elites try to conceal these discrepancies in order to maintain the integrity of the myth system. However, they often do not bear the sole responsibility for this deception in the case of a successful endeavor: many in the community "may abet the deception, avoiding the truth like someone pulling blankets over his head to avoid the cold reality of dawn",[116] which is a universal reaction, observed whatever the peculiar characteristics of any political regime. Furthermore, the deception may not be exclusively elite-induced, but more widely initiated within a community, by any of its members who believe the myth contributes to policing the group. This could be particularly true of less individualistic and more traditional societies where authority is still strictly and hierarchically organized and feared. The *UMNIP* case study (discussed in chapter 6) provides an interesting example of deception at different strata in the public, but which has recently become outdated because of excessive discrepancies.[117]

Deception, in order to conceal grave discrepancies, can take the complex form of *lex imperfecta;* it may be that prescribed norms are clear, but are supported only by the appearance of an enforcement mechanism, otherwise inadequate, understaffed or staffed "with exquisite incompetents".[118] For instance, quite many environment ministries or agencies, or review mechanisms set up in multilateral development banks show that numerous EIA requirements are instances of *lex imperfecta.*[119] Michael Reisman recalls the words of Alex Rose: "To put people in law enforcement for the purpose of non-enforcement is a very big attraction for politicians".[120] In Reisman's words, EIA norms are often Solon giving with one hand, but taking with the other.[121] EIA requirements are official obligations to carefully consider the environmental consequences of a sizeable project, but the requirements usually do not properly address timing, the necessity of independent experts and independent reviews, and sanctions. EIAS are often done too late in the decision-making process, without proper public participation, by either biased or incompetent experts and/or without

116 Id. at 23.

117 See *infra* page 283 et seq.

118 REISMAN, Folded Lies 29. 1979.

119 See *infra* chapters 4 to 6.

120 Alex Rose, Head of the Liberal Party of New York, *in* MARTIN TOLCHIN & SUSAN J. TOLCHIN, TO THE VICTOR ...: POLITICAL PATRONAGE FROM THE CLUBHOUSE TO THE WHITE HOUSE 12 (Random House. 1971); REISMAN, Folded Lies 29–30. 1979.

121 Id. at 31.

being properly reviewed. If the prescribed procedure has not been followed, judges may give short shrift to this procedural obligation.

However, EIA requirements, as part of the myth system, typically have an important effect: they generate expectations. In addition, even when an EIA is defective, it exposes the deception to affected populations who know the EIA is inaccurate. The defective EIA is an exposed discrepancy, which may naturally turn into a provocation that may generate protests. Affected populations gather, organize themselves and protest the operational code. When grave discrepancies between the myth system (EIA, environmental conservation and sustainable development) and the operational code (decisions made without an appropriate consideration of the environmental impacts) reach a tipping point, they are no longer accepted. EIAs give the means and opportunities to relevant actors to pressure for change.

EIAs are highly praised as a theoretical matter, while they seem to perform poorly in practice. Many underline that EIAs do not significantly influence the final decision, although they continue to insist that they will, sometime in the near future.[122] This despite the fact that EIAs have been in place for almost fifty years since NEPA, a duration that permits an examination of their utility and speculation about their potential. Why do EIAs often seem to be inefficient, when are they effective, how do they function, and how could they be improved?

2.2 *NEPA as Process-monger*

> *Imagine the shock of Richard Nixon and many members of Congress when, early in 1970, they discovered that these apparently innocuous words of §102 could be the basis of very real lawsuits. §102, like a snake in the grass, contained the hidden but potent impact statement requirement.*[123]

It is here necessary to go back to the time when EIAs were first introduced in the United States, by the National Environmental Policy Act (NEPA), on 1

122 "Scientific assessments often do not demonstrate significant influence on decisions affecting environmental quality", *in* Farrell & Jäger (eds.), 2. 2006. Dzidzornu, EUR. ENVT'L L. REV., 16 (2001). See also Leonard Ortolano & Anne Shepherd, *Impact Assessment*, 13 IMPACT ASSESSMENT 3 (1995); Richard K. Morgan, *Environmental impact assessment: the state of the art*, 30 IMPACT ASSESS. PROJ. APPRAIS. 5, 7 (2012).

123 ZYGMUNT J. B. PLATER, ET AL., ENVIRONMENTAL LAW & POLICY: NATURE, LAW & SOCIETY 318 (Wolters Kluwer 5th ed. 2016).

January 1970. NEPA's evolution shows the effects of this kind of procedural rule, i.e. "process-monger".[124]

2.2.1 Origins of EIS

"Congress contemplated that the Impact Statement would constitute the environmental source material for the information of the Congress as well as the Executive, in connection with the making of decisions, and would be available to enhance enlightenment of, *and by*, the public. The impact statement provides a basis for (a) evaluation of the benefits of the proposed project in light of its environmental risks, and (b) comparison of the net balance for the proposed project with the environmental risks presented by alternative courses of action".[125] NEPA represented a revolution in values, in the sense that environmental effects should be considered as well as economic effects,[126] in a comprehensive, humanistic approach, as emphasized by the bill's sponsor in the US Senate, Senator Henry M. Jackson:

> Many of the environmental controversies of recent years have, in large measure, been caused by the failure to consider all relevant points of view and all relevant values in the planning and conduct of Federal activities. Using an interdisciplinary approach that brings together the skills of [the] landscape architect, the engineer, the ecologist, the economist, the sociologist and other relevant disciplines would result in better planning, better projects, and a better environment. Too often in the past planning has been the exclusive province of the engineer and cost analyst. And, as a consequence, too often the humanistic point of view ... has been overlooked or purposely ignored.[127]

This view was embodied in the statute: "all agencies of the Federal Government shall utilize a systematic, interdisciplinary approach which will insure the integrated use of the natural and social sciences and the environmental

124 William H. Rodgers, Jr., *NEPA at Twenty: Mimicry and Recruitment in Environmental Law*, 20 ENVTL. L. 485, 493–494 (1990).

125 *Natural Resources Defense Council, Inc., et al., v. Rogers C. B. Morton, in his official capacity as Secretary of the Department of Interior, et al.*, 458 F.2d 827, 833 (DC Cir. 1972) (emphasis added).

126 Dreyfus & Ingram, NAT. RESOURCES J., 245 (1976).

127 Conference report prepared by Senator Jackson, which set out the compromise reached after disagreeing votes of the two houses on the amendments of the US House of Representatives to the bill (S.1075) to establish NEPA (*in* 115 Cong. Rec. 40415, 40419–40420 (1969)).

design arts in planning and in decision-making which may have an impact on man's environment".[128] US Senator Edmund Muskie, another prominent environmentalist, emphasized that the strong language of NEPA had been designed to apply strong pressure on federal agencies, such that they would be answerable to the demands of environmental quality.[129] The bill was passed in the Senate without debate, nor amendment, in part due to the political skills of Jackson and William Van Ness who ensured that the bill was put to a vote during the morning hours, a period reserved for routine matters.[130] In the House of Representatives, there were more difficulties. Wayne Aspinall (D-Colo.) was apprehensive about the risks of the bill hindering economic development of natural resources, which would become a standard critique of EIA requirements. As chairman of the Interior and Insular Affairs Committee and as a member of the House Rules Committee, Aspinall insisted and focused on the 'no change' disclaimer. Because of Aspinall's influence, the bill's sponsor in the House, John Dingell (D-Mich.), was forced to accept this amendment.[131]

As for the EIA requirement (called EIS in NEPA: Environmental Impact Study), recommended by Lynton Caldwell, the author of the draft NEPA bill, it was such a radical and unprecedented innovation that it was not included at first, nor in the Senate Bill No. 1075, nor in the House Resolution No. 6750. The EIS requirement was passed, thanks to Muskie's objections and late in the legislative process. Surprisingly, it passed entirely underestimated and unnoticed.[132] NEPA was deemed a sleeper, which acquired and achieved influence far beyond what Congress contemplated.[133] "Ironically, the possibility not

128 42 USC § 4332 (A).

129 115 Cong. Rec. 40425 (1969). At first, Muskie, Chairman of the Public Works Committee, had opposed the bill, for turf-protecting reasons.

130 LINDSTROM & SMITH, 40. 2002. William J. Van Ness is a Seattle attorney who worked under Senator Jackson, on the US Senate Committee on Interior and Insular Affairs from 1966 to 1977. Van Ness served as special counsel, and later (beginning in 1970) as chief counsel.

131 The no-change clause in the bill stated: "nothing in this act shall increase, decrease or change any responsibility or authority of any federal official or agency created by other provisions of law" (id. at 41).

132 For a detailed legislative history of NEPA, see RICHARD A. LIROFF, A NATIONAL POLICY FOR THE ENVIRONMENT – NEPA AND ITS AFTERMATH 34–35 (Indiana University Press. 1976). LYNN G. LLEWELLYN & CLARE PEISER, NEPA AND THE ENVIRONMENTAL MOVEMENT: A BRIEF HISTORY 24 (NBSIR 73–218. National Bureau of Standards. 1973) (report to the EPA): the EIS requirement "has probably evoked more controversy than any other aspect of NEPA, yet it appears to have been an afterthought".

133 Rodgers, ENVTL. L., 492 (1990).

discussed, mentioned, or adverted to in the legislative materials – the NEPA lawsuit – contained the seeds of the statute's explosive growth".[134] The considerable potential of a procedure that stakeholders could use to participate in the decision-making process completely escaped the Government, Congress and the commentators at first.[135] Dingell then remarked: "I have some doubts that NEPA would pass in its present form today. I very much doubt if the Section 102 provision … would be in …"[136]

But by then, it was too late. After NEPA was passed, nearly 200 bills were submitted to weaken or repeal it, all in vain.[137] Once expectations have been generated, they rarely disappear, which makes it difficult to repeal the associated acts. Senator Jackson, the very sponsor of the bill, stated clearly "The most important feature of the act, however, and probably the least recognized, is that it establishes new decision-making procedures for all agencies of the federal government. Some of these procedures are designed to establish checks and balances in order to ensure that potential environmental problems will be identified and considered early in the decision-making process and not after irrevocable commitments have been made".[138] During the discussions of the bill, Senator Muskie had warned against self-policing agencies (*Quis custodiet ipsos custodes?*[139]), and insisted on including external input.[140] "This vaguely worded statute", Justice Marshall wrote, "assiduously avoids giving any hint, either expressly or by way of legislative history, of what is meant by" its key terms, and therefore "seems designed to serve as no more than *a catalyst for*

134 Id. at 493. Congress did not discuss the enforcement mechanisms of NEPA's requirements, but lawsuits started soon after the bill was passed. Some 500 lower court cases materialized before the Supreme Court's first significant decision. What was at first "a classic symbolic response to Congressional perceptions of swelling national concern for the environment – bold in proclamation of purpose, limited in intended policy consequence – … was transformed by citizen litigation and judicial review from toothless symbolism to an action-forcing nightmare for development interests". (GEORGE HOBERG, PLURALISM BY DESIGN: ENVIRONMENTAL POLICY AND THE AMERICAN REGULATORY STATE 44 (Praeger. 1992)). The key early case interpreting NEPA's requirements is *Calvert Cliffs' Coordinating Comm., Inc. v. United States Atomic Energy Comm'n*, 449 F.2d 1109 (DC Cir. 1971).

135 On 2 January 1970, the New York Times, for instance, titled its article on Sen. Jackson, "Sponsor of the Pollution Control Bill". The EIS requirement was not even mentioned.

136 LLEWELLYN & PEISER, *supra* note 132 at 25.

137 PLATER, *supra* note 123 at 318–319.

138 Henry M. Jackson, *Foreword: Environmental Quality, the Courts, and the Congress*, 68 MICH. L. REV. 1073, 1079 (1970).

139 See *supra* note 78.

140 LINDSTROM & SMITH, 45, 46. 2002; 115 Cong. Rec. 29,053 (1969).

development of a 'common law' of NEPA".[141] In other words, procedure would effectuate substance.

2.2.2 How to Enforce a Procedural Rule Such as EIS?

Neither NEPA, nor CEQ regulations, specify the appropriate remedy when an agency carries out a project without having adequately studied its environmental impacts. Remedy formulation has been left to the courts.[142] "The particular course NEPA took in the courts owes a great deal to early judicial decisions equipping it with unexpected teeth (including a private cause of action, which Congress neither expressly provided, nor apparently considered)".[143] At first, EIS was intended to internalize the influence of environmental concerns upon agency decision-making. Its authors anticipated a hostile environment for the implementation of NEPA, but this unfavorable reception did not materialize. Changes in legislative language combined with environmental activism served to transform the impact statement process into a tool for external, public participatory policy-making.[144] The explosion of the environmental movement, the emergence of environmental law firms, and the assumption by the Council on Environmental Quality (CEQ) of the role of monitor of the EIS process turned EIS from a force operating from inside program administration into a force exerted from the outside by interest groups and by courts.[145]

Judge David L. Bazelon called this period "a new era in the history of the long and fruitful collaboration of administrative agencies and reviewing courts".[146] Bazelon was in favor of a severe judicial review of the implementation of the procedural rules imposed on agencies. He disliked having the courts

141 *Kleppe v. Sierra Club*, 427 US 390, 42021 (1976) (Marshall, J., concurring in part and dissenting in part) (emphasis added).

142 Herrmann, U. CHI. L. REV., 1269 (1992).

143 Michael Herz, *Parallel Universes: NEPA Lessons for the New Property*, 93 COLUM. L. REV. 1668, 1686, FN 86 (1993). See also FREDERICK R. ANDERSON, NEPA IN THE COURTS: A LEGAL ANALYSIS OF THE NATIONAL ENVIRONMENTAL POLICY ACT 9 – 11 and 15 – 17 (Resources for the Future; distributed by the Johns Hopkins University Press. 1973).

144 Dreyfus & Ingram, NAT. RESOURCES J., 258 (1976).

145 Id. at 256. See also "A select group of individuals trained in environmental analysis permeated the agencies, allowing for heightened environmental value in agency decision-making. However, as with the other studies, substantive changes were determined partially by internal and external factors, such as competing program objectives, disagreements between departments and agencies, threat and risk of judicial enforcement, and the resources of the commenting agencies" (TAYLOR, *supra* chapter 1 note 73, at 351–52).

146 *Environmental Defense Fund, Inc. v. Ruckelshaus*, 439 F.2d 584, 597 (DC Cir. 1971). Judge Bazelon served on the US Court of Appeals for the District of Columbia Circuit from 1949 to 1985 (Chief Judge from 1962 to 1978, then in semi-retirement from 1979 to 1985).

enmeshed in substantive or technical matters.[147] "It was the "EIS review by nongovernmental individuals and groups ... accompanied by the threat of ad hoc involvement and legal action" that contributed the most to NEPA implementation".[148] The more stakeholders are involved, the better is an EIS, and the better-accepted a project decision becomes. New property and NEPA cases are examples of the new interest representation model of US administrative law.[149] "NEPA and Goldberg were both part of a significant shift, not limited to the judiciary, toward public access to and participation in governmental decision-making. They were expressions of the new-found confidence that representation of all affected interests would enhance administrative decision-making – a confidence that characterized the 'reformation of American administrative law' ".[150] In Canada, the evolution was similarly striking. In 1989, lawsuits had had the effect of turning purely advisory guidelines, established in 1984 after a 1973 Cabinet decision, into procedural obligations enacted in a statute.[151] However, in the United States, after a first phase of crucial cases, the movement seemed to grind to a halt, and judges became reluctant to enforce procedural

147 *International Harvester Co. v. Ruckelshaus*, 478 F.2d 615, 652 (DC Cir. 1973) (Bazelon, C.J., concurring): "in cases of great technological complexity, the best way for courts to guard against unreasonable or erroneous administrative decisions is not for the judges themselves to scrutinize the technical merits of each decision. Rather, it is to establish a decision-making process which assures a reasoned decision that can be held up to the scrutiny of the scientific community and the public". See also *Monsanto Co. et al. v. Geertson Seed Farms et al.*, 561 US 139, 183 (2010), (Stevens J., dissenting), one of the last opinions Stevens authored before retiring: "Congress recognized in NEPA that complex environmental cases often require exceptionally sophisticated scientific determinations, and that agency decisions should not be made on the basis of "incomplete information". [*Marsh v. Oregon Natural Resources Council*, 490 US 360, 371 (1989)]. Congress also recognized that agencies could not fully weigh the consequences of these decisions without obtaining public comments through an EIS. See *Robertson v. Methow Valley Citizens Council*, 490 US 332, 349–350 (1989)". Lastly, see also "NEPA itself does not impose substantive duties mandating particular results, but simply prescribes the necessary process for preventing uninformed – rather than unwise – agency action (...) It ensures that the agency, in reaching its decision, will have available, and will carefully consider, detailed information concerning environmental impacts" (*Robertson*, 490 US at 333 and 349).

148 Richard N. L. Andrews, *Agency Responses to NEPA: A Comparison and Implications*, 16 NATURAL RESOURCES JOURNAL 301 (1976), concluding that "NEPA's procedures were implemented largely without reference to its substantive purposes" (p. 320).

149 Richard B. Stewart, *The Reformation of American Administrative Law*, 88 HARV. L. REV. 1669, 1669, 1722, 1759 (1975).

150 Herz, COLUM. L. REV., 1687 (1993). *Goldberg v. Kelly*, 397 US 254, 90 S. Ct. 1011, 25 L. Ed. 2d 287 (1970).

151 Christopher Wood, *What NEPA Has Wrought Abroad*, *in* ENVIRONMENTAL POLICY AND NEPA: PAST, PRESENT AND FUTURE 101 (E. Ray Clark & Larry W. Canter eds., 1997).

obligations.[152] Since then, NEPA has been implemented with a lack of guidance and needs to be better adapted to allow third-party reviews of projects.[153] Despite these difficulties and shortcomings, NEPA process generated expectations and substantive outcomes. One could expect the creation of expectations to be even more critical in the international sphere, where substantive standards cannot be easily put in place and respected.

The main purpose and benefit of an EIA is better public decision-making, which includes public participation, thus advancing better information, mutual communication and understanding. On the international plane, public participation is as paramount as it is at the domestic level. Although national agencies are supposed to act as transnational permit authorities, they appear to act exclusively on behalf of the state of origin, favoring domestic economic and financial advantages over transboundary environmental impacts. "If anyone has a problem in accepting the value of protecting another state's environment, it will be the national governmental agencies, with their institutionalized way of looking at things".[154] Because opposition is usually even more frequent and vocal in the affected state, especially when the latter benefits little if at all from the project, the project proponent will often tend to avoid that its project be submitted to an international permit process.[155] Public participation from the state of origin and/or the affected state can counter these tendencies to evade transboundary EIA obligations.

3 Public Participation is at the Heart of EIA's Efficiency and of Law-making

My hypothesis is that EIAs are effective in circumstances where there is a certain type of civil society, powerful and with their voices heard, one that can be organized, composed of integrated communities, whose members interact, support each other and where information circulates and is used influentially. Three determinative aspects of public participation can be distinguished: a

152 See *infra* page 126 et seq.

153 See, for instance, Dorothy W. Bisbee, *NEPA Review of Offshore Wind Farms: Ensuring Emission Reduction Benefits Outweigh Visual Impacts*, 31 ENVTL. AFFAIRS 349, 351–57, 374–79 (2004), and the importance of the geographic scope of an EIS.

154 Koivurova, FINNISH Y.B. INT'L L., 199 (1997).

155 Timo Koivurova, *Transboundary EIA in the North Calotte region from the perspectives of international and European Union Law*, *in* ENVIRONMENTAL IMPACT ASSESSMENT IN THE NORTH CALOTTE TRANSBOUNDARY AREAS 41 (2006).

wide understanding that civil society is the repository of exceptional knowledge; a salient, legitimate, and credible EIA process; an efficient circulation and influence of information.

3.1 *Civil Society is the Repository of Exceptional Knowledge*

> *Lorsque l'arc-en-ciel des cultures humaines aura fini de s'abimer dans le vide creusé par notre fureur*[156]

Principle 22 of the Rio Declaration emphasizes the need to permit public participation of indigenous peoples and local communities, who are uniquely knowledgeable about the environment at stake – they are home-grown experts. In chronological order, the Convention on Biological Diversity, the Arctic EIA Guidelines, the United Nations Declaration on the Rights of Indigenous Peoples and the American Declaration on the Rights of Indigenous Peoples prescribe resorting to traditional knowledge in view of an equitable and sustainable development.[157] Indigenous peoples and many local communities are environmental experts because their environment is vital to their identity and ways of life. The right to a healthy environment and to the protection of their lands has been proclaimed in the above-cited international instruments. The central and distinctive place of the environment to indigenous peoples is

---

156 CLAUDE LÉVI-STRAUSS, TRISTES TROPIQUES 497 (Plon/Terre Humaine. 1955) "when the spectrum or rainbow of human cultures has finally sunk into the void created by our frenzy" (LÉVI-STRAUSS, TRISTES TROPIQUES 415 (John Weightman and Doreen Weightman trans., Penguin. 2012)).

157 CBD, Art. 8(j) and 2006 Voluntary guidelines on biodiversity-inclusive impact assessment, Para. 5, 31(c) & 35. Arctic EIA Guidelines, Chap. 10, p. 37-38. United Nations Declaration on the Rights of Indigenous Peoples, 13 September 2007, GA Res. A/RES/61/295. Organization of American States, American Declaration on the Rights of Indigenous Peoples, 15 June 2016, AG/RES. 2888 (XLVI-O/16), its preamble has the same wording as the UN Declaration's. The Inter-American Commission on Human Rights, under the presidency of W. Michael Reisman, prepared the first draft in 1995. After the draft was sent out for comments and finalized, the Inter-American Commission on Human Rights then approved the Proposed American Declaration on the Rights of Indigenous Peoples, in 1997 (Inter-American CHR, 1333d sess., OEA/Ser/L/V/II.95, Doc. 6 (26 Feb. 1997), reprinted in 6 INT'L J. CULTURAL PROP. 364 (1997) [the OAS Draft Declaration]). Prior to the American Declaration, see the body of jurisprudence of the Inter-American Human Rights System *in* Tara Ward, *The Right to Free, Prior, and Informed Consent: Indigenous Peoples' Participation Rights within International Law*, 10 NW. J. INT'L HUM. RTS. 54 (2011). See in particular *Saramaka People v. Suriname*, Inter-Am. Ct. HR (ser. C) No. 174, para. 133 (Judgement of 28 November 2007); *Kichwa Indigenous People of Sarayaku v. Ecuador*, Inter-Am. Ct. HR (ser. C) No. 245 (Judgment of 27 June 2012).

recognized, along with the importance of traditional collective systems for the control and use of land and resources.[158] However, a long-recognized challenge has been to ensure that marginalized groups can, in practice, meaningfully and efficiently participate in decision-making processes. Vulnerable communities are usually the least likely to participate in an EIA, in part because the process is quite foreign to them. Then, even if they become acquainted with the procedure, they often lack the appropriate resources to participate, in which case, as in authoritarian regimes where public participation in an EIA is often absent or only formal, they may use the official EIA as a base from which to erect their opposition and communication, to invoke the EIA and the decision as inconsistent with the applicable legal prescriptions and to promote the preferred and best environmental policy.[159] The case studies to be presented in the ensuing chapters, and most especially the *UMNIP* case in the Sub-Mekong region (chapter 6), reveal EIAs as a beacon of hope for the most vulnerable communities, who see their land taken or washed away and their ways of life abruptly suppressed. The eradication of the inner worlds and rectitude systems of indigenous people is a profound tragedy that humanity has regularly inflicted upon itself. "In addition to the agony of the victims, the collective humanistic loss suffered in the destruction of the inner worlds of others is enormous. Entire visions of past and future, complex ways of looking at the world and the self, and repositories of rich experience are obliterated".[160] The necessity to reassert one's fragile identity through the destruction of others whose identity differs has been a striking trait of human history. The New Haven School suggests ways of adopting a stance of ongoing self-scrutiny. Well-designed and well-conducted EIAs can help this self-scrutiny process. The goal is to counter the propensity for distortion in the frequent cross-cultural inquiries of an EIA. EIAs should be conducted by a group of independent consultants, including

---

158 See the key Article XXV of the American Declaration; Articles 20, 25–27, 29, 31 and 32.3 of the UN Declaration. See also Wiessner, HARV. HUM. RTS. J., (1999).

159 O'Faircheallaigh, ENVIRONMENTAL IMPACT ASSESSMENT REVIEW, 23 (2010); see also Annie L. Booth & Norman W. Skelton, *Improving First Nations' participation in environmental assessment processes: recommendations from the field*, 29(1) IMPACT ASSESSMENT AND PROJECT APPRAISAL 49 (2011).

160 W. Michael Reisman, *International Law and the Inner Worlds of Others*, 9 ST. THOMAS L. REV. 25, 27 (1996). "The New Haven School of International Law designates this fashioning of an inner world of meaning and value in individual and collective life as the 'rectitude process.' '[R]ectitude refers to freedom of thought and religion, presumption of innocence and freedom from ex post facto laws.'[1] " [1]Philip R. Trimble, *International Law, World Order, and Critical Legal Studies*, 42 STAN. L. REV. 811, 814 (1990). *In* Reisman, ST. THOMAS L. REV., 25 (1996).

representatives and specialists of the region at stake, with public participation, and peer-reviewed. "[T]he integrity of the inner worlds of peoples – their rectitude systems or their sense of spirituality – (…) is their distinctive humanity. Without an opportunity to determine, sustain and develop that integrity, their humanity – and ours – is denied".[161]

Public participation of all affected communities is also paramount in light of the representativeness and independence of NGOs. For instance, in Central and Eastern European countries, NGOs were often perceived by authorities to be the public, thus consultation was excessively concentrated on them.[162] It is essential to include as many stakeholders as possible, not only NGOs, when the affected populations are concerned; not only does the collective input of numerous individuals tend to lead to wiser decisions than individuals deciding independently,[163] but the more general question of the representativeness of the participants in an EIA has greater chances to be solved satisfactorily. Consequently, the importance of a real consultation, in person, is essential, rather than only a collection of lists of individual answers and comments. As a whole, a combination of different methods in order to have multiple sources of data (also known as triangulation) is crucial to the EIA process.[164]

3.2 *The EIA Process Must be Salient, Legitimate and Credible*

The second and complementary aspect of public participation is that the EIA process must be salient, legitimate, and credible to be efficient.[165] An EIA is salient when it addresses the relevant issues in the eyes of any potential user of the EIA, hence the importance of early and appropriately wide public participation, starting at the scoping stage.[166] Then, engaging all affected communities provides legitimacy to the EIA. Lastly, credibility refers to the reliability of the scientific and technical information and analysis contained in the EIA. In

161 Reisman, ST. THOMAS L. REV., 35 (1996).

162 Bond, et al., Impact Assessment and Project Appraisal, 210 (2001).

163 JAMES SUROWIECKI, THE WISDOM OF CROWDS, WHY THE MANY ARE SMARTER THAN THE FEW AND HOW COLLECTIVE WISDOM SHAPES BUSINESS, ECONOMICS, SOCIETIES, AND NATIONS (Doubleday. 2004). See also *infra* page 133 et seq., especially note 214.

164 Ana Maria Esteves & Frank Vanclay, *Social Development Needs Analysis as a tool for SIA to guide corporate-community investment: Applications in the minerals industry*, 29 ENVIRONMENTAL IMPACT ASSESSMENT REVIEW 137, 141 (2009).

165 Farrell & Jäger (eds.). 2006; Mitchell, et al., 308–309, 314–324. 2006. Eva-Maria Kunseler, et al., *The reflective futures practitioner: Balancing salience, credibility and legitimacy in generating foresight knowledge with stakeholders*, 66 FUTURES 1 (2015).

166 See *supra* chapter 2. See also, for an instance of the geographic importance of the selection of public participation, Bisbee, B.C. ENVTL. AFF. L. REV., 358 (2004).

other words, scientific validity alone cannot ensure the efficiency of an EIA, as discussed above. The EIA needs to be comprehensive, easily understandable,[167] its authors renowned, as well as the institutions to which they belong.[168] An important aspect of credibility is thus the choice of experts to conduct the EIA, with whom the affected communities interact and whose report affects their fate. Only recently did the need to ensure their competence begin to be considered at the normative level.[169] Additionally, the global scientific community is often presented as a whole, without consideration for the geographical origins of the scientists. Upon closer examination, the majority of the members of the "invisible college" of experts resides in a few countries of the industrialized Northern hemisphere, whose financial dominance leaves its mark on the assessments.[170] Consequently, it has been observed that some EIAs lack a number of issues specific to Southern countries,[171] and thus do not appear as truly legitimate and credible to the affected populations. Even if Northern scientists are not suspected of deliberate bias, a greater number of independent experts that are specialized in regions of the Southern Hemisphere should be included in the expert EIA teams for EIA to better achieve its goals. Another important element is the review of the EIA by an external expert team. This peer review is highly recommended, notably by practitioners, but has only been recently required, in 2016, by the World Bank in its new Environmental and Social Safeguard Policies.[172] The role and the perception of the experts is also essential with regard to their interactions with the affected populations.

---

167 See NEPA requirements for instance, such as 40 CFR § 1502.8 (see *supra* chapter 2, page 72). See also, for a comparison of the different possible ways of presenting a project during the preliminary consultations, Olivier Labussière & André de Baere, *Entre « insertion » et « mise en situation » paysagère: la mésentente au cœur d'un projet de ligne très haute tension*, 15 COSMOPOLITIQUES 95 (2007).

168 See the point of view of some practitioners, scientists with experience in EIAs: Branko Kontic, *Why are some experts more credible than others?* 20 ENVIRONMENTAL IMPACT ASSESSMENT REVIEW 427 (2000).

169 See *supra* chapter 2, page 70 et seq.

170 Frank Biermann, *Whose Experts? The Role of Geographic Representation in Global Environmental Assessments*, *in* GLOBAL ENVIRONMENTAL ASSESSMENTS – INFORMATION AND INFLUENCE 87 and 95 (Ronald B. Mitchell, et al. eds., 2006).

171 FRANK BIERMANN, SCIENCE AS POWER IN INTERNATIONAL ENVIRONMENTAL NEGOTIATIONS: GLOBAL ENVIRONMENTAL ASSESSMENTS BETWEEN NORTH AND SOUTH (ENRP Discussion Paper E-2000–17) (John F. Kennedy School of Government, Harvard University. 2000).

172 See *infra* chapter 6, page 303 et seq. for the WB ESF, and chapter 7, page 317 et seq. for the EIA peer review.

Independent experts and coherent EIAs, where experts' disagreements are resolved, or put in perspective thanks to public participation, are key to effective EIAs. Lack of independent experts and disagreement among the evaluations lead to a decline in trust in the experts, who are considered either biased in favor of the project proponent, or excessively focused on technicalities to the detriment of a more comprehensive analysis.[173] This phenomenon worsens the difficulties in ensuring effective public participation. According to practitioners, there is a pressing need for "genuine opportunity to influence the decision … People sense very quickly when something's a done deal; then they stop participating".[174] Independent and reliable experts are crucial to incentivizing public participation.

Even then, when a high-quality EIA is being produced thanks to adequate legal provisions, "the main constraint is the limited ability of most of the actors involved to take part in a social learning process that effectively addresses complex issues".[175] Plainly and as seen above, it is difficult to motivate stakeholders to participate. One of the main obstacles is the natural belief that individual contributions do not matter. Affected populations are reluctant to participate because they are usually convinced that decisions have already been taken, or will be, without any credible possibility for them to meaningfully participate in the decision-making process.[176] It is crucial to find ways to value stakeholders as the source of an indispensable knowledge and experience, as beneficial as professional experts, and to provide informational tools so that they can feel confident enough to participate. The first step in this direction is to show that public participation can lead to decisive influence over the decision-making process. The following case studies will verify whether public participation is embodied by only a few active citizens and NGOs, or by a larger group of stakeholders.

173 Thomas Webler, et al., *Public Participation in Impact Assessment: A Social Learning Perspective*, 15 ENVIRON. IMPACT ASSES. REV. 443, 459 (1995).

174 Jennifer M. P. Stewart & A. John Sinclair, *Meaningful public participation in environmental assessment: perspectives from Canadian participants, proponents and government*, 9 J. ENV. ASSMT. POL. MGMT. 161, 168 (2007).

175 Y. Deelstra, et al., *Using knowledge for decision-making purposes in the context of large projects in The Netherlands*, 23 ENVIRON. IMPACT ASSES. REV. 517, 521 (2003).

176 Webler, et al., ENVIRON. IMPACT ASSES. REV., 459 (1995). Nicola Hartley & Christopher Wood, *Public participation in environmental impact assessment – implementing the Aarhus Convention*, 25 ENVIRON. IMPACT ASSES. REV. 319, 335 (2005).

3.3 *The Circulation and Influence of Information*

Another aspect of public participation at the core of the decision-making process is the circulation and influence of information, during and after the decision-making process.

3.3.1 How to Ensure Information is Provided?

During the EIA process and in case of deficiencies, judicial enforcement is difficult because courts generally do not fully espouse the significance of procedural rules, and do not wish to meddle in substantive decisions. In the US, for a brief time at first, "EIS review by nongovernmental individuals and groups was accompanied by the threat of ad hoc involvement and legal action. This made it the most effective action-forcing mechanism contributing to NEPA implementation during this initial period".[177] NEPA has seemingly led to more lawsuits than any other environmental statute.[178] Later, doubts arose as to what to expect from judicial enforcement of NEPA.[179] To this day, the US Supreme Court has never decided a case in favor of NEPA plaintiffs and handed down unanimous rulings in almost all cases, despite having famously emphasized that "NEPA, while establishing 'significant substantive goals for the Nation,' imposes upon agencies duties that are 'essentially procedural'";[180] in other words, "NEPA merely prohibits uninformed – rather than unwise – agency action".[181] The Supreme Court had even embraced the values of participation, unanimously: NEPA "significantly, provides a spring board for public comment".[182] Too often, agencies have tended to comply with NEPA simply by filling out some paperwork senselessly and tardily, which could have been solid grounds for successful legal actions. However, environmental groups

177 Andrews, NATURAL RESOURCES JOURNAL, 321 (1976).

178 RASBAND, et al., 260. 2009. DANIEL D. CHIRAS, ENVIRONMENTAL SCIENCE 608 (Jones & Bartlett Publishers. 2011).

179 Kenneth M. Murchison, *Does NEPA matter? – An Analysis of the Historical Development and Contemporary Significance of the National Environmental Policy Act*, 18 U. RICH. L. REV. 557, 613, 614 (1983–1984). David C. Shilton, *Is the Supreme Court Hostile to NEPA? Some Possible Explanations for a 12–0 Record*, 20 ENVTL. L. 551 (1990). Richard Lazarus, *The National Environmental Policy Act in the U.S. Supreme Court: A Reappraisal and a Peek Behind the Curtains*, 100 THE GEORGETOWN LAW JOURNAL 1507 (2012).

180 *Strycker's Bay Neighborhood Council v. Karlen*, 444 US 223 (1980) at 227 (citing *Vermont Yankee Nuclear Power Corp. v. Natural Res. Def. Council*, 435 US 519, 558 (1978)). See also *Robertson v. Methow Valley Citizens Council*, 490 US 332, 350 (1989).

181 *Robertson*, 490 US at 333 and 351.

182 *Robertson*, 490 US at 349 (quoting *Baltimore Gas & Elec. Co. v. NRDC*, 462 US 87, 97 (1983)).

have increasingly shied away from bringing cases to the US Supreme Court.[183] NEPA, like the other EIA requirements, provides a basis for enforcing substantial statutes by providing timely and adequate information. It has been widely remarked that courts lack the technical expertise to review NEPA (or any other EIA) requirements, but technical expertise is not needed to enforce procedural requirements. The role of the courts is to secure the decision-making process so that it properly takes place and develops for civil society to be informed, provide its knowledge and participate. However, courts awkwardly address the enforcement of procedural obligations. In the case concerning the pulp mills on the River Uruguay, the International Court of Justice (ICJ) has stated that EIA was now required under general international law,[184] but considered that consulting the affected populations was not a legal obligation,[185] thus undermining EIA by brushing aside an essential input for a well-informed and legitimate decision. In addition, the ICJ refused to grant provisional measures to suspend the construction. Some say that the ICJ's scrutiny from that moment on suffices,[186] but this is a risky assumption. Even in the United States, where EIAs originated, courts have had tremendous difficulties in addressing the judicial enforcement of NEPA.[187] However, a few comprehended NEPA particularities, such as the Court of Appeals for the First Circuit, in particular Judge Stephen Breyer.[188] He provided the following analysis of the purpose of an EIA statute, i.e. a certain type of decision-making process:

---

183 The number of petitions for certiorari filed by NEPA plaintiffs took a noticeable downturn after 1981 (Shilton, ENVTL. L., 556 (1990)). In almost fifty years, as of 2015, the Supreme Court had decided seventeen cases arising under NEPA, all but two of which were decided under the influence of William Rehnquist (on the Supreme Court from 1972 to 2005). See also J. Ruple & K. Race, *Measuring the NEPA Litigation Burden: A Review of 1,499 Federal Court Cases*, 50 ENVTL. L. 479 (2020).

184 *Pulp Mills on the River Uruguay* (*Argentina v. Uruguay*), Judgment, 2010 ICJ Reports 2010 14, at para. 204 (20 April).

185 Id. at para. 216.

186 Cymie R. Payne, *Pulp Mills on the River Uruguay: The International Court of Justice Recognizes Environmental Impact Assessment as a Duty under International Law* ASIL Insight (2010).

187 See *Monsanto Co. et al. v. Geertson Seed Farms et al.* (561 US 139 (2010)); the *sonar* case (*Winter v. Natural Resources Defense Council*, 555 US 7 (2008)). Herrmann, U. CHI. L. REV., 1276 (1992), emphasized what courts should have in mind: "NEPA targets the increased risk of harm to the environment that results from uninformed decision-making. Thus, the harm that an injunction under NEPA should target is the risk that the agency will make a decision to damage the environment".

188 Stephen Breyer decided *Commonwealth of Massachusetts v. Watt* 716 F.2d 946 (1st Cir. 1983) and *Sierra Club, et al. v. John O. Marsh, Jr., et al.*, 872 F.2d 497 (1st Cir. 1989), but had to withdraw from *Monsanto v. Geertson*, because his brother, Charles R. Breyer, had decided *Geertson v. Johanns and Monsanto*, 2007 WL 1302981 (ND Cal.). Charles R. Breyer had

> when a decision to which NEPA obligations attach is made without the informed environmental consideration that NEPA requires, the harm that NEPA intends to prevent has been suffered. (...) Moreover, to set aside the agency's action at a later date will not necessarily undo the harm. The agency as well as private parties may well have become committed to the previously chosen course of action, and new information – a new EIS – may bring about a new decision, but it is that much less likely to bring about a different one. It is far easier to influence an initial choice than to change a mind already made up. It is appropriate for the courts to recognize this type of injury in a NEPA case, for it reflects the very theory upon which NEPA is based – a theory aimed at presenting governmental decision-makers with relevant environmental data before they commit themselves to a course of action. This is not to say that a likely NEPA violation automatically calls for an injunction; the balance of harms may point the other way.[189]

The harm is done to the decision process itself, as an increasing commitment to the decision in the making naturally builds up:

> The way that harm arises may well have to do with the psychology of decision makers, and perhaps a more deeply rooted human psychological instinct not to tear down projects once they are built. But the risk implied by a violation of NEPA is that real environmental harm will occur through inadequate foresight and deliberation.[190]

Breyer concluded:

> The difficulty of stopping a bureaucratic steam roller, once started, still seems to us, after reading *Village of Gambell*, a perfectly proper factor for a district court to take into account in assessing that risk, on a motion for a preliminary injunction. And, it does not surprise us that, since *Village of Gambell*, other courts have reached the same conclusion.[191]

---

entered an injunction preventing future planting of altered alfalfa until APHIS prepared an EIS.

189 *Commonwealth of Massachusetts v. Watt* F.2d at 952–953, cited in *Sierra Club v. Marsh*, F.2d at 500.

190 *Sierra Club v. Marsh*, 872 F.2d at 504.

191 Ibid. See *Northern Cheyenne Tribe v. Hodel*, 851 F.2d 1152, 1156–58 (9th Cir. 1988); *Sierra Club v. United States Forest Service*, 843 F.2d 1190 (9th Cir. 1988); *Save the Yaak Committee*

In France, Jean-Marc Sauvé, Vice-President of the Council of State from 2006 to 2018, is equally wary of the bureaucratic steamroller and of the lack of proper timing for any impact assessment.[192] The powerful influence of the status quo and the reluctance to question what has already been decided have been theorized in economics.[193] Thus, in applying the equitable balancing test, courts should bear in mind the goal of a NEPA-type statute, which guarantees an informed decision in order to avoid or mitigate environmental harm. EIA procedures must be followed in a timely manner, so as to prevent the project from moving forward and bureaucratic commitment from developing without proper information, forbidding any real reconsideration of a decision already made. In this regard, all stakeholders need to be involved as early as possible. The difficulties experienced by judges when they address procedural obligations often relate to the definition of harm. Judges are used to repair a harm that is more obvious than one resulting from procedural violations. Because no damages can be requested, which is a condition of the judicial intervention, a criminalization of this branch of law may appear necessary. Judicial action is currently often counterproductive. The judges' tendency to tie up their intervention to any imminent, or impending, or probable damage seems irrepressible. They do not seem to fully comprehend that harm is done when process is not followed, and seem reluctant to address the definition of damage.

The notion of damage is at the core of the concept of civil responsibility. How can procedural obligations be enforced in international environmental law? In domestic systems, civil responsibility, which demands the existence of a prejudice, distinguishes itself from criminal responsibility on the one hand, which punishes even a simple attempt, and moral responsibility on the other

---

v. Block, 840 F.2d 714, 722 (9th Cir. 1988); *Friends of the Earth v. Hall*, 693 F.Supp. 904, 912–13, 949 (WD Wash. 1988).

192 *Audition de Jean-Marc Sauvé, Vice-Président du Conseil d'État – Groupe de travail Assemblée nationale–Sénat sur la qualité de la loi* (6 May 2010), at II, B, 2°: "even if there is no legal requirement providing specifically that the impact study be made *at the very beginning* of the law-making process, the fact that the impact study is made at a later stage, after the main choices, sometimes even after the drafting of the bill, is most regrettable. This timing betrays the spirit of the reform. Fundamentally, an impact study is a tool for improving the quality of laws. It is a useful endeavor only if it is undertaken *seriously, as soon as the thinking process begins, when all options are open, far from being an ex-post validation of decisions that have already been made and put into writing by the Government*. It is essential to convince agencies and political authorities in this regard" (author's translation and emphasis added – at https://www.conseil-etat.fr/actualites/discours-et-interventions/la-qualite-de-la-loi, accessed 17 June 2021).

193 Daniel Kahneman, et al., *Anomalies: The Endowment Effect, Loss Aversion, and Status Quo Bias*, 5 JOURNAL OF ECONOMIC PERSPECTIVES 193 (1991).

hand, which includes even guilty intentions. In international law, there is no clear distinction. Even though the objective element of damage is not required to invoke state responsibility under the ILC Draft Articles,[194] whether a state will successfully invoke another's responsibility merely because of the breach of an obligation remains to be seen. In doctrine, Roberto Ago adopted Dionisio Anzilotti's views: "international responsibility derives its *raison d'être* purely from the violation of a right of another state and every violation of a right is a damage".[195] Roberto Ago emphasized the importance of honor and dignity to justify this understanding of the concept of damage in the international sphere. A further justification is that there is no central entity to enforce international rules, so, in effect, every actor of international law is a sort of prosecutor. Damage should then be defined more broadly, so as to encompass a legal prejudice, characterized by the simple violation of an obligation.[196] Edith Brown Weiss criticized the ILC Draft Articles for their distinction between injured and non-injured states (Articles 42 and 48) whereas, if one invokes state responsibility, it is precisely because one feels injured, which means the notion of damage depends on the definition of injury.[197] James Crawford argued that it was important to distinguish between the primary beneficiaries

194 Draft Articles on the Responsibility of States for Internationally Wrongful Acts, *in* Report of the ILC, fifty-third session, UN GAOR, 56th Sess., Supp. No. 10 at 43, UN Doc. A/56/10 (2001), of which the UN GA took note in its Res. 56/83 (2001), and commended them to the attention of governments, an unusual procedure (see also GA Res. 59/35, and 62/61 of 8 January 2008, which further commended the draft articles to states and decided to examine the question of a convention on the topic). See especially Article 48. ILC Commentary: "Obligations coming within the scope of paragraph 1 (a) have to be "collective obligations", i.e. they must apply between a group of States and have been established in some collective interest. They might concern, for example, the environment or security of a region".

195 Cited *in* THIRD REPORT ON STATE RESPONSIBILITY, by Roberto Ago, THE INTERNATIONALLY WRONGFUL ACT OF THE STATE, SOURCE OF INTERNATIONAL RESPONSIBILITY (A/CN.4/246 and Add.1–3), Para. 73–74, page 223 § II(1) (1971). For similar views, see Angelo Piero Sereni, *Atti illeciti, in* DIRITTO INTERNAZIONALE – III RELAZIONI INTERNAZIONALI 1522–1523 (1962). See also Eduardo Jiménez de Aréchaga, for whom damage was a condition of international responsibility, but who defined damage as follows: "in inter-state relations the concept of damage does not, however, have an essential material or patrimonial character" (*International Responsibility, in* MANUAL OF PUBLIC INTERNATIONAL LAW 534 (Max Sørensen ed. 1968)).

196 Brigitte Stern, *Et si on utilisait la notion de préjudice juridique? Retour sur une notion délaissée à l'occasion de la fin des travaux de la CDI sur la responsabilité des Etats*, AFDI 3 (2001).

197 Edith Brown Weiss, *Invoking State Responsibility in the Twenty-First Century*, 96 AM. J. INT'L L. 798, 802 (2002).

(the right holders) and those states with a legal interest in compliance, "irrespective of how or whether the breach has affected [them]".[198] Even though Article 1 of the ILC Draft Articles does not mention the existence of a prejudice, Pierre-Marie Dupuy has deemed it necessary that a prejudice be established for the sake of identifying the victim of the violation of an international obligation. To him, a responsibility without prejudice is only virtual. However, this refers back to the definition of prejudice, and Dupuy acknowledges the notion of legal prejudice,[199] quoting Article 31(2) of the ILC Draft Articles on State Responsibility.[200]

Be that as it may, it remains that states are usually opposed to the notion of legal prejudice.[201] Moreover, state responsibility is rarely invoked. In addition to conceptual difficulties about the definition of damage or prejudice, proving a causal link is often problematic,[202] most especially in environmental matters. Lastly, reparation is, as often, nearly impossible; damage is usually irreparable in environmental cases. Consequently, invoking responsibility by posterior judicial action has not been the focus of environmental policy. Besides, taking a case to court often worsens the dispute.[203]

However, judicial enforcement of procedural obligations would make an important contribution: a credible threat of an injunction, and the delay that a lawsuit would entail, should persuade project proponents to abide by the EIA requirements in a timely fashion.[204] Furthermore, addressing the issue of

198 James R. Crawford, *Responsibility to the International Community as a Whole*, 8 IND. J. GLOBAL LEGAL STUD. 303, 320 (2001).

199 PIERRE-MARIE DUPUY, DROIT INTERNATIONAL PUBLIC 519, 522 (Dalloz 9ème ed. 2008).

200 "Injury includes *any* damage, whether material or moral, caused by the internationally wrongful act of a State" (emphasis added).

201 See, for instance, the point of view of France, *in* PROJET D'ARTICLES SUR LA RESPONSABILITÉ DES ETATS, COMMENTAIRES ET OBSERVATIONS REÇUS DES GOUVERNEMENTS, 25 mars 1998, Doc. A/CN.4/488, pages 100–101 and 138.

202 Pierre Esmein, *Le nez de Cléopâtre*, RECUEIL DALLOZ Chronique 205 (1964).

203 For this reason, NGOs were not in favor of taking the *Pulp Mills* case to the International Court of Justice. They warned that it would be of no use and feared that it would freeze the negotiation process (aimed at coming up with a better technology to produce paper), let alone the possibility that hopes would be dangerously raised (Greenpeace Argentina, *Greenpeace consideró "previsible" el resultado de La Haya* (2006) *at* http://www.greenpeace.org/argentina/es/noticias/greenpeace-consider-previsib/, accessed 17 November 2020). For an example of a pulp mill project where the EIA led to the choice of a better technology, see the Alberta-Pacific pulp mill project in Canada, *in* Tilleman, COLUM. J. TRANSNAT'L L., 347 (1995). And the REPORT OF THE ALBERTA PACIFIC FEARO REVIEW BOARD (1990).

204 See Preamble and Article 13 of the IIL Resolution on Responsibility and Liability under International Law for Environmental Damage (Strasbourg, 4 September 1997). See,

a deficient EIA at the jurisdictional phase rather than at the merits phase is also highly preferable, particularly with regard to projects in developing countries. It saves some of the rare resources these countries have at their disposal for such proceedings, "especially if the investor has resorted to corruption or other unacceptable means".[205] Lastly, NGOs, who often are key to the initiation of lawsuits, regrettably tend to focus exclusively on substantive issues and to dismiss the procedural mechanics of wide public participation. NGOs should further develop procedural strategies.[206]

EIAs set up a process comparable to trial procedure. Because the aim of an EIA is to prevent or mitigate environmental damage, a particularly difficult concept to grasp and sharply define, the subject-matter addressed in a judicial action is displaced in time.[207] EIAs move this action ahead, following the same process as a judicial one, the participants being the project proponent, affected populations, experts, and the decision-maker. However, there is a crucial difference: unlike a judge, the decision-maker is not neutral oftentimes. The capacity to make a final decision, and the desired objectivity that it promises, is already challenging enough to find in the character of a judge in a traditional lawsuit. Decision-making in general is often influenced by extraneous information and factors.[208] Since, at the project level, the ultimate decision-maker is often partial, the solution lies in having an adequate process and as wide a public participation as possible, in order to provide the relevant decision-maker with all points of view, and pressure them into being fully informed and less prejudiced.

---

more generally, JUTTA BRUNNEE, PROCEDURE AND SUBSTANCE IN INTERNATIONAL ENVIRONMENTAL LAW (2020).

205 Jorge E. Viñuales, *Foreign Investment and the Environment in International Law: An Ambiguous Relationship*, 80 BRITISH YEARBOOK OF INTERNATIONAL LAW 244, 260–261 (2010), citing the importance to not underestimate the *Inceysa* and *Fraport* decisions with regard to foreign investment and environmental protection (*Inceysa Vallisoletane, SL v. El Salvador*, ICSID No ARB/03/26, Award, 2 August 2006; *Fraport AG Frankfurt Airport Services Worldwide v. Republic of the Philippines*, ICSID Case No. ARB/03/25, Award, 16 August 2007).

206 See, for instance, in the European Union: Bond, et al., IMPACT ASSESSMENT AND PROJECT APPRAISAL, 210 (2001).

207 "Proceduralization shifts the focus of legal processes from dispute settlement toward policy formation" (CRAIK, 272. 2008).

208 Such as the hour at which the decision is taken for instance (Shai Danziger, et al., *Extraneous Factors in Judicial Decisions*, 108 PNAS 6889 (2011)). See also "the world of decision-making is determined not only by formal procedures and governmental bodies, but also consists largely of informal processes wherein various actors negotiate with each other" (Deelstra, et al., ENVIRON. IMPACT ASSES. REV., 520 (2003)).

3.3.2 The Circulation and Influence of Information

Once an EIA has been produced according to law, in an easily accessible format,[209] individuals and groups (including activists, international NGOs, local associations, international organizations and lawyers) can use this information aggressively if the EIA is reliable, or they can just as aggressively use a defective EIA to denounce its inaccuracy or lack of appropriate information. Moreover, beyond the short-term goal of deciding on a specific project, the exposure and circulation of each EIA gradually reinforces their possibility and their necessity in the long term. In 2010, 63% of Americans were convinced that global warming was a reality, but many did not understand the causes of this phenomenon, illustrating the fact that innumerable citizens of a democratic country may lack the knowledge required for informed decision-making in this field.[210] EIAs would contribute to initiating and developing social learning if their results were more widely known for educational and motivational purposes: when citizens see that influencing a decision with environmental impacts on their surroundings is possible, they feel encouraged to further inform the project proponent and the professional experts, inform themselves and participate in the decision-making process. The more EIAs are produced and publicized, the more incentives it gives to individuals to participate in public life, because they see that they could actually do so meaningfully, especially if their neighbors did. If EIAs are made early enough in the project development process and well-publicized, EIA requirements are destined to act as process-mongers. Ecological awareness can be raised in different ways. In light of the natural rivalry that often drives human beings, as Raymond Aron described in his introduction to Max Weber's lectures,[211] emulating and channeling competition can also induce civic action, in addition to self-interest since the latter does not seem to be sufficient.[212] When made

---

209 See *supra* note 16, and chapter 2, pages 71–72, regarding NEPA detailed requirements.

210 A. Leiserowitz, et al., *Americans' Knowledge of Climate Change* 3 (Yale University. New Haven, CT: Yale Project on Climate Change Communication (2010)). See also Justin Farrell, et al., *Evidence-based strategies to combat scientific misinformation*, 9 NATURE CLIMATE CHANGE 191 (2019).

211 See *supra* note 50.

212 The social proof (among five other "weapons of influence"): people will do things that they see other people are doing (ROBERT B. CIALDINI, INFLUENCE – HOW AND WHY PEOPLE AGREE TO THINGS (William Morrow & Co. 1984). Robert Cialdini was chief scientist at Opower, an energy efficiency software company (now part of Oracle), which encourages consumers to reduce their energy usage, notably via individualized home energy reports. In April 2018, after a successful experimentation in 2016, the US utility company Con Edison launched a behavioral Home Energy Report program (CONSOLIDATED EDISON, DISTRIBUTED SYSTEM IMPLEMENTATION PLAN (2020)).

aware of a developing social norm, individuals tend to adhere to it, following a primitive instinct of survival recognition – similar individuals will behave in a similar fashion. Rather than peer pressure, the new social norm is perceived as peer information and thrives in smaller communities where communication is more fluid and efficient. EIA requirements suit the argumentative theory, "When people are motivated to reason, they do a better job at accepting only sound arguments".[213] Groups are more likely to come up with better results than isolated individuals because they are exposed to the best arguments, in small, cooperative settings.[214] Hence the importance of domestic EIA requirements, local action, and the empowerment of individuals, all of which lead to global repercussions. The standard cooperation generated by EIA requirements does not take place between states, but between agencies and at the domestic level, which render actions and influence easier. Agencies are more reachable. Procedures are simpler. EIAs multiply the number of actors involved, which increases community pressure, especially where there is a strong civil society. The participation of environmentalists within agencies, NGOs or other institutions, labeled as epistemic communities, often transnational in nature,[215] has created a dynamic and constant interaction. EIA processes are efficient at channeling scientific knowledge into information useful to stakeholders and decision-makers, by means of non-technical summaries, enlightening dialogue, and by incorporating traditional knowledge and the voices of indigenous people. Not only do EIA processes facilitate cooperation, but they also lower the costs of project development, by identifying negotiation partners and issues, and by the use of domestic procedures that eliminates the necessity for states to create and finance new institutions. In the case studies, I will verify to what extent EIAs generate and resort to the power of peer information and epistemic communities.

One last and important phase of the utilization of the information produced by EIAs occurs after completion of the project, by comparing the outcomes with the predictions, and developing strategies for penalizing wrong guesses, holding proponents to promises and mitigation commitments,[216] thanks to

213 Hugo Mercier & Dan Sperber, *Why do humans reason? Arguments for an argumentative theory*, 34 BEHAVIORAL AND BRAIN SCIENCES 57, 96 (2011).

214 HUGO MERCIER & HÉLÈNE LANDEMORE, REASONING IS FOR ARGUING: UNDERSTANDING THE SUCCESSES AND FAILURES OF DELIBERATION (2010). See also *supra* page 123 and note 163.

215 Peter Haas, *Epistemic Communities*, *in* THE OXFORD HANDBOOK OF INTERNATIONAL ENVIRONMENTAL LAW (Daniel Bodansky, et al. eds., 2007).

216 In the US, see Rodgers, ENVTL. L., 503, 504 (1990).

post-monitoring programs, which also provide and develop environmental and methodological data in order to improve EIA methodology and performance. Post-monitoring programs contribute to improving scientific accuracy, on which international environmental law depends. Experiences acquired after the completion of a project should be part of future decision-making processes. Even if institutional memory of former projects naturally accrues in actual agencies or other structures, widespread formal requirements would help to develop and secure post-monitoring. Until now, such requirements have been rare. The Antarctic regime was the first to prescribe compulsory post-project monitoring.[217]

4 Conclusion

Whether during the decision-making process or after completion of the project, EIAs generate various impact mechanisms, direct and indirect, that play out in many phases. The effects of EIA are the results of numerous "interactions among diverse stakeholders across large time-frames (…) on the project design as well as the valuations, and opinions of the various stakeholders prior to, during and after the assessment process. *In many respects, the impacts of EIA are indirect and somewhat hidden in nature*".[218] By means of the case studies to be presented in this book, I will attempt to shed light on the indirect and hidden impacts of EIA requirements and show that these procedural requirements generate important incremental changes.

The role of a strong civil society is essential. Illustrations are numerous. In France, for instance, a farmers' union (*Confédération paysanne*), two environmental associations (Greenpeace and the *Faucheurs volontaires*) and a group of scientists together successfully triggered an open debate on GMOs.[219] A similar

217 Antarctic Environmental Protocol, Annex I, Article 5. See *supra* chapter 2.

218 Pölönen, et al., ENVIRONMENTAL IMPACT ASSESSMENT REVIEW, 127 (2011) (emphasis added).

219 This debate led to a de facto moratorium in Europe in 1999 (*Declaration by the Danish, Greek, French, Italian and Luxembourg Delegations concerning the suspension of new GMO authorizations*, 2194th European Council Meeting, Environment, Luxembourg, 24–25 June 1999). The moratorium ended in April 2004. Since then, NGOs, via legal proceedings, have notably safeguarded the application in France of the 2001/18/EC Directive on GMOs (CJEU, 25 July 2018, Case C-528/16, *Confédération paysanne et al. v Premier Ministre and Ministre de l'Agriculture, de l'Agroalimentaire et de la Forêt*, ECLI:EU:C:2018:583; Conseil d'Etat, 7 February 2020, No. 388649).

coalition also achieved a similar result in India.[220] Unions, environmental NGOs, scientists, dedicated individuals are usually an effective combination. Larger-scale and better-timed public participation in the decision-making process is ultimately key to improving the decision-making process and environmental policies. This role is crucial, because the natural tendency for the project proponent is to first take a decision and then conduct an EIA in a biased way with the aim of buttressing this decision. Only early intervention and early public participation by a powerful civil society, of local stakeholders that bring their expertise, will remedy this tendency towards a *faux préalable*. "Both the structure and purpose of the [Espoo] convention make clear that its implementation depends also on the involvement of the public. In other words, despite the transboundary focus of the EIA Convention, it will not be implemented effectively unless state and non-state actors – governments *and* the public – are involved in EIA procedures".[221] Within the framework of EIAs, the project proponent is generally in charge of conducting the EIA, because it usually has the advantage of professional expertise and financial resources. In addition to scientific input (especially when the project proponent's EIA is incomplete and biased),[222] the role of public participation is paramount and can take many forms. Numerous stakeholders and groups can be informed, influenced, and influence back: affected populations, consumers, companies (development of a workforce inspired by, for example, corporate social responsibility (CSR), adoption of environmental policies), and investors. Mobilizing public opinion can be far-reaching and change corporate policies, placing natural resources at the heart of business strategy.[223] Wide public participation can also be a pragmatic strategy in order to raise sufficient financial resources to initiate lawsuits and face the associated costs.[224]

Today, the reality of EIAs is a problem of post-rationalization rather than pre-analysis.[225] Too often, EIAs are still made in this spirit, toward the end of

220 "farmers, associations, and sometimes, simply charismatic and emblematic citizens are the ones that strongly mobilize against GMPs" Eric Meunier, *OGM en Inde: les industriels déçus*, 107 INF'OGM LE JOURNAL 5, 7 (2010) (author's translation).

221 Ebbesson, ENVIRONMENTAL IMPACT ASSESSMENT REVIEW, 48 (1999).

222 Dzidzornu, EUR. ENVT'L L. REV., 17–19 (2001). Dzidzornu evokes an "overriding state control and a pre-emptive determination of information accessibility".

223 See RICHARD DOBBS, ET AL., RESOURCE REVOLUTION: MEETING THE WORLD'S ENERGY, MATERIALS, FOOD, AND WATER NEEDS (McKinsey Global Institute. 2011).

224 Christian Huglo, Huglo Lepage & Associés (specialized in environmental law), 3 March 2015 interview.

225 "Courts must remember that in many cases allowing an agency to proceed makes a mockery of the EIS process, converting it from analysis to rationalization" (*Monsanto Co. et al. v. Geertson Seed Farms et al.*, 561 US 139 (2010) (Stevens, J., dissenting), citing Herrmann, U.

the decision-making process. Even when EIAs are authored by several external consultants, project proponents have tended to pick from among the findings of the consultant firms' reports, in order to accord with their already-made decision. This is a general tendency. Some external consultants readily confirm that EIAs are made in accord with their clients' needs and demands. Too often, from the beginning of a project, experts are already pressured to lean toward their client's predetermined decision. To counteract this tendency, there are two crucial elements to an effective EIA: a time element,[226] and a participatory one, the input of as many participants as possible. Meaningful public participation is composed of multiple sources of information, consultations with numerous participants with different views and interests at stake, who have a forum and a procedure that support and legitimize their collaboration with the project proponents and the decision-makers. These two crucial elements, proper timing and meaningful public participation, are precisely those most lacking usually. EIAs, and in particular public participation, are put in place with significant delay, if at all.

This problem of post-rationalization relates to a more general use of discursive rationality in the political sphere, or the lack thereof. "With respect to public institutions, a ready-made discourse is imposed, which voids the question of a meaningful expression and dialogue".[227] The Espoo and Aarhus conventions, along with numerous prescriptive norms at different levels, provide for the reintroduction of dialectics and public participation. However, EIAs often belong to a type of empty discourse, when they are done only to conform to official prescriptions, after the decision was taken, without ensuring comprehensive scientific accuracy and without sufficient public participation, if at all. Hence the fundamental importance of having the EIA procedure and proper timing respected, including public participation. EIA requirements, as *lex imperfecta*, have raised such expectations. Wide public participation helps to achieve a balance between particular interests and common interest, beyond a short-term view. With regard to the expectations raised by EIA requirements,

---

CHI. L. REV., 1289 (1992)). See also NEPA, 40 CFR §1502.5: EIS should be implemented in a manner assuring that it "will not be used to rationalize or justify decisions already made".

226 In a 2004 survey of staff from the US Department of Defense, the Department of the Interior, and the Forest Service, most respondents felt that NEPA adds value to a project, and if things were planned and started earlier, it would likely bring greater value to a project, shorten the process and may cost less (see *supra* chapter 1, note 73).

227 PIERRE LEGENDRE, JOUIR DU POUVOIR, TRAITÉ DE LA BUREAUCRATIE PATRIOTE back cover (Les éditions de Minuit. 1976) (author's translation). Original text: "Au sujet des institutions nationales est imposé un discours prêt-à-parler, qui vide la question de la parole".

Lynton Caldwell observed that "incentives and opportunity to participate in public decisions affecting well-being and security have thus grown with knowledge and its dissemination. Cause-effect relationships are better understood; for example, disasters transcending national boundaries arouse popular protest when the causes are seen as preventable. Popular pressure forces governments to respond in ways that would formerly have been considered intrusions into the internal affairs of other states (as can be seen, for example in the diverse reactions to transboundary air pollution). Popular participation has become more effective as it has become increasingly organized and facilitated through the media of communication and transportation".[228]

The effects of EIA regulations take time to develop, and prove to be effective only incrementally. Evolution in the behaviors and views of several different kinds of actors may ultimately overcome political and corporate reluctance, and common passivity. A sufficient number of relevant political actors need to perceive that their interests have been included in the common interest, which naturally solves the issue of enforcement.[229] Public participation, included within an EIA procedure, favors the pursuit of the common good, in the larger framework of law-making. International law is being prescribed continuously in a process of communication. Part of this communication process is the authority signal. The etymology of authority, *auctor – auctoritas*, refers to a combination of the credibility of the prescriber and the power to impose obedience. Successful prescription is thus best obtained by legitimate discourse, i.e. well-reasoned and justified, secured and framed by the appropriate process, which ensures credibility. This process, or discourse, is generally inscribed in a procedure: "in every society the production of discourse is at once controlled, selected, organized and redistributed according to a certain number of procedures, whose role is to avert its powers and its dangers, to cope with chance events".[230] EIA corresponds to such a procedure, the source of substantial power if correctly conducted and employed. "In appearance, speech may well be of little account, but the prohibitions surrounding it soon reveal its links with desire and power. This should not be very surprising, for psychoanalysis has already shown us that speech is not merely the medium which manifests – or dissembles – desire; it is also the object of desire. Similarly, historians have constantly impressed upon us that speech is no mere verbalisation of conflicts

228 Caldwell, COLO. J. INT'L ENVTL. L. & POL'Y, 231, 232 (1999).

229 REISMAN, The Quest for World Order and Human Dignity in the Twenty-first Century: Constitutive Process and Individual Commitment 85–87. 2013.

230 FOUCAULT, *supra* note 42 at 216.

and systems of domination, but that it is the very object of man's conflicts".[231] The outcome of the EIA procedure holds remarkable authority, generating a set of preferred prescriptions and expectations. Optimists have been in the right, the potential of the EIA process is thus immense: even when an EIA is not properly conducted, expectations are generated and remain, i.e. an EIA should be comprehensive and accurate, the affected populations should be heard and participate, proper intelligence should be gathered and disseminated, which lead to communications and social mobilization not only for a specific project, but in the longer term.

Three main problems dominate the implementation of EIAs at the moment. There is no real organization of, or motivation for, public participation (low priority has been given to environmental considerations, routinely and falsely opposed to economic benefits); EIAs are too often conducted as an ex-post rationalization of a prior decision, and relevant post-monitoring is either lacking or insufficient.

The difficulties that confront EIAs appear to be best addressed through constant interaction on the individual level within integrated communities in a strong civil society, which empowers individuals. "International law's effectiveness depends increasingly on those without direct affiliation to formal structures. It depends, in short, on you".[232]

In the following three case studies, I will expose the dynamics of the production and utilization of EIAs.

---

231 Ibid.

232 Reisman, Making International Humanitarian Law Effective: the Case for Civic Enforcement 38. 1973.

CHAPTER 4

The Vuotos Case

Finland – Sweden (1960's – 2019)

> *Consensual circumstances appear to facilitate a relatively informal use of* EIA, *for example, in Scandinavia*[1]

The Vuotos case marked a turning point in Finland, with respect to making social choices and achieving the national community's social goals. For the first time, public participation could be successfully integrated into the constitutive process, thanks in part to the early application of the Espoo Convention and the active participation of a neighboring state in the licensing procedure, on the basis of an international treaty, also a first. The project was halted exclusively for environmental reasons, but was also at the forefront of a renewed consideration of the economic aspects of environmental protection.

The Convention on Environmental Impact Assessment in a Transboundary Context was signed in Espoo, the second largest city in Finland, close to the capital, Helsinki, and part of the Helsinki Metropolitan Area. The population of Finland (5.5 million) is heavily concentrated in the south and southwest of the country, predominantly in the Helsinki Metropolitan Area (27%). The "Espoo Convention" sounds like one with which the Finns are closely associated. They consider it as an essential instrument to deal with transboundary impacts. Finland was one of the most active participants in the negotiations that led to the adoption of the convention, hence their wish on hosting the final meeting and have the convention signed in Espoo, in order to maximize visibility and show that the convention was essential to them. Since its signature, Finland has been as committed in its role as state party to the treaty. On 10 August 1995, Finland ratified the Espoo Convention, a few months after the country had joined the European Union (EU), on 1 January 1995. Almost three years later, the convention entered into force, on 10 September 1997,[2] but Finland had already begun to apply it, notably by voluntarily involving Sweden at an early stage in the Vuotos project, which consisted in the construction of a

1 Caldwell, Understanding Impact Analysis: Technical Process, Administrative Reform, Policy Principle 12. 1989. *Scandinavia* is understood as the Nordic Countries (Denmark, Finland, Iceland, Norway, Sweden) in the present book.

2 Ninety days after Poland had become the sixteenth state to ratify the convention (see Article 18.1).

 | DOI:10.1163/9789004467583_005

dam and a reservoir in Northern Finland, for hydropower purposes. Both states cooperated. Why and how was such cooperation achieved?

1 General Presentation and Historical Context of the Vuotos Case

Prior to the Espoo Convention, an important regional cooperation instrument for protecting the environment, the 1974 Nordic Environmental Protection Convention (NEPC),[3] was already in place between Denmark, Finland, Norway, and Sweden. The NEPC requires an assessment of the effects in the territory of one party of activities carried out in the territory of another party (Article 6). The convention was adopted before any national legislation on environmental impact assessments (EIA), and was the first treaty in Europe to agree on the need for preliminary consultations between neighboring states. The NEPC was part of the impetus for the Espoo Convention,[4] in the line of a long tradition of cooperation: following World War II, in 1952, Denmark, Iceland, Norway, and Sweden had established an important cooperative body, the Nordic Council, a geo-political, inter-parliamentary consultative forum, joined by Finland in 1955. In 1971, the Nordic Council of Ministers had been instituted to complement the Nordic Council, providing an intergovernmental forum. The protection of the Baltic Sea has been one of the priorities of Nordic environmental cooperation. The Baltic Sea is a unique brackish-water ecosystem, one of the largest in the world, and is very sensitive to disturbances. Save for the narrow and shallow waters of the Belt Sea and the Sound that barely connect it to the North Sea, the Baltic Sea is an enclosed sea. Over eighty-five million people live in the sea catchment area, placing severe pressure on the ecosystem; the sea has received heavy pollutant loads from the surrounding countries. On this particular issue, international cooperation is thus also based on the 1992 Helsinki Convention,[5] which obliges the riparian states to reduce emissions from all pollution sources. There are quite a few other cooperation instruments in the region.[6] In particular, the Nordic countries signed the Arctic EIA Guidelines

3 Stockholm, 19 February 1974, 1092 UNTS 279, 13 ILM 591 (1974), in force on 5 October 1976.

4 Ebbesson, ENVIRONMENTAL IMPACT ASSESSMENT REVIEW, 49 (1999).

5 The Convention on the Protection of the Marine Environment of the Baltic Sea Area, signed in 1992 and entered into force on 17 January 2000, replacing the original convention signed in 1974. The governing body of the convention is the Baltic Marine Environment Protection Commission, also called the Helsinki Commission, or HELCOM.

6 The foreign ministers of the Baltic Sea states regularly meet to promote cooperation in the Baltic Sea region through the Council of the Baltic Sea States (CBSS). In 1998, the CBSS adopted a program for sustainable development in the Baltic Sea region, Baltic 21, which

at the same time the Espoo Convention came into force, in 1997. Upon an initiative of the Finnish Minister of the Environment, Sirpa Pietikäinen, in 1994, the Arctic Environmental Ministers had asked for guidelines to be prepared, in March 1996.[7] Like the Espoo Convention, the guidelines were signed in Finland, in Rovaniemi (Lapland), as Finland acted as a lead country for their elaboration. The guidelines insist in particular on resorting to traditional knowledge, in order to better assess a project, with all the stakeholders' points of view, local communities and project proponents alike.

In spite of a common tradition of public management, environmental policy and a strongly developed planning policy, the Nordic countries at first had rather different EIA legislations, or none, partly because EIA was still new relatively to traditional planning,[8] and, worse, because it was not yet taken seriously.[9] Another reason was the affiliation, or lack thereof, to the EU when national EIA legislations were passed.[10] Norway was the first to introduce legal EIA requirements in 1985,[11] then Denmark in 1988, Sweden in 1991, Iceland in 1993,[12] and Finland in 1994.[13] Swedish regulations were formulated without any

---

provides a regional network to help with the implementation of the global Agenda 21 in the region. The Union of Baltic Cities (UBC) promotes the cooperation between cities. Another forum for cooperation is VASAB (Vision and Strategies around the Baltic Sea), which promotes intergovernmental cooperation in spatial planning and development.

7 Spurred by a Finnish initiative in 1989, the Arctic states have collaborated on environmental protection within the Arctic Environmental Protection Strategy (AEPS), adopted by Canada, Denmark/Greenland, Finland, Iceland, Norway, the Russian Federation, Sweden and the United States through a Ministerial Declaration in Rovaniemi, Finland, in 1991. The programs under the AEPS are: Sustainable Development and Utilization (SDU), Conservation of Arctic Flora and Fauna (CAFF), Arctic Monitoring and Assessment Program (AMAP), Emergency Prevention, Preparedness and Response (EPPR) and Protection of the Arctic Marine Environment (PAME). The AEPS programs have continued under the auspices of the Arctic Council since September 1996.

8 Arne Tesli & Stig Roar Husby, *EIA in a Transboundary Context: Principles and Challenges for a Coordinated Nordic Application of the Espoo Convention*, 19 ENVIRONMENTAL IMPACT ASSESSMENT REVIEW 57, 60 (1999).

9 Per Christensen, et al., THE OUTCOME OF EIA IN DENMARK 2 (Aalborg University, EU Commission, Danish Ministry of the Environment. 2003).

10 Denmark was the only EU Nordic member when the 1985 EIA Directive was adopted. Denmark had joined the EU (then called the EEC) in 1973, Finland and Sweden joined in 1995. By referendum, Norway has twice declined to join, in 1972 and in 1994.

11 As part of the Planning and Building Act, 14 June 1985, No. 77, Sections 5, 16–2, Chapter VII-A (see especially Section 33–3).

12 EIA Act No. 63/1993 (in force 1 May 1994), then replaced by Act No. 106/2000 of 25 May 2000 (in force 6 June 2000). Iceland is not part of the EU, but part of the European Economic Area (EEA), the Schengen Area and the European Free Trade Association (EFTA).

13 EIA Act, 10 June 1994, No. 468/1994. EIA is *Miljökonsekvensbedömning* (MKB) in Finnish.

EU influence, whereas the Finnish EIA Act was passed in order to abide by the 1985 EIA Directive and the Espoo Convention.

In 1996, to further develop Nordic cooperation and coordinate different EIA regulations, and to implement the Espoo Convention it had been advocating, the Nordic Council embarked upon the Coordinated Application of the Espoo Convention, managed by an Ad Hoc Group on EIA.[14] Nordic countries have always been acutely aware of forming a coherent geographical area. They wanted to develop EIA as a central planning and environmental management tool, and to apply a rational and predictable system for handling proposed development activities with potential transboundary impacts. They also wanted to coordinate the practice and application of the Espoo Convention in correspondence with the NEPC, which gives little concrete guidance.[15] Despite its decades of existence, the NEPC was poorly publicized and had been applied only a few times.[16] In the Vuotos case for instance, Sweden appealed the Finnish permit decision on the basis of the NEPC in 2000 for the first time. Insufficient awareness of the NEPC was partly due to the fact that the obligation to notify was placed on the permit authorities. This primary responsibility was thus dispersed among a very heterogeneous group of internal authorities of the origin state. During the preparatory work of the Espoo Convention, these practical problems of effective notification within the NEPC framework were kept in mind and the responsibility was placed not on permit authorities, but at the level of central governments.[17]

The Vuotos case took place during an interim period, before the entry into force of the Espoo Convention, but with the possibility of invoking the outdated and poorly functioning NEPC. Even though there were cooperation instruments for environmental protection, cooperation was only passive, mainly for the reasons stated above, that is, an insufficient awareness among

---

14 The Espoo Convention recommends that state parties produce their own, more elaborate and geographically distinct bilateral agreements to implement their obligations (Article 8).

15 Tesli & Roar Husby, ENVIRONMENTAL IMPACT ASSESSMENT REVIEW, 58 (1999).

16 JONAS EBBESSON, THE RELEVANCE AND FUTURE OF THE NORDIC ENVIRONMENT PROTECTION CONVENTION 15 (Nordic Council of Ministers. 2003). For a list of cases, see Charles Phillips, *Nordic cooperation for the protection of the environment against air pollution and the possibility of transboundary private litigation, in* TRANSBOUNDARY AIR POLLUTION 157–164 (B. Kwiatkowska, et al. eds.,1986). Besides, some open treaty violations were committed (Timo Koivurova, *The Future of the Nordic Environment Protection Convention,* NORDIC JOURNAL OF INTERNATIONAL LAW 505, 525–526 (1997)).

17 Koivurova, NORDIC JOURNAL OF INTERNATIONAL LAW, 525–526 (1997).

administrative authorities. Something else triggered actual cooperation and was crucial to the outcome of the case: public participation.

Interestingly, the two Nordic states that are the subjects of this case study, Finland and Sweden, had once formed a single entity. For six centuries, almost all of Finland belonged to the Kingdom of Sweden, from the 13th century to 1809, when the Treaty of Frederikshamn confirmed Sweden's loss of Finland to Russia in the Finnish War. The eastern third of Sweden was established as the autonomous Grand Duchy of Finland within the Russian Empire. Finland gained its independence a century later, in 1917. To this day, Finland has been a bi-lingual State (Finnish/Swedish), with its agencies of judicial administration providing service in Finnish and Swedish. Espoo appears to be a noun of Swedish origin.[18] These historical ties create a community feeling across borders that seems to augur well for cooperation, in a way more evanescent in the relations of Finland with the Russian Federation.

The Vuotos dam project was set up against the backdrop of the evolving relation to nature. In Finland, nature has been an important resource base for different industries. These different uses of nature and sources of livelihood have conflicted over time: fishing, agriculture, forestry (three-fourths of the total land area in Finland is forested), mining, hydropower, nature protection for traditional livelihoods, tourism, etc. Vuotos is situated in Lapland, a region where traditional livelihoods and nature-based activities have dominated the economy since the 1980's.[19] The Vuotos case was one of the most protracted and famous environmental struggles, stretching over a sixty-year period, and an ambitious hydropower construction project: a dam and a 43.5-mile (70 km) long reservoir of 92.67 square miles (240 km2) were planned on the upper reaches of the Vuotos River,[20] a small tributary of the Kemijoki or

18 "Before the time of the Swedish colonization, Espoo was inhabited by Tavastians, a Finnish tribe, but the city's name comes from the colonizers rather than the native inhabitants. The name of Espoo is thought to have derived from the Medieval Swedish village of *Espaby* or *Espoby* that was located in the western part of the present-day city. The name of the village has North Germanic roots. It may refer to aspens that grew on a nearby riverbank, as the archaic Swedish word for the tree is 'äspe', and the word for a river is 'å', with the suffix '-by' meaning village." (at https://en.wikipedia.org/wiki/Espoo, accessed 17 June 2021).

19 Monica Tennberg, *Arctic expertise and its social dimensions in Lapland, in* RESOURCES, SOCIAL AND CULTURAL SUSTAINABILITIES IN THE ARCTIC (Monica Tennberg, et al. eds., 2019).

20 *Vuotos* derives from the Sámi language, the word for a newly fallen snow. It also means clear tracks in the snow.

Kemi River[21] in Northern Finland, the Finnish Laponia (now called the *Province of Lapland*, which represents 30% of Finland's total area), 185 miles (300 km) from the border with Sweden, where the Swedish Norrbotten county and border town of Haparanda are located. There are numerous rivers in Finland. The longest and most impressive ones are in the north. The Kemi River is the longest of the country, with the largest network of tributaries. The river is already harnessed with many hydropower stations. The reservoir would have extended over three very sparsely populated municipalities, Savukoski,[22] Salla,[23] and Pelkosenniemi,[24] and would have covered 0.25% of the province of Lapland. The Finnish landscape is mostly flat with few hills, many lakes, extensive boreal forests and little arable land. About 75% of Finland is composed of forests and the Vuotos area is situated in the boreal forest (also called taiga). The Kemijoki rises near the Russian border, north of the Arctic Circle, and empties at Kemi, the eponymous town, into the northern part of the Gulf of Bothnia, itself the northernmost arm of the Baltic Sea, after a 345-mile (560 km) long run in a northeast to southwest direction. The catchment area of the Kemi River is about 19,846 sq mi (51,400 km2) and drains over half the Finnish province of Lapland into the Baltic Sea. The Gulf of Bothnia is not deep (200ft – 60m in average, and 965ft – 295m at its deepest), 450mi – 725km long, and 50mi-80km – 150mi-240km wide. Many rivers from both sides flow into the gulf, which creates a salinity gradient. In the south, it is the brackish water of the Baltic Sea; in the north, in the Bothnian bay, the salinity is so low that one cannot taste the salt in the water and many freshwater fish thrive in it.

---

21 Kemijoki means Kemi River (*joki* means river in Finnish).

22 Savukoski is one of the largest municipalities in Finland, in terms of area size, and the most sparsely settled. The Kemijoki runs through it. The municipality had a population of 1,005 as of 2019 and covers an area of about 2,500 square miles (6,500 km2). The population density is about 0.40 inhabitants per square mile (0.15/km2). According to the legend, Santa Claus lives in Savukoski, at the Korvatunturi Fell.

23 Salla is also one of the largest municipalities in Finland, in terms of area size. The municipality had a population of 3,400 as of 2019, and covers an area of about 2,265 square miles (5,870 km2). The population density is 1.5 inhabitants per square mile (0.58/km2).

24 Pelkosenniemi had a population of 939 as of 2019 and covers an area of about 725 square miles (1,880 km2). The population density is 1.3 inhabitants per square mile (0.5/km2).

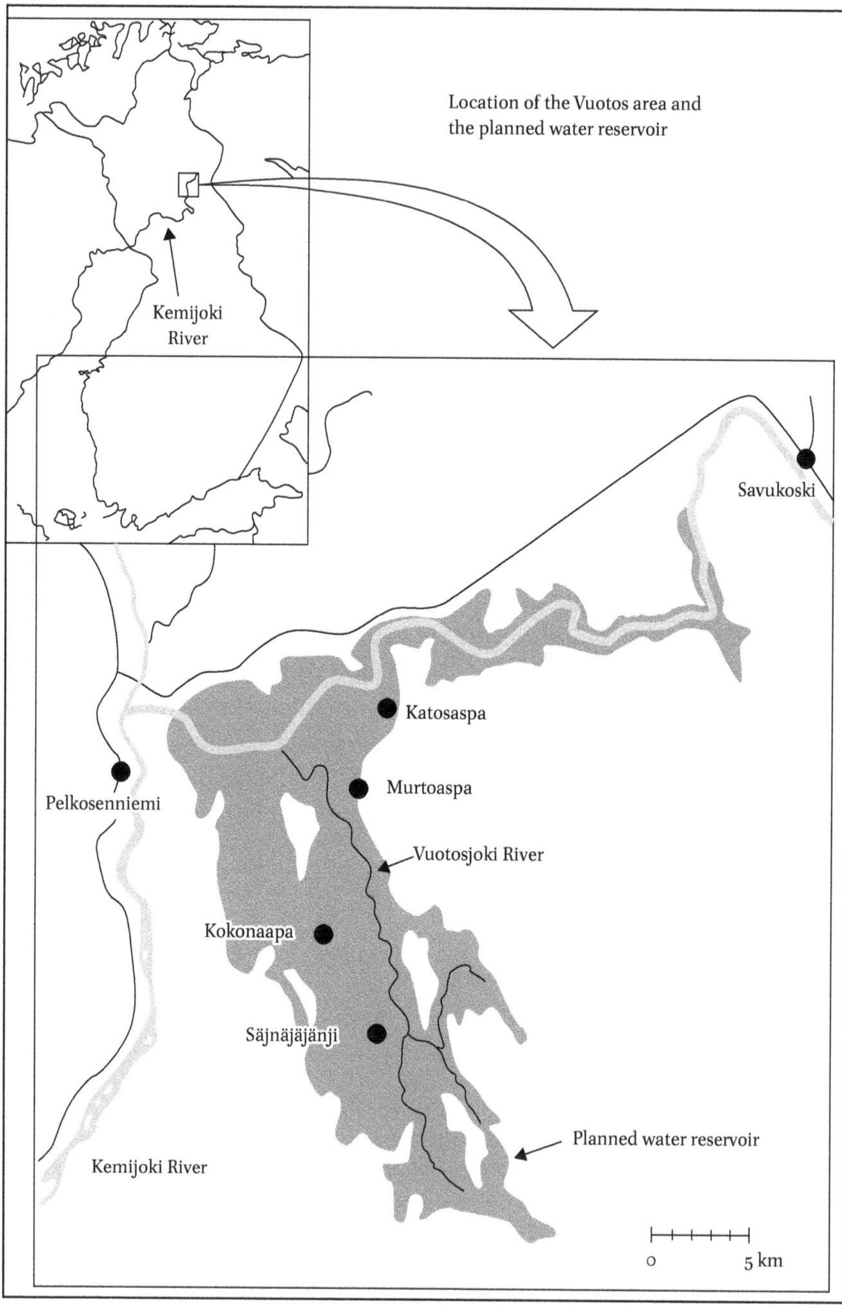

MAP 1 Location of the Vuotos area and the planned dam and water reservoir (Maija Ahvenniemi, et al., *A 15 Channel TM Classification of Bog Types in Finnish Lapland*, Department of Physics, University of Oulu (1998), http://www.metla.fi/tapahtumat/rt98/presentations/Ojala-K/aVuotosPaper.html (accessed 18 June 2021). Illustration reproduction courtesy of Maija Ahvenniemi and Kai Ojala. Note: please disregard the map scale)

The Kemi River has always been shaped and reshaped by hegemonic uses. Salmon fishing with long weirs, the use of the dominant river use since the 16th century, was displaced by timber floating in the beginning of the 20th century. Even before hydropower construction, both the growing Finnish central state and industry regarded Lapland as a resource periphery for industrial development and had, in particular, turned its rivers into a large-scale means of transport for wood-processing enterprises.[25] After World War II, Finland began to utilize the natural resources of Lapland even more extensively. The country had to endure extensive damage during the war. Furthermore, in 1940, a large part of Karelia, representing one third of Finland's hydropower capacity, had been ceded to the Soviet Union. As a result, there was a significant lack of available energy and environmental protection was ignored in the first decades after the war. To regain power capacity, sustain economic growth, industrial development, and secure energy independence, the harnessing of the longest river in Finland began, as well as of the others in the region (the southern rivers were already in hydropower production), by two energy companies, Kemijoki Oy and Pohjolan Voima Oy.[26] A law was passed in 1952 (No. 458/1952), which enabled integrated and systematic construction on the Kemi River, exploitation of its hydropower resources, and allowed the creation of Kemijoki Oy, established in 1954 and mainly state-owned to this day. In 2019, Kemijoki Oy's plants on the Kemi River produced a total of 4,338 GWh, i.e. about one third of Finland's total hydroelectric production, which itself represents 22% of Finland's electricity generation. After the rivers ceased to be used as a means of transportation, they were exploited by the state for hydroelectric generation. In parallel with the tourism industry, Lapland currently provides wood products, hydropower for the national grid and is a fertile source for mining interests.

The first suggestion of an artificial lake and hydroelectric plant near Pelkosenniemi arose in the 1960's, under the name of the *Kemihaara Project*, chosen because of the name of the mires situated there. At the time, two other

25 Franz Krause, *Shaping and Reshaping the Kemi River: Notes on the Perpetual Genesis of the Major Catchment Basin in Finnish Lapland*, *in* SOCIETY, ENVIRONMENT, AND PLACE IN NORTHERN REGIONS 33 (Mark Nuttal, et al. eds., 2011).

26 Pohjolan Voima Oy is the second largest Finnish energy company. Along with 2 large reservoirs on the upper course of the river, 21 power plants have been built on the Kemijoki and its tributaries, of which Pohjolan Voima Oy owns 2 (https://www.pohjolanvoima.fi/en/production, accessed 17 June 2021) and Kemijoki Oy, 16. Kemijoki Oy is an electric utility company principally engaged in generating electricity with hydropower. It owns and operates 20 hydropower plants total (https://www.kemijoki.fi/en/kemijoki-oy-in-brief.html, accessed 17 June 2021). The company is headquartered in Rovaniemi, the capital of Lapland, at the confluence of the Kemijoki and its tributary Ounasjoki, less than 6 miles (10 km) away from the Arctic Circle.

reservoirs in the area, those of Lokka and Porttipahta, connected by the Vuotso channel, were built at the headwaters of the Kemijoki on neighboring tributaries, without much done for environmental protection. A special act, passed in 1960, allowed permits to be specially granted for these two reservoirs.[27] This created an inundation of 2,433 sq mi (6,300 km2). Almost 600 people (farmers, reindeer herders and fishermen) lost their homes and were forced to move away.[28] There was no real opposition to those reservoirs, because they were part of Finland's overall reconstruction policy, which was then the utmost priority, a time with almost no environmental awareness. The area was considered wasteland. For these reasons, no preliminary study was made.

The power company wanted the Vuotos reservoir as an energy reserve for times of peak electric consumption. In the spring, when the snow melts, existing hydroelectric plants are forced to let large amounts of water through the floodgates, past the turbines, in order to prevent flooding. Instead, a large reservoir would have allowed water, here synonymous of energy, to be stored for later utilization. Besides, the additional hydropower plant on the Kemi River was also strongly needed to secure the operation of nuclear power plants in the country. The latter require regular maintenance and go offline regularly; when they do, hydropower plants are needed to replace them in the meantime.

In the 1970's, public controversy arose about the exploitation of natural resources in Lapland, both locally and with the support of an emerging national environmental movement. Civil society pressure began to be effective, especially because of the success of local movements,[29] even though Lapland is sparsely populated.[30] However, people organized themselves efficiently in face of an evolution they disliked. A combination of small-scale farming, subsistence economy and seasonal forest work had been replaced by mechanization and large-scale utilization of natural resources. A specific trait of the

---

27 Kemijoki River Regulation Act (No. 62/1960).

28 Leena Suopajärvi, *Competing Industries and Contested Nature in Finnish Lapland after World War II, in* ENCOUNTERING THE NORTH: CULTURAL GEOGRAPHY, INTERNATIONAL RELATIONS AND NORTHERN LANDSCAPES 212 (Frank Möller & Samu Pehkonen eds., 2003).

29 Id. at 216. In parallel, social impact studies began in the 1970's, such as studies of the opinions and expected changes among local residents caused by the construction of the Kemihaara/Vuotos reservoir, conducted by Timo Järvikoski in 1975 (STEFANOS FOTIOU, ET AL., SUSTAINABLE ECOTOURISM – INTEGRATION OF CONSERVATION AND USAGE IN NATURA 2000 AREAS (WORKSHOP IN YLLÄSJÄRVI, FINLAND) 25 (2003)).

30 As of early 2020, population density was 4.6/sq mi – 1.8/km2 (EU average is about 116/km2). Approximately 3.4% of the population of Finland live in Lapland. 178,000 inhabitants (among whom less than 9,000 indigenous Sámi) live on about 38,224 square miles (99,000 km2).

agricultural sector in Lapland is reindeer herding, a defining part of Laplanders' way of life, especially in the remote eastern and northern areas of Lapland, where the Vuotos area is located. Although most Laplanders now make their living in the services industry, nature continues to have an important role in northern life. Nature-based activities are popular – hunting, fishing, berry-picking, etc. An important concept in Finland, and in the Scandinavian countries in general, is *jokamiehenoikeus* (*everyman's right*), which reveals the importance of nature. This age-old notion gives everyone the basic right to roam freely in the countryside, without having to obtain permission, no matter who owns or occupies the land. This concept remains paramount in a country that, although urbanization has significantly increased, is still one of the least urbanized OECD member countries. For years, people in Lapland had seen changes happening in their surroundings, but without having any real possibility of influencing decisions. Authoritarian planning and decision-making by the state and powerful companies had embittered the minds of Laplanders. An instance of the hydropower companies' dismissal of the consequences of their projects in Lapland is the maps used in the planning process on the Ounas River project. The scale of these maps was so large that entire villages were inadvertently included within the new waterline. Inhabitants were also not informed about the environmental impacts.[31] The Vuotos case crystalized Laplanders' awareness and their determination to finally participate in decisions that affect them.

Lastly, from a legal scholarship perspective, the Vuotos case is interestingly complex because of the interaction of the two main legal procedures, domestic and European. On the domestic level, the legal procedure included the inspection proceedings and the licensing procedure under the Finnish Water Act. On the European level, the European Commission seems to have quite heavily influenced how this case was decided and how environmental issues were addressed in Finland (in particular because of the infringement proceedings against the Finnish state), but the extent of this influence is still a matter of speculation.

2 The Vuotos Dam/Reservoir Project

The National Board of Waters published a new plan for Vuotos in 1974.[32] The previously planned Kemihaara reservoir was quite significantly larger than the

31 Suopajärvi, 215. 2003.

32 The National Board of Waters (1970–1986), then National Board of Waters and the Environment (1986–1995), is now the Finnish Environment Institute (Finnish acronym: SYKE), appointed by the ministry of the environment as the center for environmental

new project, named after the Vuotos River. Despite this name change, people had not forgotten what the project was about, and the opposition movement was born at about that time. In 1979 and in 1980, inhabitants in the Ounasjoki Valley and eastern Lapland, where the Vuotos reservoir was planned, organized themselves in local committees. They began an active campaign against hydropower projects. Laplanders wanted to defend their home areas and traditional sources of livelihood. They began to criticize the bureaucratic state and the national discourse about a unanimous Finnish nation that had prevailed since the war.[33] At the regional and national level, public concern about environmental issues arose as well and associations strengthened their organization, such as *Suomen Luonnonsuojeluliitto* – the Finnish Association for Nature Conservation (FANC).[34] In 1981, the Agriculture and Forestry Ministry proposed the construction of the Vuotos reservoir and the Minister of Trade and Industry, Esko Ollila, from the Centre Party, supported the motion.[35] Nonetheless, the following year, in September 1982, the government decided to abandon the reservoir project and to revive the area instead, thanks to a renovation program (roads, farms, forests). The Ministry of the Interior stated that the reservoir would be unprofitable to the economy, disadvantageous in terms of population policy, compete temporarily with better employment projects, destroy valuable environment and be harmful to the primary sector production.[36] The decision of the government (named the Council of State in Finland) to withdraw the Vuotos project was declared as binding on future planning authorities and future administrations.[37] Environmental issues had

---

monitoring, development and research. SYKE is also in charge of Finland's reporting obligations under European and international agreements.

33 "People had to obey, because they were that war-time generation who had to do what they were told. But then, when we heard examples of what happened there, we here [in the Ounasjoki valley] did not obey anymore. We had learned that you have to fight for yourself, and they'll take everything if you don't." (Suopajärvi, 216. 2003).

34 The FANC is one of the oldest Finnish environmental NGOs. Its central organization was founded in 1938.

35 The Centre Party, one of the largest parties in Finland, was founded as the Agrarian Party in 1906, to represent the interests of rural communities, small farmers in the east and the north of the country.

36 Pirjo-Riitta Oinaala, *The Vuotos Reservoir, in* THE LEGAL STATUS OF THE INDIVIDUAL IN NORDIC ENVIRONMENTAL LAW 187 (Tuula Tervashonka ed. 1994). The Minister of the Interior, Matti Ahde (Social Democratic Party) was from the same party as the Prime Minister, Kalevi Sorsa, and of the President, Mauno Koivisto, who had been elected in January 1982 and was the first Social Democrat in office. Matti Ahde would later become Minister of the Environment (October 1983 – April 1987).

37 Executive power in Finland is exercised by the Cabinet, officially termed Council of State (in Finnish: *valtioneuvosto*), led by the Prime Minister.

become part of the political agenda in Finland. The Finnish Ministry of the Environment (FME) was founded in 1983 and the Green League had two representatives elected to the parliament for the first time that same year. The first protected areas in Finland had been founded in the early 1900's, but environmental legislation increased rapidly only at the start of the 1980's. To protect the country's water systems, the Finnish Parliament passed a special act for two specific rivers, in 1983 for the Ounasjoki, and in 1991 for the Kyrönjoki, as well as a general act for most of the other water systems in 1987, all three of which forbid the construction of hydropower plants in the designated areas. To exploit large amounts of new hydropower was not possible any longer, because most waterfalls that could be exploited for hydropower generation had already been harnessed, and almost all the remaining ones became protected by law,[38] except the Kemijoki.

The Vuotos project resumed very soon, in the mid-1980's, under the pressure of the powerful Kemijoki Oy company, at the same time timber floating came to be widely seen as problematic, thus opening the way to hydropower projects. The project was fully revived in 1987, with the support of the Minister of Trade and Industry, Ilkka Suominen (National Coalition Party). Kemijoki Oy began to buy up land in the area and more than 93% of the land went into its possession.[39] People were discouraged and migrated away from the area, as often seems to be the case in such environmental disputes.[40] The dam project was nevertheless put on hold again, until 1991. After the floating season that year, the Floating Association decided that they would discontinue timber floating on the Kemi River, the last active free-floating route.[41] Hydro-electricity production and flood control took precedence. At the same time as the decision of the Floating Association, a conservative government had just been elected, led by Prime Minister Esko Aho (Centre Party).[42] Sirpa Pietikäinen (National

38 Act on the Special Protection of the Ounasjoki (No. 703/1983). Act on the Special Protection of the Kyrönjoki (No. 1139/1991). The general Act on the Protection of Falls (No. 35/1987) forbids the construction of hydropower plants on fifty-two other water systems or parts of water systems.

39 As mentioned in *Supreme Administrative Court denies building permit for Vuotos reservoir*, HELSINGIN SANOMAT, 19 December 2002.

40 In 2000, a short documentary was made about the last couple living in Vuotos, by Mika Ronkainen (*Before the flood: the last couple in Vuotos* (Filmpool Nord, Yleisradio (YLE, 2000). It illustrates the deep feelings of those resisting the construction of the dam and the reservoir.

41 Free-floating was replaced by a rail shuttle in 1992.

42 Esko Aho, Chairman of the Centre Party, was appointed on 26 April 1991 (he left office on 13 April 1995).

Coalition Party) was the Minister of the Environment, from 1991 to 1995. The Aho government was a coalition government, as often happens in Finland, a center-right one, composed of the Centre Party, the National Coalition Party, the Christian Democrats, and the Swedish People's Party. Pietikäinen was deeply involved in negotiating the government's program and composition and says that the Vuotos project was never mentioned at that stage. However, only five days after the establishment of the government, in September 1991, the Minister of Trade and Industry, Kauko Juhantalo (Centre Party), put forward a governmental proposal with respect to the Vuotos project, without any EIA, or any study to show that there was some consideration for the environment. According to Pietikäinen, Kemijoki Oy had lobbied in favor of its project. Pietikäinen thought that Juhantalo's proposal was ill-justified and ill-prepared. It took her by surprise; she was not in a favorable position to argue against it.[43] The majority of the cabinet members supported the project. During the whole duration of the Vuotos dispute, many cabinet members never faltered in their support because more employment, even if only temporary, could be secured in the short run and a powerful economic actor tried to influence the decision. When asked about what stood out for her in that case, Pietikäinen emphasized that she had to confront massive business interests irrespective of environmental protection, represented by a powerful state-owned company that had continually resurrected the project since the 1960's.[44]

2.1 *Ecological and Economic Aspects of the Vuotos Project*

There were two main ecological aspects of the impacts of the dam/reservoir project:

1/ The project threatened the water quality of the lower reaches of the Kemi River and ultimately the Bothnian Bay. Hydropower is often presented as a clean energy, but the emissions of carbon dioxide and methane, and the levels of mercury would have been excessive in this case,[45] as well as the levels of nitrogen and phosphorus in the water (and the correlatively low oxygen levels

43 Sirpa Pietikäinen, 22 March 2012 interview.

44 Ibid. More generally, Satu Hassi, the Environment Minister from 1999 to 2002, testifies to the same effect: in Paavo Lipponen's second cabinet (from 15 April 1999 to 17 April 2003), there were only two representatives of the Green League in the five-party governmental coalition and it was no easy task to support environmental causes. Whenever there was a conflict between the economic versus environmental benefits of a project, "we are the only ones who opt for the environment" (*in* Usha Rai, *In Tandem with Nature*, THE HINDU, 7 October 2001).

45 Satu Hassi, 27 March 2012 interview. Bep Weijand, email of 3 April 2013.

that would result), as in the two existing reservoirs of Lokka and Porttipahta.[46] It was estimated that the phosphorus load into the Bothnian Bay would have increased by fifty tons per year, increasing the total load discharging into the Bothnian Bay from Finland by 5%.[47] This phenomenon is due to the degradation of organic matter from the bottom, since the flooded areas are mostly peatlands and forests. Carbon dioxide and methane are held latent in the plants. Experts reckoned that the greenhouse impacts of the methane emissions from the reservoir would have been, for at least fifty years, comparable to the impacts of the emissions of fossil energy producing the same amount of electricity; the general claim, often put forward by energy companies, that hydroelectric dams are a clean source of energy is not accurate.[48]

2/ The Vuotos project would have significantly altered biodiversity. The reservoir was supposed to cover not only the Kemihaara mires, but also part of the unique Kemijoki ecosystem environment, with impacts on birds and fish. A large number of birds nest in the planned reservoir area. The mires of northern Finland are the most important breeding grounds in the European Union.[49] According to some estimations, the construction of the reservoir would have meant the destruction of the habitats of 45,000 nesting pairs.[50]

---

46 Regarding these two reservoirs, see S. K. Hellsten, et al., *Relative Importance of Internal Sources of Phosphorus and Organic Matter in Northern Finnish Reservoirs*, 28 WATER SCIENCE & TECHNOLOGY, A JOURNAL OF THE INTERNATIONAL ASSOCIATION ON WATER POLLUTION RESEARCH 85 (1993).

47 *Coalition Clean Baltic*, CCB YEARBOOK 12 (CCB. 2002).

48 Satu Hassi, 27 March 2012 interview; when she appealed the 2000 permit decision in this case, one of Hassi's arguments was that, alone, the quantity of heavy metals released in the water would have been larger than what was allowed in any industrial installation under the then-current legislation. Hassi is a MSc in Electrical Power Engineering (Helsinki University of Technology), and a Licentiate of Technology in Energy Technology (Tampere University of Technology). She worked for two years for an industrial company (Oy Tampella Ab, from 1979 to 1981) as the first female engineer in their metal industry section. She also taught at Tampere University of Technology. See also, about the negative effects of dams more generally, WCD, DAMS AND DEVELOPMENT – A NEW FRAMEWORK FOR DECISION-MAKING – THE REPORT OF THE WORLD COMMISSION ON DAMS (World Commission on Dams. 2000).

49 For example, the smew (*Mergus albellus*), a species of duck, the only member of the genus *Mergellus*, with a typical cracked ice and panda appearance; hen harrier (*Circus cyaneus*), a bird of prey, called northern harrier in North America; common crane (*Grus grus*), also known as the Eurasian crane, a medium-sized species of the *Gruidae* family; greater scaup (*Aythya marila*), a mid-sized diving duck, called bluebill in North America; peregrine falcon (*Falco peregrinus*), a widespread bird of prey in the *Falconidae* family, called duck hawk in North America.

50 *Coalition Clean Baltic*, CCB YEARBOOK 12 (CCB. 2002).

About twenty of the bird species breeding in the area are included in Annex I of the Birds Directive of the European Union.[51] In 1991, the Vuotos area had already become the Kemihaara Wilderness Area (covering 119 square miles, or 31,000 hectares)[52] and an Important Bird Area (IBA).[53] The Vuotos project also might have risked to result in impacts on the unique Baltic salmon population.[54] Both Sweden and Finland have expended efforts for the protection of this indigenous wild Baltic salmon population. Lastly, the high level of nutrients from the drowned vegetation would have posed an important risk of algal

---

51 The Birds Directive was adopted in 1979 (Council Directive 79/409/EEC of 2 April 1979 on the Conservation of Wild Birds (OJ L 103, 25 April 1979, p. 1–18), replaced by Directive 2009/147/EC of 30 November 2009 (OJ L 20, 26 January 2010, p. 7–25), complemented by the Habitats Directive in 1992 (Council Directive 92/43/EEC of 21 May 1992 on the Conservation of Natural Habitats and of Wild Fauna and Flora(OJ L 206, 22 July 1992, p. 7–50). At the heart of both these directives is the creation of a network of protected sites called Natura 2000. The Birds Directive requires the establishment of Special Protection Areas (SPAs) for rare and vulnerable birds. The Habitats Directive similarly requires Special Areas of Conservation (SACs) to be designated for other species.

52 There is a total of twelve wilderness areas in Finland, all located in Lapland, governed by *Metsähallitus* ("Administration of Forests"), a state-owned enterprise. Metsähallitus manages most of the protected areas of Finland and supplies wood to the Finnish forest industry. It administers some 46,000 sq mi (119,139 km2) of state-owned land, and water areas (about 35% of Finland's surface area). Wilderness reserves were set up to preserve their wilderness character, the Sámi culture and their natural form of livelihood. The Kemihaara mires and forests are an important area for boreal avifauna, especially for waders. Breeding birds include fourteen out of the fifteen species in Europe that are restricted to the boreal biome (when breeding). The site is a very large complex of aapa mires, riverside forests, herb-rich mires and forested hills and ridges (BirdLife International, *Kemihaara (Vuotos) mires and forests*, at http://datazone.birdlife.org/site/factsheet/kemihaara-(vuotos)-mires-and-forests-iba-finland/text, accessed 17 June 2021).

53 An Important Bird Area (IBA) is an area recognized as being significant for the long-term viability of naturally occurring bird populations. To date, 10,000 IBAs have been identified worldwide. The program was developed and the sites are identified by BirdLife International, the world's largest partnership of conservation organizations that strive to conserve birds.

54 "During and after the last ice age, a unique type of salmon evolved from the Atlantic salmon when the Baltic lost its connection with the North Sea and the Atlantic Ocean. They lost their urge to swim into the Atlantic and kept this trait even when, after the last ice age, the Baltic was connected with the North Sea again". They are genetically different from the Atlantic Salmon. For about sixty years, the population has been declining, and one of the reasons is the construction of dams (at www.eaa-europe.org/positions/baltic-salmon-2009.html, accessed 17 June 2021). See also the HELCOM Recommendation 32–33/1 adopted on 15 June 2011: *Conservation of Baltic Salmon (Salmo Salar) and Sea Trout (Salmo Trutta) Populations by the Restoration of their River Habitats and Management of River Fisheries*.

blooming.[55] Kemijoki Oy contested the extent of these various environmental impacts of its project.

On the economic level, the project would have provided temporary jobs, during the time of the construction, and only forty-six definitive ones in the end, at most, according to some estimates, because this kind of facility is almost entirely automated.[56] In April 1992, the Government Institute for Economic Research (VATT) released a report, which did not consider the project to be socio-economically viable, without even beginning to consider its environmental impact.[57] This conclusion differed greatly from the report that had been released by a Government Working Group a few months before, which estimated the project to be most profitable, with only the Environment Ministry dissenting.[58] The Ministry of Trade and Industry, at the origins of the Government Working Group, had tried, in vain, to have its report coated with some undisputable credibility and legitimacy by resorting to the VATT, an independent governmental agency under the auspices of the Ministry of Finance. Aware of the sensitive context and of the importance of the project, the authors of the VATT report explained that they carefully presented their report in the most objective possible manner, displaying the relevant numbers with comments reduced to a bare minimum so that readers could draw their own conclusions.[59] Nonetheless, the numbers were clear enough to the readers of the VATT report. For some of them, the VATT report even underestimated the economic costs of the project.[60] As a result, Kauko Juhantalo, the Minister

55 Bep Weijand, email of 3 April 2013; Arto Inkala, et al., *Integrated 3D Modelling of Water Circulation and the Dynamics of Phytoplankton; the Effects of a Planned Reservoir*, 83 INTERNAT. REV. HYDROBIOL. 681 (1998).

56 Bep Weijand, *Economic Backlash Due to Negative Publicity in the Construction of the Vuotos Reservoir. More or Fewer Jobs?* (2000) *at* http://personal.fimnet.fi/luonto/vapaavuotos/bebinvalitus.htm (accessed 17 June 2021).

57 VATT, *Socio-Economic Viability of the Vuotos Project*, available in Finnish at https://www.doria.fi/handle/10024/148225 (accessed 17 June 2021).

58 *Vuotos-työryhmän raportti*, 1991, *Kauppa- ja teollisuusministeriö, energiaosasto* (Report of the Vuotos Working Group, 18 October 1991, Ministry of Trade and Industry, Energy Department). This report itself had been preceded by a report issued by a consulting firm, Energia-Ekono Oy, at the request of Kemijoki Oy. Energia-Ekono Oy had concluded that the project was profitable, both in terms of energy production and economic viability (*The Energy-Economic Significance of the Vuotuos Basin*, mentioned *in* the VATT report, *supra* note 57 at 45).

59 Esko Mustonen, Esko Niskanen, *Vastaus Varjosen jatkokommenttiin*, KAK 411, 412–413 (March 1993), at http://www.taloustieteellinenyhdistys.fi/images/stories/kak/KAK31993/KAK31993Mustonen.pdf, accessed 17 June 2021.

60 "The results obtained differ radically from the calculations of the Vuotos Working Group and Kemijoki Oy (…) Demonstrating and correcting the Working Group's serious

of Trade and Industry, was quite discontent and resorted to discrediting the VATT report by publicly uttering some dismissive comments.[61] Kemijoki Oy similarly tried to ridicule and intimidate the local opposition, as the latter was composed of individuals and NGOs supposedly without the means to produce professional studies at the same level of expertise.[62] During his time as Prime Minister of Finland (1991–1995), Esko Aho had to face the deep economic depression of the early 1990's. Because of the crisis, the government and local authorities were very keen on having the project completed and the associated jobs that it entailed, even temporary ones. Economic development was slower in Lapland than in Southern Finland. Unemployment had increased considerably and the economic crisis had created a feeling of total hopelessness. Local politicians presented the Vuotos reservoir as an employment project. In local discussions, nature conservation was presented as inherently opposed to economic development.

2.2 *Development of the Opposition Movement to the Vuotos Project*

In June 1992, the municipality of Pelkosenniemi, which had persistently opposed the reservoir plans for over three decades, found itself with a new majority of pro-reservoir municipal councilmen. In the municipalities around the planned reservoir area, decision-makers seemed to build the future of their municipalities on the compensation offered for the damage caused by

error is one of the undeniable merits of the report (…) The calculations of the return on investment clearly yield negative figures (…) Anything that is identified as a negative environmental impact will only aggravate the projected loss (…) the study clearly underestimates the real costs of the loss of recreation and leisure uses" (Markku Ollikainen, *Vihdoin selkeyttä Vuotos-vyyhteen*, KAK 562, 563, 566 (April 1992) (at https://www.taloustieteellinenyhdistys.fi/images/stories/kak/KAK41992/KAK41992Ollikainen.pdf, accessed 17 June 2021), author's translation). The opposition's lawyer underlined that, based on the VATT report, "The Vuotos project is narrowly profitable in energy production but it is not profitable in social economy" (Oinaala, 196. 1994.) See also Jaakko Tahkolahti, *Vuotoksen altaasta keskusteltu jo kymmenlä vuosia* (*Vuotos reservoir under consideration for decades*), HELSINGIN SANOMAT, 16 October 2006.

61 According to Juhantalo, the report had been written by bird-house men (*linnunpönttömiehistä*), the equivalent of the derogatory term "tree-huggers" in English, which sparked some outrage (Ollikainen, *supra* note 60 at 566; interventions of Hautala and Riitta Myller, members of parliament, *in* Parliament Record, 17 June 1992, p. 2761–2762, at https://www.eduskunta.fi/FI/vaski/Poytakirja/Documents/ptk_88+1992.pdf, accessed 17 June 2021).

62 Sirpa Pietikäinen (Minister of the Environment from April 1991 to April 1995), 22 March 2012 interview. In another project on the Kemi River, the Sierilä hydropower plant, the local population was also deemed not sufficiently competent (Huttunen, ACTA BOREALIA: A NORDIC JOURNAL OF CIRCUMPOLAR SOCIETIES, 27 (1999)).

the planned dam/reservoir. As for private landowners, they felt that they had no other choice than selling their land. They believed that the reservoir would be built eventually and that fighting it was pointless, a fairly common feeling.[63] Moreover, they thought that the compensation ordered by the Water Rights Court if the reservoir project were approved would be lower than the price they had been offered for their land if they sold beforehand. Kemijoki Oy negotiated with the inhabitants as an influential economic actor, the largest employer in the area, with the support of local officials and on the basis of the Council of State's decision. People thought that the final decision had been made, and that they had no say. However, this state of affairs angered some of them enough to organize an effective protest movement. The government granted no legal aid, but opponents still fought on all levels: in court through numerous legal proceedings,[64] in the media and by other actions like popular rowing celebrations.[65] The key actors were, in Finland, Helena Tiihonen, a doctor who lives in Kemijärvi, near the Vuotos area, 30 miles (50 km) south of Pelkosiennemi, and Pirjo-Riitta Oinaala, a lawyer who was working for the Finnish Association for Nature Conservation (FANC). Tiihonen comes from Pelkosiennemi. She remembers when the Lokka and Porttipahta reservoirs were built there, when people were forced out of their home and did not question the decision that had been made. She set up the *Vapaa Vuotos* (Free Vuotos) movement in Lapland, mainly because she wanted people to have their say, to participate in the decisions that affected their lives.[66] This local base and network was essential for the fight against the Vuotos project, as a unifying force for NGOs, politicians, media, local activists and researchers. Helena Tiihonen was regularly in contact with the Finnish Ministry of the Environment (FME). In Sweden, a few local activists devoted themselves to alerting the populace of the dangers posed by the Vuotos project. Tiihonen had contacted Urpo Taskinen, whose parents came from Finland in the 1950's, and who speaks Finnish. She informed Taskinen about the Vuotos project and

63 In the Sierilä project as well, some thought that there was nothing to be done, because there were already quite a few hydro-power plants on the river (id. at 36).

64 For the detailed list, see Oinaala, 196. 1994. An application (No. 24579/94) was also filed with the European Commission of Human Rights (which declared the application inadmissible, on 18 October 1995), as well as an appeal to the European Parliamentary Assembly.

65 Every year, every 23 June, people would come from all over Finland to the little village of Savukoski, for a two-day rowing trip, a peaceful demonstration on the Kemi River against the Vuotos dam project.

66 Helena Tiihonen & Sylvi Inez Liljegren, *Let the river run free*, *in* WOMAN IN A NORTHERN LANDSCAPE 79 (Sylvi Inez Liljegren ed. 1999).

asked him to gather support. Taskinen is a biologist and a coordinator at the Norrbotten branch of the Swedish Society for Nature Conservation (SSNC).[67] He then asked Bep Weijand, a biologist from The Netherlands, chairman of the Haparanda branch of the SSNC (*Haparanda Naturskyddsförening*). Haparanda is Sweden's easternmost settlement, in Norrbotten County, a coastal locality situated on the international border, next to Tornio in Finland. Weijand was also on the board of the regional branch of the SSNC. She would then become the legal representative of the Norrbotten SSNC in the judicial proceedings. Per Lundbäck, a fisherman, participated as well. He was already fighting against the declining and damaged fish population in the Tornio River, an impact of the Outokumpu Group's largest production site (a ferrochrome and stainless steel works), in Tornio. Lundbäck wanted to halt any additional pollution. Another participant was Vesa Tolpannen, from Pelkosiennemi in Finland, who had moved to Sweden and worked at the Swedish Environmental Protection Agency (SEPA). Tolpannen was the son of a Vuotos opponent in Finland, Annikki Tolpannen, a friend of Tiihonen's.

Helena Tiihonen and Pirjo-Riitta Oinala were the main coordinators and the heads of the movement, both in Finland and in Sweden. The Free Vuotos movement would succeed in getting the Swedish Norrbotten County Administrative Board officially involved in the licensing process. Some German speaking local activists also became involved, convincing German media to inquire about the Vuotos project. Two important German environmental NGOs, NABU[68] and Verkehrsclubs Deutschland e.V. (VCD), submitted a petition to the Finnish Prime Minister and some other ministers (including Economy, Finance, and Labor) on 20 November 1995 and again in 1998. In 1998, Kemijoki Oy dismissed them as probably commissioned by the Green League.

Following the construction of power plants on the Kemijoki, the local population had struggled since the 1950's to obtain compensation from the state. Laplanders felt helpless against the alliance of the state and large-scale industry, which attempted to justify the exploitation of the river in the name of national interest.[69] Members of protest movements believed that most of

67 *Naturskyddsföreningen* is the largest environmental NGO in Sweden. It was founded in 1909.

68 Founded in 1899, NABU (Naturschuntzbund – Nature and Biodiversity Conservation Union) is one of the oldest and largest environment associations in Germany. The association encompasses more than 820,000 members and supporters (at en.nabu.de/about/index.html, accessed 17 June 2021).

69 The powerful Prime Minister Urho Kekkonen (Centre Party), who would later become the longest serving president (1956–1982), had written a program to develop Lapland in 1952,

the benefit derived from Lapland's natural resources had mainly profited the industry and the state, with residents suffering all the disadvantages;[70] "we began to ask, for example, among the people who were against the building of Vuotos, if it really is in the public interest and what the public interest is that tramples on the local people's possibilities to earn their livelihood, and even hinders the local decision-making. The decisions are made elsewhere, not locally by local people … and things are promoted that have not been proven to be useful for the local people".[71] On the national level, the popularity of hydro-power had persisted for a fairly long time, until the early 1990's. Then, mentalities evolved,[72] and the general opinion turned against the Vuotos dam project.

2.3 *The Legal Proceedings*

Kauko Juhantalo, the Minister of Trade and Industry, had to step down on 2 August 1992, but the following two Trade and Industry Ministers in the same government, Pekka Tuomisto and Seppo Kääriäinen, both from the Centre Party, were also strongly in favor of the Vuotos project. After the preparatory work was completed, the Finnish Parliament granted Kemijoki Oy a license to file a tender with the North Finland Water Conservancy, for the construction of the dam. On 25 September 1992, the energy company applied to the Water Court of Northern Finland, the examining authority, for a permit to construct a dam and a reservoir. In Finland, permit applications for waterway construction projects were managed by a special Water Rights Court. The Water Court was presided by a chairman, who was a lawyer trained on the bench, and two expert members (non-lawyer), typically an engineer and a natural scientist.[73]

---

where he argued strongly that the goal was to develop, industrialize and modernize the region.

70 LEENA SUOPAJÄRVI, THE DISPUTES OVER HARNESSING THE OUNASJOKI AND BUILDING THE VUOTOS RESERVOIR. FIELDS AND MEANINGS IN LAPLAND (University of Lapland. 2001), at lauda.ulapland.fi/handle/10024/61734 (accessed 17 June 2021).

71 Suopajärvi, 212. 2003.

72 PENTTI KILJUNEN, ENERGY ATTITUDES 2004, RESULTS OF A FOLLOW-UP STUDY CONCERNING FINNISH ATTITUDES TOWARDS ENERGY ISSUES 1983–2004 1.2 (Finnish Energy Industries. 2005), at http://www.sci.fi/~yhdys/eas_03/english/etaustat.htm (accessed 17 June 2021). This study series followed the attitudes towards energy policy issues for twenty-two years (1983–2004).

73 There have been environmental courts in Finland for decades. Water legislation, intended to preserve economic interests at first, has then also long embodied some environmental principles. "Beginning with the medieval Nordic laws banning the pollution of bodies of water, this tradition has been further developed in the water legislation of 1902 and 1961 [See the Water Rights Act of 26 August 1902 (No. 51/1902); The 1961 Water Act (No. 264/1961)]. Since the ban was designed to protect both public interests as well as the private interests of the land and water owners, and adjacent real estate owners, the regulation

The application that Kemijoki Oy submitted to the Water Court made no reference to any significant transboundary impact on the Swedish maritime areas.[74] Legal proceedings were mainly comprised of the licensing procedure under the 1961 Water Act,[75] with Sweden's participation, and the Natura 2000 process – they thus involved national, international and community law, which is characteristic of environmental law. There was no national EIA legislation in Finland at the time when Kemijoki Oy applied for a permit (the EIA Act was adopted on 10 June 1994[76]). The major procedure was the licensing of the Vuotos project under the Water Act. The initial judgment by the Water Court of Northern Finland, in February 2000, was appealed to the Administrative Court of Vaasa, the decision (June 2001) of which was appealed to the Supreme Administrative Court of Finland, which decided the case in December 2002.[77]

I will now expose in detail the legal procedures. We will follow the stages of the main procedure (stipulated in the Finnish Water Act), which came to involve Sweden by application of international treaties. There was another key procedure, at the level of community law, initiated by the European Commission under the Wild Birds and the Habitats Directives (Natura 2000 network), which will be integrated in the developments related to the decision of the Finnish court of appeals, since the latter based its decision in part on EU law and was aware of the European Commission's procedures against Finland. The last developments of the Natura 2000 process then coincide with the ultimate developments of the Vuotos project, as the latter's final nemesis.

---

could not be classified solely as private law or public law, which led to the creation of the Water Courts pursuant to the 1961 Water Act. The Water Court's jurisdiction was concentrated on a wide range of judicial and administrative matters, with its role as a permit authority being the most prominent. At present, Regional State Administrative Agencies act as the state permit authorities in the field of the Environmental Protection Act, and the Water Act". (Erkki J. Hollo, et al., *Environmental Law and Administrative Courts in Finland*, 3 JOURNAL OF COURT INNOVATION 51, 53 (2010)).

74 TIMO KOIVUROVA, ENVIRONMENTAL IMPACT ASSESSMENT IN THE ARCTIC: A STUDY OF INTERNATIONAL LEGAL NORMS 276, FN 1053 (Ashgate. 2002).

75 Act No. 264/1961 of 19 May 1961. A new Water Act (No. 584/2011) was passed in the spring of 2011, to make the handling of water permits more effective and clarify the relation with other environmental regulation, but the main principles have not changed. The new act has come into force on 1 January 2012.

76 Act on Environmental Impact Assessment Procedure (No. 468/1994), hereinafter the 1994 EIA Act. The act entered into force three months later, on 1 September 1994. It could not be applied to projects for which there had been a public announcement before 14 January 1994 (Section 27).

77 See *infra* page 181: Figure 1 Timeline of the main legal proceedings related to the planned construction of the Vuotos reservoir, until 2002.

2.3.1 Proceedings before the Water Court and the Decision for an Early Application of the Espoo Convention

For all large-scale projects, the Water Act required an inspection proceedings phase, to determine their environmental and social impacts and to draw up recommendations for the Water Court. To this end, on 16 March 1993, the Water Court of Northern Finland appointed a panel composed of an engineer, two trustees, and an additional engineer because of the size of this particular project. Trustees were to be neutral people from the area. The procedural requirements seemed to warrant that all opinions would be heard.[78] Furthermore, in December 1992, Kemijoki Oy voluntarily submitted an EIA, drawn up by a consulting firm, Ekono, the same firm that had previously produced a report on the energy-economic significance of the Vuotos Basin (at the basis of the VATT report, along with the report of the Government Working Group).[79] The Water and Environment District of Lapland proposed to the Water and Environment Council that Kemijoki Oy's voluntary EIA be included in the permit procedure.[80] However, on 1 July 1993, the Water and Environment Council refused, after consultation with the Ministry of the Environment. Sirpa Pietikäinen, the Environment Minister, wanted the Espoo Convention to be applied with the production of a non-partial EIA, made with as much public participation as possible. The only EIA that existed had been made at the request of the project proponent and Pietikäinen thought it was a tailor-made study. If Kemijoki Oy had made a proper EIA, it might have changed her opinion, but their study appeared to her as having been done only to justify the viability and feasibility of the project. The Ministry of the Environment did not consider the energy company reliable in EIA matters, but because the EIA Act was not yet in existence, the FME had no legal basis to ask the project proponent for a proper EIA.[81] The Minister of the Environment cared to apply a proper EIA process

78 Kaj Hellsten, *Hydro-power Plants in the North*, *in* THE LEGAL STATUS OF THE INDIVIDUAL IN NORDIC ENVIRONMENTAL LAW 181 (Tuula Tervashonka ed. 1994). Hellsten was Kemijoki Oy's senior legal counsel. Some inspection meetings, at which the public could present comments, took place between 7 and 17 February 1994. The final hearings, during which private individuals and governmental authorities could comment upon and object to the results of the inspection, were held between 2 and 11 July 1996.

79 See *supra* page 155. Ekono Inc. is a consulting engineering firm incorporated in the State of Washington (USA). Ekono has worked with the North American pulp and paper industry since 1959 and is a subsidiary of Duoplan Oy, a Helsinki, Finland-based consulting engineering firm (www.ekono.com, accessed 17 June 2021).

80 The Water and Environment District of Lapland was part of the Lapland Regional Environment Centre, a regional antenna of the Finnish environmental administration.

81 Sirpa Pietikäinen, 22 March 2012 interview.

extensively, in the broader sense of the term, which meant that all stakeholders be consulted, including Sweden, as the latter had expressed some concerns on the basis of studies. Sweden asked for information and to be involved in a new EIA. Even though the Vuotos dam was rather far from Swedish territorial waters (about 185 miles – 300 km), Sweden presented studies showing potential impacts. Only one international treaty applied at the time, the 1974 Nordic Environmental Protection Convention (NEPC). However, Finland also chose to apply the Espoo Convention to involve Sweden, even though the convention was not yet in force (it came into force on 10 September 1997). The Espoo Convention had the advantage to allow for early participation, whereas the NEPC required Swedish participation only at a later stage. Importantly, a large part of the efficacy of an EIA is a proper timing. Consultations and studies should be made as early as possible. The NEPC did not provide for adequate time to prepare; its Article 5 required notification, if need be, after the completion of the inspection proceedings in Finland, when the permit authority was in the process of examining the permit request. The Espoo Convention had a more adequate timing requirement, i.e. notifying the affected state as early as possible (Article 3).

There is no definitive answer about the reasons why an anticipated application of the Espoo Convention was decided. Two explanations were suggested: either Finland simply followed the requirements of the 1991 Resolution of the Parties, in a rather positivistic view,[82] or the Environment Ministry also expected some additional support to fight against the reservoir project, which it had consistently opposed from the start.[83] Even if not yet enforceable, international law can indeed be used to support domestic policy goals.[84] Another reason may be that Finland was contemplating setting an example and expectations from which it could benefit in the future. There are, perhaps, several reasons for the decision, but the main motivation indeed appears to be the desire to implement the best decision-making process for Finland and neighboring states. The 1991 Resolution of the Parties was a soft-law instrument.

---

82 Timo Koivurova, *The Case of Vuotos: Interplay Between International, Community and National Environmental Law*, 13 RECIEL 47, 52 (2004). Upon signing the convention in 1991, the parties asserted their "resolve to strive for the entry into force of the Convention as soon as possible and to seek to implement the Convention to the maximum extent possible pending its entry into force" (Para. 1 of the Resolution on Environmental Impact Assessment in a Transboundary Context (ECE/ENVWA/19)). See also Article 18 of the 1969 Vienna Convention on the Law of Treaties.

83 Koivurova, FINNISH Y.B. INT'L L., 199 (1997).

84 Oona A. Hathaway, *Between Power and Principle: An Integrated Theory of International Law*, 72 U. CHI. L. REV. 469, FN 66 (2005).

There was no binding legal obligation. Finland wanted to apply the Espoo Convention immediately in order to show how committed to EIAs they were, as the best decision-making process in their view, which they had long promoted. The Environment Minister was an ardent proponent of EIA. Finland had urged that the Espoo Convention be adopted. Sirpa Pietikäinen had taken, and continued to pursue, several initiatives to introduce procedural requirements in her domain, especially the national EIA Act, where she also introduced Transboundary EIA (TEIA) requirements.[85] Pietikäinen had reasons both on the national and international level to pressure for an early implementation of the Espoo Convention: internationally, Pietikäinen wanted to signal that Finland cared to be respectful and respected. Because Finland is a rather small country, Pietikäinen tended to consider it important that they respect their commitments; she expected the other states to do the same in return. She wanted to set an example in order to encourage the application of the Espoo Convention as widely as possible.[86] In exchange to responding to the concerns of Finland's immediate neighbors, the FME expected them to reciprocate. Pietikäinen convinced the Minister of Foreign Affairs (Paavo Väyrinen, Centre Party, interestingly from a farmer family in Lapland) and the Prime Minister, while almost all of the rest of the government remained strongly against the application of the Espoo Convention. Pietikäinen emphasized that it was important to implement the convention, because there were several ongoing projects affecting Finland in neighboring countries – for instance, a bridge between Denmark and Sweden, the Øresund Bridge, the construction of which later began in 1995. The FME wanted to consult with Sweden about the fluctuations in the Baltic Sea induced by the bridge, and in 1992, Sweden had applied the Espoo Convention before its entry into force as well, with respect to the proposed fixed link across the Øresund.[87] The Finnish Prime Minister and the

85 1994 EIA Act, Chapter 3, Section 14, §3 (now Chapter 5 of the 2017 EIA Act, No 252/2017, in force 16 May 2017).

86 Interview of 22 March 2012. Civil servants at the Minister of the Environment, like Ulla-Riitta Soveri (Senior Adviser from 1980 to 2019), testify to the same effect (interview of 26 March 2012). Finland continued to implement the Espoo Convention diligently. By the end of 2010, it had applied the convention to 38 projects. Finland was the state of origin in the majority of them (22 projects), the affected state in 17 and in one project (the Baltic sea gas pipeline), both the origin and affected state (TIMO KOIVUROVA, ET AL., VALTIOIDEN RAJAT YLITTÄVIEN YMPÄRISTÖVAIKUTUSTEN ARVIOINTI SUOMESSA, YVA-LAIN TOIMIVUUS KANSAINVÄLISTÄ KUULEMISTA KOSKEVIEN VELVOITTEIDEN NÄKÖKULMASTA (EIA IN A TRANSBOUNDARY CONTEXT IN FINLAND) 11 (Ympäristöministeriön (Finnish Ministry of the Environment). 2012)).

87 Sweden sent the EIA documentation on 22 September 1992 to all countries around the Baltic Sea, together with a notification in accordance with Article 3 of the convention.

Minister of Foreign Affairs agreed to the application of the Espoo Convention in the Vuotos case.

Probably for the same reasons (to show their commitment to TEIA, induce their neighbors to reciprocate in other projects, develop a European support network and improve the decision-making process by involving all stakeholders for better decisions and projects), the FME applied the Espoo Convention before its entry into force in two other cases: the Outokumpu Group steel factories in Tornio, next to Sweden,[88] and the Vattenfall gas power station near Imatra, close to the Russian border.[89] The Finnish-Russian border is very long, in terms of European standards (833 miles – 1 340 km), more than twice the length of the Finnish-Swedish one, exposing Finland to the risks of many projects with transboundary impacts. In both cases, Finland's neighboring states had asked for their involvement in the decision-making process and the FME accepted, out of principle and reciprocity concerns. In its turn, Finland later wished to be consulted about the construction of two harbors in the Russian Federation.[90] However, Russia, a signatory to the Espoo Convention, responded

---

The documents were in English. Translation in other languages was discussed, but was finally regarded as not necessary, which is naturally a crucial aspect of cooperation (it is less expensive and more efficient when the same language can be used). Importantly, Sweden invited all countries to propose experts for a panel that would examine and evaluate the effects of the Øresund link on the marine environment in the Baltic sea and in the Øresund (UNECE, CURRENT POLICIES, STRATEGIES, AND ASPECTS OF ENVIRONMENTAL IMPACT ASSESSMENT IN A TRANSBOUNDARY CONTEXT 19 (United Nations. 1996)). The Øresund Bridge opened in July 2000. The bridge is the longest road and rail bridge in Europe (nearly 8 miles/5 km).

88 Koivurova, FINNISH Y.B. INT'L L., 195 (1997). The extension of Outokumpu's largest production site was only 1,3 miles (2 km) away from Sweden. "[In the Outokumpu case,] the Ministry decided to apply the [Espoo] Convention as fully as possible even before it was in force – for gaining experience on the application, but, more importantly, for taking the transboundary impacts into account, and to hear Sweden's view, the authorities', and the public's. Outokumpu is very close to Sweden, and the contacts between our countries are tight in general, especially in that region. But I think any activity with likely significant transboundary impact would have triggered the discussion with the potentially affected country, and the developer to apply the Convention" (Seija Rantakallio (Ministerial Adviser at the Environment Ministry since 1996), email of 20 March 2012).

89 The Environment Ministry had the EIA translated into Russian and sent to the contact authority of the Russian Federation on 21 November 1996. The Russian Federation did not respond before the deadline set in the notification (See Art. 3.4 of the Espoo Convention), but Finland extended the deadline. Russia eventually responded, and later issued a statement on the EIA documentation.

90 The two harbors, Primorsk and Ust-Luga, were under construction during the second half of the 1990's. In December 2001, Primorsk started to operate as an oil harbor and a terminus of an oil pipeline, the Baltic Pipeline System. The second harbor is Ust-Luga, where a

that they had not ratified the convention and could not accommodate Finland (in disregard for the general law of treaties as well as the 1991 resolution of the parties).[91] Nevertheless, the FME has continued this policy of applying the Espoo Convention to the Russian Federation and the latter applied the convention in the Nord Stream project (a system of offshore natural gas pipelines) in 2006 and 2013, albeit only to the extent permitted by its own national law.[92]

In the Vuotos case, Sirpa Pietikäinen wanted to set an example on the national level too, where she was attempting to have the EIA bill adopted. Even though the concept had already been under consideration at the beginning of the 1980's, due to the influence of the international discourse, the EIA legislation developed rather late in Finland because of the opposition of the industry and agriculture sectors, in fear of the economic consequences of compulsory EIAS. EIA legislation was eventually adopted in view of Finland's integration into the European Union. Before the 1994 EIA Act, the main issue with Finnish environmental legislation was that environmental impacts were assessed within the limits of sectorial permit laws, similarly to the United States before NEPA. The 1994 EIA Act was the first Finnish environmental statute that would call for a comprehensive assessment. Its adoption would lead to the increase of environmental information available to the public and the opportunity to participate in the early stages of project development. Finland had to undertake complex reforms to introduce EIA in its planning system.[93] The Vuotos case was a good opportunity to start training in this new type of decision-making process.

---

coal and fertilizer terminal was inaugurated that same year (later, it would also become the second terminus of the Baltic Pipeline System, in 2011).

91 See Article 18 of the Vienna Convention, which reflects customary international law, and Para. 1 of the 1991 Resolution on Environmental Impact Assessment in a Transboundary Context (ECE/ENVWA/19) (see *supra* note 82). In another project (the Leningrad Nuclear Power Plant II, in Sosnovyi Bor), Russia did not answer Finland's request, in 2008.

92 See, about Nord Stream I, Chapter 3 of the ESPOO REPORT (2009), page 62, at https://www.nord-stream.com/the-project/permits/, accessed 17 June 2021; About Nord Stream II, see ESPOO REPORT (2017), page 543, at https://web.archive.org/web/20210531072713/https://www.nord-stream2.com/media/documents/pdf/en/2018/07/espoo-report-en.pdf, accessed 17 June 2021. See also Timo Koivurova & Ismo Pölönen, *Transboundary Environmental Impact Assessment in the Case of the Baltic Sea Gas Pipeline*, 25 INT J MAR COAST LAW 151, 160 (2010)). More generally, the Russian Federation has also provided a point of contact in accordance with Article 3 of the Espoo Convention (at https://unece.org/environment-policyenvironmental-assessment/points-contact-regarding-notification, accessed 17 June 2021).

93 Finnish EIA regulations implied great changes in legal structure, reallocation of the role as competent authority and changes in procedural aspects (Tesli & Roar Husby, ENVIRONMENTAL IMPACT ASSESSMENT REVIEW, 60, FN7 (1999)).

For all these reasons, the FME succeeded in involving Sweden in the Vuotos case. On 1 July 1993, the Finnish Water and Environment Council informed the Water and Environment District of Lapland of the potential consequences to the Swedish territorial waters. Because the EIA bill provided for the Finnish Ministry of Foreign Affairs to be consulted by the FME,[94] and the FME wanted to abide by the bill it was pushing forward, a consultation with the Ministry of Foreign Affairs took place before the FME notified Sweden of the Vuotos project. It was agreed that the Espoo Convention be invoked provided that it did not exceed the obligations set forth in the applicable treaty, the NEPC. The latter provides for any person who may be affected to have standing before the permit authority of the state of origin, and to bring an appeal against its decision if necessary (Article 3). The FME also informally consulted the Water Court, the authority in charge of notifying Sweden by virtue of Article 5 of the NEPC. The Water Court agreed. On the basis of Article 3 of the Espoo Convention, the 1991 Resolution of the signatories to the convention, and the NEPC (in order to secure a valid legal basis), the FME gave notification, in Swedish, to *Naturvårdsverket* (the Swedish Environmental Protection Agency (SEPA)) on 22 June 1995, long before the conclusions of the inspection proceedings. The FME and SEPA are the Espoo Convention points of contact, whereas the NEPC requires notification from the examining authorities of the state parties, i.e. the Water Court in Finland at the time. By mutual agreement, the FME, with better resources and know-how, acted in lieu of the Water Court. Kemijoki Oy later argued that this transfer of internal competence was illegal, because the Espoo Convention was not yet into force. However, Section 14 of the 1994 Finnish EIA act would grant the competence to notify foreign states to the FME. Even though Section 27 restricted the application of the EIA Act to those activities initiated after 14 January 1994, which excluded the Vuotos case, Section 14 (in Chapter 3, dedicated to TEIA) granted the FME competence with regard not only to the Espoo Convention, but any other international treaty as well, after the entry into force of the EIA Act (1 September 1994).[95] Once the application of the Espoo Convention and the conduct of a TEIA as early as

94 Section 14(3) of the 1994 Act would read: "The Ministry of the Environment shall request a Ministry for Foreign Affairs opinion on the matter". In 1999, it was amended to a simple notification and the new EIA Act of 2017 still has the same basic requirement, for information purposes only (Para. 29).

95 Section 14: "(1) The provisions of this act (...) shall also apply if enforcement of an international agreement binding on Finland requires an EIA procedure to be arranged in cooperation with another state in the case of a project being carried out in Finland. (2) The ministry of the environment shall see to notification and consultation (...)".

possible were decided, the lower levels of the FME, along with local authorities, took charge.

Sweden was officially informed that the Vuotos Project might result in an overload of phosphorus in the maritime area of Sweden, in the Gulf of Bothnia. SEPA was asked to respond by 1 September 1995. It answered on 30 August 1995, requesting that studies be carried out on the possible impacts on the Swedish parts of the Gulf.

On 24 May 1996, the inspection proceedings ended and the report was delivered to the Water Court. According to the inspection panel, no obstacle was implied by Article 2(5) of the Water Act, which sets out the criteria by which a permit may be denied, if important public interests are at stake. They also stated that the transboundary impacts in Sweden would be minor, despite the studies stating the opposite. They supported the Vuotos project on the basis of Article 2(6) of the Water Act, because its benefits greatly exceeded its costs.[96]

In parallel, the public and Sweden could submit their opinion to the Finnish Water Court until 11 September 1996. SEPA sent its objections to the project two days after the deadline set by the Water Court, on 13 September 1996, but the FME added the Swedish submissions to their own and submitted them to the Water Court.[97] In addition, the Swedish authorities had requested further information on the project, which the FME delivered to SEPA on 25 June 1997. Three months later, on 14 September 1997, SEPA addressed its comments to the FME, where it referred to the application of the NEPC. Eventually, the FME delivered the information collected from Sweden to the Water Court on 2 October 1997. As for the local protest movement, Helena Tiihonen had had a brilliant idea: she had arranged for as many people as possible, Finnish and Swedish alike, to buy a piece of land in the Vuotos area, so that they could all have standing. Some farmers in the area affected by the project had even donated part of their land to the FANC.[98]

---

96 By an estimated 1,800 million Finnish marks (almost US$405 million, €310 million, at the time, in 1996). See Water Court decision, at 84–85, part II. According to Article 2(6), in its 1987 version then applicable, the licensing authority may grant a permit if a project is required by significant public interests. In addition, the provision stipulates that if the benefits of a proposed activity clearly outweigh its negative costs, a permit may also be granted.

97 Ulla-Riitta Soveri is rather certain that Sweden was not negligent, quite the contrary. There were a great many documents, so it took time to handle all of them and have them translated (26 March 2012 interview. Soveri was Senior Adviser at the FME from 1980 to 2019).

98 In the second half of the 1990's, around 600 persons and nine associations owned a part of land in the project area (Tiihonen & Liljegren, 81. 1999).

On 29 February 2000, the Water Court decided as the inspection proceedings had recommended. The Water Court did not examine the Swedish submissions, because the transboundary effects were minor, according to the court, and it denied standing.[99] It followed that the court did not inform the supervisory authority of Sweden. SEPA heard of the Water Court decision from the Swedish regional authority, the Norrbotten County Administrative Board.[100] The court also considered that the Wild Birds and the Habitats Directives[101] were irrelevant because Finland had excluded the Kemihaara mires from its Natura 2000 proposal.[102] Nevertheless, it remains that the FME's initiative had placed the court in a new position: for once, it had to consider the applications of various parties from abroad.

Sirpa Pietikäinen and the FME were not really surprised at the report or at the Water Court decision. While many studies showed that there were important potential environmental impacts, the Water Court seemed biased in favor of the project. Local officials wanted the dam project to proceed and the court members might have been concerned about local economic interests as well. Furthermore, Kemijoki Oy was a powerful lobbyist for its projects.[103] Similarly to EDF in France (see *infra* chapter 5), Kemijoki Oy has been

---

99 "According to the inspection proceedings, the effects of the project on the area of Sweden would be minor, an evaluation which has been confirmed by the ministry of the environment in an oral hearing" (cited *in* KOIVUROVA, Environmental Impact Assessment in the Arctic: A Study of International Legal Norms 285. 2002). The FME argued then, before the court of appeals, that the Water Court had misunderstood its presentation (id. at 280).

100 In February 2000; then the FME, on 3 April 2000, provided further information to SEPA after the latter had contacted the ministry to this effect (Helen Lindgren (Legal Adviser at SEPA since 1999), email of 23 November 2012). A County Administrative Board is a Swedish Government agency in each of the counties of Sweden, tasked with implementing national policies and developing the county.

101 See *supra* note 51.

102 According to the Water Court, "the nature protection values in the area of Vuotos had been examined very carefully during the inspection proceedings. When making its Natura 2000 network decision, the government had had very extensive material at its disposal, including the letter of formal notice by the commission of the Council of Europe [sic] referring to the Kemihaara mires. In addition, even though the ministry of the environment had proposed that the Vuotos area should be included in the Natura 2000 network, these areas had been excluded from the government's decision" (See Water Court Decision, at 264 (part II) *in* Koivurova, RECIEL, 55 (2004)).

103 See, for instance, in another project (the Sierilä hydropower plant project on the Kemi River): Huttunen, ACTA BOREALIA: A NORDIC JOURNAL OF CIRCUMPOLAR SOCIETIES, 30 (1999). The Sierilä project also has had a long history, starting in the late 1940's when it was included in the construction plan for the Kemi River. It is still at the development phase at this writing.

very influential in Lapland, to a point that it has been likened to a state within the state there.[104]

2.3.2 The Appeal to the Administrative Court of Vasaa

After the Water Court decision, major pressure was applied on the Minister of the Environment, Satu Hassi (Green League), for her not to make use of her right of appeal. Within the five-party coalition government, a tense discussion took place among party leaders. Save for Suvi-Anne Siimes (chair of the Left Alliance), who remained ambiguous, all clearly supported the Vuotos project and demanded that Hassi do not appeal.[105] Her predecessor, Pekka Haavisto (1995–1999), then suggested that all five past and present Ministers of the Environment write a letter to *Helsingin Sanomat*, the most prominent newspaper in Finland, to alert the general public regarding the Vuotos project. Pekka Haavisto was counting on the positive effects of their common, apolitical stance since they were members of different political parties. Their public appeal to renounce the Vuotos project was published in Helsingin Sanomat on 22 March 2000, signed by Matti Ahde (Social Democratic Party), Kaj Bärlund (Social Democratic Party), Sirpa Pietikäinen (National Coalition Party), Pekka Haavisto (Green League), and Satu Hassi (Green League).[106] Thereupon, the pressure on Satu Hassi stopped. She would have appealed the Water Court decision anyway, but she then could appeal without political pressure from the rest of the government.[107]

---

104 Satu Hassi, 27 March 2012 interview. Hassi was the Environment Minister from 1999 to 2002. She was the leader of the Green League in Finland from 1999 to 2001. In 2002, she resigned from the government in protest of its decision to build a fifth nuclear power plant. She was elected to the European Parliament as the sole Finnish Green representative in the 2004 election (she was a member of the Group of the Greens/European Free Alliance). Hassi was a member of the European Parliament until 2014. In April 2015, she was elected to the Finnish Parliament and became the chairperson of the Environment Committee.

105 Ibid.

106 *Time to Abandon the Vuotos Reservoir Project* (the original publication in Finnish is on file with the Päivälehti Archives. A translation in English is available at http://personal.fimnet.fi/luonto/vapaavuotos/, accessed 17 June 2021); Satu Hassi, 27 March 2012 interview. The Ministers of the Environment, during the Vuotos case, were Sirpa Pietikäinen, from 1991 to 1995 (now a member of the European Parliament since April 2008 (Group of the European People's Party (Christian Democrats)), Pekka Haavisto (for the first time, a member of the Green League had become a minister), from 1995 to 1999, in the Paavo Lipponen government, and then Satu Hassi (Green League), from 1999 to 2002, in the second cabinet of Paavo Lipponen.

107 Satu Hassi, 27 March 2012 interview.

The importance of public participation is paramount. In this case, it was essential from the beginning and remained so all along. Without the affected inhabitants and NGOs, the Vuotos case would not have reached such a high level of political controversy.[108] The case also took on a new dimension when private and public parties from another state participated in the Finnish national licensing procedure. Swedish parties argued that the Vuotos dam should not be built because of its significant environmental impacts on Swedish waters in the Gulf of Bothnia. Their participation would have a clear effect on the manner in which the Vuotos Case was later decided by the court of appeals.[109]

More than sixty parties appealed the Water Court decision to the Administrative Court of Vaasa, the only administrative court competent in environmental and water law in Finland.[110] On the bench, there were both judges trained in the law (justices) and full-time expert members (non-lawyers) with technical and ecological expertise.[111] The complainants included Sweden (SEPA, Norrbotten County Administrative Board, the Norrbotten SSNC represented by Bep Weijand, the municipality of Haparanda, and a fisherman, Per Lundbäck).[112] SEPA had previously requested the opinions of the Norrbotten County Administrative Board and the municipality of Haparanda. Both had recommended an appeal. For the first time, Sweden appealed a decision on the grounds of the NEPC. The court held a public hearing in Pelkosienniemi from 6 to 8 February 2001. Both the FME and SEPA demanded that appelants from Sweden be given the status of injured parties. The administrative court first responded that the Swedish authorities could be heard, but that their status as injured parties would be decided later.

On 14 June 2001, the administrative court of Vaasa overturned the licensing decision of the Water Court and rejected Kemijoki Oy's application, on the basis of Article 2(5) of the Water Act.[113] It was the first time that this part of the Water Act had served as legal grounds to refuse a permit. For the Vasaa court,

108 Sirpa Pietikäinen, 22 March 2012 interview.

109 Koivurova, RECIEL, 53 (2004).

110 The Vaasa Administrative Court was founded in 1999. The court is a regional administrative court, and a national court in environmental matters. It is located in Vaasa, a coastal town on the Gulf of Bothnia.

111 Hollo, et al., *supra* note 73 at 54.

112 Timo Koivurova, *Transboundary Environmental Impact Assessment: The Nordic Environmental Protection Convention, in* THEORY AND PRACTICE OF TRANSBOUNDARY IMPACT ASSESSMENT 85, 86 (Kees Bastmeijer & Timo Koivurova eds., 2008).

113 A copy of the decision can be requested from the court (in Finnish). The Administrative Court's decision includes the judgment of the Water Court, the findings of the inspection proceedings, and Kemijoki Oy's application.

the criterion for one of the three absolute prohibitions had been fulfilled, i.e. causing widespread and harmful consequences to the environment. The court further mentioned the rise of environmental protection values, as well as the requirements of EU law. The court found that damaging effects on the Swedish waters were probable and, subsequently, that SEPA was a supervisory authority under Article 4 of the NEPC, with legal standing.[114] The court did not consider Swedish local authorities as independent injured parties, but their statements were included in SEPA's claims. Kemijoki Oy had argued that SEPA had not respected the deadline, 11 September 1996, and was two days late. The administrative court nevertheless deemed it unreasonable to deny SEPA the right to appeal, in light of the fact that the Water Court and the FME had agreed on a special procedure for the participation of Sweden, as organized by the FME, and it was the FME that had transmitted the document to the court.[115] As for Per Lundbäck, he was given the status of an injured party even though his complaint had been filed late, because he had not been properly informed.[116]

Article 2(5) of the 1961 Water Act listed three distinct criteria, the fulfillment of any one of which prohibited granting a permit. According to the 1987 Amendment, which applied to the case, a permit could not be given if (1) the construction work endangered public health; (2) caused significant and wide-ranging negative changes in the natural conditions of the environment or the aquatic environment and its functioning; or (3) seriously impacted the livelihood or settlement conditions.[117] The court decided that the second criterion was fulfilled. For the administrative court, Article 2(5) was a flexible norm, which could be interpreted according to prevailing social values at any given time:

> Society and its values have significantly changed from when the Water Act was enacted in 1961. Also, the environmental sciences have developed

114 Article 4 stipulates that the supervisory authority has "the right to appeal against the decision of the court or the administrative authority in accordance with the procedures and rules of appeal applicable to such cases in the state concerned". For a more detailed presentation, see Timo Koivurova, *The Case of Vuotos*, *in* ARCTIC GOVERNANCE 186, 194 (Timo Koivurova, et al. eds., 2004).

115 Court's decision at 49–53.

116 However, the court did not consider the Norrbotten branch of the SSNC (*Länsförbundet Naturskyddsföreningen*) as an injured party, the appeal of which also had arrived too late (Court's decision at 51–52). Bep Weijand (their legal representative) explained that a technicality was the unfortunate reason of the delay (her email of 4 April 2013).

117 Amendment to the Water Act No. 467/1987 (Koivurova's translation, *in* Koivurova, RECIEL, 54 (2004)).

> considerably during this period. The societal and legal relevance of environmental and nature protection values has increased nationally as well as internationally in the recent decades, especially during the last ten years.[118]

The court reviewed the legislation, both in Finland as well as in the EU, and concluded that it reflected the evolution of these societal values. The court emphasized Section 20 of the Finnish Constitution, which promotes the protection of the environment and public participation in decision-making processes.[119] The court particularly insisted on the scientific progress made in relation to the environment. Instead of relying solely on the recommendations of the inspection proceedings, it "(...) base[d] its conception regarding the nature potentially affected by the activity, and the impacts potentially caused by the activity on the studies made in the inspection proceedings, on the additional studies done during the procedure in the administrative court, and on its own on-site observations".[120] The court applied the precautionary principle and stated that there was not enough information on the impacts of the Vuotos project. As regards the information that was submitted, the court viewed the models used for studying the likely impacts as unreliable.[121] It also considered the effects more broadly. The Water Court had studied only the flooded area, whereas the administrative court considered the reservoir as part of an ecosystem interconnected with the Luiro and Kilpiaava mires.[122] For the administrative court, the model calculations showing that the potential effects extended no further than the waters near the Finnish town of Kemi were not credible. The court found that "the effects on the Gulf of Bothnia would extend to Swedish maritime areas as well, but noted that the ecological impacts on those areas would, in all likelihood, be obscured by natural variations, and would

118 Court's decision at 56 (Koivurova's translation *in* id. at 55).

119 Court's decision at 56–57. In the 1999 Constitution (a new Constitution had been adopted after the accession of Finland to the European Union), Section 20, titled "Responsibility for the environment", reads as follows: "Nature and its biodiversity, the environment and the national heritage are the responsibility of everyone. The public authorities shall endeavor to guarantee for everyone the right to a healthy environment and for everyone the possibility to influence the decisions that concern their own living environment". The former Constitution had a similar provision (Section 14a of the 1919 Constitution, as amended in 1995 by Act No. 969/1995). The court also mentioned (at 57) that the recent case law related to water management in Finland had strongly emphasized environmental values.

120 At 57 (Koivurova's translation *in* Koivurova, RECIEL, 56 (2004)).

121 Court's decision at 59–60 and 68–69 (part I) (id. at 56).

122 Court's decision at 61 and 64 (id. at 56).

therefore be hard to measure".[123] The administrative court also reasoned with European Union law, under a particular angle. The court argued that: "Article [2(5)] must also be interpreted through the loyalty principle enshrined in the Founding Treaty of the European Community, meaning that the protection objectives of the above-mentioned directives [the Wild Birds and the Habitats Directives] are to be taken into account".[124]

Even though the European Commission could not intervene in the Vuotos project *per se*,[125] it had been quite concerned, hence the institution of two supervisory procedures against Finland. For the commission, the Kemihaara mires, situated in the Vuotos area and partly immersed if the project were implemented, should have been classified by Finland as a Special Protection Area (SPA) in the Natura 2000 network. Article 3 of the Habitats Directive established an ecological network of sites to protect biodiversity in Europe, titled Natura 2000. Despite the FME, which had recommended them on 21 March 1997, the Finnish government had decided, on 20 August 1998, not to include the mires in the Natura 2000 sites, precisely because of the Vuotos project. The proposed reservoir would have included about 39 sq mi (100 km2) of the Kemihaara mires. Apparently, the government had been convinced by information provided by Kemijoki Oy, which had downplayed the avifaunal significance of the area on the basis of data presented in a book by an ornithologist, who subsequently denounced the misuse of the statistics he had presented.[126] On 1 July 1999, the European Commission brought an action against Finland before the European Court of Justice (ECJ) for not having fully and definitively notified the commission of its SPA sites. Since the Water Court's decision, three significant events had convinced the Finnish administrative court to take the Wild Birds and Habitats Directives into consideration. Firstly, the Finnish Supreme Administrative Court had remanded the Kemihaara mires case to the

123 Court's Decision at 68 (part I) (Koivurova's translation *in* Koivurova, RECIEL, 52 (2004)).

124 Court's Decision at 58 (Koivurova's translation *in* id. at 56).

125 In response to a written question, the commission had answered, on 8 May 2000, that the 1985 EIA directive was not applicable and that Sweden had been informed (*Written Question No. E-0728/00 by Jonas Sjöstedt* (GUE/NGL) *to the Commission. Vuotos dam construction project in northern Finland.* OJ C 113E, 18 April 2001, p. 2–3).

126 The book was RISTO A. VÄISÄNEN, MUUTTUVA PESIMÄLINNUSTO (DISTRIBUTION, NUMBERS AND POPULATION CHANGES OF FINNISH BREEDING BIRDS) (Otava, Helsinki 1998). See also Jukka Halonen, *Linnutkin lasketaan tekoallaskiistassa*, EUROPA, EUROOPAN KOMISSION SUOMEN EDUSTUSTON LEHTI 16–18 (5/1999). Väisänen protested at Kemijoki Oy's interpretation: Risto A. Väisänen, *Kemijoki Oy: llä väärä käsitys Vuotoksen lintuarvoista*, EUROPA, EUROOPAN KOMISSION SUOMEN EDUSTUSTON LEHTI 4–5 (1/2000), available in English at personal.fimnet.fi/luonto/vapaavuotos/newvaisanen.htm, accessed 17 June 2021.

government for additional preparation, on 14 June 2000. Consequently, in the Vuotos case, the Vasaa Administrative Court ruled that there was insufficient information to review the legality of the 1998 Finnish decision not to include the Vuotos area in the Natura 2000 list. Secondly, on 15 June 2000, the ECJ had registered the European Commission's case against Finland for failing to classify SPAs fully and definitively, with the Kemihaara mires cited as one example of an area that should have been classified as a SPA. Thirdly, on 12 September 2000, the European Commission had started a new supervisory procedure against Finland focusing directly on the Kemihaara mires, because, in its view, Finland was on the verge of being in breach of the Wild Birds and the Habitats Directives by authorizing the Vuotos project.[127]

The decision of the Administrative Court of Vaasa was met with a barrage of criticism in Finland because it asserted a change in societal values. It was generally felt that, in doing so, the court had exceeded its authority. The court's approach was lambasted as a departure from the traditional view of the role of the judiciary in the Finnish understanding of the separation of powers, even though the court based its reasoning firmly on the development of the Finnish and EU legal systems. Supporters of the dam project were disappointed at the decision of the administrative court. At the time, Finnish Lapland had eight representatives in Parliament. Only one of them, Esko-Juhani Tennilä (Left Alliance) was opposed to the Vuotos reservoir.[128] The others resolved to find another way for proceeding with the project. The Minister of Trade and Industry (Sinikka Mönkäre – Social Democratic Party) declared she was confident that the Vuotos reservoir would be built and emphasized that the European Union would not determine the outcome of this dispute.[129]

2.3.3 The Supreme Court Decision

Kemijoki Oy appealed the decision of the administrative court to the Supreme Administrative Court, which upheld the decision to refuse a permit by a

127 Letter of formal notice of 12 September 2000, arguing that the Vuotos reservoir project would breach Article 4(4) of the Wild Birds Directive, and Article 6(2), (3) and (4) of the Habitats Directive because it would significantly harm the ecosystems and bird populations there. In fact, for the European Commission, the Kemihaara mires were the best SPA site (opinion of 10 April 2001). Regarding all three events and their influence, see Koivurova, The Case of Vuotos 202. 2004.

128 Born in 1947, Tennilä was from Lapland. He was a member of the Finnish Parliament from 1975 until 2011, and a member of the Communist Party before turning to the Left Alliance in 1990.

129 Aleksi Vakkuri, *News from Finland*, 2 CENTRAL EUROPE REVIEW 36 (2000), at www.pecina.cz/files/www.ce-review.org/00/36/finlandnews36.html (accessed 17 June 2021).

6–1 vote, on 18 December 2002, also on the basis of Article 2(5) of the 1961 Water Act, but with a different justification.[130] The Supreme Court explained that it was the first time a project could have such devastating environmental impacts, including in Sweden, and that the project could have altered the entire ecosystem (with the rise of mercury levels in the water for instance). It did not cite environmental values *per se*, but argued that the Water Act had to be interpreted within the bounds of legal discretion.[131] In cases involving the Water Act, the Supreme Court bench includes technical and ecological experts (five justices and two expert members). Unlike their colleagues in Vaasa, the Supreme Court experts, mainly renowned scientists, only hold part-time positions. Nevertheless, their role is usually crucial.[132] Similarly to the administrative court, the Supreme Court regarded Article 2(5) as a flexible norm, but, however, without considering that its interpretation should be justified by a change in societal values. In its view, judges had discretion because of the semantic openness of Article 2(5). "For the Supreme Court, this discretion meant legal discretion – the interpretation of an individual norm thanks to other sources of law".[133] The court underlined the amendment made to Article 2(5) in 1987, which added "in the aquatic environment and its functioning". According to the court, this amendment had inserted ecological values, in light of the *travaux préparatoires*. The court also stated that Article 2(5) needed to be interpreted in reference to Section 20 of the Constitution, which proclaims the right to a healthy environment and to public participation. Its decision established a significant precedent. The Supreme Court also based its decision on the constitutional right to property and a general principle – the principle of legal certainty.[134] The court showed how EU law was to be applied in Finland, in the wake of the case law of the ECJ. The Supreme Court mentioned the importance of the interpretative effect of directives in response to the argument of the applicant, Kemijoki Oy. Otherwise, the court found it sufficient to apply national law (the Water Act), which simplified the case and gave importance and visibility to Finnish environmental provisions.[135] Again, Article 2(5) of the Water Act was applied for the first time in forty years.

130 The decision of the Supreme Administrative Court (KHO 2002:86, taltionumero 3339) can be found on its website, in Finnish.

131 Para. 6.2.2.1 of its decision.

132 Hollo, et al., *supra* note 73 at 55.

133 Koivurova, RECIEL, 57 (2004).

134 Supreme Administrative Court's decision at para. 6.2.2.4.(a) (*in* ibid.).

135 "even though article 4, paragraphs 1 and 2, are sufficiently clear and unconditional in content for them to have at least in some cases a direct effect binding on the officials of the member states, the Supreme Administrative Court views that … it is not necessary to

3 Final Developments of the Vuotos Project and Conclusion

The Prime Minister, the Regional Council of Lapland,[136] the three municipalities of the Vuotos area (Pelkosienniemi, Savukoski, and Salla), two members of parliament from Finnish Lapland (Timo E. Korva and Hannes Manninen, both from the Centre Party), the Minister of Trade and Industry (Sinikka Mönkäre – Social Democratic Party) expressed their disappointment at the ruling.[137] Advocates of the project started to plan legislative initiatives to counter the judicial outcome of the case – a special law, which would be a derogation from the Water Act.[138] Parliamentary elections were held in March 2003 and a new government was formed in April. Matti Vanhanen was elected Prime Minister. The main parties of the governmental coalition, especially the Prime Minister's Centre Party, vehemently advocated for the construction of the Vuotos dam/reservoir.[139]

However, the ECJ, on 6 March 2003, decided that Finland had breached its obligations under the Wild Birds Directive, by failing to fully and definitely notify its SPAs, in particular by failing to classify as SPAs all the most suitable sites within the meaning of Article 4(1) and (2).[140] In mid-April 2003, the FME proposed again that the Kemihaara mires be designated both as SPA (in accordance with the Wild Birds Directive) and SCI (Site of Community Importance, in accordance with the Habitats Directive). Various Centre Party ministers opposed the FME's proposal. The Kemihaara mires were nonetheless classified on 22 January 2004 and are now in the Natura 2000 network, as both SPA

determine in the context of this permit application whether the obligations of the Wild Birds Directive mentioned would form an obstacle to granting a permit" (para. 6.2.2.2 (*in* Koivurova, RECIEL, 58 (2004)).

136 A joint municipal board, composed of the twenty-one municipalities of Lapland.

137 *Supreme Administrative Court denies building permit for Vuotos reservoir*, HELSINGIN SANOMAT, 19 December 2002. Quoted in that same article, Kemijoki Oy CEO Markku Autti asserted that the coming generations would take up the project again, if dry conditions continued and the greenhouse effect became stronger: "The negative decision on the reservoir did not eliminate the need for regulation power. The location of the Vuotos reservoir would have been ideal. In addition, the construction of the reservoir's power plant would have given jobs to at least 500 people for five years".

138 Governor of Lapland, Hannele Pokka, *Vuotos-päätökseen ei pitäisi tyytyä*, KALEVA (3 January 2003), as mentioned *in* Koivurova, RECIEL, 59 (2004).

139 The vice-chairman of the Centre Party, a member of parliament from Lapland, Hannu Takkula, supported amendments to the Water Act so that the Vuotos Project could be implemented (*Keskusta pitää Vuotosta mukana*, LAPIN KANSA, 4 April 2003; Koivurova, RECIEL, 59 (2004).

140 *Commission v. Finland*, Case C-240/00, ECR 2003 I-02187, ECLI:EU:C:2003:126.

and SCI. Today, about 90% of the conservation areas in Finland are situated in Lapland. The European Union Natura 2000 conservation program encompasses more than 2.9 million hectares of conservation areas in Lapland, i.e. about one-third of the province.

Despite the fact that the area became a Natura 2000 site, the Vuotos project still continued to be supported by some. Four years later, in 2008, the Ministry of Employment and the Economy stated that the project was under consideration.[141] The Minister of Justice, Tuija Brax (Green League), emphasized that the legislation did not allow the construction of a dam in the Vuotos area. The Employment and Economy Minister, Mauri Pekkarinen (Centre Party), favored an overhaul of water management legislation. However, the Council of State stated in a long-term climate and energy strategy, issued at the end of 2008, that the government led by Matti Vanhanen would not, during its term in office, put forward a proposal aimed at amending the Water Act in favor of the Vuotos dam and reservoir project.[142] Kemijoki Oy and the Regional Council of Lapland persisted in their attempt to plan a multifunctional dam (including flood prevention, fishing and windmills). However, the FANC did not consider their plan as a threat because of the state of the law, the classification of the Kemihaara mires as SPA in particular.[143] In later years, further talks took place, locally and within the Centre Party, about changing the law. In 2011, the possibility was once more excluded from the government's program with Jyrki Katainen as Prime Minister, as a strict condition posed by the Green League.[144] The debate has continued unabated, especially in view of the development of nuclear power-based energy. In contrast, hydropower continues to be presented as a cleaner energy source. Nevertheless, no new dam has been constructed since 2001.[145] Furthermore, attempts to reverse the legislation

141 Petteri Kuuva, *The EU goals for Finland and their implementation in Finnish climate and energy strategies*, in NORDIC ENERGY SCENARIOS: SIGNIFICANT IMPACTS ON THE NORDIC ENERGY SYSTEM OF THE EU CLIMATE AND ENERGY POLICY PACKAGE (conference in Helsinki, 14 May 2008).

142 KIM TALUS, et al., ENERGY LAW IN FINLAND 71 (Kluwer Law International. 2010).

143 Tapani Veistola, email of 12 January 2012.

144 Jyrki Katainen (chairman of the National Coalition Party) held office from 22 June 2011 to 24 June 2014. His cabinet was formed after some long and difficult negotiations, which is often the case. It was a right-left coalition of the National Coalition Party, Social Democratic Party, Left Alliance, Green League, Swedish People's party, and Christian Democrats.

145 The last dam was built by Kemijoki Oy in Kelukoski (Lapland) in 1999–2001. As of January 2021, there are about 190 hydropower dams in Finland (in the broadest sense of the term), of which 56 are large dams. Only one large dam/reservoir construction project is currently ongoing (still at the planning phase), the already and farther mentioned Sierilä

on the protection of waterways in view of facilitating dam building served as an impetus for the public to start protesting hydropower and advocating for restoring free-flowing rivers and migratory fish stocks, during the parliamentary elections in 2015. Finland has adopted a dam removal policy since then. Still, in 2016, yet another attempt to revive the Vuotos dam project was made. The Regional Council of Lapland filed an application for a derogation from Natura 2000, which the government rejected on 1 February 2018. This decision was upheld by the Supreme Administrative Court on 11 April 2019.[146]

The primary reasons for the cancellation of the Vuotos project were ecological. Economic arguments were barely touched upon.[147] Economic considerations have only recently been introduced into the political discourse against a proposed hydropower project in Sierilä, on the main course of the Kemi River. The absence of large infrastructure projects like a large reservoir, it is argued, will benefit the region in ecological terms, but also in economic terms because of the important development of nature-based tourism or ecotourism.[148] Protecting the environment has become an immediate necessity in economic terms. This new utilization of nature (nature conservation and tourism) has been evident in the discussions about whether to construct the Sierilä dam. The 2008 expert survey concluded against the project, especially because of its negative repercussions with respect to nature-based tourism.[149] Hitherto, Kemijoki Oy has maintained the Sierilä project, over which disputes are pending in court as of 2020.

The Vuotos case demonstrates that, even in democratic states with a strong consensus regarding the necessity of environmental protection such as in Scandinavia, EIAs may still serve as a useful facilitator of public participation, albeit in a rather informal fashion, like Lynton Caldwell observed.[150] The Vuotos case is an example of the process that took place for developing direct participation in Finland during the 1990's. The decade saw many regulatory

dam, which may be the last project of this type to be allowed. The only other dam project is a medium-sized dam on the Kuhankoski in Laukaa (in central Finland), beside an existing one.

146 Decision No. 1453/2019, ECLI:FI:KHO:2019:T1453 (in Finnish).

147 For instance, the 1992 VATT report was not mentioned in the Vasaa Administrative Court decision (see *supra* page 155).

148 Tourism in Lapland, as a percentage of Lapland GDP and employment, is twice the national average. Tourism contributed 2.6% to the national GDP in 2017. International visitors in Finland have doubled since 2000 (OECD TOURISM TRENDS AND POLICIES 166 (OECD. 2020).

149 Krause, *supra* note 25 at 40.

150 See epigraph *supra* page 140.

reforms that enhanced citizens' participation opportunities, partly due to the legitimacy crisis of representative democracy and political parties. Since then, the importance of public participation in environmental regulations has been limited. For instance, in 2006, the EIA Act became more specific with respect to the parties that have standing;[151] and EIA documents have not been easy to understand for non-experts. Improvements are necessary in order for EIAs to be useful informational documents at the disposal of the general public, which has been a common issue in other countries as well. However, EIAs and TEIAs seem successful even if the participation is quite often limited to a small number of highly motivated activists, who can influence public opinion and gather its support, like in the Vuotos case, where two women successfully acted locally, two others did on the national level, and all four on the international level. Furthermore, there is a growing, general awareness of the fact that anyone can now act and play an important role in protecting the environment and influence the decision-making process.[152]

With respect to the Espoo Convention and international cooperation in environmental matters, the Vuotos case is a striking example of Finland's commitment as well as the facile and historical collaboration with Sweden, which has been quite active because of regular projects near the border. On the institutional plane, states from the Baltic Sea Subregion actively work together to promote the ratification of the Espoo Convention, improve its implementation, general and bilateral cooperation, capacity-building, good practices, etc. through subregional workshops and workplan activities, as well as a close cooperation with the European Union (of which all state members are parties to the Espoo Convention).

The role of local activists, public participation and public opinion was crucial in the Vuotos case. This case seems exemplary also because it took place, not only before the entry into force of the Espoo Convention and the Finnish EIA Act, but also before the Finnish Environmental Protection Act (EPA),

151 Only those whose circumstances or interests may be affected can now participate (1994 EIA Act, Chapter 1, Section 1 – Aim, after amendment 458/2006, restated in EIA Act No. 252/2017, Para. 2 (7)). Does it include national NGOs for instance (with a broader geographical basis than of the related project)? In 1994, the original EIA Act did not specify. It broadly stated "The aim of this Act is to further the assessment of environmental impact and consistent consideration of this impact in planning and decision-making, and at the same time to increase the information available to citizens and their opportunities to participate".

152 See for instance the European Commission survey, *Special Eurobarometer 468: Attitudes of European citizens towards the environment* 45 (2017), where 83% of the respondents in Finland were of this opinion, an improvement from 2014 (+ 9 points).

passed on 4 February 2000 (No. 86/2000). Since the Finnish EPA, the substantive norms that apply to project development have required that the relevant information contained in the EIA be taken into account by the permit decision. A large number of the projects that fall under the EIA Act also entail an integrated environmental permit under the EPA.[153] In the Vuotos case, procedural obligations led to the cancellation of the hydropower project. Despite the chain of endless political compromises and reversals, as well as pressure from major economic actors, the growing efficacy of procedural dynamics has become a powerful and practical instrument in the fight to protect the environment, by raising expectations and guaranteeing that the concerns of stakeholders and affected parties, from states to individuals, be voiced and environmental protection be taken into account, regarding sizeable projects with potential negative impacts of significance.

153 Ismo Pölönen, *Quality control and the substantive influence of environmental impact assessment in Finland*, 26 ENVIRONMENTAL IMPACT ASSESSMENT REVIEW 481, 487 (2006).

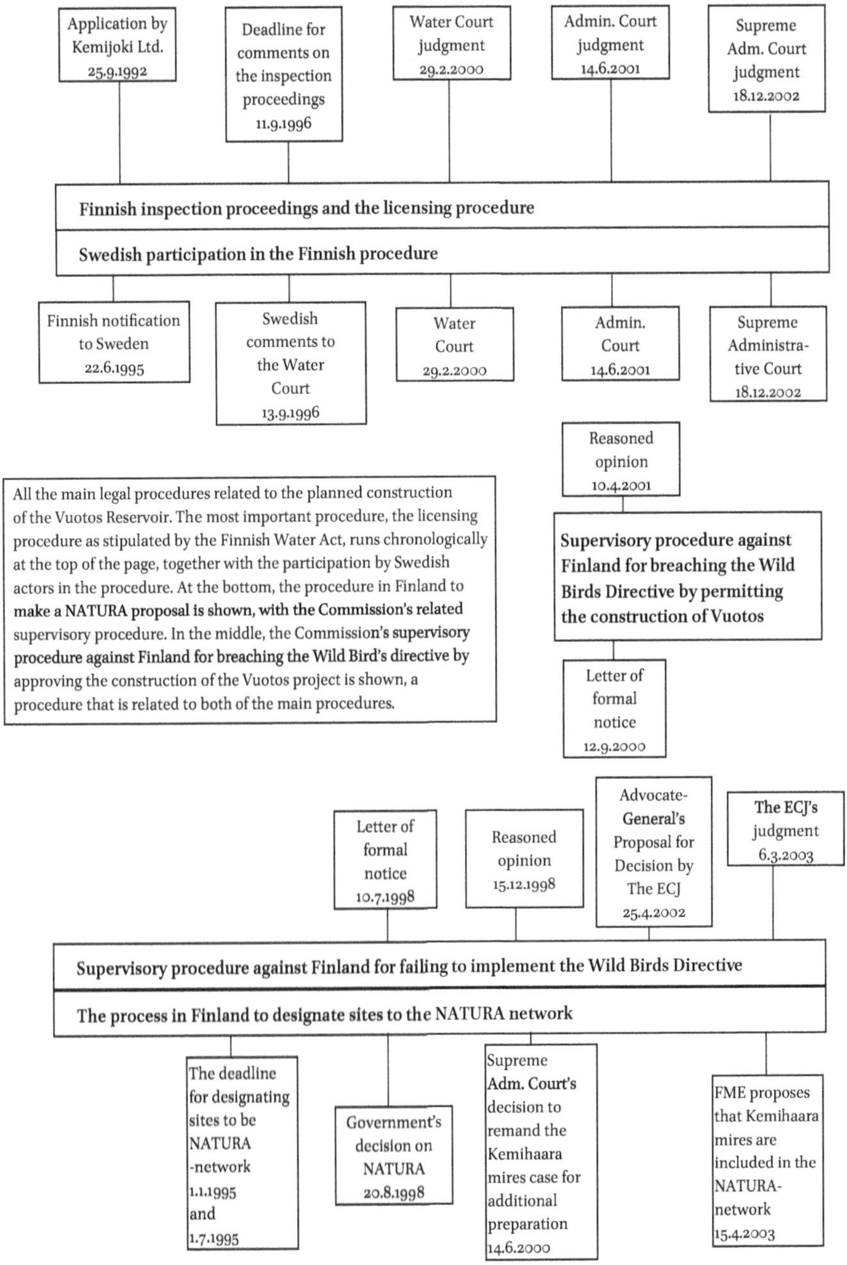

FIGURE 1 Timeline of the main legal proceedings related to the planned construction of the Vuotos reservoir, until 2002.
(Koivurova, The Case of Vuotos 190. 2004. Illustration reproduction courtesy of Timo Koivurova.)

CHAPTER 5

France – Spain Interconnection

1982 – 2015

"Je ne comprends rien à ce que vous dites.
Vous parlez entre vous seulement, pas à nous.
Tout ce que vous dites n'a pas de cœur."
Elle est partie sur ces entrefaites.
Cette dame avait trois fois raison.[1]

∴

On 20 February 2015, in the French Eastern Pyrenees, near the Mediterranean Sea, French and Spanish Prime Ministers Manuel Valls and Mariano Rajoy unveiled what was proudly proclaimed the world's longest onshore, underground Extra High Voltage in Direct Current (EHVDC) electric power line (40 mi – 64.5 km), in addition to some other technological innovations.[2] After an initial test period, the 320,000-volt line began operations on 5 October 2015, with a carrying capacity of 1,400 Mega-Watts (MW), doubling the transmission capacity between the two nations, bringing it to 2,800 MW in total. After more than thirty years, the interconnection project, ultimately called INELFE (*INterconnexion ELectrique France Espagne*),[3] was finally achieved. As of 2021, five interconnections have been established between France and Spain. While

1 "'I understand nothing of what you are saying. You only speak to each other, not to us. Everything you say is heartless.' And then she left. On all three counts, she was right" (author's translation), Michel Badré (President of the French Environmental Authority from 2009 to 2014), when asked what impressed him the most during the public debates that he attended during his mandate (15 March 2016 interview).

2 It was the first time that two times 1,000 MW VSC stations (Voltage Sourced Converter) had been built, as well as a cross-linked polyethylene (XLPE) cable in direct current (DC) at 320kV. It led to manage a DC interconnector embedded in an alternate current (AC) grid, which was also a first (Yves Decœur, CEO of INELFE, 1 April 2015 interview).

3 INELFE was also the name of the project proponent as later decided, in 2008 (see *infra* note 148).

 | DOI:10.1163/9789004467583_006

Extra-High Voltage (EHV) power lines[4] built overhead have been the target of systematic opposition, these protests were largely unsuccessful in France until the temporary cancellation of this EHV line project in 1996 and its subsequent modification, which came as a watershed moment for environmental law in France.

France and its public company, *Electricité de France* (EDF), has been among the leading countries in the electricity sector. For the project studied in this chapter, the proponent in Spain was ENDESA at first, followed by *Red Eléctrica de España* (REE) in 1985. In France, it was initially EDF, then RTE (in 2000, when transmission activities were separated from power generation ones) and then INELFE (a joint venture with Spain, created in 2008 as a temporary entity for this particular project), both subsidiaries of EDF.[5] EDF has excelled in its field since its inception in 1946, the product of the nationalization of about 1,700 smaller energy companies. The state-owned company held a monopoly until 2007.[6] Nevertheless, EDF still enjoys a factual monopoly because consumers either are unaware of, or do not yet trust, the new energy companies that have been created since 2007. With its interlocutors (government members, local officials, elected representatives on all levels, NGOs, inhabitants, etc.), EDF's and its subsidiaries' attitude has dramatically marked the decision-making process. French engineers are aware of their degree of excellence and have had difficulties to accept the necessity of public participation.[7] Despite some progress and some new obligations, EDF has still tended to behave as if able to decide unilaterally what is the general interest, at times challenging the government.[8] This is in keeping with a deeply engrained tradition

4 It is generally agreed that *Low Voltage* is up to 1,000V; *Medium Voltage*: 1,000V to 35kV; *High Voltage*: 35kV to 230kV; *Extra High Voltage*: above 220kV; *Ultra High Voltage*: above 800kV.

5 Historically, the utility companies involved in trans-Pyrenean projects were in France, UPEPO (*Union des Producteurs d'Electricité des Pyrénées Orientales*) between 1922 and 1946, then EDF (Electricité de France) until 2000, then RTE (*Réseau de Transport d'Electricité*) until 2008, a wholly subsidiary of EDF, exclusively in charge of the transmission/distribution activities, and lastly INELFE for this particular project at first, then for all subsequent projects.

6 Its monopoly was repealed in application of Directive 2003/54/EC of the European Parliament and of the Council of 26 June 2003 concerning common rules for the internal market in electricity, and repealing Directive 96/92/EC (OJ L 176, 15 July 2003, p. 37–56). In December 2015, EDF also lost its place in the CAC40 stock index mainly because it traded too thinly (only 14.5% of its capital) and because its shares had lost 45% due to the end of its monopoly.

7 Michel Badré, former President of the French Environmental Authority, has emphasized that French engineers' reluctance in this regard was a real issue (15 March 2016 interview).

8 See Alain Juppé's comment about when he found himself pitted against EDF as Prime Minister in 1996, *in* RAPHAËLLE BACQUÉ, L'ENFER DE MATIGNON 169–170 (Albin Michel. 2008). See *infra* page 214.

reaching back to the French Revolution. French high civil servants, those in EDF included, have been charged with determining the general interest.[9] EDF has been described as a state within the state (in a manner comparable to Kemijoki Oy in Finland, see *supra* chapter 4), which has, as such, inevitably provoked and irritated many. Besides, EDF often moves quite rapidly to complete its power line projects, possibly for the two following reasons: to benefit from the principle of intangibility of public works,[10] and perhaps also because, once a power line is in place, nearby residents tend to accustom themselves to it apace, which usually puts an end to their protests.[11] What was different in the INELFE case? Why did it take decades to build this EHV line, find a suitable route, and why did affected residents in France succeed in having the line built underground, at great expense?

1 General Presentation and Historical Context of the Interconnection Case

1.1 *History of the Electrical Infrastructure in the Pyrenees*

Historically, the Pyrenees were modernized at the beginning of the 20th century thanks to abundant and cheap electricity, by virtue of hydropower (nicknamed *houille blanche*, which means "white coal", by contrast with the main source of energy then, i.e. coal). The landscape of the Pyrenees was dramatically altered by numerous dams as a result, which became touristic attractions and remain so to this day. Nearly all mountain valleys were heavily equipped with hydro-electrical installations, including not only dams, but also the

9 See Alphonse de Lamartine's speech, *Intervention du 9 mai 1838 à la Chambre des députés sur l'organisation des chemins de fer*, *in* LA POLITIQUE DE LAMARTINE, CHOIX DE DISCOURS ET ECRITS POLITIQUES 173 (Hachette. 1878); PIERRE ROSANVALLON, LE MODÈLE POLITIQUE FRANÇAIS, LA SOCIÉTÉ CIVILE CONTRE LE JACOBINISME DE 1789 À NOS JOURS 395–401 (Seuil. 2004).

10 See Conseil d'Etat, 7 July 1853, *Robin de la Grimaudière*. However, this principle has been on the decline when it comes to private land that was built upon by mistake (Conseil d'Etat, 19 April 1991, No. 78275, *Epoux Denard*; Cour de cassation, Ass. plén., 6 January 1994, No. 89-17049, *Cts Baudon de Mony c/ EDF*; Tribunal des Conflits, 6 May 2002, *M. & Mme Binet*; Conseil d'Etat, 29 January 2003, No. 245239, *Syndicat départemental de l'électricité et du gaz des Alpes-Maritimes*; Conseil d'Etat, 14 October 2011, No. 320371, *Commune de Valmeinier*).

11 Caroline Gagnon, *Paysage, transport d'électricité et esthétique du quotidien. De la confrontation au moins pire*, *in* LES PAYSAGES DE L'ÉLECTRICITÉ. PERSPECTIVES HISTORIQUES ET ENJEUX CONTEMPORAINS (XIXE–XXIE SIÈCLES) 233–234 (Christophe Bouneau, et al. eds., 2012).

extensions or formation of lakes, aqueducts, access roads, pipes and tunnels. Dams and overhead transmission lines were quite naturally seen and featured as a positive sign of progress then. They meant light, heating, the development of easy transportation, by road and by train, hence also the development of tourism especially, all of which favored the economic prosperity of the Pyrenees. At first, railroads and power lines usually followed the old Roman and pilgrimage roads (such as the *Via Domitia* or the *Via Vallesperi*). The roads built for construction works are still in service today and are used to connect villages.[12] Roman architectural sites were rediscovered and put on display. The sites built during the original construction of the energy infrastructure also continue to provide service (for instance, cable cars, site buildings now used as hotels or shelters for hikers). Thanks to the electric utility companies' investments, tourism developed considerably, for several reasons: the beauty of the natural landscape, availability of outdoor sport activities, abundant cultural heritage and imposing hydropower installations (dams and lakes). At first, the power lines chiefly served two local purposes: providing electricity for railroad lines and transporting the rest of the electricity for light and heating, fulfilling a public service mission. Other needs have since emerged. Public service has been gradually replaced by the marketization of electricity, conducted on a grander scale than the areas where EHV power lines are being installed. These new lines do not serve local needs, but form a critical part of the European electrical grid. Besides, EHV power lines represent a considerably more imposing and noticeable apparatus in the landscape – gone are the days of simple cables on plain wood poles.

The Pyrenees are 267 miles (430 km) long, cover 7,336 square miles (19,000 km2), have more than two hundred summits higher than 9,842 feet (3,000 meters).[13] These mountains mark the French/Spanish border. From time immemorial, the inhabitants of the different valleys progressively and rather peacefully agreed on border delimitation, thanks to agreements they called *lies et passeries* ("alliance and peace/passage/pasturage"). Later treaties followed (the 1659 Pyrenees Treaty and the 1856–1866 Bayonne Treaties).[14] The

12 At present, any of the remotest hamlets is at most a half-hour away from the nearest town; highways and airports are also close.

13 The highest peak is the Aneto, in Spain (11,168 feet – 3,404 meters).

14 The frontier was also signaled by a change in track gauges until recently. French track gauge is standard (1,435 mm –4' 8 1/2") whereas in Spain, the track gauge is 1,674 mm (about 5'6"). The Spanish railroad network was achieved in 1870. As in Russia, a wider track gauge was dictated as a defensive measure in light of the then recent Napoleonic invasions, but later became an obstacle to international trade. Besides, building such wide railroads was expensive, especially in the mountainous regions where railroads with

inhabitants have always felt strongly about their valleys and the whole chain, which is quite typical of mountain residents.

Trans-Pyrenean railroad/electric line projects began in 1907. When this latest interconnection project started in the 1970's, it was for the same usual reason: interconnection was generally needed because electricity could not be effectively stored. Another reason had gained importance: building an electrical network makes it possible to secure supply and adjust it to demand, which in turn limits the number of power generation sites that are necessary. EHV power lines enable the formation of a wide-area synchronous electrical grid. The grid in Continental Europe is currently the largest in the world, with a synchronized frequency of 50 hertz (Hz) since the 1960's (it is 60 Hz in North America). Since the inter-war period, engineers have conducted studies showing the advantages of interconnection, which developed at the end of the 1940's in Europe. Engineers from the lead countries in the domain of electricity (Belgium, France, Germany, Italy, Switzerland) had been interested in the French-Spanish interconnection since the 1930's, because it addresses a structural challenge brought about by complementary capacities: France has substantial hydro-electrical capabilities during summer whereas Spain has more of these in winter. However, the latter was excluded from the Marshall plan at the time, because of the Francoist regime. Consequently, interconnection between France and Spain developed later than in the rest of Europe. Driven by economic considerations, and in particular to fight off the American influence, France began normalizing relationships with Spain. As a result, the first interconnection was agreed upon in 1952, in the Basque country, between Hendaye and Hernani (about 14 miles – 23 km). It was a long-term contract, over twenty years, according to which electricity would be provided by Spain in winter and by France in summer. Cooperation was thus launched in this domain between the two countries. A first HV line (220 kV) was built in the Central Pyrenees in 1954, between the hydropower plant of Pragnères in France and Sabiñanigo in Spain, with absolutely no consideration for the landscape.[15] The French *Service*

a smaller width were built, which isolated them even more. By the end of the 1960's, an adaptation system allowed some trains to go to France, in addition to a conversion system that spared all passengers to change trains. Recently, high-speed railroads with the same standard track gauge in both countries were built.

15 Situated on the territory of the town of Gèdre, the Pragnères hydropower plant is the most complex and powerful one of the Pyrenees. About thirty water connections get water from three mountain ranges (Néouvielle, Vignemale and Ardiden). There are several reservoirs: a main reservoir at Cap-de-Long, three annex ones (Aumar, Aubert, Escoubous) and a daily one, Ossoue. There is a 0.78-mile-high penstock on the right bank (1,250-meter high).

de protection des sites ("Sensitive Areas Protection Department") had protested the chosen route, via the *Cirque de Gavarnie*, home of the legendary Roland's Breach in the anticipated Pyrenees National Park. Addressing the concerns of the *Service de protection des sites* would have multiplied the cost by four. EDF thus built the line by the cirque and through the future Pyrenees National Park. Aesthetic or ecological reasons were simply dismissed at the time.[16] However, decades later, in 1996, EDF would offer to dismantle the Pragnères-Sabiñanigo overhead power line to compensate for the new 400 kV line project (the object of this case study) when it was being planned between Cazaril and Aragón in the Central Pyrenees. EDF ultimately did not proceed with this offer because the Cazaril-Aragón project was cancelled. As a result, the Pragnères-Sabiñanigo power line stayed in place. Nowadays, hikers often mention this HV line that they see and hear from the famous GR10 hiking trail. In 1956, a third power line, of 150 kV, was built between Luchon and Benós, through the Aran Valley in the Central Pyrenees, close to the Pragnères- Sabiñanigo line. Spain became one of the main partners of France, its second source of electricity imports. In addition to the Pragnères- Sabiñanigo line in the Central Pyrenees, another 220 kV line was built in the Western Pyrenees in the early 1960's (between Cantegrit in the Landes department, and Ormáiztegui in the Spanish Basque country). In 1961, cooperation between France and Spain was institutionalized with the UFEPTE (called UFIPTE after the inclusion of Portugal the year after).[17] In 1964, the Eastern Pyrenees were also interconnected with an EHV (380 kV) line between La Gaudière (near Perpignan) and Rubí, in the suburb of Barcelona – the interconnection has now become the Baixas-Vic 400 kV-line, as a result of the connection with Baixas.

During the 1970's, Spain resorted less to France for its power needs. To address this slowdown, the UFIPTE suggested the development of daily exchanges, not only seasonal ones, by taking advantage of the time gap in the electricity consumption between the two countries; peak of consumption is at around 7 pm in France, whereas it is at around 10 pm in Spain. To this end, in 1972, the Cantegrit-Ormáiztegui line was raised to 380 kV (the line is now 400 kV). Until the 1980's, France was mostly an electricity importer, from Switzerland first,

---

16 The same had happened in 1951, with a 110 kV transmission line between Hendaye and Mouguerre in the Basque country. The inhabitants and the Architecture Department at the Education Ministry had vigorously protested, in vain.

17 *Union Franco-Espagnle (Franco-Ibérique) Pour la coordination de la Production et du Transport d'Electricité* (Franco-Spanish, then Franco-Iberian, Union for Coordinating the Production and Transmission of Electricity), composed of representatives of the electricity industry from the three countries.

then Spain. In the 1980's, France became the first exporter in Europe, thanks to the development of its nuclear industry. Consequently, interconnection development also dates back to the development of this French nuclear industry, especially after the 1973 oil shock and the need to monetize via export the electricity produced in excess of domestic needs. EDF has had a competitive advantage because of its nuclear power plant complex, the second largest in the world, composed of fifty-six reactors as of 2021, producing almost 71% of French electricity (it was already 70% in 1986). The country is the largest net exporter thanks to low generation costs, but environmental costs are generally not included.[18] EDF has emphasized that increasing exports meant cheaper prices for domestic consumers. However, to this end, EDF needs to build costly EHV transmission lines, sometimes through beautiful virgin mountain valleys like in this case study. Spain has also increasingly needed these sorts of lines since the early 2000's, as its renewable energy (solar and wind) production occasionally yields a surplus. Spain has been the second-largest European wind power producer, behind Germany. Thus, since the first half of the 20th century and until recently, for the majority of engineers, the constant development of interconnection had been seen a natural and inevitable progression for the greater good,[19] and the influence of engineers within the French state has been quite compelling.

At present, as part of the completion process of the European Union Internal Energy Market (IEM), the new interconnection, the object of this case study, has been mostly dedicated to commercial trade between France and Spain, but also Portugal and North Africa. The European Union (EU), of which France is a founding member and which Spain joined in 1986, has long worked intensively

18 ECOFYS, SUBSIDIES AND COSTS OF EU ENERGY SUMMARY, p. i (European Commission. 2014).

19 "All the electrical engineers that work for the UPEPO are subject to the same industrial discipline and take communion in what truly is a blind belief in interconnection. *Mysticism* is not too strong a word to describe their state of mind. They consider themselves as an elite" (CHRISTOPHE BOUNEAU, MODERNISATION ET TERRITOIRE. L'ÉLECTRIFICATION DU GRAND SUD-OUEST DE LA FIN DU XIXÈME SIÈCLE À 1946 299 (Fédération historique du Sud-Ouest. 1997) (author's translation)). See also Christophe Bouneau, *Les réseaux de transport d'électricité en Europe occidentale depuis la fin du XIXe siècle: de la diversité des modèles nationaux à la recherche de la convergence européenne*, 2 ANNALES HISTORIQUES DE L'ÉLECTRICITÉ 23, 30 (2004). In the 1950's, some, like Giovanni Silva (UNIPEDE Interconnection Committee President), went as far as saying "Far beyond technical considerations, and as silently as tirelessly, we will always strive to secure a future of peace and happiness" (author's translation) *in* RENAN VIGUIÉ, LA TRAVERSÉE ÉLECTRIQUE DES PYRÉNÉES – HISTOIRE DE L'INTERCONNEXION ENTRE LA FRANCE ET L'ESPAGNE 14–15 (P.I.E. Peter Lang. 2014).

towards building an integrated and competitive common energy market, also for energy independence reasons, thanks to a well-interconnected grid.[20] The benefits of integration (as opposed to national self-sufficiency) were projected to represent an annual cost saving of up to 35 billion euros in 2015 compared to 2012,[21] and up to 40 billion by 2030.[22] It took decades to approach completion of the EU electricity market[23] for four main reasons: resistance to opening up national monopolies' territories to outsiders; an absence of a wave of technological innovation – as was the case with the telecoms – to challenge the incumbent energy giants; the difficulties associated with trading electricity as a commodity (numerous technical, legal and economical rules and standards must be agreed upon before it being tradeable); the diverse national agreements between industry actors and public authorities which hindered a merger into a common project of interoperable markets.[24] The revolution in information and communication technologies (the ICT revolution) made new market arrangements in the electricity sector possible. New technologies have provided the means to register electricity production and consumption alike – thus enabling bilateral trading. The 1996 Electricity Directive and its transposition into national law by EU member states constituted one of the first steps towards the IEM.[25] The Electricity Directive set up common rules in

20 In this view, on the institutional level, ENTSO-E (European Network of Transmission System Operators for Electricity) replaced UCPTE (*Union pour la Coordination de la Production et de la Transmission d'électricité*, which had become UCTE in 1991), in 2009.

21 EUROPEAN COMMISSION, ENERGY CHALLENGES AND POLICY – COMMISSION CONTRIBUTION TO THE EUROPEAN COUNCIL OF 22 MAY 2013 5 (2013). (Estimation made by the Agency for the Cooperation of Energy Regulators (ACER)).

22 Booz&COMPANY, FINAL REPORT – BENEFITS OF AN INTEGRATED EUROPEAN ENERGY MARKET 4, 78 & 89 (Directorate-General Energy – European Commission. 2013).

23 Launched in 1985, see WHITE PAPER ON "COMPLETING THE INTERNAL MARKET" FOR THE EUROPEAN COUNCIL OF JUNE 1985 (COM (85) 310 final)). Incidentally, one may observe that the term "single market" would have been preferable to "internal market" (MARIO MONTI, A NEW STRATEGY FOR THE SINGLE MARKET, AT THE SERVICE OF EUROPE'S ECONOMY AND SOCIETY, REPORT TO THE PRESIDENT OF THE EUROPEAN COMMISSION, JOSÉ MANUEL BARROSO 13, FN 1 (2010)).

24 "This very demanding market arrangement meant that electricity was considered to be a typical "anti-market" product for decades, which was best suited to monopolies or cartels" (Jean-Michel Glachant, *The three ages of Europe's single electricity market*, *in* EU'S INTERNAL ENERGY MARKET: TOUGH DECISIONS AND A DAUNTING AGENDA 34 (Friends of Europe ed., 2013)).

25 Directive 96/92/EC of the European Parliament and of the Council of 19 December 1996 concerning common rules for the internal market in electricity (OJ L 27, 30 January 1997, p. 20–29). See also Directive 2009/72/EC of the European Parliament and of the Council of 13 July 2009 concerning common rules for the internal market in electricity and repealing Directive 2003/54/EC (OJ L 211, 14 August 2009, p. 55–93).

this regard. Unbundling was required in order to achieve equal access to the different networks and to avoid conflicts of interest. Consequently, upstream and downstream activities (production and supply) had to be separated from transmission/distribution network operations.[26] France transposed the Electricity Directive in 2000,[27] and consequently transferred the transmission activities of EDF to a new company, *Réseau de Transport d'Electricité* (RTE), which then became the project proponent in the case under study here.[28] The construction of a transmission line to expand the interconnection grid is a long, technical process, which supplements the four reasons for the slow development of the European IEM mentioned above. In February 2015, the Italian Borders Market Coupling was launched a few days after the inauguration of the latest France-Spain interconnection, marking another significant step towards the IEM. The majority of the EU power markets are now linked, which allows the simultaneous calculation of electricity prices and cross-border flows. Since 1994, France-Spain electrical interconnection has been thus a priority of the European Union. To further progress, in 2014, the European Council established an interconnection target throughout the EU, with all member states having been encouraged to attain an interconnection capacity equivalent to at least 10% of their national generation capacity by 2020, and 15% by 2030. With the new EHV power line, France's and Spain's interconnection capacity dramatically increased.[29] France and Spain each paid half of the total cost of the latest power line (700 million euros) with the help of the

26 *Transmission* refers to the transport of electricity on the extra-high (230,000 volts and above) and high-voltage (from 35kV to 230kV) interconnected systems; *distribution* refers to the transport of electricity on medium-voltage and low-voltage distribution systems (between 1,000 volts and 35kV).

27 *Loi No. 2000–108 du 10 février 2000 relative à la modernisation et au développement du service public de l'électricité.*

28 RTE was created on 1 July 2000. Wholly subsidiary of EDF, RTE fulfils a public service mission for international connections. It serves as the French electricity transmission system operator. At first, RTE's supervisory authority was the *Direction du Gaz, de l'Electricité et du Charbon* (DIGEC), part of the Industry Ministry. Since 2008, RTE's supervisory authority has been the *Direction Générale de l'Energie et du Climat* (DGEC), part of the Environment Ministry.

29 Each country should have in place electricity cables that allow at least 10%, then 15% of the electricity produced by its power plants to be transported across its borders to neighboring countries (at https://eur-lex.europa.eu/legal-content/EN/ALL/?uri=CELEX%3A52014DC0330, accessed 17 June 2021). The calculation of interconnection rates is complex and in constant evolution, depending on the installed capacity and the different kinds of power generation systems. Moreover, import and export capacities may differ in certain cases.

EU.[30] Both France and Spain faced strong opposition from their citizens, environmental NGOs and local authorities when it became known that the proposed 400,000-volt line was to be built overhead, suspended by 70-meter (76.5 yard) high pylons carrying several cables, placed every 500 meters (0.3 miles or more, depending on the terrain), along a path 15-meters (16 yards) wide. In each of the two countries, people joined and united to protest for the same mix of reasons, both procedural and substantial.

1.2 *Emergence of the Opposition to Interconnection Power Lines*

The Spanish opposition emphasizes the crucial role of the opposition in France in obtaining successful results in their common fight against the overhead EHV power line project.[31] Some have argued that Spain experienced fewer protests because it was at an earlier stage of economic development, it had a greater need for additional electricity, the impacts of such a project were not well advertised and there were less regulation and fewer environmental protection concerns.[32] In Catalonia, it seems true that they opposed the line at too late a stage, there were fewer procedural requirements for public participation, a stronger sense of urgency and locally elected officials were more obedient to their political parties. However, the opposition in Aragón and then later in Catalonia was as strong as in France.[33] In any case, if international cooperation was conclusive at the grassroots level, and at the project proponent level (INELFE) ultimately, the decisive outcome came from France.

As for the reasons of the opposition, they were of two different sorts. Firstly, in procedural terms, the population was upset about the absence of an inclusive decision-making process and felt deprived of the chance to having their say. Since the 1970's, they have demanded that project proponents provide

---

30 The breakdown of the 700M€ was as follows: 230 for the cables and the installation works, 350 for the two converter substations, 110 for the tunnel, 10 for overhead costs. RTE bore some additional 20 million euros for the adaptation of the electrical station in Baixas, which needed to be linked to the converter substation.

31 Josefina Loste, Mayor of San Juan de Plan, in the Chistau Valley, from 1983 to 1995 (5 August 2015 interview). Jose Maria Fantova Aused, head of the most active Spanish association against the EHV power line project, and later Mayor of Plan (from 1997 to 2005), one of the few other villages of the Chistau Valley (26 October 2015 email).

32 VIGUIÉ, 137 & 144. 2014.

33 Michel Geoffre, 9 June 2015 interview. Olivier Fillieule, *Local Environmental Politics in France: Case of the Louron Valley, 1984–1996*, 1 FRENCH POLITICS 305 (2003). Manuel Escolá Hernando, *Question écrite E-3609/98 posée à la Commission européenne*, JOURNAL OFFICIEL DES COMMUNAUTÉES EUROPÉENNES 89 (1999). José Villanueva, *El acuerdo para mejorar la conexión eléctrica con Francia reaviva la amenaza de la Aragón-Cazaril*, HERALDO DE ARAGÓN, 14 October 2014.

some clear justification for any project that affect them. This is especially true in the case of power lines because they are often situated quite close to residences and are visible from much farther away. The Pyrenees were already well-equipped in terms of electricity, so Pyreneans questioned what the French state and EDF had determined to be the common good in this case. They no longer trusted the expertise of public officials and EDF representatives, and educated themselves on the subject. Additionally, thanks to the decentralization process in France that had begun in the 1980's, French locally elected officials had more power, as well as more responsibilities. Both inhabitants and their elected representatives on the municipal, departmental, and regional levels wanted to participate in the decision-making process. Finally, a power struggle had been brewing between EDF and national political authorities. The difficulties to dialog with EDF, its lofty attitude and sheer power eventually irritated citizens and elected officials alike.

Substantially, at first, people protested because of the detrimental effects the construction would bring to the landscape. The first route was planned through beautiful valleys, which were among the very few that had been preserved from any alteration. The French Louron Valley and the Aragonese Chistau Valley were still pastoral and pristine, devoid of any visible modern equipment. They were among the last preserved valleys and many wanted to defend their wilderness status.[34] Later, no matter where the line was planned, citizens also wanted to defend the interests of the tourism and viticulture sectors that they had developed, or had planned to develop significantly. Populations were also concerned about their health. Even though the reality of their effects on human health still seems uncertain and remains controversial, overhead EHV power lines are usually feared as a cause of cancer. For these three reasons, French regional authorities had already begun effort to bury local power lines. They were thus upset at EDF for not planning to do the same with the new interconnection line. Regarding the necessity of the EHV line, people were ready to accept it for reasons of mutual assistance and grid security, but certainly not for trade. They were well aware that the line was no longer destined to deliver local service, but to trade power on the European Union market without any immediate benefit for the region, only extensive inconveniences. When it became known the line was being planned not far from some villages or towns, the strongest opposition was triggered by health concerns. People feared the low frequency ElectroMagnetic Field (EMF) of an overhead

34 Jacques Guiu, President of the Pyrenees National Park in France from 1982 to 1989 (4 August 2015 interview). Josefina Loste, 5 August 2015 interview. Jose Maria Fantova Aused, 26 October 2015 email. See *infra* Marc-Ambroise Rendu, note 37.

line, especially for their young children. Numerous studies linking EMF exposure to leukemia were debated. Many experts explained that, because this disease has so many possible causes, it is difficult to isolate the effects of an EHV line, if any. The EMF decreases quite rapidly as one moves away from the line. After twenty years of research, at the actual norm that has been set for the magnetic field, i.e. no more than 100 microteslas (100µT),[35] these experts were positively convinced that there were no effects on health (underneath a power line, magnetic fields can be about 25µT maximum. 100µT is the magnetic field when a person is right by the line). Residents were not convinced, however. The French project proponent insisted that the electromagnetic field would pose no more danger than coffee, according to the WHO,[36] but opponents did not trust the WHO or any expert who concluded that EMFs were harmless. A few other experts reckoned that there was evidence of high risks of cancer. In light of this controversy, residents invoked the precautionary principle, insisting that the line be buried. In case of an underground line in alternative current (AC), some technical adjustments would have been required: while the ground provides protection from the effects of the electrical field, it does not provide such protection from the magnetic one. The solution was to increase the voltage, which generates the electrical field, and decrease the intensity, which generates the magnetic field, resulting in the same amount of electricity that is transmitted (electricity = intensity x voltage). In case of an underground line in direct current (DC), there is no EMF. In this case, DC was adopted eventually. Activists emphasized health issues to gather as much opposition as possible since health issues usually and obviously gather the most support for environmental protection.

As for the landscape, its beauty was defended independently, as a legitimate cause for concern in and of itself.[37] Some emphasized that it was being

---

35 European Council Recommendation 1999/519/EC of 12 July 1999 on the limitation of exposure of the general public to electromagnetic fields. In France, *décret* No. 2002–775 of 3 May 2002. In Spain, *Real Decreto No. 1066/2001, de 28 de septiembre 2001.*

36 WHO, *Electromagnetic fields and public health – Exposure to extremely low frequency fields* (2007) *at* http://www.who.int/peh-emf/publications/facts/fs322/en/# (accessed 17 June 2021). The WHO declared that it was sympathetic to the difference between what experts conclude and what the public think, which would be taken into account in its reports. This was all the more important considering the fact that the most extended research had already been done and, as a result, research budgets would decrease in this field, to be allocated to the most apparent credible causes of leukemia (CPDP, COMPTE-RENDU DU DÉBAT PUBLIC SUR LE PROJET DE LIAISON ÉLECTRIQUE THT ENTRE LA FRANCE ET L'ESPAGNE 27 (2003)).

37 "nobody dares to defend the French landscape, for it is not possible to appraise it in monetary terms. Everybody forgets that it is a unique source of tourism. An old cultural and

unfairly sacrificed in poor areas. Both in France and in Spain, the two main valleys affected by the power line project had been preserved to a point that they had not yet seen substantial tourism. They were quite poor, still very rural and used to the old ways of living. From an economic standpoint, no matter where the line was then planned in the Pyrenees, the landscape and its integrity were critical especially to viticulture and tourism.[38] It was widely and repeatedly noted that the landscape was truly exceptional and unique to the region both in terms of identity and economy.[39] Once they have arrived, tourists do not stay in one place, they move around, by car mostly (not by plane), which makes the landscape of the whole region even more essential to a prosperous tourism sector. An overhead transmission line would have spoiled many panoramic views. As regards tourism, France ranks first worldwide and the Pyrenees are one of the most touristic areas of the country. On the other hand, the nuclear industry, which produces almost 72% of the electricity in France, also represents a major part of the French GDP. Pyreneans defended their regional economic prosperity against the interests of EDF and the nuclear energy industry. They argued that France needed to protect all its landscapes if it wanted to continue attracting tourists. In addition, they expressed that they had already suffered enough national equipment that had been installed and damaged their region.[40]

Even though they accepted that an additional interconnection was necessary to maintain lower electricity prices, activists were against the new line as a means of development of an electricity market based on the continuous development and exploitation of the nuclear plants in France, which carries the additional burden of nuclear waste disposal. Activists in both France and Spain were against nuclear energy in general and in favor of local renewable energy production plants. When the opposition movement spread, the IEM

---

social heritage? Not a word. It being irreplaceable? No one cares. Government officials in charge of culture, urban planning, or the environment feel no responsibility for the 'decor' ". (Marc Ambroise-Rendu, *"Haute tension" au-dessus des Pyrénées*, LE MONDE, 20 August 1985) (author's translation).

38 Numbers were provided: in 2001, tourism represented one billion euros per year, a 12% increase over ten years, and one job out of two (CPDP, 24. 2003).

39 Rey, *Conclusions du commissaire du gouvernement sous le jugement Tribunal administratif de Pau, 16 décembre 1994*, CAHIERS JURIDIQUES DE L'ELECTRICITÉ ET DU GAZ (CJEG) 109, 112–113 (Mars 1994); Le Délégué Régional à l'Architecture et à l'Environnement (DRAE) de Midi-Pyrénées, *Avis sur le dossier établi par EDF pour la déclaration d'utilité publique et comprenant l'étude d'impact du tronçon Cazaril-Port de la Pez d'une ligne à 2 circuits 400kV Cazaril-Aragon* (1985); CPDP, 24. 2003.

40 High-Speed Rail (HSR) line, aqueduct project between the Rhône River and Spanish Catalonia, highway expansion, gas pipeline project … (CPDP, 17. 2003).

and nuclear energy became the main reasons of the opposition of the green activist leaders.[41] In France, part of the interconnection plan was also to put the Golfech nuclear plant into service, but one of the presidential candidates, François Mitterrand had promised not to build this nuclear plant. However, once elected (in 1981 and again in 1988), Mitterrand did not keep his promise and the plant was commissioned in 1991. Deceived by electoral promises, opponents were all the more motivated. They argued that France should not bear most of the burden of electricity production and that Spain should build enough of its own power plants to serve its domestic needs. Spanish opponents were of the same opinion. Later in the process, most of them accepted that a new line was necessary for the security of the grid and the enhancement of the production. They also realized that Spain not only imports, but also exports considerable quantities of electricity to France, thanks to its excess production of renewable energy. Nonetheless, they still rejected the trade aspects of the project.

In a nutshell, in both countries, people vigorously objected to a central government and a national utility company that were trying to impose their will without taking their concerns into account and appeared to be serving national mercantile interests to the detriment of their region – its physical integrity, the health of its inhabitants and its local economy. For these reasons, they firmly refused any compensation. Any such offer even irritated them. They did not want any overhead power line under any circumstances.

2 The Fifth Interconnection between France and Spain

Building the latest interconnection between France and Spain took a considerable amount of time. Over more than two decades (from 1982 to 2008), EDF consistently refused to amend its project to have the line built in direct current or buried underground, at first claiming it was technically impossible,[42] then that it was too expensive. At times, EDF offered superficial, almost ludicrous

41 Interestingly, the first time that civil society successfully mobilized against a major infrastructure project in France had been against a nuclear power plant project (in Plogoff, Brittany). Launched in 1974, the project was cancelled in 1981 by François Mitterrand, the newly elected French President, fulfilling an electoral promise.

42 In 1986, EDF had built the EHVDC Cross-Channel power line (270kV) between France and the United Kingdom, which was 45mi (73km) long, but this line connects two non-synchronous grids. The technical possibility to connect in DC two synchronous grids, such as France's and Spain's, in parallel with AC links, took longer to achieve (Yves Decœur, 1 April 2015 interview).

responses: they would install the line in the shade and paint the pylons in green. Christian Huglo, the opposition lead counsel, protested the incongruity and asked what EDF would do in wintertime, when it snows ...[43] EDF and REE insisted on having an overhead line because underground lines are singularly expensive (about ten times the price of an overhead line). Over long distances, power lines need to be in DC. As they are usually inserted in an AC grid, the two necessary converter substations (to transform the current from DC to AC and vice versa) are the reason for the high cost. In this particular case, the converter substations eventually cost 350 million euros, i.e. half of the line budget. They are actual power plants spanning several hectares.[44] Underground power lines are considered to have some important advantages: they have no impact on the avifauna, no disturbing EMF when in DC and, of course, no impact on the landscape. Additionally, maintenance on these lines tends to be cheaper (they are protected from the weather and other external events that affect overhead power lines).

The project of building a fifth trans-Pyrenean line began long ago, in the 1970's. As described above, the interconnection grid across France and Spain then consisted of four trans-Pyrenean lines. Two of them are EHV lines (Cantegrit-Argia-Hernani and Baixas-Vic). Since 1976, EDF had been studying the possibility of increasing exchanges with Spain. The construction of a fifth trans-Pyrenean line was part of the scheduled increase in transmission capacity in the region. The first formal agreement took place in 1982 between the two heads of state, François Mitterrand and Felipe González, followed in France by a decision of the Prime Minister, Laurent Fabius, in 1984. EDF started to plan an overhead 380 kV power line in the Basque country in the Western Pyrenees. This project was then dropped because of the risks of attacks from the separatist group ETA.[45] As early as 1983, EDF was also aware of the increasing risks of easily-launched attacks on the pylons from green activists, all over France, as a matter of fact. After the Western Pyrenees project was abandoned, it took three

43 Interview of 3 March 2015. See also Marie-France Verdier, *Cour administrative d'appel de Bordeaux, 11 janvier 1996 Electricité de France (No. 95BX00203), Avec note*, REVUE JURIDIQUE DE L'ENVIRONNEMENT 555, 569 (1997), doi.org/10.3406/rjenv.1997.3463. See also, about the visual impacts, Brenier, *Conclusions du commissaire du gouvernement en vue de l'arrêt du 11 janvier 1996 de la Cour administrative d'appel de Bordeaux* 9 (Document provided by the Court. 1995); Rey, Cahiers Juridiques de l'Electricité et du Gaz (CJEG), 112 (Mars 1994).

44 The converter substations are made of associated filters and thousands of semiconductors, called thyristors, which are silicon pucks (of 15cm or 6' diameter) that act exclusively as a bistable switch.

45 *Euskadi Ta Askatasuna* (ETA), i.e. Basque Country and Freedom.

project proposals to finally come to a mutual agreement: the first proposal, an overhead EHV line planned in the Central Pyrenees (Cazaril-Aragón, through the Louron and Chistau Valleys); the second, an overhead EHV line planned between Baixas and Bescanó in the Eastern Pyrenees; the third, between Baixas and Santa Llogaia (which is en route to Bescanó), but underground, and after the mediation and financial aid of the European Union.

2.1 *Cazaril-Aragón – The Louron Valley Project – 1984–1996*

The original planned route was moved from the Southwest of France to the Central Pyrenees, in the Midi-Pyrénées region, not only because of separatist claims, but also because the Spanish project proponent, *Empresa Nacional de Electricidad* (then called ENDESA), wanted to connect its power station in Aragón, near Zaragoza, as it was the only possible station for the company to connect directly to the EDF grid. Otherwise, ENDESA would have had to resort to other Spanish companies' grids. A power line between Cazaril, a village in the Haute-Garonne department in France, and the region of Aragón in Spain was decided upon. To link Cazaril and Aragón, a first route was considered through the Aran Valley, but Spain asserted that it would have had some environmental impacts. The rumor had it that the line would have been visible from a famous ski resort, Baqueira-Beret, where the Spanish royal family liked to vacation. As a matter of fact, the planned route was 15.5 miles (25 km) away, but it remained that the whole Aran Valley was a touristic area. Moreover, as later revealed, the line would also have gone in part through Catalonia, which did not care to sacrifice its landscape for the sole benefit of Aragón and bluntly refused. For these reasons, Spain had opposed this route from the start. It was thus abandoned, like some others, for the same reason: the planned power line route was going through landscapes with touristic appeal.

2.1.1 The Louron Valley Project and Its Opponents

Then, on 20 January 1984, EDF officially presented a Cazaril- Aragón route through the Louron Valley in the Hautes-Pyrénées Department (also home of the Pragnères –Sabiñanigo EHV power line of 225 kV). In Spain, the route was planned through the Chistau Valley (its name in Aragonese; the valley is called *Gistaín* in Castilian). The French government approved this route in July, supposedly because it was the shortest route from Cazaril to Aragón,[46]

46 Cazaril was the starting point, in the Haute-Garonne department. A few miles/kilometers there, then the main French part was in the Hautes-Pyrénées department, going through the territory of eighteen municipalities, through the Neste, Nistos and Louron valleys, until the Port de la Pez, on the Bachimale Crest, the frontier with Spain, then through the

and perhaps because it was the easiest and the less costly. This choice would later be analyzed as "the least worst".[47] It sparked outrage. When the Cazaril-Aragón route had been discussed for the first time, at the beginning of the 1980's, there had been such strong an opposition to the Louron/Chistau Valleys option that the French state searched for another one. After having consulted with the inhabitants, associations and local officials, the state representatives in the relevant departments and the region had proposed to EDF another route, which was actually the shortest possible route through France and had considerably smaller visual impacts, both in France and Spain. Additionally, it was also the easiest route (since no pylons at high altitudes were required), hence the cheapest. It was difficult to understand why EDF eventually rejected this route on which everybody else had agreed. It seems that it was because of Spain: the route was going in part through Catalonia and the Catalan Government did not want to allow any Aragonese pylons on its territory. The autonomous communities of Aragón and Catalonia were too strongly opposed, on this and other issues too, to come to an agreement on this project.[48] EDF did not reveal its reasons, perhaps for fear it would fuel even more the opposition in France. It preferred to emphasize its own expertise, asserting that its project was the best route, confident that its judgment would be trusted, as usual. With the approval of the French government, the Cazaril-Aragón route ended up as an agreement between the two electricity companies, EDF and ENDESA, which dismissed public participation, local officials and the administrative departments that had already worked extensively on this project. In Spain, ENDESA also dismissed the opposition of the regional government of Aragón.[49] EDF and ENDESA (REE later on) seemingly behaved as if they took for granted that no significant opposition could effectively defend two nearly-deserted valleys eventually. They disappointed and irritated all who had participated in planning the power line, ultimately in vain. In France, EDF planned the line through the Nistos Forest in spite of the fact that this forest was supposed to be protected,[50] and through the Louron

Chistau Valley. In Spain, the route was much longer than in France (115 mi/185km vs. 37 mi/60km).

47 Brenier *supra* note 43 at 4.

48 Michel Geoffre (16 July 2015 email).

49 AURELIO BIARGE LÓPEZ & TERESA DÍAZ GARCÍA, INFORME SOBRE LA LÍNEA DE TRANSPORTE DE ENERGÍA ELÉCTRICA ARAGÓN-CAZARIL – ANÁLISIS DE ALTERNATIVAS (Comercio y Turismo Departamento de Industria ed., Diputación General de Aragón. 1990).

50 *Décret du 22 mars 1927*, signed by President Gaston Doumergue. However, the Agriculture Minister, Henri Queuille, who had countersigned the decree and was in charge of its

Valley in spite of the fact that the Environment Minister at the time, Huguette Bouchardeau, opposed this decision, and that a previous ministerial committee had decided to protect the valley because of the beauty of the area.[51] Ironically, the request to register the Louron Valley had been made in 1982 by the Midi-Pyrénées Regional Architecture and Environment Department (DRAE, a regional division of the Minister of the Environment) in exchange for granting the permission to develop a ski resort (Peyragudes).[52] EDF reneged on its earlier promise. It was still behaving as it did in the 1950's, at the time of the Pragnères – Sabiñanigo line, when it could simply ignore the concerns of the *Service de protection des sites* and of all those advocating for the preservation of the landscape. The new EHV power line was planned through some beautiful and quasi-virgin valleys. For the first time however, EDF would have to face a strong opposition that eventually led to the demise of its project in the Central Pyrenees.

In Spain, no EIA was made because there was no legal requirement to this effect.[53] In France, in 1984, EDF made an EIA, in accordance with the 1976 Nature Protection Act.[54] This EIA was highly criticized, especially in a stern report by the Ministry of the Environment, because:
- it studied only one route, without giving any plausible explanation for excluding the others, especially the first route that had already been suggested and agreed upon;[55]
- it gravely underestimated the real visual impacts of the EHV line;

official publication, had omitted to proceed to the latter. Consequently, the protection was not enforceable.

51 On 26 August 1983, the Secretary of State for the Environment had asked the *préfet des Hautes-Pyrénées* (the state representative in this department) to start the proceedings to protect the Louron Valley (cited in a letter of the Industry Minister to the CPDP President, dated 17 February 2003, available at http://cpdp.debatpublic.fr/cpdp-tht-france-espagne/Lettre_de_Mme_la_Ministre.pdf, accessed 17 June 2021).

52 Fillieule, FRENCH POLITICS, 307 & 327 FN2 (2003).

53 The first EIA requirements for HV power lines were adopted in 1997 (Act No. 54/1997 about the electricity sector, BOE-A-1997-25340). In 2008, a general EIA Act was passed, which now is Act No. 9/2018 of 5 December 2018 (it modified Act No. 21/2013).

54 EDF, *Etude d'impact du tronçon Cazaril – Port de la Pez – Accroissement des échanges d'énergie électrique avec l'Espagne – Ligne à deux circuits à 400 000 volts Cazaril-Aragon* (1984) (on file with the Hautes-Pyrénées Departmental Archives). See Act No. 76-629, 10 July 1976, and its implementation decree No. 77-1141, 12 October 1977.

55 See the EDF EIA: "The necessity to find a common border crossing point led to a compromise, including the environmental interests of both countries in the best possible manner: Port de la Pez was the only possible solution. The EIA was based on this unique choice". (EDF EIA, *supra* note 54 at 6) (author's translation).

– it was not precise enough – it referred to subsequent documents, after the project was eventually completed, for any substantial information about the line and the pylons. For instance, because the line would be sited at a rather high altitude (1.5 mile – 2,400 meters) for a large part of its route, the pylons would have had to be even larger and sturdier than the usual ones, hence even more visible, but EDF did not address this issue in its EIA.[56]

In April 1985, the law governing public inquiries (*enquêtes publiques*), i.e. compulsory consultations with the public, had just passed, but was not applicable to ongoing projects.[57] A sort of rudimentary public inquiry, then called *instruction administrative*, was held about the Cazaril-Aragón EHV line project.[58] For two months, from 25 April to 25 June 1985, concerned citizens could go to a few administrative facilities, consult the file at their disposal and write their observations and requests in an official register. Only the EIA seems to have been included in the available documents, not the other reports, such as the June 1985 opinion of the Environment Ministry, which were not communicated, despite the express request of the opponents, on the grounds that they were preparatory documents for a decision not yet taken.[59] A long tradition of secrecy has cloaked administrative decisions and has been lifted only gradually, starting in 1978 with an important statute that recognized the right of any citizen to access administrative documents.[60] As of this writing, until the end of the decision-making process at stake, the principle still stands in France that preparatory documents cannot be accessed, albeit with an important

56 Le Délégué Régional à l'Architecture et à l'Environnement (DRAE) de Midi-Pyrénées, *Avis sur le dossier établi par EDF pour la déclaration d'utilité publique et comprenant l'étude d'impact du tronçon Cazaril-Port de la Pez d'une ligne à 2 circuits 400kV Cazaril-Aragon*. 5 June 1985 (on file with the DREAL Occitanie Archives). The DRAE was part of the Minister of the Environment. See also Brenier *supra* note 43 at 4.

57 Act No. 83-630, 12 July 1983 (JO, 13 July 1983, p. 2156) and its implementation decree No. 85-453, 23 April 1985 (JO, 24 April 1985, p. 4753).

58 In application of Article 7 of the governmental decree No. 70-492 of 11 June 1970, and the government *circulaire* of 12 May 1978 relating to EIAs of non-underground means of electricity transportation. *Circulaires* (circulars) in this chapter are governmental instructions.

59 See CADA's decision of 14 November 1985 (4ÈME RAPPORT D'ACTIVITE DE LA CADA, 327 (1986)). Set up in 1978, the *Commission d'Accès aux Documents Administratifs* (CADA) is an independent administrative authority, tasked with facilitating access to executive and administrative documents.

60 Act No. 78-753 of 17 July 1978, on various measures for improved relations between the Civil Service and the public. See also SENAT, RAPPORT D'INFORMATION SUR L'ACCES AUX DOCUMENTS ADMINISTRATIFS ET AUX DONNEES PUBLIQUES (2014).

exception since 2005: when the decision at stake pertains to the environmental domain.[61]

After the end of the 1985 administrative instruction of the Louron project, EDF did not address the concerns therein expressed and did not alter its plan. Later, in the course of the legal proceedings, a judge would underline that the absence of a public inquiry explained the lack of information about the impacts of the power line.[62]

Despite the evident deficiencies of the EIA, on 26 August 1988, the Minister of the Industry, Roger Fauroux, issued the *Déclaration d'Utilité Publique* (DUP), an administrative act that officially acknowledges that the project is for the common good, which allows the necessary expropriations and public utility easements, and paves the way for the building permit. EDF had asked for the DUP three years and a half before, in December 1984. Fauroux was from Montpellier, in the South of France near the Mediterranean Sea. He held a deep affection for the Pyrenees, where he hiked regularly. Five years later, he would become the mayor of Saint-Girons, his ancestral home in the neighboring Ariège department, less than a hundred km (62 miles) away from Cazaril.[63] A good friend of Roger Fauroux's, Jacques Guiu, happened to be the President of the National Pyrenees Park (from 1982 to 1989). Guiu immediately contacted the Industry Minister.[64] Fauroux was unfamiliar with the case and Guiu alerted him of the consequences of his DUP in a region that the minister held in such high esteem. The latter decided to cancel his DUP, on 12 April 1989, and order some additional studies. Fauroux himself went to the valleys in question with Guiu, discreetly, without any media coverage. He agreed with Guiu's proposal and supported it: instead of building a new line, simply upgrade the existing Pragnères-Sabiñanigo line to 400 kV. However, EDF failed to be convinced

61 CADA, 24 November 2005, No. 20054612; Conseil d'Etat, *Association des habitants du littoral du Morbihan*, 7 August 2007, No. 266668. Both decisions made the necessary distinction between documents under completion and those that are preparatory, the latter being communicable. See Articles L. 124-1, 124-3 and 124-4 of the Environmental Code. Another exception exists in matters of urban planning (Art. L. 300–2 et seq. of the Urban Code). The general rule of non-communicability has been criticized, with calls to reform and enlarge access to preparatory documents that are helpful to the decision-making process (ASSEMBLEE NATIONALE, NUMERIQUE ET LIBERTES: UN NOUVEL AGE DEMOCRATIQUE, RAPPORT NO. 3119, 36 (2015)).

62 See Brenier *supra* note 43 at 4.

63 Fauroux was elected mayor of Saint-Girons in 1989 and held this position until 1995. He was the Industry Minister from 1988 to 1991 in the government led by Prime Minister Michel Rocard, with François Mitterrand as President (Socialist Party).

64 A mountain guide, Patrice de Bellefon, had informed Jacques Guiu about the EHV power line project (Jacques Guiu, 4 August 2015 interview).

(later studies actually confirmed that a new line was truly needed for grid security reasons – if one of the existing lines failed, the other ones would not be able to withstand the necessary transportation and distribution of electricity). Fauroux reenacted his DUP, on 15 December 1989, but on the condition that in exchange, EDF dismantle the Pragnères-Sabiñanigo overhead power line, which traverses the National Pyrenees Park, and build it underground. At the same time, out of prudence, Fauroux also privately evoked the potential illegality of his reinstatement of the DUP with the opponents and the fact that they could perhaps attack his decision in court, where it might be annulled (once a DUP had been cancelled, it could not be revived). In the meantime, regardless of the outcome of the lawsuit contesting the 15 December 1989 ministerial decision, a year and a half had already been gained thanks to the intervention of only a few persons, which would later prove decisive.

In the wake of Jacques Guiu's actions, local opposition efficiently continued to organize itself. It was composed of elected officials (mayors of small and larger cities like Toulouse (Dominique Baudis[65]), general councilors, house representatives, senators), farmers' unions and environmental NGOs. A local politician, Michel Pélieu, mayor of a small town in the Louron Valley,[66] took the lead. Pélieu wanted to protect his valley for tourism purposes. NGOs joined to work with him, led by Michel Geoffre. A retired engineer,[67] Geoffre had been an active environmentalist in the region for a while (he was the head of a Green political party – *Bigorre Ecologie*). Geoffre lives in Tarbes (Hautes-Pyrénées department), a town that is also the headquarters of the National Pyrenees Park, which was headed by Jacques Guiu. On 3 December 1985, Geoffre merged twenty-three associations into a county federation called UMINATE 65, part of UMINATE, the most important environmental NGO in the Midi-Pyrénées region, where it represented *France Nature Environnement* (FNE), itself the largest environmental NGO federation in France.[68] Geoffre was also in close

65 Mayor of Toulouse from 1983 to 2001, President of the Regional Council of Midi-Pyrénées from 1986 to 1988, house representative from 1988 to 1994, and from 1997 to 2001.

66 Mayor of Loudenvielle from 1977 to 2011, then President of the Hautes-Pyrénées General Council to this day. Pélieu belongs to the PRG (*Parti Radical de Gauche*), a center-left, social-liberal party.

67 Michel Geoffre was educated at the *Conservatoire des Arts et Métiers*, one of the French engineer elite schools. For eleven years, he was a control engineer in heavy industry, specialized in the regulation and control of physical and chemical phenomena, before setting up his own company in electronic repair and maintenance services, in the early 1970's. Geoffre also received some training in Group Dynamics.

68 UMINATE-65 stands for: *Union MIdi Pyrénées NATure Environnement*. 65 is the French administrative number for the Hautes-Pyrénées department. In 2010, the association changed its name to FNE 65 (*France Nature Environnement 65*). As for UMINATE,

contact with the Spanish opposition movement, which was organized by some friends of his. In a federation called *Conseil International Associatif pour la Protection des Pyrénées* (CIAPP), Geoffre united more than twenty Spanish associations. The same type of institutional mobilization occurred in Spain. The main association was *La Coordinadora de Defensa y Desarrollo del Valle de Chistau*, headed by Jose Maria Fantova Aused, later the mayor of Plan (from 1997 to 2005), one of the few small villages of the affected valley, with fewer than 700 inhabitants in total. In France, Geoffre was also involved in politics. He would later be elected to the Regional Council of Midi-Pyrénées, from March 1992 to May 1995, during which time he was also the coordinator of the *Commission environnement transfrontière franco-andorrane-espagnole* (French-Andorran-Spanish Transfrontier Environment Commission). Together, Michel Pélieu and Michel Geoffre had important connections in all domains (politics, engineering, administration, NGOs ...), especially some at the top decision-making level. Geoffre had friends that worked at EDF, who were from the region and who were anonymous members of his NGO. Their contribution would prove decisive. As for journalists, local newspapers sided with the opposition on the EHV line project. Their readers accounted for a large segment of that opposition, including local officials.[69] On the national level, the journalist in charge of the environment section at *Le Monde* from 1974 to 1995, Marc Ambroise-Rendu, was the son of the president and founder of UMINATE, Jean Ambroise-Rendu. He supported the opposition to the EHV line.[70] In short, since 1984, the opposition to the EHV power line had organized regular French-Spanish demonstrations, were technically and legally quite competent and had secured media coverage. They had educated themselves on the subject and proposed some solid alternative options,[71] but EDF

established on 5 March 1974 in Toulouse, it is now called FNE Midi-Pyrénées. Lastly, FNE was instituted in 1968, and now groups together fifteen national associations and fifty-two regional associations or federations (such as, for instance, FNE Midi-Pyrénées and FNE 65).

69 In some other cases, when the opponents are from the outside, they tend not to get any sympathy from the local media (see, for instance, the Somport tunnel in the Atlantic-Pyrenees, opened in 2003).

70 "Nowadays, France has an electric power export policy. It still has no landscape policy (...) Spain has joined the European Union. The Pyrenees no longer exist". (author's translation) (Ambroise-Rendu, *supra* note 37).

71 In June 1985, the Permanent Regional Council of Environmental Associations in the Midi-Pyrenees region (French acronym: COPRAE) published a report that put forward two different solutions: the reinforcement of existing lines (upgrade the existing Pragnères-Sabiñanigo line to 400 kV), and the first route that had been planned through the Garonne and Aran valleys. At a press conference in April 1987, UMINATE presented a line

had refused even to consider them. EDF was still operating from a stance of superiority – they knew better than the populace in matters of power lines and electrical grids. EDF represented the French state and was composed of some of the best engineers in the world. They were probably sincerely convinced that their project was the best one and that it could not be otherwise. They had not yet acknowledged that a project could no longer be authoritatively imposed from above, but had to be explained, justified and negotiated in a process respectful of all stakeholders.

In Spain, the DUP (*Declaración de Utilidad Pública*) was published on 25 February 1989, the same year as in France. A year later, the government of Aragón strongly and officially expressed its opposition. It protested that the power line was built only for international commercial trade, with no compensation for the region. It emphasized that the authorizations were void, and that the power line should be built in Catalonia in any event. However, the same year, Spain adopted a national energy plan,[72] which was based on an increase in electricity consumption of 3.5% per year. According to this plan, 12% of the electricity was supposed to come from France within the next ten years, whereas only 2% of Spanish electricity was then currently being imported, which meant that Spain needed to reinforce and develop its interconnections even more. Thus, the regional opposition to the EHV line was dismissed in Spain as well.

2.1.2 The Legal Proceedings

In January 1990, a Parisian law firm specialized in environmental law, Huglo-Lepage, started to litigate on behalf of the opponents to the Cazaril-Aragón line.[73] They petitioned the DUP, which had been just reinstated by the Industry Minister, to the Council of State, the highest court in administrative law matters. Christian Huglo, Michel Pélieu and Michel Geoffre gathered together a range of municipalities, associations and other entities from the region, to

proposal through the Boucharo Pass, near the Gavarnie Circus. Not only did this proposal provide all the guarantees of reliability and expertise, but Geoffre also announced that the local officials of the Luz-Gavarnie Valley approved the line, as did the DDE (*Direction Départementale de l'Equipement*, i.e. the local branch of the Ministry of Infrastructure) and there would be no opposition from the Board of the National Pyrenees Park Board (where Gavarnie is situated), headed by Guiu (Fillieule, FRENCH POLITICS, 309 (2003)).

72 *Plan Energético Nacional* (PEN) 1991–2000, approved by Parliament in 1992.

73 The *Fédération Française des Sociétés de Protection de l'Environnement* (the French federation of environmental associations, future *France Nature Environnement* – FNE) recommended the local association (UMINATE-65) to hire this law firm. Established in 1978, Huglo-Lepage had famously defended the victims of the Amoco Cadiz oil spill.

have more weight and to cover the costs of the procedures, typically expensive because of the highly technical subject-matter, the interests at stake and the formidable means of the project proponent. Locally elected officials (regional and general councils, mayors) as well as some members of parliament united unanimously, across party lines, to oppose the Cazaril-Aragón project. This unanimous opposition was also remarkable in consideration of the fact that EDF used to grant generous compensations to municipalities, financing the creation or the modernization of ski resorts for instance.[74] EDF was accustomed to lobbying local town officials actively. Up to 10% of a power line budget can be devoted to lobbying activities, in view of authorizations and early settlements.[75] As far as they were concerned, most farmers left the opposition movement because of EDF's financial compensations.[76] Even though they were opposed to the line, elected officials did not refuse outright this traditional financial help from EDF. Instead, the Hautes-Pyrénées General Council tried to find a solution for EDF to build the line and for the affected municipalities to be compensated: it ordered a feasibility study to Omnitech, an independent engineering consulting firm located in Pau. In March 1991, Omnitech confirmed the possibility and the advantages of building the EHV line in direct current. It recommended that the line be underground in the Louron Valley. Omnitech also underlined that the European Union would most probably lend their support for the additional costs. Omnitech thus confirmed what the opposition had been suggesting for a while, an underground line with the EU's financial aid. EDF refused.

In December 1989, the Environment Secretary, Brice Lalonde, had reactivated the procedure to register the Louron Valley as a protected land, but his attempt was met with the opposition of the Prime Minister and failed

74 E.g. Nistos ski resort had been built thanks to EDF's funding (Fillieule, FRENCH POLITICS, 315 (2003)).

75 EDF Public Service Contract (*Contrat de service public entre l'Etat et EDF*), 36 (2005). Lobbying can be accomplished through lawful programs such as the *Fonds d'Amortissement des Charges d'Electrification* (FACE), set up by an act of 31 December 1936 *portant fixation du budget général de l'exercice 1937* (under President Léon Blum's Administration). In another EHV line project (the Cotentin-Maine power line – construction started in 2012), out of the sixty-four towns involved, thirty-five were against the project, but then only five after EDF offered its financial incentives (Jean-Claude Bossard, *in Sur la route*, a France-Culture radio show, 18 October 2013, at https://www.franceculture.fr/emissions/sur-la-route/sur-la-route-d-une-ligne-tres-haute-tension-en-basse-normandie, accessed 17 June 2021; Audrey Garric, *Cotentin-Maine, une ligne électrique sous très haute tension*, LE MONDE, 6 March 2012).

76 Michel Geoffre, 9 June 2015 interview.

eventually.[77] The Cazaril-Aragón line project resumed. On 13 June 1990, the local representative of the French government, titled the department prefect (*préfet des Hautes-Pyrénées*), delivered the building permit for the construction of the power line.[78] The legality of the permit was challenged in court, before the Administrative Tribunal of Pau, and the opposition to the power line won its case. Firstly, on 5 November 1991, the tribunal stayed the decision of the prefect because there seemed to be a serious argument to be made against it and because the damage would be irreparable, as only monetary damages could be paid (because of the intangibility of public works once they are in place[79]). Indeed, the same tribunal would later annul the building permit, on 16 December 1994. EDF appealed the 1991 preliminary injunction to the *Conseil d'Etat* (CE or Council of State),[80] the supreme administrative court in France. EDF also reminded the government that, because contracts had been signed according to which France had committed to provide electricity to Spain and Portugal, it could not cancel the project. Dominique Strauss-Kahn, the Industry Minister, asked for a technical comparison between the construction of a new power line and an enhancement of the existing ones. The UCPTE confirmed that a fifth power line was the only solution (if one of the existing four lines failed, the other three could not sustain sufficient power to provide the electricity needed in both countries). Meanwhile, Spain was advancing in constructing its part of the power line. About two thirds were finished in 1993. Legislative elections took place in France in March 1993, which led to a change of majority in favor of the right-wing party. Gérard Longuet, the new Industry Minister, was at first in favor of EDF's project. In May 1993, he conveyed his opinion to the Council of State, where the decisions on the building permit and the DUP were pending. He emphasized the European aspects of the project

77 See also Alain Monferrand, *D'une décentralisation à l'autre de 1973 à 1985, souvenirs d'un DRE devenu DRAE*, 6 "POUR MÉMOIRE" REVUE DU COMITÉ D'HISTOIRE DU MINISTÈRE DE L'ÉCOLOGIE, DE L'ÉNERGIE, DU DÉVELOPPEMENT DURABLE ET DE LA MER 29, 31 (2009), as a testimony of the Environment Ministry's difficulties when faced with powerful economic interests.

78 Not without qualms apparently: "the line will be a slash in a wonderful landscape, but private interests must yield to the general interest" (*in* Jean-François Podevin, *Louron: feu vert à la THT*, LA NOUVELLE RÉPUBLIQUE DES PYRENEES, 17 September 1991) (author's translation)).

79 See *supra* note 10.

80 It is important to emphasize here that *Council of State* in this chapter means the French supreme administrative court, and should not be confused with the same term in use for the government of Finland (previous chapter).

and its beneficial consequences on the environment, because Spain would not need to build new thermal power plants.[81]

On 29 April 1994, the opponents to the new line lost before the Council of State,[82] which on the one hand confirmed the legality of the DUP, and reversed the 5 November 1991 preliminary injunction on the other hand, hence reinstating the building permit, which had been suspended by this injunction. Regarding the DUP, the Council of State decided on the basis of a cost-benefit analysis:[83] the advantages of the overhead power line (national economic interests) outweighed the disadvantages (harm done to the beauty and to the economic interests of the concerned areas, especially the Louron Valley, without any benefit for them in return). The Council of State aligned itself with its *commissaire du gouvernement* (equivalent to an advocate-general), Patrick Frydman.[84] Frydman had emphasized the comparable importance of the French-Spanish opposition and of the economic issues at stake, bending in favor of the latter and the necessity of allowing EDF to respect its agreements with REE. He had also deemed the EIA valid, on the surprising ground that it had satisfactorily studied several options (even though the EIA itself clearly stated that it did not[85]) and that it was respectful of not only French law (*décrets* No. 70-492 of 11 June 1970 and No. 77-1141 of 12 October 1977), but also European law (Directive 85/337/CEE of 27 June 1985), as the Council of State deemed French law "not incompatible" with the 1985 EIA Directive.[86] As for the building permit, Frydman had mentioned that EDF would position the pylons in the shade (*sic*) and that the permit should be validated in light of the validation of the DUP, even though the two were independent. He had also

81 VIGUIÉ, 120. 2014.

82 Conseil d'Etat, 29 April 1994, cases No. 112910 and 115044 for the DUP; For the building permit: case No. 131674. See Marie-France Verdier's comments, *in Cour administrative d'appel de Bordeaux, 11 janvier 1996 Electricité de France (No. 95BX00203), Avec note*, REVUE JURIDIQUE DE L'ENVIRONNEMENT 555, 569 (1997) (doi.org/10.3406/rjenv.1997.3463).

83 It had been an accepted method of analysis for power lines projects since its 24 January 1975 decision, *Gorlier et Bonifay*, case No. 91074.

84 Patrick Frydman, *Conclusions du commissaire du gouvernement sous l'arrêt Conseil d'Etat, 29 avril 1994*, Juillet – Août CAHIERS JURIDIQUES DE L'ELECTRICITÉ ET DU GAZ (CJEG) 443 (1994).The *commissaire du gouvernement* is the judge in charge of marshalling the arguments of the parties, and sharing her/his impartial assessment of the facts and the applicable law, as well as her/his opinion on the solution to the dispute (Conseil d'Etat, 29 July 1998, No. 179635, *Mme Esclatine*).

85 See *supra* note 55.

86 CE, *Ville d'Amiens et autres*, 3 December 1990, case No. 111677, where the Council of State deemed that French law (*décret* No. 77-1141 of 12 October 1977 and Code of Urbanism) did not ignore the goals assigned by the EIA Directive.

minimized the aesthetic appeal of the Louron Valley. EDF and the Industry Minister seemed to have thus convinced the Council of State of the primacy of EDF's choice, understood as furthering the economic interests of EDF and France. The *commissaire du gouvernement* then resolved the legal issues in favor of EDF. For Frydman, the DUP had to be validated because of the trade balance surplus, the promise of cheaper electricity prices for domestic consumers and job creations, which outweighed the rest.

However, two months later, in June 1994, the Industry Minister, Gérard Longuet, changed his mind and with the Environment Minister, Michel Barnier, asked EDF to halt its project, in the broader context of another highly controversial infrastructure project in the Central Pyrenees (the Somport tunnel). Not only was the opposition to the Somport tunnel in the Aspe Valley equally vehement, but it was also fueled by similar concerns – the preservation of the beauty of the landscape and the existence of alternative solutions.[87] Therefore, the government had become wary of these projects. Furthermore, Barnier, supported by Longuet, had organized on behalf of the government a national debate on energy and environment, which was then in progress. Barnier was determined to wait for its results before proceeding further with the line: "EDF must abide by the government's policy, not the other way around".[88] In the meantime, Barnier and Longuet insisted on verifying whether having an EHV power line carrying direct current along an existing railroad might provide a better solution. Following Roger Fauroux' attempt, environmental concerns were again expressed politically at the governmental level. Longuet explains that he eventually came to doubt that EDF had France's best overall interests at heart and that EDF had too often built too many power lines throughout France, which it had disfigured without any consideration for the affected parties and the landscape. He wanted to be sure that EDF had considered all possible options and that there was no other solution than the Louron Valley route, especially in terms of protecting the environment and the landscape. More generally, Longuet found EDF overconfident regarding its power and influence.[89] However, he had to resign from his ministerial position four months

87 The Aspe Valley is part of the Pyrenees National Park. The Pau administrative tribunal had cancelled the DUP on 2 December 1992, on the grounds that the EIA was insufficient (See Marie-Laure Lambert, *Construction du tunnel routier du Somport, Tribunal administratif de Pau, 2 décembre 1992, FNE et autres c/ Préfet des Pyrénées Atlantiques*, REVUE JURIDIQUE DE L'ENVIRONNEMENT 91 (1993/1)).

88 *Michel Barnier: « Impulser un nouveau projet économique »*, LES ECHOS, 10 June 1993 (author's translation). The consultations of the national debate took place from May to October 1994.

89 Gérard Longuet (20 October 2015 interview).

later, in October 1994, and the study he had requested never came to light. Nonetheless, Barnier and Longuet helped to buy time; even these few months would later prove decisive. Mid-December 1994, the national debate on energy and environment initiated by Michel Barnier came to an end, and the final report was handed down (*Rapport Souviron*). It underlined that French energy policy was not the result of transparent and democratic enough a process, and that there was too much of a confusion between the two roles of the French state: regulator on the one hand, operator on the other (EDF). With respect to infrastructure and power line projects in particular, Jean-Pierre Souviron recommended that their necessity, characteristics and route be clearly established and justified, as well as the alternatives, with a second, independent expert opinion.[90] The report mentioned the Cazaril-Aragón line project as exemplary of the existing issues. It stressed the deadlock, the fierceness of the opposition and that greater consultations would have prevented the difficulties. The conclusion of the report on this point disappointed the opposition, however. For Souviron, absent another route on which all parties would rapidly agree, the Louron Valley project then would need to proceed because of the French state's national and international commitments.[91]

On 16 December 1994, the administrative tribunal of Pau decided to proceed with the annulment of the building permit decision that it had previously suspended, regardless of the April 1994 decision of the Council of State, which had confirmed the legality of the DUP. The tribunal based its decision on the fact that the state had dismissed urban and rural planning regulations regarding public works: in particular, that the latter should not hurt the character or the attractiveness of the neighboring areas, the landscape and perspectives, in reference to Article R. 111-21 of the French Urbanism Code. Because the power line route was planned through wilderness areas and areas of cultural heritage that were highly valued by a vast majority of inhabitants and that had been a constant object of conservation and preservation efforts, the tribunal decided that the prefect had made a manifest error of assessment. This resulted in an annulment of the prefect's decision to grant a building permit, irrespective of

90 After the report, at the final conference, the Prime Minister, Edouard Balladur, acknowledged the necessity of a wide public participation and a departure from the previous, firmly entrenched convictions and persistent mistakes (*La clôture du débat national Energie et Environnement*, LE MONDE, 17 December 1994; Declaration of the Prime Minister, 15 December 1994, at https://www.vie-publique.fr/discours/142875-declaration-de-m-edouard-balladur-premier-ministre-sur-la-prise-en-co, accessed 17 June 2021).

91 JEAN-PIERRE SOUVIRON, DÉBAT NATIONAL ÉNERGIE & ENVIRONNEMENT, RAPPORT DE SYNTHÈSE (December 1994). On file with the *Agence De l'Environnement et de la Maîtrise de l'Energie* (ADEME).

the validity of the DUP (the two bodies of rules are independent) and contrary to what the advocate-general, Patrick Frydman, had asserted in this regard before the Council of State in April of that same year. The advocate-general before the tribunal duly cited Frydman on one hand and the opposition of the Environment Ministry (in the 1985 DRAE's report) on the other hand. He also alluded to the fact that the EIA was insufficient, contrary to what the Council of State had decided. Lastly, he criticized the pleadings of the *préfet des Hautes-Pyrénées* (the state representative in the department and at the trial), literally identical to EDF's, as another example of the confusion between the role of the state as a regulator/permit authority on the one hand, and as an operator/project proponent on the other hand, citing in this regard the Souviron report concluding the national debate on energy and environment, which had just denounced this problematic and recurrent issue.[92]

Nevertheless, EDF continued to refuse to reinforce the existing lines, insisting on building a new overhead line. The energy company appealed the judgment of the Pau administrative tribunal. In the meantime, on 18 May 1995, Corinne Lepage was appointed the Environment Minister, in the new government led by Alain Juppé.[93] Following her nomination, Huglo-Lepage announced that they would withdraw from all their cases related to the protection of the environment.[94]

On 11 January 1996, EDF won its appeal before the administrative appeal court of Bordeaux,[95] which reversed the December 1994 judgment of the administrative tribunal of Pau regarding the building permit. Interestingly, in a rare move, the court decided against its advocate-general, who had deemed EDF's route unreasonable.[96] The advocate-general had emphasized that the Louron Valley in particular was too narrow to bear such an imposing power line and that its wilderness had been preserved intact thus far; also, that EDF could

92 See the judgment, and the conclusions of the advocate-general *in* Rey, CAHIERS JURIDIQUES DE L'ELECTRICITÉ ET DU GAZ (Mars 1994).

93 Corinne Lepage's political engagement had started in 1981. She became Deputy-Mayor of Cabourg in 1989 (she held this mandate until 2001). In 1990, Lepage had been among the founders (notably with Brice Lalonde and Jean-Louis Borloo) of a new green party, *Génération Ecologie*, which she had then left not long after. Upon entering the government in May 1995, she was without any political affiliation.

94 Corinne Lepage, 19 February 2015 interview. Christian Huglo, 3 March 2015 interview. *Corinne Lepage, Du prétoire au ministère, toujours nature*, LIBERATION, 14 July 1995; Olivier Razemon, *Plaideur pour l'environnement contre les pollueurs*, PETITES AFFICHES, 2 May 2013.

95 *Cour administrative d'appel de Bordeaux*, 11 January 1996, case No. 95BX00203.

96 See Brenier *supra* note 43 at 6–7.

not prove the required imperative technological necessity to go through protected mountains:[97] an underwater solution had been studied and set aside for purely financial reasons. Lastly, the *commissaire du gouvernement* had emphasized that the Council of State itself had already decided that Article R.111-21 of the Code of Urbanism unambiguously applied to projects that alter valuable, virgin landscapes.[98] However, the court of appeals seems to have been under pressure from EDF and the French state authorities and the majority was eventually very slight. The decision of the court of appeals confirmed the Council of State's bias. As the opposition put it, paradoxically, they were right in legal terms, but not in economic terms.[99]

On 29 January 1996, the opposition movement appealed to the Council of State, but with little hope in view of the previous unfavorable Council's decision in the same case, in April 1994. As for Spain, the Supreme Court had also validated the project.[100] As in the case of Finland in the previous chapter, the higher and lower courts were clearly opposed to each other on this project. However, unlike Finland, it was the lower court (Pau administrative tribunal) that decided against the project in France, whereas the higher courts were the ones in favor of the national energy company's plans. The lower court was composed of judges that lived in the concerned area, and some had naturally become attached to it. They hiked and appreciated the landscape.[101] There was no local economic benefit. At the higher level, judges were far from local problematics and closer to national political power and its concerns about traditional economic and energetic issues on the national and European planes. They still deferred to EDF's expertise and did not think possible to reconcile all stakeholders' interests.

97 Mountain ranges are protected in France by Act No. 85-30 of 9 January 1985. See in particular Article L.145-8 of the Urbanism Code, in its 1985 version applicable to this case.

98 CE, *SCI Résidence du Castillon*, 9 May 1979, No. 08864. This precedent was about private real estate investments, not about a public project like EDF's power line.

99 See also "EDF was legally right because they were economically right" (Marie-France Verdier, *Cour administrative d'appel de Bordeaux, 11 janvier 1996 Electricité de France (No. 95BX00203). Avec note*, REVUE JURIDIQUE DE L'ENVIRONNEMENT 555, 570 (1997) (doi .org/10.3406/rjenv.1997.3463) author's translation).

100 *Tribunal Supremo*, 2 December 1994, No. 705/90. Rey, CAHIERS JURIDIQUES DE L'ELECTRICITÉ ET DU GAZ, 115 (Mars 1994).

101 Pau is on the northern edge of the Pyrenees, the capital of the Pyrénées-Atlantiques department in the region of Aquitaine. It has one of the most beautiful panoramic viewpoints on the Pyrenees mountain range. Alphonse de Lamartine found Pau "*la plus belle vue de terre comme Naples est la plus belle vue de mer*" (ANGELA THIRLWELL, WILLIAM AND LUCY: THE OTHER ROSSETTIS 291 (Yale University Press. 2003).

In addition to the French Council of State, the opponents brought an action before the European Commission on the basis of Article 169 of the Treaty on European Union (also known as the Maastricht Treaty) and an action before the European Court of Justice for violation of the 1985 EIA Directive.

2.1.3 The Cancellation of the Louron Valley Project

Because the opposition did not trust the Council of State and because lawsuits before European institutions were usually quite long, Michel Pélieu resorted to go to Paris to plead his cause at the highest political level. He asked Philippe Douste-Blazy, the Culture Minister, to arrange an appointment with the Prime Minister, Alain Juppé. Douste-Blazy was one of the prominent personalities of the governmental majority. He had been a key supporter of President Jacques Chirac in his successful election the year before, in 1995. The Midi-Pyrenees region was Douste-Blazy's home region. He was the mayor of Lourdes, a beautiful and historic small town in the Hautes-Pyrénées department, a famous place of pilgrimage for Roman Catholics. Douste-Blazy was also against the power line.[102]

On 24 January 1996, Alain Juppé received Michel Pélieu, in the company of Philippe Douste-Blazy – a meeting ultimately confined to three men from Southwestern France.[103] The Prime Minister decided that Douste-Blazy should discuss this power line project with the Industry Minister, Franck Borotra. However, the latter was in favor of the project. A few days later, EDF began construction of the EHV power line. Pélieu called Douste-Blazy, who told the Prime Minister immediately. In the meantime, Juppé had also consulted with the Environment Minister, Corinne Lepage. In one last development, the day after, on 1 February 1996, the Prime Minister officially announced that he had decided to cancel the Cazaril-Aragón EHV power line project for aesthetic and economic/touristic reasons, pleading, in a rather emotional speech at the French Senate, for sustainable development, denouncing the disfiguration of

102 Douste-Blazy was born in Lourdes (less than 62 mi/100 km away from the power line project), in the Hautes-Pyrénées department. He is the grandson of a mayor of Lourdes and had himself been mayor of this city from 1989 to 2000. He had been a house representative from Hautes-Pyrénées and would be minister several times (Health (twice), Culture, and Foreign Affairs), then mayor of Toulouse and house representative from the Haute-Garonne department, neighboring the Hautes-Pyrénées, from 2001 to 2004.

103 Michel Pélieu, 19 October 2015 interview; Alain Juppé's testimony *in* BACQUÉ, supra note 8 at 169; Fillieule, FRENCH POLITICS, 312 (2003). Juppé was born in Mont-de-Marsan, in the Landes, about 124 miles (200 km) away from the power line project.

France, and announcing an ambitious program for developing underground transmission lines.[104]

The Louron Valley was saved *in extremis*. Furthermore, Corinne Lepage ensured that it would not be threatened in the future and gave the necessary instructions for its protection.[105] Furthermore, in 1992, some of the Louron and Chistau Valleys' defenders, among whom Patrice de Bellefon, Roger Fauroux, Michel Geoffre, Jacques Guiu, had founded an association for the protection of the nearby Mont Perdu (*Mont Perdu Patrimoine Mondial* – MPPM), along with some local mayors, with Guiu as its first president and Geoffre as its general-secretary for thirty years (1987–2018). At approximately the same time than the official protection was granted to the Louron Valley, the Mont Perdu area was declared a World Heritage site for the same reasons. UNESCO declared the area straddling the border between France and Spain an outstanding cultural landscape, which combined scenic beauty with a socio-economic structure that has had deep roots in the past and is home to mountain communities and a way of life that has become rare in Europe.[106] Spain had also decided to preserve the area by creating a national natural park,[107] protected by various environmental regimes: the Spanish Natural Park Act[108] and the EU Birds and Habitat Directives.[109] Consequently, the whole area that had been threatened by the EHV power line project in both France and Spain became protected at the national, European and international level.[110]

104 "I am shocked when I see admirable landscapes ruined by EHV lines, which inflict long-term damage on the environment" (author's translation), decision announced at the Senate, on 1 February 1996, under the explicit title "*Enfouissement des lignes électriques*" (Burial of Power Lines) (JO, 2 February 1996, *Sénat – débats parlementaires, session ordinaire de 1995–1996*, page 362; *Communiqué des services du Premier ministre sur la suspension des travaux de construction d'une ligne électrique à 400 000 volts à travers les Pyrénées* (1996), at https://www.vie-publique.fr/discours/132746-communique-des-services-du-premier-ministre-en-date-du-1er-fevrier-1996, accessed 17 June 2021).

105 *Décret du 14 janvier 1998 portant classement d'un site*, NOR: ATEN9750097D (Lepage was Environment Minister until June 1997, when the Prime Minister's party lost the legislative elections, but Lepage's successor, Dominique Voynet, approved her decision and gave it full effect).

106 At whc.unesco.org/en/list/773, accessed 17 June 2021. The transboundary area comprises two national parks, the entire Ordesa y Monte Perdido National Park in Spain, and the eastern part of the Pyrenees National Park in France.

107 Act No. 3/1994, 23 June 1994, *de creación del Parque Posets-Maladeta* (*Boletín Oficial del Aragón*, No. 80, p. 3116–3119).

108 Act No. 4/1989, 27 March 1989 (BO, No. 74, p. 8262–8269).

109 See *supra* chapter 4, note 51.

110 To go further, see about the Pyrenees' dilemma between the imperatives of natural conservation and the interests of tourist development *in* MARTYN LYONS, THE PYRENEES IN THE MODERN ERA – REINVENTIONS OF A LANDSCAPE, 1775–2012 (Bloomsbury. 2018).

When later asked about his memories as Prime Minister, Alain Juppé specifically mentioned the Louron Valley and notably recalled:

> I decided that we would not have the line. Cataclysm at the Industry Ministry and EDF: "*irresponsible decision! etc*". For once, I held my ground; after all, I felt like it. (…) It is also necessary to free oneself from the technicians sometimes. How often did I see them asserting, on this or that issue "*It is not possible!*" Very often, you defer to them, since you are not a technician yourself. But then, from time to time, you decide "*actually, we need that it be possible.*" And I saw that in 99% of the time, two weeks later, it had become possible …[111]

At the time of the cancellation of the project, Juppé was highly criticized by some, who denounced the money wasted on a nonexistent power line. The complete list of reasons for Juppé's decision was never quite unearthed. As noted already, the concern about preserving landscapes, wilderness and tourism dated back a long time and had been raised from the start of this particular project. Juppé was a convinced environmentalist and the beauty of the valley undoubtedly moved him.[112] When Michel Pélieu and Philippe Douste-Blazy offered him the seeming possibility, should Juppé decide to cancel the EHV line project, to be the protector of the beauty and the environment of France, he weighed the political costs carefully, especially in consideration of the signed contracts between France and Spain. Importantly, it also gave Juppé the opportunity to fight off the overwhelming power and influence of EDF,[113] which two previous industry ministers, Roger Fauroux and Gérard Longuet, had also tried, but in vain. Besides, Spain no longer needed electricity imports in Aragón, but instead farther southeast, in Catalonia, and in smaller quantities (incidentally, in Spain, the cancellation of the power line project was also quite popular during the campaign for the general elections of 3 March 1996). Consequently, everything had coalesced for Alain Juppé to take this unexpected and courageous political decision. Parenthetically, it might also have come as a relief of some sort: he had recently become Prime Minister (on 17 May 1995) and had

Lyons evokes the role of Michel Geoffre in warning about the risks of uncontrolled tourist development (p. 200).

111 BACQUÉ, *supra* note 8 at 168–170.

112 Id. at 168–169.

113 "We cannot accept that engineers impose an all-or-nothing choice on elected officials" (author's translation) (*Questions d'actualité au gouvernement, 1 February 1996*, Sénat – débats parlementaires, session ordinaire de 1995–1996, page 363, JO, 2 February 1996).

quickly been confronted, during the autumn of 1995, with one of the worst strikes since 1968.[114] In this case at last, Juppé could take a popular decision, concretely act for environmental protection, assert his power and restore some balance. His decision moved and marked many in France – for the first time, the French landscape and the environment had been meaningfully protected at the highest level.

The Cazaril-Aragón case was later mentioned, in 2003, in a commission of inquiry headed by Philippe Douste-Blazy, which dealt with the management of public companies, in order to improve their decision-making process. Before the commission, EDF emphasized the existing contracts with Spain at the time of Juppé's decision and seemingly dismissed the fact that the decision had been in favor of finding a better route, since Spain no longer needed the line in Aragón.[115] Only two years before, in 1994, Aragón had even created a natural park that included the area of the planned route of the EHV line, where various environmental protection regimes were in place.[116] Then, in the wake of the Prime Minister's decision, more stringent rules were imposed on EDF, because it did not sufficiently respect its environmental commitments. Following a senate report, the French government and EDF had decided on a program to enhance the protection of the French landscape. EDF's first commitments had been specified in a protocol concerning the placement of electrical grids in the environment and introducing the possibility of compensation for visual damage to the inhabitants, signed on 25 August 1992 in exchange for higher selling prices, since the government decided what these prices would be. France was late in this regard at the time. Only a small part of its electrical grid was underground compared with some other European countries. The first protocol was reinforced and amended following the cancellation of the Cazaril-Aragón project, in 1997.[117] EDF agreed to bury at least 20% of future EHV lines. Similar

114 After his nomination, on 17 May 1995, Alain Juppé wanted to jumpstart several structural reforms so that they could be achieved before his departure. He faced a very strong opposition to his pension and Social Security reform plans. Juppé was proposing to apply the same plan to the public sector as what had been imposed to the private sector by the 1993 pension reform (led by the previous Prime Minister, Edouard Balladur). Juppé was thus quite unpopular early 1996.

115 ASSEMBLÉE NATIONALE, RAPPORT NO. 1004, FAIT AU NOM DE LA COMMISSION D'ENQUÊTE SUR LA GESTION DES ENTREPRISES PUBLIQUES AFIN D'AMÉLIORER LE SYSTÈME DE PRISE DE DÉCISION (2003). Edmond Alphandéry, the CEO of EDF from 1995 to 1998 (and a former Economy Minister, from 1993 to 1995), recalled the Louron episode as a painful memory (Assemblée Nationale, Tome II (Hearings), part 3, page 17. 2003).

116 See *supra* page 213 and notes 107 and 108.

117 *Réseaux électriques et environnement* annexed to the *Contrat d'entreprise 1997–2000*, signed by EDF and the French government.

agreements followed until the last one to date, in 2005, still in force at present. A new agreement has yet to be signed. Consequently, the existing provisions are outdated, such as the one according to which 30% of the new HV power lines must be underground. As a matter of fact, more than 90% of these new HV lines are now being built underground. It remains that barely 6% of the totality of RTE's electrical grid is underground.[118] There was also a 1995 act that compelled EDF to bury power lines in protected areas,[119] but there were as yet no such areas on the projected route of the new interconnection line between France and Spain at the time of the Louron route. However, after the Louron Valley case, EDF and RTE committed to never increase the length of existing overhead power lines.[120]

As for Spain, many benefits flowed from Alain Juppé's decision. Not only did Spain need the line in Catalonia, as opposed to Aragón, it also needed to import less electricity than planned in the original contracts because of its investments and the rise of its own power generation capacity. In addition to having the line's location changed, it renegotiated the quantities and obtained high damages. It had already built quite a few pylons and displayed major discontentment with the cancellation decision. Spain wished to be compensated and did not admit publicly that it no longer needed electricity in Aragón. In January 1997, a transaction occurred and financial compensation was finally paid, amounting to about 552 million euros with an additional 12 million euros per year from 1996 to 2004, for as long as the power line remained not built.[121] Ten years later, the CEO of REE, Jorge Fabra Utray, confirmed how beneficial the cancellation had been to Spain.[122] Juppé was naturally aware of the financial consequences of his decision, but he had deemed imperative to send a

---

118 2005 EDF public service contract (*Contrat de service public entre l'Etat et EDF*), page 36. RTE, ELECTRICITY REPORT 2020, 90–91, 93 (2020).

119 Act No. 95-101 of 2 February 1995, Article 91. See MICHEL PRIEUR, DROIT DE L'ENVIRONNEMENT, Para. 809 (Dalloz 8th ed. 2019).

120 *Accord "Réseaux électriques et environnement", EDF-RTE – Etat, 2001–2003*, followed by the *Circulaire Fontaine*, Ministerial Circular of 9 September 2002, according to which consultations on project development must aim at providing information of high quality and at conducting altogether project design as well as mitigation measures. See also 2005 EDF public service contract (*Contrat de service public entre l'Etat et EDF*), page 37. If a landscape is worthy of protection, a protection directive can also be adopted to grant landmark status (Act No. 93-24, 8 January 1993, and its implementation decree No. 94-283, 11 April 1994, now articles L.350-1 and R.350-9 of the Environment Code).

121 REE, EL LIBRO DE LOS 20 ANOS, 1985–2005, 46 (REE. 2005); CPDP, 18. 2003; VIGUIÉ, 125. 2014.

122 " 'the results were spectacular', confirms Fabra, 'but it went unnoticed' " (author's translation), *in* REE, *supra* note 121 at 46. Fabra was CEO of REE from 1988 to 1997.

strong signal about the absolute necessity of environmental protection and a more balanced and inclusive decision-making process.

It remained that contracts had been signed between France, Spain and Portugal. The three countries still needed to exchange electricity and the European Union was adding pressure to this end. The EU was highly critical of Juppé's decision, because developing the IEM was a priority and Spain was developing its grid (Spain finished building an EHV power line between Morocco and Spain in 1997 for instance). In November 1996, the French President, Jacques Chirac, announced that the French-Spanish interconnection project would resume. Several new sites were considered along the Pyrenees Chain, but they were abandoned because of an overwhelming opposition each time. The vast majority of Pyreneans had heard of the new EHV line project and none of them wanted it anywhere in the Pyrenees, in a wave of solidarity. Consequently, the Industry Minister, Franck Borotra, asked EDF to evaluate the cost of an offshore power line. However, EDF kept answering that underground lines were too expensive: an offshore line would have cost 1.9 billion euros, and even an onshore underground line would have represented ten times the cost of an overhead power line.[123]

2.2 *The Baixas-Bescanó Project – 2001–2003*

Consequently, the planned route was moved as far from the center of controversy as possible, to the Eastern Pyrenees near the Mediterranean Sea, where Spain had come to need more electricity. The new plan, presented by RTE (which had succeeded EDF in 2000) on 11 December 2001, was to build an overhead power line between Baixas near Perpignan in France, and Bescanó in the province of Gerona in Spain, at a cost of eighty-three million euros. The prefect of the Eastern Pyrenees department began to consult with locally elected officials.

2.2.1 The Public Debate

This time, an official public debate was organized so that inhabitants could really make their voices heard. The public debate procedure had been created in 1993, but was optional at the time.[124] On 28 November 2001, the main French

123 RTE, LE PROJET DE RENFORCEMENT DES ÉCHANGES ÉLECTRIQUES ENTRE LA FRANCE ET L'ESPAGNE, SYNTHÈSE DU DOSSIER DU MAÎTRE D'OUVRAGE POUR LE DÉBAT PUBLIC 17–18 (March 2003), at https://cpdp.debatpublic.fr/cpdp-tht-france-espagne/Synthese_RTE.pdf, accessed 17 June 2021.

124 *Circulaire Billardon*, 14 January 1993, *relative aux procédures d'instruction des projets d'ouvrages électriques d'EDF*. See also Article 2 of Act No. 95-101 of 2 February 1995.

federative NGO in the environmental domain, FNE, had decided to submit the EHV line project to the *Commission Nationale du Débat Public* (CNDP – National Commission for Public Debate), which was free to then decide whether or not to organize a public debate. The CNDP had been created in 1995, in view of securing and facilitating public participation in large public development projects with significant socio-economic and/or environmental impacts.[125] On 14 February 2002, the CNDP agreed, approving FNE's request, at exactly the same time a new bill was about to be passed on proximity democracy, in the wake of the Aarhus Convention, ratified by France that same year. According to this bill, seizing the CNDP for this type of project would become compulsory. However, once seized, the CNDP would remain free to organize or not a public debate.[126] The opposition to the EHV power line project was so strong that the CNDP felt naturally compelled to organize a public debate, also for fear to discredit itself otherwise.[127] The CNDP voluntarily abided by the new law, not yet in force, for the organization of the debate, which cost about 1.2 million euros. The project proponent, RTE, paid all the expenses. The commission obtained all the necessary credits easily.[128] A special commission is created for each case, called *Commission Particulière du Débat Public* (CPDP). In this instance, the CPDP was presided by Georges Mercadal, the CNDP Vice-President and an ardent advocate of procedural obligations over substantial requirements, especially in technological fields.[129] The CPDP was composed of engineers, academics, a former industry senior executive, an expert, a judge (seven members in total).[130] The CPDP President intentionally chose all of them from the

125 Article 2 of Act No. 95-101, 2 February 1995 ("Barnier law") on the reinforcement of environmental protection.

126 Articles L.121-8 and L. 121-9 of the Environment Code, created by Act No. 2002-276 of 27 February 2002; Article 1, 4° and the annex of the implementation decree No. 2002-1275 of 22 October 2002 (see point 4 of the chart: creation of electrical power lines, equal or superior to 400 kV, of more than 10 km – 6.2 miles).

127 Pierre Zémor (CNDP President at the time), according to Georges Mercadal (29 February 2016 interview). Mercadal was the CPDP President for this particular case, and the CNDP Vice-President from September 2002 to September 2007. The documents of the CNDP debate are available at https://www.archives.debatpublic.fr/projet-ligne-a-tres-haute-tension-entre-france-lespagne, accessed 18 June 2021.

128 Article L.121-9 of the Environment Code. Georges Mercadal emphasized that RTE had always accepted all his requests without any difficulty (5 March 2016 email).

129 Georges Mercadal, *Garantir le débat*, 297 PROJET 4 (2007).

130 The seven members of the CPDP were: Georges Mercadal, President of the CPCP and Vice-President of the CNDP (civil engineer – a *Polytechnique* and *Ponts et Chaussées* graduate), Georges Demouchy (landscaper, professor at *Ecole Nationale Supérieure du Paysage de Versailles* – he had already participated in many landmark commissions in the region), Louis Domenjo (former senior executive in the industrial sector, in the Eastern Pyrenees),

region at stake. The debate took place over three months, in the spring of 2003. Before it started, the opposition was clear: as it had already stated, it categorically refused any new overhead power line, for the same reasons the previous Cazaril-Aragón project in the Louron Valley had been contested. The EHV line had not been built in the Central Pyrenees and they naturally did not want it in the Eastern Pyrenees either. The opposition was very suspicious, of the CNDP included.

Spain participated in the debate as well, represented by REE on the one hand, and by some NGOs on the other hand, united under the banner *400,000 volts: No Gracias*. However, the Spanish NGOs were not very involved eventually, because of the language issue. French NGOs came together under the same explicit slogan *Non à la THT* (there were twenty-three French NGOs). A representative of the World Health Organization (WHO) was also in attendance. The debate took place from 21 March to 27 June 2003:

- 1,380 in total went to seven public hearings, which lasted about five hours each;
- eight specific panels (between three and six hours each), with 110 persons in attendance on average (the most attended panel was the health panel – 216 persons);
- partnerships with the press – weekly two pages in the two main local newspapers, *L'Indépendant* (225,000 readers) and *Midi-Libre* (110,000 readers). The eight issues of this newsletter were also published independently, distributed in city halls and during meetings. More than 250 articles were published in the press (almost three per day on average), plus radio and TV segments. As in the Cazaril-Aragón case, the vast majority of the media sided with the opposition to the EHV line project;
- a website (active from 21 March 2003 to 15 March 2004). During the three-month debate, there were 3,362 connections (about 33 per day);
- 275 written questions were sent to the CPDP. All were answered;
- a 10,000-person demonstration, on 31 May 2003, in Perpignan, France, a prominent city near Baixas, the starting point of the proposed new route for the EHV line.

Some EIAs were made by RTE, which resorted to a consultant firm, Geokos. RTE explained that it could not build an underground 400 kV transmission

Paul Llamas (former civil servant, expert to the administrative tribunal of Montpellier), Jacques Percebois (Dean of Montpellier University, professor of economics, specialist in the energy markets), Gérard Porcell (vice-president of the administrative tribunal of Paris, president for the Boutre-Carros case public debate, in the South-East, see *infra* note 168), Pierre Torrès (agricultural engineer, head of a vineyard in the region).

line. The environmental impact of an underground line was limited to the construction phase, but RTE emphasized the hydrogeological risks and the extensive footprint of the construction site: fifteen hectares (179,000 square yards), compared to the permanent six hectares (7,180 square yards) maximum of the total area of an overhead transmission line.[131] Some other EIAs were made by a major independent consultancy firm from Italy, *Centro Elettrotecnico Sperimentale Italiano* (CESI), specialized in the electricity industry sector. The prefect of the Eastern Pyrenees department had requested these additional and independent studies, also paid for by the project proponent in application of the public service agreement between RTE and the French State. On 31 December 2002, the first EIA made by CESI was handed in. It concluded that a new line was imperative, if only for grid security reasons.[132] As for the technique to be employed, according to CESI, an overhead line seemed to be preferable since it had the least impact on the environment, with the exception of visual impacts; building underground lines was much more invasive (due to the high volume of excavated soil and dust it would produce) and presented some risks of hydrogeological impacts; an offshore line was considered the most harmful to the environment (because of the electromagnetic field, electrolysis effects and heat generation) and there was concern that its electromagnetic field could disrupt ship navigation systems. In its second EIA, CESI simply emphasized that doubling the actual Baixas-Vic line was not secure and that a new line was imperative in the Eastern Pyrenees, but no longer necessary in the Central Pyrenees.[133] In its third report, CESI confirmed that reinforcing the existing lines was not a secure option because, if one of them was out of order, the others could not take over and bear the extra burden.[134] This actually convinced some expert activists like Michel Geoffre.

The EIAs did not satisfy the opponents, however. They questioned their neutrality, as the government representative in the department (the prefect of the Eastern Pyrenees) was the one who had requested the studies from CESI. They thought that the EIAs had dismissed the effects on the 200,000 inhabitants

131 CPDP, 23. 2003.

132 CESI, 1ER RAPPORT (A2/038822) – SYNTHÈSE DE L'ÉTUDE DE FAISABILITÉ TECHNICO-ÉCONOMIQUE D'ALTERNATIVES À LA RÉALISATION D'UNE LIGNE À TRÈS HAUTE TENSION ENTRE LA FRANCE ET L'ESPAGNE 12 (2002), at https://cpdp.debatpublic.fr/cpdp-tht-france-espagne/Synthese_CESI_1.pdf, accessed 17 June 2021.

133 CESI, 2ÈME RAPPORT (A3/006235), COMPARAISON AU POINT DE VUE ELECTRIQUE DES DIVERSES SOLUTIONS DE PASSAGE DE LA CHAINE DES PYRENEEES (SYNTHESE) (2002), at https://cpdp.debatpublic.fr/cpdp-tht-france-espagne/Synthese_CESI_2.pdf, accessed 17 June 2021.

134 CESI, RAPPORT SUPPLÉMENTAIRE (A3/014524) (2003), on file with the CNDP.

who lived along the proposed route of the power line project.[135] NGOs asked that the EIAs be verified by two independent experts, chosen by RTE and by themselves. This appraisal, paid for by the CNDP,[136] found that the CESI EIAs were reliable.[137]

However, two incidents prevented a compromise on how and where to build the EHV power line. Firstly, the project proponent tried to justify the necessity of the line for rather confusing or unsubstantiated reasons.[138] In particular, RTE contended that the line was necessary to provide power more effectively to the existing high-speed railroad. Railroad transportation in France is quite efficient, well-developed and widely appreciated. RTE hoped to convince the affected inhabitants by means of an appeal to a popular and necessary service. However, a CESI study revealed that the operation of the HS railroad did not need the extra power.[139] Secondly, and independently from the public debate, upon a meeting in Spain, the French and Spanish Industry Ministers, Nicole Fontaine and José Folgado, publicly announced that the interconnection objective was 4,000 MW, which implied that yet another transmission line, in addition to the new line under debate, would be necessary, whereas the debate in progress had been based on a 2,800 MW objective and only one new power line. As a result, trust was lost and the opposition became radicalized. About a hundred persons attended the last meeting, on 27 June 2003. The conclusion was clear: the line would be accepted only if it went underground, along existing routes. This proved acceptable because the line could easily be built along the high-speed railway and because engineers had assured that they knew how to address hydrogeological risks. The overhead EHV transmission line proposed by RTE was flatly rejected. For the CPDP, while it was clear that it was only a matter of cost, these costs were significant: at the time and according to the project proponent, an underground line would have cost ten times more than an overhead line. RTE seemed to think that the results of the debate were predetermined. Undeniably, the opposition said "no" from the beginning, through the end of the public debate.[140] However, the CPDP observed that ultimately, actors without a formal power base gained

135 CPDP, 27 & 28. 2003.

136 Article L.121-9 of the Environment Code.

137 CPDP, 33. 2003. Antoine Bonduelle & Jean-Marie Delincé, *Renforcement des interconnexions entre la France et l'Espagne: rapport d'expertise complémentaire* (CPDP. 31 May 2003), on file with the CNDP.

138 Antoine Bonduelle, *Commentaires en complément de la contre-expertise CESI* (CPDP. 31 May 2003), on file with the CNDP.

139 CESI, 2ÈME RAPPORT, *supra* note 133 at 4.

140 CPDP, 14. 2003.

legitimacy through process, and that an opposition initially based mostly on instinct and intuition was transformed into a fully-reasoned one. The goal of the public debate was, on the one hand, to inform civil society and allow it to express itself, and, on the other, to supply exhaustive information to the project proponent, in order to take a decision in an enlightened way. This goal was achieved.[141] Inhabitants had educated themselves on the subject and had some experts on their side.[142] Even though not all of them attended the public debate, this process had taken place, such that even those who did not attend were aware of it. The possibility of expressing oneself and being heard was crucial to the inhabitants.

2.2.2 The Stalemate

On 3 July 2003, as soon as she heard of the first conclusions of the public debate, the French Industry Minister, Nicole Fontaine, immediately asked RTE to propose alternatives. She was the third Industry Minister to oppose the national company's plan, this time with success, in spite of the increased financial stakes (the cost of the lack of interconnection *per se*, plus the associated yearly compensation to be paid to REE since 1997). Fontaine had previously negotiated the new agreement between EDF/RTE and the French state, in the wake of which she had issued a ministerial circular, on 9 September 2002, which still regulates project development in the domain of electricity transmission today.[143] According to the Fontaine ministerial circular, power line projects must be the object of consultations with local authorities and affected populations before the project proponent requests the necessary authorizations. The public inquiry procedure that was in place up until that time engaged with civil society only at a later stage, once the EIA had been made. Since the Fontaine circular, it has been necessary to inform inhabitants about the necessities of the project and involve them in its design and route at an earlier stage (see its Para. 3). These consultations may take the form of a public debate as in the Baixas-Bescanó project case. An EIA is submitted by the project proponent, who must bear the costs of counter studies if they are requested. With these renewed and improved procedural obligations in place, the tide had turned.

141 Id. at, 38–41. PRESIDENT DU CNDP, BILAN DU DÉBAT PUBLIC SUR LE PROJET DE LIGNE THT FRANCE – ESPAGNE 5 (15 July 2003), at https://www.archives.debatpublic.fr/projet-ligne-a-tres-haute-tension-entre-france-lespagne, accessed 18 June 2021.

142 VIGUIÉ, 139. 2014.

143 *Accord Réseaux électriques et environnement, EDF – Etat 2001–2003. Circulaire sur le développement des réseaux publics de transport et de distribution de l'électricité*, also known as *Circulaire Fontaine*, 9 September 2002. See *supra* note 120.

The French Industry Minister ensured that RTE had to include the affected populations in the decision-making process, at an early stage.

RTE offered to bury the line only partially, which was refused by the French government. In view of the fact that the new RTE-REE proposal was still not satisfactory, the opposition heightened its organizational efforts. All NGOs, French and Spanish, covering the whole Pyrenees, joined together in September 2003 (15,000 activists in total). The opposition was strong enough for locally elected officials to decide, across a rather large spectrum of political parties and institutions (including the mayors of small and large communes, president of the general council, a senator ...), to side with it. In October 2003, they all united in an association, *Sydeco THT 66* (representing all the communes included in the territorial area of the project), led by Jean-Claude Péralba, the mayor of a little town, Villemolaque. The longevity of the most charismatic leaders also played an important role in the stability and the strength of the opposition.[144] Unlike some other French power line projects,[145] locally elected officials were powerfully united against the EHV line. The project was stalled.

2.3 *The Final Route (Baixas – Santa Llogaia) – 2007–2015*

After the end of the public debate in 2003, four years passed, during which time France and Spain failed to find a suitable new route. Both countries decided to pass on the responsibility for the project. EU mediation would take over.

2.3.1 The Mediation of the European Union

On 12 September 2007, the European Commission chose Mario Monti as a European coordinator.[146] His first report duly noted that local opposition was forceful and determined, criticized France and Spain for their poor communication about the necessity of the project and for having, until then, failed to create a joint coordination mechanism. Until that time, both sides had worked

144 Jean-Claude Péralba, Mayor of Villemolaque from 2001 to 2020, president of SYDECO THT 66; Christian Bourquin, President of the Eastern Pyrenees General Council from 1998 to the end of 2010 (Socialist Party); Jean-Paul Alduy, Mayor of Perpignan from 1993 to 2009 and senator from 2001 to 2011 (UMP, the major right-wing party at the time).

145 See *supra* note 75 and *infra* note 169.

146 Mario Monti is an Italian economist. He graduated from Bocconi University (Milan, Italy), of which he would later become the president, and then pursued some graduate studies at Yale University. Monti served as European Commissioner in charge of the Internal Market, Financial Services, and Taxation from 1995 to 1999, and as European Commissioner for Competition from 1999 to 2004. He was an international advisor to Goldman Sachs from 2005 to 2011. Monti was the Prime Minister of Italy from 2011 to 2013.

largely in isolation on either side of the border.[147] As a matter of fact, the only organizations working together were the French and Spanish opposition, at the local level. Following Monti's first report, the French and Spanish governments agreed on conducting studies on an underground EHV line, and on setting up a common structure exclusively in charge of the project from then on. REE and RTE created INELFE, a joint venture, in October 2008.[148] It was the first time that a joint Transmission System Operator (TSO) company had been created to implement this kind of project (since then, others have followed suit). Monti then decided to focus on identifying possible justifications for the project. He ordered a new, complete and independent study to CESI, the consulting firm that had already been in charge of the EIAs for the Baixas-Bescanó project in 2002–2003. Between March and June 2008, CESI produced six reports. CESI presented the same justifications as before, and Monti was satisfied that no doubt remained as to the necessity of a new EHV line. He reached the same conclusion as the French CPDP, which had organized the public debate in 2003: the new EHV power line was necessary, but could not be built overhead. Monti recommended that the line be entirely underground, in direct current and along existing infrastructure.[149] Monti explained the advantages of direct current: there is no intermediary compensation station (DC is the only possibility for underground power lines that are longer than 25 mi (40 km)), the technique is well understood, less invasive environmentally and the EMF is equivalent to the Earth's natural EMF.[150] An underground EHVDC

147 MARIO MONTI, PREMIER RAPPORT D'ÉTAPE DU COORDONNATEUR EUROPÉEN SUR L'INTERCONNEXION ÉLECTRIQUE FRANCE-ESPAGNE, PROJET D'INTÉRÊT EUROPÉEN EL3 (Brussels. 12 December 2007), at ec.europa.eu/ten/energy/coordinators/doc/2008_01_10_interim_report_mm_fr.pdf, accessed 17 June 2021.

148 INELFE is a joint stock company governed by French law, incorporated on 1 October 2008 as a joint investment by Spain's and France's electric grid managing companies, REE and RTE. Each one of the two owns 50%. INELFE was created with the aim of carrying out the new electrical connection between Baixas (France) and Santa Llogaia (Spain). The French part is a 100% subsidiary of RTE, itself a wholly subsidiary of EDF. As for its Spanish part, INELFE is a wholly subsidiary of REE.

149 MARIO MONTI, RAPPORT DU COORDONNATEUR EUROPÉEN, PROJET D'INTÉRÊT EUROPÉEN EL3, INTERCONNEXION ÉLECTRIQUE FRANCE-ESPAGNE, 14 (Brussels. September 2008), at https://ec.europa.eu/ten/energy/coordinators/doc/annual/1_monti_fr.pdf, accessed 17 June 2021.

150 Today, direct current is the only possible solution for the transmission of electricity over long distance (beyond 25 mi / 40 km) and with regard to the quantities that are needed, which are considerably increasing. For instance, a 2,113 miles (3,400 km) UHV DC line (1,100kV) with a 12 GW capacity was built in China (Jinping-Sunan) in 2018, one in twenty-two already in existence, with eleven others under way in that country. The next step is

power line was the only solution. Monti suggested that the EU cover at least 10% of the extra cost.[151]

2.3.2 The New Interconnection Line (Baixas – Santa Llogaia)

At the Saragosse Summit on 27 June 2008, the French and Spanish governments announced that they would follow Mario Monti's recommendations: the interconnection was to be underground, in direct current, along already existing infrastructure. A High-Speed Railroad (HSR) was already in place between Perpignan and Figueres. The power line was planned along this HSR, running entirely underground. This could be achieved thanks to a new technology (notably, the VSC – Voltage Source Converter) according to INELFE, who explained that an underground line was not possible until then.[152] Besides, albeit in a rather circular logic, the French government promised that, absent future interconnection needs, there would not be another electrical interconnection on the territory of the *Pyrénées Orientales* department.[153] As a matter of fact, the next one will be offshore (past the West side of the Pyrenees, across the Biscay Gulf, further increasing French-Spanish interconnection capacity to 5,000 MW).

Opposition had become minimal.[154] At that point, there were only technicalities to agree upon. Consequently, in France, the CNDP decided that no expensive public debate was necessary, but simply a consultation procedure with an independent supervisor. The president of the previous public debate, Georges Mercadal, was chosen once again. The consultation took place in two phases (January – April 2009, and November 2009 – March 2010), during which time INELFE decided on the new route together with local officials,

1.1 million volts. During the War of Currents (late 1880's) in the United States, Thomas Edison fought for a DC based power distribution network, but Nikola Tesla and its lower cost AC power distribution prevailed. Today, engineers are working on a DC grid idea, in parallel to the AC one.

151 MONTI, *supra* note 149 at 17.

152 Yves Decœur, 1 April 2015 interview. VSC replaced thyristors with IGBTs (Insulated Gate Bipolar Transistor), more flexible and compact (massive filters are no longer required), which are operated by elaborate software.

153 Article 3 of the cooperation agreement on the electrical interconnection between the governments of France and Spain, signed in Saragosse, 27 June 2008 (*Décret No. 2008-1087 du 23 octobre 2008*).

154 There were only 163 questions from January 2009 to March 2010 (GEORGES MERCADAL, CONSULTATION REPORT 23 (7 April 2010), at https://www.archives.debatpublic.fr/file/1210/download?token=S5p9vVGZ, accessed 18 June 2021).

NGOs, and inhabitants, based on documents from both France and Spain (especially EIAs).[155]

The French Environmental Authority (AE) delivered a favorable opinion on the project. The AE had been created in 2005, in order to abide by Article 6 of the 1985 EIA European Directive. Since 2009, its opinion has been compulsory, as part of the EIA procedure.[156] In both states, the DUPs were pronounced in 2011 and early 2012.[157] EU financial aid was officially granted in their wake. The European Union proved essential to the completion of the project, in helping to cover not only 10%, but in fact more than 80% of the costs in the end, with 225-million euro in funding under the European Energy Programme for Recovery (more than 32% of the total cost) and a 350-million-euro loan from the European Investment Bank (EIB), i.e. half of the total cost, also the maximum authorized to the EIB. The European Union decided to participate for two reasons: the completion of the IEM, and the ongoing financial crisis. 700 million euros was the final cost of the EHV DC line that was built, i.e. almost eight times the cost of an overhead power line, to which should be added the compensations paid by France to Spain for the delays. Construction began mid-2011 and finished at the end of 2014. The underground power line is more than 40 mile-long (64.5 km) between Baixas in France and Santa Llogaia in Spain. The tunnel under the Pyrenees is more than 5 mile-long (8.5 km) and 11.5 ft in diameter (3.5 m). On both sides of the mountains, the line runs through two covered trenches.[158]

---

155 The documents of the public consultation are available at https://www.archives.debatpublic.fr/projet-renforcement-echanges-electriques-entre-france-lespagne, accessed 18 June 2021.

156 Act No. 2005-1319 of 26 October 2005 (Article L.122-1 of the Environment Code), together with its implementation decree No. 2009-496 of 30 April 2009. In France, the administrative authority for environmental matters is, according to project types, either the Environment Minister, or the *Autorité Environnementale* (an entity lodged within the *Conseil Général de l'Environnement et du Développement Durable* (CGEDD)). See Article R.122-6 of the Environment Code. In this particular case, in which three DUPs were necessary, both the *Autorité Environnementale* on 8 July 2010 (Recommendation No. 2010-26) and the region prefect (Claude Baland, Languedoc-Roussillon Region) on 19 July 2010 handed down a recommendation (the region prefect was the competent authority at the time, along with the AE).

157 In France, ministerial order of 22 April 2011 *portant déclaration d'utilité publique d'un ouvrage d'énergie électrique*, NOR: EFIR1111294A, published in the *Journal Officiel* of 4 May 2011. In Spain, 21 May 2011 for the line itself, and 28 February 2012 for the converter substation in Santa Llogaia.

158 The total width of the two trenches, including the gap between them, is about 10 ft (3 m) and the depth is 5 ft (1.5 m). Two parallel cables were laid in each of the trenches.

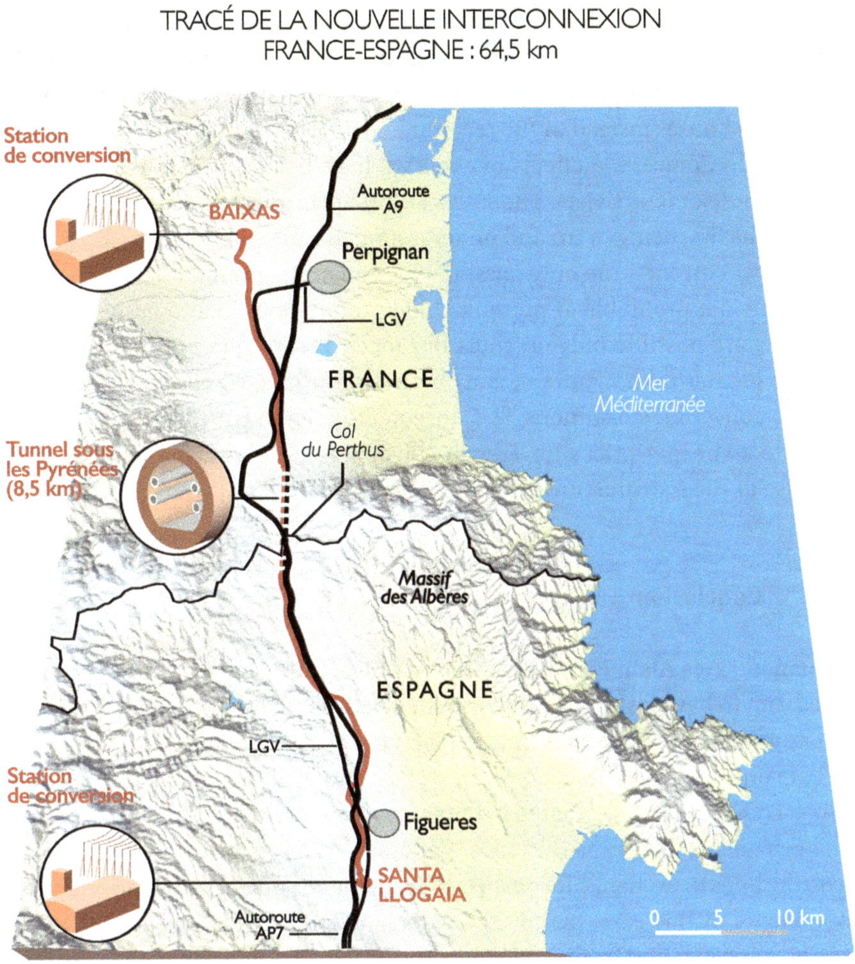

MAP 2 Final route of the new French-Spanish transmission line, between Baixas and Santa Llogaia, along the high-speed railway and the highway, underground (Jean-Claude Bourbon, *Une nouvelle ligne électrique relie la France et l'Espagne*, LA CROIX, 19 February 2015.)
ILLUSTRATION REPRODUCTION COURTESY OF ART PRESSE.
Note: please disregard the map scale

In 2001, Spain had begun adopting electromagnetic field regulations.[159] The Spanish 2008 act that applied allowed lines to be built starting only 5.5 yards

159 See *supra* note 35.

(5 m) away from a residence.[160] As a result, in Spain, where the line between Santa Llogaia and Bescanó is no longer an interconnection, but a domestic power line, the EHV power line runs overhead, sometimes only a few meters away from houses instead of the recommended 328 yards (300 m) or 437 yards (400 m). In France, the effects of the EMF have been continually monitored by RTE and some activists. The latter still suspect there is a significant EMF despite the line being in DC and underground. Because of the technology chosen (direct current – the only possibility for an underground line of this size), the line is not profitable at present. Underground lines in alternative current (EHVAC) are possible only on short distances. EHVDC lines are profitable at lengths greater than 155mi (250km) because of the fixed costs of associated AC/DC converter substations.[161] Consequently, contrary to what EDF had predicted, cheaper prices for French consumers did not materialize, in part because of the transmission network costs.[162]

3 Conclusion

In France, since Alain Juppé's decision to cancel their project in 1996, EDF and RTE seem to have lost some of their influence. They are now forced to communicate and make occasional compromises. In 2003, the same year as the public debate on the Baixas-Bescanó route, RTE had to abandon an EHV power line project (*Quercy Blanc*), situated in the same Midi-Pyrénées region, between the Golfech nuclear plant and the city of Cahors.[163] RTE agreed instead to reinforce existing lines in exchange for an electricity demand control mechanism.[164] The opponents in this case, mainly the association *Quercy Blanc Environnement* (QBE), were inspired by the 1996 outcome in the Cazaril-Aragón line case (the

160 *Real Decreto 223/2008*, 15 February 2008. Until 2008, there was no minimum distance between a power line and human dwellings (*Decreto 3151/1968*, 28 November 1968).

161 Jean-François Lesigne (Environmental Advisor at RTE), 31 March 2015 interview. See also *supra* note 150.

162 As a matter of fact, retail electricity prices have risen, for diverse reasons (see SENAT, RAPPORT SUR LE COUT REEL DE L'ELECTRICITE AFIN D'EN DETERMINER L'IMPUTATION AUX DIFFERENTS AGENTS ECONOMIQUES (2012); Commission de Régulation de l'Energie, Decision No. 2019-028 of 7 February 2019).

163 It was a 25-mile (40 km), 225kV power line project (public debate page at https://www.archives.debatpublic.fr/projet-ligne-tht-renforcement-electrique-du-lot-dit-quercy-blanc (accessed 18 June 2021).

164 DANIEL BOY & MATHIEU BRUGIDOU, LE DÉBAT PUBLIC, UN RISQUE DÉMOCRATIQUE? L'EXEMPLE DE LA MOBILISATION AUTOUR D'UNE LIGNE HAUTE TENSION 144 (Lavoisier. 2008).

Louron Valley project), which convinced them that their actions might not be in vain. Prominent opponents to the Cazaril-Aragón line project came to lend their support, such as Michel Geoffre. The founder and head of QBE, Charles Farreny (a mathematics teacher and an elected municipal official), was the brother of Geoffre's colleague, Henri Farreny, at the Midi-Pyrénées Regional Council. Here again, Geoffre, Charles and Henri Farreny united all those that opposed the project under an umbrella association, called *Coordination Lignes Electriques Midi-Pyrénées* (CLEM). The solution that was eventually adopted for the Quercy Blanc power line project was suggested in a report made by a consultancy firm (INESTENE) headed by Pierre Radanne, who became Deputy Chief of Staff to the Environment Minister, Dominique Voynet,[165] and then head of the ADEME, the French governmental agency in charge of the reforms in the combined environment and energy domains.[166] Radanne was highly respected and in a position to provide financial aid for this proposal.[167] As for RTE, one might speculate that they preferred to avoid having two controversial ongoing projects in the same region. Moreover, unlike the INELFE project, the Quercy Blanc project had no international trade aspect and the nuclear plant was already connected. Radanne's solution proved thus acceptable to them. Three years later, in 2006, another EHV power line project was cancelled, this time by the French Council of State, which was a first. On 2 May 2006, the Council of State visited the relevant area, itself an exceptional move. The *Conseil d'Etat* decided that its beauty and wilderness (the natural regional park of Verdon in Southeastern France) forbade the installation of any new power lines.[168] Since the Cazaril-Aragón (Louron) case, when other

165 Environment Minister from June 1997 to July 2001, in the government of Lionel Jospin (Socialist Party).

166 *Agence De l'Environnement et de la Maîtrise de l'Energie*, created in 1990 (Act No. 90-1130, 19 December 1990). Pierre Radanne was its president from 1998 to 2003.

167 INESTENE was as competent as EDF/RTE engineers and more trusted than the latter (Alban Bouvier, *La dynamique des relations de confiance et d'autorité au sein de la démocratie dite « participative » et « délibérative »*, 45 REVUE EUROPÉENNE DES SCIENCES SOCIALES 181, 215 (2007)). INESTENE stands for INstitut d'Evaluation des STratégies sur l'Energie et l'ENvironnement en Europe (created in 1987, it ceased to exist in 2006).

168 There are two HV power lines that already run through the park. They were supposed to be dismantled and replaced by a new 400kV line. CE, 10 July 2006, *Boutre-Carros*, case No. 288108, cancelled the DUP: "the affected region is of exceptional value, as such already protected by diverse legal regimes. The project will inflict new and significant environmental harm, superior to its benefits, which deprives it from any public interest quality" (author's translation). In November 2008, a serious outage finally led to the decision to build new 225kV power lines, but underground (by segments of 40 mi (65 km) each), and in parallel with existing infrastructure, similarly to the Baixas-Santa Llogaia power line.

EHV overhead power line projects have been successful despite local opposition, RTE has explained this was because it was truly impossible to have the line in direct current for technical and financial reasons. Some were domestic projects, with no European dimension.[169] Additionally, and importantly, the opposition is often significantly less united than in the Pyrenees.

Like the Vuotos Dam case (see previous case study, in Finland with potential impacts in Sweden), the French-Spanish Interconnection case marked a turning point in making social choices and achieving community's goals in France, in particular as regards environmental matters. For the first time in Finland and in France, in the energy sector, public participation and environmental concerns were successfully integrated in the constitutive process. Many factors came into play. The combination of civil society activism, lawsuits, tourism industry special interests, personal political clout and power struggles between a public company and the government together led to the cancellation of the project in both these European cases, and to the subsequent, substantial modification of the project in the Interconnection case. Both cases are emblematic, insofar as the affected populations were able to successfully oppose the project. They categorically refused any compensation. They wanted to be heard and to participate in the decision-making process that would affect them. They vigorously rejected the government's attempts to impose its will without considering them and to serve economic interests to the detriment of their region. The Interconnection project took a considerable amount of time because EDF/RTE refused originally to engage in dialogue and amend its project. Then, all three agents of the common good – state, citizens and technicians[170] – contributed effectively to the decision that was ultimately taken.

The Vuotos and Interconnection cases differ regarding the role of international cooperation, local authorities and legal proceedings: except with regard to NGOs, international cooperation was nonexistent in the Interconnection case until 2008. It was then imposed by the European Union; for the first time, a joint TSO company was created, INELFE (French-Spanish). INELFE was

169 See for instance the Cotentin-Maine EHV line, in Normandy, commissioned in 2013 (101 mi (163km) long, 414 pylons, one every 437 yards (400 m)). A mayor (Jean-Claude Bossard) and his council resigned to protest against the lack of respect for his order imposing a minimum distance between pylons and dwellings or farms (municipal order of Chefresne on the protection of the inhabitants and their livestock, No. 04-2008, 19 February 2008). Out of the thirty-five municipalities that first opposed the project (sixty-four were affected in total), there were only five left after EDF offered its financial compensations. See *supra* note 75.

170 René-Jean Dupuy, *L'organisation internationale et l'expression de la volonté générale*, REVUE GÉNÉRALE DE DROIT INTERNATIONAL PUBLIC 527, 578 (1957).

supposed to be dissolved at the end of the EHVDC line project, but instead, it stayed in existence for future other projects, for both the French and Spanish companies (RTE and REE) were quite satisfied with their cooperation.[171] As for locally elected representatives, they were in favor of the project proponent in Finland, but not in France. Lastly, the opposition to the interconnection project ultimately lost in court, unlike the Vuotos case, but achieved its goal nonetheless. EIAs played a significant part, combined with the other procedural rules that were followed, notably those about public participation. In regulating EIAs, the key issue is to determine the optimum moment to consult and to produce the studies. Since EIAs have been put in place, project proponents, engineers and investors have frequently seen them as a source of delays. Moreover, they have endeavored to preserve their authority and influence. Consequently, EIAs are often made late in the decision-making process, only to validate retrospectively decisions that have already been taken. Even though EIAs purport to identify environmental impacts and integrate affected populations into the decision-making process, the two are dissociated in France. EIAs are made before informing concerned citizens. The Interconnection case has contributed to having public participation included earlier in the project development process. Reforms are underway and project proponents now often take the initiative to inform and consult early because experience shows they run higher risks of costly delays otherwise.

In this case, the first EIA, in 1984, clearly showed an absence of justification for the route chosen by the project proponent (EDF), in disregard of the preparatory work done with the Environment Minister and local officials. EDF alone had already taken its decision and the EIA was conducted only to justify its choice. Such disregard was typical in the past, but thanks to the EIA, it became public this time, thus laying the groundwork for subsequent reasoned discussions and legal proceedings. More generally, faced with increasing opposition with regard to all its projects, the French public utility company agreed, in 1992, to systematically consult affected populations during the decision-making process. EDF/RTE implemented this commitment only incrementally. Nevertheless, from the beginning, the opposition in this case was very well-organized and efficient, and used all possible means, which drove the decision-making authorities to hesitate and then retreat. The opposition gained precious time. There were two pivotal moments: the

171 Following the Madrid Summit on 4 March 2015 (*Energy Interconnections Links Summit – Spain – France – Portugal – European Commission – EIB*), INELFE was made responsible for the construction and start-up of the electricity interconnections between France and Spain aimed at increasing the electricity interchange capacity between the two countries.

decision of the French Prime Minister, Alain Juppé, in February 1996, and the decision of the French Industry Minister after the CNDP report in 2003. In 1996, when Juppé decided to support the opposition and cancel the first project (the Cazaril-Aragón route through the Louron Valley), he acted without the full support of his government, as he was shattering an engrained French tradition. For the first time, the national energy company was no longer the only dominant actor. In broader terms, the Prime Minister's decision signaled a deep change in the determination of the common good. Since the French Revolution, engineers from the *grands corps de l'Etat* had been accustomed to embodying the continuity of the French state and of the general interest. However, in situations where the French state is both the project proponent and the competent authority, confidence had been gradually lost, beginning in the 1970's.[172] Juppé's decision signaled a change in the decision-making process. In addition, the Aarhus Convention led to a new law on democracy of proximity, in 2002.[173] In particular, the CNDP, in charge of organizing a public debate before the public inquiry procedure since 1995, was transformed into an independent administrative authority. Heightened public participation in determining the common interest has tended to restore trust among the populations affected by a project – trust in the possibilities to participate effectively. When RTE attempted to have its project approved elsewhere in the Pyrenees, with the same type of overhead power line, it lost again in 2003, after a public debate organized by the CNDP. This was followed by a decision of the Industry Minister to take the outcome of the debate into account. No compromise had been found mainly because of the obstruction of the project proponent, who provided inaccurate information. For the first time, an Industry Minister was able to decide not to support the national public utility company, in the broader context of renewed and improved environmental obligations for such project proposals, with the support of the President and the government. The 2003 public debate was the first to be held in France after the CNDP had become an independent administrative authority. Public debates organized by the CNDP have been a welcome additional procedure for civil society to inform, be informed, and gain legitimacy earlier on in an improved decision-making process. In the Interconnection project, no solution could be found

172 In the Louron Valley case, in the wake of the Souviron Report, the advocate-general did not fail to mention this problematic confusion caused by the two roles of the French state (Rey, CAHIERS JURIDIQUES DE L'ELECTRICITÉ ET DU GAZ, 111 (Mars 1994)).

173 Act No. 2002-276, 27 February 2002. The Aarhus Convention was ratified by France in 2002 (Act No. 2002-285, 28 February 2002 and executive order No. 2002-1187, 12 September 2002).

in 2003, because neither the project proponent, nor the state representatives had shown sufficient consideration for the public debate process, misstating the justifications of the EHV power line. The project was then stalled for four entire years, which was quite significant in terms of financial costs. Only the EU mediation solved the deadlock. The project was then completed in accord with the wishes of the inhabitants, thanks to the overwhelming financial help of the European Union and because of existing infrastructure. The last consultation was a remarkable achievement, the outcome of decades of resolute opposition, which led to an atypical instance of a project proponent deciding on the route of its project together with the affected populations. In the end, the final route of the EHV power line benefited the common good in both France and Spain.

Procedural obligations (EIAs with public participation), through diverse effects, reduced the overwhelming power of the French national public utility company and changed the relationship dynamics between the actors involved. Since then, multiple actors have substantially participated in the decision-making processes. Similarly to Finland, there is a growing, general awareness of the fact that anyone can now act and play an important role in protecting the environment and influence the decision-making process.[174] Moreover, the French Environmental Authority (AE), which is an independent administrative authority like the CNDP, firmly asked that, in the future, international obligations impose a unique EIA for transnational projects, which would apply to the entire area covered by a project, in all concerned states. The AE also recommended that obligations under international law provide for the transmission of the observations of the public in one state to the authorities of the other state(s) in a timely fashion, early in the process, before any decision be made.[175] France had already ratified such international provisions, notably the Espoo Convention.[176] The AE's comments applied beyond

174 See for instance the European Commission survey, *Special Eurobarometer 468: Attitudes of European citizens towards the environment* 45 (2017), where 85% of the respondents in France were of this opinion, an improvement from 2014 (+ 5 points); in Spain: 89% (+1 point). About Finland, see *supra* chapter 4, note 152.

175 *Avis No. 2010-26 – Avis délibéré de l'Autorité environnementale relatif à l'étude d'impact du projet de ligne électrique souterraine entre Baixas et la frontière franco-espagnole au Perthus* (Conseil général de l'Environnement et du Développement Durable – Autorité environnementale. 8 July 2010).

176 Articles 2.6, 3.8 and 6.1 of the Espoo Convention. France ratified the convention on 14 April 2000 (Act No. 2000-328). The convention was published in the Official Journal of the French Republic by effect of the executive order No. 2001-1176 of 5 December 2001.

this particular interconnection case and drew attention to this oft-neglected aspect.[177] Interestingly, Michel Badré, the President of the AE from 2009 to 2014, also established new rules to shield the AE from external pressure. He systematically chose its members from among senior candidates nearing the end of their careers, and he decided to publish the AE's decisions immediately after its deliberations.[178]

In France, at the same time the interconnection was achieved, in 2015, the increased pressure of public concern and public participation in environmental matters led to a large number of stalled projects in different sectors (about 170 projects). The government and the national assembly decided to remedy the situation by improving public participation procedures. On 19 February 2015, the government appointed a special commission to this end.[179] In June 2015, the commission's report was clear: the main reason projects were opposed and blocked was because public participation was organized at too late a stage (after EIAs were made[180]), when the project was quite advanced and even already decided by the project proponent alone. It had become evident that public participation needed to be organized as early as possible in project development.[181] The French Government decided to follow through with the Richard Commission's report. In August 2015, inspired by this report, a law was passed on its initiative, to prepare for improved regulations.[182] In April and August 2016, ordinances were thus passed. They were disappointing, but still provided for slightly better timing of public participation, the increased use of information technologies and a better articulation between SEAs and EIAs.[183]

177 Michel Badré remembers the AE's willingness to take the opportunity to comment more generally about this issue, beyond the Interconnection case under review (15 March 2016 interview).

178 Michel Badré, 15 March 2016 interview. See also Michel Badré, *L'Autorité environnementale et la participation du public à l'élaboration de ses décisions*, 81 ANNALES DES MINES – RESPONSABILITÉ ET ENVIRONNEMENT 30, 32–33 (2016).

179 *Commission spécialisée du Conseil national de la transition écologique sur la démocratisation du dialogue environnemental présidée par Alain Richard* (the Richard Commission, presided by Alain Richard).

180 Articles L.122-1-1 and L.123-10 of the Environmental Code.

181 See the commission's report: COMMISSION RICHARD, RAPPORT: DÉMOCRATIE ENVIRONNEMENTALE – DÉBATTRE ET DÉCIDER (3 June 2015), which was in line with the 1994 Souviron report (see *supra* page 209).

182 See Article 106 of Act No. 2015-990, 6 August 2015, allowing future ordinances in the matter.

183 Ordinance No. 2016-488, 21 April 2016, relating to local consultations for projects that are likely to have environmental impacts; Ordinance No. 2016-1060, 3 August 2016, on the reform of procedures to ensure information and public participation in decisions that may have environmental impacts.

The Richard Commission had insisted on this latter point. The three case studies under review in this book show that this articulation is at the core of a more efficient project development process. With an SEA, conducted by both French and Spanish project proponents, EDF may not have insisted on building the interconnection in Central Pyrenees. Catalonia, rather than Aragón, would have been identified as the relevant region earlier in the process.

Importantly, French law prescribes that rules in matters of public participation, including EIAs, must be equally followed as regards an affected State, by virtue of the 1985 EIA Directive and the Espoo Convention.[184] Consequently, any domestic improvement in these rules is automatically applied to transboundary projects. In France, EIAs alone may have limited effects, but in a broader sense, i.e. combined with the other procedural obligations in matters of public participation, they lead to the involvement of the affected populations, who exert pressure through diverse means (including legal proceedings, elections, studies and media campaigns). The competent authorities in democratic regimes can no longer ignore this pressure. EIAs are slowly being developed and improved in France, so that they can be made in a timely and comprehensive fashion and form the basis of a fully informed and inclusive decision-making process. In both the Vuotos Dam and the Interconnection cases, civil society successfully prevented the construction for decades. Both cases are emblematic of the evolution of EIAs and public participation in a democratic context. To think of procedural obligations as an inefficient source of delays because of a lack of required substantive outcomes appears to be misleading. State law-making institutions cannot keep pace with the rapidity of change in a science-based and technological society. Hard law would be unworkable. Soft law performs important functions in this regard. Both cases illustrate the complexity of positive modifications to the constitutive process. They took place in the European Union, which decisively intervened. Regional systems have been described as the best way to achieve common goals through international organizations with general competency.[185] So far, in the Vuotos case, Natura 2000 regulations (EU nature protection areas) have prevented any subsequent Finnish government from reversing its position and attempting to pass a new law in order to have the dam built. In the Interconnection case, the power line was finally built along the best route because of EU mediation and financial aid. Beyond the Interconnection case, environmental experts involved in this case have emphasized the crucial role of international and

184 Articles L.123-7, L.123-8, R.122-4, and R.122-10 of the Environmental Code.

185 Dupuy, REVUE GÉNÉRALE DE DROIT INTERNATIONAL PUBLIC (1957).

regional obligations in this regard, such as the Espoo and Aarhus Conventions, as well as the EIA Directive.[186] Furthermore, as all three case studies in this book demonstrate, and as the Espoo Convention emphasizes, the efficiency of EIAs starts at the domestic level. It is a national procedure, a participatory one.

We will now turn to the last case study, in a different part of the world, South-East Asia – the Mekong region more precisely.

186 BONDUELLE, *supra* note 138 at 1; Badré, ANNALES DES MINES – RESPONSABILITÉ ET ENVIRONNEMENT (2016).

CHAPTER 6

The Upper Mekong Navigation Improvement Project (UMNIP)

China – Myanmar – Thailand – Laos (1989 – 2020)

在少数民族中，流传着一个古老的民间传说，说澜沧江是太阳的第十个儿子[1]

La navigabilité du Mékong ! … il y a là une œuvre digne de passionner notre siècle amoureux des grandes entreprises et de tenter nos ingénieurs pour qui il n'y a pas d'impossible … Mais une entreprise aussi colossale doit être préparée par de laborieuses études … il faut avant tout connaître le fleuve, s'y avancer pas à pas, le théodolite et le niveau à la main[2]

Die Philosophen haben die Welt nur verschieden interpretiert; es kommt aber darauf an, sie zu verändern[3]

∴

1 "There was an old folk legend among ethnic minorities that Lancang Jiang is the tenth son of the Sun" (Pu Chaozhu, *Preface*, *in* 钱杰林、杨选民："话说澜沧江"，云南民族出版社1988年版 (Qian Jielin & Yang Xuanmin, DISCOVERING THE LANCANG JIANG 1 (Yunnan Nationality Press. 1988) (Wang Zhiqiang's translation)). Pu is a former governor of Yunnan Province.

2 CONTRE-AMIRAL PAUL-EMILE RÉVEILLÈRE, LE HAUT-MÉKONG OU LE LAOS OUVERT 17 (Librairie Fischbacher. 1892). "The navigability of the Mekong! … there is a task worthy of raising the passions of our century with its love for great undertakings, tempting our engineers for whom nothing is impossible. … However, such an endeavor must be meticulously prepared by comprehensive studies. … First and foremost, we must know the river well, carefully advance there, with a theodolite and a level in hand" (author's translation). Réveillère (1829–1908) was a French admiral who served in Asia. He was the first foreigner to pass the Khone Rapids, on a 44-torpedo boat in 1885.

3 "Philosophers have hitherto only interpreted the world in various ways; the point, however, is to change it", Karl Marx, Theses on Feuerbach (appendix to Ludwig Feuerbach and the End of Classical German Philosophy, by Friedrich Engels) (1888).

 | DOI:10.1163/9789004467583_007

New technological possibilities have led to an ever-increasing alteration of the planet that sustains human life. This case study concerns the daunting attempt to transform one of its mightiest and most tormented rivers, which flows through six states, into a tranquil navigation canal. It further considers the extent to which the international constitutive process can be shaped by the existence of a pressing common interest – i.e. the conservation of the Mekong River, a body of water that has long secured the livelihood of the tens of million inhabitants of its basin.

The People's Republic of China, where the Lancang Jiang (the Chinese name of the river) has its source, borders fourteen states and has the greatest number of international rivers and lakes in the world – over a hundred.[4] The country holds the headwaters for most of these, and possesses a significant part of each before the rivers finally reach a neighboring state's territory. Consequently, in the crucial domain of water management, China has a tremendous impact on downstream countries. In addition, as a prominent investor in many of these countries, it also has considerable persuasive power in carrying out the projects of its choice on their territories. The economic and geopolitical order is thus highly skewed in favor of China.

Concerns related to Chinese dams on these international rivers have been growing since the mid-1990's. Hydropower on the whole Mekong River and its tributaries has become the most contentious environmental issue in mainland Southeast Asia. Less attention has been given to the environmental impacts that have resulted from attempts to improve and increase navigation on the Mekong River, the last attempt being the Upper Mekong Navigation Improvement Project (UMNIP), conducted by the People's Republic of China (China) on the territories of Myanmar, Thailand, and the Lao People's Democratic Republic (Lao PDR, or Laos).

1 General Presentation and Historical Context of the UMNIP Case

To date, remarkably, the UMNIP is the only case of a joint Environmental Impact Assessment (EIA) in the Mekong region.[5] At present, EIA is the principal procedure by which the Greater Mekong Subregion (GMS) states account for the

4 About 110, i.e. 42% of all the international rivers and lakes in the world. Beyond China, of all continents, Asia is the one that possesses the most international waters.

5 QI GAO, A PROCEDURAL FRAMEWORK FOR TRANSBOUNDARY WATER MANAGEMENT IN THE MEKONG RIVER BASIN – SHARED MEKONG FOR A COMMON FUTURE 248 (Stephen McCaffrey ed., Brill / Nijhoff. 2014).

social and environmental impacts of their numerous development activities. The UMNIP has entailed significant transboundary environmental impacts. As in the Interconnection case (see previous chapter), more than one state of origin was involved. In the previous case study, both France and Spain were states of origin and affected states. In this case, the four states that decided on the UMNIP (China, Myanmar, Thailand, Laos) were in a similar dual position. In addition to those four, two other states were affected (Cambodia and Vietnam), but were left aside. Rather strikingly, considering its role in the project, China represented only 9% of the length of the targeted stretch, which was also shared in part with Myanmar, as their common frontier. First and foremost, China was the project proponent, and the only beneficiary, as we will see farther below. China had already started to clear the river on its own territory long before, as early as the 1960's, without informing the downstream countries and before any EIA was made. It would continue to do so in parallel with the UMNIP and after the interruption of the project. Since China had begun a massive blasting campaign on the Mekong River on its own territory, it was (and has remained for any given project so far) unwilling to conduct any Transboundary EIA (TEIA),[6] and declined to follow the principle of prior consultations regarding water management, as first set out in the *Lake Lanoux* arbitration.[7] Furthermore, China did not need external financial funding – nor does it generally for any project – which removes opportunities to exert external pressure on the country.

The Lancang-Mekong River links six countries (China, Myanmar, Thailand, Laos, Cambodia, and Vietnam). It originates from the Nyenchen Tanglha mountains in Tibet, from what is now the Sanjiangyan National Nature Reserve (established to protect the headwaters of the Yellow, Yangtze, and Mekong rivers). The Mekong watershed is about 307,000 sq mi (800,000 km2), which makes the Mekong the largest international river in Southeast Asia – its catchment covers 38% of this region. About seventy million people live in the Mekong River Basin. Already at the time of the UMNIP, the population of the basin was expected to increase by more than 60% by 2025, which would ultimately represent more than a 100 million inhabitants. The Mekong River feeds and provides livelihoods for these millions of people. In 2014, the lower

6 Eric W. Sievers, *Transboundary Jurisdiction and Watercourse Law: China, Kazakhstan, and the Irtysh*, 37 TEXAS INTERNATIONAL LAW JOURNAL 1 (2002); Simon Marsden, *Developing Approaches to Trans-boundary Environmental Impact Assessment in China: Co-operation through the Greater Tumen Initiative and in the Pearl River Delta Region*, 9 CHINESE JOURNAL OF INTERNATIONAL LAW 393 (2010); Nadia Sanchez Castillo & Yongmin Bian, *China's Obligation to Conduct Transboundary Environmental Impact Assessment (TEIA) in Utilizing Its Shared Water Resources*, 55 NATURAL RESOURCES JOURNAL 105 (2014).

7 See *supra* page 15.

Mekong countries (Myanmar, Laos, Thailand, Cambodia, and Vietnam) produced about 15% of the world's total production of rice. The region's fertile soil depends on nutrient-rich sediment that the Mekong carries downriver, mainly during the rainy season, from June to October. The river and its nutrients also support the world's largest inland fishery, accounting for over 15% of the global freshwater catch (down from 20% in 1990). The river's name changes depending on the countries and regions through which it flows. In China, it is Lancang Jiang (Turbulent River), in Laos, Mènam Khong, or Mae Nam Khong in Thailand (Mother of Rivers), Tonle Thom (Great Water) in Cambodia, and Cuu Long (Nine Dragons) in Vietnam, where it divides itself into nine rivers and innumerable waterways, which form its delta. The Mekong River is about 3,000 miles long (4,800 km), with 1,320 miles (2,130 km) in China, 20 miles (31 km) along the China-Myanmar boundary, 145 miles (234 km) along the Laos-Myanmar border (this stretch includes the infamous Golden Triangle, where Myanmar, Thailand and Laos meet), 606 miles (976 km) between Laos and Thailand, 483 miles (777 km) in Laos, 312 miles (502 km) in Cambodia, and 143 miles (230 km) in Vietnam.[8]

Fueling vivid dreams of river trade, the hopes of forging a navigable route along the Mekong River have long existed, despite obstacles of all sorts along its course. As the Mekong leaves Laos and passes into Cambodia, it flows over the spectacular Khone Falls, a six-mile stretch of rapids near the legendary area of Four Thousand Islands, undergoing a drop in elevation of 23 yards (21 meters), which prevents vessel passage entirely. Over time, there were plans and attempts, including the UMNIP, to eliminate those falls, all in vain. In 1866, a two-year French expedition set off upriver from the Mekong Delta. Its mission was to find an inland water route to China for trade purposes and to bypass the British Hong Kong. Besides, the expedition was not devoid of political intentions: a prominent motive was to assert the French presence and to counter the British expansion in the north of the Mekong region. However, France's ambitions were thwarted, as navigation proved too difficult.[9] The French Mekong

8 JOINT EXPERTS GROUP ON EIA OF CHINA LAOS MYANMAR THAILAND, EXECUTIVE SUMMARY OF THE ENVIRONMENTAL IMPACT ASSESSMENT OF THE NAVIGATION CHANNEL IMPROVEMENT PROJECT OF THE LANCANG-MEKONG RIVER FROM THE CHINA-MYANMAR BOUNDARY MARKER 243 TO BAN HOUEI SAI IN LAOS, September 2001 (at http://www.livingriversiam.org/4river-tran/4mk/mek_rapid_eia_summary.pdf, accessed 17 June 2021).

9 In April 1865, with the support of Napoleon III, the French Navy Minister, Prosper de Chasseloup-Laubat (also head of the Geographical Society), had approved the Mekong expedition, led by Ernest Doudart de Lagrée and Francis Garnier. The expedition lasted two years (1866–1868), but failed to find a navigable waterway to China. However, the scientific

Exploration Commission ended up simply building a small portage railway to bypass Khone Falls.[10] From its source on the Tibetan plateau, the river winds southeast along a riverbed dotted with looming sandbars, reefs, serrated rocks, shoals, and fatal whirlpools, which have made the navigation almost impossible, especially during the dry season (November to May), except for the traditional boats – long, slender, flat-bottomed – used by Lao traders, which can carry a maximum of sixty deadweight tons (DWT). These boats are designed to slip through the rapids, if guided by experienced boatmen, who can navigate the river all year long. When British Naval Intelligence produced a handbook on the Indochinese region, the information provided on the Mekong as a navigable route was explicit and concise. Despite the French railway, "at the end of the 1930's, it still took longer to travel by river from Saigon to Luang Prabang [in Laos] than by sea from Saigon to Marseilles [France]. The golden route to China did not lie along the Mekong".[11]

The river never belonged to any one single political entity after the fall of the Khmer empire in the 15th century, but became an international border for countries often at war or unwilling to cooperate. The river evolved into a Cold-War frontier, dividing the communist countries of the region from Thailand. Consequently, until recently, the Mekong remained one of the least developed, hence one of the best preserved, of the world's major rivers. In the early 1990's, with the end of the Cold War and a settlement of the conflict in Cambodia, came talk of a "peace dividend" in Southeast Asia. This was the era of "turning battlefields to marketplaces", in the words of a former Thai Prime Minister.[12] After war and turmoil, there were hopes for regional cooperation and economic development. China revived the notion of the Mekong River as an international trade route, with reports often describing the Mekong as the "Danube of the East"[13] (perhaps a somewhat inapt comparison to make, in view of the

---

discoveries were numerous, and the first precise map of the Mekong River was drawn. Garnier expressed his admiration: "Without doubt, no other river, over such a length, has a more singular or remarkable character". (MILTON OSBORNE, RIVER ROAD TO CHINA: THE SEARCH FOR THE SOURCE OF THE MEKONG – 1866-73, 238 (Atlantic Monthly Press. 1997).

10 The Don Det – Don Khon railway was 4.3-mile long (7 km). It opened in 1893, and closed in the 1940's.

11 OSBORNE, *supra* note 9 at 217.

12 Chatichai Choonhavan, Prime Minister from August 1988 to February 1991, *in* Steven Erlanger, *Thailand Seeks to Shape a 'Golden Peninsula'*, THE NEW YORK TIMES, 30 April 1989.

13 See, for instance (in Chinese), MA SHUHONG, THE ORIENTAL DANUBE: A STUDY ON THE DEVELOPMENT OF THE LANCANG JIANG-MEKONG RIVER BASIN (Yunnan People's Press. 1995), prefaced by Liu Shusheng, a former chairman of the People's Consultative Conference of Yunnan Province.

severe disputes between Hungary and Slovakia over dams and environmental issues[14]). Improving the navigation on the Mekong River was an integrated part of substantial economic development plans for the entire Mekong region, putting considerable pressure on the ecosystem of the river, if not disrupting it entirely in due course.

In 1989–1990, China initiated specific plans for waterway alterations that would open up northern segments of the Mekong River to year-round navigation by larger passenger and cargo ships in Myanmar, Thailand, and Laos, from its border with Myanmar to Luang Prabang in Laos. From February to May 1993, a joint investigation on waterway transport on the Lancang-Mekong was conducted, according to which a significant economic potential lay with the river, in terms of commercial navigation. The findings were that the watercourse was navigable for vessels of 60-DWT, but if channel improvement were carried out, the river would be navigable for vessels from 100 to 500 DWT for at least 95% of the year. The Mekong River was an important waterway for China in view of the economic development of its landlocked, impoverished rural southern province of Yunnan. To prevent looming social and political unrest in this peripheral province, spurred in part by envy of the fast-growing East Coast cities, the Chinese government was anxious to direct Yunnan's trade southerly to the neighboring countries in the Mekong region and to improve sea access for its exports. Neglected for some time, this rural province was to be transformed into a bridgehead to Asia. The navigation project was thus not only about Sino-Thai trade, but also about southwest China's access to the rest of the world. At the time, most export cargo from Yunnan was shipped via river or rails to the Chinese East Coast ports. That trip could take from two weeks to a month or more, as opposed to an expected two-day trip when shipped down the Mekong River to a port in Bangkok. The Mekong River reaches Thailand at Chiang Saen port, which provides the first link between the river and the efficient Thai transportation network.

Some regional institutional developments have put increased pressure on the Mekong River as a waterway infrastructure of prime importance. The Greater Mekong Subregion (GMS), home to 340 million people, was designated, with the launch of a development project formed in 1992 by the Asian Development Bank (ADB), to bring together Cambodia, Laos, Myanmar, Thailand, Vietnam, Yunnan and Guangxi in China into a program of economic cooperation, shifting from subsistence farming to open, market-based systems.

---

14 MATTHEW Z. WHEELER, BLASTED RIVER: DILEMMAS OF MEKONG NAVIGATION 6 (Institute of Current World Affairs. 2004). See *Gabčíkovo-Nagymaros Project (Hungary v. Slovakia)*, Judgment, 1997 ICJ Reports 7 (25 September), reprinted in 37 ILM 162 (1998).

With support from the Japan-led ADB and some other donors, the GMS Program has helped the implementation of high priority regional projects in infrastructure (superhighways, large dams, power transmission grids, etc.), trade, private sector investment, mass tourism and agriculture. The UMNIP became a component of the GMS North-South Economic Corridor Flagship Program, approved in 2002. That same year, China signed the ASEAN–China Free Trade Area (ACFTA or CAFTA) initial framework agreement, creating a free trade area among the ten member-states of the Association of Southeast Asian Nations (ASEAN) and China. The ACFTA came into effect on 1 January 2010. There is a dozen institutional embodiments of the cooperation and development plans for the Mekong region, among which the ASEAN Mekong Basin Development Cooperation established in 1996, the American-led Lower Mekong Initiative (LMI) launched in 2009 (called the Mekong-US Partnership since 2020), and the recent Lancang-Mekong Cooperation Mechanism (LMC) led by China and set up in 2015 in parallel and notably in support of its global infrastructure development project, the Road and Belt Initiative.[15] The Mekong region is of significant interest to many.

In the 1990's and 2000's, transforming the Mekong River into a water-highway became rather urgent because of the disastrous state of the road links between Yunnan's capital, Kunming, and Chiang Rai in northern Thailand, via Shan State in Myanmar and Luang Namtha in northern Laos. In 1989, talks started to be held between the provincial government of Yunnan and the government of Laos. China, Laos, Myanmar, and Thailand then conducted some joint investigations about improving the navigation on the Mekong River in May-June and in October-November 1990. China had already planned to rebuild the roads and add more of them, but in the meantime, the UMNIP was considerably less expensive and swifter. The Mekong River certainly offered the shortest distance between Yunnan and Thailand's fine highways and ports, and the world beyond. In its plea for the UMNIP, China emphasized the frequency of boat accidents, the loss of lives and cargo because of the presence of rocks especially between Jinghong in Yunnan and Chiang Saen in Thailand, resulting in a prolonged lull in shipping during the dry season, when the water level is low and the rocks more protuberant.[16] Although, as mentioned above, experienced boatmen could navigate year-round in the long and slender 60-DWT boats used by Lao traders, or in up to 200-DWT boats during the rainy

15 The Mekong-US Partnership and LMC are both a multinational partnership between Cambodia, Laos, Myanmar, Thailand, Vietnam on the one hand and, on the other hand, the United States in the case of the Mekong-US Partnership, China in the case of the LMC.

16 WHEELER, 4. 2004.

season, these boats either were not considered, or deemed insufficient by Chinese authorities.

Apart from China's reasons for dramatically altering the Mekong River, the downstream states had their own incentives, which led their representatives to agree to the UMNIP.

As for Myanmar (population of more than 55 million), given its isolation at the time, its relationship with China was essential and the country was in no position to refuse. Furthermore, the Mekong River is far from Myanmar's center and its basin represents only a small part of the territory (3.5%). In addition, the UMNIP seemed to have offered the military government the possibility to assert, for the first time, direct control of Shan State's Mekong banks.[17] The military and business elites were keen on profiting from increased trade and tourism. For instance, quite a few luxurious casinos were then built on Burmese territory along the Mekong.

With regard to Laos (population of 7.3 million), the UMNIP was exclusively in favor of China and its larger ships. Laos was content with navigation as it was. For ages, Lao boatmen had known perfectly well how to make the most of the river with their well-designed 60-DWT boats. However, Laos is a one-party communist state and the small country could ill-afford to stand in the way of China, a major investor. Mountainous and landlocked, Laos is the poorest country in Southeast Asia. It is widely covered by largely unspoiled tropical forest. Less than 5% of the land is suitable for subsistence agriculture (most of it along the shores of the Mekong), which nevertheless provides around 75% of employment. Laos is the country with the largest share of the Mekong River Basin territory (78,000 square miles – 202,000 km2, 25% of the river's catchment area), which itself covers 85% of Lao territory, where more than 95% of the Lao total population lives. The communist Lao People's Revolutionary Party (LPRP – formerly Pathet Lao) has ruled the country since 1975. After a long period of isolation, Laos reopened itself to the world in the 1990's. It is plagued by corruption, but corruption does not seem to have played a direct role in this particular case. The UMNIP was conducted in the broader context of the tremendous influence that China has upon Laos. Furthermore, Laos did not think that the UMNIP would have negative impacts, quite the contrary: by opening the Mekong River to increased trade, the majority of the government hoped to benefit indirectly from China's economic growth and to steer its population away from a subsistence farming economy. However, international

17 Senior General Than Shwe was the head of state from 1992 to 2011, as chairman of the State Peace and Development Council (SPDC), the military regime that had seized power in 1988.

NGOs and the local population, informed at a later stage, after the work had begun, dreaded the disruptive consequences that the UMNIP could, and eventually did, trigger. The villagers in Laos (and in Thailand, for that matter) feared that the incoming Chinese vessels would flood local markets with goods much cheaper than domestic ones, undermining local shopkeepers and farmers. Residents and some government officials also worried that local agriculture could be further undercut by changes to the river current, which could accelerate the already severe erosion of the shores. "Without the reefs, the flow in the Mekong is likely to be much stronger, and big waves caused by huge ships would destroy the country's river banks," warned Thongpho Vongsriprasom of the Lao Ministry of Agriculture and Forestry.[18] Farmers relied on the fertile, sediment-enriched riverbanks for their annual harvests of rice, lettuce, cabbage and other crops. More generally, the seventy million people that live along the Mekong shores and in the whole Mekong Basin have relied heavily on the river as a vital source of protein. The Mekong supplied about 80% of the dietary protein consumed in the Mekong Basin, and more than 80% of its population was dependent on the river for their livelihood at the time of the UMNIP, in the 1990's. Reefs in the area, some as long as two kilometers, were the breeding ground for many migratory fish and there were fears that fish stocks be destroyed.

The government of Laos downplayed these concerns. Chinese investments in Laos alone totaled US$87 million in 1999, whereas foreign investments from other sources were in decline. Laos has continued to deepen its involvement with China as the latter has increased its economic and infrastructure investments, even though Laos has risked going heavily into debt as a result. "Right now we don't have transportation, so Laos gets nothing," declared the Laotian Trade Minister, Soulivong Daravong. "But this link will increase revenue. By having the possibility of transporting goods, people can buy and sell. It's much better than being isolated". Soulivong said the project would have a small effect on fisheries. "We're not blowing up whole rapids, just some stones that could break the boats when they come. [...] Of course we're making some harm to nature, but that can be accepted because it is not big harm".[19]

From the perspective of the government of Thailand (population of 70 million), the UMNIP meant a welcome expansion of trade with China, through the use of its river, road and port infrastructure. The Prime Minister at the

18 Lisa Mastny, *Messing with the Mekong*, November/December WORLD WATCH MAGAZINE 21, 24 (2003).

19 Dominic Whiting, *Chinese reef blasts send waves down Mekong River*, REUTERS, 28 April 2003.

time, Thaksin Shinawatra, was of Chinese origin.[20] He was strongly in favor of the UMNIP. He was also suspected of taking advantage of conflicts of interest. NGOs tried to argue that Thailand's expectations of a major increase in exports to China thanks to the UMNIP were unrealistic (they eventually proved to be right). However, China was a major investor and the Thai government led by Thaksin had had a steady pro-China policy.[21] Lastly, environmental protection at the governmental level was only at a nascent stage. As for the Mekong River itself, the average politician had no real interest in those matters, unless perhaps his constituency bordered the river.

2 The UMNIP

Entirely funded and carried out by China (i.e. by the Yunnan Province and by the Chinese Central Government), the UMNIP involved dynamiting and excavating a navigation channel through twenty-one of the most treacherous shoals, rapids and reefs along the 205 miles (331 km) of the stretch of the river that represented the worst navigability for boats beyond 60-DWT, along the border running successively between China and Myanmar, Myanmar and Laos, and Thailand and Laos – precisely from the China-Myanmar Boundary Marker number 243 to Ban Houei Sai in Laos. The Chinese stretch of the river was not formerly part of the UMNIP, as China conducted the works on its territory early and without informing the downstream countries. The UMNIP was expected to make this section much easier to navigate for large cargo and passenger ships, and secure a convenient waterway between the port of Simao in China (the city of Simao is now called Pu'Er) and Luang Prabang in Laos. The goal was to dramatically increase the annual shipping capacity of the Mekong – from four million tons in 2001 to ten million tons by 2007 – with the passage of up to a dozen 500-ton ships on a daily basis, for an estimated budget of only 5.3 million US dollars,[22] which was quite a modest amount for an infrastructure project.

20 Thaksin Shinawatra was Prime Minister of Thailand from February 2001 to September 2006. Thaksin's great grandfather, Seng Saekhu, was an immigrant from Meizhou, Guangdong, who arrived in Siam in the 1860's, and later settled in Chiang Mai. Thaksin's father adopted a Thai surname in 1938 because of anti-Chinese sentiment in the country.

21 Beyond the UMNIP, developing exchanges with China was Thailand's international trade policy. In 1990, China did not count among Thailand's top trading partners. Ten years later, China ranked 4th. At present, Thailand is the 22nd largest export economy in the world, China is its top export destination, as well as its top import origin.

22 JOINT SURVEY GROUP, JOINT SURVEY REPORT ON THE FEASIBILITY OF THE WATERWAY IMPROVEMENT PROJECT ON THE UPPER MEKONG RIVER FROM CHINA-MYANMAR

MAP 3 The Mekong River in South China (Yunnan) and downstream countries
MASTNY, WORLD WATCH MAGAZINE, 23 (2003). ILLUSTRATION REPRODUCTION COURTESY OF WORLDWATCH INSTITUTE. Note: please disregard the map scale

On 20 April 2000, China, Myanmar, Thailand, and Lao PDR signed an international navigation agreement, the Quadripartite Agreement on Commercial Navigation on the Lancang-Mekong River (hereinafter the Navigation Agreement). It has allowed, since 2005, commercial ships registered with any of the four signatories to freely sail and use designated ports along the Mekong River over 550 miles (886 km), from the southern Chinese port of Pu'er (formerly Simao) to Luang Prabang in Laos.[23] Even though Article 17 of the Navigation Agreement prescribes that no hazardous materials shall be transported on the river, one of China's goals in widening it was to access oil from Thai refineries.[24] On 15 March 2001, the Navigation Agreement was completed by a memorandum of understanding, which added six annexes to the original agreement. Annex 3 in particular provided some guidelines to maintain and improve navigation, increase the tonnage of ships and reduce transportation costs. In addition to this regulatory apparatus, cooperation for navigation on the Mekong was institutionalized with the establishment of the Joint Committee on Coordination of Commercial Navigation on the Lancang-Mekong River (JCCCN), in June 2001.

At first, in 2000, a technical working group was set up for the implementation of the Navigation Agreement (named the Technical Working Group on the Implementation of the Quadripartite Agreement on Commercial Navigation on the Lancang-Mekong River – TWG), with China as its coordinator. On 18–22 September 2000, the second meeting of the TWG, held in Kunming, the capital of Yunnan Province in China, unanimously decided to undertake all necessary measures to dramatically improve the navigability of the 206-mile/331km long section cited above, starting with another joint survey on the feasibility of the project. The survey was released soon after, in November of that same year; it concluded not only that the project was feasible (it would not change the thalweg, flow discharge, nor the boundaries of the river), but also that it was "imperative and imminent to carry out the project".[25]

BOUNDARY MARKER 243 TO BAN HOUAYXAI OF LAOS (The Technical Working Group on the Implementation of the Quadripartite Agreement on Commercial Navigation on the Lancang-Mekong River. 2000), at http://www.livingriversiam.org/4river-tran/4mk/mek_rapid_fs.pdf, accessed 17 June 2021.

23 The Navigation Agreement is available at https://www.jcccn.org/images/rule/Agreement.pdf (accessed 17 June 2021).

24 Article 17 cites examples "… such as toxic chemicals, explosives and radioactive material", the list of which is not exhaustive. Consequently, transporting oil on such a restricted water area can be considered as hazardous, according to the agreement.

25 JOINT SURVEY GROUP, *supra* note 22 at 10.

Thereupon, the Chinese Premier formally announced the launch of the UMNIP, in November 2000.[26]

2.1 *The First Phase – 2000–2003*

The UMNIP was to be conducted in three phases. The first phase, mostly along the Myanmar-Lao stretch of the river, would remove eleven major rapids, one shoal, and ten scattered reefs to give access to 150-DWT ships. The second phase was supposed to remove fifty-one rapids and shoals, to upgrade the channel up to a capacity to take 300-ton vessels. The last phase involved canalization, to allow trains of four 500-DWT Chinese barges to be towed, almost all year long.[27] In parallel, each party to the Navigation Agreement was to build or improve port infrastructure. China even announced that the long-term and ultimate goal was, at last, to have the Lancang-Mekong River navigable all the way down to its delta and the South-China Sea.

2.1.1 The Preparatory Stage

The Technical Working Group (TWG) third meeting, held in Beijing on 14–15 March 2001, decided to carry out an EIA, with China as the coordinator. It was then speculated that an EIA was most probably decided upon because it was an international project, of which China needed to have a proper and favorable presentation, respectful of Lao law, in order to appear as granting proper consideration to its neighbors and not attract international criticism. The EIA regulations in Laos had been recently introduced by the Environmental Protection Law (EPL) in 1999, followed by the Environmental Agency (STEA) regulation in 2000.[28] The history of EIA requirements in Laos had started in 1993 with the first National Environmental Action Plan, which

---

26 Zhu Rongji announced that he wished to strengthen infrastructure building in the Mekong River Basin, to invest in its development in view of the development of the Western part of China. China would fund the dredging of the Mekong River and improve its navigation, as it had already done on Chinese territory (Zhu Rongji, *Speech by His Excellency Zhu Rongji Premier of the State Council of The People's Republic of China At the Fourth ASEAN+ China Summit* (*10+1*) (2000), at https://www.fmprc.gov.cn/zdjn/eng/zywj/t270549.htm (accessed 17 June 2021)).

27 JOINT SURVEY GROUP, *supra* note 22 at 10.

28 EIA Regulation No. 1770/STEA, 3 October 2000, referring to the Environmental Protection Law No. 02-99/NA, 3 April 1999, of which Article 8.3 read: "Development projects and activities that have or will have the potential to affect the environment shall submit an EIA report (…) to the concerned environmental management and monitoring unit for issuance of an environment compliance certificate before starting the project".

had set up a framework for the EIA adoption process. Then, this process took years due to concerns about economic development and what was perceived as costly environmental protection. The EPL was developed under the influence of the Asian Development Bank and based in part on Thailand's. Secondly, Laos understandably also asked for an EIA because Vietnam, along with Cambodia, had expressed its concerns about the UMNIP. At the time, Vietnam still had significant influence over Laos (this is no longer so, as China has become Laos' main investor). While the Thai EIA law had been in place the longest, there was no EIA requirement applicable to the UMNIP in Thailand: the first mandatory provisions for EIA were issued in 1975, as part of the Improvement and Conservation of National Environmental Quality Act (NEQA), which was amended a few times, most notably in 1992 by The Enhancement and Conservation of National Environmental Quality Act. According to Section 46, what is now the Ministry of Natural Resources and Environment (MoNRE), had the power to specify the type and size of projects or activities requiring an EIA, provided it had the approval of the National Environment Board (NEB). Twenty-two types of projects had been listed. Navigational improvements were not on the NEQA list of projects, as Thai authorities would later emphasize. In Myanmar, there was no EIA requirement at the time. With the assistance of the Asian Development Bank, EIA requirements were developed and adopted in late 2015.[29] Besides, as regards transboundary impacts, no domestic law in any relevant country considered them. Thus, Lao regulations, introduced because of the influence of a development bank, are the reason why China decided to make the so-called "joint EIA". Nonetheless, no matter what the outcome of the EIA might be, there were already signs of China's readiness to disregard any negative reaction to the idea of the UMNIP.

Consequently, in the meantime, Thai activists, NGOs, and the press made the UMNIP public. Already very active for some time, prominent Thai NGOs had moved from focusing on national issues to a wider regional standpoint. Notably, the Southeast Asia International Rivers Network (SEARIN, now called Living River Siam Association – LRS) and the Towards Ecological Recovery and Regional Alliance (TERRA) both vividly denounced the UMNIP, but the most active group with respect to the UMNIP was a local NGO in northern Thailand, the Chiang Khong Conservation Group (Rak Chiang Khong), which had been established in 1996. Chiang Khong is a trading port and a town composed of a group of linked villages strung out along the Mekong River, across Huay Xai in

29 The EIA Procedure Act (No. 616/2015) was issued on 29 December 2015.

Laos, along the route of the UMNIP.[30] Rak Chiang Khong obtained its information on the navigation project thanks to the NGO network. It was informed of the UMNIP in 2001 by another NGO, the Northern Development Foundation, based in Chiang Mai (186 miles – 300 km away). The Thai government had presented the UMNIP to locally elected representatives only. There had been no public participation, but the press strongly echoed the NGOs in denouncing the project. In contrast with Thailand, critical civil society was only nascent in the other countries of the region.[31] Only once the UMNIP had been made public, did Cambodia and Vietnam raise the issue to the Mekong River Commission Joint Committee (MRC JC). At first, Laos relayed China's position, responding that the UMNIP was a bilateral issue and that the MRC was not to be involved. More generally, whenever there is a controversial project, the state of origin usually does not want the MRC to be involved and claims it as a bilateral issue. The UMNIP was no exception. However, when the UMNIP came to the attention of the MRC, its CEO, Joern Kristensen, was a powerful and influential figure.[32] As already mentioned with respect to the decision to make an EIA, Laos was also sensitive to Vietnam's concerns and pressure. On 30 April – 1 May 2001, Thailand and Laos agreed to each provide their separate evaluation of the environmental impacts of the UMNIP, to be submitted to China at a proposed meeting scheduled for 6–16 August. The MRC provided experts to assist with the study. These experts emphasized that Laos was potentially the most affected country by far, and that there were serious implications for downstream countries (Cambodia and Vietnam) to consider as well. Despite the technical help of the MRC, the promised evaluations were never submitted. On 6–7 July 2001, at the suggestion of the MRC secretariat, the MRC joint

30 For a broader account of the dynamics in the northern borderlands, and the extent of collaboration between borderland communities in particular, see ANDREW WALKER, THE LEGEND OF THE GOLDEN BOAT – REGULATION, TRADE AND TRADERS IN THE BORDERLANDS OF LAOS, THAILAND, CHINA AND BURMA (University of Hawaii Press. 1999).

31 Louis Lebel, et al., *The Politics of Scale, Position, and Place in the Governance of Water Resources in the Mekong Region*, 10 ECOLOGY & SOCIETY 18 (2005).

32 Joern Kristensen, of Danish nationality, had arrived at the MRC in October 1999, with a mission to regain donors' trust. Denmark had been the most important donor since 1995. The 1997 Asian financial crisis started in Thailand in July, with the collapse of the Thai baht. The MRC was supposed to keep its budget in US dollars, but, when the financial crisis broke out, it announced that it had previously converted it in Thai baht, thus losing the major part of it. In addition, also in 1997, the MRC decided to move its headquarters to Phnom Penh (because Bangkok is not in the Mekong River Basin). As a result, it had lost much of its professional staff, which impacted its competence. Some major donors were thus quite upset.

committee agreed to at least review the upcoming joint EIA led by China. At this point, it appears necessary to pause and focus on the MRC.

2.1.2 The Mekong River Commission (MRC)

The Mekong River Commission was established on 5 April 1995 and includes Cambodia, Lao PDR, Thailand, and Vietnam as its member states. On that day, the four countries signed the Agreement on the Cooperation for the Sustainable Development of the Mekong River Basin (hereinafter the 1995 Agreement) for the joint management of their shared water resources and development of the economic potential of the river. The MRC consists of three permanent bodies: the council, the joint committee (MRC JC) and the secretariat (MRCS). Every year, the MRC Council, composed of the environment and water ministers of the four member states, meets to discuss emerging issues related to the Lower Mekong Basin. The MRC Joint Committee, which comprises senior officials, implements the council's decisions. Lastly, the MRCS is the technical and operational unit of the MRC, headquartered in Vientiane, with a branch located in Phnom Penh – the Regional Flood and Drought Management Center.[33] National Mekong Committees (NMCs) were set up in each member state, to act as liaison between the MRC and national governments. NMCs are government agencies tasked with facilitating regional cooperation. Neither China, nor Myanmar belongs to the MRC. Since 1996, they have only been dialogue partners. China has always refused to adhere to the MRC,[34] which has considerably limited the MRC's possibilities from the start.

The MRC emanates from the defunct Committee for the Coordination of the Comprehensive Development of the Lower Mekong Basin (hereinafter the Mekong Committee (MC)), based in Bangkok, established in 1957 by the same four states under the auspices of the United Nations regional office in Bangkok and the UN Economic Commission for Asia and the Far East (ECAFE – today known as ESCAP). China was not a member of ECAFE, hence not a member of the Mekong Committee. The MC ceased to exist in the late 1970's. It was devoid of any environmental mandate. However, it seems worth noting that, in 1975,

33 The MRCS has about sixty staff members at present. The secretariat facilitates regional meetings of the member countries and provides scientific and technical advice on joint planning, coordination, and cooperation. It also works closely with the four countries' coordinating bodies, the National Mekong Committees (NMCs) and other state agencies (www.mrcmekong.org/about-mrc/organisational-structure/, accessed 17 June 2021).

34 In 1995, China stated that it wanted "to study in-depth the effect of the MRC's water usage rule on China's capacity to utilize upstream water. We want to find out the limitations that China will be subject to under this new rule." (Andrew Nette, *Mekong River Commission: Going with the money*, 2 WATERSHED 31, 32 (1997)).

the MC had adopted a water usage rule, according to which its member states had to present, well in advance, detailed studies of all potential detrimental effects resulting from a mainstream project. Each member state also had veto rights on any major unilateral appropriation.[35] Paradoxically, compared with the 1975 MC rules (although they were never applied), the current MRC water usage rule is weaker. Only inter-basin diversion projects from the mainstream during the dry season must be agreed upon,[36] and member states are simply required to consult with the aim of arriving at an agreement only in the case of:

- intra-basin use of the mainstream during the dry season[37]
- inter-basin diversion from the mainstream during the wet season
- inter-basin diversion of surplus quantities of water during the dry season[38]

In these three cases, a transboundary EIA has been required since the MRC Procedures for Notification, Prior Consultation and Agreement (PNPCA), adopted in 2003.[39]

The role of the MRC could be summarized as follows: providing scientific knowledge and data on the basin, impact assessments in order for member states to make informed decisions and accommodate common interests;[40] serving as a forum for member states to convene and discuss; capacity-building.[41] The first two are its main role – a regional knowledge hub and water diplomacy platform. MRC is an intergovernmental body. All decisions must be unanimous.[42] The rule is to reach a consensus on any issue that member states have accepted to discuss within the MRC. The MRC cannot criticize or contradict any of the four governments by itself. It has only advisory and coordination roles, must respect national decisions made by its members, and has limited ability to settle internal struggles between them. Since the

35 Joint Declaration of Principles for Utilization of the Waters of the Lower Mekong Basin, signed in Vientiane, on 31 January 1975. See in particular Articles 10, 11, 17, 20.

36 Article 5 B.2.b of the 1995 Agreement combined with Article 6 of the 2003 Procedures for Notification, Prior Consultation and Agreement (PNPCA). The PNPCA were adopted by a Council Resolution of 13 November 2003.

37 Article 5.B.2.a of the 1995 Agreement and Article 5.1.b of the PNPCA. See also the Guidelines on Implementation of the Procedures for Notification, Prior Consultation and Agreement (MRC Joint Committee Resolution of 31 August 2005).

38 1995 Agreement, Article 5 B, combined with Article 5.1 of the PNPCA.

39 Article 5.2.1 of the PNPCA. In addition, Article 4.2.1 requires a feasibility study report to accompany the simple notification of intra-basin use and inter-basin diversion on the tributaries, including Tonle Sap, and of intra-basin use during the wet season on the mainstream.

40 1995 Agreement, Article 24 C, D and E, and Article 30 C and E.

41 1995 Agreement, Article 24 G.

42 1995 Agreement, Articles 20 and 27.

2003 PNPCA, member states must notify the MRC about any development plans that might have regional implications, but the MRC cannot force them to comply, nor can it object to their final decision to proceed with a project. The MRC is not endowed with enforcement mechanisms. Even if it were, the member states would have to be willing and able to deploy the force at their disposal, as for any sanction in any international instrument. With regard to the four member states themselves, their collective history seems to have prevented trust building. The MRC has been plagued by significant tension from the start. Instead of facilitators, National Mekong Committees became more of an an additional bureaucratic hurdle. Laos especially, with its ambitious hydropower policy, considers that there have been unfair attempts at preventing the full exercise of its sovereign rights. At play is not only the self-interest of riparian states, but also the overwhelming influence of China as well. The MRC and its donors, and downstream countries individually do not weigh much in comparison with China, nor with important international financial institutions such as the ADB, which encouraged the UMNIP (the World Bank has had a similar influence in regard to large hydropower development projects[43]).

As a result of these limitations, from the Mekong Committee until 2009, the MRC received only 28 notifications related to hydropower development whereas there were 110 ongoing dam projects;[44] the MRC thus received only 25% of the notifications that were required. Despite the possibility offered by Article 26 of the 1995 Agreement, the MRC has not yet transformed its procedures for water utilization and inter-basin diversions into enforceable rules.[45]

With respect to the other main role of the MRC, scientific research began in the early 1990's, including research on the local ecological knowledge of the communities living in the Mekong River Basin. At the time of the UMNIP, the ecosystem of the river and its basin was still not well understood. Because of decades of war and turmoil, scientific knowledge of the river's ecology had remained scarce. Much baseline data was lacking and studies of the traditional human use of the Mekong Basin's natural resources were fragmented. Today,

43 See *infra* page 281 et seq.

44 Diana Suhardiman, et al., *Between interests and worldviews: the narrow path of the Mekong River Commission*, 33 ENVIRONMENT AND PLANNING C: GOVERNMENT AND POLICY 199, 204 (2015). For current data starting in 1998, see the MRC website at https://portal.mrcmekong.org/pnpca/map, accessed 17 June 2021.

45 Simon Marsden, *Developing Agreements for Transboundary Environmental Impact Assessment and Strategic Environmental Assessment in Asia*, *in* TRANSBOUNDARY ENVIRONMENTAL GOVERNANCE. INLAND, COASTAL, AND MARINE PERSPECTIVES 154 (Robin Warner & Simon Marsden eds., 2012).

a considerable amount of scientific knowledge has been provided, to which the MRC has contributed greatly since 1995. A crucial potential strength of the MRC lies in its advanced technical competence, should its member states wish to use it.

With respect to the UMNIP, apart from the decision to review the joint EIA, the MRC was excluded from the preparation of the navigation improvement project due to China's demand, relayed by Laos. As regards the MRC rules, only the 1995 Agreement was applicable at the time, and only to Thailand and Laos. China and Myanmar were dialogue partners, not members of the MRC. The member states viewed Article 5 (especially Article 5.B.2.a: intra-basin use of the mainstream during the dry season) and the obligation of prior consultation as pertaining to the use of water that would apply to water extraction or reducing dry season flows, not to navigational use. During the July 2001 MRC JC meeting, when the review of the joint EIA was decided, the Lao delegation assured that Laos would take into consideration the potential adverse effects on downstream countries, and the Thai delegation assured that any harmful effect in those countries would be avoided. This would mean that member states were thinking in terms of Article 7 on harmful effects rather than Article 5, but no article was specifically mentioned. Besides, in case of a potential violation of the 1995 Agreement, the member states had no enforcement mechanism at their disposal, should they have been willing to use it. Nonetheless, the MRC could have provided data and some solid scientific support, or at least guidance, to improve planning, but, presumably for this reason, China categorically refused any involvement of the MRC. It probably preferred to be unhampered in order to plan and execute the UMNIP as it wished. Even before the joint EIA was completed, China organized the UMNIP inauguration, in Jinghong Port in China, on 26–27 June 2001. At the inauguration, all countries officially expressed their serious concerns about the environmental impacts of the UMNIP, but China officially reassured them all.

2.1.3 The Joint EIA

The Joint Expert EIA Group of China, Laos, Myanmar, and Thailand was composed of six representatives from China, three from Laos, one from Myanmar, and four from Thailand. China headed the expert group and wrote its report – *Report on Environmental Impact Assessment: The Navigation Channel Improvement Project of the Lancang-Mekong River from China- Myanmar Boundary Marker 243 to Ban Houei Sai of Laos* (referred hereinafter as the joint EIA, or Navigation Project EIA). Completed in September 2001, the joint EIA concluded that the project was acceptable under the environmental protection laws of the four countries and that there would be only minor possible impacts on the ecology of the river, limited to the construction period.[46] Neither Cambodia, nor Vietnam had been associated with the Navigation Project EIA despite obvious potential downstream effects.

There was considerable opposition to the competence of the joint EIA from environmentalists. Cambodia and Vietnam kept expressing their concerns. The adequacy of the EIA was substantially questioned. Not only was it one-sided (involving mainly hydro-engineers, but not fishery experts or social scientists), but it was also completed in under six months and represented only two days of actual field investigations (the expert group went on site on 18 April and on 29 April 2001, not even two weeks apart),[47] whereas the Mekong River was famously under-studied at the time, represented the livelihood and well-being of tens of millions of people, and was the world's largest and most productive inland fishery.[48]

More generally, as regards the process followed from 1989 up until the production of the supposedly joint EIA, China had always been the only stakeholder to propose and decide, and had asked the three other countries only whether or not they agreed. The latter had always agreed. When it had come to the joint EIA, the Chinese members of the joint expert group had led it entirely. Worse, according to some reviewers, they did not even share the data they collected. Under Chinese pressure, the other experts seemed to have assented to the EIA without having been fully informed. Eventually, "joint EIA" may have been a misleading title.

At the MRC JC meeting of July 2001, the MRC member states had accepted to have the Navigation Project EIA reviewed, but these meetings were not held publicly and their decision was not yet known. In October 2001, it was finally

---

46 THE JOINT EXPERT GROUP ON EIA OF CHINA, LAOS, MYANMAR AND THAILAND, REPORT ON ENVIRONMENTAL IMPACT ASSESSMENT: NAVIGATION CHANNEL IMPROVEMENT PROJECT OF THE LANCANG-MEKONG RIVER FROM CHINA-MYANMAR BOUNDARY MARKER 243 TO BAN HOUEI SAI OF LAOS 121 (September 2001), on file with the MRC.

47 Id. at ii & 4.

48 And to the value of the fishing sector itself should be added the numerous enterprises of the fishing communities, ranging from the shops and food stalls, to boat builders and suppliers of fishing gear. Furthermore, fishing was crucial for household economies. In 2010, the MRC explained that "In Lao PDR, more than 50% of people fish, and fishing provides 20% of household income; in the south of the country, fishing is even more important and, there, 80% of people fish. Of special importance is the linkage between fisheries and other sectors. For example, income from fisheries provides cash to buy rice seed at the end of the long dry season." (Patrick Dugan, *Mainstream dams as barriers to fish migration: international learning and implications for the Mekong*, 14 CATCH AND CULTURE 9, 10 (2010)).

Laos (in the person of its President of the Lao National Mekong Committee and Minister to the Prime Minister's Office, Somphong Mongkhonvilay) that officially proposed that the Mekong River Commission review the controversial Navigation Project EIA. To respect national sensitivities, and to avoid directly and openly criticizing member states, the MRC asked independent experts to confidentially review the joint EIA. A series of reports were produced and transmitted to the MRC.

Chris Cocklin and Monique Hain of the Monash Environment Institute in Australia, in charge of reviewing the socio-economic impacts as assessed by the Navigation Project EIA, were harshly critical in their evaluation, claiming the EIA to be "substantively inadequate and in many places fundamentally flawed". "Much of the analysis ... appears to be based on little more than speculation, subjective judgments, or unsubstantiated research". Then they went on to articulate precisely forty-five flaws of the joint EIA.[49] Another reviewer, in charge of the impacts on fisheries, also voiced his concerns about the project's consequences, as the fisheries were already in decline along many stretches of the river: Robert M. McDowall, with the New Zealand's National Institute of Water & Atmospheric Research, noted that the EIA lacked not only published lists of fish species and descriptions of their habitats and life histories, but also investigation of their biological values. "Put plainly, the EIA is manifestly totally inadequate".[50] Brian Finlayson, of the University of Melbourne's Centre for Environmental Applied Hydrology, in charge of reviewing the impacts on geomorphology and hydrology, observed that "the haste with which this EIA has been prepared is obvious in the paucity of basic data and information and the sketchy and unsupported nature of the analyses carried out. A much

---

49 CHRIS COCKLIN & MONIQUE HAIN, EVALUATION OF THE EIA FOR THE PROPOSED UPPER MEKONG NAVIGATION IMPROVEMENT PROJECT – REPORT PREPARED FOR THE MRC – ENVIRONMENT PROGRAM 2, 5-8 (Monash Environment Institute, Monash University, Australia. December 2001), available at https://www.irn.org/files/programs/mekong/021018.socialimpacts.pdf, accessed 17 June 2021.

50 "Reading of the EIA makes it clear that no explicit effort has been made to determine the fish fauna and its ecology in the development zone nor to measure the potential impacts of channelization on such biological values. " (ROBERT M. MCDOWALL, EVALUATION OF: REPORT ON ENVIRONMENTAL IMPACT ASSESSMENT: THE NAVIGATION CHANNEL IMPROVEMENT PROJECT OF THE LANCANG-MEKONG RIVER FROM CHINA-MYANMAR BOUNDARY MARKER 243 TO BAN HOUEI SAI OF LAOS, PREPARED BY THE JOINT EXPERT GROUP ON EIA OF CHINA, LAOS, MYANMAR AND THAILAND, SEPTEMBER 2001: THE FISHERIES IMPACTS REVIEWED 6 (Prepared for the Mekong River Commission) (National Institute of Water & Atmospheric Research. January 2002)), available at https://www.irn.org/files/programs/mekong/021018.critiquefisheries.pdf, accessed 17 June 2021.

more substantial analysis is necessary". Finlayson emphasized that the joint EIA was incomplete, especially in regard to the 2000 Science, Technology and Environment Agency Assessment Regulation of Lao PDR, Article 12, item 2,[51] which required that "the [EIA] report shall identify and describe the environmental impacts of the project and compare them to the impacts of one or more reasonable alternatives to the project … These are not considered in the EIA as required by the Lao regulations". He noted that a minimum of a year of study was needed for an adequate EIA, given the lack of data about the river. Finlayson also observed that the Navigation Project EIA was focused almost entirely on the construction phase, rather than on long-term effects of the project. He further argued that although the joint EIA did not address possible impacts of phases two and three, there would likely be pressure to pursue those stages after the first phase is completed.[52] In Laos, the Navigation Project EIA also violated domestic requirements regarding public involvement.[53] In Thailand, even though Thai EIA law did not require an EIA, the UMNIP process were in violation of the constitution, which recognized the rights of traditional communities to participate in the management of, and the decision-making processes related to their local natural resources.[54] Even if these constitutional

51 Regulation on Environment Assessment in the Lao PDR, 1770/STEA, 3 October 2000, available at https://portal.mrcmekong.org/assets/v1/documents/Lao-Law/Regulations-on-EIA-(2000).pdf, accessed 17 June 2021.

52 BRIAN FINLAYSON, REPORT TO THE MEKONG RIVER COMMISSION ON THE "REPORT ON ENVIRONMENTAL IMPACT ASSESSMENT – THE NAVIGATION IMPROVEMENT PROJECT OF THE LANCANG-MEKONG RIVER FROM CHINA-MYANMAR BOUNDARY MARKER 243 TO BAN HOUEI SAI OF LAOS" PREPARED BY THE JOINT EXPERTS GROUP ON EIA OF CHINA, LAOS, MYANMAR AND THAILAND (Centre for Environmental Applied Hydrology, School of Anthropology, Geography and Environmental Studies, University of Melbourne. 2002).

53 Article 6 of the Regulation on Environment Assessment in the Lao PDR (No. 1770/STEA), 3 October 2000: "Public involvement shall include at least the following activities:
- notification of stakeholders
- dissemination of information about the project and its impacts
- consultation with the affected parties and parties interested in the project regarding their opinions, and
- invitation to affected parties and parties interested in the project to attend hearings or other meetings when (i) DPRA is reviewing an IEE report, (ii) STEA is reviewing and approving an EIA report, (iii) responding to affected and interested parties' concerns during project planning and implementation".

54 See 1997 Constitution of the Kingdom of Thailand, Sections 46, 56, 69, and 79. The 1997 Constitution was repealed on 19 September 2006, after a successful military coup (see the text of the 1997 Constitution at www.asianlii.org/th/legis/const/1997/1.html#S046, accessed 17 June 2021).

provisions were brief and general by nature, and, in truth, had been adopted to compensate for NEQA's lack of public participation requirements in the EIA process, it remains that they were in place and project developments could be gauged against them.

The MRC sent out the confidential reports, which ended up being leaked to the public in parallel. Laos, Myanmar, and Thailand did not react to these critics. It became evident that the Navigation Project EIA had been made only to validate the decision that had already been made a long time before, in the early 1990's. The reviews communicated by the MRC were the most recent example of environmental information disregarded by the project proponent. Since the start of the UMNIP, the series of surveys made by China had persisted with little change despite subsequent information.

2.1.4 Final Project Approval and Construction Stage

On 29 January 2002, the entire Thai cabinet approved the UMNIP. Six months later, on 31 July 2002, the Thai authorities incidentally admitted that the Navigation Project EIA was not comprehensive enough, but claimed that the UMNIP was not listed among the projects that required an EIA according to Thai law. Then, only a few weeks after it had been established, The Ministry of Natural Resources and Environment (MoNRE) of Thailand committed itself to supporting the controversial infrastructure project. In November 2002, it announced that the project should be implemented because the joint EIA indicated that there would be no negative impacts, in blatant denial of the negative reviews sent by the MRC.

Following Thailand, in March 2002, the Lao PDR was the last country to approve the EIA and the UMNIP. Laos had let Thailand be the first to announce its decision, because Thailand was the only country capable of resisting China. Furthermore, in the wake of Thailand's approval, Laos would appear, from Vietnam's perspective, to have its hands tied and therefore shielded from criticism. The Lao government members that had asked for the joint EIA to be reviewed were not the most influential – this kind of opposition within a government is frequent; it happened in the Vuotos dam and the Interconnection cases too (see previous chapters). Since the beginning of the project, Laos had agreed to every step taken by China. The existence of the joint EIA allowed the Lao government to show that they had supposedly met the legal requirements, irrespective of content and subsequent reviews. As for downstream countries, that same year, in 2002, China canceled US$200 million of Cambodian debt and granted millions of dollars in aid to the Hun Sen government. As is generally the case, these kinds of gestures made it obviously more difficult for downstream countries to oppose Chinese plans, notwithstanding weak and indirect protests.[55] In conclusion, at this stage, the MRC, even with a powerful secretariat, could not counter China's influence. The MRC member states did not reach a consensus on the continuation of the project and maintained that dynamiting the Mekong River was not a transboundary issue in any case, but rather a local one that had to be addressed within each country. The UMNIP illustrates the failure of the MRC to play a prominent mediating role in achieving better governance.[56]

In 2002, following Laos' approval, Chinese teams started the first phase of the UMNIP during the dry season. As planned in parallel, the four countries involved in the UMNIP also built and improved their port infrastructure.[57] In Myanmar and Thailand, protests continued and amplified. In June 2002, more than 12,000 people gathered in the North of Thailand to demonstrate against the UMNIP, mostly out of environmental concerns. In Myanmar, more than fifty organizations petitioned the Thai and Lao governments in December 2002, arguing that the project would benefit only business elites and the military, urging officials to pressure China to renounce its plans. In Laos, resistance to the navigation project had emerged too, but only slowly because the Communist government deterred public opposition. "People directly affected by the blasting have been excluded from the planning process, with no forum to express their opinions or influence decision-making".[58] In Laos, the public information process, as required by law,[59] apparently lasted only five days and excluded the general public, interest groups and even local government agencies. Local residents were not aware of the UMNIP until the explosions commenced in 2002. Inhabitants started to notice increased erosion, higher sediment levels and strange disruptions of the water flow.[60] In some places,

55 Prime Minister Hun Sen warned that Mekong development could dry up the vital Tonle Sap Lake, but without naming those responsible (Ker Munthit, ASSOCIATED PRESS, 12 February 2003, at web.archive.org/web/20160901235145/http://www.terraper.org/web/en/node/1057, accessed 17 June 2021). Hun Sen has been Prime Minister of Cambodia since 1985.

56 For other examples, see Marsden, *Developing Agreements for Transboundary Environmental Impact Assessment and Strategic Environmental Assessment in Asia* 154–155. 2012.

57 China upgraded three ports: Simao (now called Pu'Er), which opened for operation in March 2001, Jinghong (opened in December 2002), and Guanlei (opened in 2004). Myanmar designated two ports for international traffic, Wan Seng and Wan Pong, and built a third port at Soploi, opened in 2002. Thailand built two ports in Chiang Saen and Chiang Kong, both completed in 2003, as well as some terminals in Chiang Rai Province. Laos set up a new economic development zone near the Golden Triangle area, which consisted of construction of the Ban Mom Port, a new urban area development, and some bank protection.

58 Aviva Imhof (International Rivers) *in* Mastny, WORLD WATCH MAGAZINE, 26 (2003).

59 Notably, Article 4 of the 1999 EPL and Article 6 of the 2000 EIA Act.

60 See *infra* note 100 for references.

the Lao government was then forced to boost its military presence following local protests.

The International Union for Conservation of Nature (IUCN) conducted some diplomatic negotiations with China, Laos, and Thailand, which are members of the IUCN, in order to pressure them to stop violating different international commitments that they had undertaken or renewed recently.[61] Despite the affirmation in the joint EIA that the UMNIP abided by the environmental regulations of all four countries, the IUCN emphasized that without an adequate EIA process, the governments were failing to meet their obligations under the 1992 Convention on Biological Diversity (for China, Myanmar and Laos[62]) and the 1971 Ramsar Convention (for China),[63] both of which oblige state parties to prevent species extinction. The Mekong riparian states had also just agreed to use sustainably and conserve biodiversity at the World Summit on Sustainable Development (WSSD) in 2002, in order to reduce the loss of biodiversity by 2010.[64] Lastly, the UMNIP directly contradicted the commitments that all signatories had undertaken in Article 21 of the 2000 Quadripartite Navigation Agreement, in terms of cooperation to protect the environment. As part of the IUCN's diplomatic negotiations, in February 2003, the IUCN, the Laotian government (through its National Mekong Committee) and the Thai-based NGO SEARIN (now called Living River Siam – LRS) sponsored a biodiversity scoping study, which concluded that the UMNIP presented a high risk of increased negative impacts and no further implementation should be done without an adequate EIA, with full consultation of local people, consideration of all options for improving trade communications and constant monitoring.[65]

61 The IUCN was founded on 5 October 1948 at an international conference in Fontainebleau, France, at the initiative of the Director General of UNESCO, the British biologist Julian Huxley. The IUCN is a global environmental organization with over 1,400 members, including more than 200 government organizations and more than a thousand NGOs as members, among which the Ministry of Natural Resources of China, the Foreign Affairs Ministry of Laos, the Department of National Parks, Wildlife and Plant Conservation of Thailand, the Ministry of Natural Resources and Environmental Conservation of Myanmar.

62 Thailand ratified the CBD only later, on 31 October 2003, and became a party on 1 January 2004.

63 Thailand accessed the convention only later, on 17 November 2004, and Lao PDR on 28 May 2010.

64 See Point 44 (g) of the WSSD Plan of Implementation.

65 PETER-JOHN MEYNELL (ed.), SCOPING STUDY FOR BIODIVERSITY ASSESSMENT OF THE MEKONG RIVER IN NORTHERN LAO PDR AND THAILAND (IUCN Mekong Water and Nature Initiative and Mekong Wetlands Biodiversity Conservation and Sustainable Use Programme, Bangkok. August 2003). See also a follow-up survey: PIERRE DUBEAU (ed.), FOLLOW-UP SURVEY FOR BIODIVERSITY ASSESSMENT OF THE MEKONG RIVER

2.2 *Cancellation and Outcome of the UMNIP*

There was no tangible result from the IUCN's interventions. The organization was thus surprised by the sudden turn taken by the UMNIP, which surpassed their hopes.

2.2.1 Cancellation

The UMNIP was interrupted in April 2003. Officially, this was neither because of local opposition to the project, nor because of environmental concerns, but rather for national security concerns: the destruction of the last rapids of the phase 1 section (the Khon Phi Luang Rapids) was averted because the Defense Ministry of Thailand became concerned that the blasting might complicate even further the Thai-Lao border demarcation negotiations that had started in 1996.[66] On 8 April 2003, the Thai Cabinet issued a resolution suspending the plan to blast the rapids. The Lao government had warned about the UMNIP and its implications for the border demarcation process.[67] Nevertheless, because the border demarcation negotiations were already well in progress when the UMNIP was decided by both Thailand and Laos, Thailand's official statement regarding the interruption of the UMNIP was not entirely convincing. There

---

IN NORTHERN LAO PDR (IUCN Water and Nature Initiative and Mekong Wetlands Biodiversity Conservation and Sustainable Use Programme, Bangkok. October 2004).

66 When the Pathet Lao came to power in 1975 after years of civil war in Laos, there was a flood of refugees into Thailand, whence some continued to fight the Lao communist regime. Their presence, in addition to unresolved border disputes, strained relations between Laos and Thailand until diplomatic relations ceased entirely. There were armed border clashes until 1976 and a few incidents in June 1982. In June 1984, some incidents resumed and intensified gradually until late 1987. A brief war erupted then, between December 1987 and February 1988. In 1996, the Thai-Lao Joint Boundary Commission was established to settle the border dispute, the origins of which are to be found in the delimitation set up in the southern Luang Prabang range mountain area by the Boundary Treaty between French Indochina and Siam, signed on 23 March 1907, and by the 25 August 1926 French Indochina and Siam Convention. Thailand has then considered the river boundary line unreasonable, especially when it comes to islands on the Mekong River. Border demarcation is still in process. As of 2018, 420 miles (676 km), i.e. 60%, had been delimited since the two countries began the border survey in May 1997. The border is 1,125 mile-long (1,810 km), of which 436 miles (702 km) is on land (at https://www.mfa.go.th/en/content/5d5bd0e815e39c3060022073?cate=5d5bcb4e15e39c306000683e, accessed 17 June 2021).

67 In 2001, "what worried Laos, Somphong Mongkhonvilay said, were some possible ecological changes as a result of the clearance and widening, including depletion of fishery and other resources, and a change in the river's course. Disruption to the Mekong could also hamper the resolution of the river boundary" *in* Saritdet Marukatat, *Laos upset about channel widening plan*, BANGKOK POST, 2 November 2001.

was speculation as to what extent another reason played a role in the Thai government's decision: there had been strong local protests in the Chiang Khong area. The Thai government may have wanted to avoid acknowledging them officially, in order not to set a precedent and raise hopes that environmental issues could be used against its projects. Not only did the Thai Cabinet resolution suspend the UMNIP, but it also required the Office of Natural Resources and Environmental Policy and Planning (part of MoNRE) to conduct a new EIA along the Thai-Lao PDR border. The new EIA began in September 2003 and was completed in June 2004. However, Chainarong Srethachua (director of SEARIN-LRS) said, "It's bad. In fact, it is quite similar to the Chinese EIA. It has almost nothing to say about social impacts".[68] This would tend to attest to the fact that this last EIA was made simply to counter surveys like the IUCN's, and assuage local concerns in Thailand.

In truth, rather than diplomatic or environmental concerns, or even local opposition, Thailand's reason for halting the UMNIP may have been simply that China had unilaterally taken that decision, but chose to let Thailand announce it first. In June 2003, MRC CEO Joern Kristensen announced that China had decided to stop the navigation project after completion of the first phase. That same month, China itself declared that it would reduce the extent of its project, abandoning after the first stage rather than continuing with the more invasive widening that would eventually clear the river and allow 500-DWT vessels to navigate it. Consequently, some said that there were signs that China might also be listening to critics. In late 2002, the country had adopted a new national law requiring comprehensive environmental impact assessments for large infrastructure projects,[69] which led some to think that China was becoming environmentally conscious even for projects abroad. Prospects for a solution to the blasting conflict looked bright. The IUCN had brought the UMNIP and similar projects conducted in China to the attention of the Chinese environmental authorities, which had not known about it. The IUCN supposed that these authorities might apply pressure to stop the project. China claimed that, in any event, they were satisfied with the navigation channel that had resulted from the completion of the first phase. 90% of the boats plying the Mekong River were then Chinese. New ports had been built, and some were developed significantly, especially Chiang Saen in Thailand.[70] The Thai government even continued to work on port facilities. China's main goal, i.e. to provide Yunnan with quick and easy access to downstream countries and the

68 WHEELER, 11. 2004.

69 The new EIA law was adopted on 28 October 2002 and took effect on 1 September 2003.

70 See *supra* note 57.

sea, had been sufficiently accomplished. Ships up to 300-DWT could navigate the river between China and the Golden Triangle port of Chiang Saen all year long, proving that, in fact, after the official interruption of the project, additional dredging and other construction projects had been carried out beyond phase 1, under the rubric of "maintenance", and that phase 2 had also been completed. Even though China was still far from having its commercial ships be able to navigate the Mekong River all the way down to the South-China Sea, or even through Laos, that was deemed sufficient. In 2004, by all accounts, the project was definitively stopped.

To explain its decision, China cited increased public and international scrutiny, including the growing concerns of downstream countries about livelihood impacts as well as calls from the Mekong River Commission to halt the project until a more comprehensive environmental assessment was made available. China had everything to gain in reputational terms with such proclamations. However, it had other reasons for stopping the UMNIP, the main one being that some cheaper alternatives had materialized (China had started to work on these options at the same time as the UMNIP): roads, bridges and railroads were preferred to river transportation.[71] In addition, the fear that the current would become too strong may have played a certain role. According to several testimonies, dredging the river actually increased the current to a point that it became dangerous, as the EIA reviews, environmental organizations and some Lao officials had said it would.[72] The waters also remained too shallow, or became even shallower, as some had tried to warn here again; at an MRC technical meeting, a hydraulics engineer had made a presentation detailing this very outcome. After a few months of work, it had become evident that the UMNIP had been poorly conceived and could not achieve its ultimate goal. Laos was of the same opinion, finally in accord with what then-president of its NMC, Somphong Mongkhonvilay, had tried to voice in 2001.[73] One last

71 Not long after, in 2008, the whole "north-south economic corridor", a network of roads linking Kunming to Bangkok spanning 1,100 miles (1,800 km) was inaugurated, including the Kunming-Bangkok (via Laos) expressway.

72 FINLAYSON, REPORT TO THE MEKONG RIVER COMMISSION ON THE "REPORT ON ENVIRONMENTAL IMPACT ASSESSMENT – THE NAVIGATION IMPROVEMENT PROJECT OF THE LANCANG-MEKONG RIVER FROM CHINA-MYANMAR BOUNDARY MARKER 243 TO BAN HOUEI SAI OF LAOS" PREPARED BY THE JOINT EXPERTS GROUP ON EIA OF CHINA, LAOS, MYANMAR AND THAILAND 6, 2002. Thongpho Vongsriprasom of the Lao Ministry of Agriculture and Forestry, *in* Mastny, WORLD WATCH MAGAZINE, 24 (2003). Tyson R. Roberts, *Downstream ecological implications of China's Lancang Hydropower and Mekong Navigation project, in* Biodiversity Management and Sustainable Development in the Lancang-Mekong River in the New Millennium 48 (Cao Min, et al. eds., 2001).

73 See *supra* note 67.

important reason for not pursuing the UMNIP to the end is that intense hydroelectric use of the river had already become the priority, as opposed to navigation concerns. Upstream of a dam, navigation is made easy, but a great many dams have been built on the Mekong River. Their exploitation provokes frequent and severe water level fluctuations, which make navigation downstream too dangerous or prevent it entirely,[74] to which must be added the obvious impossibility of continuing farther down the river, past each dam. No costly bypasses were planned at the time.

2.2.2 Outcome and Appraisal of the UMNIP

As a result of China's endeavors, navigation improved only temporarily (2001–2004). In 2007, as navigation had severely declined, Laos planned to resume the improvement of the navigation channels of the Mekong River, this time simply by installing concrete poles to indicate water channels for boats to follow. This persistence in improving navigation was due to the fact that ships carry more goods and require less fuel than trucks, and because Lao people have had a long experience with building and operating boats rather than with trucks. However, navigation still remains quite undeveloped as an integrated transport sector, due to irregular river flows. During the dry season, the river is not deep enough and boats are stranded. Because of the current, the fluctuations in water levels and the ever-greater number of dams, there were severe doubts as to whether the UMNIP would be resumed. Moreover, after a criminal incident in October 2011 (two Chinese ships were attacked, and thirteen Chinese crewmen were killed), China completely stopped navigation on the river, which was ultimately more of a symbolic political gesture: navigation was already limited in reality, precisely because of a long history of drug-related violence and occasional resistance to the Laotian government by members of the Hmong ethnic minority.

The UMNIP failed entirely. The lack of timely, proper assessment and subsequent planning generated significant environmental and socio-economic damage in return for a poor, even negative, result as regards the grandiose goal of the project.

At first, SEARIN, other NGOs and the IUCN monitored the problems that occurred through regular consultations with villagers who lived by the river. At the time, given the scarcity of scientific studies on the impacts of dams and

74 In 2010, there were severe droughts and China's dams were accused on this account. Paradoxically, it was the year ACFTA came into effect. Whereas the Mekong had been intended to be a transport route for the expected increase in trade of goods between China and ASEAN, the shallow waters prevented cargo ships from plying the route.

rock removals on the ecology of the Mekong River, this kind of surveys and random information was the best indicator of what was happening to the river and the populations it sustained. They have since been confirmed. In view of the consequences of the implementation of the UMNIP, the environmental groups' main criticisms of the Navigation Project EIA can be summarized as follows:

- *Water level fluctuations*. The joint EIA noted that they would be small and limited.[75] In reality, significant sporadic changes, even flash floods in the worst cases, were observed and attributed to the combination of water damming and release from upstream dams, and blasting for the UMNIP, which removed rapids and other obstacles to navigation. Such activities have also caused adverse fluctuation in the Mekong tributaries. In the past, the river level rose and lowered only seasonally, whereas now it can suddenly fluctuate daily, preventing fishing, disrupting the migratory and breeding patterns of the fish, eventually leading to the decline or the disappearance of fish populations.[76]
- *Water velocity*. The Navigation Project EIA observed that there would be very small impacts and that they would be positive.[77] As a matter of fact, the speed of the current increased. Chinese engineers had to stop the blasting, for fear that the river flow would become too rapid. Navigation became dangerous.[78]
- *Soil loss and erosion*. According to the joint EIA, "no soil erosion will happen at the reef blasting places"; "On the contrary, [the UMNIP] will lead to the protection of the land".[79] In reality, altered river flows have resulted in soil erosion, floods and landslides. The villagers lost their riverbank gardens and paddy fields.[80] Villagers who were formerly self-sufficient in rice

75 JOINT EXPERTS GROUP ON EIA, *supra* note 46 at 73–74.

76 Carl E. Bruch, et al., *Assessing the Assessments: Improving Methodologies for Impact Assessment in Transboundary Watercourses*, 23 WATER RESOURCES DEVELOPMENT 391, 397 (2007). IUCN, LARGE SHIPS OR LARGE FISH? BLASTING OF SHOALS AND RAPIDS IN THE UPPER MEKONG RIVER MAY SERIOUSLY ENDANGER FISH SPECIES (IUCN – The World Conservation Union. 13 January 2003).

77 JOINT EXPERTS GROUP ON EIA, *supra* note 46 at 74–76.

78 See *supra* page 264 et seq.; LNDO, *Blasting the Mekong – The navigation scheme is making trade easier – but for whom? in* UNDERCURRENTS – MONITORING DEVELOPMENT ON BURMA'S MEKONG 4 (2005), at http://burmariversnetwork.org/images/stories/publications/english/undercurrents1.pdf, accessed 17 June 2021.

79 JOINT EXPERTS GROUP ON EIA, *supra* note 46 at 72–76.

80 Naho Mirumachi & Mikiyasu Nakayama, *Improving Methodologies for Transboundary Impact Assessment in Transboundary Watercourses: Navigation Channel Improvement Project of the Lancang-Mekong River from China- Myanmar Boundary Marker 243 to Ban Houei Sai of Laos*, 23 INT. J. WATER RESOUR. DEV. 411, 416, 419 (2007); Bruch, et al.,

growing were then forced to purchase it due to the destruction of the riverbank fields, and also lost a significant source of income. Many even lost their homes.[81]

- *Fish.* The Navigation Project EIA stated that blasting would "bring very limited injuries to the fish" and only during the initial period of work. One proposed mitigation measure was that construction would be conducted between December and March (during the dry season, which, in any case, was the easiest time for the work), thus avoiding fish migration and reproduction. The EIA also proposed a short-term relocation of fish to avoid shocks from blasting, by initiating small explosions to scare away the fish. It asserted that the fish would temporarily leave the concerned areas with this method and that few, if any, fish would be injured by the blasting. The EIA predicted minor impacts on fish from shock waves, also because of the relatively small impact range and the biological characteristics of some fish species: "fish living at the bottom of the river are normally small in size, flat-shaped, or their swimming bladders are protected by their bone". In the long term, the EIA acknowledged that fish species would lose their habitat due to the removal of reefs, shoals and rapids, but the blasting areas were said to be relatively small compared to the entire river. In some cases, the EIA stated that the removal of river obstacles might actually facilitate fish migration. Hence, "the living environment for fish can be gradually resumed" upon project completion and "macroscopically, this project will not change the ecological environment of the 331 km [206 miles] reach".[82] In reality, the blasting, subsequent water fluctuations, the reduction of deep pools, alteration of the rapids and increased navigation, even if temporary, dramatically altered the ecosystem of the river, a major wildlife habitat, and caused a decline in biodiversity and depletion of the fish stocks. Countless testimonies to this effect soon materialized.[83]

WATER RESOURCES DEVELOPMENT, 397 (2007). SEARIN, SUMMARY OF THAI BAAN (VILLAGERS') RESEARCH AT CHIANG KHONG (LRS. 2004). SEARIN, MEKONG RAPIDS UNDER FIRE 40 (SEARIN 2nd ed. 2003).

81 LNDO, *supra* note 79 at 8. WHEELER, 8. 2004; Bruch, et al., WATER RESOURCES DEVELOPMENT, 397 (2007). SEARIN, Mekong rapids under fire 38. 2003. SEARIN, Summary of Thai Baan (Villagers') Research at Chiang Khong. 2004.

82 JOINT EXPERTS GROUP ON EIA, *supra* note 46 at 70–72.

83 SEARIN, Summary of Thai Baan (Villagers') Research at Chiang Khong. 2004. LNDO, *supra* note 79 at 4. Whiting, *supra* note 19. Bounsaw Jinarat, et al., *"If we lost our environment and suffer the impacts, can anyone return our original environment?"* 8 WATERSHED 34 (2002). WHEELER, 8. 2004.

- *Seaweed.* There would be "no damage to the nearby animals and plants on the river banks" because the blasting was in submerged areas and limited in noise, shockwaves and substance scattering, according to the Navigation Project EIA.[84] In reality, numerous plants were affected, plants upon which the self-sufficiency of local communities depended. One such plant, a type of Mekong seaweed called *Kai*, a well-known, flavorsome food among communities along the river, grows from the Burmese-Lao border down to Luang Prabang in Laos. Kai was grown in the riverbank gardens and harvested for family consumption and for trade. It was also a significant source of food for fish. Dramatic changes in river fluctuation have diminished Kai growth from the tri-border point of China, Laos and Thailand down to Chiang Khong, Thailand. In addition, the harvest days and amount of Kai in areas where it is still grown have decreased.[85]
- *Biodiversity at large.* The Navigation Project EIA summarily noted that the Mekong Giant Catfish for instance was "the most important fish of Mekong River",[86] whereas the Mekong is second only to the Amazon in terms of biological diversity. Scientists had already estimated that more than 1,200 species of fish live in the Mekong[87] and yet the full diversity of fish, plant, mollusk and other aquatic life was still unknown, and still is. This contrasts with the observation made by the EIA, according to which there were 124 species in the Mekong River.[88] Together, freshwater ecosystems barely cover 1% of the Earth's surface and, while holding a mere 0.008% of its water, support almost 10% of known animal species (more than 100,000) – a disproportionately large number for their size relative to marine and terrestrial habitats. Freshwater systems bestow underappreciated benefits on populations, whose lives and economies have depended on them. The value of all the services that freshwater ecosystems provide worldwide, such as drinking water, food security, irrigation, nutrients for agriculture, and climate regulation, has been estimated in the trillions of US dollars (assuming

84 JOINT EXPERTS GROUP ON EIA, *supra* note 46 at 72.

85 SEARIN, Summary of Thai Baan (Villagers') Research at Chiang Khong. 2004. KATE LAZARUS, et al., AN UNCERTAIN FUTURE: BIODIVERSITY AND LIVELIHOODS ALONG THE MEKONG RIVER IN NORTHERN LAO PDR 13 & 20 (IUCN. 2006). MILTON OSBORNE, RIVER AT RISK – THE MEKONG AND THE WATER POLITICS OF CHINA AND SOUTHEAST ASIA 29–30 (Lowy Institute for International Policy. 2004). SEARIN, Mekong rapids under fire 36–37. 2003. WHEELER, 8. 2004. Jinarat, et al., WATERSHED, 35 (2002).

86 JOINT EXPERTS GROUP ON EIA, *supra* note 46 at 57.

87 WALTER J. RAINBOTH, FAO SPECIES IDENTIFICATION FIELD GUIDE FOR FISHERY PURPOSES – FISHES OF THE CAMBODIAN MEKONG 5 & 14 (FAO. 1996).

88 JOINT EXPERTS GROUP ON EIA, *supra* note 46 at 70.

one could purchase the services elsewhere if they became unavailable in nature).[89] Freshwater organisms rank among the world's most threatened species, as freshwaters are increasingly impacted by anthropogenic modifications. The rocks and rapids near Chiang Khong in Thailand, just south of the Golden Triangle, were the only known spawning grounds of the critically endangered Mekong giant catfish (*pangasianodon gigas*), one of the largest freshwater fish in the world, which can weigh more than 661 pounds (300 kg) and reach 10 ft (3 m) in length. In recent years, Cambodia, Laos and Thailand have outlawed its harvest, but the efficacy of these bans remains to be seen. According to the design plans for the navigation channel, the thousands of tons of rock blasted out of the rapids were supposed to be dumped in the deep pools of the river. The deep pools are critically important dry-season habitats for the fish of the upper Mekong, and are therefore the best fishing grounds for nearby local communities. Filling the deep pools with the blasted rocks had a severe and permanent impact on the fisheries of the upper Mekong River and on the thousands of fishing families living along the river. None of this had been considered by the EIA. Not only did fish lose their habitat and spawning grounds, but the changing water flow disturbed their patterns of migration and reproduction.[90]

- *Pollution*. The Navigation Project EIA only predicted that ship accidents were expected to decrease by 90% thanks to the UMNIP, hence the quasi-end of oil pollution.[91] As navigation increased in 2001–2004, pollution from larger cargo boats became so severe that the MRC concluded that one of the most urgent environmental issues facing the navigation on the Mekong River was the need for harmonized rules for carrying dangerous and noxious goods such as fuel. In some places, tanker barges would still even land directly on shore. Even as the overt goal of the UMNIP was to dramatically increase commercial navigation, there were no protection measures at the time to ensure the correct handling of dangerous substances and a safe navigation.[92]

---

89 UNITED NATIONS, ET AL., WORLD RESOURCES 2000–2001: PEOPLE AND ECOSYSTEMS: THE FRAYING WEB OF LIFE 104 (Elsevier Science. 2000). As a whole, biological resources contribute over 66% to the Laos' GDP (FAO, *Laos at a glance*, at http://www.fao.org/laos/fao-in-laos/laos-at-a-glance/en/, accessed 17 June 2021).

90 SEARIN, Mekong rapids under fire 39. 2003.

91 JOINT EXPERTS GROUP ON EIA, *supra* note 46 at 12, 87.

92 PETER STARR, THE PEOPLE'S HIGHWAY: PAST, PRESENT AND FUTURE TRANSPORT ON THE MEKONG RIVER SYSTEM 37 (Mekong Development Series No. 3. Mekong River Commission. 2004).

- *Socio-economic impacts.* Although the Navigation Project EIA mentioned that economic impacts had not been studied, they were actually addressed under the category of impacts on sustainable development, scenery, and of social impacts. The EIA forecast that the completion of the project would improve the quality of life in communities along the river, including "higher waterway transport capacity, lower transport cost, lower energy consumption, less pollution impacts on the environment, less investment, less land acquisition etc". The only negative impact noted was that "some local epidemic diseases may be distributed to other areas through the transportation in the River", which were described as minor impacts. The EIA appeared to place great importance on the increased opportunities for tourism, noting that the clearing of rapids would make the "natural scenery at both sides of the channel more attractive", allowing "tourists … [to] arrive at the scenic spots directly", hence promoting tourism in the whole catchment area. This time, the EIA was correct, at least in the short run, when it asserted that the UMNIP would satisfy the needs of economic development of the concerned parts of China and would provide convenient and fast access to the advanced areas of Southeast Asia.[93] The UMNIP did provide Yunnan Province with convenient sea access and improved trade between this Chinese province and Thailand, the port value of which doubled immediately (by 2001).[94] 90% of the boats plying the Mekong were then Chinese. However, the EIA failed to address the disappearance of the fishing communities. About 85% of the Mekong River Basin's population lived in rural areas. The ecosystem of the river was fundamental to the viability of their natural resource-based livelihoods. Over 60% of the economically active population had water-related occupations that were vulnerable to water-related shocks and degradation. Local communities were accustomed to being self-sufficient (one-third of the population lived on less than US$2 per day). Population in the Mekong Basin was estimated to be 97% of the population of Laos, 37% in Thailand, 90% in Cambodia, 20% in Vietnam.[95] Soon, fishing disappeared as a viable means of income generation for many of the local inhabitants.[96] The outcome of the UMNIP damaged the local economy, as well as local knowledge about fishing, navigation and agriculture.

93 JOINT EXPERTS GROUP ON EIA, *supra* note 46 at 89–97, 104–105.
94 From US$43 million to US$88 million (STARR, *supra* note 92 at 26).
95 FAO, MEKONG RIVER BASIN – WATER REPORT 37, 1–4 (2011).
96 Mirumachi & Nakayama, INT. J. WATER RESOUR. DEV., 419 (2007).

The Mekong posed new dangers to fishermen, caused a loss of income to Lao and Thai populations, in addition to the above-mentioned pollution,[97] for which the local populations received no compensation. If the EIA had emphasized navigation safety and the reduced number of accidents after completion of the UMNIP, it had kept silent about the fact that traditional 60-DWT boats had been able to navigate all year long without any difficulty from time immemorial. As far as local boatmen were concerned, accidents dramatically increased with the UMNIP because of the Chinese cargo boats. Lao boatmen regularly capsized during encounters with these boats, often losing their engines as a result. These losses were usually catastrophic to the boatmen, as the cost of the engine replacement was typically prohibitive.[98] In conclusion, with respect to local communities, the economic impacts were vastly negative, contrary to the assertions of the EIA. The usual justification for projects of this type, i.e. the primacy of economic growth, ignored and concealed the fact that the UMNIP, along with hydropower plants, tipped the balance towards economic decline for the fishing communities across the entire Mekong River system – in other words, for the vast majority of the population of the Mekong River Basin.

- *Failure to include local participation.* As mentioned above and despite the assertions of the Navigation Project EIA,[99] local populations were not consulted, nor even informed. They learnt about the UMNIP upon seeing the Chinese teams come into their areas and hearing the explosions on the river.[100]

As feared upon reviewing the joint Navigation Project EIA, the consequences of the Chinese engineers' accomplishments were not what their EIA had predicted.

And yet, there were alternatives to blasting the river. The Navigation Project EIA could and should have looked at signalization, maps of the rapids, training of boat captains and crew and enhanced standards in boat design to improve the navigation conditions. In other words, boats used on the river should be adapted to the natural environment, rather than the other way

97 MEYNELL (ed.), 21–22. August 2003.

98 OSBORNE, 29. 2004; Mastny, WORLD WATCH MAGAZINE, 26 (2003); SEARIN, Mekong rapids under fire 39. 2003. LNDO, *supra* note 78 at 4. Whiting, *supra* note 19.

99 JOINT EXPERTS GROUP ON EIA, *supra* note 46 at 98–107.

100 Jinarat, et al., WATERSHED, 34 (2002). LNDO, *supra* note 78 at 3–4. TERRA, The Upper Mekong Navigation Improvement Project 48 (2004). Mastny, WORLD WATCH MAGAZINE, 26 (2003). See *supra* page 260–261.

around. As Somkiat Khuanchiangsa (from the Chiang Khong Conservation Group, or Rak Chiang Khong) explained, "Nobody is saying you can't use the river for commercial transport. You can, but during the dry season boats shouldn't be larger than 50 tons, and in the rainy season, no larger than 200 tons. If they really want 500-ton vessels operating 95% of the year, they'll have to blast away constantly, as maintenance".[101] The Navigation Project EIA should also have looked at alternative ways to improve transport between countries in the Greater Mekong Subregion. As the outcome of the UMNIP showed, improving road and especially rail transportation between China, Lao PDR, Myanmar, and Thailand considerably reduced the need, if any, for major river transport improvements. Opponents of the blasting scheme had pointed to the road links being developed between Yunnan and Chiang Rai through Myanmar and Laos, and a proposed bridge over the Mekong (between Chiang Khong in Thailand and Huay Xai in Laos – finally in operation in December 2013), as alternatives to river-shipping. "When the roads are finished and they've built the bridge, the blasting will be like a monument (…) With decent roads, it will have been a waste", Somkiat Khuanchiangsa had predicted.[102]

2.3 *Last Attempt*

In spite of the negative outcome of the UMNIP and the existence of dams, further destruction of the Mekong rapids seemed only a matter of time. In 2004, the director-general of Thailand's Marine Department, Wanchai Sarnthoontat, declared that the navigation-improvement project would continue to be implemented once the border with Laos was demarcated and the new EIA process completed.[103] China continued to push for further clearance of the Mekong River as well. Road transport corridors are shorter, but more expensive.[104] As

101 WHEELER, 12. 2004.

102 Id. at. 12.

103 Id. at 11.

104 The river stretches 367 miles (590 km) from the port of Simao in China through Huay Xay in Laos to Chiang Kong in Thailand. The equivalent road route is 280 miles (450 km). In 2015, transporting cargo by road from Simao to Chiang Kong cost US$39.47 per ton, compared to US$23.22 by river. The distance by river from Simao to Luang Prabang in Laos is 553 miles (890 km); by road, it is 317 miles (510 km). Road transport between these two locations was US$34.56/ton vs. US$12.76 by river. From Simao to Vientiane, the capital of Laos, the distance is 857 miles (1,380km) by river, and 553 miles (890km) by road (MRC, DESIGN OF A MASTER PLAN FOR REGIONAL WATERBORNE TRANSPORT IN THE MEKONG RIVER BASIN – FINAL REPORT 15 (2015)).

one Thai-based diplomat had warned: "They'll use the roads, the river, they'll use it all".[105]

The coordination mechanism of the Navigation Agreement, the Joint Committee on Coordination of Commercial Navigation on the Lancang-Mekong River (JCCCN), issued a development plan in 2014,[106] openly criticized by the MRC for its failure to adequately consider the environmental and social impacts.[107] This time, China appeared to be determined to coordinate dams and increased international commercial navigation on the Mekong River.[108] The new UMNIP planned to build dams equipped with ship locks, along with the further development of port capacity. The goal was to have a 553 mile-long (890 km) navigation channel for 500-DWT cargo ships and large passenger ships by 2025. From US$5 million in 2001, the budget went to US$655 million, which China seemed unwilling to fund by itself this time (even though it probably would have if necessary, as the project served first and foremost Chinese interests). Phase I of the new project targeted 146 rapids this time, which would have been "improved and maintained" on the 392 miles (631 km) river section between China-Myanmar Boundary Marker 243 and Luang Prabang in Laos (to be compared with the 11 rapids that were previously removed between the same starting point and Ban Houei Sai in Laos, in 2002/2004). By 2025, China was planning for more than six million tons of cargo (plus diverse oil products potentially) and about three million passengers transported per year, according to the JCCCN's previsions.

NGOs were aware of the new UMNIP and started to protest this new attempt with the support of the press. If the MRC and the Thai Government informed locally elected officials and NGOs this time, they did so only briefly and still without any public participation. They did not solicit any traditional ecological knowledge. After its launch by the JCCCN at its 14th meeting in January

---

105 WHEELER, 12. 2004.

106 The last version of the development plan is available on the JCCCN website at https://www.jcccn.org/images/rule/Plan-29-6-2015.pdf, accessed 17 June 2021.

107 MRC, FINAL REPORT, *supra* note 104 at 85.

108 "hydropower development of the Lancang River can improve navigation conditions", Song Tao, Vice Minister of Foreign Affairs of the People's Republic of China, in his statement at the 1st summit of the MRC (Hua Hin, Thailand) in April 2010 (at http://www.mrcsummit.org/assets/previous-summits/1st-summit/statements/4e33940111/China-Statement.pdf, accessed 17 June 2021). See also Nathanial Matthews & Stew Motta, *Chinese State-Owned Enterprise Investment in Mekong Hydropower: Political and Economic Drivers and Their Implications across the Water, Energy, Food Nexus*, 7 Water 6269, 6274 (2015), doi.org/10.3390/w7116269.

2016, the new plan (framework and preliminary studies) was approved by the Thai Government in December 2016. A Chinese company, CCCC Second Harbor Consultants Co. Ltd, was put in charge of surveying the Mekong River for completion of the new UMNIP. With regard to the EIA, the same consulting firm that had carried it out in 2004 was chosen, TEAM Consultant Engineering and Management Co., Ltd. The Thai Cabinet resolution triggered renewed opposition. Associations regrouped and united their efforts, issuing joint public statements. Early January 2017, Niwat Roikaew (head of the Rak Chiang Khong Group) submitted a petition against the decision of the government to the National Human Rights Commission (NHRC). Tuenjai Deetes, member of the NHRC, argued that the rights of the local people had not been respected (no access to information and no public participation). Deetes said she would raise the issue with the NHRC's subcommittee on human rights in natural resources and the environment, as well as with international organizations.[109] The project sputtered until 4 February 2020, when the Thai Cabinet formally announced the cancellation of the UMNIP, in the midst of a severe drought with water levels at their lowest in decades. As a matter of fact, it had been a year since China had decided not to pursue this project and stopped its funding. For several reasons, Thailand put an end to the UMNIP in its turn. The increasing recurrence of droughts due to hydropower dams and climate change rendered navigation quite often impossible. As already revealed in the 2000's, further clearing of the Mekong River would have worsened this phenomenon. In addition, the transformation of the tumultuous river into a dull canal serving as an industrial corridor, populated with 500-ton freighters would have naturally hampered tourism development, the other quite contradictory purpose of the UMNIP. Once again, because other means of transportation were being developed, notably within the Belt and Road Initiative, the negative effects of the project, including civil protests, led to its cancellation.

3 Taming and Exploiting the Mekong River – from a Free-flowing Watercourse to a Series of Stagnant Reservoirs

In parallel with the UMNIP, hydropower development was an additional threat to the river, as numerous dams had already been built in China, as well as in Laos. At a later time, sand mining compounded the devastating effects of the

---

109 Nauvarat Suksamran, *Locals slam Mekong blasting plan*, THE BANGKOK POST, 9 January 2017; Pratch Rujivanarom, *Residents stare at uncertain future as Cabinet gives nod to blasting of Mekong River rapids*, THE NATION, 16 January 2017.

inconsiderate exploitation of the river. The erosion of the riverbanks caused by the UMNIP could have replaced part of the sediments trapped behind the dams, but excessive sand mining on the other hand has cancelled out this possibility. Worse, at the current rates of extraction, the riverbed and the riverbanks are in the process of being dangerously depleted.

At present, nearly 170 dams in the Mekong Basin hold tremendous amounts of water, block the flow of sediments that nourish the floodplains and fish downstream, and disrupt the seasonal flood and fish migratory patterns, harming fish stocks and, at times, even their very existence.[110] Apart from Myanmar, which represents only a small part of the Mekong River Basin (but where hydropower has also been developed on the other rivers of the country), Mekong countries have embarked on this dam-building spree despite the proven costs of large-scale dams. As currently planned, dam development will ultimately reduce by more than 90% the sediment load in downstream Mekong waters, according to the latest estimates.[111] It has also been estimated that more than 70% of the total fish catch in the Mekong Basin is dependent on the long-distance migrants that move up the Mekong mainstream to breed, some as far upstream as China. Under the current state of knowledge, 87% of the known Mekong species are migratory. The dam cascade has increasingly blocked fish migrations. Moreover, dams may even increase flooding risks, contrary to one of the most established beliefs about their benefits. Besides, dams on the Mekong River have been built in blatant disregard of its essential flood pulse. The Mekong Basin ecosystem belongs to the category of wetlands, the productivity of which is ruled mainly by hydrology, the quality of the floodplain, and fish migration patterns. The Mekong River is endowed with the most variable hydrology in the world, characterized by its annual flood pulse during the monsoon season (May to November). Mekong fisheries depend on three hydrological factors: the level, duration and timing of the flood. About 32,500 sq mi (84,000 km2) of floodplains are inundated during the wet season. Their quality depends on three factors: their accessibility (presently at risk because of infrastructure development that fragments the habitat), the nature of the flooded vegetation, the availability of refuges during the dry season (the deep pools for migrant white fish for instance, filled up and eliminated by the UMNIP for a number of them). Fish migrations are triggered by hydrological

110 Dams are a significant threat to freshwater in general, see, for instance, K. O. Winemiller, et al., *Balancing hydropower and biodiversity in the Amazon, Congo, and Mekong*, 351 SCIENCE 128 (2016).

111 R.J.P. Schmitt, et al., *Planning dam portfolios for low sediment trapping shows limits for sustainable hydropower in the Mekong*, 5 SCI. ADV. (2019).

factors (variations in water level or discharge). The seasonal flood is indispensable to fish productivity. Consequently, dams negatively impact river connectivity. They block the migration routes, lower and shorten floods during the wet season, while they release water during the dry season, thus blurring or suppressing entirely the hydrological cues that trigger fish migrations. Besides, untimely water release during the dry season inundates some vegetation unlikely to survive permanent flooding. At present, attempts to offset declining river capture fisheries by breeding fish in reservoirs or by installing fish ladders seem mostly ineffective. Artificial fish passages can even be harmful.

Because of the controversy about the benefits of dams, the World Bank was criticized for its role in financing such projects worldwide. To confront this criticism, the World Bank and the World Conservation Union established the World Commission on Dams in May 1998. In 2000, the commission concluded in its final report that large dams have, indeed, consistently failed to deliver the benefits promised by their advocates, while exacting heavy tolls on the environment and affected communities.[112] This diagnostic has been confirmed ever since.[113] Without even taking into account social and environmental impacts, which are almost invariably negative and frequently vast, "the actual construction costs of large dams are too high to yield a positive return".[114] In the medium and long term, the Mekong dams are poised to cause an ecological disaster in the Mekong Basin. Chinese experts insist that concerns about the dams are misplaced and, thus far, have been unwilling to consult with

112 DAMS AND DEVELOPMENT – A NEW FRAMEWORK FOR DECISION-MAKING – THE REPORT OF THE WORLD COMMISSION ON DAMS (2000). With the publication of the report, the commission was disbanded, in 2001.

113 The negative impacts of dams are widely documented. See, for instance, International Rivers, *Understanding the Impacts of China's Upper Mekong Dams*, 29 WORLD RIVERS REVIEW 15 (2014), and the rest of the issue, dedicated to the Mekong River; ERIC BARAN, ET AL., FISH, SEDIMENT AND DAMS IN THE MEKONG – HOW HYDROPOWER DEVELOPMENT AFFECTS WATER PRODUCTIVITY AND FOOD SUPPLY (WorldFish-CGIAR Research Program on Water, Land and Ecosystems (WLE). 2015); Winemiller, et al., SCIENCE, (2016); MRC, THE STUDY ON THE SUSTAINABLE MANAGEMENT AND DEVELOPMENT OF THE MEKONG RIVER BASIN INCLUDING IMPACTS OF MAINSTREAM HYDROPOWER PROJECTS (MRC. 2017), known as the Council Study, conducted over six years; Valerio Barbarossa, et al., *Impacts of current and future large dams on the geographic range connectivity of freshwater fish worldwide*, 117 PNAS 3468 (2020).

114 Atif Ansar, et al., *Should we build more large dams? The actual costs of hydropower megaproject development*, 69 ENERGY POLICY 43, 44 (2014). See also Jacques Leslie, *Large Dams Just Aren't Worth the Cost*, NEW YORK TIMES, 22 August 2014, relating the experience of Thayer Scudder, one of the leading world's authorities on dams, former commissioner of the World Commission on Dams, author of LARGE DAMS – LONG TERM IMPACTS ON RIVERINE COMMUNITIES AND FREE-FLOWING RIVERS (Springer. 2019).

downstream countries about the Lancang-Mekong cascade. Grandiose public works are still in favor. "Chinese officials get promoted for building dams, not for saving fish".[115]

3.1 *China's Dam Policy*

What explains Chinese persistence in transforming the Lancang/Mekong River? Chinese leaders' legitimacy has long been linked in part to their engineering capabilities, e.g. taming the great rivers, considered as a threat because of repetitive deadly floods in their history. China has had an army of water engineers. Two recent Chinese leaders were water engineers themselves: Li Peng, Premier from 1987 to 1998 (and Congress Chairman from 1998 to 2003), under whom the Three Gorges Dam was decided, the world's largest;[116] and Hu Jintao, President from 2003 to 2013. The Communist party has had a policy of building innumerable dams (thousands since the 1940's), which has led to the emergence of the Chinese hydro-industrial complex. China ranks number one in the world for the number of large dams, and is also the world's leading contractor of large dams abroad,[117] where they indiscriminately apply their historical mindset, dismissing and suppressing local characteristics, such as the Mekong River's beneficial flood pulse, which I have just described above. Several dam projects have been regularly proposed, even though they are often not efficient, such as Xiaonanhai, a $5.2 billion dam project on the Yangzi River in Chongqing, in southwest China. Construction began in 2012. It would have produced little electricity, at the cost of the fertile soil that makes the site one of China's most productive agricultural regions; it could also have destroyed a rare fish preserve. According to Chinese regulations, one can request access to public records and demand public hearings. However, these avenues have occasionally been barred when most needed, concerning

115 According to a Bangkok-based diplomat, *in* WHEELER, 5. 2004. Paradoxically, the tremendous economic value of the Mekong fisheries has not been on the policy-makers' mind. Because of its abundance, fish in itself is of low value, nor does it have an emotional or symbolical one (Eric Baran & Chris Myschowoda, *Dams and fisheries in the Mekong Basin*, 12 AQUAT. ECOSYST. HEALTH MANAG. 227, 229 (2009)).

116 In addition, Li Peng's daughter, Li Xiaolin, was the head of a publicly listed arm of one of the five leading state-owned power companies, China Power International. In July 2015, she became the Vice-President of China Datang Corporation, another one of the five companies. Li Xiaolin was trained as a power generation engineer.

117 As of 2015, Chinese companies and banks were involved in about 330 dam projects in 74 countries, according to International Rivers, a global pressure group established in 1985, which focuses on Latin America, Africa and Asia (International-Rivers, *China's Global Role in Dam Building* (2015)), available at https://archive.internationalrivers.org/campaigns/china-s-global-role-in-dam-building (accessed 17 June 2021).

controversial projects, such as this one.[118] Even if China has had environmental authorities very well aware of crucial issues in that domain, their voices have not been readily heard.[119] The Water Resources Ministry, whose staff is highly educated in environmental matters, seems to have no real influence. Local governments have often proceeded with no need for higher-level authorization, and construction of some projects has even been started without final approval. Moreover, during the 1990's, China increased the number of gigantic mega-dams as clean energy, in response to its economic development and air pollution.[120] Sometimes, but rarely, environmental concerns seem to prevail: Wen Jabao, Prime Minister from 2003 to 2013, halted the construction of a thirteen-dam cascade project in 2004, in order to protect the environment, because the project proponent had failed to comply with the most recent EIA law. The Xiaonanhai dam was cancelled too, by the Ministry of Environmental Protection, on 30 March 2015.[121] However, sixty-five dams have already been built on the Lancang River and its tributaries, including eleven mega-dams on its mainstream, the so-called *Lancang Cascade*, and twenty-three more are currently planned,[122] without any EIA being made, or made meaningfully, despite

118 Authorities have rejected requests for public records on Xiaonanhai, and did not grant a public hearing (*The politics of dam-building – Opening the flood gates*, THE ECONOMIST, 21 September 2013).

119 In 2005, Pan Yue (China's Vice Minister of the Environment from 2008 to 2015) strikingly framed China's environmental outlook: "Our raw materials are scarce, we don't have enough land, and our population is constantly growing. Currently, there are 1.3 billion people living in China; that's twice as many as 50 years ago. In 2020, there will be 1.5 billion people in China. Cities are growing, but desert areas are expanding at the same time; habitable and usable land have been halved over the past 50 years. (...) [China's GDP miracle] will end soon because the environment can no longer keep pace. Half of the water in our seven largest rivers is completely useless, while one fourth of our citizens does not have access to clean drinking water. One third of the urban population is breathing polluted air, and less than 20 percent of the trash in cities is treated and processed in an environmentally sustainable manner." *in* Andreas Lorenz, *Interview with China's Deputy Minister of the Environment – "The Chinese Miracle Will End Soon"*, DER SPIEGEL, 7 March 2005.

120 Charlton Lewis, *China's Great Dam Boom: A Major Assault on Its Rivers*, YALE ENVIRONMENT 360, 4 November 2013.

121 Following the arrest of the governor of Chongqing, Bo Xilai, convicted of corruption (Edward Wong, *China Blocks Yangtze Dam Project, Activists Say*, THE NEW YORK TIMES, 10 April 2015). The project was situated on protected areas, designated as such in compensation for the Three Gorges Dam, farther downstream.

122 In China, the exploitation of the Lancang River Basin for its hydroelectric power potential commenced on a modest scale more than seventy years ago. The Tianshengqiao hydropower station (400 kW) was completed in 1946 on the Xi'er River, a tributary of the Lancang. See International Rivers, *Dams on the Mekong Mainstream*, at https://drive.google.com/file/d/1njKmrKml-9Y_MClJa-XkaNCFj4G3XNqp/view, accessed 17 June

legal requirements, which, moreover, seem flawed and outdated. Some 70% of the whole Mekong hydroelectric possibilities are concentrated in China, where the Lancang plunges 875 yards (800 meters) through narrow gorges over a 466-mile (750-km) stretch. Some of the cascade's electricity is sold to Thailand, which, with its investment in the Jinghong Dam, was the first foreign country with a stake in a Chinese hydroelectric project. Often, China does not issue warnings when it opens the floodgates, generating unexpected floods. Moreover, the country has long been suspected of withholding some increasingly large amounts of water, responsible for droughts. On 1 April 2002, China signed a limited agreement on the seasonal provision of hydrological information on the Lancang-Mekong River.[123] Nevertheless, despite its repeated commitment to increase data sharing, under international pressure exacerbated by worsening droughts, China has considered in truth that daily flow data on transboundary rivers were a matter of national secrecy, and has insisted on its absolute right to pursue development on waters within its sovereign territory without consulting with its neighbors.[124] Some evidence of increasingly larger amounts of water withheld upstream has recently come to light, however, pointing to China's responsibility for the severe droughts that have now repeatedly plagued the downstream countries for years. China has denied and claimed low precipitations as the real cause. It remains that the evidence appears indisputable this time, and widely shared, which might alter China's stance eventually.[125]

More generally, the Chinese government has officially taken environmental issues into consideration. In 2015, new environmental regulations, including in the area of international investment, have been passed. To reassure an increasingly worried population, Chinese authorities can no longer rely solely on economic growth. Some Chinese investors have apparently been potentially amenable to a corporate social responsibility approach. However, the new comprehensive environmental law does not seem sufficient to address the current issues. As it is already well documented, a chronic lack of enforcement,

---

2021. ALAN BASIST & CLAUDE WILLIAMS, MONITORING THE QUANTITY OF WATER FLOWING THROUGH THE UPPER MEKONG BASIN UNDER NATURAL (UNIMPEDED) CONDITIONS 11-12 (Sustainable Infrastructure Partnership, Bangkok. 2020).

123 Under this agreement, China is supposed to provide water level data during the flood season. This information is fed into the MRC's flood forecasting system.

124 Contrary to the principle of prior consultations regarding international water management, as first set out in the *Lake Lanoux* arbitration in 1957 (see *supra* page 15 et seq.).

125 BASIST & WILLIAMS, *supra* note 122; Brian Eyler, *Science Shows Chinese Dams Are Devastating the Mekong*, FOREIGN POLICY, 22 April 2020.

implementation mechanisms and accountability regimes have remained as an impediment to an efficient environmental policy in the country.[126]

3.2 *Laos' Dam Policy*

As for Laos, its ambition has been to become the "battery of South-Asia", with the support of many economists and international financial institutions like the World Bank and the Asian Development Bank. Most of the power produced by actual and planned dams is destined to be exported to neighboring countries. The government of Laos intends that hydropower become its major source of revenue, as the Greater Mekong Subregion (GMS) program develops a regional grid. The ultimate development objective of the GMS Power Trade Project is the realization of an integrated GMS power grid, fueled primarily by hydropower.[127] As of 2021, there were seventy-eight operational dams in the country, and Laos announced that they would build an additional hundred, despite its crippling debt to China, which recently resulted in Laos' loss of majority control of its national power grid to the latter.[128]

For their part, Lao authorities are insistent on asserting their sovereign rights to use natural resources as they wish. In addition, the Lao government emphasizes the country's need to steer away from poverty. Land-locked and with most of its trading links with China, Thailand and Vietnam only, Laos' prospects of economic growth are limited to debt-accruing infrastructure development and hydropower generation. In its view, environmental and social impacts are generally exaggerated, and procedural obligations deter potential investors. An independent observer noted that the government of Laos "does not respond well to external pressure, they respond much more to their own opportunities

---

126 The Environmental Protection Law was promulgated by the Standing Committee of the National People's Congress on 24 April 2014 (effective 1 January 2015). See Zhang, et al., *A New Environmental Protection Law, Many Old Problems? Challenges to Environmental Governance in China*, 28 JEL 325 (2016).

127 The GMS power grid project is based on a 1994 report to the ADB by a Norwegian consulting firm, Norconsult. Since this report, the ADB and the World Bank have encouraged and supported the establishment of a regional power market.

128 Luke Hunt, *Laos Presses Ahead with 4 More Mekong Dams amid Drought*, VOICE OF AMERICA, 12 December 2020. More generally, about the downstream countries, see Brian Eyler, *2020 Status of Lower Mekong Mainstream and Tributary Dams* (Stimson Center. 10 January 2020), at https://www.stimson.org/2020/2020-status-of-lower-mekong-mainstream-and-tributary-dams/, accessed 17 June 2021. For a comprehensive source of information about infrastructure projects in the Mekong Basin, including energy infrastructure, see Stimson Center, *Mekong Infrastructure Tracker*, at https://www.stimson.org/2020/mekong-infrastructure-tracker-tool/, accessed 17 June 2021.

that they identify by themselves".[129] Corruption also plays an important role in having the environmental and social impacts ignored.[130] In addition, China, Laos' main investor, exerts a tremendous influence on the country. With regard to international financial institutions, despite the earlier criticisms and the WCD's findings, the World Bank soon began to explore a resumption of funding for large dams. In Laos, the World Bank accepted to provide funding for a large dam, the Nam Theun 2 hydropower project, in 2005.[131] In 2013, it fully resumed encouraging and supporting large-dam projects globally, despite the evidence of their negative impacts.[132] Furthermore, the implementation of the Lao EIA requirements can be deficient as in the UMNIP case, or utterly absent. As for the MRC, Laos took no notice of its important Strategic Environmental Assessment (SEA) in 2010, which called for the suspension of dam building on the Mekong for ten years, to allow for a number of different courses of action so that better-informed decisions can be taken.[133] Soon after, in blatant disregard of the MRC's recommendation, Laos unilaterally acted on a mega-dam project, the Xayaburi dam, now in service.[134] The 2010 SEA was a donor-funded project, in view of reasserting the MRC's role as a forum for dam project development and as the source of presumably neutral technical expertise, but, in

129 Andrew Wells-Dang, *Prospects for Regional Cooperation on Environmental Impact Assessment in Mainland Southeast Asia*, 37 CONTEMPORARY SOUTHEAST ASIA 406 (2015).

130 More generally, about corruption in foreign investment, see ALOYSIUS P. LLAMZON, CORRUPTION IN INTERNATIONAL INVESTMENT ARBITRATION (Oxford University Press. 2014).

131 See, for a critical analysis, Ian G. Baird, et al., *The People and their River, the World Bank and its Dam: Revisiting the Xe Bang Fai River in Laos*, 46 DEV. CHANGE 1080 (2015).

132 "Large hydro is a very big part of the solution for Africa and South Asia and Southeast Asia ... I fundamentally believe we have to be involved," said Rachel Kyte, the WB's vice president for sustainable development and an influential voice among Jim Yong Kim's top staff members. The earlier move out of hydropower "was the wrong message ... That was then. This is now. We are back", *in* Howard Schneider, *World Bank turns to hydropower to square development with climate change*, THE WASHINGTON POST, 8 May 2013. Then President of the World Bank (2012–2019), Jim Yong Kim, confirmed this policy in favor of large dams (statements at the Union Theological Seminary on "The Principle of Mercy", New York, 6 April 2016).

133 INTERNATIONAL CENTRE FOR ENVIRONMENTAL MANAGEMENT (ICEM), STRATEGIC ENVIRONMENTAL ASSESSMENT OF HYDROPOWER ON THE MEKONG MAINSTREAM 138 (Mekong River Commission. 2010). The 10-year suspension was proposed not so much because of scientific concerns, as knowledge of the ecosystem of the Mekong had already significantly progressed. Rather, the suspension was suggested in order for decision-makers to pause and take the time to better inform themselves. The long duration (ten years) was expected to be striking enough to draw their attention.

134 See *infra* page 284 et seq.

the end, the MRC failed to take a formal position on mainstream dam policy and the recommendation on deferment was not adopted, nor even discussed, partly due to internal struggles within the MRC – the four member states have had different views on mainstream dam development.[135] Nonetheless, the manner in which the SEA was presented and released as a consultant report accelerated the dissemination of the findings, and eliminated the possibility of the report being rejected by Laos. Had it been required to follow the review and approval process as an official MRC report, it is unlikely that the SEA would have ever been released publicly. Beyond its limited power from the start, the MRC is now highly criticized for failing its mission to protect the Mekong River's ecosystem, partly because of the overbearing and undue influence of Laos since its offices have been relocated in part to Vientiane, fifteen years ago. The number of independent observers to the MRC meetings has been reduced to two (from more than fifteen).[136] Because of the weakness of the MRC, and particularly because the MRC rarely encouraged public participation, the Mekong People's Forum, a regional federation of NGOs and local communities, put into question the very existence of the commission in 2015. Similarly, the MRC donors had questioned its role.[137] They have called for independent audits and significantly reduced their contributions. In reaction, the MRC has initiated a long transition from a primarily donor-funded to a self-sustainable organization.[138] As a result, the government of Laos has repeatedly denied the real consequences of its use of, and alterations to, the Mekong River without encountering much resistance. Lao authorities have regularly refused to take into account scientific studies, or to allow effective public participation, before deciding on their projects. Furthermore, the government of Laos has ignored alternatives that yield the same hydropower benefits and secure sustainable development, with a higher budget. For instance, the Nam Theun

135 Suhardiman, et al., ENVIRONMENT AND PLANNING C: GOVERNMENT AND POLICY, 206 (2015).

136 Joern Kristensen, former CEO of the MRC (1999–2003) had taken care of increasing the number of independent observers to the meetings of the joint committee.

137 Mekong-People's-Forum, *6,400 Signatures and Thumbprints Submitted in Support of Local People's Statement On Mekong Dams at Mekong People's Forum* (2015) at https://mangroveactionproject.blogspot.com/2015/11/6400-signatures-and-thumbprints.html, accessed 17 June 2021. In 2009, the government of Finland, of Germany and AusAid representatives in particular had questioned the MRC's actual role in the region, urging that the MRC should make sure it received notifications from its member states (Suhardiman, et al., ENVIRONMENT AND PLANNING C: GOVERNMENT AND POLICY, 206 (2015)).

138 In 2019, 67% of the MRC income came from development partners: Australia, Belgium, the European Union, Finland, France, Germany, Japan, Luxembourg, the Netherlands, Sweden, Switzerland, and the World Bank (MRC, 2019 ANNUAL REPORT).

2 Dam releases waters into the Xe Bang Fai River, with vast negative ecological and social impacts, all of which had been predicted by independent EIAs years earlier.[139] The EIA team working at the request of the MRC had tried to suggest building a channel between the Nam Theun River and the Mekong River, instead of diverting the waters into a shorter channel leading to the Xe Bang Fai River. Villagers and the environment that sustains them would have been protected. This alternative was disregarded. More generally, investment has increased so considerably that it has outpaced the ability of the government to regulate it,[140] in the rare circumstances where a strong willingness to adopt such regulations exists. Lao authorities have operated with short-term considerations, in a very secluded fashion, at the opposite end of an inclusive decision-making process. They have cracked down on dissent, as attested for instance by the disappearance of Sombath Somphone, who was last seen at a police checkpoint in Vientiane on 15 December 2012. Somphone is a US-trained agriculture specialist and a renown, peaceful and respected activist.[141] Nevertheless, local villagers have become increasingly assertive in making complaints about perceived land and environmental violations, far from the deference to authority that marked traditional public participation when the ruler was believed to be benevolent.[142] Discrepancies between the myth system (the official norms)

139 TYSON R. ROBERTS, FLUVICIDE: AN INDEPENDENT ENVIRONMENTAL ASSESSMENT OF THE NAM THEUN 2 HYDROPOWER PROJECT IN LAOS, WITH PARTICULAR REFERENCE TO AQUATIC BIOLOGY AND FISHES (1996), at https://www.irn.org/files/programs/mekong/tysonfluvicide0904.pdf, accessed 17 June 2021; DAVID J.H. BLAKE, A REVIEW OF THE NAM THEUN 2 ENVIRONMENTAL ASSESSMENT AND MANAGEMENT PLAN (EAMP) AS IT PERTAINS TO IMPACTS ON XE BANG FAI FISHERIES (International Rivers Network. 2005). The Nam Theun 2 Power Company (NTPC) is 40% owned by Electricité de France (EDF), 35% by Electricity Generating Public Company (EGCO) in Thailand and 25% by the Lao Government. The role of the World Bank was essential, and a number of European banks, export credit agencies and the Asian Development Bank (ADB) also provided financing. Construction began in 2005, and operation in 2010.

140 Andrew Wells-Dang, et al., *A Political Economy of Environmental Impact Assessment in the Mekong Region*, 9 WATER ALTERNATIVES 33, 50 (2016).

141 Sebastian Strangio, *Eight Years, and Still No Answers on Lao Activist's Disappearance*, THE DIPLOMAT, 16 December 2020. More generally, about intimidation, see Ian G. Baird, et al., *The People and their River, the World Bank and its Dam: Revisiting the Xe Bang Fai River in Laos*, 46 DEVELOPMENT AND CHANGE 1080, 1099 (2015); HUMAN RIGHTS FOUNDATION, VOICES SILENCED: THE IMPACT OF FOREIGN INVESTMENTS ON HUMAN RIGHTS IN LAOS (February 2021).

142 Prachoom Chomchai, *Public Participation in Watershed Management in Theory and Practice: a Mekong River Basin Perspective*, in PUBLIC PARTICIPATION IN THE GOVERNANCE OF INTERNATIONAL FRESHWATER RESOURCES 140–141 (Carl E. Bruch, et al. eds., 2005).

and the operational code (effective behavior of relevant actors) are no longer accepted. Deceptions to conceal these discrepancies have been exposed. There are dissensions and pressure to respect the key values and policies embodied in the official norms.[143] As a member of the Lao government stated, "villagers are not the same as before. They raise concerns to the National Assembly [and] to the government … they didn't do this before".[144]

3.3 *Thailand's Dam Policy*

In Thailand, civil society has increasingly organized itself in order to be effectively heard. In the UMNIP area, Rak Chiang Khong established the Mekong River Councils, in parallel with some education programs, so that traditional ecological knowledge could be preserved and included in project developments.[145] The Chiang Khong Conservation Group is savvy and well connected to academia and to the NGO network in the Mekong Basin. However, the Thai Government does not seem to accommodate their concerns. Despite the progress of the NGO movement and the development of some environmental legislation, influential economic interests and the centralized government have opposed public participation. Environmental activism can be dangerous; according to the 2014 statistics from Union for Civil Liberty, a Bangkok-based NGO, a grass-roots activist had disappeared and thirty-three had been killed in the past twenty-five years.[146] In several instances, including the UMNIP, the Thai Government did not respect its obligations in matters of EIA and public participation under domestic and international law.[147] On these grounds, about forty villagers, led by Niwat Roikaew (Rak Chiang Khong), brought a suit against five Thai Governmental Bodies (including the MoNRE) in August 2012. It was the first lawsuit concerning transboundary impacts of dams and community rights. The plaintiffs have challenged the validity of the Power

143 See *supra* chapter 3, page 112 et seq.

144 Wells-Dang, et al., WATER ALTERNATIVES, 43 (2016).

145 *The Chiang Khong Mekong School on Local Knowledge.* For twenty-five years, a team of researchers in Chiang Khong has undertaken "Tai Baan" Research. The goal is to spread the adoption of a collaborative learning process that can empower inhabitants to conserve their natural resources and culture. The Chiang Khong Mekong School was established to pass on local knowledge to younger generations and visitors.

146 Anchalee Kongrut, *At the Borders of Ecological Destruction*, BANGKOK POST, 18 January 2016. Union for Civil Liberty (UCL) was founded in 1973 after the downfall of the military regime. See also AMNESTY INTERNATIONAL, "THEY CANNOT KEEP US QUIET" THE CRIMINALIZATION OF ACTIVISTS, HUMAN RIGHTS DEFENDERS, AND OTHERS IN THAILAND (Amnesty International. 2017).

147 See *supra* pages 258–259 (and note 54), and page 261.

Purchase Agreement (PPA), signed in October 2011, between Xayaburi Power Company Ltd (XPCL, headquartered in Laos) and the Thai national electric utility company – Electricity Generating Authority of Thailand (EGAT), for purchase of power from the $3.5 billion Xayaburi project, the first dam project on the Mekong mainstream in Laos. This dam is exemplary of the tensions and risks of environmental conflict that can rise between states. In 2012, when Laos declared that construction was on schedule, the president of Vietnam, Truong Tan Sang, warned that "tensions over water resources are not only threatening economic growth in many countries, but also presenting a source of conflict".[148] The dam started to operate in October 2019. It was financed and built by Thai entities, to satisfy Thai needs in energy. According to the agreement between the Thai developers and EGAT, 95% of the power that is generated is to be sold exclusively to the latter. Activists have accused the Thai Government of displacing controversial energy projects in neighboring countries (Cambodia, Laos, Myanmar) with weaker legal institutions and lower environmental standards. Thailand's main role in the region has transformed into that of an investor and developer abroad. In the water management domain, no large dams have been built in Thailand since the 1990's, but EGATi (the international branch of EGAT) is a major actor in regional hydropower development.[149] The plaintiffs in the Xayaburi case have asked that the definition of state project include projects in which the government enters into a contractual arrangement with a private developer. They hope to set a precedent for the responsibilities of state-owned companies making investments in projects abroad, and to create uncertainty for investors.[150] The case was also brought in solidarity with communities in other riparian countries, who may not be able to access their justice system so readily. Plaintiffs have argued that the transboundary impacts should have led to the application of Thai environmental obligations, as stated in the 2007 Thai Constitution, the 1995 MRC Agreement and the 2003 MRC Procedures (the PNPCA). The Xayaburi project was devoid of any proper TEIA, EIA, notification, consultations. In 2011, the MRC member states had agreed on conducting EIAs, but the PPA was already signed and construction began without any previous proper study, nor public participation. The PPA stipulated that XPCL would have had to pay heavy penalties to Thailand in case of any

148 *River elegy – Damming the Mekong River*, THE ECONOMIST, 3 November 2012.

149 See Nathanial Matthews, *Water Grabbing in the Mekong Basin – An Analysis of the Winners and Losers of Thailand's Hydropower Development in Lao PDR*, 5 WATER ALTERN. 392 (2012).

150 Pianporn Deetes, *Thai Court Holds Hope for Transboundary Justice in the Mekong*, INTERNATIONAL RIVERS, 23 July 2015.

delay, hence XPCL's haste. On 15 February 2013, the Thai administrative court of first instance decided that it had no jurisdiction to hear the case because the plaintiffs could not be considered injured persons, and the PPA was not an administrative act.[151] On 17 April 2014, the Supreme Administrative Court reversed the lower court's decision and ruled that the latter had jurisdiction to hear the case. The court stated that "Evidence suggests relevant authorities have failed to adequately listen to the opinions of people and to comply with the PNPCA";[152] "It is widely known that the project may cause impacts to the environment, water quality and quantity, the flow of water, ecological balances of the Mekong Basin and other transboundary impacts in riparian countries, particularly local communities in the eight riparian provinces of the Kingdom of Thailand, which may bear extensive impacts on environmental quality, public health, sanitation, livelihoods, or community interests".[153] The Supreme Court remanded the lower court's decision. On 25 December 2015, the administrative court of first instance dismissed the case on the merits this time, on the grounds that information disclosure had been sufficient, EIA and public participation requirements did not apply to the PPA, and the 2003 MRC PNPCA rules imposing notification and prior consultations had been respected.[154] In the meantime, on 22 July 2014, the 2007 Thai Constitution had been repealed and replaced by an Interim Constitution, in the wake of a *coup d'Etat* staged by a military junta two months before. The army tried to intimidate the plaintiffs in this case, but the latter have persevered, undeterred.[155] In January 2016, the plaintiffs decided to appeal the administrative court's decision to the

151 Decision No. 59/2556. See *The Court Dismissed the Case against EGAT*, PRACHATAI. 25 December 2015, at https://prachatai.com/journal/2015/12/63167 (in Thai) accessed 14 June 2021, with photos of the decision.

152 *In* Business & Human Rights Resource Center, *Xayaburi dam lawsuit* (*re Laos & Thailand*) (2016) *at* http://business-humanrights.org/en/xayaburi-dam-lawsuit-re-laos-thailand, accessed 17 June 2021. The decision (in Thai) is available at http://www.livingriversiam.org/4river-tran/4mk/mek_n176.pdf (accessed 14 June 2021).

153 *In* Sor Rattanamanee Polkla, *Mekong Villagers in Fight for Their Rights*, BANGKOK POST, 30 November 2015. Polkla is one of the plaintiffs' counsels in the Xayaburi PPA case. She has been a public interest lawyer for fifteen years. In 2010, with Prashant Singh, she co-founded the Community Resource Centre (CRC), an NGO working with communities who face the impacts of development projects.

154 Supreme Administrative Court of Thailand, 25 December 2015, available in English at https://media.business-humanrights.org/media/documents/files/documents/CourtDecisionXayaburi25_12_2015ENG.pdf (summary – unofficial translation), and in Thai at https://thaipublica.org/wp-content/uploads/2015/12/คำพิพากษา-คดีไฟฟ้าเขื่อนไซยะบุรี-คำ-ส493-2555.pdf (both accessed 14 June 2021).

155 *Military interrupts private meeting of lawyer with clients in Isan*, PRACHATAI, 11 December 2014.

Administrative Supreme Court. However, the dam was built and started operation in October 2019. Consequently, the plaintiffs have submitted additional evidence of environmental damage, and also filed an injunction in parallel on 26 July 2019, for the suspension of the PPA until the evidence has been properly assessed. At this writing, the case is still pending.

Both the UMNIP and the Xayaburi dam cases exemplify poor planning. EGAT acknowledged it did not need the electricity generated by the Xayaburi hydropower plant. Independent studies have found that EGAT had grossly over-estimated the amount of electricity needs in Thailand, and that it had not studied potentially cheaper or greener electricity generation options.[156] Moreover, Laos' best interests were put into question, as the PPA was denounced as an unbalanced agreement in favor of Thai interests.[157] Laos has recently built another mega dam on the Mekong mainstream, under the same conditions.[158] Cambodia and Vietnam have kept expressing their concerns, to little avail.

As for Myanmar, with respect to environmental protection at large, civil society is also trying to make itself heard, but projects have usually proceeded without proper EIAs (some EIA regulations were issued only at the end of December 2015[159]), with scarce information disclosure, and without any consultation with the affected populations.[160]

Practical solutions exist, however. The efficiency and environmental impacts of existing dams could be improved. Small-scale hydropower and solar power could be developed. According to a 2013 study, an appropriate combination of renewables could, by 2025, be significantly more productive than the proposed

156 Pianporn Deetes, *Right way forward for the Mekong River*, BANGKOK POST, 3 May 2016.

157 ASHWINI CHITNIS, THE XAYABURI POWER PURCHASE AGREEMENT – AN INDEPENDENT REVIEW (International Rivers. 2013).

158 The Don Sahong Dam, close to the Cambodian border, which started to operate in January 2020. Most of the electricity is to be exported abroad.

159 Environmental Impact Assessment Procedure, Notification No. 616/2015 (29 December 2015), issued by the Ministry of Environmental Conservation and Forestry, based on Article 7 (m) of the Environmental Conservation Law (30 March 2012).

160 See, for instance, the Myitsone Dam project on the Irrawaddy River (Aung, et al., *Evaluation of the environmental impact assessment (EIA) of Chinese EIA in Myanmar: Myitsone Dam, the Lappadaung Copper Mine and the Sino-Myanmar oil and gas pipelines*, IMPACT ASSESS. PROJECT APPRAIS. (2018), doi.org/10.1080/14615517.2018.1529948; Laur Kiik, *Confluences amid Conflict: How Resisting China's Myitsone Dam Project Linked Kachin and Bamar Nationalisms in War-Torn Burma*, 24 Journal of Burma Studies 229 (2020); Laur Kiik, *Inter-National Conspiracy? Speculating on the Myitsone Dam Controversy in China, Burma, Kachin, and a Displaced Village*, Geopolitics (2020) doi.org/10.1080/14650045.2020.1808886).

dams.[161] Developing energy efficiency in combination with environmental protection could lead to substantial savings. Yet mega-dams have tended to attract all the support because, paradoxically at first glance, they are capital-intensive. They boost foreign direct investment and stimulate GDP growth, temporarily, but for long enough a time to accommodate short-term interests. They allow host governments to collect money swiftly by granting construction rights to private developers. In countries where the rule of law is weak, large-dam projects have provided quick and easy opportunities for skimming and cronyism. All this leads to the absence of EIAs, or of proper ones. Project proponents and relevant authorities are often not interested in alternatives laid out in EIAs. They have already decided on the specifics of the project. Adding to the trouble is the involvement of major financial institutions, such as the World Bank or the Asian Development Bank. Mega-dams, like any large and costly project, seem to have allowed the World Bank to increase its visibility by displaying shiny showcase projects and to make full use of its budget, thus pleasing its 189 members by appearing to fulfill its role in a very public way. In 2016, the World Bank seemed to reverse direction again, but only to diminish its support.[162] Furthermore, the World Bank was relegated to second place, as China overtook it as the world's leader in the domain of hydropower financing.

4 Conclusion and Recommendations

The UMNIP case casts a stark light on EIA practices in the Greater Mekong Subregion. Instead of examining alternatives to proposed projects objectively and early on in the process, and considering the environmental and socio-economic impacts of all options, most EIAs are made, if at all, when the project is already well advanced and decided. This case study attests to the fact that EIAs,

161 See ADB, et al., *Ensuring Sustainability of the GMS Regional Power Development* (2013) *at* http://icem.com.au/portfolio-items/ensuring-sustainability-of-the-greater-mekong-subregion-regional-power-development-final-reports/, accessed 17 June 2021.

162 *Can the World Bank Lead by Example in Moving Away from Large Dams?* INTERNATIONAL RIVERS, 13 October 2016. About the persistent involvement of the World Bank, see, for instance, the 2018 SEA in Myanmar, conducted by the IFC, which does not take into account cumulative and transboundary impacts, and considers mega-dam projects as a starting point without considering the alternatives (at https://www.ifc.org/wps/wcm/connect/industry_ext_content/ifc_external_corporate_site/hydro+advisory/resources/sea+of+the+hydropower+sector+in+myanmar+resources+page, accessed 17 June 2021). For a longer-term perspective, see Jacques Leslie, *After a Long Boom, an Uncertain Future for Big Dam Projects*, YALE ENVIRONMENT 360, 27 November 2018.

when they are made and disclosed, are used by Chinese, Thai, or Lao authorities only so that they will appear as if they have abided by the applicable regulations, and to validate a decision that has already been taken. Transboundary impacts are usually dismissed. There is not yet any effective regional cooperation between the riparian states in terms of environmental protection. The current EIA system as practiced in the Greater Mekong Subregion does not lead to sustainable development. EIAs are usually made at too late a stage, in the form of technical reports of poor quality, which are inaccessible to non-experts, not publicly available and without public participation (either because the latter is dismissed, or because of pressure and intimidation that silence the affected populations[163]). In the short run, consultancy firms appear to have a vested interest in having EIAs approved, as they want to secure more clients.[164] Choosing an independent consulting company presents the risk of not having the EIA approved rapidly, whereas choosing the consulting company with adequate government ties allows an expedited process. Some project proponents at times even contract staff of government agencies responsible for approving the EIA as consultants to carry out the EIA, which is a case of conflict of interest. Besides, EIA systems have been developed and regulated over a short period of time, which has led to an overload, because the capacities of ministries have not been appropriately developed. In addition to a general lack of coordination between the actors of the decision-making process, the review agencies, from the provinces to the relevant central government ministries, lack authority and resources. External pressure, political or economic, easily derail the EIA process.[165] As a result, as of the mid-2010's, no EIA had ever been rejected by the approval authorities in Thailand, Laos or Vietnam.[166] Devoid of their *raison d'être*, EIAs are reduced to being little more than administrative hurdles, made in haste, if at all. Often, the consulting company and/or the approval authority,

163 In addition to the other examples already mentioned, see the case of the China Western Poverty Reduction Project (see *infra* notes 217 and 229), as witnessed by the World Bank Inspection Panel team: "The Inspection Team's short field visit, though it recorded many positive comments about the proposed Project, also yielded some disturbing and dramatic examples of what can only be described as a climate of fear, through which some individuals nevertheless managed, at great perceived risk, to express their opposition to this Project" (The Inspection Panel, *Investigation Report – The Qinghai Project, a component of the China: Western Poverty Reduction Project* (Credit No. 3255-CHA and Loan No 4501-CHA) 52 (IBRD-IDA (World Bank). 2000).

164 On the issue of independence of EIA practitioners, see *supra* chapter 2, page 70 et seq.

165 Sengdeuane Wayakone & Inoue Makoto, *Evaluation of the Environmental Impacts Assessment (EIA) System in Lao PDR*, 3 JOURNAL OF ENVIRONMENTAL PROTECTION 1655, 1663 (2012).

166 Wells-Dang, et al., WATER ALTERNATIVES, 37–38 (2016).

which are sometimes the same entity, view EIAs as little more than opportunities to extract funds from the developer. The lack of EIAs, or properly conducted ones, combined with the absence of genuine public participation, has led the Mekong countries to an improper use of the river with consequences for its inhabitants' livelihoods, the full scale of which is still unknown, but can be expected to be formidable. Economic development is based on extraction and depletion of natural resources, from which only a minority seems to benefit. Short-term financial interests have overridden environmental laws and procedures in selecting projects. Environmental and social impacts have not been factored into appraisal decisions.

The UMNIP case is striking because a proper EIA would have shown that blasting obstacles on the Mekong River was, first and foremost, simply not the appropriate way to fulfill the goal of the project. Contrary to large dams, this project had a small budget. For all the states involved, benefits of all kinds were negligible in the end, even the short-term ones (apart perhaps from the temporary value increase of the ports). Combined with the dam effect and contrary to its goal, the UMNIP eventually made navigation even more difficult than it was before the start of the project. Large boats could not navigate the Mekong, and traditional boats began having serious difficulties to ply the river.[167] As for large dams, the short-term benefits of which are a given for some privileged authorities, China and Laos were resolute in refusing to consider any critical data. As a result, the environmental consequences of the UMNIP have been disproportionately negative.

The following recommendations will focus on the role of financial institutions and civil society.

4.1 *Financial Institutions*

Despite its obligations and declarations in favor of a comprehensive environmental policy, the World Bank has been regularly and harshly criticized for the detrimental environmental consequences of some of the projects it helps to finance.[168] In light of the crucial role of the World Bank, its reversal in dam

---

167 "Boat owner Odd Boontha is one of the millions who make their living on the Mekong. The sunburned 38-year-old in the northern Thai port of Chiang Khong has his own way of gauging the health of the river. Passengers who a few years ago used concrete steps to reach his shallow-draught vessel must now scramble over rocks to reach it. The water level is at its lowest in 20 years, Odd says, and Chinese dams upstream are to blame.", *in* Barry Wain, *River at Risk*, 167 FAR EASTERN ECONOMIC REVIEW 48, 48 (2004).

168 For instance, see the Nam Theun II dam in Laos (*supra* pages 281–283). See also the Sardar Sarovar dam in India (Bruce Rich, *The Emperor's New Clothes: The World Bank and*

policy in 2013, its subsequent and renewed support for mega-dam projects (albeit in a reduced fashion lately),[169] improving the role of banks (multilateral and private) seems paramount among the recommendations for more effective environmental protection in developing economies, especially under authoritarian regimes. Their role is essential for securing sustainable development and supporting civil society's endeavors. Because financial institutions are in a unique position of powerful influence, they must be more active in terms of environmental protection. There has been insufficient progress thus far. Recommendations consist in applying external pressure on the banks (the first two parts below will address lender environmental liability and accountability), so that they continue to improve their internal organization (the third part will address the role of bank sustainability and environment departments in the decision-making process).

4.1.1 Lender Environmental Liability (LEL)

A radical recommendation would be to enact national legislation imposing derivative responsibility for environmental harm on the banks extending loans (Lender Environmental Liability – LEL), as an incentive for them to forestall such responsibility by ensuring EIAs are effective. Many World Bank stakeholders insisted on the ultimate responsibility of the World Bank and similar institutions.[170] International regulations and domestic laws imposing derivative responsibility on lenders for environmental harm would force the banks to protect themselves with effective EIAs. The more actors engaged in the project are concerned and liable, the better the quality of interaction and information. Because lenders have deep pockets and because they are uniquely positioned to press borrowers for environmental compliance, their derivative responsibility has imposed itself in a few countries.

Environmental Reform, 7 WORLD POLICY JOURNAL 305 (1990)). Under tremendous external pressure, the World Bank set up an independent commission to investigate its alleged violations, review the project and make recommendations. After the report of the Morse Commission, the World Bank withdrew from the Sardar Sarovar project, in 1993. The dam project was then financed by India.

169 See *supra* page 276, 281, 288 and note 162.

170 World Bank, *Review and Update of the World Bank's Environmental and Social Safeguard Policies – Summary of input submitted by stakeholders*, Question 1, Management Plan and Impact Assessment, point 2; Q10, Monitoring and compliance, pt 4; Q11, Other issues, pt 2 (October 2012-April 2013).

4.1.1.1 *Domestic Financial Institutions*

LEL has been developed in a few countries only, at varying degrees. In the European Union, under the 2004 Environmental Liability Directive (ELD),[171] banks do not have a duty to avoid financing environmentally harmful projects, but only a possible role in environmental protection, which mainly consists in conducting EIAs.[172] In the United States, in 1980, the Comprehensive Environmental Response, Compensation and Liability Act (CERCLA – also commonly known as *Superfund*) provided for liability of persons responsible for contaminated properties.[173] Under CERCLA, potentially responsible parties (PRPs) can be required to carry out, or pay for, the cleanup of the contaminated sites. Any current owner or operator of a vessel or a facility can be designated a PRP, whose liability would be pronounced if it participated in the management of the activities in question. In 1990, a seminal case (*United States v. Fleet Factors Corp.*) decided that the mere ability to exercise control, regardless of the actual exercise of such control, counted as participating in management,[174] bringing lenders within the reach of CERCLA. Liability under CERCLA is both strict, joint and several. There is no cap. However, in 1996, the Asset Conservation, Lender Liability, and Deposit Insurance Protection Act (the 1996 Amendments) amended CERCLA to set up some lender liability

171 Directive 2004/35/CE of the European Parliament and of the Council of 21 April 2004 on environmental liability with regard to the prevention and remedying of environmental damage (OJ L 143, 30 April 2004, p. 56–75). The directive "ended up as a very complicated, uncertain and impractical tool" (Kleoniki C. Pouikli, *Overview of the implementation of the directive 2004/35/EC on environmental liability with regard to the prevention and remedying of environmental damage at European level*, 57 DESALINATION AND WATER TREATMENT 11520 (2016)).

172 In the own words of the European Union itself, see EUROPEAN COMMISSION, ENVIRONMENTAL LIABILITY DIRECTIVE – PROTECTING EUROPE'S NATURAL RESOURCES 9 (European Union. 2013). Nonetheless, some decidedly construe the EU concept of operator as potentially encompassing lenders (see RÔMULO S. R. SAMPAIO, et al., LENDERS AND INVESTORS ENVIRONMENTAL LIABILITY – HOW MUCH IS TOO MUCH? 6 (UNEP. 2016)). Under the ELD, "operator means any natural or legal, private or public person who operates or controls the occupational activity or, where this is provided for in national legislation, to whom decisive economic power over the technical functioning of such an activity has been delegated, including the holder of a permit or authorisation for such an activity or the person registering or notifying such an activity" (Article 2.6).

173 42 USC §§ 9601 et seq.

174 *United States v. Fleet Factors Corp.*, 901 F. 2d 1550, 1558 (11th Cir. 1990): "A secured creditor will be liable if its involvement with the management of the facility is sufficiently broad to support the inference that it could affect hazardous waste disposal decisions if it so chose".

protection. The 1996 Amendments stated which activities do not qualify as "participation in the management activity". In other words, they list a set of objective criteria to allow for a liability defense. Under the 1996 Amendments definition of participation in management, the secured creditor exemption has consisted in a two-prong test: firstly, a person must qualify as a lender. And they must be deemed as not having participated in management. The mere capacity to influence an activity, or an unexercised right to control this activity can no longer be regarded as participation in management.[175]

At present, Brazil is the only country with a comprehensive LEL regime. In 2009, the Superior Court of Justice (STJ) decided, in an *obiter dictum*:

> … For the purpose of determining the existence of a causal link in the urban and environmental damage and possible joint and several liability, anyone who does, who does not do, who does not do when something should be done, who does not care if someone else does, who remains silent instead of denouncing, who finances for something to be done or who benefits from what the others do are all equal for the purpose of liability.[176]

Two weeks later, the Superior Court of Justice handed down another similar decision, in the case of a lender.[177] Lenders can be held to be indirect polluters under a strict, joint and several liability regime.[178] In addition, environmental groups have standing.[179] Soon after the 2009 decisions, more lawsuits started

---

175 However, the secured creditor exemption under CERCLA has not provided an absolute protection from environmental liability, see Matthew H. Ahrens & David S. Langer, *Lender Liability under CERCLA—Environmental Risks for Lenders under Superfund: A Refresher for the Economic Downturn*, 3 BLOOMBERG CORPORATE LAW JOURNAL 482, 489–491 (2008).

176 STJ-T2, Resp 650728, Relator: Min. Benjamin Herman, 23 October 2007, Revista do Superior Tribunal de Justiça [RSTJ], 1 December 2009 (Braz.).

177 "Regarding BNDES, the simple fact that it is the financial institution responsible for financing the mining activities … at a first analysis, does not establish that it can be a defendant in the case. However, if there is evidence that this government-owned corporation [BNDES] was even aware of serious and severe environmental harm [and] … has released intermediate or final disbursements to the mining project … in this case, [BNDES] shall be under a joint and several liability for damages" (STJ, Resp 995321, Relator: Min. Benedito Gonçalves, 15 October 2007, Revista do Superior Tribunal de Justiça [RSTJ], 15 December 2009 (Braz.)).

178 Brazil National Environmental Policy Act, Article 14, para. 1 (Act No. 6938, 31 August 1981, DOU 2 September 1981). STJ, Resp. 1056540, Relator: Min. Eliana Calmon, 16 May 2008, RSTJ, 14 September 2009 (Braz.).

179 Article 5 of Public Civil Action Law (*Lei de Ação Civil Pública*), Act No. 7347, 24 July 1985, DOU 25 July 1985 (Braz.).

to be filed, but a solid trend of precedents has failed to appear.[180] Nonetheless, public prosecutors and NGOs (whether international or local) have already grasped what power was at their disposal. Early in project development, they can warn the IFIs that are involved that they will sue in case of environmental damage, with a high probability of success.[181] This tactic has proved efficient in the short run. However, the threat of judicial enforcement has been limited, usually reserved for politically astute plaintiffs, equipped with the adequate financial and legal means. In Brazil, LEL has been criticized as a deliberate weak substitute for preventive environmental policy (EIAs and environmental permits). In the long run and as a general principle, LEL should indeed only complement a strong and effective public administration, because environmental issues are complex and require systematic enforcement, rather than scattered lawsuits. Brazilian LEL is expected to follow the same evolution as the US CERCLA.

Apart from the United States and Brazil, some tentative liability regimes have existed in a few countries where they have faced the same hurdles and limitations, such as Germany,[182] Paraguay,[183] South Africa,[184] United Kingdom,[185] Portugal.[186] In the European Union, many member states transposed the ELD (EU Directive 2004/35/EC), which includes an apparent broad concept of "operator" (Article 2.6), but its concrete implications with respect to financial institutions remain to be seen. It follows that LEL would need to be prudently adjusted in view of its potential repercussions on the availability of

---

180 Antônio José Maristrello Porto, et al., *Lenders Environmental Liability in Brazil: How Much is Too Much?*, 6 ECONOMIC ANALYSIS OF LAW REVIEW 128, 135 (2015).

181 Three examples are mentioned *in* Bianca Zambão, *Brazil's Launch of Lender Environmental Liability as a Tool to Manage Environmental Impacts*, 18 U. MIAMI INT'L & COMP. L. REV. 47, 75–77 (2010).

182 SAMPAIO, et al., 8. 2016.

183 Mario Peña Chacón, *Responsabilidad por daño ambiental de las entidades financieras*, REVISTA IBEROAMERICANA DE DERECHO AMBIENTAL Y RECURSOS NATURALES, No. 8 (Mayo 2013).

184 The 1998 National Water Act (NWA) and the 1998 National Environmental Management Act (NEMA) consider persons who "indirectly contribute to" or benefit from pollution or degradation as liable, but in the absence of direct intervention, it seems unlikely that a lender be held liable (Claire Tucker, *Environment & Climate Change Law 2016 – South Africa*, *in* ENVIRONMENT & CLIMATE CHANGE LAW 2016 (Daniel Lawrence & John Blain eds., 2016)).

185 Liability could be incurred if the lender exercised sufficient direction. Specific legislation can stipulate wider liability, such as the 1998 Petroleum Act regarding the decommission of offshore installations (LOUISE MOORE, ENVIRONMENTAL RISKS FOR MAJOR PROJECTS 354–355 (Sweet & Maxwell. 2012)).

186 Decree-law No. 147/2008 regulating environmental damages liability (passed in 2008).

investment capital.[187] In addition to direct consequences (including cleanup and compensation costs, i.e. liability risks), environmental liability has some indirect consequences for banks. The borrower's environmental liability can affect its capacity to service its debt, with no or little recourse to insurance (credit risks), and the environmental consequences of its activities can affect the value of its assets held as collateral (security risks). The United States is an interesting illustration: in the wake of the *Fleet Factors* case, banks were reluctant to fund environmental sensitive projects and insurance companies reduced their coverage.[188] Moreover, if banks are liable, risks are shared, resulting in a weaker incentive for borrowing companies to invest in risk prevention, leading potentially to investments with greater negative externalities for the environment.[189] As regards financial institutions, they incur a precautionary cost if they incorporate environmental risk management analysis into their decision processes. If there is no LEL, their dominant strategy is not to undertake precautionary measures, except when there is a credit risk associated with the lack of environmental precaution, i.e. when there is a high repair cost imposed in case of environmental harm. As borrowers' environmental liability develops, so do the relevant credit default risks. Consequently, regulators have another way of incentivizing banks to be cautious and adopt precautionary measures: developing an accurate remediation regulation based on the cost of recovery (for instance by imposing a high repair cost, adding fines and other administrative penalties, such as a ban on engaging in similar financial operations for a limited period of time), which will make the precautionary cost appear small in comparison with the costs associated with the default risk. The combination of high interest rates and high costs of repair results in strong incentives for both actors (the bank and the borrower) to adopt precautionary measures. If there is an additional strong potential LEL for this regulation scheme (LEL should only come in addition to the above-cited regulations), incentives would be at their maximum without deterring financial institutions from lending. LEL may be especially efficient in emerging economies that lack compliance and enforcement mechanisms. There is less of an LEL need in stabler economies with solid and influential environmental agencies. When

187 See Christopher Murgatroyd, *The World Bank: A Case for Lender Liability?* 1 REV. EUR. COMMUN. INT'L ENVTL. L. 436, 438 (1992); Benoît Mayer, *Development is no excuse for Human Rights Abuses: Framing the Responsibility of International Development Agencies*, 5 TRADE, LAW AND DEV. 286, 340 (2013).

188 Richard Hooley, *Lender Liability for Environmental Damage*, 60 CAMB. L. J. 405, 416 (2001).

189 KARINE GOBERT & MICHEL POITEVINS, ENVIRONMENTAL RISKS: SHOULD BANKS BE LIABLE? CIRANO – Cahiers de recherche – Scientific Series No. 98s-39 (1998).

LEL is established, a financial institution determines a lower interest rate if the borrower has had a record of acting in an environmentally responsible fashion, which is an incentive for borrowers to behave responsibly. The recommended legal arrangement is a general environmental liability regime reinforced by detailed regulations imposed by the regulatory body of the financial sector in combination with other regulations, such as the 2014 resolution of the Central Bank of Brazil, requiring all financial institutions to conduct an EIA before any financial operation,[190] or such as the resolution of the Association of Mexican Banks establishing a Sustainability Committee to improve their environmental safeguard policies and procedures.[191] Beyond national legislation and regulations, some important initiatives have focused on harmonizing standards for due diligence: the Equator Principles and UNEP Financial Initiative (UNEP FI).[192] Lastly, a bare authorization from an environmental authority may not be sufficient for complex project finance operations. The environmental permit should include periodic compliance reports as well as external and independent environmental audits. In a nutshell, depending on its degree of involvement, if the indirectly responsible party may be held liable, it should be able to waive this liability by demonstrating compliance with appropriate EIA legal and regulatory requirements.

4.1.1.2 *Multilateral Development Banks* (*MDBs*)

When it comes to the responsibility of Multilateral Development Banks (MDBs), International Organizations (IOs), a category to which they belong, are established by treaty and are therefore subjects of, and must conform to, international law.

> The responsibility of IOs derives from community expectation about their personality as subjects of international law, designed for specific objectives, and provided with only such authority, resources, and bases of power as are necessary to such objectives. (…)
>
> Because IOs are created to promote public order, it would be perverse, even destructive, to postulate a community expectation that IOs need not conform to the principles of public order.[193]

---

190 Resolution No. 4.327/2014 of 28 April 2014 – Guidelines for the Social and Environmental Responsibility Policies (SERP) of Financial Institutions.

191 Which led to the adoption of the *Protocolo de Sustentabilidad de la Banca* in 2016.

192 See *supra* chapter 2, page 58 et seq.

193 Arsanjani, YALE JOURNAL OF WORLD PUBLIC ORDER, 132,134 (1981).

The initial mandate of the World Bank was to support the reconstruction of Europe. It later evolved to promoting development throughout the world. At first, development was understood as a purely economic notion, but is now expressly defined as sustainable development.[194] MDBs, however, enjoy immunity from domestic jurisdiction, which in particular bars claims from non-state third parties.[195] A growing trend has challenged absolute immunity. Immunity from jurisdiction should indeed evolve because IOs have now developed sufficiently to warrant their submission to the imperatives of justice.[196] In cases that cannot be decided by domestic courts because there has been no waiver of immunity decided by the head of the IO, the IO remains bound by its obligation to provide adequate alternative procedures for settling the dispute, and should faithfully comply with this obligation.[197] To this end, IOs regularly waive their immunity by agreeing to arbitration, but this choice remains discretionary. When they do agree to defer to an arbitral tribunal, arbitration can become a means to protect populations. It should be noted, however, that arbitration was first conceived to protect investors. For disputes involving third parties, in the current state of affairs, ensuring an effective recourse to arbitration would amount to extending the waiver to the establishment of the arbitral tribunal, and to the review of the arbitral award.[198] There must be a real possibility of enforcement of the award. Lastly, the accusatorial nature of the procedure followed in arbitration may not suit the asymmetrical positions of the respective parties in such claims, which calls for a more inquisitorial

194 UNGA Res. 47/191, Institutional arrangements to follow up the United Nations Conference on Environment and Development (A/Res/47/191), 22 December 1992, para. 23. See, for instance, World Bank, *Making Development Sustainable: The World Bank Group and the Environment* (1994); *Advancing Sustainable Development: The World Bank and Agenda 21* (1997); *Making Sustainable Commitments. An Environment Strategy for the World Bank*, 17 July 2001. See also *supra* chapter 2, page 53 et seq.

195 See the Convention on the Privileges and Immunities of the Specialized Agencies (New York) 21 November 1947, 33 UNTS 261, in force 2 December 1948. As of August 2021, 129 states are parties to this convention. See also, for instance, Article 50 of the Agreement Establishing the Asian Development Bank (Manila) 4 December 1965, 571 UNTS 123, in force 22 August 1966 (the ADB Charter).

196 Arsanjani, YALE JOURNAL OF WORLD PUBLIC ORDER, (1981); Gaillard & Pingel-Lenuzza, INTERNATIONAL AND COMPARATIVE LAW QUARTERLY, 2 (2002); Steven Herz, *Rethinking International Financial Institution Immunity*, *in* INTERNATIONAL FINANCIAL INSTITUTIONS AND INTERNATIONAL LAW (Daniel D. Bradlow & David Hunter eds., 2010).

197 See International Law Association (ILA), Committee on Accountability of International Organizations, *Final Report* (2004), page 48.

198 Gaillard & Pingel-Lenuzza, INTERNATIONAL AND COMPARATIVE LAW QUARTERLY, 12–15 (2002).

procedure. Arbitration should be reformed to accommodate those claims that significantly deviate from the usual investment disputes.[199]

Furthermore, states are bound by their own human rights obligations, which impose a proper administration of justice. Granting immunity to an IO in the absence of adequate alternative remedial mechanisms violates human right obligations, i.e. access to justice. Some cases have been decided on these grounds by some courts.[200]

4.1.2 Accountability of the MDBs

Nonetheless, because of the above-cited procedural bars and the prevalent practice of abstention,[201] the focus has been on accountability rather than on responsibility. Contrary to responsibility, the term accountability is not well defined. For the International Law Association, accountability is an umbrella concept that comprises three levels: 1. Internal and external scrutiny and monitoring, 2. Tortious liability for injurious consequences arising out of acts or omissions not involving a breach of any rule of international and/or institutional law, 3. Responsibility arising out of acts or omissions that do constitute a breach of a rule of international and/or institutional law.[202] The first level of the accountability of IOs has been achieved in particular by means of internal rules, information dissemination, public participation, reports and internal review mechanisms. Until the late 1980's, the World Bank and other IOs preferred to preserve their autonomy by operating in secrecy. This temptation has resurfaced at times.[203] However, under external pressure, the World Bank

199 Mayer, TRADE, LAW AND DEV., 338 (2013).

200 International Law Association (ILA), Committee on Accountability of International Organizations, *Final Report* 48 (2004); August Reinisch & Jakob Wurm, *International Financial Institutions before National Courts, in* INTERNATIONAL FINANCIAL INSTITUTIONS AND INTERNATIONAL LAW (Daniel D. Bradlow & David B. Hunter eds., 2010); Mayer, TRADE, LAW AND DEVELOPMENT, 333–334 (2013). These cases have usually been related to employment disputes. See, for instance, *African Development Bank v. Haas*, Cour de Cassation, 25 January 2005, No. 04-41012 (France); *Drago v. International Plant Genetic Resources Institute (IPGRI)*, Final Appeal Judgment, Case No. 3718, Giustizia Civile Massimario, 2007, 2, ILDC 827 (IT 2007), 19 February 2007 (Italy).

201 NB: such practices of abstention cannot alone be a proof of customary law (Arsanjani, YALE JOURNAL OF WORLD PUBLIC ORDER, 171 (1981)). See also DANIEL D. BRADLOW & DAVID B. HUNTER, INTERNATIONAL FINANCIAL INSTITUTIONS AND INTERNATIONAL LAW 394 (Kluwer Law International 2010).

202 International Law Association (ILA), Committee on Accountability of International Organizations, *First Report* 600–601 (1998).

203 See, for instance, William E. Holder, *Can International Organizations be Controlled? Accountability and Responsibility*, 97 ASIL PROCEEDINGS 231 (2003). Holder was the IMF Deputy General Counsel.

gradually shifted and led the way by setting up a legal and policy framework for transparency and public participation. In 1993, the World Bank also created an internal review mechanism, the Inspection Panel,[204] which allows third party non-state actors to bring claims concerning the bank's non-compliance with its internal policies, rules and procedures. Subsequently, other MDBs have set up similar independent accountability mechanisms,[205] which have been regularly improved for some. Before the WB Inspection Panel and the like, non-state actors who were not in a contractual relationship with IFIs, but nonetheless were directly affected by their operations, could not hold IFIs accountable. As Mahnoush Arsanjani emphasized, this was a paradox, as affected populations are naturally among those whom the actions of IOs are supposed to protect.[206] The standards and rules of the MDBs have the significant advantage of being preventive in nature as they apply to the preparation and appraisal of loan projects, which is the optimal time for the careful consideration of all the aspects of a project. Procedures that must be followed during the evaluation of a project derive from these environmental policies and standards, which are also found in the environmental covenants inserted in the loan agreements.

Until recently, Western multilateral banks were setting the rules, but green credit policies have now also been developed in Brazil, India, and China, for

---

204 Resolutions IBRD 93-10 and IDA 93-6, 22 September 1993, 34 ILM 520 (1995). The Inspection Panel modeled itself on the Morse Commission, which the World Bank had recently set up to review the Sardar Sarovar Dam Project, and which report led to the cancellation of the bank's participation in the project. The findings of the Morse Commission revealed that the WB had deliberately violated its social and environmental policies and guidelines (B. MORSE & T. R. BERGER, SARDAR SAROVAR: REPORT OF THE INDEPENDENT REVIEW (1992); T. R. Berger, *The World Bank's Independent Review of India's Sardar Sarovar Projects*, 9 AM. U. INT'L L. REV. 33 (1993)). On 8 September 2020, the World Bank adopted Resolutions No. IBRD 2020-0004 and No. IDA 2020-0003 (Inspection Panel Resolution), and Resolutions No. IBRD 2020-0005 and No. IDA 2020-0004 (Accountability Mechanism Resolution), establishing the WB Accountability Mechanism that houses the Inspection Panel and a new Dispute Resolution Service.

205 For instance, the Inter-American Development Bank (in 1994), the Asian Development Bank (in 1995), the EBRD (in 2003), the African Development Bank (in 2004), the EIB (in 2008). For a comparison of the different independent accountability mechanisms, see Daniel D. Bradlow, *Private Complainants and International Organizations: A Comparative Study of the Independent Inspection Mechanisms in International Financial Institutions*, 36 GEO. J. INT'L L. 403 (2005); DANIEL D. BRADLOW, EXTERNAL REVIEW OF THE INSPECTION PANEL'S TOOLKIT 2 et seq. (Prepared for the Committee on Development Effectiveness (World Bank). 2018).

206 "It would be fantastic to assume that United Nations officials and agencies are authorized to violate the principles they were established to serve"; consequently, private parties are potential claimants (Arsanjani, YALE JOURNAL OF WORLD PUBLIC ORDER, 133, 136 (1981)).

instance. In China, the national policy framework (green credit) has encouraged Chinese banks to consider the environmental aspects of their lending activities,[207] but has not been coordinated with other policies. China often layers policies over each other.[208] A green regulatory framework is gradually being put in place, but still remains to prove effective.[209]

In conclusion about LEL and accountability, only private banks could be subject to claims in national courts for environmental harm arising out of their lending activities, but their liability proves difficult to put in place. Besides, private banks tend to follow, not drive investment projects. "They are project enablers, making business decisions".[210] Similarly to MDBs, with which they may be in competition, they are pressed to fulfill their statutory activity. Nonetheless, the looming probability of their environmental liability has already led to promising developments and reinforcements of EIAs. As for MDBs, their independent review mechanisms have provided limited means of accountability, as the review is confined to the exclusive purview of the bank's internal rules. Inspection panels are also not entitled to grant compensation for any harm that was suffered, nor can they issue recommendations on further actions. They are often excluded from the follow-up of remedial measures.[211]

---

207 See Green Credit Guidelines (banks must end their credit if some major risks or hazards appear) and credit blacklists (companies that pose major environmental risks because of their record of environmental violations) (Qiang Wang & Yong Chen, *Energy saving and emission reduction revolutionizing China's environmental protection*, 14 RENEW. SUSTAIN. ENERGY REV. 535, 539 (2010)).

208 Motoko Aizawa & Chaofei Yang, *Green Credit, Green Stimulus, Green Revolution? China's Mobilization of Banks for Environmental Cleanup*, 19 J.E.D. 119, 136 (2010). For instance, the green policy can come into conflict with policies encouraging banks to lend to employment-intensive sectors (Bruce Gilley, *Authoritarian environmentalism and China's response to climate change*, 21 ENV. POLIT. 287, 297 (2012)).

209 FRIENDS OF THE EARTH, EMERGING SUSTAINABILITY FRAMEWORKS – CHINA DEVELOPMENT BANK AND CHINA EXPORT-IMPORT BANK (Friends of the Earth. 2016); Bing Zhang, et al., *Tracking the implementation of green credit policy in China: Top-down perspective and bottom-up reform*, 92 JOURNAL OF ENVIRONMENTAL MANAGEMENT 1321 (2011).

210 A director for Infrastructure & Energy Structured Finance at a major private bank (interview of 25 May 2016, anonymity required). See also Laurence Pessez, Head of Corporate Social Responsibility for BNP Paribas Group: "States are the ones who decide on energy policies. Banks must remain neutral." *in* Sophie Gauvent, *Développement durable: les efforts des banques observés à la loupe*, 312 BANQUE & STRATÉGIE 3 (2013) (author's translation).

211 See, for instance, Para. 15 and 16 of the Clarification of the Board's Second Review of the World Bank Inspection Panel (1999). Although the 2020 Accountability Mechanism Resolution now allows the IP to verify the actions taken by Management, the efficiency of the new supervisory role of the IP remains to be seen (Diane Desierto, et al., *The 'New'*

The findings of the World Bank Inspection Panel are not binding. Due process is rather deficient.[212] Consequently, one may reasonably doubt the existence of a deterrent effect on MDB managers. Such mechanisms appear to have been established "to promote the good management of the organization and not for the sake of the third parties",[213] i.e. the affected populations. These review mechanisms are not entirely independent, nor do they provide truly effective remedies. Third parties affected by all types of WB-financed investments should have full access to information, participation in decision-making and access to redress.[214] Review mechanisms in IFIs are an example of *lex imperfecta*, passed in order to address some grave discrepancies between the myth system (the official norm system based on key values) and the operational code (the effective behavior). The tension generated by these discrepancies can become sufficiently high to be ultimately conducive to progressive change. If not deterrence, review mechanisms have raised awareness and greater compliance within IFIs, even if a concrete appraisal of this outcome proves delicate. Accountability mechanisms, such as the WB Inspection Panel, are among the factors that have provoked a gradual shift in the balance of power between the IFIs and the affected populations, and they have helped "to diminish the culture of impunity".[215] Aware of the operational code and testing it against the standards of the myth system,[216] some determined citizens and civil society groups have exercised a constant and increasing pressure on IFIs, which has led to the installation of these inspection mechanisms, which in turn help to exert pressure as soft law instruments. The findings of the Inspection Panel can heighten public pressure on a project,[217] and contribute to the improvement

World Bank Accountability Mechanism: Observations from the ND Reparations Design and Compliance Lab, EJIL:TALK! (11 November 2020)).

212 See, for instance, with regard to equality of arms, Resolution IBRD 93-10 and IDA 93-6, The World Bank Inspection Panel, 22 September 1993, 34 ILM 520 (1995), Para. 21. and the Updated Operating Procedures (April 2014), Para. 54–57. For an appraisal of the reform of the World Bank Inspection Panel, see Desierto, et al., EJIL:TALK! (11 November 2020).

213 Mayer, TRADE, LAW AND DEV., 319 (2013).

214 See for instance World Bank, *Review and Update of the World Bank's Environmental and Social Safeguard Policies – Summary of input submitted by stakeholders*, Q6, Internal reforms, point 2 (October 2012-April 2013); Desierto, et al., EJIL:TALK!, (11 November 2020).

215 Dana Clark, *The World Bank Inspection Panel*, *in* SOCIAL RIGHTS JURISPRUDENCE – EMERGING TRENDS IN INTERNATIONAL AND COMPARATIVE LAW 629 (Malcolm Langford ed., 2008).

216 See *supra* chapter 3, page 112 et seq. On dissensions and unstable discrepancies between myth and practice in periods of social change, see REISMAN, Folded Lies 18 and 36. 1979.

217 For instance, in 2000, the Inspection Panel found that the World Bank was in violation of several provisions of six of its most important social and environmental policies in

of the WB's rules and procedures, and of international law more generally. These mechanisms have been periodically improved insofar as they are closer to being truly independent, more effective and to increasingly provide satisfactory recourse. Nevertheless, the people affected by the IFIs' operations and the civil society groups that represent them have questioned the IFIs' position toward the applicability of international law to their operations and the extent of their immunity. In addition, some have suggested the establishment of a Safeguards Committee by the United Nations General Assembly as a subsidiary body, similar to the UN Human Rights Committee. This committee would be truly independent.[218] Presently, the actions of the MDBs have evolved from operating *en vase clos* to being subject to accountability standards. This heightened accountability is bridging the gap "between arbitrariness and responsibility",[219] in particular thanks to the establishment of the WB Inspection Panel and similar compliance mechanisms. Whether this evolution will endure with the emergence of new MDBs and the new WB environmental safeguards (ESF) remains to be seen. If accountability proves insufficient, then responsibility will remain the ultimate goal, as with private banks. Here again, the pace of progress has not been aligned with the pace of development projects plagued with negative environmental consequences.

4.1.3 The Essential Role of Banks' Sustainability/Environment Departments

Because of the inherent limits of LEL, the focus also needs to be on significant risk reductions, thanks to safe lending practices of a preventive nature. Empowering the internal environment department of banks and increasing

---

the design and appraisal of the Qinghai Project (a dam and irrigation project), including the EIA according to OD 4.01 (China Western Poverty Reduction Project – *The Inspection Panel, Investigation Report – The Qinghai Project, a component of the China: Western Poverty Reduction Project (Credit No. 3255-CHA and Loan No 4501-CHA)* (IBRD-IDA (World Bank). 2000)). Subsequently, the Board of Executive Directors rejected Management's recommendations and support for the project, a rare move. Faced with heated opposition, China preferred to withdraw before a looming cancellation (Kay Treakle & Liz Sweet, *Summary of events leading to the cancellation of the China Western Poverty Reduction Project*, BANK INFORMATION CENTER (BIC), 20 July 2000)). Another example is a project in Ecuador where, upon the Panel's findings, the WB Management agreed to further improve the consultation and participation processes (World Bank, *Management Report and Recommendation in Response to the Inspection Panel Investigation Report-Ecuador Development and Environmental Control Technical Assistance Project (Loan No. 3655-EC)*, 23 February 2001).

218 Mayer, TRADE, LAW AND DEV., 341–342 (2013).

219 Id. at 340.

their role with regard to loan project approvals is essential. Concretely, IFIs and domestic financial institutions should embrace a more active and aggressive role by empowering their internal environment department, securing competent and properly trained staff, demanding reliable EIAs as preconditions, developing environmental covenants, adequate guarantees and associated events of default.[220] In 2016, the World Bank updated its environmental policy for investment project financing. The new Environmental and Social Framework (ESF) also aims at further harmonizing the WB's environmental protections with other development institutions. At first, the imperative necessity of EIAs had been well-received among IFIs. They complied with US domestic legislation (NEPA) at great length, as a matter of practice, since the United States has been a major shareholder.[221] Then, formal procedures were established, tailored and improved.[222] However, at the moment, banks too often content themselves with defective EIAs. The new ESF of the World Bank has been met with sharp disappointment and criticisms from NGOs, and reserves from the US government, especially with regard to a pronounced shift towards borrower ownership.[223] Nevertheless, if the World Bank emphasizes that it is the borrower's responsibility to provide all relevant information for the bank to fulfill its own responsibility, the World Bank also acknowledges that, in cases in which the borrower has limited information capacity, it would conduct the EIA itself and assess the risks of the gaps in information.[224] The new ESF has gradually entered into force since October 2018. The manner in which it unfolds in this regard remains to be seen.

220 Hooley, CAMB. L. J., 416–417 (2001).

221 William V. Kennedy, *EIA and Multi-lateral Financial Institutions*, *in* HANDBOOK OF ENVIRONMENTAL IMPACT ASSESSMENT, VOLUME 2, IMPACTS AND LIMITATIONS 113 (Judith Petts ed. 1999). Kennedy was a Senior Environmental Specialist at the EBRD.

222 See *supra* chapter 2.

223 US Department of the Treasury, *US Position on the Review and Update of the World Bank's Safeguard Policies* (2016); Press Release, *NGO response to the World Bank's proposed Environmental and Social Framework: Proposed World Bank standards represent dangerous set-back to key environmental and social protections* (2016). See Bugalski, AM. U. INT'L L. REV., (2016); Cristina Passoni, et al., *Empowering the Inspection Panel: the Impacts of the World Bank's New Environmental and Social Safeguards*, 49 N.Y.U. J. INT'L LAW & POL. 921 (2017); Priester, GEO. INT'L ENVTL. L. REV. (2020). See *supra* chapter 2, pages 56–57.

224 World Bank, *World Bank Environmental and Social Policy for Investment Project Financing*, *in* ENVIRONMENTAL AND SOCIAL FRAMEWORK – SETTING ENVIRONMENTAL AND SOCIAL STANDARDS FOR INVESTMENT PROJECT FINANCING Para. 32 and 33 (2016).

4.2 *Recommendations with Respect to Financial Institutions and EIAs*

The quality of an EIA depends on the competence of its authors. Independence and competence of EIA experts should be better verified and ensured. Another crucial factor of a proper EIA is the extent of public participation. Banks should demand that EIAs be produced by proficient EIA experts with local knowledge combined with adequate consultations of the affected populations. It has been observed that when the local World Bank team is involved with local counterparts (thanks to training opportunities and regular consultations), the implementation of environmental policies is more successful.[225] Financial institutions should also ensure and develop the competence of their staff that supervise and appraise EIAs, through appropriate hires and trainings. To assist its staff in conducting due diligence and implementation support, the World Bank announced that it would issue non-mandatory guidance and information tools in the wake of its new ESF of 2016. The need to have better trained bank internal staff for adequate preparation, supervision and follow-up was not considered at first, regrettably, but was included eventually, in 2020.[226]

Another significant improvement would be a regional EIA standard in the Mekong Subregion. International investors and IFIs should find it favorable to accept this standard if it reduced administrative formalities, increased predictability and clarity in state behavior and regulation, and lowered costs.

When an EIA has been produced, many warn about the evident fact that it should be reviewed before a final appraisal is made during the decision-making process. In 2016, the World Bank took this necessity into account in its new ESF Policies; for projects that are high risk (this threshold has yet to be defined) or contentious, or that involve serious multidimensional risks or impacts, the borrower may be required to hire internationally recognized independent experts who will provide independent advice and oversight of the project (Paragraph 33 of ESS1), including the conduct of the EIA by the expert team already mentioned in Paragraph 25.[227] Considering the important role of the

---

225 World Bank, *Review and Update of the World Bank's Environmental and Social Safeguard Policies – Summary of input submitted by stakeholders*, Question 3, point 5 (October 2012-April 2013).

226 World Bank, *Overview of the World Bank Environmental and Social Framework*, *in* Environmental and Social Framework – Setting Environmental and Social Standards for Investment Project Financing Para. 9 (2017); *The World Bank ESF – Implementation Update*, 8 (October 2020). This necessity had been emphasized during the consultations that led to the ESF, *in* World Bank, *Review and Update of the World Bank's Environmental and Social Safeguard Policies – Summary of input submitted by stakeholders*, Question 2, Capacity, point 4; Q4, Monitoring and oversight, point 3 and 4 (October 2012-April 2013).

227 World Bank, *ESS1. Assessment and Management of Environmental and Social Risks and Impacts*, *in* ENVIRONMENTAL AND SOCIAL FRAMEWORK – SETTING ENVIRONMENTAL

World Bank and the like in the Lower Mekong Region, ensuring a second independent expert review of EIAs is a welcome improvement. This necessity does not seem to have been debated by other banks, but the World Bank has had a leading role. EIA reviews may thus follow at other banks in the near future. For dam projects in particular, the World Bank's stakeholders themselves insisted that its existing safeguards policies have not been sufficient,[228] despite the use of environmental covenants. Environmental covenants impose environmental obligations on the borrower. However, if the borrower defaults, the World Bank rarely suspends disbursement, let alone cancels the loan.[229] Moreover, compliance with the covenant is often not assessed before the project is completed, and sometimes not even before the project has been in operation for some time. Post-project monitoring needs to be more stringent and effective. Furthermore, if proper procedures for project development prove to be crucial, so does a larger perspective of the kind provided by Strategic Environmental

---

AND SOCIAL STANDARDS FOR INVESTMENT PROJECT FINANCING Para. 25 and 33, (2016); World Bank, ESS10. Stakeholder Engagement and Information Disclosure para. 12. 2016; World Bank, World Bank Environmental and Social Policy for Investment Project Financing para. 35. 2016.

228 World Bank, *Review and Update of the World Bank's Environmental and Social Safeguard Policies – Summary of input submitted by stakeholders*, Question 3, point 10 (page 7) (Oct. 2012-Apr. 2013). In 2001 already, an external Advisory Panel was highly critical of the World Bank's performance on the environment (Gowlland Gualtieri, BRITISH YEARBOOK OF INTERNATIONAL LAW, 217–218 & FN 28 (2001). See also OED – OPERATIONS EVALUATION DEPARTMENT, REPORT NO. 22441 – OED REVIEW OF THE BANK'S PERFORMANCE ON THE ENVIRONMENT (World Bank. 2001).

229 Since the use of environmental covenants has been in place, and upon the findings of the Inspection Panel, the World Bank cancelled a loan project partly for environmental concerns in four instances:
- a dam in Nepal (Inspection Panel, Request for Inspection: Panel Investigation Report-Nepal Arun III Proposed Hydroelectric Project (INSP/SecM95-J), 22 June 1995; World Bank, *Nepal Arun III Proposed Hydroelectric Project-Management Response to the Inspection Panel's Investigation Report* (INSP/SecM95-S), 5 August 1995);
- a poverty reduction / dam and irrigation project in China. The Board of Executive Directors resisted the insistence of the Bank's Management in favor of the project (*Chinese Government's Statement on the Inspection Panel Investigation Report for the China: Western Poverty Reduction Project (Qinghai Component)* Press Release, 6 July 2000; World Bank, *China to Implement Qinghai Component of the China Western Poverty Reduction Project with its Own Resources,* Press Release, 7 July 2000; Kay Treakle & Liz Sweet, *Summary of events leading to the cancellation of the China Western Poverty Reduction Project,* BANK INFORMATION CENTER (BIC), 20 July 2000);
- a road project in Uganda (*World Bank Statement on Cancellation of the Uganda Transport Sector Development Project* (TSDP), Press Release, 21 December 2015);
- a dam in Lebanon (*World Bank Statement on Cancellation of Water Supply Augmentation Project* (Bisri Dam Project), 5 September 2020).

and Social Assessments (SESAs). The Bank's stakeholders insisted on the necessity that countries have a coherent development policy, appraised by SESAs, before engaging in programs and projects, lest the latter be piecemeal rather than coherent.[230] IFIs should continue to promote the further development of SESAs.[231]

In conclusion about financial institutions, when projects are financed by foreign private banks or MDBs, these financial institutions can help support sustainable development in regions such as the Sub-Mekong region if they adopt proper decision-making processes, accountability mechanisms or if some LEL regulations are passed. If a leading bank, such as the World Bank, withdraws from a loan project because of its potential environmental consequences, it can also discourage other potential lenders, be they private or public. However, in the case of China and other major economic powers, the majority of projects within their territory or area of influence can be financed without the involvement of foreign banks.[232] Countries in the Sub-Mekong region have had two main options at their disposal for financing their infrastructure projects: China, or other foreign financial institutions. Lower costs associated with the appearance of fewer and less stringent conditions, let alone the corruption of some governmental elites, often led these countries to prefer China's loans and involvement. The possibility of external pressure in favor of environmental protection through other foreign banks has been removed by China, while the severity of the Chinese debt trap has revealed itself over time. Heavily indebted countries have become vulnerable to China's influence and intrusion.[233] However, China has started to withdraw from funding projects on its own, as

---

230 World Bank, *Review and Update of the World Bank's Environmental and Social Safeguard Policies – Summary of input submitted by stakeholders*, Question 4, Changing development context, point 2; Q12, Harmonization and country systems (October 2012-April 2013).

231 ASIAN DEVELOPMENT BANK, STRATEGIC ENVIRONMENTAL ASSESSMENT IN THE GREATER MEKONG SUBREGION (ADB. 2015); Iain Watson, *Promoting Good Practice in SEA in the Greater Mekong Subregion* (International Association for Impact Assessment (IAIA). 2016).

232 For instance, in 2000, when the World Bank suspended its loan for the poverty reduction/dam and irrigation project in China, the latter announced it would resort to its own resources (see *supra* notes 163, 217, 229). In 2008, because of the cancellation of the WB loan for a hydro-electric project (Arun III) in Nepal in 1995, India announced it would fund the project itself, through its joint venture Public Sector SJVN Limited (*in* Gowlland Gualtieri, BRITISH YEARBOOK OF INTERNATIONAL LAW, 242, 249–250 (2001)).

233 ANNA GELPERN, et al., HOW CHINA LENDS, A RARE LOOK INTO 100 DEBT CONTRACTS WITH FOREIGN GOVERNMENTS (Peterson Institute for International Economics, Kiel Institute for the World Economy, Center for Global Development, AidData at William & Mary. 2021).

in the case of the UMNIP. This has reinstated the participation of IFIs in project development back into the region. In this respect, China has been carrying out some hydro-diplomacy. In 2013, it proposed the creation of a new MDB, which materialized in 2015 – the Asian Infrastructure Investment Bank (AIIB), of which China is the major shareholder.[234] The AIIB is destined to finance infrastructure projects in Asia. China is also part of another new MDB, the New Development Bank (NDB), established in 2014.[235] Furthermore, in order to secure an even tighter grip on the downstream states and to further drive away Western and Japanese influence in the region, China has spearheaded the creation of a new regional intergovernmental organization, the Lancang-Mekong Cooperation Mechanism (LMC), with the strong support of Thailand. The LMC comprises all six Mekong countries.[236] It is intended to overshadow the American-led Lower Mekong Initiative (LMI – now called the Mekong-US Partnership since 2020), Japan's ADB-led Greater-Mekong Subregion (GMS) programs, as well as the Mekong River Commission (MRC), of which the LMC is the equivalent, save for the inclusion of China and Myanmar. Amidst this whirlwind of Chinese influence, whether the new MDBs will set up, and abide by, adequate environmental standards remains to be seen. Moreover, the World Bank has reacted to new rivals by reverting to more flexible and discretionary environmental safeguards, in order to compete efficiently and still attract borrowers. In the near future, the consequences of Chinese involvement may be too disproportionate a burden on the Mekong Basin countries. Only if proper environmental regulations are dutifully applied by financial institutions, in

234 Established by treaty signed in Beijing, on 29 June 2015, in force 25 December 2015. At present, there are 89 member states. China represents almost 27% of the voting shares, far ahead of the second shareholder, India, with less than 8% (Russia ranks third with 6%). The bank was established with US$100 billion in capital, which is equivalent to half of the World Bank's and two-thirds of the ADB's. The United States refused membership and tried to dissuade other countries in part because of some environmental concerns (for a critical appraisal of the US opposition, see Amitai Etzioni, *The Asian Infrastructure Investment Bank: A Case Study of Multifaceted Containment*, 40 ASIAN PERSPECTIVE 173 (2016)). The AIIB is headquartered in Beijing, China. In September 2020, it appointed Swedish economist Erik Berglof as its first chief economist. Berglof was the chief economist of the EBRD from 2006 to 2015.

235 The treaty was signed on 15 July 2014, in force a year later, in July 2015. The New Development Bank is headquartered in Shanghai, China. The five member states (Brazil, Russia, India, China, South Africa (BRICS)) represent each 20% of the actual shares. The NDB was established with US$50 billion in capital (see *supra* note 234 for a comparison with the AIIB, World Bank, and ADB).

236 The LMC was created in 2015. The first leaders' meeting took place on 23 March 2016, co-chaired by China and Thailand.

combination with NGO active participation, could the Sub-Mekong region then be headed in the direction of sustainable development.

4.3 *Expectations Regarding the Role of Civil Society: Supporting the Increase of NGO Activity Where it Thrives, and Advancing International NGO Agitation*

> *A large number of individuals, operating on their own behalf and through non-governmental organizations, [can play] an important role in reinforcing the demand for a more effective regime, setting out the contours of what such a regime might be and drafting and then agitating for the inclusion of precise language in such a regime.*[237]

To counter an overwhelming power like China and achieve some degree of real environmental protection in the Mekong Subregion, the solution seems for the most part to lie with civil society, public accountability and procedural requirements. The populations in the Mekong River Basin share inclusive concerns, which have gradually led them to organize and unite within civil groups, in order to try to influence decisions that affect their fate.

Procedural requirements empower individual and NGO agitation. Even if such requirements appear, at first glance, to have played a small role in the UMNIP case, the joint EIA made because of Lao regulations did provide an opportunity for several actors to convene, discuss, produce more studies, work together and improve the NGO network. If Laos had had no EIA law, the UMNIP would probably have been considerably more secretive. Procedural requirements build up and lay out the ground, slowly, for future, more powerful actions. Developing procedures is key to favoring meaningful participation, building trust and increasing the ability of civil society to assemble and express itself in order to pressure decision-makers. Procedures should be further developed at all levels, in all settings. Moreover, harmonizing EIA regulations throughout the region would help tremendously with regional cooperation so that transboundary impacts can be addressed. The MRC has attempted to have an EIA

---

237 W. Michael Reisman, *Private International Declaration Initiatives*, *in* LA DÉCLARATION UNIVERSELLE DES DROITS DE L'HOMME 1948–98: AVENIR D'UN IDÉAL COMMUN – ACTES DU COLLOQUE DES 14, 15 ET 16 SEPTEMBRE 1998 À LA SORBONNE, PARIS 81 (Commission nationale consultative des droits de l'Homme ed. 1999). See also Myres S. McDougal, et al., *The World Community: A Planetary Social Process*, 21 U.C. DAVIS L. REV. 807 (1988); Steve Charnovitz, *How Nongovernmental Actors Vitalize International Law*, *in* LOOKING TO THE FUTURE – ESSAYS IN INTERNATIONAL LAW IN HONOR OF W. MICHAEL REISMAN (Mahnoush H. Arsanjani, et al. eds., 2011).

standard adopted in the Mekong Subregion, but to little avail so far. In 2018, the MRC issued the latest and most comprehensive version of its Guidelines for Transboundary Environmental Impact Assessment in the Lower Mekong Basin, but as a working document only.[238] It remains to be seen if they will be implemented. In parallel with these attempts, suggestions were made to proceed in the broader context of regional cooperation, at the ASEAN level, but they have stalled as well.[239] None of the Mekong countries have signed up to the Espoo Convention.

Consequently, the most promising prospects are based on a bottom-up approach to influence the preparation and the outcome of projects with potential significant environmental impacts. In the Mekong region, the isolation of states still appears to be much more natural than a common and uniting will among them. National governments tend to dismiss the benefits of regional cooperation in socio-economic and environmental matters. There is a tension between sovereignty, which often seems to constitute a convenient screen for short-term interests, and the necessity of cooperation induced by geostrategic interdependence. Including public participation in the decision process as early as possible is critical. In the whole Mekong River Basin, pressure is mounting as the population is increasingly suffering from the consequences of the infrastructure projects conducted on the Mekong River system. Instead of an economic hydro-boom as anticipated by many, continuous dam building on the Mekong and its tributaries has resulted in severe disruptions such as droughts, critical food shortages, destruction of livelihoods, economic hardships, displaced populations and large irregular movements of people. Will environmental disruptions have a positive influence on states' cooperation, in addition to, or in place of, an awareness of a common interest in a preventive environmental policy? This case study shows that the governments of Laos and Thailand do not appear to be moved by such incentives.

---

238 MRC, *Guidelines for Transboundary Environmental Impact Assessment in the Lower Mekong Basin* (*Working Document*), at https://www.mrcmekong.org/assets/Publications/TbEIA-Guidelines-Final-version-25-9-2018.pdf, accessed 17 June 2021.

239 Such as the ASEAN Economic Community (AEC), and the Mekong Partnership for Environment (MPE). The MPE project has been funded by USAID since 2013 as a regional project with the goal of improved application of social and environmental safeguards (SES) in regional development projects. The project works across all countries in the Lower Mekong Subregion (LMS) including Myanmar, Thailand, Cambodia, Laos and Vietnam with some outreach to China. See MATTHEW BAIRD, AN EXAMINATION AND EVALUATION OF EXISTING TRANSBOUNDARY, REGIONAL, AND INTERGOVERNMENTAL MODELS FOR A POTENTIAL REGIONAL EIA STANDARD IN ASEAN 29–31 (Pact – Mekong Partnership For the Environment. 2014).

However, across the Mekong River Basin, civil society has organized and united itself to demand proper TEIAs and public participation, including in Myanmar. There has been increasing NGO activity. Key regional illustrations of dauntless civil society action have been provided by the Save the Mekong Coalition, the Mekong People's Forum,[240] The Rak Chiang Khong Group, by activist groups in Myanmar (such as the Dawei Development Association – DDA), by regional cooperation against the Xayaburi Dam and hopes related to the pending lawsuit, and by community-level action research such as Thai Baan Research, the Sustainable Mekong Research Network (Sumernet), and the Mekong Program on Water, Environment and Resilience (M-Power). Thanks to their persistence, small local groups are gaining some valuable exposure, such as Rak Chiang Khong with respect to the Mekong River and the UMNIP.[241] Rak Chiang Khong has kept expanding its reach and reputation. Multiple networks gather at regular workshops and conferences at venues such as the annual ASEAN People's Forum (APF) or the Earth Rights International Mekong School. International NGO agitation has also increased. For instance, International Rivers, one of the leading organizations, has led numerous actions and has helped in filing a lawsuit endowed with some success, in the high-profile Xayaburi Dam case.[242] There are tangible signs that some progress is under way, but nonetheless, its pace stands in stark contrast with the velocity with which environmental damage is occurring, too often irreversibly.

240 PREMRUDEE DAOROUNG, FROM THE LOSS OF FISH TO CLIMATE CHANGE: A LOOK INTO THE RECENT DAM MOVEMENT IN THE MEKONG REGION (World Rainforest Movement. 2016).

241 See, for instance, Richard Bernstein, *China's Mekong Plans Threaten Disaster for Countries Downstream*, FOREIGN POLICY. 27 September 2017.

242 See the decision of the Thai Supreme Administrative Court, 24 June 2014 (see *supra* page 284 et seq.).

CHAPTER 7

Conclusion

Civic enforcement will have achieved a significant victory if it sustains expectations of the effectiveness of certain norms, even though, in particular cases, it has not succeeded in securing the full implementation of those norms. And civic enforcement will become a major strut of international order if it can, by recruiting more and more private individuals, mobilize increasing support for the basic prescriptions of a world order of human dignity.[1]

∴

1 Procedural Requirements, Such as EIA, Lead to Substantive Law in International Environmental Law

Collecting evidence from state practice, in order to identify customary international law, is a difficult, herculean even, task.[2] The International Law Association, for instance, concluded that the duty to notify was a norm of customary international law, but cited only seven examples of state practice.[3]

1 Reisman, Making International Humanitarian Law Effective: the Case for Civic Enforcement 37–38. 1973.

2 Daniel Bodansky, *Customary (and Not So Customary) International Environmental Law*, 3 IND. J. GLOBAL LEGAL STUD. 105, 113 (1995), by reference to Ronald Dworkin who named his ideal judge "Hercules", "a lawyer of superhuman skill, learning, patience and acumen" (RONALD DWORKIN, TAKING RIGHTS SERIOUSLY 105 (Harvard University Press. 1977)). Some observed that "perhaps only an International Law Commission in permanent session with armies of researchers could gather and sift through all the relevant evidence to establish, in a manner acceptable to social scientists, the existence of a rule of customary international law" (Stephen Zamora, *Is There Customary International Economic Law?* 32 GERMAN Y.B.INT'L L. 9, 38 (1989)). "[T]he immense material from which [international custom] may be gathered has hardly yet been touched by international lawyers" (Georg Schwarzenberger, *The Inductive Approach to International Law*, 60 HARV. L. REV. 539 (1947). These statements seem to still ring true nowadays. See Bodansky, *Prologue to a Theory of Non-Treaty Norms*. 2011.

3 Daniel G. Partan, *The "Duty to Inform" in International Environmental Law*, 6 B.U. INT'L L.J. 43, 51 (1988). Three of these seven examples of notification were based on treaty. Moreover, as regards the four examples that were not based on treaty, Partan explained that their real motivation was "problematical" and "entirely speculative" (Id. at 54). See also, more

 | DOI:10.1163/9789004467583_008

Still, custom has been extolled in international law. In reality, this praise has heralded a setback in international legislation. The new definition of custom has concealed a power shift:

> the new use of the word "custom" camouflages a constitutive shift in two aspects of the politics of international lawmaking. What is being signalled is opposition to the quantity and the style of formal international legislation as it has developed in the last twenty years. The setting of necessary legislation is being shifted from the most inclusive and open international arenas, such as the General Assembly and universal conferences, to more limited alliance, regional and, within them, value sectoral conferences from which most of the new majority in the United Nations will be excluded. The "all states" trend of the last forty years, seeking to bring everyone into an inclusive conference arena, is being reversed in favor of a network of restrictive-access legislative arenas. Because this shift from the floors of the world legislatures to back rooms elsewhere is inconsistent with venerated international legal myth, it is more convenient, if less accurate, to describe it as the resurgence of custom.[4]

Consequently, the most desirable way to rebuild an international legislative system is the return of inclusive fora.[5] In the meantime, rather than proclaiming customary law on dubious grounds, emphasis should be placed on the various multilateral and bilateral treaties in which putative customary norms have appeared.[6] More importantly, the remarkable ubiquity of domestic EIA systems,[7] many of which include transnational EIA requirements, provides an efficient, albeit nascent, international legal system, in which states can concur

generally, regarding the debate over the legal status of international environmental norms, OWEN MCINTYRE, ENVIRONMENTAL PROTECTION OF INTERNATIONAL WATERCOURSES UNDER INTERNATIONAL LAW 192 et seq. (Routledge. 2016).

4 W. Michael Reisman, *The Cult of Custom in the Late 20th Century*, 17 CAL. W. INT'L L.J. 133, 135 (1987).

5 Id. at 143–145.

6 Partan, B.U. INT'L L.J., 51, 53 (1988); MCINTYRE, 196. 2016. See also Robert Jennings, *Need for Environmental Court?* 22 ENVIRONMENTAL POLICY AND LAW 312, 313 (1992).

7 See *supra* chapter 2, note 10. Apart from a few states, all UN members now have EIA requirements in place. Already at the end of the 1990's, there were more than a hundred countries with national EIA systems. If autonomous provincial jurisdictions were added, the number of EIA systems would have been about 200 (UNEP TIE (DIVISION OF TECHNOLOGY, INDUSTRY AND ECONOMICS), EIA FOR INDUSTRY: STATUS REPORT ON UNEP TIE INITIATIVE TO IMPROVE INDUSTRIAL PROJECT PLANNING 5 (UNEP. 1999)).

on standards and principles, while relying on local expertise to develop a specific approach to EIAs and to achieve environmental protection and sustainable development worldwide. This domestic focus could remedy the absence of sufficiently precise multilateral environmental legislation. For decades, EIA requirements have straddled international and local realms.[8] The main international EIA agreement, the Espoo Convention, insists on the inherently domestic nature of EIAs. A domestic focus favors flexibility, which is key in the field of environmental protection. Over time, adjustments to commitments ensure the longevity of a legislative process for protecting the environment.[9] In this regard, EIA procedures are adapted to different and evolutive political, economic, and social contexts.

In addition to domestic requirements, and in case of the absence, or because of the vagueness, of international agreements, soft law is of paramount importance,[10] especially since there have been few interactions in judicial fora. However, the legal status of norms is not monolithic.[11] Furthermore, a unitary model of legal education no longer exists. Mosaics in Byzantine art reflected the same foundational concept as the Justinian codification, based on "NeoPlatonic, and in particular Plotinian motifs: the attainment and the contemplation of the truth of the whole, of oneness, as a redemption made possible by the actuation of a divine plan in opposition to the chaotic and deceptive multiplicity of human life and experience".[12] This model has vanished. Upon closer look, hard and soft law are terms that have become rather inadequate to describe international prescriptions.[13] Consequently, the development of procedures such as EIAs has been crucial in the democratization

8 Yang, HASTINGS LAW JOURNAL, 532–533 (2019).

9 For instance, it assured the longevity of the Long-Range Transboundary Air Pollution (LRTAP) Convention, which set up its status as a "permanent negotiating process", see Alexander E. Farrell & Terry J. Keating, *Dissent and Trust in Multilateral Assessments – Comparing LRTAP and OTAG*, *in* ASSESSMENTS OF REGIONAL AND GLOBAL ENVIRONMENTAL RISKS – DESIGNING PROCESSES FOR THE EFFECTIVE USE OF SCIENCE IN DECISIONMAKING 78, 79, (Alexander E. Farrell & Jill Jäger eds., 2006).

10 Reisman, AM. SOC'Y INT'L L. PROC., (1988); Pierre-Marie Dupuy, *Overview of the Existing Customary Legal Regime Regarding International Pollution*, *in* INTERNATIONAL LAW AND POLLUTION 61–62 & 69 (Daniel B. Magraw ed. 1991).

11 Prosper Weil, *Towards Relative Normativity in International Law?* 77 AM. J. INT'L L. 413, 421 (1983).

12 ALDO SCHIAVONE, THE INVENTION OF LAW IN THE WEST 8 (see also 17–18) (Jeremy Carden & Antony Shugaar trans., Harvard University Press. 2012).

13 REISMAN, The Quest for World Order and Human Dignity in the Twenty-first Century: Constitutive Process and Individual Commitment 151–155. 2013.

of international law-making. As seen in the case studies, EIAs have facilitated and encouraged the participation of individuals and civic groups so that they may embrace their ever more essential role in international environmental law. Many have started to build upon the empowerment potential of EIA requirements. Ultimately, back-room and high-level negotiations and accords may, to some important extent, be superseded by the actions of civil society in the environmental protection domain. As evoked in the introduction and verified in the Vuotos case, the Espoo Convention has contributed to a partial shift in decision-making, from central governments to a transnational EIA system.[14] Even in Southeast Asia, where Espoo-like commitments are much weaker, a similar trend toward transnational networks has arisen. In parallel to a myriad of EIA requirements, case studies establish that expectations are now commonly and widely set on the necessity of such assessments, in view of environmental protection and sustainable development. As also seen in the case studies, evidence is conversely found in the efforts with which some project proponents and competent authorities try to circumvent EIA obligations (exploiting bureaucratic loopholes, leading and pressuring consultants, and short-circuiting public participation).

It remains that, when an EIA is produced, even if it is inaccurate, it will often at least serve as a useful base for protests and for further organizing opposition movements, as the three case studies demonstrate (*supra* chapters 4 to 6). "The conception that the dignity of every human individual includes a right to participate in all value processes finds repeated expression in contemporary international law. Such participation ultimately depends upon relatively unrestricted access to pertinent intelligence by all who seek it".[15] Progressively, either EIAs have granted such access, or concerned citizens have sought pertinent intelligence by demanding that proper EIAs be produced, or have denounced vehemently the lack thereof. Civil society is becoming ever more active, and increasingly equipped with effective communication tools. The determination and experience of activists such as Helena Tiihonen, Michel Geoffre, Niwat Roikaew, Chak Kineesee, Pai Deetes, and their ability to develop efficient networks, in great part based on EIA requirements, are exemplary and have led to some remarkable and encouraging developments. Consequently, the role of procedure in secreting substantive law may also be accomplished through the idiosyncratic legal system of public international law, though at a pace that does not seem adequate to address the rapidity of environmental

14 See *supra* chapter 1, page 23, and chapter 4.

15 McDougal, et al., TEMPLE LAW QUATERLY, 396 (1973).

degradation. This discrepancy could be addressed by means of recommendations to be presented below.

sono pessimista con l'intelligenza, ma ottimista per la volontà[16]

2 Recommendations

Scientific accuracy (given the state of the art in any particular domain at any given time) and public participation are the two main pillars of a proper EIA. Naturally, coordination between states is also key, as in the case of the European Union. It is thus recommended that states create efficient supranational institutions to set up a common environmental policy.[17] In addition, when it comes to EIA, the multinational character of an institution enhances the credibility of an assessment. However, the Mekong River Commission (MRC), for instance, has not been as successful as one would have hoped, as seen in the UMNIP case study. In such an instance, national EIA systems and transnational networks can compensate for the weakness of a supranational institution, or circumvent the necessity to create and endow such entities. Absent such national EIA systems and transnational networks, or if the former are inadequate and the latter only nascent, treaties and diplomatic capital, also via multilateral development banks as seen in chapter 6, should be used to influence those states where there is also often no influential civil society, or a civil society whose development has trailed behind the cadence of environmentally harmful projects (in a top-down approach). In other states where EIA procedures are more detailed and more rigorously followed, such as in Scandinavia, there may be advantages to the absence of routinized notification and centralized procedures, in the sense that EIAs may thus avoid political roadblocks. On the other

16 "We should join together the pessimism of the intellect and the optimism of the will" (author's translation), Antonio Gramsci (1891–1937), in a letter from prison to his brother, Carlo Gramsci, dated 19 December 1929. Gramsci may have drawn inspiration from Romain Rolland. Alain also famously said "le pessimisme est d'humeur; l'optimisme est de volonté" (ALAIN, PROPOS SUR LE BONHEUR 233 (Gallimard. 1928) "Pessimism is a matter of mood; optimism is a matter of will" (author's translation)).

17 Guillaume Cheikbossian, *La coordination des politiques environnementales entre deux pays de taille asymétrique*, 61 REVUE ÉCONOMIQUE 11 (2010). DANIEL C. ESTY & MARIA H. IVANOVA, MAKING INTERNATIONAL ENVIRONMENTAL EFFORTS WORK: THE CASE FOR A GLOBAL ENVIRONMENTAL ORGANIZATION (Yale Center for Environmental Law and Policy. 2001).

hand, it then requires that civil servants and public officials, from any licensing authority that may be concerned, be aware of (T)EIA requirements.[18]

As the three case studies demonstrate, a host of challenges need to be addressed to improve the quality of EIAs such as, for instance, the necessity of broader EIAs, which systematically include cumulative impacts and longer-term impacts, or the importance of an inclusive governance framework. Infrastructure projects have been on the rise, in number and in size. They frequently entail heated struggles and suffer considerable delays as well as dramatic cost-overruns. Both project proponents and affected populations would highly benefit from better and proper EIAs. I will focus here on the following three issues: preventing ex-post rationalization, developing public participation, and improving post-monitoring programs.

2.1 *Preventing Ex-post Rationalization*

In view of preventing ex-post rationalization, as seen in the previous chapters, one cannot overstate the importance of adequate timing of an EIA because of the "difficulty of stopping a bureaucratic steam roller" .[19] If the assessment does not occur at the beginning of the decision-making process, a predilection toward a specific action rapidly crystallizes, often at the expense of identifying better alternatives, or even sound mitigation measures. Yet, the timely onset of an EIA is still most commonly overlooked. Even Sweden for instance, with advanced environmental policies and its status as one of the lead states within the international donor community, has not consistently included environmental considerations into the projects of its International Development Cooperation Agency (SIDA). In 2009, an evaluation conducted by the OECD concluded that demanding EIA regulations had backfired and discouraged the relevant authorities from observing them. Out of 89 projects from 6 countries, only 7 included the mandatory EIA. 39 contained only a brief statement. The compulsory study appeared to have been completely disregarded in half of the projects under consideration. Simpler tools for strategic and impact assessment, and for greater awareness, were recommended to mainstream environmental issues into SIDA's work.[20] EIAs have often been

---

18 Ebbesson, ENVIRONMENTAL IMPACT ASSESSMENT REVIEW, 51–52 (1999).

19 Stephen Breyer (*Sierra Club v. Marsh*, 872 F.2d at 504). See *supra* chapter 3, page 127 et seq.

20 OECD, SWEDEN – DEVELOPMENT ASSISTANCE COMMITTEE (DAC) PEER REVIEW 78 (OECD. 2009). Environmental concerns were not mentioned in the 2013 evaluation (OECD, SWEDEN – DEVELOPMENT ASSISTANCE COMMITTEE (DAC) PEER REVIEW (OECD. 2013)). Since then, Sweden has strengthened its approach to environmental policy within its development cooperation, but SIDA has experienced issues with human

criticized as a cause of delay in project development. This is part of the reason why project proponents tend to defer EIAs until late in the decision process, reducing them to rubber stamps – a meaningless bureaucratic validation of a decision that has already been made. However, factors foreign to the EIA process appear to have truly been the main cause of delays.[21] Contrary to what is too often assumed, EIAs contribute to preventing delays, and scoping is a crucial phase in this regard. An adequate original scoping is required, so that the issues to be studied can be properly identified, and further related conflicts in case of a lacunar EIA avoided. Moreover, an appropriate and complete scoping phase is instrumental in focusing consultations and public participation on project-specific issues. Otherwise, an open and ill-defined EIA opens the door to controversies not directly related to the project at stake, at the risk of turning them into "proxies in political disputes that can *never* be resolved by reference to environmental impacts alone".[22] Similarly, if an EIA is done only as a post hoc justification, worse conflicts usually arise, which tend to exceed the environmental issues related to the project, as seen, for instance, in France.[23] Another cause of late EIA timing is related to insufficient capacity to conduct EIAs properly. Developing states in particular often lack adequate personnel (such as environmental experts and departments in responsible institutions) and financial resources. Capacity building is thus essential, as underlined by development agencies.

Another important element for ensuring the quality of EIAs and avoiding ex-post rationalization is an independent evaluation of the EIA by an external expert team. While specialists highly recommend this peer review – "the yardstick applied in the normal process of science",[24] this obligation has only

---

and financial resources to meet its ambitions (OECD, SWEDEN – DEVELOPMENT ASSISTANCE COMMITTEE (DAC) PEER REVIEW 40–41, 54, 115–116 (OECD. 2019).

21 Regarding NEPA for instance, in the 2004 survey above mentioned (*Fast Tracking NEPA Documents – Tools to Overcome Delays – supra* chapter 1, note 73), depending on the agency responding, factors outside the NEPA process were identified as the cause of delay between 68% and 84% of the time (LUTHER, *supra* chapter 1, note 73 at 30).

22 Beattie, ENVIRON. IMPACT ASSESS. REV., 113 (1995).

23 See *supra* chapter 5, page 234 et seq.

24 Marcus Sheaves, et al., *Enhancing the Value and Validity of EIA: Serious Science to Protect Australia's Great Barrier Reef*, 9 CONSERVATION LETTERS 377, 379 (2016). See chapter 6, page 304 et seq. See also OLIVIER MAUREL & COMMISSION NATIONALE CONSULTATIVE DES DROITS DE L'HOMME, LA RESPONSABILITÉ DES ENTREPRISES EN MATIÈRE DE DROITS DE L'HOMME – II. ETAT DES LIEUX ET PERSPECTIVES DE L'ACTION PUBLIQUE 67 (La documentation française. 2008)). World Bank, *Review and Update of the World Bank's Environmental and Social Safeguard Policies – Summary of input submitted by stakeholders*, Question 10, Monitoring and compliance, point 1 (October 2012-April 2013).

been recently considered, for instance by the World Bank in 2016, in its new Environmental and Social Safeguard Policies.[25] Not only does such a review improve scientific accuracy, it also significantly contributes to credibility and efficiency in the decision process. Stakeholders and decision-makers are more likely to treat an assessment as credible if they hear similar findings and recommendations from a variety of sources. Consequently, reviewed assessments help secure a legitimate and reasonable decision.

2.2 *Developing Public Participation*

> *Little will be gained by an escape from the Scylla of a self-induced sense of futility to a Charybdis of vigorous quixotism*[26]

Despite the continuous development and implementation of EIA requirements over five decades, the participation of the public has been limited. Instead, a new elite has developed, composed of activists and NGOs, which begs the question of its legitimacy and representativeness. While some may argue that the legitimacy of deliberation is not dependent on the number of participants,[27] it remains that EIA requirements have failed to allow the majority of affected populations to participate in the decision-making processes. If the democratization of international law-making is underway, much remains to be accomplished.

In the European Union, in the absence of EIA legislation that would systematically require public participation at the inception of the decision-making process, the depth of experience of the participants in the EIA process (project proponents, permit authorities and consultants) was usually found to be the single most important variable for the quality of an EIA.[28] The same study emphasized that the importance of scoping, and particularly the involvement

---

CORINNE LEPAGE, "ON NE PEUT RIEN FAIRE MADAME LE MINISTRE ..." 79, 83 and 86 (Albin Michel. 1998). COMMISSION RICHARD, *supra* chapter 5, note 181 at 13 & 30.

25 World Bank, ESS1. Assessment and Management of Environmental and Social Risks and Impacts Para. 25 and 33. 2016; World Bank, ESS10. Stakeholder Engagement and Information Disclosure Para. 12. 2016; World Bank, World Bank Environmental and Social Policy for Investment Project Financing Para. 35. 2016.

26 Reisman, Making International Humanitarian Law Effective: the Case for Civic Enforcement 34. 1973.

27 Pölönen, et al., ENVIRONMENTAL IMPACT ASSESSMENT REVIEW, 126 & FN77 (2011).

28 Barker & Wood, ENVIRONMENTAL IMPACT ASSESSMENT REVIEW, 396 & 401 (1999). The eight states under evaluation were Belgium, Denmark, Germany, Greece, Ireland, Portugal, Spain and the United Kingdom.

of the public, are key determinants of the EIA report quality. Public participation determines the quality of project design.[29] Some critics of public participation have questioned the relevant expertise of civil society. Moreover, and undeniably, there is a powerful defense mechanism, a protective cognition phenomenon that prevents numerous individuals from accepting obvious scientific data.[30] At the same time, local expertise is too often dismissed. Furthermore, there is a virtuous circle of social learning and civic science, which has long been recognized and leads to information sharing and participation. Georg Simmel observed that individuals in the modern world are no longer limited to only one social circle, but belong to several of them,[31] which favors the constitution of a less biased and culturally determined individual. This plurality nuances the cognitive bias phenomena, which may diminish by relativism thanks to increasingly diverse references and sources of information, provided individuals be aware of the risks of social filter bubbles generated by social media in particular nowadays. Consequently, with the view toward making social choices, the New Haven School underlines the necessity of self-calibration and clarification of standpoint, as jurisprudential tools. In this regard, focal lenses, i.e. how observers look at pertinent data, need to be identified, along with the participants' perspectives, i.e. their patterns of identification, their expectations and values.[32] The revolution in information and communication technologies (the ICT revolution – the Internet, electronic registries and other similar digital tools) has exponentially developed the possibilities and the rapidity of the diffusion of information. Presently, the use of these technologies is limited to the dissemination of information, and has not yet been fully extended to deliberations and active public participation.[33] Soon it will, but in the meantime, in order to reach the widest possible audience, the most up-to-date technology must be accompanied, for instance, by design models that can be read on older computers,[34] or simply integrate traditional hearings and paper documents. A great many projects affect mostly populations without

29 Id. at 396, 391, 400. EIA reports in Germany were believed to be of the highest quality.

30 Kahan, *supra* chapter 3, note 74. See also ETIENNE KLEIN, LE GOÛT DU VRAI (Gallimard. 2020).

31 SIMMEL, *supra* chapter 3, note 77 at 414 et seq.

32 Reisman, AM. SOC'Y INT'L. L. PROC., 120–121 (1992).

33 A. John Sinclair, et al., *Environmental assessments in the Internet age: the role of e-governance and social media in creating platforms for meaningful participation*, 35 IMPACT ASSESS. PROJ. APPRAIS. 148 (2017). Michael B. Gerrard & Michael Herz, *Harnessing Information Technology to Improve the Environmental Impact Review Process*, 12 NYU ENVTL. LJ 18 (2003).

34 Farrell & Keating, 76. 2006.

access to modern technologies – the elderly, and/or regions with limited or no connectivity, etc. Consequently, even when modern means of communication are fully in use for e-deliberations,[35] those populations must not be left aside and traditional information channels should be maintained and integrated, not to mention that conventional interactions in person remain the most meaningful mode of exchange. Furthermore, technological innovations alone often do not suffice. Their anticipated benefits actually depend on several factors: local beliefs and value systems, institutional capacity, trusted institutions, familiarity with best-practice …[36] In order to enhance public participation, other concrete steps must be followed (for instance, identifying affected populations, points of contact and communication barriers),[37] which comes within the competence of agencies and independent consultancy firms. A further difficulty is the lack of capacity in developing countries with regard to information sharing and consultations with affected populations (such as literacy rates, insufficient communication and transportation infrastructure).[38] Here again, capacity building programs should be developed, in addition to development banks' environmental policies and compulsory EIAS.

As Michael Reisman has emphasized, to be efficient, civic groups should have a realistic focus, which entails in particular identifying the precise target ("the most appropriate pressure point") among the many composites of a state, recruit allies (including small committees within IOS, functional state agencies, NGOS, nation-state elites, domestic pressure groups, business entities), take into account their expectations, choose the optimum arena, and identify the base of control on which the individual enforcer can draw, i.e. resorting to symbols and other means to mobilize the required wealth and power and achieve the desired goal.[39] Lastly, public participation often ends too soon. Affected populations should be involved in the project implementation phase as well, in order to contribute to post-monitoring and adaptive management.[40]

35 It is already being developed in Germany, Iceland and the Netherlands (Sinclair, et al., IMPACT ASSESS. PROJ. APPRAIS., 154 (2017).

36 Beyond environmental issues, see Evan Rosevear, Michael Trebilcock, Mariana Mota Prado, *The New Progressivism and its implications for institutional theories of development*, 39 DEV POLICY REV. 644 (2021), at https://doi.org/10.1111/dpr.12517, accessed 17 June 2021.

37 EPA, *supra* chapter 1, note 75.

38 CRAIK, 43–44. 2008.

39 Reisman, Making International Humanitarian Law Effective: the Case for Civic Enforcement 34. 1973.

40 Anne Steinemann, *Improving Alternatives for Environmental Impact Assessment*, 21 ENVIRON. IMPACT ASSES. REV. 3 (2001).

2.3 *Improving Post-monitoring Programs*

> *L'action politique n'est rien si elle n'est l'inlassable effort d'agir dans la clarté et n'être pas trahie par les suites des initiatives qu'elle a prises*[41]

Post-monitoring has long been ignored. Obligations for ensuring adequate follow-up programs are now being developed, but there is still significant progress to be made with regard to tracking and storing data.[42] The effectiveness of EIAs can be fully assessed only after the proposals subject to authorizations are actually implemented. All stages, from pre- to post decision-making, represent the real life-cycle approach to EIA effectiveness.[43] However, there is currently little rigorous post-monitoring, if any. Only the naturally accumulated experience of practitioners remains available. To solve the problem of dead data in past EIAs and other related documents, the information that was collected should be placed under active management, with constant updates – a common data base, clearinghouses, repositories – which should tremendously improve EIA efficiency, while enhancing and solidifying networks and trust among scientists, experts, analysts, stakeholders, activists, NGOs, environmental organizations and institutions, project proponents, and decision-makers.[44]

Lastly, post-monitoring would also inform another planning tool, SEA, which was recommended rather soon after the introduction of EIA.[45] SEA

41 RAYMOND ARON, *Préface à Max Weber*, LE SAVANT ET LE POLITIQUE 27 (Plon. 1959). "Political action is nothing other than a tireless effort to act in an enlightened manner and to avoid being betrayed by certain consequences of that action." (Aron, Max Weber and Modern Social Science 349. 1985).

42 See *supra* chapter 2, page 82 et seq. See for instance, in the US, UNITED STATES GOVERNMENT ACCOUNTABILITY OFFICE, NATIONAL ENVIRONMENTAL POLICY ACT – LITTLE INFORMATION EXISTS ON NEPA ANALYSES § GAO-14-369 (GAO. 2014), and in the EU, UNECE, FOURTH REVIEW OF IMPLEMENTATION OF THE CONVENTION ON ENVIRONMENTAL IMPACT ASSESSMENT IN A TRANSBOUNDARY CONTEXT (2010–2012) (UN. 2015), which underlined the following weakness in the implementation of the Espoo Convention: "A lack of experience in carrying out post-project analysis (art. 7)" (p. 2, 12–13). According to the following and most recent review, this lack of post-project analysis remains a persistent issue (UNECE, FIFTH REVIEW OF IMPLEMENTATION OF THE ESPOO CONVENTION, 2, 28, 38 (2018)).

43 SADLER, 39. 1996.

44 Nicholas A. Robinson, *Legal Systems, Decisionmaking, and the Science of Earth's Systems: Procedural Missing Links*, 27 ECOLOGY L. Q. 1077 (2001); Joseph F.C. DiMento & Helen Ingram, *Science and Environmental Decision Making: The Potential Role of Environmental Impact Assessment in the Pursuit of Appropriate Information*, 45 NATURAL RESOURCES JOURNAL 283, 300–303 (2005).

45 Will A. Irwin, *Impact Assessment – First Session of the Working Group of Experts*, 13 ENVTL. POL'Y & L. 51, 53 (1984).

should continue to develop, in order to ensure comprehensive planning and EIA at an early stage. The three case studies in this book patently demonstrate this necessity. SEA has been vigorously promoted as a way to extend impact assessment to a higher-level decision-making at the policy, program and plan levels, as a reaction to the project-level orientation of most EIA applications.[46]

As a final note, despite their critics, EIAs have chalked up substantial successes and achievements. Harold Lasswell "advocated a search of symbols which are expressive of common aspirations around the world, speak of the 'World Minimum' and find sentiments for crystallizing it". Mahnoush Arsanjani also recalls that "Lasswell saw the development of 'a common cultural experience as a seed bed for the emergence of common symbols and practices' [[47]] essential for world unity".[48] Arsanjani underlines the decisive illusion of unity created by international organizations and world governance, through the provision of legal and non-legal common symbols. "The most striking aspects of these common symbols are related to the value and the place of the individual vis-a-vis others and vis-a-vis their governments".[49] EIA is such a symbol. In promoting and prescribing informed and reasoned political decisions, it has emerged as a common procedural experience and facilitated the empowerment of individuals and the creation of transnational environmental networks. Substantive law is being gradually secreted in the interstices of the EIA procedures. EIA and procedural law, in arming individuals with tools to express their preferred social choices have tended to bend the arc toward less arbitrariness and secrecy, in order for the confrontation of competing interests to unfold within expectations of effective norms of environmental protection, in view of sustainable development worldwide.

46 Morgan, IMPACT ASSESS. PROJ. APPRAIS., 7 (2012); Barry Sadler, *Taking Stock of SEA*, *in* HANDBOOK OF STRATEGIC ENVIRONMENTAL ASSESSMENT (Barry Sadler, et al. eds., 2011).

47 Lasswell, 187. 1935.

48 Arsanjani, The Uses and Abuses of Illusion in International Politics 56. 2011.

49 Id. at 58.

Appendices

APPENDIX 1

Convention on Environmental Impact Assessment in a Transboundary Context (Espoo Convention)

25 February 1991, 30 ILM 802 (1991), in force 10 September 1997

NB: Although in force since 2014, the first amendment is not yet operational, pending the missing ratifications: Decision II/14 of the Meeting of the Parties, 7 August 2001, UN Doc. ECE/MP.EIA/4

The second amendment came into force on 23 October 2017: Decision III/7 of the Meeting of the Parties, 13 September 2004, UN Doc. ECE/MP.EIA/6

The first amendment appears in *italics* and the second amendment in **bold**

The Parties to this Convention,

Aware of the interrelationship between economic activities and their environmental consequences,

Affirming the need to ensure environmentally sound and sustainable development,

Determined to enhance international co-operation in assessing environmental impact in particular in a transboundary context,

Mindful of the need and importance to develop anticipatory policies and of preventing, mitigating and monitoring significant adverse environmental impact in general and more specifically in a transboundary context,

Recalling the relevant provisions of the Charter of the United Nations, the Declaration of the Stockholm Conference on the Human Environment, the Final Act of the Conference on Security and Co-operation in Europe (CSCE) and the Concluding Documents of the Madrid and Vienna Meetings of Representatives of the Participating States of the CSCE,

Commending the ongoing activities of States to ensure that, through their national legal and administrative provisions and their national policies, environmental impact assessment is carried out,

Conscious of the need to give explicit consideration to environmental factors at an early stage in the decision-making process by applying environmental impact assessment, at all appropriate administrative levels, as a necessary tool to improve the quality of information presented to decision makers so that environmentally sound decisions

 | DOI:10.1163/9789004467583_009

can be made paying careful attention to minimizing significant adverse impact, particularly in a transboundary context,

Mindful of the efforts of international organizations to promote the use of environmental impact assessment both at the national and international levels, and taking into account work on environmental impact assessment carried out under the auspices of the United Nations Economic Commission for Europe, in particular results achieved by the Seminar on Environmental Impact Assessment (September 1987, Warsaw, Poland) as well as noting the Goals and Principles on environmental impact assessment adopted by the Governing Council of the United Nations Environment Programme, and the Ministerial Declaration on Sustainable Development (May 1990, Bergen, Norway),

Have agreed as follows:

Article 1 – Definitions

For the purposes of this Convention,

(i) "Parties" means, unless the text otherwise indicates, the Contracting Parties to this Convention;

(ii) "Party of origin" means the Contracting Party or Parties to this Convention under whose jurisdiction a proposed activity is envisaged to take place;

(iii) "Affected Party" means the Contracting Party or Parties to this Convention likely to be affected by the transboundary impact of a proposed activity;

(iv) "Concerned Parties" means the Party of origin and the affected Party of an environmental impact assessment pursuant to this Convention;

(v) "Proposed activity" means any activity or any major change to an activity subject to a decision of a competent authority in accordance with an applicable national procedure;

(vi) "Environmental impact assessment" means a national procedure for evaluating the likely impact of a proposed activity on the environment;

(vii) "Impact" means any effect caused by a proposed activity on the environment including human health and safety, flora, fauna, soil, air, water, climate, landscape and historical monuments or other physical structures or the interaction among these factors; it also includes effects on cultural heritage or socio-economic conditions resulting from alterations to those factors;

(viii) "Transboundary impact" means any impact, not exclusively of a global nature, within an area under the jurisdiction of a Party caused by a proposed activity the physical origin of which is situated wholly or in part within the area under the jurisdiction of another Party;

(ix) "Competent authority" means the national authority or authorities designated by a Party as responsible for performing the tasks covered by this Convention and/or the authority or authorities entrusted by a Party with decision-making powers regarding a proposed activity;

(x) "The Public" means one or more natural or legal persons *and, in accordance with national legislation or practice, their associations, organizations or groups.*

Article 2 – General Provisions

1. The Parties shall, either individually or jointly, take all appropriate and effective measures to prevent, reduce and control significant adverse transboundary environmental impact from proposed activities.
2. Each Party shall take the necessary legal, administrative or other measures to implement the provisions of this Convention, including, with respect to proposed activities listed in Appendix I that are likely to cause significant adverse transboundary impact, the establishment of an environmental impact assessment procedure that permits public participation and preparation of the environmental impact assessment documentation described in Appendix II.
3. The Party of origin shall ensure that in accordance with the provisions of this Convention an environmental impact assessment is undertaken prior to a decision to authorize or undertake a proposed activity listed in Appendix I that is likely to cause a significant adverse transboundary impact.
4. The Party of origin shall, consistent with the provisions of this Convention, ensure that affected Parties are notified of a proposed activity listed in Appendix I that is likely to cause a significant adverse transboundary impact.
5. Concerned Parties shall, at the initiative of any such Party, enter into discussions on whether one or more proposed activities not listed in Appendix I is or are likely to cause a significant adverse transboundary impact and thus should be treated as if it or they were so listed. Where those Parties so agree, the activity or activities shall be thus treated. General guidance for identifying criteria to determine significant adverse impact is set forth in Appendix III.
6. The Party of origin shall provide, in accordance with the provisions of this Convention, an opportunity to the public in the areas likely to be affected to participate in relevant environmental impact assessment procedures regarding proposed activities and shall ensure that the opportunity provided to the public of the affected Party is equivalent to that provided to the public of the Party of origin.
7. Environmental impact assessments as required by this Convention shall, as a minimum requirement, be undertaken at the project level of the proposed activity. To the extent appropriate, the Parties shall endeavour to apply the principles of environmental impact assessment to policies, plans and programmes.
8. The provisions of this Convention shall not affect the right of Parties to implement national laws, regulations, administrative provisions or accepted legal

practices protecting information the supply of which would be prejudicial to industrial and commercial secrecy or national security.

9. The provisions of this Convention shall not affect the right of particular Parties to implement, by bilateral or multilateral agreement where appropriate, more stringent measures than those of this Convention.

10. The provisions of this Convention shall not prejudice any obligations of the Parties under international law with regard to activities having or likely to have a transboundary impact.

11. **If the Party of origin intends to carry out a procedure for the purposes of determining the content of the environmental impact assessment documentation, the affected Party should to the extent appropriate be given the opportunity to participate in this procedure.**

Article 3 – Notification

1. For a proposed activity listed in Appendix I that is likely to cause a significant adverse transboundary impact, the Party of origin shall, for the purposes of ensuring adequate and effective consultations under Article 5, notify any Party which it considers may be an affected Party as early as possible and no later than when informing its own public about that proposed activity.

2. This notification shall contain, *inter alia*:
   (a) Information on the proposed activity, including any available information on its possible transboundary impact;
   (b) The nature of the possible decision; and
   (c) An indication of a reasonable time within which a response under paragraph 3 of this Article is required, taking into account the nature of the proposed activity; and may include the information set out in paragraph 5 of this Article.

3. The affected Party shall respond to the Party of origin within the time specified in the notification, acknowledging receipt of the notification, and shall indicate whether it intends to participate in the environmental impact assessment procedure.

4. If the affected Party indicates that it does not intend to participate in the environmental impact assessment procedure, or if it does not respond within the time specified in the notification, the provisions in paragraphs 5, 6, 7 and 8 of this Article and in Articles 4 to 7 will not apply. In such circumstances the right of a Party of origin to determine whether to carry out an environmental impact assessment on the basis of its national law and practice is not prejudiced.

5. Upon receipt of a response from the affected Party indicating its desire to participate in the environmental impact assessment procedure, the Party of origin shall, if it has not already done so, provide to the affected Party:
   (a) Relevant information regarding the environmental impact assessment procedure, including an indication of the time schedule for transmittal of comments; and
   (b) Relevant information on the proposed activity and its possible significant adverse transboundary impact.
6. An affected Party shall, at the request of the Party of origin, provide the latter with reasonably obtainable information relating to the potentially affected environment under the jurisdiction of the affected Party, where such information is necessary for the preparation of the environmental impact assessment documentation. The information shall be furnished promptly and, as appropriate, through a joint body where one exists.
7. When a Party considers that it would be affected by a significant adverse transboundary impact of a proposed activity listed in Appendix I, and when no notification has taken place in accordance with paragraph 1 of this Article, the concerned Parties shall, at the request of the affected Party, exchange sufficient information for the purposes of holding discussions on whether there is likely to be a significant adverse transboundary impact. If those Parties agree that there is likely to be a significant adverse transboundary impact, the provisions of this Convention shall apply accordingly. If those Parties cannot agree whether there is likely to be a significant adverse transboundary impact, any such Party may submit that question to an inquiry commission in accordance with the provisions of Appendix IV to advise on the likelihood of significant adverse transboundary impact, unless they agree on another method of settling this question.
8. The concerned Parties shall ensure that the public of the affected Party in the areas likely to be affected be informed of, and be provided with possibilities for making comments or objections on, the proposed activity, and for the transmittal of these comments or objections to the competent authority of the Party of origin, either directly to this authority or, where appropriate, through the Party of origin.

Article 4 – Preparation of the Environmental Impact Assessment Documentation

1. The environmental impact assessment documentation to be submitted to the competent authority of the Party of origin shall contain, as a minimum, the information described in Appendix II.

2. The Party of origin shall furnish the affected Party, as appropriate through a joint body where one exists, with the environmental impact assessment documentation. The concerned Parties shall arrange for distribution of the documentation to the authorities and the public of the affected Party in the areas likely to be affected and for the submission of comments to the competent authority of the Party of origin, either directly to this authority or, where appropriate, through the Party of origin within a reasonable time before the final decision is taken on the proposed activity.

Article 5 – Consultations on the Basis of the Environmental Impact Assessment Documentation

The Party of origin shall, after completion of the environmental impact assessment documentation, without undue delay enter into consultations with the affected Party concerning, *inter alia*, the potential transboundary impact of the proposed activity and measures to reduce or eliminate its impact. Consultations may relate to:

(a) Possible alternatives to the proposed activity, including the no-action alternative and possible measures to mitigate significant adverse transboundary impact and to monitor the effects of such measures at the expense of the Party of origin;

(b) Other forms of possible mutual assistance in reducing any significant adverse transboundary impact of the proposed activity; and

(c) Any other appropriate matters relating to the proposed activity.

The Parties shall agree, at the commencement of such consultations, on a reasonable time-frame for the duration of the consultation period. Any such consultations may be conducted through an appropriate joint body, where one exists.

Article 6 – Final Decision

1. The Parties shall ensure that, in the final decision on the proposed activity, due account is taken of the outcome of the environmental impact assessment, including the environmental impact assessment documentation, as well as the comments thereon received pursuant to Article 3, paragraph 8 and Article 4, paragraph 2, and the outcome of the consultations as referred to in Article 5.
2. The Party of origin shall provide to the affected Party the final decision on the proposed activity along with the reasons and considerations on which it was based.
3. If additional information on the significant transboundary impact of a proposed activity, which was not available at the time a decision was made with respect to that activity and which could have materially affected the decision, becomes

available to a concerned Party before work on that activity commences, that Party shall immediately inform the other concerned Party or Parties. If one of the concerned Parties so requests, consultations shall be held as to whether the decision needs to be revised.

Article 7 – Post-Project Analysis

1. The concerned Parties, at the request of any such Party, shall determine whether, and if so to what extent, a post-project analysis shall be carried out, taking into account the likely significant adverse transboundary impact of the activity for which an environmental impact assessment has been undertaken pursuant to this Convention. Any post-project analysis undertaken shall include, in particular, the surveillance of the activity and the determination of any adverse transboundary impact. Such surveillance and determination may be undertaken with a view to achieving the objectives listed in Appendix V.
2. When, as a result of post-project analysis, the Party of origin or the affected Party has reasonable grounds for concluding that there is a significant adverse transboundary impact or factors have been discovered which may result in such an impact, it shall immediately inform the other Party. The concerned Parties shall then consult on necessary measures to reduce or eliminate the impact.

Article 8 – Bilateral and Multilateral Co-Operation

The Parties may continue existing or enter into new bilateral or multilateral agreements or other arrangements in order to implement their obligations under this Convention and under any of its protocols to which they are a Party. Such agreements or other arrangements may be based on the elements listed in Appendix VI.

Article 9 – Research Programmes

The Parties shall give special consideration to the setting up, or intensification of, specific research programmes aimed at:

(a) Improving existing qualitative and quantitative methods for assessing the impacts of proposed activities;
(b) Achieving a better understanding of cause-effect relationships and their role in integrated environmental management;
(c) Analysing and monitoring the efficient implementation of decisions on proposed activities with the intention of minimizing or preventing impacts;

(d) Developing methods to stimulate creative approaches in the search for environmentally sound alternatives to proposed activities, production and consumption patterns;
(e) Developing methodologies for the application of the principles of environmental impact assessment at the macro-economic level.

The results of the programmes listed above shall be exchanged by the Parties.

Article 10 – Status of the Appendices

The Appendices attached to this Convention form an integral part of the Convention.

Article 11 – Meeting of Parties

1. The Parties shall meet, so far as possible, in connection with the annual sessions of the Senior Advisers to ECE Governments on Environmental and Water Problems. The first meeting of the Parties shall be convened not later than one year after the date of the entry into force of this Convention. Thereafter, meetings of the Parties shall be held at such other times as may be deemed necessary by a meeting of the Parties, or at the written request of any Party, provided that, within six months of the request being communicated to them by the secretariat, it is supported by at least one third of the Parties.
2. The Parties shall keep under continuous review the implementation of this Convention, and, with this purpose in mind, shall:
   (a) Review the policies and methodological approaches to environmental impact assessment by the Parties with a view to further improving environmental impact assessment procedures in a transboundary context;
   (b) Exchange information regarding experience gained in concluding and implementing bilateral and multilateral agreements or other arrangements regarding the use of environmental impact assessment in a transboundary context to which one or more of the Parties are party;
   (c) ~~Seek, where appropriate, the services of competent international bodies and scientific committees in methodological and technical aspects pertinent to the achievement of the purposes of this Convention;~~
   (c) **Seek, where appropriate, the services and cooperation of competent bodies having expertise pertinent to the achievement of the purposes of this Convention;**
   (d) At their first meeting, consider and by consensus adopt rules of procedure for their meetings;

(e) Consider and, where necessary, adopt proposals for amendments to this Convention;
(f) Consider and undertake any additional action that may be required for the achievement of the purposes of this Convention;
(g) Prepare, where appropriate, protocols to this Convention;
(h) Establish such subsidiary bodies as they consider necessary for the implementation of this Convention.

Article 12 – Right to Vote

1. Each Party to this Convention shall have one vote.
2. Except as provided for in paragraph 1 of this Article, regional economic integration organizations, in matters within their competence, shall exercise their right to vote with a number of votes equal to the number of their member States which are Parties to this Convention. Such organizations shall not exercise their right to vote if their member States exercise theirs, and vice versa.

Article 13 – Secretariat

The Executive Secretary of the Economic Commission for Europe shall carry out the following secretariat functions:
(a) The convening and preparing of meetings of the Parties;
(b) The transmission of reports and other information received in accordance with the provisions of this Convention to the Parties; and
(c) The performance of other functions as may be provided for in this Convention or as may be determined by the Parties.

Article 14 – Amendments to the Convention

1. Any Party may propose amendments to this Convention.
2. Proposed amendments shall be submitted in writing to the secretariat, which shall communicate them to all Parties. The proposed amendments shall be discussed at the next meeting of the Parties, provided these proposals have been circulated by the secretariat to the Parties at least ninety days in advance.
3. The Parties shall make every effort to reach agreement on any proposed amendment to this Convention by consensus. If all efforts at consensus have been exhausted, and no agreement reached, the amendment shall as a last resort be

adopted by a three-fourths majority vote of the Parties present and voting at the meeting.

4. Amendments to this Convention adopted in accordance with paragraph 3 of this Article shall be submitted by the Depositary to all Parties for ratification, approval or acceptance. ~~They shall enter into force for Parties having ratified, approved or accepted them on the ninetieth day after the receipt by the Depositary of notification of their ratification, approval or acceptance by at least three fourths of these Parties.~~ **They shall enter into force for Parties having ratified, approved or accepted them on the ninetieth day after the receipt by the Depositary of notification of their ratification, approval or acceptance by at least three fourths of the number of Parties at the time of their adoption.** Thereafter they shall enter into force for any other Party on the ninetieth day after that Party deposits its instrument of ratification, approval or acceptance of the amendments.
5. For the purpose of this Article, "Parties present and voting" means Parties present and casting an affirmative or negative vote.
6. The voting procedure set forth in paragraph 3 of this Article is not intended to constitute a precedent for future agreements negotiated within the Economic Commission for Europe.

Article 14 bis – Review of Compliance

1. **The Parties shall review compliance with the provisions of this Convention on the basis of the compliance procedure, as a non-adversarial and assistance-oriented procedure adopted by the Meeting of the Parties. The review shall be based on, but not limited to, regular reporting by the Parties. The Meeting of Parties shall decide on the frequency of regular reporting required by the Parties and the information to be included in those regular reports.**
2. **The compliance procedure shall be available for application to any protocol adopted under this Convention.**

Article 15 – Settlement of Disputes

1. If a dispute arises between two or more Parties about the interpretation or application of this Convention, they shall seek a solution by negotiation or by any other method of dispute settlement acceptable to the parties to the dispute.
2. When signing, ratifying, accepting, approving or acceding to this Convention, or at any time thereafter, a Party may declare in writing to the Depositary that for a dispute not resolved in accordance with paragraph 1 of this Article, it accepts

one or both of the following means of dispute settlement as compulsory in relation to any Party accepting the same obligation:
(a) Submission of the dispute to the International Court of Justice;
(b) Arbitration in accordance with the procedure set out in Appendix VII.

3. If the parties to the dispute have accepted both means of dispute settlement referred to in paragraph 2 of this Article, the dispute may be submitted only to the International Court of Justice, unless the parties agree otherwise.

Article 16 – Signature

This Convention shall be open for signature at Espoo (Finland) from 25 February to 1 March 1991 and thereafter at United Nations Headquarters in New York until 2 September 1991 by States members of the Economic Commission for Europe as well as States having consultative status with the Economic Commission for Europe pursuant to paragraph 8 of the Economic and Social Council resolution 36 (IV) of 28 March 1947, and by regional economic integration organizations constituted by sovereign States members of the Economic Commission for Europe to which their member States have transferred competence in respect of matters governed by this Convention, including the competence to enter into treaties in respect of these matters.

Article 17 – Ratification, Acceptance, Approval and Accession

1. This Convention shall be subject to ratification, acceptance or approval by signatory States and regional economic integration organizations.
2. This Convention shall be open for accession as from 3 September 1991 by the States and organizations referred to in Article 16.
3. *Any other State, not referred to in paragraph 2 of this Article, that is a Member of the United Nations may accede to the Convention upon approval by the Meeting of the Parties. The Meeting of the Parties shall not consider or approve any request for accession by such a State until this paragraph has entered into force for all the States and organizations that were Parties to the Convention on 27 February 2001.*
4. The instruments of ratification, acceptance, approval or accession shall be deposited with the Secretary-General of the United Nations, who shall perform the functions of Depositary.
5. Any organization referred to in Article 16 which becomes a Party to this Convention without any of its member States being a Party shall be bound by all the obligations under this Convention. In the case of such organizations, one or more of whose member States is a Party to this Convention, the organization and its member States shall decide on their respective responsibilities for the

performance of their obligations under this Convention. In such cases, the organization and the member States shall not be entitled to exercise rights under this Convention concurrently.

6. In their instruments of ratification, acceptance, approval or accession, the regional economic integration organizations referred to in Article 16 shall declare the extent of their competence with respect to the matters governed by this Convention. These organizations shall also inform the Depositary of any relevant modification to the extent of their competence.

7. *Any State or organization that ratifies, accepts or approves this Convention shall be deemed simultaneously to ratify, accept or approve the amendment to the Convention set out in decision II/14 taken at the second meeting of the Parties.*

Article 18 – Entry into Force

1. This Convention shall enter into force on the ninetieth day after the date of deposit of the sixteenth instrument of ratification, acceptance, approval or accession.
2. For the purposes of paragraph 1 of this Article, any instrument deposited by a regional economic integration organization shall not be counted as additional to those deposited by States members of such an organization.
3. For each State or organization referred to in Article 16 which ratifies, accepts or approves this Convention or accedes thereto after the deposit of the sixteenth instrument of ratification, acceptance, approval or accession, this Convention shall enter into force on the ninetieth day after the date of deposit by such State or organization of its instrument of ratification, acceptance, approval or accession.

Article 19 – Withdrawal

At any time after four years from the date on which this Convention has come into force with respect to a Party, that Party may withdraw from this Convention by giving written notification to the Depositary. Any such withdrawal shall take effect on the ninetieth day after the date of its receipt by the Depositary. Any such withdrawal shall not affect the application of Articles 3 to 6 of this Convention to a proposed activity in respect of which a notification has been made pursuant to Article 3, paragraph 1, or a request has been made pursuant to Article 3, paragraph 7, before such withdrawal took effect.

Article 20 – Authentic Texts

The original of this Convention, of which the English, French and Russian texts are equally authentic, shall be deposited with the Secretary-General of the United Nations.

IN WITNESS WHEREOF the undersigned, being duly authorized thereto, have signed this Convention.

DONE at Espoo (Finland), this twenty-fifth day of February one thousand nine hundred and ninety-one.

Appendix I – List of Activities

1. Crude oil refineries (excluding undertakings manufacturing only lubricants from crude oil) and installations for the gasification and liquefaction of 500 metric tons or more of coal or bituminous shale per day.
2. (a) Thermal power stations and other combustion installations with a heat output of 300 megawatts or more, and
   (b) Nuclear power stations and other nuclear reactors, including the dismantling or decommissioning of such power stations or reactors[1] (except research installations for the production and conversion of fissionable and fertile materials, whose maximum power does not exceed 1 kilowatt continuous thermal load).
3. (a) Installations for the reprocessing of irradiated nuclear fuel;
   (b) Installations designed:
   - For the production or enrichment of nuclear fuel;
   - For the processing of irradiated nuclear fuel or high-level radioactive waste;
   - For the final disposal of irradiated nuclear fuel;
   - Solely for the final disposal of radioactive waste; or
   - Solely for the storage (planned for more than 10 years) of irradiated nuclear fuels or radioactive waste in a different site than the production site.
4. Major installations for the initial smelting of cast iron and steel and for the production of non-ferrous metals.
5. Installations for the extraction of asbestos and for the processing and transformation of asbestos and products containing asbestos: for asbestos-cement

1 For the purposes of this Convention, nuclear power stations and other nuclear reactors cease to be such an installation when all nuclear fuel and other radioactively contaminated elements have been removed permanently from the installation site.

products, with an annual production of more than 20,000 metric tons finished product; for friction material, with an annual production of more than 50 metric tons finished product; and for other asbestos utilization of more than 200 metric tons per year.

6. Integrated chemical installations.

7. (a) Construction of motorways, express roads[2] and lines for long-distance railway traffic and of airports[3] with a basic runway length of 2,100 metres or more;

   (b) Construction of a new road of four or more lanes, or realignment and/or widening of an existing road of two lanes or less so as to provide four or more lanes, where such new road, or realigned and/or widened section of road, would be 10 km or more in a continuous length.

8. Large-diameter pipelines for the transport of oil, gas or chemicals.

9. Trading ports and also inland waterways and ports for inland-waterway traffic which permit the passage of vessels of over 1,350 metric tons.

10. (a) Waste-disposal installations for the incineration, chemical treatment or landfill of toxic and dangerous wastes;

    (b) Waste-disposal installations for the incinration or chemical treatment of non-hazardous waste with a capacity exceeding 100 metric tons per day.

11. Large dams and reservoirs.

12. Groundwater abstraction activities or artificial groundwater recharge schemes where the annual volume of water to be abstracted or recharged amounts to 10 million cubic metres or more.

13. Pulp, paper and board manufacturing of 200 air-dried metric tons or more per day.

14. Major quarries, mining, on-site extraction and processing of metal ores or coal.

---

2 For the purposes of this Convention:

- "Motorway" means a road specially designed and built for motor traffic, which does not serve properties bordering on it, and which:
  (a) Is provided, except at special points or temporarily, with separate carriageways for the two directions of traffic, separated from each other by a dividing strip not intended for traffic or, exceptionally, by other means;
  (b) Does not cross at level with any road, railway or tramway track, or footpath; and
  (c) Is specially signposted as a motorway.
- "Express road" means a road reserved for motor traffic accessible only from interchanges or controlled junctions and on which, in particular, stopping and parking are prohibited on the running carriageway(s).

3 For the purposes of this Convention, "airport" means an airport which complies with the definition in the 1944 Chicago Convention setting up the International Civil Aviation Organization (annex 14).

15. Offshore hydrocarbon production. Extraction of petroleum and natural gas for commercial purposes where the amount extracted exceeds 500 metric tons/day in the case of petroleum and 500 000 cubic metres/day in the case of gas.
16. Major storage facilities for petroleum, petrochemical and chemical products.
17. Deforestation of large areas.
18. (a) Works for the transfer of water resources between river basins where this transfer aims at preventing possible shortages of water and where the amount of water transferred exceeds 100 million cubic metres/year; and
    (b) In all other cases, works for the transfer of water resources between river basins where the multi-annual average flow of the basin of abstraction exceeds 2 000 million cubic metres/year and where the amount of water transferred exceeds 5 per cent of this flow.

    In both cases transfers of piped drinking water are excluded.
19. Waste-water treatment plants with a capacity exceeding 150 000 population equivalent.
20. Installations for the intensive rearing of poultry or pigs with more than:
    - 85 000 places for broilers;
    - 60 000 places for hens;
    - 3 000 places for production pigs (over 30 kg); or
    - 900 places for sows.
21. Construction of overhead electrical power lines with a voltage of 220 kV or more and a length of more than 15 km.
22. Major installations for the harnessing of wind power for energy production (wind farms).

Appendix II – Content of the Environmental Impact Assessment Documentation

Information to be included in the environmental impact assessment documentation shall, as a minimum, contain, in accordance with Article 4:

(a) A description of the proposed activity and its purpose;
(b) A description, where appropriate, of reasonable alternatives (for example, locational or technological) to the proposed activity and also the no-action alternative;
(c) A description of the environment likely to be significantly affected by the proposed activity and its alternatives;
(d) A description of the potential environmental impact of the proposed activity and its alternatives and an estimation of its significance;
(e) A description of mitigation measures to keep adverse environmental impact to a minimum;

(f) An explicit indication of predictive methods and underlying assumptions as well as the relevant environmental data used;
(g) An identification of gaps in knowledge and uncertainties encountered in compiling the required information;
(h) Where appropriate, an outline for monitoring and management programmes and any plans for post-project analysis; and
(i) A non-technical summary including a visual presentation as appropriate (maps, graphs, etc.).

Appendix III – General Criteria to Assist in the Determination of the Environmental Significance of Activities Not Listed in Appendix I

1. In considering proposed activities to which Article 2, paragraph 5, applies, the concerned Parties may consider whether the activity is likely to have a significant adverse transboundary impact in particular by virtue of one or more of the following criteria:
   (a) *Size*: proposed activities which are large for the type of the activity;
   (b) *Location*: proposed activities which are located in or close to an area of special environmental sensitivity or importance (such as wetlands designated under the Ramsar Convention, national parks, nature reserves, sites of special scientific interest, or sites of archaeological, cultural or historical importance); also, proposed activities in locations where the characteristics of proposed development would be likely to have significant effects on the population;
   (c) *Effects*: proposed activities with particularly complex and potentially adverse effects, including those giving rise to serious effects on humans or on valued species or organisms, those which threaten the existing or potential use of an affected area and those causing additional loading which cannot be sustained by the carrying capacity of the environment.
2. The concerned Parties shall consider for this purpose proposed activities which are located close to an international frontier as well as more remote proposed activities which could give rise to significant transboundary effects far removed from the site of development.

Appendix IV – Inquiry Procedure

1. The requesting Party or Parties shall notify the secretariat that it or they submit(s) the question of whether a proposed activity listed in Appendix I is likely

to have a significant adverse transboundary impact to an inquiry commission established in accordance with the provisions of this Appendix. This notification shall state the subject-matter of the inquiry. The secretariat shall notify immediately all Parties to this Convention of this submission.

2. The inquiry commission shall consist of three members. Both the requesting party and the other party to the inquiry procedure shall appoint a scientific or technical expert, and the two experts so appointed shall designate by common agreement the third expert, who shall be the president of the inquiry commission. The latter shall not be a national of one of the parties to the inquiry procedure, nor have his or her usual place of residence in the territory of one of these parties, nor be employed by any of them, nor have dealt with the matter in any other capacity.
3. If the president of the inquiry commission has not been designated within two months of the appointment of the second expert, the Executive Secretary of the Economic Commission for Europe shall, at the request of either party, designate the president within a further two-month period.
4. If one of the parties to the inquiry procedure does not appoint an expert within one month of its receipt of the notification by the secretariat, the other party may inform the Executive Secretary of the Economic Commission for Europe, who shall designate the president of the inquiry commission within a further two-month period. Upon designation, the president of the inquiry commission shall request the party which has not appointed an expert to do so within one month. After such a period, the president shall inform the Executive Secretary of the Economic Commission for Europe, who shall make this appointment within a further two-month period.
5. The inquiry commission shall adopt its own rules of procedure.
6. The inquiry commission may take all appropriate measures in order to carry out its functions.
7. The parties to the inquiry procedure shall facilitate the work of the inquiry commission and, in particular, using all means at their disposal, shall:
   (a) Provide it with all relevant documents, facilities and information; and
   (b) Enable it, where necessary, to call witnesses or experts and receive their evidence.
8. The parties and the experts shall protect the confidentiality of any information they receive in confidence during the work of the inquiry commission.
9. If one of the parties to the inquiry procedure does not appear before the inquiry commission or fails to present its case, the other party may request the inquiry commission to continue the proceedings and to complete its work. Absence of a party or failure of a party to present its case shall not constitute a bar to the continuation and completion of the work of the inquiry commission.

10. Unless the inquiry commission determines otherwise because of the particular circumstances of the matter, the expenses of the inquiry commission, including the remuneration of its members, shall be borne by the parties to the inquiry procedure in equal shares. The inquiry commission shall keep a record of all its expenses, and shall furnish a final statement thereof to the parties.
11. Any Party having an interest of a factual nature in the subject-matter of the inquiry procedure, and which may be affected by an opinion in the matter, may intervene in the proceedings with the consent of the inquiry commission.
12. The decisions of the inquiry commission on matters of procedure shall be taken by majority vote of its members. The final opinion of the inquiry commission shall reflect the view of the majority of its members and shall include any dissenting view.
13. The inquiry commission shall present its final opinion within two months of the date on which it was established unless it finds it necessary to extend this time limit for a period which should not exceed two months.
14. The final opinion of the inquiry commission shall be based on accepted scientific principles. The final opinion shall be transmitted by the inquiry commission to the parties to the inquiry procedure and to the secretariat.

Appendix v – Post-Project Analysis

Objectives include:

(a) Monitoring compliance with the conditions as set out in the authorization or approval of the activity and the effectiveness of mitigation measures;
(b) Review of an impact for proper management and in order to cope with uncertainties;
(c) Verification of past predictions in order to transfer experience to future activities of the same type.

Appendix vi – Elements for Bilateral and Multilateral Co-Operation

1. Concerned Parties may set up, where appropriate, institutional arrangements or enlarge the mandate of existing institutional arrangements within the framework of bilateral and multilateral agreements in order to give full effect to this Convention.
2. Bilateral and multilateral agreements or other arrangements may include:
   (a) Any additional requirements for the implementation of this Convention, taking into account the specific conditions of the subregion concerned;

(b) Institutional, administrative and other arrangements, to be made on a reciprocal and equivalent basis;
(c) Harmonization of their policies and measures for the protection of the environment in order to attain the greatest possible similarity in standards and methods related to the implementation of environmental impact assessment;
(d) Developing, improving, and/or harmonizing methods for the identification, measurement, prediction and assessment of impacts, and for post-project analysis;
(e) Developing and/or improving methods and programmes for the collection, analysis, storage and timely dissemination of comparable data regarding environmental quality in order to provide input into environmental impact assessment;
(f) The establishment of threshold levels and more specified criteria for defining the significance of transboundary impacts related to the location, nature or size of proposed activities, for which environmental impact assessment in accordance with the provisions of this Convention shall be applied; and the establishment of critical loads of transboundary pollution;
(g) Undertaking, where appropriate, joint environmental impact assessment, development of joint monitoring programmes, intercalibration of monitoring devices and harmonization of methodologies with a view to rendering the data and information obtained compatible.

3. **Paragraphs 1 and 2 may be applied, mutatis mutandis, to any protocol to the Convention.**

Appendix VII – Arbitration

1. The claimant Party or Parties shall notify the secretariat that the Parties have agreed to submit the dispute to arbitration pursuant to Article 15, paragraph 2, of this Convention. The notification shall state the subject-matter of arbitration and include, in particular, the Articles of this Convention, the interpretation or application of which are at issue. The secretariat shall forward the information received to all Parties to this Convention.
2. The arbitral tribunal shall consist of three members. Both the claimant Party or Parties and the other Party or Parties to the dispute shall appoint an arbitrator, and the two arbitrators so appointed shall designate by common agreement the third arbitrator, who shall be the president of the arbitral tribunal. The latter shall not be a national of one of the parties to the dispute, nor have his or her usual place of residence in the territory of one of these parties, nor be employed by any of them, nor have dealt with the case in any other capacity.

3. If the president of the arbitral tribunal has not been designated within two months of the appointment of the second arbitrator, the Executive Secretary of the Economic Commission for Europe shall, at the request of either party to the dispute, designate the president within a further two-month period.
4. If one of the parties to the dispute does not appoint an arbitrator within two months of the receipt of the request, the other party may inform the Executive Secretary of the Economic Commission for Europe, who shall designate the president of the arbitral tribunal within a further two-month period. Upon designation, the president of the arbitral tribunal shall request the party which has not appointed an arbitrator to do so within two months. After such a period, the president shall inform the Executive Secretary of the Economic Commission for Europe, who shall make this appointment within a further two-month period.
5. The arbitral tribunal shall render its decision in accordance with international law and in accordance with the provisions of this Convention.
6. Any arbitral tribunal constituted under the provisions set out herein shall draw up its own rules of procedure.
7. The decisions of the arbitral tribunal, both on procedure and on substance, shall be taken by majority vote of its members.
8. The tribunal may take all appropriate measures in order to establish the facts.
9. The parties to the dispute shall facilitate the work of the arbitral tribunal and, in particular, using all means at their disposal, shall:
   (a) Provide it with all relevant documents, facilities and information; and
   (b) Enable it, where necessary, to call witnesses or experts and receive their evidence.
10. The parties and the arbitrators shall protect the confidentiality of any information they receive in confidence during the proceedings of the arbitral tribunal.
11. The arbitral tribunal may, at the request of one of the parties, recommend interim measures of protection.
12. If one of the parties to the dispute does not appear before the arbitral tribunal or fails to defend its case, the other party may request the tribunal to continue the proceedings and to render its final decision. Absence of a party or failure of a party to defend its case shall not constitute a bar to the proceedings. Before rendering its final decision, the arbitral tribunal must satisfy itself that the claim is well founded in fact and law.
13. The arbitral tribunal may hear and determine counter-claims arising directly out of the subject-matter of the dispute.
14. Unless the arbitral tribunal determines otherwise because of the particular circumstances of the case, the expenses of the tribunal, including the remuneration of its members, shall be borne by the parties to the dispute in equal shares. The tribunal shall keep a record of all its expenses, and shall furnish a final statement thereof to the parties.

15. Any Party to this Convention having an interest of a legal nature in the subject-matter of the dispute, and which may be affected by a decision in the case, may intervene in the proceedings with the consent of the tribunal.
16. The arbitral tribunal shall render its award within five months of the date on which it is established unless it finds it necessary to extend the time limit for a period which should not exceed five months.
17. The award of the arbitral tribunal shall be accompanied by a statement of reasons. It shall be final and binding upon all parties to the dispute. The award will be transmitted by the arbitral tribunal to the parties to the dispute and to the secretariat. The secretariat will forward the information received to all Parties to this Convention.
18. Any dispute which may arise between the parties concerning the interpretation or execution of the award may be submitted by either party to the arbitral tribunal which made the award or, if the latter cannot be seized thereof, to another tribunal constituted for this purpose in the same manner as the first.

Available at https://unece.org/environment-policyenvironmental-assessment/text-convention (accessed 17 June 2021)

APPENDIX 2

Annex I to the Protocol on Environmental Protection to the Antarctic Treaty Environmental Impact Assessment

4 October 1991, 30 ILM 1461 (1991), in force 14 January 1998

Article 1 – *Preliminary Stage*

1. Protocol shall, before their commencement, be considered in accordance with appropriate national procedures.
The environmental impacts of proposed activities referred to in Article 8 of the
2. If an activity is determined as having less than a minor or transitory impact, the activity may proceed forthwith.

Article 2 – *Initial Environmental Evaluation*

1. Unless it has been determined that an activity will have less than a minor or transitory impact, or unless a Comprehensive Environmental Evaluation is being prepared in accordance with Article 3, an Initial Environmental Evaluation shall be prepared. It shall contain sufficient detail to assess whether a proposed activity may have more than a minor or transitory impact and shall include:
   (a) a description of the proposed activity, including its purpose, location, duration and intensity; and
   (b) consideration of alternatives to the proposed activity and any impacts that the activity may have, including consideration of cumulative impacts in the light of existing and known planned activities.
2. If an Initial Environmental Evaluation indicates that a proposed activity is likely to have no more than a minor or transitory impact, the activity may proceed, provided that appropriate procedures, which may include monitoring, are put in place to assess and verify the impact of the activity.

 | DOI:10.1163/9789004467583_010

Article 3 – *Comprehensive Environmental Evaluation*

1. If an Initial Environmental Evaluation indicates or if it is otherwise determined that a proposed activity is likely to have more than a minor or transitory impact, a Comprehensive Environmental Evaluation shall be prepared.
2. A Comprehensive Environmental Evaluation shall include:
   (a) a description of the proposed activity including its purpose, location, duration and intensity, and possible alternatives to the activity, including the alternative of not proceeding, and the consequences of those alternatives;
   (b) a description of the initial environmental reference state with which predicted changes are to be compared and a prediction of the future environmental reference state in the absence of the proposed activity;
   (c) a description of the methods and data used to forecast the impacts of the proposed activity;
   (d) estimation of the nature, extent, duration, and intensity of the likely direct impacts of the proposed activity;
   (e) consideration of possible indirect or second order impacts of the proposed activity;
   (f) consideration of cumulative impacts of the proposed activity in the light of existing activities and other known planned activities;
   (g) identification of measures, including monitoring programmes, that could be taken to minimise or mitigate impacts of the proposed activity and to detect unforeseen impacts and that could provide early warning of any adverse effects of the activity as well as to deal promptly and effectively with accidents;
   (h) identification of unavoidable impacts of the proposed activity;
   (i) consideration of the effects of the proposed activity on the conduct of scientific research and on other existing uses and values;
   (j) an identification of gaps in knowledge and uncertainties encountered in compiling the information required under this paragraph;
   (k) a non-technical summary of the information provided under this paragraph; and the name and address of the person or organization which prepared the Comprehensive Environmental Evaluation and the address to which comments thereon should be directed.
   (l) The draft Comprehensive Environmental Evaluation shall be made publicly
3. The draft Comprehensive Environmental Evaluation shall be made publicly available and shall be circulated to all Parties, which shall also make it publicly available, for comment. A period of 90 days shall be allowed for the receipt of comments.

4. The draft Comprehensive Environmental Evaluation shall be forwarded to the Committee at the same time as it is circulated to the Parties, and at least 120 days before the next Antarctic Treaty Consultative Meeting, for consideration as appropriate.
5. No final decision shall be taken to proceed with the proposed activity in the Antarctic Treaty area unless there has been an opportunity for consideration of the draft Comprehensive Environmental Evaluation by the Antarctic Treaty Consultative Meeting on the advice of the Committee, provided that no decision to proceed with a proposed activity shall be delayed through the operation of this paragraph for longer than 15 months from the date of circulation of the draft Comprehensive Environmental Evaluation.
6. A final Comprehensive Environmental Evaluation shall address and shall include or summarise comments received on the draft Comprehensive Environmental Evaluation. The final Comprehensive Environmental Evaluation, notice of any decisions relating thereto, and any evaluation of the significance of the predicted impacts in relation to the advantages of the proposed activity, shall be circulated to all Parties, which shall also make them publicly available, at least 60 days before the commencement of the proposed activity in the Antarctic Treaty area.

Article 4 – *Decisions to be Based on Comprehensive Environmental Evaluations*

Any decision on whether a proposed activity, to which Article 3 applies, should proceed, and, if so, whether in its original or in a modified form, shall be based on the Comprehensive Environmental Evaluation as well as other relevant considerations.

Article 5 – *Monitoring*

1. Procedures shall be put in place, including appropriate monitoring of key environmental indicators, to assess and verify the impact of any activity that proceeds following the completion of a Comprehensive Environmental Evaluation.
2. The procedures referred to in paragraph 1 above and in Article 2 (2) shall be designed to provide a regular and verifiable record of the impacts of the activity in order, inter alia, to:
   (a) enable assessments to be made of the extent to which such impacts are consistent with the Protocol; and

(b) provide information useful for minimising or mitigating impacts, and, where appropriate, information on the need for suspension, cancellation or modification of the activity.

Article 6 – *Circulation of Information*

1. The following information shall be circulated to the Parties, forwarded to the Committee and made publicly available:
   (a) a description of the procedures referred to in Article 1;
   (b) an annual list of any Initial Environmental Evaluations prepared in accordance with Article 2 and any decisions taken in consequence thereof;
   (c) significant information obtained, and any action taken in consequence thereof, from procedures put in place in accordance with Articles 2 (2) and 5; and
   (d) information referred to in Article 3 (6).
2. Any Initial Environmental Evaluation prepared in accordance with Article 2 shall be made available on request.

Article 7 – *Cases of Emergency*

1. This Annex shall not apply in cases of emergency relating to the safety of human life or of ships, aircraft or equipment and facilities of high value, or the protection of the environment, which require an activity to be undertaken without completion of the procedures set out in this Annex.
2. Notice of activities undertaken in cases of emergency, which would otherwise have required preparation of a Comprehensive Environmental Evaluation, shall be circulated immediately to all Parties and to the Committee and a full explanation of the activities carried out shall be provided within 90 days of those activities.

Article 8 – *Amendment or Modification*

1. This Annex may be amended or modified by a measure adopted in accordance with Article IX (1) of the Antarctic Treaty. Unless the measure specifies otherwise, the amendment or modification shall be deemed to have been approved, and shall become effective, one year after the close of the Antarctic

Treaty Consultative Meeting at which it was adopted, unless one or more of the Antarctic Treaty Consultative Parties notifies the Depositary, within that period, that it wishes an extension of that period or that it is unable to approve the measure.

2. Any amendment or modification of this Annex which becomes effective in accordance with paragraph 1 above shall thereafter become effective as to any other Party when notice of approval by it has been received by the Depositary.

Available at https://www.ats.aq/e/protocol.html (accessed 17 June 2021)

APPENDIX 3

Directive 2011/92/EU of the European Parliament and of the Council of 13 December 2011 on the Assessment of the Effects of Certain Public and Private Projects on the Environment (Codification of the 1985 EIA Directive)

(OJ L 26, 28 January 2012, p. 1)
As amended by Directive 2014/52/EU of the European Parliament and of the Council of 16 April 2014 (OJ L 124, 25 April 2014, p. 1)
The following is an informal consolidated version

The European Parliament and the Council of the European Union,

Having regard to the Treaty on the Functioning of the European Union, and in particular Article 192(1) thereof,

Having regard to the proposal from the European Commission,

After transmission of the draft legislative act to the national parliaments, Having regard to the opinion of the European Economic and Social Committee, After consulting the Committee of the Regions,

Acting in accordance with the ordinary legislative procedure,

Whereas:

(1) Council Directive 85/337/EEC of 27 June 1985 on the assessment of the effects of certain public and private projects on the environment has been substantially amended several times. In the interests of clarity and rationality the said Directive should be codified.

(2) Pursuant to Article 191 of the Treaty on the Functioning of the European Union, Union policy on the environment is based on the precautionary principle and on the principles that preventive action should be taken, that environmental damage should, as a priority, be rectified at source and that the polluter should pay. Effects on the environment should be taken into account at the earliest possible stage in all the technical planning and decision-making processes.

(3) The principles of the assessment of environmental effects should be harmonised, in particular with reference to the projects which should be subject to assessment, the main obligations of the developers and the content of the assessment. The Member States may lay down stricter rules to protect the environment.

(1) *Directive 2011/92/EU of the European Parliament and of the Council(4) has harmonised the principles for the environmental impact assessment of projects by*

 | DOI:10.1163/9789004467583_011

introducing minimum requirements, with regard to the type of projects subject to assessment, the main obligations of developers, the content of the assessment and the participation of the competent authorities and the public, and it contributes to a high level of protection of the environment and human health. Member States are free to lay down more stringent protective measures in accordance with the Treaty on the Functioning of the European Union (TFEU).

(4) In addition, it is necessary to achieve one of the objectives of the Union in the sphere of the protection of the environment and the quality of life.

(2) *The Commission Communication of 30 April 2007, entitled 'The mid-term review of the sixth Community Environment Action Programme' and the Report from the Commission of 23 July 2009 on the application and effectiveness of Council Directive 85/337/*EEC(5), *the predecessor to Directive 2011/92/EU, stressed the need to improve the principles of environmental impact assessment of projects, and to adapt Directive 85/337/*EEC *to the policy, legal and technical context, which has evolved considerably.*

(3) *It is necessary to amend Directive 2011/92/EU in order to strengthen the quality of the environmental impact assessment procedure, align that procedure with the principles of smart regulation and enhance coherence and synergies with other Union legislation and policies, as well as strategies and policies developed by Member States in areas of national competence.*

(6) *Directive 2011/92/EU should also be revised in a way that ensures that environmental protection is improved, resource efficiency increased and sustainable growth supported in the Union. To this end, the procedures it lays down should be simplified and harmonised.*

(5) The environmental legislation of the Union includes provisions enabling public authorities and other bodies to take decisions which may have a significant effect on the environment as well as on personal health and well-being.

(21) *Member States have several options for implementing Directive 2011/92/EU as regards the integration of environmental impact assessments into national procedures. Accordingly, the elements of those national procedures can vary. Due to this fact, the reasoned conclusion by which the competent authority finalises its examination of the environmental impact of the project may be part of an integrated development consent procedure or may be incorporated in another binding decision required in order to comply with the aims of this Directive.*

(6) General principles for the assessment of environmental effects should be laid down with a view to supplementing and coordinating development consent procedures governing public and private projects likely to have a major effect on the environment.

(25) *The objectivity of the competent authorities should be ensured. Conflicts of interest could be prevented by, inter alia, a functional separation of the competent authority*

from the developer. In cases where the competent authority is also the developer, Member States should at least implement, within their organisation of administrative competences, an appropriate separation between conflicting functions of those authorities performing the duties arising from Directive 2011/92/EU.

(7) Development consent for public and private projects which are likely to have significant effects on the environment should be granted only after an assessment of the likely significant environmental effects of those projects has been carried out. That assessment should be conducted on the basis of the appropriate information supplied by the developer, which may be supplemented by the authorities and by the public likely to be concerned by the project in question.

(22) *In order to ensure a high level of protection of the environment and human health, screening procedures and environmental impact assessments should take account of the impact of the whole project in question, including, where relevant, its subsurface and underground, during the construction, operational and, where relevant, demolition phases.*

(23) *With a view to reaching a complete assessment of the direct and indirect effects of a project on the environment, the competent authority should undertake an analysis by examining the substance of the information provided by the developer and received through consultations, as well as considering any supplementary information, where appropriate.*

(8) Projects belonging to certain types have significant effects on the environment and those projects should, as a rule, be subject to a systematic assessment.

(9) Projects of other types may not have significant effects on the environment in every case and those projects should be assessed where the Member States consider that they are likely to have significant effects on the environment.

(26) *In order to enable the competent authority to determine whether projects listed in Annex II to Directive 2011/92/EU, their changes or extensions, are to be subject to an environmental impact assessment (screening procedure), the information which the developer is required to supply should be specified, focussing on the key aspects that allow the competent authority to make its determination. That determination should be made available to the public.*

(27) *The screening procedure should ensure that an environmental impact assessment is only required for projects likely to have significant effects on the environment.*

(10) Member States may set thresholds or criteria for the purpose of determining which of such projects should be subject to assessment on the basis of the significance of their environmental effects. Member States should not be required to examine projects below those thresholds or outside those criteria on a case-by-case basis.

(11) When setting such thresholds or criteria or examining projects on a case-by-case basis, for the purpose of determining which projects should be subject to

assessment on the basis of their significant environmental effects, Member States should take account of the relevant selection criteria set out in this Directive. In accordance with the subsidiarity principle, the Member States are in the best position to apply those criteria in specific instances.

(28) *The selection criteria laid down in Annex III to Directive 2011/92/EU, which are to be taken into account by the Member States in order to determine which projects are to be subject to environmental impact assessment on the basis of their significant effects on the environment, should be adapted and clarified. For instance, experience has shown that projects using or affecting valuable resources, projects proposed for environmentally sensitive locations, or projects with potentially hazardous or irreversible effects are often likely to have significant effects on the environment.*

(29) *When determining whether significant effects on the environment are likely to be caused by a project, the competent authorities should identify the most relevant criteria to be considered and should take into account information that could be available following other assessments required by Union legislation in order to apply the screening procedure effectively and transparently. In this regard, it is appropriate to specify the content of the screening determination, in particular where no environmental impact assessment is required. Moreover, taking into account unsolicited comments that might have been received from other sources, such as members of the public or public authorities, even though no formal consultation is required at the screening stage, constitutes good administrative practice.*

(12) For projects which are subject to assessment, a certain minimal amount of information should be supplied, concerning the project and its effects.

(31) *The environmental impact assessment report to be provided by the developer for a project should include a description of reasonable alternatives studied by the developer which are relevant to that project, including, as appropriate, an outline of the likely evolution of the current state of the environment without implementation of the project (baseline scenario), as a means of improving the quality of the environmental impact assessment process and of allowing environmental considerations to be integrated at an early stage in the project's design.*

(32) *Data and information included by the developer in the environmental impact assessment report, in accordance with Annex IV to Directive 2011/92/EU, should be complete and of sufficiently high quality. With a view to avoiding duplication of assessments, the results of other assessments under Union legislation, such as Directive 2001/42/EC of the European Parliament and the Council (15) or Directive 2009/71/Euratom, or national legislation should, where relevant and available, be taken into account.*

(33) *Experts involved in the preparation of environmental impact assessment reports should be qualified and competent. Sufficient expertise, in the relevant field of the project concerned, is required for the purpose of its examination by the competent*

authorities in order to ensure that the information provided by the developer is complete and of a high level of quality.

(13) It is appropriate to lay down a procedure in order to enable the developer to obtain an opinion from the competent authorities on the content and extent of the information to be elaborated and supplied for the assessment. Member States, in the framework of this procedure, may require the developer to provide, inter alia, alternatives for the projects for which it intends to submit an application.

(30) *In order to improve the quality of an environmental impact assessment, to simplify the procedures and to streamline the decision-making process, the competent authority should, where requested by the developer, issue an opinion on the scope and level of detail of the environmental information to be submitted in the form of an environmental impact assessment report ('scoping').*

(14) The effects of a project on the environment should be assessed in order to take account of concerns to protect human health, to contribute by means of a better environment to the quality of life, to ensure maintenance of the diversity of species and to maintain the reproductive capacity of the ecosystem as a basic resource for life.

(7) *Over the last decade, environmental issues, such as resource efficiency and sustainability, biodiversity protection, climate change, and risks of accidents and disasters, have become more important in policy making. They should therefore also constitute important elements in assessment and decision-making processes.*

(8) *In its Communication of 20 September 2011 entitled 'Roadmap to a Resource Efficient Europe', the Commission committed itself to including broader resource efficiency and sustainability considerations in the context of the revision of Directive 2011/92/EU.*

(9) *The Commission Communication of 22 September 2006 entitled 'Thematic Strategy for Soil Protection' and the Roadmap to a Resource-Efficient Europe underline the importance of the sustainable use of soil and the need to address the unsustainable increase of settlement areas over time ('land take'). Furthermore, the final document of the United Nations Conference on Sustainable Development held in Rio de Janeiro on 20–22 June 2012 recognises the economic and social significance of good land management, including soil, and the need for urgent action to reverse land degradation. Public and private projects should therefore consider and limit their impact on land, particularly as regards land take, and on soil, including as regards organic matter, erosion, compaction and sealing; appropriate land use plans and policies at national, regional and local level are also relevant in this regard.*

(10) *The United Nations Convention on Biological Diversity ('the Convention'), to which the Union is party pursuant to Council Decision 93/626/EEC(9), requires assessment, as far as possible and as*

appropriate, of the significant adverse effects of projects on biological diversity, which is defined in Article 2 of the Convention, with a view to avoiding or minimising such effects. Such prior assessment of those effects should contribute to attaining the Union headline target adopted by the European Council in its conclusions of 25–26 March 2010 of halting biodiversity loss and the degradation of ecosystem services by 2020 and restoring them where feasible.

(11) *The measures taken to avoid, prevent, reduce and, if possible, offset significant adverse effects on the environment, in particular on species and habitats protected under Council Directive 92/43/EEC and Directive 2009/147/EC of the European Parliament and of the Council, should contribute to avoiding any deterioration in the quality of the environment and any net loss of biodiversity, in accordance with the Union's commitments in the context of the Convention and the objectives and actions of the Union Biodiversity Strategy up to 2020 laid down in the Commission Communication of 3 May 2011 entitled 'Our life insurance, our natural capital: an EU biodiversity strategy to 2020'.*

(12) *With a view to ensuring a high level of protection of the marine environment, especially species and habitats, environmental impact assessment and screening procedures for projects in the marine environment should take into account the characteristics of those projects with particular regard to the technologies used (for example seismic surveys using active sonars). For this purpose, the requirements of Directive 2013/30/EU of the European Parliament and of the Council could also facilitate the implementation of the requirements of this Directive.*

(13) *Climate change will continue to cause damage to the environment and compromise economic development. In this regard, it is appropriate to assess the impact of projects on climate (for example greenhouse gas emissions) and their vulnerability to climate change.*

(14) *Following the Commission Communication of 23 February 2009 entitled 'A Community approach on the prevention of natural and man-made disasters', the Council, in its conclusions of 30 November 2009, invited the Commission to ensure that the implementation, review and further development of Union initiatives, take into consideration disaster risk prevention and management concerns as well as the United Nations Hyogo Framework for Action Programme (2005–2015) adopted on 22 January 2005, which stresses the need to put in place procedures for assessment of the disaster risk implications of major infrastructure projects.*

(15) *In order to ensure a high level of protection of the environment, precautionary actions need to be taken for certain projects which, because of their vulnerability to major accidents, and/or natural disasters (such as flooding, sea level rise, or earthquakes) are likely to have significant adverse effects on the environment. For such projects, it is important to consider their vulnerability (exposure and resilience) to major accidents and/or disasters, the risk of those accidents and/or disasters*

occurring and the implications for the likelihood of significant adverse effects on the environment. In order to avoid duplications, it should be possible to use any relevant information available and obtained through risk assessments carried out pursuant to Union legislation, such as Directive 2012/18/EU of the European Parliament and the Council and Council Directive 2009/71/Euratom, or through relevant assessments carried out pursuant to national legislation provided that the requirements of this Directive are met.

(16) *For the protection and promotion of cultural heritage comprising urban historical sites and landscapes, which are an integral part of the cultural diversity that the Union is committed to respecting and promoting in accordance with Article 167(4) TFEU, the definitions and principles developed in relevant Council of Europe Conventions, in particular the European Convention for the Protection of the Archaeological Heritage of 6 May 1969, the Convention for the Protection of the Architectural Heritage of Europe of 3 October 1985, the European Landscape Convention of 20 October 2000, the Framework Convention on the Value of Cultural Heritage for Society of 27 October 2005 can be useful. In order to better preserve historical and cultural heritage and the landscape, it is important to address the visual impact of projects, namely the change in the appearance or view of the built or natural landscape and urban areas, in environmental impact assessments.*

(17) *When applying Directive 2011/92/EU, it is necessary to ensure smart, sustainable and inclusive growth, in line with the objectives set out in the Commission's Communication of 3 March 2010 entitled 'Europe 2020 – A strategy for smart, sustainable and inclusive growth'.*

(15) It is desirable to lay down strengthened provisions concerning environmental impact assessment in a transboundary context to take account of developments at international level. The European Community signed the Convention on Environmental Impact Assessment in a Transboundary Context on 25 February 1991, and ratified it on 24 June 1997.

(4) *In order to coordinate and facilitate the assessment procedures for cross-border projects, and, in particular, to conduct consultations in accordance with the Convention on Environmental Impact Assessment in a Transboundary Context of 25 February 1991 (Espoo-Convention), the Member States concerned may set up, on the basis of equal representation, a joint body.*

(5) *The mechanisms set out in Regulations (EU) No 347/2013, (EU) No 1315/2013 and (EU) No 1316/2013 of the European Parliament and of the Council, which are relevant for Union co-financed infrastructure projects, may also facilitate the implementation of the requirements of Directive 2011/92/EU.*

(16) Effective public participation in the taking of decisions enables the public to express, and the decision-maker to take account of, opinions and concerns which may be relevant to those decisions, thereby increasing the accountability

and transparency of the decision-making process and contributing to public awareness of environmental issues and support for the decisions taken.

(17) Participation, including participation by associations, organisations and groups, in particular non- governmental organisations promoting environmental protection, should accordingly be fostered, including, inter alia, by promoting environmental education of the public.

(18) The European Community signed the UN/ECE Convention on Access to Information, Public Participation in Decision-Making and Access to Justice in Environmental Matters (the Aarhus Convention) on 25 June 1998 and ratified it on 17 February 2005.

(19) Among the objectives of the Aarhus Convention is the desire to guarantee rights of public participation in decision-making in environmental matters in order to contribute to the protection of the right to live in an environment which is adequate for personal health and well-being.

(20) Article 6 of the Aarhus Convention provides for public participation in decisions on the specific activities listed in Annex I thereto and on activities not so listed which may have a significant effect on the environment.

(18) With a view to strengthening public access to information and transparency, timely environmental information with regard to the implementation of this Directive should also be accessible in electronic format. Member States should therefore establish at least a central portal or points of access, at the appropriate administrative level, that allow the public to access that information easily and effectively.

(21) Article 9(2) and (4) of the Aarhus Convention provides for access to judicial or other procedures for challenging the substantive or procedural legality of decisions, acts or omissions subject to the public participation provisions of Article 6 of that Convention.

(22) However, this Directive should not be applied to projects the details of which are adopted by a specific act of national legislation, since the objectives of this Directive, including that of supplying information, are achieved through the legislative process.

(24) In the case of projects adopted by a specific act of national legislation, Member States should ensure that the objectives of this Directive relating to public consultation are achieved through the legislative process.

(19) Experience has shown that in cases of projects, or parts of projects, serving defence purposes, including projects related to activities by allied forces on the territory of Member States in accordance with international obligations, the application of Directive 2011/92/EU could result in the disclosure of relevant confidential information which would undermine defence purposes. Provision should therefore be made to authorise Member States not to apply that Directive in such cases, where appropriate.

(20) *Experience has shown that, as regards projects having as their sole purpose the response to cases of civil emergency, compliance with Directive 2011/92/EU could have adverse effects inter alia on the environment, and provision should therefore be made to authorise Member States not to apply that Directive in such cases, where appropriate.*

(23) Furthermore, it may be appropriate in exceptional cases to exempt a specific project from the assessment procedures laid down by this Directive, subject to appropriate information being supplied to the Commission and to the public concerned.

(34) *With a view to ensuring transparency and accountability, the competent authority should be required to substantiate its decision to grant development consent in respect of a project, indicating that it has taken into consideration the results of the consultations carried out and the relevant information gathered.*

(35) *Member States should ensure that mitigation and compensation measures are implemented, and that appropriate procedures are determined regarding the monitoring of significant adverse effects on the environment resulting from the construction and operation of a project, inter alia, to identify unforeseen significant adverse effects, in order to be able to undertake appropriate remedial action. Such monitoring should not duplicate or add to monitoring required pursuant to Union legislation other than this Directive and to national legislation.*

(36) *In order to stimulate more efficient decision-making and increase legal certainty, Member States should ensure that the various steps of the environmental impact assessment of projects are carried out within a reasonable period of time, depending on the nature, complexity, location and size of the project. Such time-frames should, under no circumstances, compromise the achievement of high standards for the protection of the environment, particularly those resulting from Union legislation on the environment other than this Directive, and effective public participation and access to justice.*

(37) *In order to improve the effectiveness of the assessments, reduce administrative complexity and increase economic efficiency, where the obligation to carry out assessments related to environmental issues arises simultaneously from this Directive and Directive 92/43/EEC and/or Directive 2009/147/EC, Member States should ensure that coordinated and/ or joint procedures fulfilling the requirements of these Directives are provided, where appropriate and taking into account their specific organisational characteristics. Where the obligation to carry out assessments related to environmental issues arises simultaneously from this Directive and from other Union legislation, such as Directive 2000/60/EC of the European Parliament and of the Council (16), Directive 2001/42/EC, Directive 2008/98/EC of the European Parliament and of the Council (17), Directive 2010/75/EU of the European Parliament and of the Council (18) and Directive 2012/18/EU, Member States should be able*

to provide for coordinated and/ or joint procedures fulfilling the requirements of the relevant Union legislation. Where coordinated or joint procedures are set up, Member States should designate an authority responsible for performing the corresponding duties. Taking into account institutional structures, Member States should be able to, where they deem it necessary, designate more than one authority.

(38) *Member States should lay down rules on penalties applicable to infringements of the national provisions adopted pursuant to this Directive. Member States should be free to decide the kind or form of those penalties. The penalties thus provided for should be effective, proportionate and dissuasive.*

(24) Since the objectives of this Directive cannot be sufficiently achieved by the Member States and can therefore, by reason of the scale and effects of the action, be better achieved at Union level, the Union may adopt measures in accordance with the principle of subsidiarity as set out in Article 5 of the Treaty on European Union. In accordance with the principle of proportionality, as set out in that Article, this Directive does not go beyond what is necessary in order to achieve those objectives.

(41) *Since the objective of this Directive, namely to ensure a high level of protection of the environment and of human health, through the establishment of minimum requirements for the environmental impact assessment of projects, cannot be sufficiently achieved by the Member States but can rather, by reason of the scope, seriousness and transboundary nature of the environmental issues to be addressed, be better achieved at Union level, the Union may adopt measures, in accordance with the principle of subsidiarity as set out in Article 5 of the Treaty on European Union. In accordance with the principle of proportionality, as set out in that Article, this Directive does not go beyond what is necessary in order to achieve that objective.*

(25) This Directive should be without prejudice to the obligations of the Member States relating to the time limits for transposition into national law of the Directives set out in Annex v, Part B,

(39) *In accordance with the principles of legal certainty and proportionality and in order to ensure that the transition from the existing regime, laid down in Directive 2011/92/EU, to the new regime that will result from the amendments contained in this Directive is as smooth as possible, it is appropriate to lay down transitional measures. Those measures should ensure that the regulatory environment in relation to an environmental impact assessment is not altered, with regard to a particular developer, where any procedural steps have already been initiated under the existing regime and a development consent or another binding decision required in order to comply with the aims of this Directive has not yet been granted to the project. Accordingly, the related provisions of Directive 2011/92/EU prior to its amendment by this Directive should apply to projects for which the screening procedure has been initiated, the scoping procedure has been initiated, (where*

scoping was requested by the developer or required by the competent authority) or the environmental impact assessment report is submitted before the time-limit for transposition.

(40) *In accordance with the Joint Political Declaration of Member States and the Commission of 28 September 2011 on explanatory documents(19), Member States have undertaken to accompany, in justified cases, the notification of their transposition measures with one or more documents explaining the relationship between the components of a directive and the corresponding parts of national transposition instruments. With regard to this Directive, the legislator considers the transmission of such documents to be justified.*

(42) *Directive 2011/92/EU should therefore be amended accordingly,*

Have adopted this directive:

Article 1

1. This Directive shall apply to the assessment of the environmental effects of those public and private projects which are likely to have significant effects on the environment.
2. For the purposes of this Directive, the following definitions shall apply:
   (a) "project" means:
   - the execution of construction works or of other installations or schemes,
   - other interventions in the natural surroundings and landscape including those involving the extraction of mineral resources;

   (b) "developer" means the applicant for authorisation for a private project or the public authority which initiates a project;

   (c) "development consent" means the decision of the competent authority or authorities which entitles the developer to proceed with the project;

   (d) "public" means one or more natural or legal persons and, in accordance with national legislation or practice, their associations, organisations or groups;

   (e) "public concerned" means the public affected or likely to be affected by, or having an interest in, the environmental decision-making procedures referred to in Article 2(2). For the purposes of this definition, non-governmental organisations promoting environmental protection and meeting any requirements under national law shall be deemed to have an interest;

   (f) "competent authority or authorities" means that authority or those authorities which the Member States designate as responsible for performing the duties arising from this Directive.

   (g) *"environmental impact assessment" means a process consisting of:*

(*i*) *the preparation of an environmental impact assessment report by the developer, as referred to in Article 5(1) and (2);*
(*ii*) *the carrying out of consultations as referred to in Article 6 and, where relevant, Article 7;*
(*iii*) *the examination by the competent authority of the information presented in the environmental impact assessment report and any supplementary information provided, where necessary, by the developer in accordance with Article 5(3), and any relevant information received through the consultations under Articles 6 and 7;*
(*iv*) *the reasoned conclusion by the competent authority on the significant effects of the project on the environment, taking into account the results of the examination referred to in point (iii) and, where appropriate, its own supplementary examination; and*
(*v*) *the integration of the competent authority's reasoned conclusion into any of the decisions referred to in Article 8a.*

3. Member States may decide, on a case-by-case basis *and* if so provided under national law, not to apply this Directive to projects, *or parts of projects, having* defence *as their sole* purpose, *or to projects having the response to civil emergencies as their sole purpose,* if they deem that such application would have an adverse effect on those purposes.

Article 2

1. Member States shall adopt all measures necessary to ensure that, before *development* consent is given, projects likely to have significant effects on the environment by virtue, inter alia, of their nature, size or location are made subject to a requirement for development consent and an assessment with regard to their effects *on the environment.* Those projects are defined in Article 4.
2. The environmental impact assessment may be integrated into the existing procedures for *development* consent to projects in the Member States, or, failing this, into other procedures or into procedures to be established to comply with the aims of this Directive.
3. *In the case of projects for which the obligation to carry out assessments of the effects on the environment arises simultaneously from this Directive and from Council Directive 92/43/EEC and/or Directive 2009/147/EC of the European Parliament and the Council, Member States shall, where appropriate, ensure that coordinated and/or joint procedures fulfilling the requirements of that Union legislation are provided for.*

In the case of projects for which the obligation to carry out assessments of the effects on the environment arises simultaneously from this Directive and Union legislation other than the Directives listed in the first subparagraph, Member States may provide for coordinated and/or joint procedures.

Under the coordinated procedure referred to in the first and second subparagraphs, Member States shall endeavour to coordinate the various individual assessments of the environmental impact of a particular project, required by the relevant Union legislation, by designating an authority for this purpose, without prejudice to any provisions to the contrary contained in other relevant Union legislation.

Under the joint procedure referred to in the first and second subparagraphs, Member States shall endeavour to provide for a single assessment of the environmental impact of a particular project required by the relevant Union legislation, without prejudice to any provisions to the contrary contained in other relevant Union legislation.

The Commission shall provide guidance regarding the setting up of any coordinated or joint procedures for projects that are simultaneously subject to assessments under this Directive and Directives 92/43/EEC, 2000/60/EC, 2009/147/EC or 2010/75/EU.

4. Without prejudice to Article 7, Member States may, in exceptional cases, exempt a specific project from the provisions laid down in this Directive, *where the application of those provisions would result in adversely affecting the purpose of the project, provided the objectives of this Directive are met.*

   In that event, the Member States shall:

   (a) consider whether another form of assessment would be appropriate;

   (b) make available to the public concerned the information obtained under other forms of assessment referred to in point (a), the information relating to the decision granting exemption and the reasons for granting it;

   (c) inform the Commission, prior to granting consent, of the reasons justifying the exemption granted, and provide it with the information made available, where applicable, to their own nationals.

   The Commission shall immediately forward the documents received to the other Member States.

   The Commission shall report annually to the European Parliament and to the Council on the application of this paragraph.

5. *Without prejudice to Article 7, in cases where a project is adopted by a specific act of national legislation, Member States may exempt that project from the provisions relating to public consultation laid down in this Directive, provided the objectives of this Directive are met.*

   Member States shall inform the Commission of any application of the exemption referred to in the first subparagraph every two years from 16 May 2017.

Article 3

1. The environmental impact assessment shall identify, describe and assess in an appropriate manner, in the light of each individual case, the direct and indirect *significant* effects of a project on the following factors:
   (*a*) *population and human health;*
   (*b*) *biodiversity, with particular attention to species and habitats protected under Directive 92/43/EEC*
   and Directive 2009/147/EC;
   (*c*) *land*, soil, water, air and climate;
   (*d*) material assets, cultural heritage *and the landscape*;
   (*e*) *the interaction between the factors referred to in points (a) to (d).*
2. *The effects referred to in paragraph 1 on the factors set out therein shall include the expected effects deriving from the vulnerability of the project to risks of major accidents and/or disasters that are relevant to the project concerned.*

Article 4

1. Subject to Article 2(4), projects listed in Annex I shall be made subject to an assessment in accordance with Articles 5 to 10.
2. Subject to Article 2(4), for projects listed in Annex II, Member States shall determine whether the project shall be made subject to an assessment in accordance with Articles 5 to 10. Member States shall make that determination through:
   (a) a case-by-case examination;
   or
   (b) thresholds or criteria set by the Member State.
   Member States may decide to apply both procedures referred to in points (a) and (b).
3. Where a case-by-case examination is carried out or thresholds or criteria are set for the purpose of paragraph 2, the relevant selection criteria set out in Annex III shall be taken into account. *Member States may set thresholds or criteria to determine when projects need not undergo either the determination under paragraphs 4 and 5 or an environmental impact assessment, and/or thresholds or criteria to determine when projects shall in any case be made subject to an environmental impact assessment without undergoing a determination set out under paragraphs 4 and 5.*
4. *Where Member States decide to require a determination for projects listed in Annex II, the developer shall provide information on the characteristics of the project and*

its likely significant effects on the environment. The detailed list of information to be provided is specified in Annex IIA. The developer shall take into account, where relevant, the available results of other relevant assessments of the effects on the environment carried out pursuant to Union legislation other than this Directive. The developer may also provide a description of any features of the project and/or measures envisaged to avoid or prevent what might otherwise have been significant adverse effects on the environment.

5. *The competent authority shall make its determination, on the basis of the information provided by the developer in accordance with paragraph 4 taking into account, where relevant, the results of preliminary verifications or assessments of the effects on the environment carried out pursuant to Union legislation other than this Directive. The determination shall be made available to the public and:*
   (*a*) *where it is decided that an environmental impact assessment is required, state the main reasons for requiring such assessment with reference to the relevant criteria listed in Annex III; or*
   (*b*) *where it is decided that an environmental impact assessment is not required, state the main reasons for not requiring such assessment with reference to the relevant criteria listed in Annex III,*

   and, where proposed by the developer, state any features of the project and/or measures envisaged to avoid or prevent what might otherwise have been significant adverse effects on the environment.

6. *Member States shall ensure that the competent authority makes its determination as soon as possible and within a period of time not exceeding 90 days from the date on which the developer has submitted all the information required pursuant to paragraph 4. In exceptional cases, for instance relating to the nature, complexity, location or size of the project, the competent authority may extend that deadline to make its determination; in that event, the competent authority shall inform the developer in writing of the reasons justifying the extension and of the date when its determination is expected.*

Article 5

1. *Where an environmental impact assessment is required, the developer shall prepare and submit an environmental impact assessment report. The information to be provided by the developer shall include at least:*
   (*a*) *a description of the project comprising information on the site, design, size and other relevant features of the project;*
   (*b*) *a description of the likely significant effects of the project on the environment;*

(c) *a description of the features of the project and/or measures envisaged in order to avoid, prevent or reduce and, if possible, offset likely significant adverse effects on the environment;*

(d) *a description of the reasonable alternatives studied by the developer, which are relevant to the project and its specific characteristics, and an indication of the main reasons for the option chosen, taking into account the effects of the project on the environment;*

(e) *a non-technical summary of the information referred to in points (a) to (d); and*

(f) *any additional information specified in Annex IV relevant to the specific characteristics of a particular project or type of project and to the environmental features likely to be affected.*

Where an opinion is issued pursuant to paragraph 2, the environmental impact assessment report shall be based on that opinion, and include the information that may reasonably be required for reaching a reasoned conclusion on the significant effects of the project on the environment, taking into account current knowledge and methods of assessment. The developer shall, with a view to avoiding duplication of assessments, take into account the available results of other relevant assessments under Union or national legislation, in preparing the environmental impact assessment report.

2. *Where requested by the developer, the competent authority, taking into account the information provided by the developer in particular on the specific characteristics of the project, including its location and technical capacity, and its likely impact on the environment, shall issue an opinion on the scope and level of detail of the information to be included by the developer in the environmental impact assessment report in accordance with paragraph 1 of this Article.* The competent authority shall consult the authorities referred to in Article 6(1) before it gives its opinion. Member States may also require the competent authorities to give an opinion *as referred to in the first subparagraph,* irrespective of whether the developer so requests.

3. *In order to ensure the completeness and quality of the environmental impact assessment report:*

(a) *the developer shall ensure that the environmental impact assessment report is prepared by competent experts;*

(b) *the competent authority shall ensure that it has, or has access as necessary to, sufficient expertise to examine the environmental impact assessment report; and*

(c) *where necessary, the competent authority shall seek from the developer supplementary information, in accordance with Annex IV, which is directly relevant to reaching the reasoned conclusion on the significant effects of the project on the environment.*

4. Member States shall, if necessary, ensure that any authorities holding relevant information, with particular reference to Article 3, make this information available to the developer.

Article 6

1. Member States shall take the measures necessary to ensure that the authorities likely to be concerned by the project by reason of their specific environmental responsibilities *or local and regional competences* are given an opportunity to express their opinion on the information supplied by the developer and on the request for development consent, *taking into account, where appropriate, the cases referred to in Article 8a(3)*. To that end, Member States shall designate the authorities to be consulted, either in general terms or on a case-by-case basis. The information gathered pursuant to Article 5 shall be forwarded to those authorities. Detailed arrangements for consultation shall be laid down by the Member States.
2. *In order to ensure the effective participation of the public concerned in the decision-making procedures*, the public shall be informed *electronically and by public notices or by other appropriate means*, of the following matters early in the environmental decision-making procedures referred to in Article 2(2) and, at the latest, as soon as information can reasonably be provided:
   (a) the request for development consent;
   (b) the fact that the project is subject to an environmental impact assessment procedure and, where relevant, the fact that Article 7 applies;
   (c) details of the competent authorities responsible for taking the decision, those from which relevant information can be obtained, those to which comments or questions can be submitted, and details of the time schedule for transmitting comments or questions;
   (d) the nature of possible decisions or, where there is one, the draft decision;
   (e) an indication of the availability of the information gathered pursuant to Article 5;
   (f) an indication of the times and places at which, and the means by which, the relevant information will be made available;
   (g) details of the arrangements for public participation made pursuant to paragraph 5 of this Article.
3. Member States shall ensure that, within reasonable time-frames, the following is made available to the public concerned:
   (a) any information gathered pursuant to Article 5;
   (b) in accordance with national legislation, the main reports and advice issued to the competent authority or authorities at the time when the public concerned is informed in accordance with paragraph 2 of this Article;

(c) in accordance with the provisions of Directive 2003/4/EC of the European Parliament and of the Council of 28 January 2003 on public access to environmental information, information other than that referred to in paragraph 2 of this Article which is relevant for the decision in accordance with Article 8 of this Directive and which only becomes available after the time the public concerned was informed in accordance with paragraph 2 of this Article.

4. The public concerned shall be given early and effective opportunities to participate in the environmental decision-making procedures referred to in Article 2(2) and shall, for that purpose, be entitled to express comments and opinions when all options are open to the competent authority or authorities before the decision on the request for development consent is taken.

5. The detailed arrangements for informing the public, (for example by bill posting within a certain radius or publication in local newspapers), and for consulting the public concerned, (for example by written submissions or by way of a public inquiry), shall be determined by the Member States. *Member States shall take the necessary measures to ensure that the relevant information is electronically accessible to the public, through at least a central portal or easily accessible points of access, at the appropriate administrative level.*

6. Reasonable time-frames for the different phases shall be provided *for*, allowing sufficient time for:
   (*a*) *informing the authorities referred to in paragraph 1 and the public; and*
   (*b*) *the authorities referred to in paragraph 1 and the public concerned to prepare and participate effectively in the environmental decision-making, subject to the provisions of this Article.*

7. *The time-frames for consulting the public concerned on the environmental impact assessment report referred to in Article 5(1) shall not be shorter than 30 days.*

Article 7

1. Where a Member State is aware that a project is likely to have significant effects on the environment in another Member State or where a Member State likely to be significantly affected so requests, the Member State in whose territory the project is intended to be carried out shall send to the affected Member State as soon as possible and no later than when informing its own public, inter alia:
   (a) a description of the project, together with any available information on its possible transboundary impact;
   (b) information on the nature of the decision which may be taken.

The Member State in whose territory the project is intended to be carried out shall give the other Member State a reasonable time in which to indicate whether it wishes to participate in the environmental decision-making procedures referred to in Article 2(2), and may include the information referred to in paragraph 2 of this Article.

2. If a Member State which receives information pursuant to paragraph 1 indicates that it intends to participate in the environmental decision-making procedures referred to in Article 2(2), the Member State in whose territory the project is intended to be carried out shall, if it has not already done so, send to the affected Member State the information required to be given pursuant to Article 6(2) and made available pursuant to points (a) and (b) of Article 6(3).

3. The Member States concerned, each insofar as it is concerned, shall also:
   (a) arrange for the information referred to in paragraphs 1 and 2 to be made available, within a reasonable time, to the authorities referred to in Article 6(1) and the public concerned in the territory of the Member State likely to be significantly affected; and
   (b) ensure that the authorities referred to in Article 6(1) and the public concerned are given an opportunity, before development consent for the project is granted, to forward their opinion within a reasonable time on the information supplied to the competent authority in the Member State in whose territory the project is intended to be carried out.

4. The Member States concerned shall enter into consultations regarding, inter alia, the potential transboundary effects of the project and the measures envisaged to reduce or eliminate such effects and shall agree on a reasonable time-frame for the duration of the consultation period.
Such consultations may be conducted through an appropriate joint body.

5. The detailed arrangements for implementing *paragraphs 1 to 4 of* this Article, *including the establishment of time-frames for consultations, shall* be determined by the Member States concerned, *on the basis of the arrangements and time-frames referred to in Article 6(5) to (7)*, and shall be such as to enable the public concerned in the territory of the affected Member State to participate effectively in the environmental decision-making procedures referred to in Article 2(2) for the project.

Article 8

The results of consultations and the information gathered pursuant to Articles 5 to 7 shall be *duly* taken into *account* in the development consent procedure.

Article 8a

1. *The decision to grant development consent shall incorporate at least the following information:*
   (*a*) *the reasoned conclusion referred to in Article 1(2)(g)(iv);*
   (*b*) *any environmental conditions attached to the decision, a description of any features of the project and/or measures envisaged to avoid, prevent or reduce and, if possible, offset significant adverse effects on the environment as well as, where appropriate, monitoring measures.*
2. *The decision to refuse development consent shall state the main reasons for the refusal.*
3. *In the event Member States make use of the procedures referred to in Article 2(2) other than the procedures for development consent, the requirements of paragraphs 1 and 2 of this Article, as appropriate, shall be deemed to be fulfilled when any decision issued in the context of those procedures contains the information referred to in those paragraphs and there are mechanisms in place which enable the fulfillment of the requirements of paragraph 6 of this Article.*
4. *In accordance with the requirements referred to in paragraph 1(b), Member States shall ensure that the features of the project and/or measures envisaged to avoid, prevent or reduce and, if possible, offset significant adverse effects on the environment are implemented by the developer, and shall determine the procedures regarding the monitoring of significant adverse effects on the environment.*
   The type of parameters to be monitored and the duration of the monitoring shall be proportionate to the nature, location and size of the project and the significance of its effects on the environment.
   Existing monitoring arrangements resulting from Union legislation other than this Directive and from national legislation may be used if appropriate, with a view to avoiding duplication of monitoring.
5. *Member States shall ensure that the competent authority takes any of the decisions referred to in paragraphs 1 to 3 within a reasonable period of time.*
6 *The competent authority shall be satisfied that the reasoned conclusion referred to in Article 1(2)(g)(iv), or any of the decisions referred to in paragraph 3 of this Article, is still up to date when taking a decision to grant development consent. To that effect, Member States may set time-frames for the validity of the reasoned conclusion referred to in Article 1(2)(g)(iv) or any of the decisions referred to in paragraph 3 of this Article.*

Article 9

1. When a decision to grant or refuse development consent has been taken, the competent authority or authorities shall *promptly* inform the public *and the*

authorities referred to in Article 6(1) thereof, in accordance with the *national* procedures, and shall *ensure that the following information is* available to the public *and to the authorities referred to in Article 6(1), taking into account, where appropriate, the cases referred to in Article 8a(3)*:

(a) the content of the decision and any conditions attached thereto *as referred to in Article 8a(1) and (2)*;

(b) the main reasons and considerations on which the decision is based, including information about the public participation process. *This also includes the summary of the results of the consultations and the information gathered pursuant to Articles 5 to 7 and how those results have been incorporated or otherwise addressed, in particular the comments received from the affected Member State referred to in Article 7.*

2. The competent authority or authorities shall inform any Member State which has been consulted pursuant to Article 7, forwarding to it the information referred to in paragraph 1 of this Article.

The consulted Member States shall ensure that that information is made available in an appropriate manner to the public concerned in their own territory.

Article 9a

Member States shall ensure that the competent authority or authorities perform the duties arising from this Directive in an objective manner and do not find themselves in a situation giving rise to a conflict of interest.

Where the competent authority is also the developer, Member States shall at least implement, within their organisation of administrative competences, an appropriate separation between conflicting functions when performing the duties arising from this Directive.

Article 10

Without prejudice to Directive 2003/4/EC, the provisions of this Directive shall not affect the obligation on the competent authorities to respect the limitations imposed by national laws, regulations and administrative provisions, and accepted legal practices with regard to commercial and industrial confidentiality, including intellectual property, and the safeguarding of the public interest.

Where Article 7 applies, the transmission of information to another Member State and the receipt of information by another Member State shall be subject to the limitations in force in the Member State in which the project is proposed.

Article 10a

Member States shall lay down rules on penalties applicable to infringements of the national provisions adopted pursuant to this Directive. The penalties thus provided for shall be effective, proportionate and dissuasive.

Article 11

1. Member States shall ensure that, in accordance with the relevant national legal system, members of the public concerned:
   (a) having a sufficient interest, or alternatively;
   (b) maintaining the impairment of a right, where administrative procedural law of a Member State requires this as a precondition;

   have access to a review procedure before a court of law or another independent and impartial body established by law to challenge the substantive or procedural legality of decisions, acts or omissions subject to the public participation provisions of this Directive.
2. Member States shall determine at what stage the decisions, acts or omissions may be challenged.
3. What constitutes a sufficient interest and impairment of a right shall be determined by the Member States, consistently with the objective of giving the public concerned wide access to justice. To that end, the interest of any non-governmental organisation meeting the requirements referred to in Article 1(2) shall be deemed sufficient for the purpose of point (a) of paragraph 1 of this Article. Such organisations shall also be deemed to have rights capable of being impaired for the purpose of point (b) of paragraph 1 of this Article.
4. The provisions of this Article shall not exclude the possibility of a preliminary review procedure before an administrative authority and shall not affect the requirement of exhaustion of administrative review procedures prior to recourse to judicial review procedures, where such a requirement exists under national law. Any such procedure shall be fair, equitable, timely and not prohibitively expensive.
5. In order to further the effectiveness of the provisions of this Article, Member States shall ensure that practical information is made available to the public on access to administrative and judicial review procedures.

Article 12

1. The Member States and the Commission shall exchange information on the experience gained in applying this Directive.

2. *In particular, every six years from 16 May 2017 Member States shall inform the Commission, where such data are available, of:*
   - (a) *the number of projects referred to in Annexes I and II made subject to an environmental impact assessment in accordance with Articles 5 to 10;*
   - (b) *the breakdown of environmental impact assessments according to the project categories set out in Annexes I and II;*
   - (c) *the number of projects referred to in Annex II made subject to a determination in accordance with Article 4(2);*
   - (d) *the average duration of the environmental impact assessment process;*
   - (e) *general estimates on the average direct costs of environmental impact assessments, including the impact from the application of this Directive to SMEs.*
3. On the basis of that exchange of information, the Commission shall if necessary submit additional proposals to the European Parliament and to the Council, with a view to ensuring that this Directive is applied in a sufficiently coordinated manner.

Article 13

Member States shall communicate to the Commission the texts of the provisions of national law which they adopt in the field covered by this Directive.

Article 2

1. *Without prejudice to Article 3, Member States shall bring into force the laws, regulations and administrative provisions necessary to comply with this Directive by 16 May 2017.*
   When Member States adopt those provisions, they shall contain a reference to this Directive or be accompanied by such a reference on the occasion of their official publication. Member States shall determine how such reference is to be made.
2. *Member States shall communicate to the Commission the text of the main provisions of national law which they adopt in the field covered by this Directive.*

Article 3

1. *Projects in respect of which the determination referred to in Article 4(2) of Directive 2011/92/EU was initiated before 16 May 2017 shall be subject to the obligations referred to in Article 4 of Directive 2011/92/EU prior to its amendment by this Directive.*
2 *Projects shall be subject to the obligations referred to in Article 3 and Articles 5 to 11 of Directive 2011/92/EU prior to its amendment by this Directive where, before 16 May 2017:*

(*a*) *the procedure regarding the opinion referred to in Article 5(2) of Directive 2011/92/EU was initiated; or*
(*b*) *the information referred to in Article 5(1) of Directive 2011/92/EU was provided.*

Article 14

Directive 85/337/EEC, as amended by the Directives listed in Annex V, Part A, is repealed, without prejudice to the obligations of the Member States relating to the time limits for transposition into national law of the Directives set out in Annex V, Part B.

References to the repealed Directive shall be construed as references to this Directive and shall be read in accordance with the correlation table in Annex VI.

Article 15

This Directive shall enter into force on the 20th day following its publication in the Official Journal of the European Union.

Article 4

This Directive shall enter into force on the twentieth day following that of its publication in the Official Journal of the European Union.

Article 16

This Directive is addressed to the Member States.

Article 5

This Directive is addressed to the Member States.

Annex I – Projects Referred to in Article 4(1)

1. Crude-oil refineries (excluding undertakings manufacturing only lubricants from crude oil) and installations for the gasification and liquefaction of 500 tonnes or more of coal or bituminous shale per day.

2. (a) Thermal power stations and other combustion installations with a heat output of 300 megawatts or more;
   (b) Nuclear power stations and other nuclear reactors including the dismantling or decommissioning of such power stations or reactors[1] (except research installations for the production and conversion of fissionable and fertile materials, whose maximum power does not exceed 1 kilowatt continuous thermal load).
3. (a) Installations for the reprocessing of irradiated nuclear fuel;
   (b) Installations designed:
      (i) for the production or enrichment of nuclear fuel;
      (ii) for the processing of irradiated nuclear fuel or high-level radioactive waste;
      (iii) for the final disposal of irradiated nuclear fuel;
      (iv) solely for the final disposal of radioactive waste;
      (v) solely for the storage (planned for more than 10 years) of irradiated nuclear fuels or radioactive waste in a different site than the production site.
4. (a) Integrated works for the initial smelting of cast iron and steel;
   (b) Installations for the production of non-ferrous crude metals from ore, concentrates or secondary raw materials by metallurgical, chemical or electrolytic processes.
5. Installations for the extraction of asbestos and for the processing and transformation of asbestos and products containing asbestos: for asbestos-cement products, with an annual production of more than 20 000 tonnes of finished products, for friction material, with an annual production of more than 50 tonnes of finished products, and for other uses of asbestos, utilisation of more than 200 tonnes per year.
6. Integrated chemical installations, i.e. those installations for the manufacture on an industrial scale of substances using chemical conversion processes, in which several units are juxtaposed and are functionally linked to one another and which are:
   (a) for the production of basic organic chemicals;
   (b) for the production of basic inorganic chemicals;
   (c) for the production of phosphorous-, nitrogen- or potassium-based fertilisers (simple or compound fertilisers);
   (d) for the production of basic plant health products and of biocides;

1 Nuclear power stations and other nuclear reactors cease to be such an installation when all nuclear fuel and other radioactively contaminated elements have been removed permanently from the installation site.

(e) for the production of basic pharmaceutical products using a chemical or biological process;

(f) for the production of explosives.

7. (a) Construction of lines for long-distance railway traffic and of airports[2] with a basic runway length of 2 100 m or more;

(b) Construction of motorways and express roads;[3]

(c) Construction of a new road of four or more lanes, or realignment and/or widening of an existing road of two lanes or less so as to provide four or more lanes, where such new road or realigned and/or widened section of road would be 10 km or more in a continuous length.

8. (a) Inland waterways and ports for inland-waterway traffic which permit the passage of vessels of over 1 350 tonnes;

(b) Trading ports, piers for loading and unloading connected to land and outside ports (excluding ferry piers) which can take vessels of over 1 350 tonnes.

9. Waste disposal installations for the incineration, chemical treatment as defined in Annex I to Directive 2008/98/EC of the European Parliament and of the Council of 19 November 2008 on waste under heading D9, or landfill of hazardous waste, as defined in point 2 of Article 3 of that Directive.

10. Waste disposal installations for the incineration or chemical treatment as defined in Annex I to Directive 2008/98/EC under heading D9 of non-hazardous waste with a capacity exceeding 100 tonnes per day.

11. Groundwater abstraction or artificial groundwater recharge schemes where the annual volume of water abstracted or recharged is equivalent to or exceeds 10 million cubic metres.

12. (a) Works for the transfer of water resources between river basins where that transfer aims at preventing possible shortages of water and where the amount of water transferred exceeds 100 million cubic metres/year;

(b) In all other cases, works for the transfer of water resources between river basins where the multi-annual average flow of the basin of abstraction exceeds 2 000 million cubic metres/year and where the amount of water transferred exceeds 5 % of that flow.

In both cases transfers of piped drinking water are excluded.

13. Waste water treatment plants with a capacity exceeding 150 000 population equivalent as defined in point 6 of Article 2 of Council Directive 91/271/EEC of 21 May 1991 concerning urban waste-water treatment.

---

2 For the purposes of this Directive, 'airport' means an airport which complies with the definition in the 1944 Chicago Convention setting up the International Civil Aviation Organisation (Annex 14).

3 For the purposes of this Directive, 'express road' means a road which complies with the definition in the European Agreement on Main International Traffic Arteries of 15 November 1975.

14. Extraction of petroleum and natural gas for commercial purposes where the amount extracted exceeds 500 tonnes/day in the case of petroleum and 500 000 cubic metres/day in the case of gas.
15. Dams and other installations designed for the holding back or permanent storage of water, where a new or additional amount of water held back or stored exceeds 10 million cubic metres.
16. Pipelines with a diameter of more than 800 mm and a length of more than 40 km:
    (a) for the transport of gas, oil, chemicals;
    (b) for the transport of carbon dioxide (CO_2) streams for the purposes of geological storage, including associated booster stations.
17. Installations for the intensive rearing of poultry or pigs with more than: (a) 85 000 places for broilers, 60 000 places for hens;
    (b) 3 000 places for production pigs (over 30 kg); or
    (c) 900 places for sows.
18. Industrial plants for the production of:
    (a) pulp from timber or similar fibrous materials;
    (b) paper and board with a production capacity exceeding 200 tonnes per day.
19. Quarries and open-cast mining where the surface of the site exceeds 25 hectares, or peat extraction, where the surface of the site exceeds 150 hectares.
20. Construction of overhead electrical power lines with a voltage of 220 kV or more and a length of more than 15 km.
21. Installations for storage of petroleum, petrochemical, or chemical products with a capacity of 200 000 tonnes or more.
22. Storage sites pursuant to Directive 2009/31/EC of the European Parliament and of the Council of 23 April 2009 on the geological storage of carbon dioxide.
23. Installations for the capture of CO_2 streams for the purposes of geological storage pursuant to Directive 2009/31/EC from installations covered by this Annex, or where the total yearly capture of CO_2 is 1,5 megatonnes or more.
24. Any change to or extension of projects listed in this Annex where such a change or extension in itself meets the thresholds, if any, set out in this Annex.

Annex II – Projects Referred to in Article 4(2)

1. AGRICULTURE, SILVICULTURE AND AQUACULTURE
    (a) Projects for the restructuring of rural land holdings;
    (b) Projects for the use of uncultivated land or semi-natural areas for intensive agricultural purposes;

(c) Water management projects for agriculture, including irrigation and land drainage projects;
(d) Initial afforestation and deforestation for the purposes of conversion to another type of land use;
(e) Intensive livestock installations (projects not included in Annex I); (f) Intensive fish farming;
(g) Reclamation of land from the sea.

2. EXTRACTIVE INDUSTRY

(a) Quarries, open-cast mining and peat extraction (projects not included in Annex I); (b) Underground mining;
(c) Extraction of minerals by marine or fluvial dredging;
(d) Deep drillings, in particular:
   (i) geothermal drilling;
   (ii) drilling for the storage of nuclear waste material;
   (iii) drilling for water supplies;

with the exception of drillings for investigating the stability of the soil;

(e) Surface industrial installations for the extraction of coal, petroleum, natural gas and ores, as well as bituminous shale.

3. ENERGY INDUSTRY

(a) Industrial installations for the production of electricity, steam and hot water (projects not included in Annex I);
(b) Industrial installations for carrying gas, steam and hot water; transmission of electrical energy by overhead cables (projects not included in Annex I);
(c) Surface storage of natural gas;
(d) Underground storage of combustible gases; (e) Surface storage of fossil fuels;
(f) Industrial briquetting of coal and lignite;
(g) Installations for the processing and storage of radioactive waste (unless included in Annex I);
(h) Installations for hydroelectric energy production;
(i) Installations for the harnessing of wind power for energy production (wind farms);
(j) Installations for the capture of CO2 streams for the purposes of geological storage pursuant to Directive 2009/31/EC from installations not covered by Annex I to this Directive.

4. PRODUCTION AND PROCESSING OF METALS

(a) Installations for the production of pig iron or steel (primary or secondary fusion) including continuous casting;
(b) Installations for the processing of ferrous metals:
   (i) hot-rolling mills;
   (ii) smitheries with hammers;

(iii) application of protective fused metal coats;

(c) Ferrous metal foundries;

(d) Installations for the smelting, including the alloyage, of non-ferrous metals, excluding precious metals, including recovered products (refining, foundry casting, etc.);

(e) Installations for surface treatment of metals and plastic materials using an electrolytic or chemical process;

(f) Manufacture and assembly of motor vehicles and manufacture of motor-vehicle engines; (g) Shipyards;

(h) Installations for the construction and repair of aircraft;

(i) Manufacture of railway equipment;

(j) Swaging by explosives;

(k) Installations for the roasting and sintering of metallic ores.

5. MINERAL INDUSTRY

(a) Coke ovens (dry coal distillation);

(b) Installations for the manufacture of cement;

(c) Installations for the production of asbestos and the manufacture of asbestos products (projects not included in Annex I);

(d) Installations for the manufacture of glass including glass fibre;

(e) Installations for smelting mineral substances including the production of mineral fibres;

(f) Manufacture of ceramic products by burning, in particular roofing tiles, bricks, refractory bricks, tiles, stoneware or porcelain.

6. CHEMICAL INDUSTRY (PROJECTS NOT INCLUDED IN ANNEX I)

(a) Treatment of intermediate products and production of chemicals;

(b) Production of pesticides and pharmaceutical products, paint and varnishes, elastomers and peroxides;

(c) Storage facilities for petroleum, petrochemical and chemical products.

7. FOOD INDUSTRY

(a) Manufacture of vegetable and animal oils and fats;

(b) Packing and canning of animal and vegetable products; (c) Manufacture of dairy products;

(d) Brewing and malting;

(e) Confectionery and syrup manufacture;

(f) Installations for the slaughter of animals;

(g) Industrial starch manufacturing installations;

(h) Fish-meal and fish-oil factories;

(i) Sugar factories.

8. TEXTILE, LEATHER, WOOD AND PAPER INDUSTRIES

(a) Industrial plants for the production of paper and board (projects not included in Annex I);
(b) Plants for the pre-treatment (operations such as washing, bleaching, mercerisation) or dyeing of fibres or textiles;
(c) Plants for the tanning of hides and skins;
(d) Cellulose-processing and production installations.

9. RUBBER INDUSTRY

Manufacture and treatment of elastomer-based products.

10. INFRASTRUCTURE PROJECTS

(a) Industrial estate development projects;
(b) Urban development projects, including the construction of shopping centres and car parks;
(c) Construction of railways and intermodal transhipment facilities, and of intermodal terminals (projects not included in Annex I);
(d) Construction of airfields (projects not included in Annex I);
(e) Construction of roads, harbours and port installations, including fishing harbours (projects not included in Annex I);
(f) Inland-waterway construction not included in Annex I, canalisation and flood-relief works;
(g) Dams and other installations designed to hold water or store it on a long-term basis (projects not included in Annex I);
(h) Tramways, elevated and underground railways, suspended lines or similar lines of a particular type, used exclusively or mainly for passenger transport;
(i) Oil and gas pipeline installations and pipelines for the transport of CO2 streams for the purposes of geological storage (projects not included in Annex I);
(j) Installations of long-distance aqueducts;
(k) Coastal work to combat erosion and maritime works capable of altering the coast through the construction, for example, of dykes, moles, jetties and other sea defence works, excluding the maintenance and reconstruction of such works;
(l) Groundwater abstraction and artificial groundwater recharge schemes not included in Annex I;
(m) Works for the transfer of water resources between river basins not included in Annex I.

11. OTHER PROJECTS

(a) Permanent racing and test tracks for motorised vehicles;
(b) Installations for the disposal of waste (projects not included in Annex I); (c) Waste-water treatment plants (projects not included in Annex I);
(d) Sludge-deposition sites;

(e) Storage of scrap iron, including scrap vehicles;
(f) Test benches for engines, turbines or reactors;
(g) Installations for the manufacture of artificial mineral fibres;
(h) Installations for the recovery or destruction of explosive substances;
(i) Knackers' yards.

12. TOURISM AND LEISURE
(a) Ski runs, ski lifts and cable cars and associated developments;
(b) Marinas;
(c) Holiday villages and hotel complexes outside urban areas and associated developments;
(d) Permanent campsites and caravan sites;
(e) Theme parks.

13. (a) Any change or extension of projects listed in Annex I or this Annex, already authorised, executed or in the process of being executed, which may have significant adverse effects on the environment (change or extension not included in Annex I);
(b) Projects in Annex I, undertaken exclusively or mainly for the development and testing of new methods or products and not used for more than two years.

Annex II A – Information Referred to in Article 4(4)

(INFORMATION TO BE PROVIDED BY THE DEVELOPER ON THE PROJECTS LISTED IN ANNEX II)

1. A description of the project, including in particular:
(a) a description of the physical characteristics of the whole project and, where relevant, of demolition works;
(b) a description of the location of the project, with particular regard to the environmental sensitivity of geographical areas likely to be affected.

2. A description of the aspects of the environment likely to be significantly affected by the project.

3. A description of any likely significant effects, to the extent of the information available on such effects, of the project on the environment resulting from:
(a) the expected residues and emissions and the production of waste, where relevant;
(b) the use of natural resources, in particular soil, land, water and biodiversity.

The criteria of Annex III shall be taken into account, where relevant, when compiling the information in accordance with points 1 to 3.

Annex III – Selection Criteria Referred to in Article 4(3)

(*CRITERIA TO DETERMINE WHETHER THE PROJECTS LISTED IN ANNEX II SHOULD BE SUBJECT TO AN ENVIRONMENTAL IMPACT ASSESSMENT*)

1. Characteristics of projects

   The characteristics of projects must be considered, with particular regard to:

   (a) the size *and design* of the *whole* project;
   (b) cumulation with other *existing and/or approved* projects;
   (c) the use of natural resources, *in particular land, soil, water and biodiversity*;
   (d) the production of waste;
   (e) pollution and nuisances;
   (f) the risk of *major* accidents *and/ or disasters which are relevant to the project concerned, including those caused by climate change, in accordance with scientific knowledge;*
   (g) the risks to human health (for example due to water contamination or air pollution).

2. Location of projects

   The environmental sensitivity of geographical areas likely to be affected by projects must be considered, *with* particular *regard* to:

   (a) the existing *and approved* land use;
   (b) the relative abundance, *availability*, quality and regenerative capacity of natural resources (*including soil, land, water and biodiversity*) in the area *and its underground*;
   (c) the absorption capacity of the natural environment, paying particular attention to the following areas:
      (i) wetlands, *riparian areas, river mouths*;
      (ii) coastal zones *and the marine environment*;
      (iii) mountain and forest areas;
      (iv) nature reserves and parks;
      (v) areas classified or protected under *national* legislation; *Natura 2000* areas designated by Member States pursuant to Directive 92/43/EEC and Directive 2009/147/EC;
      (vi) areas in which *there has already been a failure to meet* the environmental quality standards, laid down in Union legislation *and relevant to the project, or in which it is considered that there is such a failure*;
      (vii) densely populated areas;
      (viii) landscapes *and sites* of historical, cultural or archaeological significance.

3. *Type and* characteristics of the potential impact

The *likely* significant effects of projects *on the environment* must be considered in relation to criteria set out in points 1 and 2 *of this Annex, with* regard to *the impact of the project on the factors specified in Article 3(1), taking into account*:

(a) the *magnitude and spatial* extent of the impact (*for example* geographical area and size of the population *likely to be affected*);
(*b*) *the nature of the impact;*
(*c*) *the transboundary nature of the impact;*
(*d*) the *intensity* and complexity of the impact;
(*e*) the probability of the impact;
(*f*) the *expected onset*, duration, frequency and reversibility of the impact;
(*g*) *the cumulation of the impact with the impact of other existing and/or approved projects;*
(*h*) *the possibility of effectively reducing the impact.*

Annex IV – Information Referred to in Article 5(1)

(*INFORMATION FOR THE ENVIRONMENTAL IMPACT ASSESSMENT REPORT*)

1. *Description of the project, including in particular:*
   (*a*) *a description of the location of the project;*
   (b) a description of the physical characteristics of the whole project, *including, where relevant, requisite demolition works*, and the land-use requirements during the construction and operational phases;
   (c) a description of the main characteristics of the *operational phase of the project* (*in particular any production process*), for instance, *energy demand and energy used*, nature and quantity of the materials *and natural resources* (*including water, land, soil and biodiversity*) used;
   (d) an estimate, by type and quantity, of expected residues and emissions (*such as* water, air, soil *and subsoil* pollution, noise, vibration, light, heat, radiation) *and quantities and types of waste produced during the construction and operation phases.*

2. *A description of the reasonable* alternatives (*for example in terms of project design, technology, location, size and scale*) studied by the developer, *which are relevant to the proposed project and its specific characteristics,* and an indication of the main reasons for this choice *selecting the chosen option, including a comparison of* the environmental effects.

3. *A description of the relevant aspects of the current state of the environment* (*baseline scenario*) *and an outline of the likely evolution thereof without implementation of the project as far as natural changes from the baseline scenario can be assessed with reasonable effort on the basis of the availability of environmental information and scientific knowledge.*

4. *A description* factors *specified in Article 3(1)* likely to be significantly affected by the proposed project, including in particular: population, *human health, biodiversity (for example fauna and flora), land (for example land take)*, soil (*for example organic matter, erosion, compaction, sealing*), water (*for example hydromorphological changes, quantity and quality*), air, *climate (for example greenhouse gas emissions, impacts relevant to adaptation*), material assets, *cultural heritage*, including architectural and archaeological heritage *aspects, and* landscape.
5. A description of the likely significant effects of the project on the environment resulting from, *inter alia:*
   (a) the *construction and* existence of the project, *including, where relevant, demolition works;*
   (b) the use of natural resources, *in particular land, soil, water and biodiversity, considering as far as possible the sustainable availability of these resources;*
   (c) the emission of pollutants, *noise, vibration, light, heat and radiation*, the creation of nuisances, *and the disposal and recovery of waste;*
   (*d*) *the risks to human health, cultural heritage or the environment (for example due to accidents or disasters);*
   (*e*) *the cumulation of effects with other existing and/or approved projects, taking into account any existing environmental problems relating to areas of particular environmental importance likely to be affected or the use of natural resources;*
   (*f*) *the impact of the project on climate (for example the nature and magnitude of greenhouse gas emissions) and the vulnerability of the project to climate change;*
   (*g*) *the technologies and the substances used.*

   The description of the likely significant effects on the factors specified in Article 3(1) should cover the direct effects and any indirect, secondary, cumulative, transboundary, short-term, medium- term and long-term, permanent and temporary, positive and negative effects of the project. This description should take into account the environmental protection objectives established at Union or Member State level which are relevant to the project.
6. *A* description of the forecasting methods *or evidence*, used to *identify and* assess the *significant* effects on the environment, *including details of difficulties (for example technical deficiencies or lack of knowledge) encountered compiling the required information and the main uncertainties involved.*
7. A description of the measures envisaged to *avoid*, prevent, reduce *or, if* possible, offset any *identified* significant adverse effects on the environment *and, where appropriate, of any proposed monitoring arrangements (for example the*

preparation of a post-project analysis). That description should explain the extent, to which significant adverse effects on the environment are avoided, prevented, reduced or offset, and should cover both the construction and operational phases.

8. *A description of the expected significant adverse effects of the project on the environment deriving from the vulnerability of the project to risks of major accidents and/or disasters which are relevant to the project concerned. Relevant information available and obtained through risk assessments pursuant to Union legislation such as Directive 2012/18/EU of the European Parliament and of the Council or Council Directive 2009/71/Euratom or relevant assessments carried out pursuant to national legislation may be used for this purpose provided that the requirements of this Directive are met. W here appropriate, this description should include measures envisaged to prevent or mitigate the significant adverse effects of such events on the environment and details of the preparedness for and proposed response to such emergencies.*
9. A non-technical summary of the information provided under points 1 to *8.*
10. *A reference list detailing the sources used for the descriptions and assessments included in the report.*

Annex V

PART B

List of time limits for transposition into national law
(referred to in Article 14)

Directive 85/337/EEC	3 July 1988
Directive 97/11/EC	14 March 1999
Directive 2003/35/EC	25 June 2005
Directive 2009/31/EC	25 June 2011

This document is meant purely as a documentation tool and the author does not assume any liability for its contents.
Available at: https://ec.europa.eu/environment/eia/pdf/EIA_Directive_informal .pdf (accessed 17 June 2021)

APPENDIX 4

Convention on Access to Information, Public Participation in Decision-Making and Access to Justice in Environmental Matters (Aarhus Convention)

25 June 1998, 38 ILM 517 (1999), in force 30 October 2001

The Parties to this Convention,

Recalling principle 1 of the Stockholm Declaration on the Human Environment,

Recalling also principle 10 of the Rio Declaration on Environment and Development,

Recalling further General Assembly resolutions 37/7 of 28 October 1982 on the World Charter for Nature and 45/94 of 14 December 1990 on the need to ensure a healthy environment for the well-being of individuals,

Recalling the European Charter on Environment and Health adopted at the First European Conference on Environment and Health of the World Health Organization in Frankfurt-am-Main, Germany, on 8 December 1989,

Affirming the need to protect, preserve and improve the state of the environment and to ensure sustainable and environmentally sound development,

Recognizing that adequate protection of the environment is essential to human well-being and the enjoyment of basic human rights, including the right to life itself,

Recognizing also that every person has the right to live in an environment adequate to his or her health and well-being, and the duty, both individually and in association with others, to protect and improve the environment for the benefit of present and future generations,

Considering that, to be able to assert this right and observe this duty, citizens must have access to information, be entitled to participate in decision-making and have access to justice in environmental matters, and acknowledging in this regard that citizens may need assistance in order to exercise their rights,

Recognizing that, in the field of the environment, improved access to information and public participation in decision-making enhance the quality and the implementation of decisions, contribute to public awareness of environmental issues, give the public the opportunity to express its concerns and enable public authorities to take due account of such concerns,

Aiming thereby to further the accountability of and transparency in decision-making and to strengthen public support for decisions on the environment,

 | DOI:10.1163/9789004467583_012

Recognizing the desirability of transparency in all branches of government and inviting legislative bodies to implement the principles of this Convention in their proceedings,

Recognizing also that the public needs to be aware of the procedures for participation in environmental decision-making, have free access to them and know how to use them,

Recognizing further the importance of the respective roles that individual citizens, non-governmental organizations and the private sector can play in environmental protection,

Desiring to promote environmental education to further the understanding of the environment and sustainable development and to encourage widespread public awareness of, and participation in, decisions affecting the environment and sustainable development,

Noting, in this context, the importance of making use of the media and of electronic or other, future forms of communication,

Recognizing the importance of fully integrating environmental considerations in governmental decision-making and the consequent need for public authorities to be in possession of accurate, comprehensive and up-to- date environmental information,

Acknowledging that public authorities hold environmental information in the public interest, Concerned that effective judicial mechanisms should be accessible to the public, including organizations, so that its legitimate interests are protected and the law is enforced,

Noting the importance of adequate product information being provided to consumers to enable them to make informed environmental choices,

Recognizing the concern of the public about the deliberate release genetically modified organisms into the environment and the need for increased transparency and greater public participation in decision-making field,

Convinced that the implementation of this Convention will contribute to strengthening democracy in the region of the United Nations Economic Commission for Europe (ECE),

Conscious of the role played in this respect by ECE and recalling, inter alia, the ECE Guidelines on Access to Environmental Information and Public Participation in Environmental Decision-making endorsed in the Ministerial Declaration adopted at the Third Ministerial Conference "Environment for Europe" in Sofia, Bulgaria, on 25 October 1995,

Bearing in mind the relevant provisions in the Convention on Environmental Impact Assessment in a Transboundary Context, done at Espoo, Finland, on 25 February 1991, and the Convention on the Transboundary Effects of Industrial Accidents and the Convention on the Protection and Use of Transboundary Watercourses and

International Lakes, both done at Helsinki on 17 March 1992, and other regional conventions,

Conscious that the adoption of this Convention will have contributed to the further strengthening of the "Environment for Europe" process and to the results of the Fourth Ministerial Conference in Aarhus, Denmark, in June 1998,

Have agreed as follows:

Article 1 – Objective

In order to contribute to the protection of the right of every person of present and future generations to live in an environment adequate to his or her health and well-being, each Party shall guarantee the rights of access to information, public participation in decision-making, and access to justice in environmental matters in accordance with the provisions of this Convention.

Article 2 – Definitions

For the purposes of this Convention,

1. "Party" means, unless the text otherwise indicates, a Contracting Party to this Convention;
2. "Public authority" means:
   (a) Government at national, regional and other level;
   (b) Natural or legal persons performing public administrative functions under national law, including specific duties, activities or services in relation to the environment;
   (c) Any other natural or legal persons having public responsibilities or functions, or providing public services, in relation to the environment, under the control of a body or person falling within subparagraphs (a) or (b) above;
   (d) The institutions of any regional economic integration organization referred to in article 17 which is a Party to this Convention.

   This definition does not include bodies or institutions acting in a judicial or legislative capacity;
3. "Environmental information" means any information in written, visual, aural, electronic or any other material form on:
   (a) The state of elements of the environment, such as air and atmosphere, water, soil, land, landscape and natural sites, biological diversity and its

components, including genetically modified organisms, and the interaction among these elements;

(b) Factors, such as substances, energy, noise and radiation, and activities or measures, including administrative measures, environmental agreements, policies, legislation, plans and programmes, affecting or likely to affect the elements of the environment within the scope of subparagraph (a) above, and cost-benefit and other economic analyses and assumptions used in environmental decision-making;

(c) The state of human health and safety, conditions of human life, cultural sites and built structures, inasmuch as they are or may be affected by the state of the elements of the environment or, through these elements, by the factors, activities or measures referred to in subparagraph (b) above;

4. "The public" means one or more natural or legal persons, and, in accordance with national legislation or practice, their associations, organizations or groups;

5. "The public concerned" means the public affected or likely to be affected by, or having an interest in, the environmental decision-making; for the purposes of this definition, non-governmental organizations promoting environmental protection and meeting any requirements under national law shall be deemed to have an interest.

Article 3 – General Provisions

1. Each Party shall take the necessary legislative, regulatory and other measures, including measures to achieve compatibility between the provisions implementing the information, public participation and access-to-justice provisions in this Convention, as well as proper enforcement measures, to establish and maintain a clear, transparent and consistent framework to implement the provisions of this Convention.

2. Each Party shall endeavour to ensure that officials and authorities assist and provide guidance to the public in seeking access to information, in facilitating participation in decision-making and in seeking access to justice in environmental matters.

3. Each Party shall promote environmental education and environmental awareness among the public, especially on how to obtain access to information, to participate in decision-making and to obtain access to justice in environmental matters.

4. Each Party shall provide for appropriate recognition of and support to associations, organizations or groups promoting environmental protection and ensure that its national legal system is consistent with this obligation.

5. The provisions of this Convention shall not affect the right of a Party to maintain or introduce measures providing for broader access to information, more extensive public participation in decision-making and wider access to justice in environmental matters than required by this Convention.
6. This Convention shall not require any derogation from existing rights of access to information, public participation in decision-making and access to justice in environmental matters.
7. Each Party shall promote the application of the principles of this Convention in international environmental decision-making processes and within the framework of international organizations in matters relating to the environment.
8. Each Party shall ensure that persons exercising their rights in conformity with the provisions of this Convention shall not be penalized, persecuted or harassed in any way for their involvement. This provision shall not affect the powers of national courts to award reasonable costs in judicial proceedings.
9. Within the scope of the relevant provisions of this Convention, the public shall have access to information, have the possibility to participate in decision-making and have access to justice in environmental matters without discrimination as to citizenship, nationality or domicile and, in the case of a legal person, without discrimination as to where it has its registered seat or an effective centre of its activities.

Article 4 – Access to Environmental Information

1. Each Party shall ensure that, subject to the following paragraphs of this article, public authorities, in response to a request for environmental information, make such information available to the public, within the framework of national legislation, including, where requested and subject to subparagraph (b) below, copies of the actual documentation containing or comprising such information:
   (a) Without an interest having to be stated;
   (b) In the form requested unless:
      (i) It is reasonable for the public authority to make it available in another form, in which case reasons shall be given for making it available in that form; or
      (ii) The information is already publicly available in another form.
2. The environmental information referred to in paragraph 1 above shall be made available as soon as possible and at the latest within one month after the request has been submitted, unless the volume and the complexity of the information justify an extension of this period up to two months after the request. The applicant shall be informed of any extension and of the reasons justifying it.

3. A request for environmental information may be refused if:
   (a) The public authority to which the request is addressed does not hold the environmental information requested;
   (b) The request is manifestly unreasonable or formulated in too general a manner; or
   (c) The request concerns material in the course of completion or concerns internal communications of public authorities where such an exemption is provided for in national law or customary practice, taking into account the public interest served by disclosure.
4. A request for environmental information may be refused if the disclosure would adversely affect:
   (a) The confidentiality of the proceedings of public authorities, where such confidentiality is provided for under national law;
   (b) International relations, national defence or public security;
   (c) The course of justice, the ability of a person to receive a fair trial or the ability of a public authority to conduct an enquiry of a criminal or disciplinary nature;
   (d) The confidentiality of commercial and industrial information, where such confidentiality is protected by law in order to protect a legitimate economic interest. Within this framework, information on emissions which is relevant for the protection of the environment shall be disclosed;
   (e) Intellectual property rights;
   (f) The confidentiality of personal data and/or files relating to a natural person where that person has not consented to the disclosure of the information to the public, where such confidentiality is provided for in national law;
   (g) The interests of a third party which has supplied the information requested without that party being under or capable of being put under a legal obligation to do so, and where that party does not consent to the release of the material; or
   (h) The environment to which the information relates, such as the breeding sites of rare species.

   The aforementioned grounds for refusal shall be interpreted in a restrictive way, taking into account the public interest served by disclosure and taking into account whether the information requested relates to emissions into the environment.
5. Where a public authority does not hold the environmental information requested, this public authority shall, as promptly as possible, inform the applicant of the public authority to which it believes it is possible to apply for the information requested or transfer the request to that authority and inform the applicant accordingly.

6. Each Party shall ensure that, if information exempted from disclosure under paragraphs 3 (c) and 4 above can be separated out without prejudice to the confidentiality of the information exempted, public authorities make available the remainder of the environmental information that has been requested.
7. A refusal of a request shall be in writing if the request was in writing or the applicant so requests. A refusal shall state the reasons for the refusal and give information on access to the review procedure provided for in accordance with article 9. The refusal shall be made as soon as possible and at the latest within one month, unless the complexity of the information justifies an extension of this period up to two months after the request. The applicant shall be informed of any extension and of the reasons justifying it.
8. Each Party may allow its public authorities to make a charge for supplying information, but such charge shall not exceed a reasonable amount. Public authorities intending to make such a charge for supplying information shall make available to applicants a schedule of charges which may be levied, indicating the circumstances in which they may be levied or waived and when the supply of information is conditional on the advance payment of such a charge.

Article 5 – Collection and Dissemination of Environmental Information

1. Each Party shall ensure that:
   (a) Public authorities possess and update environmental information which is relevant to their functions;
   (b) Mandatory systems are established so that there is an adequate flow of information to public authorities about proposed and existing activities which may significantly affect the environment;
   (c) In the event of any imminent threat to human health or the environment, whether caused by human activities or due to natural causes, all information which could enable the public to take measures to prevent or mitigate harm arising from the threat and is held by a public authority is disseminated immediately and without delay to members of the public who may be affected.
2. Each Party shall ensure that, within the framework of national legislation, the way in which public authorities make environmental information available to the public is transparent and that environmental information is effectively accessible, inter alia, by:
   (a) Providing sufficient information to the public about the type and scope of environmental information held by the relevant public authorities, the

basic terms and conditions under which such information is made available and accessible, and the process by which it can be obtained;

(b) Establishing and maintaining practical arrangements, such as:

(i) Publicly accessible lists, registers or files;

(ii) Requiring officials to support the public in seeking access to information under this Convention; and

(iii) The identification of points of contact; and

(c) Providing access to the environmental information contained in lists, registers or files as referred to in subparagraph (b)(i) above free of charge.

3. Each Party shall ensure that environmental information progressively becomes available in electronic databases which are easily accessible to the public through public telecommunications networks. Information accessible in this form should include:

(a) Reports on the state of the environment, as referred to in paragraph 4 below;

(b) Texts of legislation on or relating to the environment;

(c) As appropriate, policies, plans and programmes on or relating to the environment, and environmental agreements; and

(d) Other information, to the extent that the availability of such information in this form would facilitate the application of national law implementing this Convention, provided that such information is already available in electronic form.

4. Each Party shall, at regular intervals not exceeding three or four years, publish and disseminate a national report on the state of the environment, including information on the quality of the environment and information on pressures on the environment.

5. Each Party shall take measures within the framework of its legislation for the purpose of disseminating, inter alia:

(a) Legislation and policy documents such as documents on strategies, policies, programmes and action plans relating to the environment, and progress reports on their implementation, prepared at various levels of government;

(b) International treaties, conventions and agreements on environmental issues; and

(c) Other significant international documents on environmental issues, as appropriate.

Available to the public is transparent and that environmental is effectively accessible, inter alia, by:

Providing sufficient information to the public about the type and

6. Each Party shall encourage operators whose activities have a significant impact on the environment to inform the public regularly of the environmental impact

of their activities and products, where appropriate within the framework of voluntary eco-labelling or eco-auditing schemes or by other means.

7. Each Party shall:
   (a) Publish the facts and analyses of facts which it considers relevant and important in framing major environmental policy proposals;
   (b) Publish, or otherwise make accessible, available explanatory material on its dealings with the public in matters falling within the scope of this Convention; and
   (c) Provide in an appropriate form information on the performance of public functions or the provision of public services relating to the environment by government at all levels.
8. Each Party shall develop mechanisms with a view to ensuring that sufficient product information is made available to the public in a manner which enables consumers to make informed environmental choices.
9. Each Party shall take steps to establish progressively, taking into account international processes where appropriate, a coherent, nationwide system of pollution inventories or registers on a structured, computerized and publicly accessible database compiled through standardized reporting. Such a system may include inputs, releases and transfers of a specified range of substances and products, including water, energy and resource use, from a specified range of activities to environmental media and to on-site and off- site treatment and disposal sites.
10. Nothing in this article may prejudice the right of Parties to refuse to disclose certain environmental information in accordance with article 4, paragraphs 3 and 4.

Article 6 – Public Participation in Decisions on Specific Activities

1. Each Party:
   (a) Shall apply the provisions of this article with respect to decisions on whether to permit proposed activities listed in annex I;
   (b) Shall, in accordance with its national law, also apply the provisions of this article to decisions on proposed activities not listed in annex I which may have a significant effect on the environment. To this end, Parties shall determine whether such a proposed activity is subject to these provisions; and
   (c) May decide, on a case-by-case basis if so provided under national law, not to apply the provisions of this article to proposed activities serving national defence purposes, if that Party deems that such application would have an adverse effect on these purposes.

2. The public concerned shall be informed, either by public notice or individually as appropriate, early in an environmental decision-making procedure, and in an adequate, timely and effective manner, inter alia, of:
   (a) The proposed activity and the application on which a decision will be taken;
   (b) The nature of possible decisions or the draft decision;
   (c) The public authority responsible for making the decision;
   (d) The envisaged procedure, including, as and when this information can be provided:
      (i) The commencement of the procedure;
      (ii) The opportunities for the public to participate;
      (iii) The time and venue of any envisaged public hearing;
      (iv) An indication of the public authority from which relevant information can be obtained and where the relevant information has been deposited for examination by the public;
      (v) An indication of the relevant public authority or any other official body to which comments or questions can be submitted and of the time schedule for transmittal of comments or questions; and
      (vi) An indication of what environmental information relevant to the proposed activity is available; and
   (e) The fact that the activity is subject to a national or transboundary environmental impact assessment procedure.
3. The public participation procedures shall include reasonable time-frames for the different phases, allowing sufficient time for informing the public in accordance with paragraph 2 above and for the public to prepare and participate effectively during the environmental decision-making.
4. Each Party shall provide for early public participation, when all options are open and effective public participation can take place.
5. Each Party should, where appropriate, encourage prospective applicants to identify the public concerned, to enter into discussions, and to provide information regarding the objectives of their application before applying for a permit.
6. Each Party shall require the competent public authorities to give the public concerned access for examination, upon request where so required under national law, free of charge and as soon as it becomes available, to all information relevant to the decision-making referred to in this article that is available at the time of the public participation procedure, without prejudice to the right of Parties to refuse to disclose certain information in accordance with article 4, paragraphs 3 and 4. The relevant information shall include at least, and without prejudice to the provisions of article 4:

(a) A description of the site and the physical and technical characteristics of the proposed activity, including an estimate of the expected residues and emissions;
(b) A description of the significant effects of the proposed activity on the environment;
(c) A description of the measures envisaged to prevent and/or reduce the effects, including emissions;
(d) A non-technical summary of the above;
(e) An outline of the main alternatives studied by the applicant; and
(f) In accordance with national legislation, the main reports and advice issued to the public authority at the time when the public concerned shall be informed in accordance with paragraph 2 above.

7. Procedures for public participation shall allow the public to submit, in writing or, as appropriate, at a public hearing or inquiry with the applicant, any comments, information, analyses or opinions that it considers relevant to the proposed activity.
8. Each Party shall ensure that in the decision due account is taken of the outcome of the public participation.
9. Each Party shall ensure that, when the decision has been taken by the public authority, the public is promptly informed of the decision in accordance with the appropriate procedures. Each Party shall make accessible to the public the text of the decision along with the reasons and considerations on which the decision is based.
10. Each Party shall ensure that, when a public authority reconsiders or updates the operating conditions for an activity referred to in paragraph 1, the provisions of paragraphs 2 to 9 of this article are applied *mutatis mutandis*, and where appropriate.
11. Each Party shall, within the framework of its national law, apply, to the extent feasible and appropriate, provisions of this article to decisions on whether to permit the deliberate release of genetically modified organisms into the environment.

Article 7 – Public Participation Concerning Plans, Programmes and Policies Relating to the Environment

Each Party shall make appropriate practical and/or other provisions for the public to participate during the preparation of plans and programmes relating to the environment, within a transparent and fair framework, having provided the necessary information to the public. Within this framework, article 6, paragraphs 3, 4 and 8, shall be applied. The public which may participate shall be identified by the relevant public authority, taking into account the objectives of this Convention. To the extent appropriate, each Party shall endeavour to provide opportunities for public participation in the preparation of policies relating to the environment.

Article 8 – Public Participation during the Preparation of Executive Regulations and/or Generally Applicable Legally Binding Normative Instruments

Each Party shall strive to promote effective public participation at an appropriate stage, and while options are still open, during the preparation by public authorities of executive regulations and other generally applicable legally binding rules that may have a significant effect on the environment. To this end, the following steps should be taken:

(a) Time-frames sufficient for effective participation should be fixed;
(b) Draft rules should be published or otherwise made publicly available; and
(c) The public should be given the opportunity to comment, directly or through representative consultative bodies.

The result of the public participation shall be taken into account as far as possible.

Article 9 – Access to Justice

1. Each Party shall, within the framework of its national legislation, ensure that any person who considers that his or her request for information under article 4 has been ignored, wrongfully refused, whether in part or in full, inadequately answered, or otherwise not dealt with in accordance with the provisions of that article, has access to a review procedure before a court of law or another independent and impartial body established by law.

   In the circumstances where a Party provides for such a review by a court of law, it shall ensure that such a person also has access to an expeditious procedure established by law that is free of charge or inexpensive for reconsideration by a public authority or review by an independent and impartial body other than a court of law.

   Final decisions under this paragraph 1 shall be binding on the public authority holding the information. Reasons shall be stated in writing, at least where access to information is refused under this paragraph.
2. Each Party shall, within the framework of its national legislation, ensure that members of the public concerned

(a) Having a sufficient interest

or, alternatively,

(b) Maintaining impairment of a right, where the administrative procedural law of a Party requires this as a precondition,

have access to a review procedure before a court of law and/or another independent and impartial body established by law, to challenge the substantive and procedural legality of any decision, act or omission subject to the provisions of article 6 and, where so provided for under national law and without prejudice to paragraph 3 below, of other relevant provisions of this Convention.

What constitutes a sufficient interest and impairment of a right shall be determined in accordance with the requirements of national law and consistently with the objective of giving the public concerned wide access to justice within the scope of this Convention. To this end, the interest of any non-governmental organization meeting the requirements referred to in article 2, paragraph 5, shall be deemed sufficient for the purpose of subparagraph (a) above. Such organizations shall also be deemed to have rights capable of being impaired for the purpose of subparagraph (b) above.

The provisions of this paragraph 2 shall not exclude the possibility of a preliminary review procedure before an administrative authority and shall not affect the requirement of exhaustion of administrative review procedures prior to recourse to judicial review procedures, where such a requirement exists under national law.

3. In addition and without prejudice to the review procedures referred to in paragraphs 1 and 2 above, each Party shall ensure that, where they meet the criteria, if any, laid down in its national law, members of the public have access to administrative or judicial procedures to challenge acts and omissions by private persons and public authorities which contravene provisions of its national law relating to the environment.

4. In addition and without prejudice to paragraph 1 above, the procedures referred to in paragraphs 1, 2 and 3 above shall provide adequate and effective remedies, including injunctive relief as appropriate, and be fair, equitable, timely and not prohibitively expensive. Decisions under this article shall be given or recorded in writing. Decisions of courts, and whenever possible of other bodies, shall be publicly accessible.

5. In order to further the effectiveness of the provisions of this article, each Party shall ensure that information is provided to the public on access to administrative and judicial review procedures and shall consider the establishment of appropriate assistance mechanisms to remove or reduce financial and other barriers to access to justice.

Article 10 – Meeting of the Parties

1. The first meeting of the Parties shall be convened no later than one year after the date of the entry into force of this Convention. Thereafter, an ordinary meeting of the Parties shall be held at least once every two years, unless otherwise decided by the Parties, or at the written request of any Party, provided that, within six months of the request being communicated to all Parties by the Executive Secretary of the Economic Commission for Europe, the said request is supported by at least one third of the Parties.
2. At their meetings, the Parties shall keep under continuous review the implementation of this Convention on the basis of regular reporting by the Parties, and, with this purpose in mind, shall:
   (a) Review the policies for and legal and methodological approaches to access to information, public participation in decision-making and access to justice in environmental matters, with a view to further improving them;
   (b) Exchange information regarding experience gained in concluding and implementing bilateral and multilateral agreements or other arrangements having relevance to the purposes of this Convention and to which one or more of the Parties are a party;
   (c) Seek, where appropriate, the services of relevant ECE bodies and other competent international bodies and specific committees in all aspects pertinent to the achievement of the purposes of this Convention;
   (d) Establish any subsidiary bodies as they deem necessary;
   (e) Prepare, where appropriate, protocols to this Convention;
   (f) Consider and adopt proposals for amendments to this Convention in accordance with the provisions of article 14;
   (g) Consider and undertake any additional action that may be required for the achievement of the purposes of this Convention;
   (h) At their first meeting, consider and by consensus adopt rules of procedure for their meetings and the meetings of subsidiary bodies;
   (i) At their first meeting, review their experience in implementing the provisions of article 5, paragraph 9, and consider what steps are necessary to develop further the system referred to in that paragraph, taking into account international processes and developments, including the elaboration of an appropriate instrument concerning pollution release and transfer registers or inventories which could be annexed to this Convention.
3. The Meeting of the Parties may, as necessary, consider establishing financial arrangements on a consensus basis.

4. The United Nations, its specialized agencies and the International Atomic Energy Agency, as well as any State or regional economic integration organization entitled under article 17 to sign this Convention but which is not a Party to this Convention, and any intergovernmental organization qualified in the fields to which this Convention relates, shall be entitled to participate as observers in the meetings of the Parties.
5. Any non-governmental organization, qualified in the fields to which this Convention relates, which has informed the Executive Secretary of the Economic Commission for Europe of its wish to be represented at a meeting of the Parties shall be entitled to participate as an observer unless at least one third of the Parties present in the meeting raise objections.
6. For the purposes of paragraphs 4 and 5 above, the rules of procedure referred to in paragraph 2 (h) above shall provide for practical arrangements for the admittance procedure and other relevant terms.

Article 11 – Right to Vote

1. Except as provided for in paragraph 2 below, each Party to this Convention shall have one vote.
2. Regional economic integration organizations, in matters within their competence, shall exercise their right to vote with a number of votes equal to the number of their member States which are Parties to this Convention. Such organizations shall not exercise their right to vote if their member States exercise theirs, and vice versa.

Article 12 – Secretariat

The Executive Secretary of the Economic Commission for Europe shall carry out the following secretariat functions:

(a) The convening and preparing of meetings of the Parties;
(b) The transmission to the Parties of reports and other information received in accordance with the provisions of this Convention; and
(c) Such other functions as may be determined by the Parties.

Article 13 – Annexes

The annexes to this Convention shall constitute an integral part thereof.

Article 14 – Amendments to the Convention

1. Any Party may propose amendments to this Convention.
2. The text of any proposed amendment to this Convention shall be submitted in writing to the Executive Secretary of the Economic Commission for Europe, who shall communicate it to all Parties at least ninety days meeting of the Parties at which it is proposed for adoption.
3. The Parties shall make every effort to reach agreement on any proposed amendment to this Convention by consensus. If all efforts at consensus have been exhausted, and no agreement reached, the amendment shall as a last resort be adopted by a three-fourths majority vote of the Parties present and voting at the meeting.
4. Amendments to this Convention adopted in accordance with paragraph 3 above shall be communicated by the Depositary to all Parties for ratification, approval or acceptance. Amendments to this Convention other than those to an annex shall enter into force for Parties having ratified, approved or accepted them on the ninetieth day after the receipt by the Depositary of notification of their ratification, approval or acceptance by at least three fourths of these Parties. Thereafter they shall enter into force for any other Party on the ninetieth day after that Party deposits its instrument of ratification, approval or acceptance of the amendments.
5. Any Party that is unable to approve an amendment to an annex to this Convention shall so notify the Depositary in writing within twelve months from the date of the communication of the adoption. The Depositary shall without delay notify all Parties of any such notification received. A Party may at any time substitute an acceptance for its previous notification and, upon deposit of an instrument of acceptance with the Depositary, the amendments to such an annex shall become effective for that Party.
6. On the expiry of twelve months from the date of its communication by the Depositary as provided for in paragraph 4 above an amendment to an annex shall become effective for those Parties which have not submitted a notification to the Depositary in accordance with the provisions of paragraph 5 above, provided that not more than one third of the Parties have submitted such a notification.
7. For the purposes of this article, "Parties present and voting" means Parties present and casting an affirmative or negative vote.

Article 15 – Review of Compliance

The Meeting of the Parties shall establish, on a consensus basis, optional arrangements of a non-confrontational, non-judicial and consultative nature for reviewing compliance with the provisions of this Convention. These arrangements shall allow for appropriate public involvement and may include the option of considering communications from members of the public on matters related to this Convention.

Article 16 – Settlement of Disputes

1. If a dispute arises between two or more Parties about the interpretation or application of this Convention, they shall seek a solution by negotiation or by any other means of dispute settlement acceptable to the parties to the dispute.
2. When signing, ratifying, accepting, approving or acceding to this Convention, or at any time thereafter, a Party may declare in writing to the Depositary that, for a dispute not resolved in accordance with paragraph 1 above, it accepts one or both of the following means of dispute settlement as compulsory in relation to any Party accepting the same obligation:
   (a) Submission of the dispute to the International Court of Justice;
   (b) Arbitration in accordance with the procedure set out in annex II.
3. If the parties to the dispute have accepted both means of dispute settlement referred to in paragraph 2 above, the dispute may be submitted only to the International Court of Justice, unless the parties agree otherwise.

Article 17 – Signature

This Convention shall be open for signature at Aarhus (Denmark) on 25 June 1998, and thereafter at United Nations Headquarters in New York until 21 December 1998, by States members of the Economic Commission for Europe as well as States having consultative status with the Economic Commission for Europe pursuant to paragraphs 8 and 11 of Economic and Social Council resolution 36 (IV) of 28 March 1947, and by regional economic integration organizations constituted by sovereign States members of the Economic Commission for Europe to which their member States have transferred competence over matters governed by this Convention, including the competence to enter into treaties in respect of these matters.

Article 18 – Depositary

The Secretary-General of the United Nations shall act as the Depositary of this Convention.

Article 19 – Ratification, Acceptance, Approval and Accession

1. This Convention shall be subject to ratification, acceptance or approval by signatory States and regional economic integration organizations.
2. This Convention shall be open for accession as from 22 December 1998 by the States and regional economic integration organizations referred to in article 17.
3. Any other State, not referred to in paragraph 2 above, that is a Member of the United Nations may accede to the Convention upon approval by the Meeting of the Parties.
4. Any organization referred to in article 17 which becomes a Party to this Convention without any of its member States being a Party shall be bound by all the obligations under this Convention. If one or more of such an organization's member States is a Party to this Convention, the organization and its member States shall decide on their respective responsibilities for the performance of their obligations under this Convention. In such cases, the organization and the member States shall not be entitled to exercise rights under this Convention concurrently.
5. In their instruments of ratification, acceptance, approval or accession, the regional economic integration organizations referred to in article 17 shall declare the extent of their competence with respect to the matters governed by this Convention. These organizations shall also inform the Depositary of any substantial modification to the extent of their competence.

Article 20 – Entry into Force

1. This Convention shall enter into force on the ninetieth day after the date of deposit of the sixteenth instrument of ratification, acceptance, approval or accession.
2. For the purposes of paragraph 1 above, any instrument deposited by a regional economic integration organization shall not be counted as additional to those deposited by States members of such an organization.
3. For each State or organization referred to in article 17 which ratifies, accepts or approves this Convention or accedes thereto after the deposit of the sixteenth instrument of ratification, acceptance, approval or accession, the Convention shall enter into force on the ninetieth day after the date of deposit by such State or organization of its instrument of ratification, acceptance, approval or accession.

Article 21 – Withdrawal

At any time after three years from the date on which this Convention has come into force with respect to a Party, that Party may withdraw from the Convention by giving written notification to the Depositary. Any such withdrawal shall take effect on the ninetieth day after the date of its receipt by the Depositary.

Article 22 – Authentic Texts

The original of this Convention, of which the English, French and Russian texts are equally authentic, shall be deposited with the Secretary-General of the United Nations.

IN WITNESS WHEREOF the undersigned, being duly authorized thereto, have signed this Convention.

DONE at Aarhus (Denmark), this twenty-fifth day of June, one thousand nine hundred and ninety-eight.

Annex I – List of Activities Referred to in Article 6, Paragraph 1 (a)

1. Energy sector
   - Mineral oil and gas refineries;
   - Installations for gasification and liquefaction;
   - Thermal power stations and other combustion installations with a heat input of 50 megawatts (MW) or more;
   - Coke ovens;
   - Nuclear power stations and other nuclear reactors including the dismantling or decommissioning of such power stations or reactors[1] (except research installations for the production and conversion of fissionable and fertile materials whose maximum power does not exceed 1 kW continuous thermal load);
   - Installations for the reprocessing of irradiated nuclear fuel;
   - Installations designed:
     - For the production or enrichment of nuclear fuel;
     - For the processing of irradiated nuclear fuel or high-level radioactive waste;

1 Nuclear power stations and other nuclear reactors cease to be such an installation when all nuclear fuel and other radioactively contaminated elements have been removed permanently from the installation site.

- For the final disposal of irradiated nuclear fuel;
- Solely for the final disposal of radioactive waste;
- Solely for the storage (planned for more than 10 years) of irradiated nuclear fuels or radioactive waste in a different site than the production site.

2. Production and processing of metals:
   - Metal ore (including sulphide ore) roasting or sintering installations;
   - Installations for the production of pig-iron or steel (primary or secondary fusion) including continuous casting, with a capacity exceeding 2.5 tons per hour;
   - Installations for the processing of ferrous metals:
     (i) Hot-rolling mills with a capacity exceeding 20 tons of crude steel per hour;
     (ii) Smitheries with hammers the energy of which exceeds 50 kilojoules per hammer, where the calorific power used exceeds 20 MW;
     (iii) Application of protective fused metal coats with an input exceeding 2 tons of crude steel per hour;
   - Ferrous metal foundries with a production capacity exceeding 20 tons per day;
   - Installations:
     (i) For the production of non-ferrous crude metals from ore, concentrates or secondary raw materials by metallurgical, chemical or electrolytic processes;
     (ii) For the smelting, including the alloying, of non-ferrous metals, including recovered products (refining, foundry casting, etc.), with a melting capacity exceeding 4 day for lead and cadmium or 20 tons per day for all metals;
   - Installations for surface treatment of metals and plastic materials using an electrolytic or chemical process where volume of the treatment vats exceeds 30 m3.

3. Mineral industry:
   - Installations for the production of cement clinker in rotary kilns with a production capacity exceeding 500 tons per day or lime in rotary kilns with a production capacity exceeding 50 tons per day or in other furnaces with a production capacity exceeding 50 tons per day;
   - Installations for the production of asbestos and the manufacture of asbestos-based products;
   - Installations for the manufacture of glass including glass fibre with a melting capacity exceeding 20 tons per day;
   - Installations for melting mineral substances including the production of mineral fibres with a melting capacity exceeding 20 tons a day;

- Installations for the manufacture of ceramic products by firing, in particular roofing tiles, bricks, refractory bricks, tiles, stoneware or porcelain, with a production capacity exceeding 75 tons per day, and/or with a kiln capacity exceeding 4 m3 and with a setting density per kiln exceeding 300 kg/m3.

4. Chemical industry: Production within the meaning of the categories of activities contained in this paragraph means the production on an industrial scale by chemical processing of substances or groups of substances listed in subparagraphs (a) to (g):
 (a) Chemical installations for the production of basic organic chemicals, such as:
  (i) Simple hydrocarbons (linear or cyclic, saturated or unsaturated, aliphatic or aromatic);
  (ii) Oxygen-containing hydrocarbons such as alcohols, aldehydes, ketones, carboxylic acids, esters, acetates, ethers, peroxides, epoxy resins;
  (iii) Sulphurous hydrocarbons;
  (iv) Nitrogenous hydrocarbons such as amines, amides, nitrous compounds, nitro compounds or nitrate compounds, nitriles, cyanates, isocyanates;
  (v) Phosphorus-containing hydrocarbons;
  (vi) Halogenic hydrocarbons;
  (vii) Organometallic compounds;
  (viii) Basic plastic materials (polymers, synthetic fibres and cellulose-based fibres);
  (ix) Synthetic rubbers;
  (x) Dyes and pigments;
  (xi) Surface-active agents and surfactants;
 (b) Chemical installations for the production of basic inorganic chemicals, such as:
  (i) Gases, such as ammonia, chlorine or hydrogen chloride, fluorine or hydrogen fluoride, carbon oxides, sulphur compounds, nitrogen oxides, hydrogen, sulphur dioxide, carbonyl chloride;
  (ii) Acids, such as chromic acid, hydrofluoric acid, phosphoric acid, nitric acid, hydrochloric acid, sulphuric acid, oleum, sulphurous acids;
  (iii) Bases, such as ammonium hydroxide, potassium hydroxide, sodium hydroxide;
  (iv) Salts, such as ammonium chloride, potassium chlorate, potassium carbonate, sodium carbonate, perborate, silver nitrate;
  (v) Non-metals, metal oxides or other inorganic compounds such as calcium carbide, silicon, silicon carbide;

(c) Chemical installations for the production of phosphorous-, nitrogen- or potassium-based fertilizers (simple or compound fertilizers);
(d) Chemical installations for the production of basic plant health products and of biocides;
(e) Installations using a chemical or biological process for the production of basic pharmaceutical products;
(f) Chemical installations for the production of explosives;
(g) Chemical installations in which chemical or biological processing is used for the production of protein feed additives, ferments and other protein substances.

5. Waste management:
– Installations for the incineration, recovery, chemical treatment or landfill of hazardous waste;
– Installations for the incineration of municipal waste with a capacity exceeding 3 tons per hour;
– Installations for the disposal of non-hazardous waste with a capacity exceeding 50 tons per day;
– Landfills receiving more than 10 tons per day or with a total capacity exceeding 25 000 tons, excluding landfills of inert waste.

6. Waste-water treatment plants with a capacity exceeding 150 000 population equivalent.

7. Industrial plants for the:
(a) Production of pulp from timber or similar fibrous materials;
(b) Production of paper and board with a production capacity exceeding 20 tons per day.

8. (a) Construction of lines for long-distance railway traffic and of with a basic runway length of 2 100 m or more; airports[2]
(b) Construction of motorways and express roads;[3]
(c) Construction of a new road of four or more lanes, or realignment and/or widening of an existing road of two lanes or less so as to provide four or more lanes, where such new road, or realigned and/or widened section of road, would be 10 km or more in a continuous length.

2 For the purposes of this Convention, "airport" means an airport which complies with the definition in the 1944 Chicago Convention setting up the International Civil Aviation Organization (Annex 14).

3 For the purposes of this Convention, "express road" means a road which complies with the definition in the European Agreement on Main International Traffic Arteries of 15 November 1975.

9. (a) Inland waterways and ports for inland-waterway traffic which permit the passage of vessels of over 1 350 tons;
   (b) Trading ports, piers for loading and unloading connected to land and outside ports (excluding ferry piers) which can take vessels of over 1 350 tons.
10. Groundwater abstraction or artificial groundwater recharge schemes where the annual volume of water abstracted or recharged is equivalent to or exceeds 10 million cubic metres.
11. (a) Works for the transfer of water resources between river basins where this transfer aims at preventing possible shortages of water and where the amount of water transferred exceeds 100 million cubic metres/year;
    (b) In all other cases, works for the transfer of water resources between river basins where the multiannual average flow of the basin of abstraction exceeds 2 000 million cubic metres/year and where the amount of water transferred exceeds 5% of this flow.

    In both cases transfers of piped drinking water are excluded.
12. Extraction of petroleum and natural gas for commercial purposes where the amount extracted exceeds 500 tons/day in the case of petroleum and 500 000 cubic metres/day in the case of gas.
13. Dams and other installations designed for the holding back or permanent storage of water, where a new or additional amount of water held back or stored exceeds 10 million cubic metres.
14. Pipelines for the transport of gas, oil or chemicals with a diameter of more than 800 mm and a length of more than 40 km.
15. Installations for the intensive rearing of poultry or pigs with more than:
    (a) 40 000 places for poultry;
    (b) 2 000 places for production pigs (over 30 kg); or
    (c) 750 places for sows.
16. Quarries and opencast mining where the surface of the site exceeds 25 hectares, or peat extraction, where the surface of the site exceeds 150 hectares.
17. Construction of overhead electrical power lines with a voltage of 220 kV or more and a length of more than 15 km.
18. Installations for the storage of petroleum, petrochemical, or chemical products with a capacity of 200 000 tons or more.
19. Other activities:
    - Plants for the pretreatment (operations such as washing, bleaching, mercerization) or dyeing of fibres or textiles where the treatment capacity exceeds 10 tons per day;
    - Plants for the tanning of hides and skins where the treatment capacity exceeds 12 tons of finished products per day;
    - (a) Slaughterhouses with a carcass production capacity greater than 50 tons per day;

(b) Treatment and processing intended for the production of food products from:

(i) Animal raw materials (other than milk) with a finished product production capacity greater than 75 tons per day;

(ii) Vegetable raw materials with a finished product production capacity greater than 300 tons per day (average value on a quarterly basis);

(c) Treatment and processing of milk, the quantity of milk received being greater than 200 tons per day (average value on an annual basis);

- Installations for the disposal or recycling of animal carcasses and animal waste with a treatment capacity exceeding 10 tons per day;
- Installations for the surface treatment of substances, objects or products using organic solvents, in particular for dressing, printing, coating, degreasing, waterproofing, sizing, painting, cleaning or impregnating, with a consumption capacity of more than 150 kg per hour or more than 200 tons per year;
- Installations for the production of carbon (hard-burnt coal) or electrographite by means of incineration or graphitization.

20. Any activity not covered by paragraphs 1–19 above where public participation is provided for under an environmental impact assessment procedure in accordance with national legislation.

21. The provision of article 6, paragraph 1 (a) of this Convention, does not apply to any of the above projects undertaken exclusively or mainly for research, development and testing of new methods or products for less than two years unless they would be likely to cause a significant adverse effect on environment or health.

22. Any change to or extension of activities, where such a change or extension in itself meets the criteria/thresholds set out in this annex, shall be subject to article 6, paragraph 1 (a) of this Convention. Any other change or extension of activities shall be subject to article 6, paragraph 1 (b) of this Convention.

Annex II – Arbitration

1. In the event of a dispute being submitted for arbitration pursuant to article 16, paragraph 2, of this Convention, a party or parties shall notify the secretariat of the subject matter of arbitration and indicate, in particular, the articles of this Convention whose interpretation or application is at issue. The secretariat shall forward the information received to all Parties to this Convention.

2. The arbitral tribunal shall consist of three members. Both the claimant party or parties and the other party or parties to the dispute shall appoint an arbitrator,

and the two arbitrators so appointed shall designate by common agreement the third arbitrator, who shall be the president of the arbitral tribunal. The latter shall not be a national of one of the parties to the dispute, nor have his or her usual place of residence in the territory of one of these parties, nor be employed by any of them, nor have dealt with the case in any other capacity.

3. If the president of the arbitral tribunal has not been designated within two months of the appointment of the second arbitrator, the Executive Secretary of the Economic Commission for Europe shall, at the request of either party to the dispute, designate the president within a further two-month period.

4. If one of the parties to the dispute does not appoint an arbitrator within two months of the receipt of the request, the other party may so inform the Executive Secretary of the Economic Commission for Europe, who shall designate the president of the arbitral tribunal within a further two-month period. Upon designation, the president of the arbitral tribunal shall request the party which has not appointed an arbitrator to do so within two months. If it fails to do so within that period, the president shall so inform the Executive Secretary of the Economic Commission for Europe, who shall make this appointment within a further two-month period.

5. The arbitral tribunal shall render its decision in accordance with international law and the provisions of this Convention.

6. Any arbitral tribunal constituted under the provisions set out in this annex shall draw up its own rules of procedure.

7. The decisions of the arbitral tribunal, both on procedure and on substance, shall be taken by majority vote of its members.

8. The tribunal may take all appropriate measures to establish the facts.

9. The parties to the dispute shall facilitate the work of the arbitral tribunal and, in particular, using all means at their disposal, shall:
   (a) Provide it with all relevant documents, facilities and information;
   (b) Enable it, where necessary, to call witnesses or experts and receive their evidence.

10. The parties and the arbitrators shall protect the confidentiality of any information that they receive in confidence during the proceedings of the arbitral tribunal.

11. The arbitral tribunal may, at the request of one of the parties, recommend interim measures of protection.

12. If one of the parties to the dispute does not appear before the arbitral tribunal or fails to defend its case, the other party may request the tribunal to continue the proceedings and to render its final decision. Absence of a party or failure of a party to defend its case shall not constitute a bar to the proceedings.

13. The arbitral tribunal may hear and determine counter-claims arising directly out of the subject matter of the dispute.
14. Unless the arbitral tribunal determines otherwise because of the particular circumstances of the case, the expenses of the tribunal, including the remuneration of its members, shall be borne by the parties to the dispute in equal shares. The tribunal shall keep a record of all its expenses, and shall furnish a final statement thereof to the parties.
15. Any Party to this Convention which has an interest of a legal nature in subject matter of the dispute, and which may be affected by a decision in case, may intervene in the proceedings with the consent of the tribunal.
16. The arbitral tribunal shall render its award within five months of the date on which it is established, unless it finds it necessary to extend the time limit for a period which should not exceed five months.
17. The award of the arbitral tribunal shall be accompanied by a statement of reasons. It shall be final and binding upon all parties to the dispute. The award will be transmitted by the arbitral tribunal to the parties to the dispute and to the secretariat. The secretariat will forward the information received to all Parties to this Convention.
18. Any dispute which may arise between the parties concerning the interpretation or execution of the award may be submitted by either party to the arbitral tribunal which made the award or, if the latter cannot be seized thereof, to another tribunal constituted for this purpose in the same manner as the first.

Available at https://unece.org/DAM/env/pp/documents/cep43e.pdf (accessed 17 June 2021)

Selective Bibliography

Matthew H. Ahrens & David S. Langer, *Lender Liability under CERCLA- Environmental Risks for Lenders under Superfund: A Refresher for the Economic Downturn*, 3 BLOOMBERG CORPORATE LAW JOURNAL 482 (2008).

Motoko Aizawa & Chaofei Yang, *Green Credit, Green Stimulus, Green Revolution? China's Mobilization of Banks for Environmental Cleanup*, 19 J.E.D. 119 (2010).

James R. Allum, *"An Outcrop of Hell": History, Environment, and the Politics of the Trail Smelter Dispute*, *in* TRANSBOUNDARY HARM IN INTERNATIONAL LAW: LESSONS FROM THE TRAIL SMELTER ARBITRATION (2009).

FREDERICK R. ANDERSON, NEPA IN THE COURTS: A LEGAL ANALYSIS OF THE NATIONAL ENVIRONMENTAL POLICY ACT (Resources for the Future; distributed by the Johns Hopkins University Press. 1973).

Richard N. L. Andrews, *Agency Responses to NEPA: A Comparison and Implications*, 16 NATURAL RESOURCES JOURNAL 301 (1976).

Atif Ansar, et al., *Should we build more large dams? The actual costs of hydropower megaproject development*, 69 ENERGY POLICY 43 (2014).

Raymond Aron, *Max Weber and Modern Social Science*, *in* HISTORY, TRUTH, LIBERTY – SELECTED WRITINGS OF RAYMOND ARON (Franciszek Draus ed. 1985).

Mahnoush H. Arsanjani, *Claims Against International Organizations: Quis custodiet ipsos custodes*, 7 YALE JOURNAL OF WORLD PUBLIC ORDER 131 (1981).

Mahnoush H. Arsanjani, *The Uses and Abuses of Illusion in International Politics*, *in* LOOKING TO THE FUTURE – ESSAYS IN INTERNATIONAL LAW IN HONOR OF W. MICHAEL REISMAN (Mahnoush H. Arsanjani, et al. eds. 2011).

Eric Ashby, *Background to environmental impact assessment*, *in* ENVIRONMENTAL IMPACT ASSESSMENT (Timothy O'Riordan & Richard D. Hey eds. 1976).

Karin Bäckstrand, *Civic Science for Sustainability: Reframing the Role of Experts, Policy-Makers and Citizens in Environmental Governance*, 3 GLOBAL ENVIRONMENTAL POLITICS 24 (2003).

Michel Badré, *L'Autorité environnementale et la participation du public à l'élaboration de ses décisions*, 81 ANNALES DES MINES – RESPONSABILITÉ ET ENVIRONNEMENT 30 (2016).

Ian G. Baird, et al., *The People and their River, the World Bank and its Dam: Revisiting the Xe Bang Fai River in Laos*, 46 DEVELOPMENT AND CHANGE 1080 (2015).

MATTHEW BAIRD, AN EXAMINATION AND EVALUATION OF EXISTING TRANS-BOUNDARY, REGIONAL, AND INTERGOVERNMENTAL MODELS FOR A POTENTIAL REGIONAL EIA STANDARD IN ASEAN (Pact – Mekong Partnership For the Environment. 2014).

Adam Barker & Christopher Wood, *An Evaluation of EIA System Performance in Eight EU Countries*, 19 ENVIRONMENTAL IMPACT ASSESSMENT REVIEW 387 (1999).

Kees Bastmeijer & Timo Koivurova, *Transboundary Environmental Impact Assessment: An Introduction*, *in* THEORY AND PRACTICE OF TRANSBOUNDARY IMPACT ASSESSMENT (Kees Bastmeijer & Timo Koivurova eds., 2008).

Robert B. Beattie, *Everything you already know about EIA (But don't often admit)*, 15 ENVIRON. IMPACT ASSESS. REV. 109 (1995).

Daniel Bodansky, *Customary (and Not So Customary) International Environmental Law*, 3 IND. J. GLOBAL LEGAL STUD. 105 (1995).

Daniel Bodansky, *Legitimacy*, *in* THE OXFORD HANDBOOK OF INTERNATIONAL ENVIRONMENTAL LAW (Daniel Bodansky, et al. eds. 2008).

Daniel Bodansky, *Prologue to a Theory of Non-Treaty Norms*, *in* LOOKING TO THE FUTURE – ESSAYS IN INTERNATIONAL LAW IN HONOR OF W. MICHAEL REISMAN (Mahnoush H. Arsanjani, et al. eds. 2011).

James P. Boggs, *Procedural vs. Substantive in NEPA Law: Cutting the Gordian Knot*, 15 THE ENVIRONMENTAL PROFESSIONAL 25 (1993).

Annie L. Booth & Norman W. Skelton, *Improving First Nations' participation in environmental assessment processes: recommendations from the field*, 29(1) IMPACT ASSESSMENT AND PROJECT APPRAISAL 49 (2011).

Christophe Bouneau, *Les réseaux de transport d'électricité en Europe occidentale depuis la fin du XIXe siècle: de la diversité des modèles nationaux à la recherche de la convergence européenne*, 2 ANNALES HISTORIQUES DE L'ÉLECTRICITÉ 23 (2004).

Ian A. Bowles & Cyril F. Kormos, *Environmental Reform at the World Bank: The Role of the U.S. Congress*, 35 VA. J. INT'L L. 777 (1995).

DANIEL BOY & MATHIEU BRUGIDOU, LE DÉBAT PUBLIC, UN RISQUE DÉMOCRATIQUE? L'EXEMPLE DE LA MOBILISATION AUTOUR D'UNE LIGNE HAUTE TENSION (Lavoisier. 2008).

Alan Boyle, *The Gabcikovo-Nagymaros Case: New Law in Old Bottles*, 8 YBIEL 13 (1997).

Alan Boyle, *Transboundary air pollution: a tale of two paradigms*, *in* TRANSBOUNDARY POLLUTION – EVOLVING ISSUES OF INTERNATIONAL LAW AND POLICY (S. Jayakumar, et al. eds. 2015).

Daniel D. Bradlow, *Private Complainants and International Organizations: A Comparative Study of the Independent Inspection Mechanisms in International Financial Institutions*, 36 GEO. J. INT'L L. 403 (2005).

DANIEL D. BRADLOW, EXTERNAL REVIEW OF THE INSPECTION PANEL'S TOOLKIT (Prepared for the Committee on Development Effectiveness (World Bank, 2018).

Carl E. Bruch, et al., *Assessing the Assessments: Improving Methodologies for Impact Assessment in Transboundary Watercourses*, 23 WATER RESOURCES DEVELOPMENT 391 (2007).

JUTTA BRUNNEE, PROCEDURE AND SUBSTANCE IN INTERNATIONAL ENVIRONMENTAL LAW (2020).

Natalie Bugalski, *The Demise of Accountability at the World Bank?*, 31 AM. U. INT'L L. REV. 1 (2016).

Lynton K. Caldwell, *NEPA Revisited: A Call for a Constitutional Amendment*, 6 THE ENVIRONMENTAL FORUM 18 (1989).

Lynton K. Caldwell, *Understanding Impact Analysis: Technical Process, Administrative Reform, Policy Principle*, *in* POLICY THROUGH IMPACT ASSESSMENT – INSTITUTIONALIZED ANALYSIS AS A POLICY STRATEGY (Robert V. Bartlett ed. 1989).

Lynton K. Caldwell, *Analysis–Assessment–Decision: the Anatomy of Rational Policymaking*, 9 IMPACT ASSESSMENT 81 (1991).

LYNTON K. CALDWELL, THE NATIONAL ENVIRONMENTAL POLICY ACT: AN AGENDA FOR THE FUTURE (Indiana University Press. 1998).

Lynton K. Caldwell, *Is World Law an Emerging Reality? Environmental Law in a Transnational World*, 10 COLO. J. INT'L ENVTL. L. & POL'Y 227 (1999).

Lynton K. Caldwell, *An Interview with Lynton Caldwell on the National Environmental Policy Act (NEPA)*, 5 ENVTL. PRAC. 281 (2003).

Laura Carlan Battle, *A Transnational Perspective on Extending Nepa: The Convention on Environmental Impact Assessment in a Transboundary Context*, 5 DUKE ENV L & POL'Y F 1 (1995).

Matthew Cashmore, *The role of science in environmental impact assessment: process and procedure versus purpose in the development of theory*, 24 ENVIRONMENTAL IMPACT ASSESSMENT REVIEW 403 (2004).

Matthew Cashmore, et al., *Introduction: The effectiveness of impact assessment instruments*, 27 IMPACT ASSESSMENT AND PROJECT APPRAISAL 91 (2009).

Matthew Cashmore, et al., *The interminable issue of effectiveness: substantive purposes, outcomes and research challenges in the advancement of environmental impact assessment theory*, 22 IMPACT ASSESSMENT AND PROJECT APPRAISAL 295 (2004).

Steve Charnovitz, *How Nongovernmental Actors Vitalize International Law*, *in* LOOKING TO THE FUTURE – ESSAYS IN INTERNATIONAL LAW IN HONOR OF W. MICHAEL REISMAN (Mahnoush H. Arsanjani, et al. eds. 2011).

Prachoom Chomchai, *Public Participation in Watershed Management in Theory and Practice: a Mekong River Basin Perspective*, *in* PUBLIC PARTICIPATION IN THE GOVERNANCE OF INTERNATIONAL FRESHWATER RESOURCES (Carl E. Bruch, et al. eds. 2005).

Robin R. Churchill & Geir Ulfstein, *Autonomous Institutional Arrangements in Multilateral Environmental Agreements: A Little-Noticed Phenomenon in International Law*, 94 AMERICAN JOURNAL OF INTERNATIONAL LAW 623 (2000).

Robert G. Connelly, *The UN Convention on EIA in a Transboundary Context: A Historical Perspective*, 19 ENVIRON. IMPACT ASSESS. REV. 37 (1999).

CPDP, COMPTE-RENDU DU DÉBAT PUBLIC SUR LE PROJET DE LIAISON ÉLECTRIQUE THT ENTRE LA FRANCE ET L'ESPAGNE (2003).

NEIL CRAIK, THE INTERNATIONAL LAW OF ENVIRONMENTAL IMPACT ASSESSMENT, PROCESS, SUBSTANCE AND INTEGRATION (Cambridge University Press. 2008).

Y. Deelstra, et al., *Using knowledge for decision-making purposes in the context of large projects in The Netherlands*, 23 ENVIRON. IMPACT ASSES. REV. 517 (2003).

Diane Desierto, et al., *The 'New' World Bank Accountability Mechanism: Observations from the ND Reparations Design and Compliance Lab*, EJIL:TALK! (11 November 2020).

John F. Devlin & Nonita T. Yap, *Contentious politics in environmental assessment: blocked projects and winning coalitions*, 26 IMPACT ASSESSMENT AND PROJECT APPRAISAL 17 (2008).

Alan Diduck & Bruce Mitchell, *Learning, Public Involvement and Environmental Assessment: A Canadian Case Study*, 5 JOURNAL OF ENVIRONMENTAL ASSESSMENT POLICY AND MANAGEMENT 339 (2003).

Joseph F.C. DiMento & Helen Ingram, *Science and Environmental Decision Making: The Potential Role of Environmental Impact Assessment in the Pursuit of Appropriate Information*, 45 NATURAL RESOURCES JOURNAL 283 (2005).

Daniel A. Dreyfus & Helen M. Ingram, *The National Environmental Policy Act: A View of Intent and Practice*, 16 NAT. RESOURCES J. 243 (1976).

PIERRE DUBEAU (ED.), FOLLOW-UP SURVEY FOR BIODIVERSITY ASSESSMENT OF THE MEKONG RIVER IN NORTHERN LAO PDR (IUCN Water and Nature Initiative and Mekong Wetlands Biodiversity Conservation and Sustainable Use Programme, Bangkok. October 2004).

Pierre-Marie Dupuy, *Overview of the Existing Customary Legal Regime Regarding International Pollution*, *in* INTERNATIONAL LAW AND POLLUTION (Daniel B. Magraw ed. 1991).

René-Jean Dupuy, *L'organisation internationale et l'expression de la volonté générale*, REVUE GÉNÉRALE DE DROIT INTERNATIONAL PUBLIC 527 (1957).

David M. Dzidzornu, *Environmental Impact Assessment Procedure Through the Conventions*, 10 EUR. ENVT'L L. REV. 15 (2001).

Jonas Ebbesson, *The Notion of Public Participation in International Environmental Law*, 8 YB.INT'L ENV.L. 51 (1998).

Jonas Ebbesson, *Innovative Elements and Expected Effectiveness of the 1991 EIA Convention*, 19 ENVIRONMENTAL IMPACT ASSESSMENT REVIEW 47 (1999).

JONAS EBBESSON, THE RELEVANCE AND FUTURE OF THE NORDIC ENVIRONMENT PROTECTION CONVENTION (Nordic Council of Ministers. 2003).

Jonas Ebbesson, *A Modest Contribution to Environmental Democracy and Justice in Transboundary Contexts: The Combined Impact of the Espoo Convention and Aarhus Convention*, 20 RECIEL 248 (2011).

Jonas Ebbesson, *Public Participation and Privatisation in Environmental Matters: An Assessment of the Aarhus Convention*, 4 ERASMUS LAW REVIEW 71 (2011).

Ana Maria Esteves & Frank Vanclay, *Social Development Needs Analysis as a tool for SIA to guide corporate-community investment: Applications in the minerals industry*, 29 ENVIRONMENTAL IMPACT ASSESSMENT REVIEW 137 (2009).

Daniel C. Esty, *Good Governance at the Supranational Scale: Globalizing Administrative Law*, 115 YALE L. J. 1490 (2006).

DANIEL C. ESTY & MARIA H. IVANOVA, MAKING INTERNATIONAL ENVIRONMENTAL EFFORTS WORK: THE CASE FOR A GLOBAL ENVIRONMENTAL ORGANIZATION (Yale Center for Environmental Law and Policy. 2001).

DANIEL C. ESTY & P.J. SIMMONS, GREEN TO GOLD BUSINESS PLAYBOOK: HOW TO IMPLEMENT SUSTAINABILITY PRACTICES FOR BOTTOM-LINE RESULTS IN EVERY BUSINESS FUNCTION (John Wiley & Sons, Inc. 2011).

DANIEL C. ESTY & ANDREW WINSTON, GREEN TO GOLD: HOW SMART COMPANIES USE ENVIRONMENTAL STRATEGY TO INNOVATE, CREATE VALUE, AND BUILD COMPETITIVE ADVANTAGE (Yale University Press (revised and updated edition from Wiley in 2009) (2006).

Amitai Etzioni, *The Asian Infrastructure Investment Bank: A Case Study of Multifaceted Containment*, 40 ASIAN PERSPECTIVE 173 (2016).

EUROPEAN COMMISSION, ENVIRONMENTAL LIABILITY DIRECTIVE – PROTECTING EUROPE'S NATURAL RESOURCES (European Union. 2013).

FAO, MEKONG RIVER BASIN – WATER REPORT 37 (2011).

ASSESSMENTS OF REGIONAL AND GLOBAL ENVIRONMENTAL RISKS – DESIGNING PROCESSES FOR THE EFFECTIVE USE OF SCIENCE IN DECISIONMAKING (Alexander E. Farrell & Jill Jäger eds., RFF Press. 2006).

Alexander E. Farrell & Terry J. Keating, *Dissent and Trust in Multilateral Assessments – Comparing LRTAP and OTAG*, *in* ASSESSMENTS OF REGIONAL AND GLOBAL ENVIRONMENTAL RISKS – DESIGNING PROCESSES FOR THE EFFECTIVE USE OF SCIENCE IN DECISIONMAKING (Alexander E. Farrell & Jill Jäger eds. 2006).

Olivier Fillieule, *Local Environmental Politics in France: Case of the Louron Valley, 1984–1996*, 1 FRENCH POLITICS 305 (2003).

DAVID FREESTONE, THE WORLD BANK AND SUSTAINABLE DEVELOPMENT – LEGAL ESSAYS (Martinus Nijhoff. 2013).

Patrick Frydman, *Conclusions du commissaire du gouvernement sous l'arrêt Conseil d'Etat, 29 avril 1994*, Juillet – Août CAHIERS JURIDIQUES DE L'ELECTRICITÉ ET DU GAZ (CJEG) 443 (1994).

Caroline Gagnon, *Paysage, transport d'électricité et esthétique du quotidien. De la confrontation au moins pire*, *in* LES PAYSAGES DE L'ÉLECTRICITÉ. PERSPECTIVES HISTORIQUES ET ENJEUX CONTEMPORAINS (XIXE–XXIE SIÈCLES) (Christophe Bouneau, et al. eds. 2012).

Emmanuel Gaillard & Isabelle Pingel-Lenuzza, *International Organisations and Immunity from Jurisdiction: to Restrict or to Bypass*, 51 INTERNATIONAL AND COMPARATIVE LAW QUARTERLY 1 (2002).

QI GAO, A PROCEDURAL FRAMEWORK FOR TRANSBOUNDARY WATER MANAGEMENT IN THE MEKONG RIVER BASIN – SHARED MEKONG FOR A COMMON FUTURE (Stephen McCaffrey ed., Brill / Nijhoff. 2014).

ANNA GELPERN, et al., HOW CHINA LENDS, A RARE LOOK INTO 100 DEBT CONTRACTS WITH FOREIGN GOVERNMENTS (Peterson Institute for International Economics, Kiel Institute for the World Economy, Center for Global Development, AidData at William & Mary. 2021).

Robert B. Gibson, *In full retreat: the Canadian government's new environmental assessment law undoes decades of progress*, 30 IMPACT ASSESS. PROJ. APPRAIS. 179 (2012).

Alix Gowlland Gualtieri, *The Environmental Accountability of the World Bank to Non-State Actors: Insights from the Inspection Panel*, 72 BRITISH YEARBOOK OF INTERNATIONAL LAW 213 (2001).

Monica Hakimi, *The Media as Participants in the International Legal Process*, 16 DUKE JOURNAL OF COMPARATIVE & INTERNATIONAL LAW 1 (2006).

Gunther Handl, *The Legal Mandate of Multilateral Development Banks as Agents for Change Toward Sustainable Development*, 92 AJIL 642 (1998).

Garrett Hardin, *The Tragedy of the Commons*, 162 SCIENCE 1243 (1968).

Nicola Hartley & Christopher Wood, *Public participation in environmental impact assessment – implementing the Aarhus Convention*, 25 ENVIRON. IMPACT ASSES. REV. 319 (2005).

Oona A. Hathaway, *Between Power and Principle: An Integrated Theory of International Law*, 72 U. CHI. L. REV. 469 (2005).

Leslye A. Herrmann, *Injunctions for NEPA Violations: Balancing the Equities*, 59 U. CHI. L. REV. 1263 (1992).

Michael Herz, *Parallel Universes: NEPA Lessons for the New Property*, 93 COLUM. L. REV. 1668 (1993).

Steven Herz, *Rethinking International Financial Institution Immunity*, *in* INTERNATIONAL FINANCIAL INSTITUTIONS AND INTERNATIONAL LAW (Daniel D. Bradlow & David Hunter eds. 2010).

ROSALYN HIGGINS, PROBLEMS AND PROCESS: INTERNATIONAL LAW AND HOW WE USE IT (Oxford University Press. 1994).

Mikael Hilden & Eeva Rebekka Furman, *Assessment across borders – Stumbling blocks and options in the practical implementation of the Espoo Convention*, 21 ENVIRONMENTAL IMPACT ASSESSMENT REVIEW 537 (2001).

Ann Hironaka & Evan Schofer, *Decoupling in the Environmental Arena: The Case of Environmental Impact Assessments*, *in* ORGANIZATIONS, POLICY AND THE

NATURAL ENVIRONMENT: INSTITUTIONAL AND STRATEGIC PERSPECTIVES (Andrew Hoffmann ed. 2002).

Richard Hooley, *Lender Liability for Environmental Damage*, 60 CAMB. L. J. 405 (2001).

Arja Huttunen, *The effectiveness of public participation in the environmental impact assessment process – a case study of the projected Sierilä hydropower station at Oikarainen, northern Finland*, 16:2 ACTA BOREALIA: A NORDIC JOURNAL OF CIRCUMPOLAR SOCIETIES 27 (1999).

INTERNATIONAL CENTRE FOR ENVIRONMENTAL MANAGEMENT (ICEM), STRATEGIC ENVIRONMENTAL ASSESSMENT OF HYDROPOWER ON THE MEKONG MAINSTREAM (Mekong River Commission. 2010).

Will A. Irwin, *Impact Assessment – First Session of the Working Group of Experts*, 13 ENVTL. POL'Y & L. 51 (1984).

Henry M. Jackson, *Foreword: Environmental Quality, the Courts, and the Congress*, 68 MICH. L. REV. 1073 (1970).

TRANSBOUNDARY POLLUTION – EVOLVING ISSUES OF INTERNATIONAL LAW AND POLICY (S. Jayakumar, et al. eds. 2015).

Jerzy Jendrośka, *Practice and Relevant Cases that emerged in the Context of the Espoo Convention Implementation Committee*, *in* NON-COMPLIANCE PROCEDURES AND MECHANISMS AND THE EFFECTIVENESS OF INTERNATIONAL ENVIRONMENTAL AGREEMENTS (Tullio Treves, et al. eds., 2009).

Bounsaw Jinarat, et al., *"If we lost our environment and suffer the impacts, can anyone return our original environment?"*, 8 WATERSHED 34 (2002).

Dan Kahan, *Fixing the Communications Failure*, 463 NATURE 296 (2010).

Bradley C. Karkkainen, *Toward a Smarter NEPA: Monitoring and Managing Government's Environmental Performance*, 102 COLUM. L. REV. 903 (2002).

William V. Kennedy, *EIA and Multi-lateral Financial Institutions*, *in* HANDBOOK OF ENVIRONMENTAL IMPACT ASSESSMENT, VOLUME 2, IMPACTS AND LIMITATIONS (Judith Petts ed. 1999).

ETIENNE KLEIN, LE GOÛT DU VRAI (Gallimard. 2020).

John H. Knox, *The Myth and Reality of Transboundary Environmental Impact Assessment*, 96 AJIL 291 (2002).

John H. Knox, *Assessing the Candidates for a Global Treaty on Transboundary Environmental Impact Assessment*, 12 NYU ENVT'L LJ 153 (2003).

Timo Koivurova, *The Future of the Nordic Environment Protection Convention*, NORDIC JOURNAL OF INTERNATIONAL LAW 505 (1997).

Timo Koivurova, *The Transnational EIA Procedure of the Espoo Convention*, 8 FINNISH Y.B. INT'L L. 161 (1997).

TIMO KOIVUROVA, ENVIRONMENTAL IMPACT ASSESSMENT IN THE ARCTIC: A STUDY OF INTERNATIONAL LEGAL NORMS (Ashgate. 2002).

Timo Koivurova, *The Case of Vuotos, in* ARCTIC GOVERNANCE (Timo Koivurova, et al. eds. 2004).

Timo Koivurova, *The Case of Vuotos: Interplay Between International, Community and National Environmental Law,* 13 RECIEL 47 (2004).

Timo Koivurova, *Transboundary EIA in the North Calotte region from the perspectives of international and European Union Law, in* ENVIRONMENTAL IMPACT ASSESSMENT IN THE NORTH CALOTTE TRANSBOUNDARY AREAS (2006).

Timo Koivurova, *Transboundary Environmental Impact Assessment: The Nordic Environmental Protection Convention, in* THEORY AND PRACTICE OF TRANSBOUNDARY IMPACT ASSESSMENT (Kees Bastmeijer & Timo Koivurova eds. 2008).

Timo Koivurova, *Could the Espoo Convention Become a Global Regime for Environmental Impact Assessment and Strategic Environmental Assessment?, in* TRANSBOUNDARY ENVIRONMENTAL GOVERNANCE – INLAND, COASTAL AND MARINE PERSPECTIVES (Robin Warner & Simon Marsden eds. 2012).

Timo Koivurova & Ismo Pölönen, *Transboundary Environmental Impact Assessment in the Case of the Baltic Sea Gas Pipeline,* 25 INT J MAR COAST LAW 151 (2010).

Jeffrey D. Kovar, *A Short Guide to the Rio Declaration,* 4 COLO. J. INT'L ENVTL. L. & POL'Y 119 (1993).

Douglas A. Kysar, *It Might Have Been: Risk, Precaution, and Opportunity Costs,* 22 J. LAND. USE & ENVTL. LAW 1 (2006).

JOHN H. LANGBEIN, et al., HISTORY OF THE COMMON LAW, THE DEVELOPMENT OF ANGLO-AMERICAN LEGAL INSTITUTIONS (Aspen Publishers – Wolters Kluwer. 2009).

Harold D. Lasswell, *In Quest of a Myth: the Problem of World Unity, in* WORLD POLITICS AND PERSONAL INSECURITY (1935).

KATE LAZARUS, et al., AN UNCERTAIN FUTURE: BIODIVERSITY AND LIVELIHOODS ALONG THE MEKONG RIVER IN NORTHERN LAO PDR (IUCN. 2006).

Richard Lazarus, *The National Environmental Policy Act in the U.S. Supreme Court: A Reappraisal and a Peek Behind the Curtains,* 100 THE GEORGETOWN LAW JOURNAL 1507 (2012).

Pamela Lesser & Timo Koivurova, *Impact Assessment and the New Arctic Geo-Environment, in* ARCTIC MARINE GOVERNANCE, OPPORTUNITIES FOR TRANSATLANTIC COOPERATION (Elizabeth Tedsen, et al. eds. 2014).

MATTHEW J. LINDSTROM & ZACHARY A. SMITH, THE NATIONAL ENVIRONMENTAL POLICY ACT: JUDICIAL MISCONSTRUCTION, LEGISLATIVE INDIFFERENCE, AND EXECUTIVE NEGLECT (Texas A&M University Press. 2002).

RICHARD A. LIROFF, A NATIONAL POLICY FOR THE ENVIRONMENT – NEPA AND ITS AFTERMATH (Indiana University Press. 1976).

ALOYSIUS P. LLAMZON, CORRUPTION IN INTERNATIONAL INVESTMENT ARBITRATION (Oxford University Press. 2014).

David A. Lubin & Daniel C. Esty, *The Sustainability Imperative – Lessons for leaders from previous game-changing megatrends*, 88 HARVARD BUSINESS REVIEW 42 (2010).

Antônio José Maristrello Porto, et al., *Lenders Environmental Liability in Brazil: How Much is Too Much?*, 6 ECONOMIC ANALYSIS OF LAW REVIEW 128 (2015).

Simon Marsden, *Developing Approaches to Trans-boundary Environmental Impact Assessment in China: Co-operation through the Greater Tumen Initiative and in the Pearl River Delta Region*, 9 CHINESE JOURNAL OF INTERNATIONAL LAW 393 (2010).

Simon Marsden, *Developing Agreements for Transboundary Environmental Impact Assessment and Strategic Environmental Assessment in Asia*, *in* TRANSBOUNDARY ENVIRONMENTAL GOVERNANCE. INLAND, COASTAL, AND MARINE PERSPECTIVES (Robin Warner & Simon Marsden eds. 2012).

Lisa Mastny, *Messing with the Mekong*, November/December WORLD WATCH MAGAZINE 21 (2003).

Benoît Mayer, *Development is no excuse for Human Rights Abuses: Framing the Responsibility of International Development Agencies*, 5 TRADE, LAW AND DEV. 286 (2013).

Myres S. McDougal, *Jurisprudence for a Free Society*, 1 GEORGIA LAW REVIEW 1 (1966).

Myres S. McDougal, et al., *The World Constitutive Process of Authoritative Decision*, 19 J. LEGAL EDUC. 253 (1967).

Myres S. McDougal, et al., *The Intelligence Function and World Public Order*, 46 TEMPLE LAW QUATERLY 365 (1973).

Myres S. McDougal, et al., *The World Community: A Planetary Social Process*, 21 U.C. DAVIS L. REV. 807 (1988).

Georges Mercadal, *Garantir le débat*, 297 PROJET 4 (2007).

PETER-JOHN MEYNELL (ED.), SCOPING STUDY FOR BIODIVERSITY ASSESSMENT OF THE MEKONG RIVER IN NORTHERN LAO PDR AND THAILAND (IUCN Mekong Water and Nature Initiative and Mekong Wetlands Biodiversity Conservation and Sustainable Use Programme, Bangkok. August 2003).

Garry Middle & Isaac Middle, *Professional Practice – The inefficiency of environmental impact assessment: reality or myth?*, 28(2) IMPACT ASSESS. PROJ. APPRAIS. 159 (2010).

Naho Mirumachi & Mikiyasu Nakayama, *Improving Methodologies for Transboundary Impact Assessment in Transboundary Watercourses: Navigation Channel Improvement Project of the Lancang-Mekong River from China- Myanmar Boundary Marker 243 to Ban Houei Sai of Laos*, 23 INT. J. WATER RESOUR. DEV. 411 (2007).

Ronald B. Mitchell, et al., *Information and Influence*, *in* GLOBAL ENVIRONMENTAL ASSESSMENTS – INFORMATION AND INFLUENCE (Ronald B. Mitchell, et al. eds., 2006).

GLOBAL ENVIRONMENTAL ASSESSMENTS – INFORMATION AND INFLUENCE (Ronald B. Mitchell, et al. eds., The MIT Press. 2006).

Jesse L. Moorman & Zhang Ge, *Promoting and Strengthening Public Participation in China's Environmental Impact Assessment Process: Comparing China's EIA Law and U.S. NEPA*, 8 VT. J. ENVTL. L. 281 (2007).

Richard K. Morgan, *Environmental impact assessment: the state of the art*, 30 IMPACT ASSESS. PROJ. APPRAIS. 5 (2012).

Angus Morrison-Saunders & Barry Sadler, *The art and science of impact assessment: results of a survey of IAIA members*, 28(1) IMPACT ASSESSMENT AND PROJECT APPRAISAL 77 (2010).

Kenneth M. Murchison, *Does NEPA matter? – An Analysis of the Historical Development and Contemporary Significance of the National Environmental Policy Act*, 18 U. RICH. L. REV. 557 (1983–1984).

Christopher Murgatroyd, *The World Bank: A Case for Lender Liability?*, 1 REV. EUR. COMMUN. INT'L ENVTL. L. 436 (1992).

RODNEY MUTH, et al., HAROLD D. LASSWELL: AN ANNOTATED BIBLIOGRAPHY (New Haven Press · Kluwer Academic Publishers. 1990).

MYRON H. NORDQUIST, UNITED NATIONS CONVENTION ON THE LAW OF THE SEA: A COMMENTARY (Myron H. Nordquist, et al. eds., Martinus Nijhoff. 1991).

Ciaran O'Faircheallaigh, *Public participation and environmental impact assessment: Purposes, implications, and lessons for public policy making*, 30 ENVIRONMENTAL IMPACT ASSESSMENT REVIEW 19 (2010).

Pirjo-Riitta Oinaala, *The Vuotos Reservoir*, *in* THE LEGAL STATUS OF THE INDIVIDUAL IN NORDIC ENVIRONMENTAL LAW (Tuula Tervashonka ed. 1994).

Leonard Ortolano & Anne Shepherd, *Impact Assessment*, 13 IMPACT ASSESSMENT 3 (1995).

MILTON OSBORNE, RIVER AT RISK – THE MEKONG AND THE WATER POLITICS OF CHINA AND SOUTHEAST ASIA (Lowy Institute for International Policy. 2004).

Tonis Poder & Tiit Lukki, *A critical review of checklist-based evaluation of environmental impact statements*, 29(1) IMPACT ASSESSMENT AND PROJECT APPRAISAL 27 (2011).

Ismo Pölönen, et al., *The effectiveness of the Finnish EIA system – What works, what doesn't, and what could be improved?*, 31 ENVIRONMENTAL IMPACT ASSESSMENT REVIEW 120 (2011).

Kleoniki C. Pouikli, *Overview of the implementation of the directive 2004/35/EC on environmental liability with regard to the prevention and remedying of environmental damage at European level*, 57 DESALINATION AND WATER TREATMENT 11520 (2016).

Kathryn D. Priester, *Safeguard Reforms at the World Bank: Mutual Accountability or a Race to the Bottom?*, 32 GEO. INT'L ENVTL. L. REV. 599 (2020).

Michel Prieur, *Le respect de l'environnement et les études d'impact*, 2 REVUE JURIDIQUE DE L'ENVIRONNEMENT 103 (1981).

JAMES RASBAND, et al., NATURAL RESOURCES – LAW AND POLICY (Foundation Press. 2009).

W. Michael Reisman, *Making International Humanitarian Law Effective: the Case for Civic Enforcement, in* THE UNITED NATIONS: A REASSESSMENT – SANCTIONS, PEACEKEEPING, AND HUMANITARIAN ASSISTANCE (John M. Paxman & George T. Boggs eds. 1973).

W. MICHAEL REISMAN, FOLDED LIES (Free Press. 1979).

W. Michael Reisman, *International Lawmaking: A Process of Communication*, 75 AM. SOC'Y INT'L L. PROC. 101 (1981).

W. Michael Reisman, *The Cult of Custom in the Late 20th Century*, 17 CAL. W. INT'L L.J. 133 (1987).

W. Michael Reisman, *A Hard Look at Soft Law*, 82 AM. SOC'Y INT'L L. PROC. 373 (1988).

W. Michael Reisman, *The Concept and Functions of Soft Law in International Politics, in* ESSAYS IN HONOUR OF JUDGE TASLIM OLAWALE ELIAS (Emmanuel G. Bello & Bola A. Ajibola eds. 1992).

W. Michael Reisman, *The View from the New Haven School of International Law*, 86 AM. SOC'Y INT'L. L. PROC. 118 (1992).

W. Michael Reisman, *1995 Siebenthaler Lecture – A Jurisprudence from the Perspective of the "Political Superior"*, 23 N. KY. L. REV. 605 (1995).

W. Michael Reisman, *International Law and the Inner Worlds of Others*, 9 ST. THOMAS L. REV. 25 (1996).

W. MICHAEL REISMAN, LAW IN BRIEF ENCOUNTERS (Yale University Press. 1999).

W. Michael Reisman, *Private International Declaration Initiatives, in* LA DÉCLARATION UNIVERSELLE DES DROITS DE L'HOMME 1948–98: AVENIR D'UN IDÉAL COMMUN – ACTES DU COLLOQUE DES 14, 15 ET 16 SEPTEMBRE 1998 À LA SORBONNE, PARIS (Commission nationale consultative des droits de l'Homme ed. 1999).

W. Michael Reisman, *The Democratization of Contemporary International Law-Making Processes and the Differentiation of their Application, in* DEVELOPMENTS OF INTERNATIONAL LAW IN TREATY MAKING (Rüdiger Wolfrum & Volker Röben eds. 2005).

W. Michael Reisman, *On the Causes of Uncertainty and Volatility in International Law, in* THE SHIFTING ALLOCATION OF AUTHORITY IN INTERNATIONAL LAW: CONSIDERING SOVEREIGNTY, SUPREMACY AND SUBSIDIARITY – ESSAYS IN HONOUR OF PROFESSOR RUTH LAPIDOTH (Tomer Broude & Yuval Shany eds. 2008).

W. MICHAEL REISMAN, THE QUEST FOR WORLD ORDER AND HUMAN DIGNITY IN THE TWENTY-FIRST CENTURY: CONSTITUTIVE PROCESS AND INDIVIDUAL COMMITMENT (Hague Academy of International Law. 2013).

W. Michael Reisman & Eisuke Suzuki, *Recognition and Social Change in International Law: A Prologue for Decision-making, in* TOWARD WORLD ORDER AND HUMAN

DIGNITY: ESSAYS IN HONOR OF MYRES S. MCDOUGAL (W. Michael Reisman & Burns H. Weston eds. 1976).

W. Michael Reisman, et al., *The New Haven School: A Brief Introduction*, 32 YALE J.INT'L L. 575 (2007).

Rey, *Conclusions du commissaire du gouvernement sous le jugement Tribunal administratif de Pau, 16 décembre 1994*, CAHIERS JURIDIQUES DE L'ELECTRICITÉ ET DU GAZ (CJEG) 109 (Mars. 1994).

Tyson R. Roberts, *Downstream ecological implications of China's Lancang Hydropower and Mekong Navigation project*, *in* BIODIVERSITY MANAGEMENT AND SUSTAINABLE DEVELOPMENT IN THE LANCANG-MEKONG RIVER IN THE NEW MILLENNIUM (Cao Min, et al. eds. 2001).

Nicholas A. Robinson, *Legal Systems, Decisionmaking, and the Science of Earth's Systems: Procedural Missing Links*, 27 ECOLOGY L. Q. 1077 (2001).

William H. Rodgers, Jr., *NEPA at Twenty: Mimicry and Recruitment in Environmental Law*, 20 ENVTL. L. 485 (1990).

Francesca Romanin Jacur, *Triggering Non-Compliance Procedures*, *in* NON-COMPLIANCE PROCEDURES AND MECHANISMS, AND THE EFFECTIVENESS OF INTERNATIONAL ENVIRONMENTAL AGREEMENTS (Tullio Treves, et al. eds., 2009).

Susan Rose-Ackerman, *Étude d'impact et analyse coûts-avantages : qu'impliquent- elles pour l'élaboration des politiques publiques et les réformes législatives?*, 140 REVUE FRANÇAISE D'ADMINISTRATION PUBLIQUE 787 (2011).

Susan Rose-Ackerman, *Putting Cost-Benefit Analysis in Its Place: Rethinking Regulatory Review*, 65 U. MIAMI L. REV. 335 (2011).

Emmanuel Roucounas, *The Users of International Law*, *in* LOOKING TO THE FUTURE – ESSAYS IN INTERNATIONAL LAW IN HONOR OF W. MICHAEL REISMAN (Mahnoush H. Arsanjani, et al. eds. 2011).

BARRY SADLER, INTERNATIONAL STUDY OF THE EFFECTIVENESS OF ENVIRONMENTAL ASSESSMENT – FINAL REPORT – ENVIRONMENTAL ASSESSMENT IN A CHANGING WORLD: EVALUATING PRACTICE TO IMPROVE PERFORMANCE (Canadian Environmental Assessment Agency – International Association for Impact Assessment. 1996).

Barry Sadler, *Taking Stock of SEA*, *in* HANDBOOK OF STRATEGIC ENVIRONMENTAL ASSESSMENT (Barry Sadler, et al. eds. 2011).

Salman M.A. Salman, *The Future of International Water Law: Regional Approaches to Shared Watercourses?*, *in* LOOKING TO THE FUTURE – ESSAYS IN INTERNATIONAL LAW IN HONOR OF W. MICHAEL REISMAN (Mahnoush H. Arsanjani, et al. eds. 2011).

RÔMULO S. R. SAMPAIO, et al., LENDERS AND INVESTORS ENVIRONMENTAL LIABILITY – HOW MUCH IS TOO MUCH? (UNEP. 2016).

Nadia Sanchez Castillo & Yongmin Bian, *China's Obligation to Conduct Transboundary Environmental Impact Assessment (TEIA) in Utilizing Its Shared Water Resources*, 55 NATURAL RESOURCES JOURNAL 105 (2014).

Peter H. Sand, *The Role of Domestic Procedures in Transnational Environmental Disputes*, *in* LEGAL ASPECTS OF TRANSFRONTIER POLLUTION (OECD ed. 1977).

Peter H. Sand, *The Potential Impact of the Global Environment Facility of the World Bank, UNDP and UNEP*, *in* ENFORCING ENVIRONMENTAL STANDARDS: ECONOMIC MECHANISMS AS VIABLE MEANS? (Rüdiger Wolfrum ed. 1996).

Oscar Schachter, *The Emergence of International Environmental Law*, 44 J. INT'L AFF. 457 (1991).

Wiek Schrage & Nick Bonvoisin, *Transboundary impact assessment: frameworks, experiences and challenges*, 26 IMPACT ASSESSMENT AND PROJECT APPRAISAL 234 (2008).

SEARIN, MEKONG RAPIDS UNDER FIRE (SEARIN 2nd ed. 2003).

SEARIN, SUMMARY OF THAI BAAN (VILLAGERS') RESEARCH AT CHIANG KHONG (LRS. 2004).

David C. Shilton, *Is the Supreme Court Hostile to NEPA? Some Possible Explanations for a 12-0 Record*, 20 ENVTL. L. 551 (1990).

Eric W. Sievers, *Transboundary Jurisdiction and Watercourse Law: China, Kazakhstan, and the Irtysh*, 37 TEXAS INTERNATIONAL LAW JOURNAL 1 (2002).

A. John Sinclair, et al., *Environmental assessments in the Internet age: the role of e-governance and social media in creating platforms for meaningful participation*, 35 IMPACT ASSESS. PROJ. APPRAIS. 148 (2017).

Rob Sippe, *Criteria and Standards for Assessing Significant Impact*, *in* HANDBOOK OF ENVIRONMENTAL IMPACT ASSESSMENT (Judith Petts ed. 1999).

Jennifer M. P. Stewart & A. John Sinclair, *Meaningful public participation in environmental assessment: perspectives from Canadian participants, proponents and government*, 9 J. ENV. ASSMT. POL. MGMT. 161 (2007).

Diana Suhardiman, et al., *Between interests and worldviews: the narrow path of the Mekong River Commission*, 33 ENVIRONMENT AND PLANNING C: GOVERNMENT AND POLICY 199 (2015).

Leena Suopajärvi, *Competing Industries and Contested Nature in Finnish Lapland after World War II*, *in* ENCOUNTERING THE NORTH: CULTURAL GEOGRAPHY, INTERNATIONAL RELATIONS AND NORTHERN LANDSCAPES (Frank Möller & Samu Pehkonen eds. 2003).

William Murray Tabb, *Environmental Impact Assessment in the European Community: Shaping International Norms*, 73 TULANE LAW REVIEW 923 (1999).

KIM TALUS, et al., ENERGY LAW IN FINLAND (Kluwer Law International. 2010).

TERRA, The Upper Mekong Navigation Improvement Project (2004).

Arne Tesli & Stig Roar Husby, *EIA in a Transboundary Context: Principles and Challenges for a Coordinated Nordic Application of the Espoo Convention*, 19 ENVIRONMENTAL IMPACT ASSESSMENT REVIEW 57 (1999).

Helena Tiihonen & Sylvi Inez Liljegren, *Let the river run free*, *in* WOMAN IN A NORTHERN LANDSCAPE (Sylvi Inez Liljegren ed. 1999).

William A. Tilleman, *Public Participation in the Environmental Impact Assessment Process: A Comparative Study of Impact Assessment in Canada, The United States, and the European Community*, 33 COLUM. J. TRANSNAT'L L. 337 (1995).

JEAN TIROLE, ECONOMIE DU BIEN COMMUN (PUF. 2016).

Philip R. Trimble, *International Law, World Order, and Critical Legal Studies*, 42 STAN. L. REV. 811 (1990).

EVE TRUILHÉ-MARENGO, DROIT DE L'ENVIRONNEMENT DE L'UNION EUROPÉENNE (Larcier. 2015).

UNEP, ENVIRONMENTAL IMPACT ASSESSMENT TRAINING RESOURCE MANUAL (UNEP 2nd ed. 2002).

Marie-France Verdier, *Cour administrative d'appel de Bordeaux, 11 janvier 1996 Electricité de France (No. 95BX00203). Avec note*, REVUE JURIDIQUE DE L'ENVIRONNEMENT 555 (1997).

Rob Verheem, *How to strengthen the independence of IA reviewers and practitioners*, 39 IMPACT ASSESS. PROJ. APPRAIS. 80 (2021).

RENAN VIGUIÉ, LA TRAVERSÉE ÉLECTRIQUE DES PYRÉNÉES – HISTOIRE DE L'INTERCONNEXION ENTRE LA FRANCE ET L'ESPAGNE (P.I.E. Peter Lang. 2014).

Michel Villey, *Liminaire – Données historiques*, *in* ARCHIVES DE PHILOSOPHIE DU DROIT – LA LOGIQUE DU DROIT (1966).

Michel Villey, *Histoire de la logique juridique*, *in* ANNALES DE LA FACULTÉ DE DROIT DE TOULOUSE – TOME XV (1967).

MICHEL VILLEY, PHILOSOPHIE DU DROIT (DÉFINITIONS ET FINS DU DROIT – LES MOYENS DU DROIT) (Dalloz Réédition ed. 2001).

Jorge E. Viñuales, *Foreign Investment and the Environment in International Law: An Ambiguous Relationship*, 80 BRITISH YEARBOOK OF INTERNATIONAL LAW 244 (2010).

Jorge E. Viñuales, *Legal Techniques for Dealing with Scientific Uncertainty in Environmental Law*, 43 VAND. J. TRANSNAT'L L. 437 (2010).

Jorge E. Viñuales, *The Rio Declaration on Environment and Development*, *in* THE RIO DECLARATION ON ENVIRONMENT AND DEVELOPMENT: A COMMENTARY (Jorge E. Viñuales ed. 2015).

Barry Wain, *River at Risk*, 167 FAR EASTERN ECONOMIC REVIEW 48 (2004).

Tara Ward, *The Right to Free, Prior, and Informed Consent: Indigenous Peoples' Participation Rights within International Law*, 10 NW. J. INT'L HUM. RTS. 54 (2011).

Sengdeuane Wayakone & Inoue Makoto, *Evaluation of the Environmental Impacts Assessment (EIA) System in Lao PDR*, 3 JOURNAL OF ENVIRONMENTAL PROTECTION 1655 (2012).

WCD, DAMS AND DEVELOPMENT – A NEW FRAMEWORK FOR DECISION-MAKING – THE REPORT OF THE WORLD COMMISSION ON DAMS (World Commission on Dams. 2000).

Thomas Webler, et al., *Public Participation in Impact Assessment: A Social Learning Perspective*, 15 ENVIRON. IMPACT ASSES. REV. 443 (1995).

Andrew Wells-Dang, *Prospects for Regional Cooperation on Environmental Impact Assessment in Mainland Southeast Asia*, 37 CONTEMPORARY SOUTHEAST ASIA 406 (2015).

Andrew Wells-Dang, et al., *A Political Economy of Environmental Impact Assessment in the Mekong Region*, 9 WATER ALTERNATIVES 33 (2016).

MATTHEW Z. WHEELER, BLASTED RIVER: DILEMMAS OF MEKONG NAVIGATION (Institute of Current World Affairs. 2004).

Siegfried Wiessner, *Rights and Status of Indigenous Peoples: A Global Comparative and International Legal Analysis*, 12 HARV. HUM. RTS. J. 57 (1999).

Siegfried Wiessner, *Michael Reisman, Human Dignity, and the Law*, *in* LOOKING TO THE FUTURE – ESSAYS IN INTERNATIONAL LAW IN HONOR OF W. MICHAEL REISMAN (Mahnoush H. Arsanjani, et al. eds. 2011).

K. O. Winemiller, et al., *Balancing hydropower and biodiversity in the Amazon, Congo, and Mekong*, 351 SCIENCE 128 (2016).

Christopher Wood, *What NEPA Has Wrought Abroad*, *in* ENVIRONMENTAL POLICY AND NEPA: PAST, PRESENT AND FUTURE (E. Ray Clark & Larry W. Canter eds., 1997).

CHRISTOPHER WOOD, ENVIRONMENTAL IMPACT ASSESSMENT: A COMPARATIVE REVIEW (Prentice Hall 2nd ed. 2003).

WORLD COMMISSION ON ENVIRONMENT AND DEVELOPMENT, OUR COMMON FUTURE (Oxford University Press. 1987).

Tseming Yang, *The Emergence of the Environmental Impact Assessment Duty as a Global Legal Norm and General Principle of Law*, 70 HASTINGS LAW JOURNAL 525 (2019).

Bianca Zambão, *Brazil's Launch of Lender Environmental Liability as a Tool to Manage Environmental Impacts*, 18 U. MIAMI INT'L & COMP. L. REV. 47 (2010).

Index

The text in the appendices are indicated by page numbers in *italics*.

www.ingramcontent.com/pod-product-compliance
Lightning Source LLC
LaVergne TN
LVHW020631300926
849161LV00004B/664
* 9 7 8 9 0 0 4 4 6 7 5 7 6 *